Irene C. Fountas **&** Gay Su Pinnell

The Reading
Minilessons
Book

Your Every Day Guide for Literacy Teaching

GRADE 6

HEINEMANN
Portsmouth, NH

Heinemann
145 Maplewood Avenue, Suite 300
Portsmouth, NH 03801
www.heinemann.com

Offices and agents throughout the world

The author and publisher wish to thank those who have generously given permission to reprint
borrowed material: Please see the Credits section beginning on page 659.

Library of Congress Cataloging-in-Publication Data is on file at the Library of Congress.
Library of Congress Control Number: 2019947434
ISBN: 978-0-325-09867-8

Editor: Sue Paro
Production: Cindy Strowman
Cover and interior designs: Ellery Harvey
Illustrator: Sarah Snow
Typesetter: Sharon Burkhardt
Manufacturing: Erin St. Hilaire

Printed in the United States of America on acid-free paper

2   3   4   5   6   7   BB   24   23   22   21
February 2021 Printing

CONTENTS

2 Literary Analysis

Fiction and Nonfiction

General

Messages and Themes

Style and Language

Illustrations

Book and Print Features

Nonfiction

Genre

Book and Print Features

Fiction

Genre

3   Strategies and Skills

4   Writing About Reading

Chapter 1

The Role of Reading Minilessons in Literacy Learning

THE GOAL OF ALL READING is the joyful, independent, and meaningful processing of a written text. As a competent reader, you become immersed in a fiction or nonfiction text; you read for a purpose; you become highly engaged with the plot, the characters, or the content. Focused on the experience of reading the text, you are largely unconscious of the thousands of actions happening in your brain that support the construction of meaning from the print that represents language. And, this is true whether the print is on a piece of paper or an electronic device. Your purpose may be to have vicarious experiences via works of fiction that take you to places far distant in time and space—even to worlds that do not and cannot exist! Or, your purpose may be to gather fuel for thinking (by using fiction or nonfiction) or it may be simply to enjoy the sounds of human language via literature and poetry. Most of us engage in the reading of multiple texts every day— some for work, some for pleasure, and some for practical guidance—but what we all have in common as readers is the ability to independently and simultaneously apply in-the-head systems of strategic actions that enable us to act on written texts.

Young readers are on a journey toward efficient processing of any texts they might like to attempt, and it is important every step of the way that they have successful experiences in independently reading those texts that are available at each point in time. In a literacy-rich classroom with a multitext approach, readers have the opportunity to hear written texts read aloud through interactive read-aloud, and so they build a rich treasure chest of known stories and nonfiction books that they can share as a classroom community. They understand and talk about these shared texts in ways that extend comprehension, vocabulary, and knowledge of the ways written texts are presented and organized. They participate with their classmates in the shared or performance reading of a common text so that they understand more and know how to act on written language. They experience tailored instruction in small guided reading groups using leveled texts precisely matched to their current abilities and needs for challenge. They stretch their thinking as they discuss a variety of complex texts in book clubs. They process fiction and nonfiction books with expert teacher support—always moving in the direction of more complex texts that will lift their reading abilities. *But it is in independent reading that they apply everything they have learned across all of those instructional contexts.* So the goal of all the reading instruction is to enable the reader to engage in effective, efficient, and meaningful processing of written text *every day* in the classroom. This is what it means to grow up literate in our schools.

Independent reading involves choices based on interests and tastes. Competent, independent readers are eager to talk and write about the books they have chosen and read on their own. They are gaining awareness of themselves as readers with favorite authors, illustrators, genres, and topics; their capacity for self-regulation is growing. The key to this kind of independent reading is making an explicit connection between all other instructional contexts—interactive read-aloud, shared reading, guided reading, and book clubs—and the reader's own independent work. Making these explicit links is the goal of minilessons. All teaching, support, and confirmation lead to the individual's successful, independent reading.

Making Learning Visible Through Minilessons

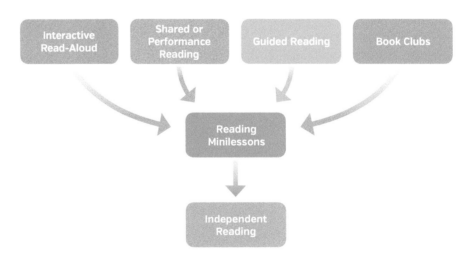

Figure 1-1: Various reading experiences supported by explicit instruction in reading minilessons lead to independent reading.

What Is a Reading Minilesson?

A reading minilesson is a concise and focused lesson on any aspect of effective reading that is important for students to explicitly understand at a particular point in time. It is an opportunity to build on all of the students' literacy experiences, make one important understanding visible, and hold learners accountable for applying it consistently in reading. These explicit minilessons place a strong instructional frame around independent reading.

A minilesson takes only a few minutes and usually involves the whole class. Because it builds on shared literary experiences that the students in your class have experienced prior to the lesson, you can quickly bring these shared texts to mind as powerful examples. Usually, you will teach only one focused lesson each day, but minilessons are logically organized to build on each other. Each minilesson is designed to engage your students in an inquiry process that leads to the discovery and understanding of a general principle that they can immediately apply. Most of the time, interactive read-aloud books that students have already heard serve as mentor texts from which they generalize the understanding. In this way, the reading minilesson provides a link between students' previous experience and their own independent reading (see Figure 1-1). The reading minilesson plays a key role in systematic, coherent teaching, all of which is directed toward each reader's developing competencies.

To help students connect ideas and develop deep knowledge and broad application of **principles**, related reading minilessons are grouped under **umbrella** concepts (see Chapter 3). An umbrella is the broad category within which several lessons are linked to each other; all minilessons contribute to the understanding of the umbrella concept. Within each umbrella, the lessons build on each other (see Figure 1-2). In each lesson, you will create an **anchor chart** with the students. This visual representation of the principle will be a useful reference tool as students learn new routines, encounter new texts, and draw and write about their reading in a reader's notebook.

Figure 1-2: Each minilesson focuses on a different aspect of the larger umbrella concept.

Four Types of Reading Minilessons

In this book, you will find 230 minilessons that are organized into four types:

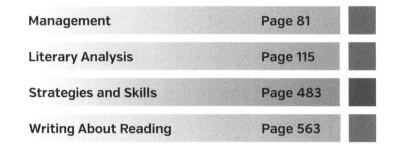

Management	Page 81
Literary Analysis	Page 115
Strategies and Skills	Page 483
Writing About Reading	Page 563

Figure 1-3: The minilessons in this book are organized into four sections.

Management Minilessons. These lessons include routines that are essential to the smooth functioning of the classroom and student-centered, independent literacy learning. The Management minilessons are designed to support students' development of independence and self-regulatory behavior. The Management minilessons for sixth graders help students learn to be respectful members of a classroom community of readers who share book recommendations, talk together about books, and write about reading on a regular basis. You'll also find minilessons that support students in reading independently at school and at home and that prepare them for living a reading life by developing their reading interests and preferences, challenging themselves to stretch and grow as readers, and dedicating time to read at home. Most of your minilessons at the beginning of the school year will focus on management. You will want to repeat any of the lessons as needed across the year. A guiding principle: teach a minilesson on anything that prevents the classroom from running smoothly and feeling like a strong community.

Literary Analysis Minilessons. These lessons build students' awareness of the characteristics of various genres and of the elements of fiction and nonfiction texts. Most of the mentor texts used to illustrate the principles are interactive read-aloud books that you have read previously to the class. However, a few mentor texts are independent reading books or guided reading books. When using these books, make sure that you have read them aloud to the whole class before the minilesson. Through these lessons, students learn how to apply new thinking to their independent reading; they also learn how to share their thinking with others.

Strategies and Skills Minilessons. Readers need to develop a robust body of in-the-head strategic actions for the efficient processing of texts. For example, they need to monitor their reading for accuracy and understanding, solve words (simple and complex), read fluently with phrasing, and constantly construct meaning. And, as they encounter more complex books in sixth grade, they need to use a variety of effective techniques when approaching texts that are difficult for them to read. The lessons not only support your students in monitoring their comprehension but also address the importance of focus and persistence in reading difficult texts. Teaching related to processing texts (decoding words, parsing language, and reading with accuracy and fluency) will best take place in guided reading and independent reading conferences. The general lessons included in this volume reinforce broad principles that every reader in your class may need to be reminded of from time to time. Included in Section Three: Strategies and Skills is Umbrella 7: Reading in Digital Environments, which is designed to help you teach students to effectively find online the information they need, evaluate its relevance and credibility, and stay focused while doing so. At sixth grade, when many students begin to spend more time reading in digital environments, these lessons provide essential teaching for the digital age.

Writing About Reading Minilessons. Throughout the sixth-grade year, students will have opportunities to use a reader's notebook to respond

Figure 1-4: Characteristics of effective minilessons

Characteristics of Effective Minilessons

Effective Minilessons . . .

- have a **clear rationale and a goal** to focus meaningful teaching
- are **relevant to the specific needs of readers** so that your teaching connects with the learners
- are **brief, concise, and to the point** for immediate application
- use **clear and specific language** to avoid talk that clutters learning
- stay **focused on a single idea** so students can apply the learning and build on it day after day
- build **one understanding on another** across several days instead of single isolated lessons
- use an **inquiry approach** whenever possible to support constructive learning
- often include **shared, high-quality mentor texts** that can be used as examples
- are **well paced** to engage and hold students' interest
- are **grouped into umbrellas** to foster depth in thinking and coherence across lessons
- provide time for students to **"try out" the new concept** before independent application
- engage students in **summarizing the new learning** and thinking about its application to their own work
- build **academic vocabulary** appropriate to the grade level
- help students become **better readers and writers**
- **foster community** through the development of shared language
- **can be assessed** as you observe students in authentic literacy activities to provide feedback on your teaching
- help **students understand what they are learning** how to do and how it helps them as readers

to what they read. These lessons introduce *Reader's Notebook: Advanced* (Fountas and Pinnell 2011) and help students use this important tool for independent literacy learning. Sixth graders will use a reader's notebook to keep track of their reading and writing (which will include new genres and forms of writing), keep a record of the principles taught in minilessons, write a weekly letter about the books they are reading, and write regularly about the thinking they do while reading.

The goal of all minilessons is to help students to think and act like readers and to build effective processing strategies while reading continuous text independently. Whether you are teaching Management lessons, Literary Analysis lessons, Strategies and Skills lessons, or Writing About Reading lessons, the characteristics of effective minilessons, listed in Figure 1-4, apply.

Constructing Anchor Charts for Effective Minilessons

Anchor charts are an essential part of each minilesson in this book (see Figure 1-5). They provide a way for you to capture the students' thinking during the lesson and reflect on the learning at the end. When you think about a chart, it helps you think through the big, important ideas and the language you will use in the minilesson. It helps you think about the sequence and your efficiency in getting down what is important.

Each minilesson in this book provides guidance for adding information to the chart. Read through each lesson carefully to know whether any parts of the chart should be prepared ahead or whether the chart is constructed during the lesson or at the end. After the lesson, the charts become resources for your students to use for reference throughout the day and on following days. They can revisit these charts as they apply the principles in reading, talking, and writing about books, or as they try out new routines in the classroom. You can refer to them during interactive read-aloud, shared and performance reading, reading conferences, guided reading, and book clubs. Anchor charts are a resource for students who need a visual representation of their learning.

Though your charts will be unique because they are built from the ideas your students share, you will want to consider some of the common characteristics among the charts we have included in this book. We have created one example in each lesson, but vary it as you see fit. When you create charts with students, consider the following:

  ▶ **Make your charts simple, clear, and organized.** The charts you create with your students should be clearly organized. Regardless of grade, it is important to keep them simple without a lot of dense text. Provide white space and write in dark, easy-to-read colors. You will notice that some of the sample charts are more conceptual. The idea is conveyed through a few words and a visual representation. Others use a grid to show how the principle is applied specifically across several texts.

▶ **Make your charts visually appealing and useful.** Many of the minilesson charts for sixth grade contain visual support, and this is especially helpful to English language learners. For example, you will see book covers, symbols, and drawings. Some students will benefit from the visuals to help them in reading the words on the chart and in understanding the concept. The drawings are intentionally simple to give you a quick model to draw yourself. English language learners might need to rely heavily on a graphic representation of the principle ideas. You might find it helpful to prepare these drawings on separate pieces of paper or sticky notes ahead of the lesson and tape or glue them on the chart as the students construct their understandings. This time-saving tip can also make the charts look more interesting and colorful, because certain parts stand out for the students.

▶ **Make your charts colorful.** Though the sample minilesson charts are colorful for the purpose of engagement or organization, be careful about the amount and types of color that you use. You may want to use color for specific purposes. For example, color can help you point out particular parts of the chart ("Look at the purple word on the chart") or support English language learners by providing a visual link to certain words or ideas. However, color can also be distracting if overused. Be thoughtful about when you choose to use colors to highlight an idea or a word on a chart so that students are supported in reading continuous text. Text that is broken up by a lot of different colors can be very distracting for readers. You will notice that the minilesson principle is usually written in black or another dark color across the top of the chart so that it stands out and is easily recognized as the focus of the lesson.

ELL CONNECTION

When you teach English language learners, you must adjust your teaching—not more teaching, but different teaching—to assure effective learning. Look for this symbol to see ways to support English language learners.

Figure 1-5: Constructing anchor charts with your students provides verbal and visual support for all learners.

Modern Fantasy
Noticings:

Always	Often
• Not originally passed down from generation to generation	• Characters with unusual traits (animals that behave like humans; characters who are eccentric, extraordinary, or magical)
• Original stories by known authors	
• People, events, and places that could not exist in the real world	• Universal truths or lessons about life
• Narrative structure that includes characters, plot, and setting	• Something unusual about the setting (imaginary things happening in the real world; imaginary, alternative, or parallel worlds)
• Conflict between good and evil	
• Magical elements (magical powers, objects, transformations)	• Hero on a quest or mission

Anchor charts support language growth in all students, and especially in English language learners. Conversation about the minilesson develops oral language and then connects that oral language to print when you write words on the chart and provide picture support. By constructing an anchor chart with your students, you provide print that is immediately accessible to them because they helped create it and have ownership of the language. After a chart is finished, revisit it as often as needed to reinforce not only the ideas but also the printed words.

Balancing Time and Inquiry

Most minilessons in this book follow an inquiry-based approach in which students discover and construct understandings of the minilesson principle. Constructing ideas through inquiry can take a lot of time if not properly structured and supported. Notice that most of the minilessons in this book start right away with focused examples from mentor texts rather than a general review of the books. Time can be lost by reviewing each mentor text used in a minilesson. Avoid starting the lesson by asking "Do you remember what this book is about?" or "What happened in this story?" Instead, choose examples from books your students know really well. Following are some helpful time-saving tips:

- Teach students to listen to one another to avoid wasting time by repeating the same information during the minilesson.

- Avoid repeating every student response yourself. Repeat (or ask the student to repeat) only if clarification is needed.

- Take a few responses and move on; you don't need to hear from everyone who has raised a hand. Over time, assure everyone has a chance to respond.

- Don't be afraid to ask a student to hold a thought for another time if it is not related or is only tangentially related. A lot of time can be lost when students share personal stories or go far away from the focus. Stay focused on building understanding of the minilesson principle and invite the sharing of personal experiences only when it is applicable to understanding the principle.

- Make sure the mentor text examples you choose are short and to the point. Usually you will not need to read more than a paragraph or a few sentences out of the mentor texts to conduct the inquiry.

- Assess your students' talk as they participate in the inquiry and omit examples you do not need. Each minilesson section generally has two or three examples. They are there if you need them, but you should judge from your students' participation whether you need to share every example or whether you can simply move on and ask students to have a try.

Using Reading Minilessons with Sixth-Grade Students

A minilesson brings to students' conscious attention a focused principle that will assist them in developing an effective, independent literacy processing system. It provides an opportunity for students to do the following:

▶ Respond to and act on a variety texts

▶ Become aware of and be able to articulate understandings about texts

▶ Engage in further inquiry to investigate the characteristics of texts

▶ Search for and learn to recognize patterns and characteristics of written texts

▶ Build new ideas on known ideas

▶ Think critically about the quality, authenticity, and credibility of texts

▶ Learn how to think about effective actions as they process texts

▶ Learn to manage their own reading lives

▶ Learn how to work together well in the classroom

▶ Learn to talk to others to share their thinking about books

▶ Learn how to write to communicate their thinking about books

Reading minilessons help readers build in-the-head processing systems. In the following chapters, you will explore how minilessons support students in using integrated systems of strategic actions for thinking *within*, *beyond*, and *about* many different kinds of texts and also how to use minilessons to build a community of readers who demonstrate a sense of agency and responsibility. You will also look in more depth at how minilessons fit within a design for literacy learning and within a multitext approach.

We conclude this chapter with some key terms we will use as we describe minilessons in the next chapters (see Figure 1-6). Keep these in mind so you can develop a common language to talk about the minilessons you teach.

Figure 1-6: Important terms used in *The Reading Minilessons Book*

Key Terms When Talking About Reading Minilessons

Umbrella	A group of minilessons, all of which are directed at different aspects of the same larger understanding.
Principle	A concise statement of the understanding students will need to learn and apply.
Mentor Text	A fiction or nonfiction text that offers a clear example of the principle toward which the minilesson is directed. Students will have previously heard and discussed the text.
Text Set	A group of fiction or nonfiction texts or a combination of fiction and nonfiction texts that, taken together, support a theme or exemplify a genre. Students will have previously heard all the texts referenced in a minilesson and had opportunities to make connections between them.
Anchor Chart	A visual representation of the lesson concept, using a combination of words and images. It is constructed by the teacher and students to summarize the learning and is used as a reference tool by the students.

Chapter 2

Using *The Literacy Continuum* to Guide the Teaching of Reading Minilessons

WE BELIEVE SCHOOLS SHOULD BE places where students read, think, talk, and write every day about relevant content that engages their hearts and minds. Learning deepens when students engage in thinking, talking, reading, and writing about texts across many different learning contexts and in whole-group, small-group, and individual instruction. Students who live a literate life in their classrooms have access to multiple experiences with texts throughout a day. As they participate in interactive read-aloud, shared and performance reading, guided reading, book clubs, and independent reading, they engage in the real work of reading and writing. They build a network of systems of strategic actions that allow them to think deeply within, beyond, and about text.

The networks of in-the-head strategic actions are inferred from observations of proficient readers, writers, and speakers. We have described these networks in *The Fountas & Pinnell Literacy Continuum: A Tool for Assessment, Planning, and Teaching* (Fountas and Pinnell 2017b). This volume presents detailed text characteristics and behaviors and understandings to notice, teach, and support for prekindergarten through middle school across eight instructional reading, writing, and language contexts. In sum, *The Literacy Continuum* describes proficiency in reading, writing, and language as it changes over grades and over levels.

Figure 2-1: Minilesson principles are drawn from the observable behaviors of proficient students as listed in *The Literacy Continuum*.

	INSTRUCTIONAL CONTEXT	BRIEF DEFINITION	DESCRIPTION OF THE CONTINUUM
1	Interactive Read-Aloud and Literature Discussion	Students engage in discussion with one another about a text that they have heard read aloud or one they have read independently.	• Year by year, grades PreK–8 • Genres appropriate to grades PreK–8 • Specific behaviors and understandings that are evidence of thinking within, beyond, and about the text
2	Shared and Performance Reading	Students read together or take roles in reading a shared text. They reflect the meaning of the text with their voices.	• Year by year, grades PreK–8 • Genres appropriate to grades PreK–8 • Specific behaviors and understandings that are evidence of thinking within, beyond, and about the text
3	Writing About Reading	Students extend their understanding of a text through a variety of writing genres and sometimes with illustrations.	• Year by year, grades PreK–8 • Genres/forms for writing about reading appropriate to grades PreK–8 • Specific evidence in the writing that reflects thinking within, beyond, and about the text
4	Writing	Students compose and write their own examples of a variety of genres, written for varying purposes and audiences.	• Year by year, grades PreK–8 • Genres/forms for writing appropriate to grades PreK–8 • Aspects of craft, conventions, and process that are evident in students' writing, grades PreK–8
5	Oral and Visual Communication	Students present their ideas through oral discussion and presentation.	• Year by year, grades PreK–8 • Specific behaviors and understandings related to listening and speaking, presentation
6	Technological Communication	Students learn effective ways of communicating and searching for information through technology; they learn to think critically about information and sources.	• Year by year, grades PreK–8 • Specific behaviors and understandings related to effective and ethical uses of technology
7	Phonics, Spelling, and Word Study	Students learn about the relationships of letters to sounds as well as the structure and meaning of words to help them in reading and spelling.	• Year by year, grades PreK–8 • Specific behaviors and understandings related to nine areas of understanding related to letters, sounds, and words, and how they work in reading and spelling
8	Guided Reading	Students read a teacher-selected text in a small group; the teacher provides explicit teaching and support for reading increasingly challenging texts.	• Level by level, A to Z • Genres appropriate to grades PreK–8 • Specific behaviors and understandings that are evidence of thinking within, beyond, and about the text • Specific suggestions for word work (drawn from the phonics and word analysis continuum)

Figure 2-2: From *The Literacy Continuum* (Fountas and Pinnell 2017b, 3)

Systems of Strategic Actions

The systems of strategic actions are represented in the wheel diagram shown in Figure 2-3 and on the inside back cover of this book. This model helps us think about the thousands of in-the-head processes that take place simultaneously and largely unconsciously when a competent reader processes a text. When the reader engages the neural network, he builds a literacy processing system over time that becomes increasingly sophisticated. Teaching in each instructional context is directed toward helping every reader expand these in-the-head networks across increasingly complex texts.

Four sections of *The Literacy Continuum* (Fountas and Pinnell 2017b)—Interactive Read-Aloud and Literature Discussion, Shared and Performance Reading, Guided Reading, and Writing About Reading—describe the specific competencies or goals of readers, writers, and language users:

Within the Text   (literal understanding achieved through searching for and using information, monitoring and self-correcting, solving words, maintaining fluency, adjusting, and summarizing) The reader gathers the important information from the fiction or nonfiction text.

Beyond the Text   (predicting; making connections with personal experience, content knowledge, and other texts; synthesizing new information; and inferring what is implied but not stated) The reader brings understanding to the processing of a text, reaching for ideas or concepts that are implied but not explicitly stated.

About the Text   (analyzing or critiquing the text) The reader looks at a text to analyze, appreciate, or evaluate its construction, logic, literary elements, or quality.

The Literacy Continuum is the foundation for all the minilessons. The minilesson principles come largely from the behaviors and understandings in the Interactive Read-Aloud continuum, but some are selected from the Shared and Performance Reading; Writing About Reading; Oral and Visual Communication; Technological Communication; Phonics, Spelling, and Word Study; and Guided Reading continua. In addition, we have included minilessons related to working together in a classroom community to assure that effective literacy instruction can take place. In most lessons, you will see a direct link to the goals from *The Literacy Continuum* called Continuum Connection.

As you ground your teaching in support of each reader's development of the systems of strategic actions, it is important to remember that these actions are never applied one at a time. A reader who comprehends a text engages these actions rapidly and simultaneously and largely without conscious attention. Your intentional talk and conversations in the various instructional contexts should support students in engaging and building their processing systems while they respond authentically as readers and enjoy the text.

Figure 2-3: All of your teaching will be grounded in support of each reader's development of the systems of strategic actions (see the inside back cover for a larger version of the Systems of Strategic Actions wheel).

Relationship of Intentional Talk to Reading Minilessons

Intentional talk refers to the language you use that is consciously directed toward the goal of instruction. We have used the term *facilitative talk* to refer to the language that the teacher uses to support student learning in specific ways. When you plan for intentional talk in your interactive read-aloud and shared and performance reading experiences, think about the meaning of the text and what your students will need to think about to fully understand and enjoy the story. You might select certain pages where you want to stop and have students turn and talk about their reading so they can engage in sharing their thinking with each other. The interactive read-aloud and shared and performance reading sections of *The Literacy Continuum* can help you plan what to talk about. For example, when you read a book like *Babu's Song*, you would likely invite talk about the characters' feelings and motivations, discuss the author's message, and analyze the author's use of symbolism (see Figure 2-4). When you read a text set of expository nonfiction, you might invite students to comment on the significance of the topic, how the author organized the information, and what they think is the theme of the book.

As you talk about texts together, embed brief and specific teaching in your read-aloud lessons while maintaining a focus on enjoyment and support for your students in gaining the meaning of the whole text. In preparation, mark a few places with sticky notes and a comment or question to invite thinking. Later, when you teach explicit minilessons about concepts such as theme, the use of symbolism, and text organization, your students will already have background knowledge to bring to the minilesson and will be ready to explore how the principle works across multiple texts.

In reading minilessons, you explicitly teach the principles you have already embedded in the students' previous experiences with text in these different instructional contexts. Intentional talk within each context prepares a foundation for this explicit focus. Through each interactive read-aloud and shared or performance reading experience, you build a large body of background knowledge, academic vocabulary, and a library of shared texts to draw on as you explore specific literary principles. You will read more about this multitext approach in Chapter 9.

Figure 2-4: Mark a few pages to invite students to think about during interactive read-aloud. Later, you might teach an explicit minilesson on one of the concepts introduced during the interactive read-aloud.

Chapter 3 **Understanding the Umbrellas and Minilessons**

Minilessons in this book are organized into conceptual groups, called "umbrellas," in which groups of principles are explored in sequence, working toward larger concepts. Within each section (Management, Literary Analysis, etc.), the umbrellas are numbered in sequence and are often referred to by *U* plus the number, for example, U1 for the first umbrella. A suggested sequence of umbrellas is presented in Figure 8-2 to assist you in planning across the year, but the needs of your students always take priority.

Umbrella Front Page

Each umbrella has an introductory page on which the minilessons in the umbrella are listed and directions are provided to help you prepare to present the minilessons within the umbrella (see Figure 3-1). The introductory page is designed to provide an overview of how the umbrella is organized and the texts from *Fountas & Pinnell Classroom™ Interactive Read-Aloud Collection, Independent Reading Collection, Guided Reading Collection,* and *Book Clubs Collection* that are suggested for the lessons (Fountas and Pinnell 2020). In addition, we provide types of texts you might select if you are not using the books referenced in the lessons. Understanding how the umbrella is designed and how the minilessons fit together will help you keep your lessons focused, concise, and brief. Using familiar mentor texts that you have previously read and enjoyed with your students will help you streamline the lessons in the umbrella. You will not need to spend a lot of time rereading large sections of the texts because the students will already know them well.

When you teach lessons in an umbrella, you help students make connections between concepts and texts and help them develop deeper understandings. A rich context such as this one is particularly helpful for English language learners. Grouping lessons into umbrellas supports English language learners in developing shared vocabulary and language around a single and important area of knowledge.

Following the umbrella front page, you will see a series of two-page lesson spreads that include several parts.

ELL CONNECTION

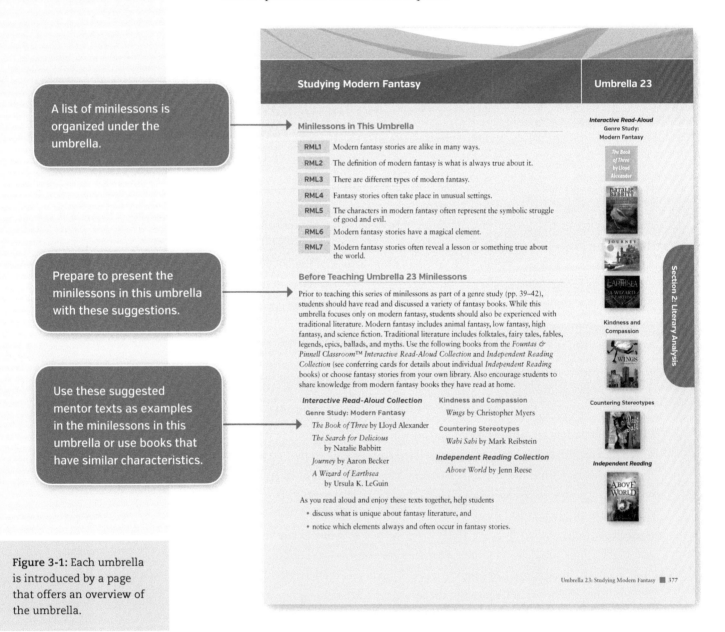

A list of minilessons is organized under the umbrella.

Prepare to present the minilessons in this umbrella with these suggestions.

Use these suggested mentor texts as examples in the minilessons in this umbrella or use books that have similar characteristics.

Figure 3-1: Each umbrella is introduced by a page that offers an overview of the umbrella.

Studying Modern Fantasy   **Umbrella 23**

Minilessons in This Umbrella

RML1   Modern fantasy stories are alike in many ways.

RML2   The definition of modern fantasy is what is always true about it.

RML3   There are different types of modern fantasy.

RML4   Fantasy stories often take place in unusual settings.

RML5   The characters in modern fantasy often represent the symbolic struggle of good and evil.

RML6   Modern fantasy stories have a magical element.

RML7   Modern fantasy stories often reveal a lesson or something true about the world.

Before Teaching Umbrella 23 Minilessons

Prior to teaching this series of minilessons as part of a genre study (pp. 39–42), students should have read and discussed a variety of fantasy books. While this umbrella focuses only on modern fantasy, students should also be experienced with traditional literature. Modern fantasy includes animal fantasy, low fantasy, high fantasy, and science fiction. Traditional literature includes folktales, fairy tales, fables, legends, epics, ballads, and myths. Use the following books from the *Fountas & Pinnell Classroom™ Interactive Read-Aloud Collection* and *Independent Reading Collection* (see conferring cards for details about individual *Independent Reading* books) or choose fantasy stories from your own library. Also encourage students to share knowledge from modern fantasy books they have read at home.

Interactive Read-Aloud Collection

Genre Study: Modern Fantasy
The Book of Three by Lloyd Alexander
The Search for Delicious by Natalie Babbitt
Journey by Aaron Becker
A Wizard of Earthsea by Ursula K. LeGuin

Kindness and Compassion
Wings by Christopher Myers

Countering Stereotypes
Wabi Sabi by Mark Reibstein

Independent Reading Collection
Above World by Jenn Reese

As you read aloud and enjoy these texts together, help students

* discuss what is unique about fantasy literature, and
* notice which elements always and often occur in fantasy stories.

Interactive Read-Aloud
Genre Study:
Modern Fantasy

Kindness and Compassion

Countering Stereotypes

Independent Reading

Section 2: Literary Analysis

Two-Page Minilesson Spread

Each minilesson includes a two-page spread that consists of several parts (see Figure 3-2). The section (for example, Literary Analysis), umbrella number (for example, U1), and minilesson number (for example, RML1) are listed at the top to help you locate the lesson you are looking for. Accordingly, the code LA.U1.RML1 identifies the first minilesson in the first umbrella of the Literary Analysis section.

Principle, Goal, Rationale

The **Principle** describes the understanding the students will need to learn and apply. The idea of the principle is based on *The Literacy Continuum* (Fountas and Pinnell 2017b), but the language of the principle has been carefully crafted to be precise, focused on a single idea, and accessible to students. We have placed the principle at the top of the lesson on the left-hand page so you have a clear idea of the understanding you will help students construct through the example texts used in the lesson. Although we have crafted the language to make it appropriate for the age group, you may shape the language in a slightly different way to reflect the way your students use language. Be sure that the principle is stated simply and clearly and check for understanding. Once that is accomplished, say it the same way every time.

The **Goal** of the minilesson is stated in the top section of the lesson, as is the **Rationale**, to help you understand what this particular minilesson will do and why it may be important for the students in your classroom. In this beginning section, you will also find suggestions for specific behaviors and understandings to observe as you assess students' learning during or after the minilesson.

Minilesson

In the **Minilesson** section of the lesson, you will find an example lesson for teaching the understanding, or principle. The example includes suggestions for teaching and the use of precise language and open-ended questions to engage students in a brief, focused inquiry. Effective minilessons include, when possible, the process of inquiry so students can actively construct their understanding from concrete examples, because *telling* is not *teaching*. Instead of simply being told what they need to know, students get inside the understanding by engaging in the thinking themselves. In the inquiry process, invite students to look at a group of texts that were read previously (for example, stories in which characters change). Choose the books carefully so they represent the characteristics students are learning about. They will have knowledge of these texts because they have previously experienced them. Invite them to talk about what they notice across all the books. As students

A Closer Look at a Reading Minilesson

The **Goal** of the minilesson is clearly identified, as is the **Rationale**, to support your understanding of what this particular minilesson is and why it may be important for the students in your classroom.

The **Reading Minilesson Principle**—a brief statement that describes the understanding students will need to learn and apply.

This code identifies this minilesson as the fourth reading minilesson (RML4) in the twenty-third umbrella (U23) in the Literary Analysis (LA) section.

Specific behaviors and understandings to observe as you assess students' learning after presenting the minilesson.

Academic Language and **Important Vocabulary** that students will need to understand in order to access the learning in the minilesson.

Suggested language to use when teaching the minilesson principle.

RML4
LA.U23.RML4

Studying Modern Fantasy

You Will Need

- several familiar fantasy stories that have something unusual about the setting, such as the following:
  - *The Book of Three* by Lloyd Alexander and *Journey* by Aaron Becker from Text Set: Genre Study: Modern Fantasy
  - *Above World* by Jenn Reese, from *Independent Reading Collection*
- chart paper prepared with three columns and headings: *Title, Setting(s), What do you notice about the setting?*
- markers
- modern fantasies students are reading or have read
- sticky notes

Academic Language / Important Vocabulary

- modern fantasy
- genre
- setting
- real world
- imaginary world
- parallel world

Continuum Connection

- Notice science fiction and fantasy settings: e.g., alternative or secondary world, futuristic setting, alternative histories, animal kingdom, fictional planet, pseudo-medieval setting [p. 80]

Reading Minilesson Principle
Fantasy stories often take place in unusual settings.

Goal
Notice unusual settings in fantasy stories.

Rationale
When students understand that the setting in a fantasy story can be real or imagined, they become aware that realistic elements coincide with fantasy elements. This enables them to engage fully with the story and understand the connection between setting, characters, and plot.

Assess Learning
Observe students when they read and discuss fantasy stories and notice if there is evidence of new learning based on the goal of this minilesson.

- Do they notice and discuss the setting in fantasy stories?
- Are they able to determine which settings are real and which are imagined?
- Can they discuss the interconnectedness of setting with characters and plot?
- Do they use the terms *modern fantasy, genre, setting, real world, imaginary world,* and *parallel world*?

Minilesson

To help students think about the minilesson principle, engage them in noticing both the real and the unusual settings of familiar fantasy stories. Here is an example.

- Show *The Book of Three.*
  What is the setting of *The Book of Three?* What do you notice about it?
- Guide the conversation so that students note that it is a magical place.
- Begin a chart that shows what is unusual about the setting and how it influences the story.
- Repeat the activity with *Journey.* Continue adding to the chart.
  Modern fantasy writers create a world in which imaginary things happen in a real setting, or they create imaginary or parallel worlds that follow different rules of physics. Why must the setting in a modern fantasy make readers suspend disbelief and accept something that couldn't actually happen?
- You may want to use some prompts as you discuss setting, such as:
  - *How does the story world differ from your own real world?*
  - *How has the author altered the secondary world?*
  - *Are there any clues that show time has been altered?*

Figure 3-2: All the parts of a single minilesson are contained on a two-page spread.

RML4
LA.U23.RML4

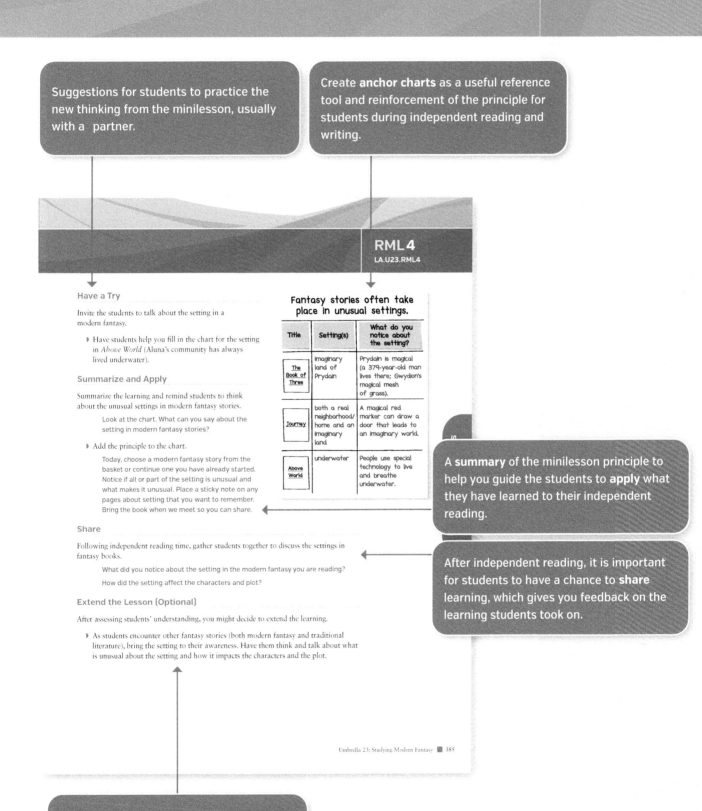

Have a Try

Invite the students to talk about the setting in a modern fantasy.

▸ Have students help you fill in the chart for the setting in *Above World* (Aluna's community has always lived underwater).

Summarize and Apply

Summarize the learning and remind students to think about the unusual settings in modern fantasy stories.

Look at the chart. What can you say about the setting in modern fantasy stories?

▸ Add the principle to the chart.

Today, choose a modern fantasy story from the basket or continue one you have already started. Notice if all or part of the setting is unusual and what makes it unusual. Place a sticky note on any pages about setting that you want to remember. Bring the book when we meet so you can share.

Share

Following independent reading time, gather students together to discuss the settings in fantasy books.

What did you notice about the setting in the modern fantasy you are reading?

How did the setting affect the characters and plot?

Extend the Lesson (Optional)

After assessing students' understanding, you might decide to extend the learning.

▸ As students encounter other fantasy stories (both modern fantasy and traditional literature), bring the setting to their awareness. Have them think and talk about what is unusual about the setting and how it impacts the characters and the plot.

Fantasy stories often take place in unusual settings.

Title	Setting(s)	What do you notice about the setting?
The Book of Three	imaginary land of Prydain	Prydain is magical (a 379-year-old man lives there; Gwydion's magical mesh of grass).
Journey	both a real neighborhood/ home and an imaginary land	A magical red marker can draw a door that leads to an imaginary world.
Above World	underwater	People use special technology to live and breathe underwater.

Umbrella 23: Studying Modern Fantasy ■ 385

explore the text examples using your questions and supportive comments as a guide, co-construct the anchor chart, creating an organized and visual representation of the students' noticings and understandings. (See the section on anchor charts in Chapter 1 for more information on chart creation.) From this exploration and the discussion surrounding it, students derive the principle, which is then written at the top of the chart.

Throughout this book, you will find models and examples of the anchor charts you co-construct with students. Of course, the charts you create will be unique because they reflect your students' thinking. Learning is more powerful and enjoyable for students when they actively search for the meaning, find patterns, talk about their understandings, and share in the co-construction of the chart. Students need to form networks of understanding around the concepts related to literacy and to be constantly looking for connections for themselves.

ELL CONNECTION

Creating a need to produce language is an important principle in building language, and reading minilessons provide many opportunities for students to express their thoughts in language and to communicate with others. The inquiry approach found in these lessons invites more student talk than teacher talk, and that can be both a challenge and an opportunity for you as you work with English language learners. In our previous texts, we have written that Marie Clay (1991) urges us to be "strong minded" about holding meaningful conversations even when they are difficult. In *Becoming Literate,* she warns us that it is "misplaced sympathy" to do the talking for those who are developing and learning language. Instead, she recommends "concentrating more sharply, smiling more rewardingly and spending more time in genuine conversation." Building talk routines, such as turn and talk, into your reading minilessons can be very helpful in providing these opportunities for English language learners in a safe and supportive way.

When you ask students to think about the minilesson principle across several texts that they have previously listened to and discussed, they are more engaged and able to participate because they know these texts and can shift to a new way of thinking about them. Using familiar texts is particularly important for English language learners. When you select examples for a reading minilesson, choose texts that you know were particularly engaging for the English language learners in your classroom. Besides choosing accessible, familiar texts, it is important to provide plenty of wait and think time. For example, you might say, "Let's think about that for a minute" before calling for responses.

When working with English language learners, value partially correct responses. Look for what the child knows about the concept instead of focusing on faulty grammar or language errors. Model appropriate language use in your responses, but do not correct a child who is attempting to use language to learn it. You might also provide an oral sentence frame to get the student response started. Accept variety in pronunciation and intonation, remembering that the more students speak, read, and write, the more they will take on the understanding of grammatical patterns and the complex intonation patterns that reflect meaning in English.

Have a Try

Because students will be asked to apply the new thinking on their own during independent literacy work, it is important to give students a chance to apply it with a partner or a small group while still in the whole-group setting. **Have a Try** is designed to be brief, but it offers you an opportunity to gather information on how well students understand the minilesson principle. In many minilessons, students are asked to apply the new thinking to another concrete example from a familiar book. In Management lessons, students quickly practice the new routine that they will be asked to do independently. You will often add further thinking to the chart after the students have had the chance to try out their new learning.

The Have a Try portion of the reading minilesson is particularly important for English language learners. Besides providing repetition and allowing for the gradual release of responsibility, it gives English language learners a safe place to try out the new idea before sharing it with the whole group. These are a few suggestions for how you might support students during the Have a Try portion of the lesson:

 **ELL CONNECTION**

- Pair students with specific partners in a way that will allow for a balance of talk between the two.

- Spend time teaching students how to turn and talk. (In Section One: Management, MGT.U2.RML1, addresses the turn and talk routine.) Teach students how to provide wait time for one another, invite the other partner into the conversation, and take turns.

- Provide concrete examples to discuss so that students are clear about what they need to talk about and are able to stay grounded in the text. English language learners will feel more confident if they are able to talk about a text that they know really well.

- Observe partnerships involving English language learners and provide support as needed.

- When necessary, you might find it helpful to provide the oral language structure or language stem for how you want your students to share. For example, ask them to start with the phrase "I think the character feels . . ." and to rehearse the language structure a few times before turning and talking.

Summarize and Apply

This part of the lesson consists of two parts: summarizing the learning and applying the learning to independent reading.

The **summary** is a brief but essential part of the lesson. It provides a time to bring together all of the learning that has taken place through the inquiry and to help students think about its application and relevance to their own learning. It is best to involve the students in constructing the minilesson principle with you. Ask them to reflect on the chart you have created together and talk about what they have learned that day. In simple, clear language, shape the suggestions. Other times, you may decide to help summarize the new learning to keep the lesson short and allow enough time for the students to apply it independently. Whether you state the principle or co-construct it with your students, summarize the learning in a way that makes the principle generative and applicable to future texts the students will read.

After the summary, the students **apply** their new understandings to their independent reading. However, before students begin their independent reading, let them know what you expect them to discuss or bring for the group sharing session so they can think about it as they read. This way, they know they are accountable for trying out the new thinking in their own books and are expected to share upon their return.

Students engaged in independent reading will choose books from the classroom library. These are genuine choices based on their interests and previous experiences. Book levels are not used in the classroom library. Some teachers choose to have students shop for books in the library at specific times and have them keep selected books in their personal literacy boxes. When you designate certain times for browsing, you maximize students' time spent on reading and are able to carve out time to assist with book selection. When needed, plan to supply independent reading books that will provide opportunities to apply the principle. For example, if you teach the umbrella on studying biographies, make sure students have access to biographies. You will notice that in some of the lessons, students are invited to read from a certain basket of books in the classroom library to ensure that there are opportunities to apply their new learning.

We know that when students first take on new learning, they often overgeneralize or overapply the new learning at the exclusion of some of the other things they have learned. The best goal when students are reading any book is to enjoy it, process it effectively, and gain its full meaning. Always encourage meaningful and authentic engagement with text. You don't want students so focused and determined to apply the minilesson principle that they make superficial connections to text that actually distract from their understanding of the book. You will likely find the opportunity in many reading conferences, guided reading lessons, or book club meetings to reinforce the minilesson understanding.

In our professional book, *Teaching for Comprehending and Fluency: Thinking, Talking, and Writing About Reading, K–8* (Fountas and Pinnell 2006), we write, "Whenever we instruct readers, we mediate (or change) the meaning they derive from their reading. Yet we must offer instruction that helps readers expand their abilities. There is value in drawing readers' attention to important aspects of the text that will enrich their understanding, but we need to understand that using effective reading strategies is not like exercising one or two muscles at a time. The system must always work together as an integrated whole." The invitation to apply the new learning must be clear enough to have students try out new ways of thinking, but "light" enough to allow room for readers to expand and express their own thinking. The application of the minilesson principle should not be thought of as an exercise or task that needs to be completed but instead as an invitation to a deeper, more meaningful response to the events or ideas in a text.

While students are reading independently, you may be meeting with small groups for guided reading or book clubs, rotating to observe students working independently, or conferring with individuals. If you have a reading conference, you can take the opportunity to reinforce the minilesson principle. We have provided two conferring record sheets (choose whichever form suits your purpose) for you to download from the online resources (see Figure 3-3) so that you can make notes about your individual conferences with students. You can use your notes to plan the content of future minilessons.

Figure 3-3: Choose one of these downloadable forms to record your observations of students' behaviors and understandings during reading conferences. Visit **resources.fountasandpinnell.com** to download this and all other online resources.

Teacher Ms. Hein   Grade 6   Week of November 5

Conferring Record 1

Minilesson Focus Studying Biography (LA U14)

Student	Monday	Tuesday	Wec
Henry		Who Was Blackbeard? Needs support critiquing authenticity and author credentials.	
Ryan			Gross about Ages. this tin Plans t biograp Middle
Aisha	Albert Einstein. Talked about the facts the author included and inferred why.		
Darius			
Tatiana			
Hasan			

Teacher Ms. Williams   Grade 6   Week of April 1–April 5

Conferring Record 2

Minilesson Focus Exploring Conflict in Fiction Texts (LA U28)

Student	Comments/Observations
Louis	The Thing About Jellyfish. Discussed whether the conflict was human vs. nature or human vs. self.
Miguel	Tracking Bigfoot. Critiqued the author's credentials.
Genevieve	The Truth About Stacey. Compared the Baby-sitters Club graphic novels to the chapter books. Loves the graphic novels.
Maeve	The War That Saved My Life. Discussed the two conflicts: war and the human vs. human conflict between the girl and her mother.
Michael	What Came from the Stars. Identified some of the elements of fantasy in this book.
Pia	Out of My Mind. Expressed empathy for main character but struggling to articulate the deeper messages of the book.
Jamai	The Omnivore's Dilemma. Connecting book to his own life—said it is making him think about his food choices.
Esperanza	Poached. Discussed the term "red herring" as it pertains to mystery. Identified a "red herring" in Poached.
Liam	The Gross Science of Bad Smells. Loving the series. Discussed taking a break from NF and trying some fiction; he might try HF next.
Leah	Hour of the Bees. Needs support identifying different types of conflict in fiction.
Liam	Home of the Brave. Read a section aloud. Needs support with intonation.
Marcos	How They Croaked. Talked about how the author conveys information and critiqued the text structure.

Share

At the end of the independent work time, students come together and have the opportunity to **share** their learning with the entire group. Group share provides an opportunity for you to revisit, expand, and deepen understanding of the minilesson principle as well as to assess learning. In Figure 3-2, you will notice that in the Share section we provide suggestions for how to engage students in sharing their discoveries. Often, students are asked to bring a book to share and to explain how they applied the minilesson principle in their independent reading. Sometimes we suggest sharing with the whole group, but other times we suggest that sharing take place among pairs, triads, or quads. As you observe and talk to students engaged in independent reading, shared and performance reading, guided reading, or book clubs, you can assess whether they are easily able to apply the minilesson principle. Use this information to inform how you plan to share. If only a few students were able to apply the minilesson to their reading (for example, if the minilesson applies to a particular book feature or genre characteristic that not all students came across in their books during independent reading), you might ask only a few students to share. Whereas if you observe most of the class applying the principle, you might have them share in pairs or small groups.

As a general guideline, in addition to revisiting the reading minilesson principle at the end of independent reading time, you might also ask students to share what they thought or wrote about their reading that day. For example, a student might share part of a letter he wrote about his reading. Another student might share a memorable line from a book or celebrate reaching the goal of trying a book in a different genre. The Share is a wonderful way to bring the community of readers and writers back together to expand their understandings and celebrate their learning at the end of the workshop time.

There are some particular accommodations you might want to consider to support English language learners during sharing:

 ELL CONNECTION

▶ Ask English language learners to share in pairs before sharing with the whole group.

▶ Use individual conferences and guided reading to help students rehearse the language structure they might use to share their application of the minilesson principle to the text they have read.

▶ Teach the entire class respectful ways to listen to peers and model how to give their peers time to express their thoughts. Many of the minilessons in the Management section will be useful for developing a peaceful, safe and supportive community of readers and writers.

Extending the Lesson

At the end of each lesson we offer suggestions for **extending** the learning of the principle. Sometimes extending the learning involves repeating the lesson over time with different examples. Sixth graders might need to experience some of the concepts more than once before they are able to transfer actions to their independent reading. Using the questions in the Assess Learning section will help you to determine if you need to repeat the lesson, move on, or revisit the lesson (perhaps in a slightly different way) in the future. Other suggestions for extending the lesson include applying the minilesson concept within other contexts, performing readers' theater, or writing and drawing in response to reading. In several cases, the suggestions will refer to a reader's notebook (see Chapter 7 for more information about writing about reading and Section Four: Writing About Reading for minilessons that teach ways to use a reader's notebook).

Umbrella Back Page

Assessment and Link to Writing

Following the minilessons in each umbrella, you will see the final umbrella page that includes **Assessment**, sometimes **Link to Writing**, and **Reader's Notebook**. The last page of each umbrella, shown in Figure 3-4, provides suggestions for assessing the learning that has taken place through the minilessons in the entire umbrella. The information you gain from observing what the students can already do, almost do, and not yet do will help inform the selection of the next umbrella you teach. (See Chapter 8 for more information about assessment and the selection of umbrellas.) In many umbrellas, this last page also provides a Link to Writing. In some cases, this section provides further suggestions for writing about reading in a reader's notebook. However, in most cases, the Link to Writing provides ideas for how students might try out some of the new learning in their own writing. For example, after learning about text features in nonfiction, you might want to teach students how to include one or more of the features, such as an infographic or sidebar, in their own nonfiction writing.

You will also find a section titled Reader's Notebook, which describes how to access and print a copy of the minilesson principles for your students to glue in a reader's notebook to refer to as needed.

Gain important information by **assessing** students' understandings as they apply and share their learning of a minilesson principle. Observe and then follow up with individuals or address the principle during guided reading.

Assessment

After you have taught the minilessons in this umbrella, observe students as they talk and write about their reading across instructional contexts: interactive read-aloud, independent reading, guided reading, shared reading, and book club. Use *The Literacy Continuum* (Fountas and Pinnell 2017) to guide observation of students' reading and writing behaviors.

▶ What evidence do you have of new understandings related to modern fantasy?

- Can students describe ways that modern fantasy stories are alike?
- Can they provide a definition of the modern fantasy genre?
- Are they able to categorize different types of modern fantasy stories?
- Do they understand that modern fantasy stories often have unusual settings?
- Are they recognizing recurring motifs in modern fantasy, such as the struggle between good and evil, magical elements, and universal truths?
- Are they using academic language, such as *modern fantasy, genre, animal fantasy, low fantasy, high fantasy, science fiction,* and *motif*?

▶ In what other ways, beyond the scope of this umbrella, are students talking about fiction genres?

- Are students talking about types of fiction, such as historical fiction?

Use your observations to determine the next umbrella you will teach. You may also consult Minilessons Across the Year (pp. 61–64) for guidance.

Read and Revise

After completing the steps in the genre study process, help students read and revise their definition of the genre based on their new understandings.

▶ **Before:** Modern fantasy stories are written by known authors and are about people, places, and events that cannot exist in the real world.

▶ **After:** Modern fantasy stories are original stories written by known authors. They are about people, places, and events that cannot exist in the real world. They typically have magical elements and show a struggle between good and evil.

Reader's Notebook

When this umbrella is complete, provide a copy of the minilesson principles (see resources.fountasandpinnell.com) for students to glue in the reader's notebook (in the Minilessons section if using *Reader's Notebook: Advanced* [Fountas and Pinnell 2011]), so they can refer to the information as needed.

Wrap up the umbrella by engaging students in an activity that uses their expanded understanding of the umbrella concept.

Figure 3-4: The final page of each umbrella offers ways to wrap up new learning from the umbrella: questions to use in assessing students' learning, sometimes suggestions for linking new learning to writing, sometimes suggestions for revising the definition of a genre, and a reference to online resources for downloading the umbrella's principles.

Online Resources for Planning

We have provided examples in this book of how to engage your sixth-grade students in developing the behaviors and understandings of competent readers, as described in *The Literacy Continuum* (Fountas and Pinnell 2017b). Remember that you can modify the suggested lesson or construct new lessons using the goals of the continuum as needed for your particular students. The form shown in Figure 3-5 will help you plan each part of a new minilesson. For example, you can design a minilesson that uses a different set of example texts from the ones suggested in this book or you can teach a concept in a way that fits the current needs of your students. The form shown in Figure 3-6 will help you plan which minilessons to teach over a period of time so as to address the goals that are important for your students. You can find both forms at **resources.fountasandpinnell.com**.

Teacher Mr. Randolph   Grade 6   Year

Planning a Minilesson

Umbrella:	LA U14 Studying Biography
Minilesson Principle:	Biographers choose to include facts that reveal something important about the subject's personality traits and motivations.
Continuum Goal(s):	Notice that a biography is built around significant events, problems to overcome, and the subject's decisions (pp. 591, 603, 615)

Minilesson:	**Examples:** Show *Marvelous Mattie* and ask: 1. How would you describe Margaret Knight? 2. What examples does the biographer include that show you what Mattie was like? 3. What do those facts tell you about her personality traits and motivations?	**Chart:** On chart, identify subject's traits and how they are revealed by biographer.

Principle

Title and subject	What is subject like?	How is this revealed?

| Have a Try |
| Summarize and Apply |
| Share |

© 2020 by Irene C. Fountas and Gay Su Pinnell. Port...

Figure 3-5: Use this downloadable form to plan your own minilessons.

Teacher Ms. Vahle   Grade 6   Year

Curriculum Plan: Reading Minilessons

Month April	Umbrella/Minilesson	Comments/Observations	✓ or Date
Week 1	LA U24: Studying Epic Tales RML1: noticing characteristics of epics RML2: creating definition of epics RML3: hero's quest RML4: epic tales reflect cultural values RML5: written as poetry or in a poetic way	• U24: Strong understanding of the characteristics of epics. Able to develop a clear definition.	4/8 4/9 4/10 4/11 4/12
Week 2	LA U11: Studying Illustrators RML1: illustrator study—K. Y. Craft LA U25: Understanding Myths RML1: characteristics of myths RML2: written to explain things RML3: gods and goddesses	• U25 RML3: Check in with Willem and Celia—are they understanding the cultural and symbolic elements of myths?	4/15 4/17 4/18 4/19
Week 3	LA U23 Studying Modern Fantasy RML1: characterisitcs of modern fantasy RML2: definition of modern fantasy RML3: different types of modern fantasy RML4: unusual settings	• RML3: Need more examples of high and low fantasy; repeat with different examples.	4/29 4/30 5/1–2 5/3
Week 4	LA U23 Studying Modern Fantasy (continued) RML5: struggle between good and evil RML6: magical elements RML7: reveals a lesson or truth LA U28 Exploring Conflict in Fiction Texts RML1: people vs. nature	• RML 7: Check in with Dina and Calvin.	5/6 5/7 5/8 5/10

© 2020 by Irene C. Fountas and Gay Su Pinnell. Portsmouth, NH: Heinemann. All rights reserved.

Figure 3-6: Use this downloadable form to make notes about specific minilessons for future planning.

Chapter 3   27

Chapter 4 Management Minilessons: Building a Literacy Community

MANAGEMENT MINILESSONS FOCUS ON ROUTINES for thinking and talking about reading and working together in the classroom. Good management allows you to teach effectively and efficiently; use these lessons to create an orderly, busy classroom in which students know what is expected as well as how to behave responsibly and respectfully in a community of learners. They learn how the classroom library is organized, how to choose books and return them, how to use their voices in the classroom, and how to engage in independent reading. You can use these minilessons to teach your students the routines for independent reading, how to use and return materials, and how to solve problems independently. Classroom management is important in implementing a multitext approach to literacy learning. You want your students to grow in the ability to regulate their own behavior and to sustain reading and writing for increasing periods of time.

Altogether, there are thirteen minilessons in the Management section for your use. Teach the Management minilessons in the order that fits your class, or consult the suggested sequence in Figure 8-2. You may need to reteach some Management minilessons across the year, especially as students encounter more complex situations and routines. Sometimes when there is a schedule change or other disruption in classroom operations, a refresher Management minilesson will be needed. Any management problem in your classroom should be addressed through a Management minilesson.

The Physical Space

Before students enter your classroom, prepare the physical space in a way that provides maximum support for learning (see Figure 4-1). Remember that this relatively small room must support the productive work of some 20 to 30 people, 6 or 7 hours a day, 180-plus days a year. Each Management umbrella will help your students become acquainted with different parts of the classroom, which will make them feel secure and at home. Make sure that the classroom is:

▶ **Welcoming and Inviting.** Pleasing colors and a variety of furniture will help. There is no need for commercially published posters or slogans. The room can be filled with the work that students have produced beginning on day one. The classroom library should be as inviting as a bookstore or a public library. Place books in baskets and tubs on shelves to make the front covers of books visible and accessible for easy browsing. Clear out old, dated, poor-quality, inaccurate, or tattered books that students never choose. Clearly label (or, even better, have students label) the tub or basket with the topic, author, series, genre, or illustrator. Add new books to the library all year and retire books that are no longer of interest or that perpetuate stereotypes and inaccuracies. Once you have taught LA.U5.RML1, you can use the list to evaluate the classroom library collection for diversity and fair representation.

▶ **Organized for Easy Use.** The first thing you might want to do is to take out everything you do not need. Clutter increases stress and noise. Using scattered and hard-to-find materials increases student dependence on the teacher. Consider keeping supplies for reading, writing, and word study in designated areas. For example, some teachers designate a writing area where they keep paper, highlighters, staplers, etc. Every work area should be clearly organized with necessary, labeled materials and nothing else. The work that takes place in each area should be visible at a glance;

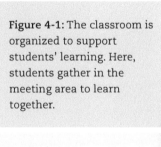

Figure 4-1: The classroom is organized to support students' learning. Here, students gather in the meeting area to learn together.

all materials needed for the particular activity should be available. See Figure 4-2 for a list of some suggested materials to keep accessible in the different areas in your classroom.

▶ **Designed for Whole-Group, Small-Group, and Individual Instruction.** Minilessons are generally provided as whole-class instruction and typically take place at an easel in a meeting space that is comfortable and large enough to accommodate all students in a group or circle. It will be helpful to have a colorful rug with some way of helping students find an individual space to sit without crowding one another. Often, the meeting space is adjacent to the classroom library so books are handy. The teacher usually has a larger chair or seat next to an easel or two so that he can display the mentor texts, make anchor charts, do shared writing, or place materials for shared or performance reading. This space is available for all whole-group instruction; for example, the students come back to it for group share. In addition to the group meeting space, there should be designated tables and spaces in the classroom for small-group reading instruction. The guided reading table is best located in a quiet corner of the room that keeps the group focused on reading, talking, and listening and at the same time allows you to scan the room to identify students who may need help staying on task independently. The table (round or horseshoe) should be positioned so the students in the group are turned away from the activity in the classroom. You might also designate a place to meet with book clubs. Provide a space that allows everyone to comfortably see one another and engage in conversation (ideally a circle of chairs). Students also need tables and spaces throughout the classroom where they can work independently and where you can easily set a chair next to a student for a brief, individual conference.

Figure 4-2: Adapted from *Guided Reading: Responsive Teaching Across the Grades* (Fountas and Pinnell 2017c)

Classroom Areas	Materials
Classroom Library	Organize books by topic, author, illustrator, genre, and series. Spaces for students to read comfortably and independently.
Writing Materials	Pencils, different types of paper for first and final drafts, markers, stapler, scissors, glue, sticky notes, colored pencils, and highlighters.
Word Work Materials	Blank word cards; magnetic letters; games; folders for Look, Cover, Write, Check; word study principles; place for students' individualized lists.
Listening Area or Media Center	Computers, audio players (e.g., iPod®, iPhone®, tablet), clear sets of directions for the activity and/or technology, multiple copies of books organized in boxes or plastic bags.

▶ **Respectful of personal space.** Sixth-grade students do not necessarily need an individual desk. Desks can be pushed together to make tables. But they do need a place to keep a personal box, including items such as their book of choice (or several that they plan to read) and a reader's notebook. These containers can be placed on a shelf and labeled for each student. A writer's notebook, writing folder, and word study folder may be stored in the same place or in groups by themselves to be retrieved easily. If students have personal poetry books (colorfully decorated by them and growing out of the shared reading of poetry and poetry workshop), they can be placed face out on a rack for easy retrieval. Artifacts like these add considerably to the aesthetic quality of the classroom.

A Peaceful Atmosphere for a Community of Readers and Writers

The minilessons in this book will help you establish a classroom environment where students can become confident, self-determined, and kind members of the community. They are designed to contribute to an ambiance of peaceful activity and shared responsibility in the sixth-grade classroom. Through the Management minilessons, students will make agreements, or set norms, about working together as a community of readers and writers. They will learn how to find help when the teacher is busy, listen to and show empathy for one another, and make everyone feel included. The lessons in this section are designed to help you develop a community of readers and writers who use multiple resources to find interesting and enjoyable books, are excited to share book recommendations, and challenge themselves and one another to stretch and grow in their reading tastes, preferences, and goals. The overall tone of every classroom activity is respectful. Sixth-grade students who enter your classroom for the first time will benefit from learning your expectations and being reminded of how to work with twenty to thirty others in a small room day after day. These minilessons are designed to help you establish the atmosphere you want. Everything in the classroom reflects the students who work there; it is their home for the year.

Figure 4-3: A readers' workshop structure as shown in *Guided Reading: Responsive Teaching Across the Grades* (Fountas and Pinnell 2017c, 565)

Structure of Readers' Workshop		
Book Talks and Minilessons		5–15 minutes
Students: • Independent Reading • Writing in a Reader's Notebook	**Teacher:** • Guided Reading Groups (about 20–25 minutes each) • Book Clubs (about 20–25 minutes each) • Individual Conferences (3–5 minutes each)	45–50 minutes
Group Share		5 minutes

Getting Started with Independent Reading: A Readers' Workshop Structure

Many of the minilessons in the Management section will be the ones that you address early in the year to establish routines that students will use to work at their best with one another and independently. In Umbrella 2: Getting Started with Independent Reading, you will teach students the routines and structure for independent reading. We recommend a readers' workshop structure for Grade 6 in which students move from a whole-class meeting, to individual reading and small-group work, and back to a whole-class meeting (see Figure 4-3). The minilessons in this book are designed with this structure in mind, providing a strong instructional frame around independent reading and regular opportunities for students to share their thinking with each other. Your use of time will depend on the amount of time you have for the entire class period. As we explain in Chapter 23 of *Guided Reading: Responsive Teaching Across the Grades* (Fountas and Pinnell 2017c), ideally you will have seventy-five to ninety minutes, though many teachers have only sixty minutes. You will need to adjust accordingly. The minilessons in this umbrella are focused on promoting independence and supporting students in making good book choices for independent reading, including knowing when to abandon a book. Students also learn how to keep their materials for independent reading organized and ready to use. It is possible that you will spend several days reviewing the minilessons in this umbrella until you feel students are able to choose books and read independently for a sustained period of time. It's worth the effort and will benefit the learning community all year. At the beginning of the year, make independent reading time relatively short and circulate around the room to help students select books, write about their reading, and stay engaged. As students become more self-directed, you can increase independent reading time, and this should happen quickly with sixth graders. When you determine that students can sustain productive independent behavior, you can begin to meet with guided reading groups.

Figure 4-4: Readers' workshop begins with a minilesson and, often, a book talk.

Book Talks and Minilessons

The minilessons in the Management section will help you establish routines for your students that they will use throughout the year. In addition to these lessons, you will want to teach the students to sit in a specific place during book talks and reading minilessons. They might sit on a carpet or in chairs. Be sure everyone can see the chart and hear you and each other. Teachers with larger classes sometimes find it helpful to have a smaller circle sitting on the carpet and the remaining students sitting behind them in chairs. Be sure each student has sufficient personal space. Everyone should have enough space so as not to distract others. Most importantly, make it a comfortable place to listen, view, and talk.

Teachers often start readers' workshop with a few short book talks. Book talks are an effective way to engage students' interest in books, enriching independent reading. Consider giving two or three very short book talks before your reading minilesson a few times a week. Students can write titles in their notebooks for later reference (see Writing About Reading minilessons). Book talks are an important part of creating a community of readers and writers who talk about and share books. Once you have set the routines for book talks, you can turn this responsibility over to the students. Minilessons in Management Umbrella 3: Living a Reading Life are designed to teach students how to craft an interesting book talk.

Whether you are engaging your students in a reading minilesson, a book talk, or another whole-group instruction, you will need to teach them how to listen and talk when the entire class is meeting. Management minilessons lay the foundation for this whole-group work.

Figure 4-5: While some students read and write independently, you can work with small groups or hold individual conferences.

Independent Reading, Individual Conferences, and Small-Group Work

After the reading minilesson, work with students individually and in small groups (e.g., in guided reading and book clubs) while other students are engaged in independent reading and writing in the reader's notebook. To establish this as productive independent time, spend time on the minilessons in Management Umbrella 1: Being a Respectful Member of the Classroom Community and Umbrella 2: Getting Started with Independent Reading. Independent reading and the reader's notebook, while highly beneficial in themselves, also act as your management system. Students are engaged in reading and writing for a sustained period of time, freeing you to have individual conferences and to meet with small groups. You will find minilessons in Section Four: Writing About Reading to help you introduce and use the reader's notebook.

Students will have plenty of time during the share and small-group work to express their thinking about books. During independent reading time, there should be limited opportunity for distraction. The only voices heard should be your individual conferences with students and your work with small groups. In MGT.U1.RML2, students have the opportunity to establish agreements or norms for working together, including using the appropriate voice level during readers' workshop.

Consider the space in your classroom and position yourself during small-group work in a way that you can scan the room frequently. This thoughtful positioning will allow you to identify problems that arise and make notes to use in individual conferences. However, if you spend the time to set and practice these routines and expectations, students will learn to self-regulate and change inappropriate behavior with little intervention. When they are taught to make good book choices and are members of a community that share and recommend books with one another, they look forward to this quiet time of the day to read books of their own choosing.

When you first start readers' workshop, you will spend all or most of your time engaging in individual conferences to get to know your students. Conferences allow you time to evaluate whether they are making good book choices and help them become self-managed. Students who have persistent difficulty in selecting books might benefit from working with a limited selection of just-right books, which you can assemble in a temporary basket for this purpose.

Sharing Time

The readers' workshop ends with the community of readers and writers coming together for a short time to share discoveries made during independent reading time. Whatever is taught in the minilesson (management routines, literary analysis, strategies and skills, or writing about reading) guides the independent work time and is revisited during group share. Besides using sharing time to revisit the minilesson principle, you can use this time for your students to self-evaluate how the whole class is working together. The charts you create together during Management minilessons can be a source for self-evaluation. For example, you might ask students to review the list of agreements they made for working together and evaluate the class's behavior based on the chart criteria.

In addition to evaluating independent work time, you might also ask students to evaluate the quality of their sharing time. Is everyone able to see and hear each other? Does everyone transition well from turning and talking with a partner back to the whole group? Is everyone using an appropriate voice level? Do enough students have an opportunity to share their thinking?

In *Guided Reading: Responsive Teaching Across the Grades* (Fountas and Pinnell 2017c), we wrote the following: "The readers' workshop brings together both individual interests and the shared experiences of a literate community. Students read at a sharper edge when they know they will be sharing their thoughts with peers in their classroom. They are personally motivated because they have choice. In addition to providing an excellent management system, the workshop engages students in massive amounts of daily reading and in writing about reading" (p. 571). The Management minilessons in this book are designed to set a management system in motion in which choice and independence are guiding principles. Students develop into a community of readers and writers that respect and look forward to listening to and responding to each other's ideas.

Chapter 5

Literary Analysis Minilessons: Thinking and Talking About Books

LITERARY ANALYSIS MINILESSONS SUPPORT STUDENTS in a growing awareness of the elements of literature and the writer's and illustrator's craft. Use these lessons to help students learn how to think analytically about texts and identify the characteristics of fiction and nonfiction genres. Invite them to notice characters and how they change, critique whether a story's plot is believable, and analyze how nonfiction writers present and organize information as well as how they use graphics and other nonfiction features. Prior to each Literary Analysis minilesson, students will have listened to texts read aloud or will have experienced them through shared or performance reading. You will have read the texts aloud and taught specific lessons that encourage students to discuss and explore concepts and to respond in writing, art, or drama. This prior knowledge will be accessed as they participate in the minilesson and will enable them to make the understanding explicit. They then can apply the concepts to their own reading and share what they have learned with others.

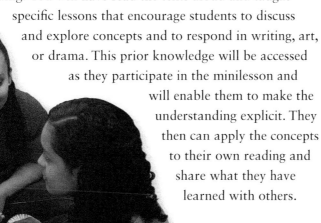

Organization of Literary Analysis Umbrellas and the Link to *The Literacy Continuum*

There are 151 Literary Analysis minilessons in Section Two of this book. These minilessons are divided into categories according to *The Literacy Continuum* (Fountas and Pinnell 2017b), and the order of presentation in this book follows that of *The Literacy Continuum*. The categories of fiction and nonfiction are listed below.

- ▶ Fiction and Nonfiction
  - General
  - Genre
  - Messages and Themes
  - Style and Language
  - Illustrations
  - Book and Print Features
- ▶ Nonfiction
  - Genre
  - Organization
  - Topic
  - Illustration/Graphics
  - Book and Print Features
- ▶ Fiction
  - Genre
  - Setting
  - Plot
  - Character
  - Style and Language

As you can tell from the suggested sequence in Minilessons Across the Year (Figure 8-2), you will want to use simpler concepts (such as recognizing that characters have feelings and motivations) before more sophisticated concepts (such as critiquing a character's authenticity).

Echoes of the Literary Analysis minilessons reverberate across all the instruction for the year in instructional contexts for reading (interactive read-aloud, shared and performance reading, guided reading, book clubs, and independent reading) as well as for writing. The students continue to develop their understanding of the characteristics of fiction and nonfiction texts.

Genre Study

Within the Literary Analysis section you will find three umbrellas that bring students through a process of inquiry-based study of the characteristics of a particular genre. The genre study umbrellas are identified by the word *Studying:* Studying Biography, Studying Modern Fantasy, and Studying Epic Tales. We chose to feature these genres because sixth graders are often engaged in reading them. Other umbrellas also address genre (e.g., memoir, historical fiction, and myths) but do not model all the steps of the genre study process. Genre study gives students the tools they need to navigate a variety of texts with deep understanding. When readers understand the characteristics of a genre, they know what to expect when they begin to read a text. They use their knowledge of the predictable elements within a genre as a road map to anticipate structures and elements of the text. They make increasingly more sophisticated connections between books within the same genre and build on shared language for talking about genre. In our professional book *Genre Study: Teaching with Fiction and Nonfiction Books* (Fountas and Pinnell 2012c), we designed a six-step approach for learning about a variety of genres. The six broad steps are described in Figure 5-1. The first two steps of the genre study process take place before and during interactive read-aloud. Steps 3–5 are accomplished through reading minilessons. Step 6 is addressed on the last page of each genre study umbrella.

Figure 5-3 is an overview of how we categorize various fiction and nonfiction genres. As students progress through the grades, they will revisit some genres to gain a deeper understanding and be introduced to new genres. Fiction genres are divided into two categories: realism and and fantasy. Realism is broken down into historical and realistic fiction. Fantasy

Figure 5-1: Adapted from *Genre Study* (Fountas and Pinnell 2012c)

Steps in the Genre Study Process	
1	**Collect** books in a text set that represent good examples of the genre you are studying.
2	**Immerse.** Read aloud each book using the lesson guidelines. The primary goal should be enjoyment and understanding of the book.
3	**Study.** After you have read these mentor texts, have students analyze characteristics or "noticings" that are common to the texts, and list the characteristics on chart paper.
4	**Define.** Use the list of characteristics to create a short working definition of the genre.
5	**Teach** specific minilessons on the important characteristics of the genre.
6	**Read and Revise.** Expand students' understanding by encouraging them to talk about the genre in appropriate instructional contexts (book club, independent reading conferences, guided reading lessons, and shared or performance reading lessons) and revise the definition.

Epic Tales

Noticings:

Always	Often
The stories are imagined and feature characters and events that could not exist in the real world.	The hero is on a quest or journey.
Epics are long stories or a series of stories.	There is a series of tasks or tests in which the hero triumphs.
They have a hero.	The characteristics of the hero reveal what was valued at that time in the culture of origin.
They were originally told orally by storytellers for many years.	Epics are written as poetry or in a poetic way.
The moral values of the society are expressed through the epic.	Epics exaggerate the qualities of the hero.
	Epics are connected to myths.

Sometimes

There are gods and human heroes.

Figure 5-2: On this anchor chart, the teacher has recorded what the students noticed was always, often, or sometimes true about several epic tales that they had read.

is more complicated because it encompasses several different genres, categorized as either traditional literature or modern fantasy. Within traditional literature are several genres including folktales. Folktales include the following subgenres: tall tales, beast tales, cumulative tales, porquoi tales, trickster tales, noodlehead (or fool) tales. Epic tales are also considered traditional literature. Epic tales present significant concrete themes for students to think and talk about. Because modern fantasy is rooted in traditional literature, the same themes, ideas, or subjects, called motifs (e.g., the struggle between good and evil, the presence of magic, and the concept of a hero's quest), are found in both.

These motifs are often embedded in one's mind as part of a cultural experience. Students who are not familiar with traditional European motifs may, however, be familiar with others.

It is important to make connections between straightforward traditional literature and the more challenging literature that students will be expected to understand later on. Early experiences with these motifs in traditional literature provide a strong foundation for understanding the more complex

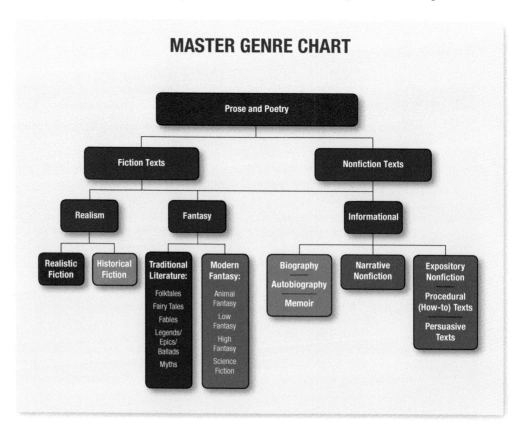

MASTER GENRE CHART

Figure 5-3: Master Genre Chart from *Genre Study: Teaching with Fiction and Nonfiction Books* (Fountas and Pinnell 2012c)

types of fantasy, such as high fantasy and science fiction. The steps in the genre study process allow students to discover these characteristics through inquiry.

It's also important for students to read nonfiction. Nonfiction genres include narrative genres (e.g., biographies, autobiographies, memoirs, and narrative nonfiction) and non-narrative genres (e.g., expository nonfiction, procedural, and persuasive texts).

The first step in the genre study process, **Collect,** involves collecting a set of texts. The genre study minilessons in this book draw on texts sets from the *Fountas & Pinnell Classroom™ Interactive Read-Aloud Collection* (Fountas and Pinnell 2020). Use these texts if you have them, but we encourage you to collect additional texts within each genre to immerse your students in as many texts as possible. Students will enjoy additional examples of the genre placed in a bin in the classroom library. You can use the texts listed in the Before Teaching section of each umbrella as a guide to making your own genre text set if you do not have access to the *Interactive Read-Aloud Collection.*

As you engage students in step 2 of the genre study process, **Immerse,** be sure that the students think and talk about the meaning of each text during the interactive read-aloud. The imperative is for students to enjoy a wonderful book, so it is important for them to respond to the full meaning of the text before focusing their attention on the specific characteristics of the genre.

After immersing students in the books through interactive read-aloud, it is time to teach minilessons in the appropriate genre study umbrella. The first minilesson in each genre study umbrella addresses step 3 in the process, **Study.** During this initial minilesson, help students notice characteristics that are common across all of the texts. As students discuss and revisit books in the genre, list their noticings on chart paper. Distinguish between what is *always* true about the genre and what is *often* true about the genre.

The second minilesson in each genre study umbrella addresses step 4 in the process, **Define.** Use shared writing to co-construct a working definition of the genre based on the students' previous noticings. Help students understand that you will revisit and revise this definition as they learn more about the genre over the next few days.

Next, as part of step 5, **Teach,** provide specific minilessons related to each of your students' noticings about the genre. In each genre study umbrella, we offer minilessons that we think would develop out of most sixth graders' noticings. Pick and choose the lessons that match your own students' noticings or use these lessons as a model to develop your own minilessons. In the minilessons and throughout a genre study, support your teaching with prompts for thinking, talking, and writing about reading. Prompts and definitions for each genre are included in *Fountas & Pinnell Genre Prompting Guide for Fiction* (2012a) and *Fountas & Pinnell Genre Prompting Guide for Nonfiction, Poetry, and Test Taking* (2012b).

S. D. Nelson

Noticings:

Always	Often
• Writes about people struggling in hard times or who have been treated poorly	• Writes about the conflict between the Lakota and Wasichu
• Includes messages of hope for the future	• Writes biographies from the point of view of the subject
• Writes historical fiction or biographies	• Is both the author and illustrator
• Writes about a setting in the United States, set in the past	
• Illustrates his own books	

Figure 5-4: This chart shows what students noticed about the work of author and illustrator S. D. Nelson.

Figure 5-5: Minilessons address step 3 of an author/illustrator study.

At the end of the umbrella, work with the students to **Read and Revise** the class definition of the genre based on the minilessons that have been taught. Using shared writing, make changes to the definition so it reflects your students' understanding of the genre.

Author and Illustrator Studies

Section Two: Literary Analysis also includes two umbrellas of minilessons for conducting inquiry-based author and illustrator studies. They are Umbrella 3: Studying Authors and Their Processes and Umbrella 11: Studying Illustrators and Analyzing an Illustrator's Craft. Author and illustrator studies allow students to make connections to the people behind the books they love. For an author or illustrator study, be sure that the students think and talk about the full meaning of each text in interactive read-aloud before identifying characteristics specific to the author or illustrator.

Students will need plenty of opportunities to explore the texts during read-aloud time, on their own, or in groups or pairs. As they become more familiar with the steps in an author or illustrator study, they learn how to notice characteristics common to a particular author's or illustrator's work. The steps in an author/illustrator study are described in Figure 5-5.

In the first minilesson in Umbrella 3: Studying Authors and Their Processes, you provide a demonstration of step 3 by working with your students to create a chart of noticings about an author. In this lesson, we model a study of S. D. Nelson from the *Fountas & Pinnell Classroom™ Interactive Read-Aloud Collection* (Fountas and Pinnell 2020). For this

Steps in an Author/Illustrator Study

1   Gather a set of books and read them aloud to the class over several days. The goal is for students to enjoy the books and discuss the full meaning.

2   Take students on a quick tour of all the books in the set. As you reexamine each book, you might want to have students do a brief turn and talk with a partner about what they notice.

3   Have students analyze the characteristics of the author's or illustrator's work, and record their noticings on chart paper.

4   You may choose to read a few more books by the author and compare them to the books in this set, adding to the noticings as needed.

author study, we have chosen an author who is also an illustrator. In RML1 of Umbrella 11: Studying Illustrators and Analyzing an Illustrator's Craft, students develop noticings about S. D. Nelson as an illustrator. The other minilessons in Umbrella 3: Studying Authors and Their Processes help students understand that authors engage in research for their writing and develop their own unique styles. If you choose different authors and illustrators, choose ones that students are familiar with and love. Teach these umbrellas across the year as you conduct author or illustrator studies, instead of consecutively (see Minilessons Across the Year, Figure 8-2). Collect books by a particular author or illustrator and follow the steps listed in Figure 5-5. Use the same language and process modeled in the minilessons in these umbrellas, but substitute the authors and illustrators of your choice.

Developing Critical Thinking

In the age of social media and biased media views, it is imperative for students to be able to evaluate the accuracy, authenticity, and quality of the information they read. They need to be able to identify the sources of the information they read in both digital and print forms and evaluate an author's credibility and expertise. Throughout the Literary Analysis umbrellas, you will find several minilessons designed to foster the deep analysis of text and to develop the ability of students to think critically. For example, Umbrella 15: Exploring Persuasive Texts and Umbrella 17: Thinking About the Topic of Expository Nonfiction have lessons that help students evaluate the accuracy and quality of texts, consider an author's qualifications and sources, and notice both overt and subtle persuasive techniques. In Umbrella 18: Reading and Evaluating Multiple Sources, students learn how to cross-check information in more than one source and begin to notice that authors carefully select the facts they include in their nonfiction texts. Through inquiry, they develop a foundational understanding of how to use multiple texts to compare and contrast information to answer larger research questions.

It is also important for students to be able to critique texts for bias, stereotyping, and representation (or omission) of race, gender, socioeconomic levels, disability, and different family structures. In Umbrella 5: Thinking Critically About Texts, students are taught to evaluate how characters are portrayed in fiction, critique how different groups of people are represented in illustrations and graphics, and think about how stories are affected by an author's choice of a character's gender, race/culture, and socioeconomic status.

In the next section on Strategies and Skills, you will read more about teaching students to apply these critical thinking skills in meeting the challenges of reading in digital environments.

Chapter 6 Strategies and Skills Minilessons: Teaching for Effective Processing

STRATEGIES AND SKILLS minilessons will help students continue to strengthen their ability to process print by searching for and using information from the text, self-monitoring their reading, self-correcting their errors, and solving multisyllable words. You'll notice the students engaging in these behaviors in your interactive read-aloud, shared or performance reading, and guided reading lessons. Strategies and skills are taught in every instructional context for reading, but guided reading is the most powerful one. The text is just right to support the learning of all the readers in the group, enabling them to learn how to solve words and engage in the act of problem solving across a whole text.

The Strategies and Skills minilessons in this book may serve as reminders and be helpful to the whole class. They can be taught any time you see a need. For example, as students engage in independent reading, they may need to realize that a reader

- uses context to understand vocabulary,

- breaks apart a new word to read it,

- understands how connectives work in sentences, and

- applies different techniques to monitor comprehension when reading a difficult text.

The minilessons in Section Three: Strategies and Skills are designed to bring a few important strategies to temporary, conscious attention so that students are reminded to think in these ways as they problem solve in independent reading. By the time students participate in these minilessons, they should have engaged these strategic actions successfully in shared or guided reading. In the minilessons, they will recognize the strategic actions; bring them to brief, focused attention; and think about applying them consistently in independent reading. Some Strategies and Skills minilessons require students to see the print from a page of text. For these lessons, we recommend you use a document camera or write the word, sentence, or phrase from the text on a piece of chart paper.

Through the reading of continuous text, students develop an internal sense of in-the-head actions; for example, monitoring and checking, searching for and using information, and using multiple sources of information to solve words. They have a sense of how to put words together in phrases and use intonation to convey meaning. They are thinking more deeply about how a character would speak the dialogue. And, they are learning to check their comprehension by summarizing the most important parts and the big ideas and messages of a fiction or nonfiction text. The minilesson, the application, and the share help them better understand what they do and internalize effective and efficient reading behaviors.

Reading in Digital Environments

Sixth graders increasingly use the internet to research topics they are investigating, read reviews, participate in online communities, and compare information from multiple sources. A 2015 report by Common Sense Media, (https://www.commonsensemedia.org/sites/default/files/uploads/research/census_researchreport.pdf, 21) found that eight- to twelve-year-old children spend about two and a half hours per day using digital media (e.g., computers, tablets, and smart phones) outside of school. It is important for students to learn to navigate digital environments safely and critically. Umbrella 7: Reading in Digital Environments is designed to provide an overview of some of these crucial skills; however, we encourage you to become informed about the safety features and policies that your school district uses to safeguard students as they navigate the digital world. The minilessons in this umbrella help students learn how to use search engines efficiently and effectively, evaluate the credibility and sources of the information they find, and stay focused in a reading environment that provides link after link to related and sometimes unrelated information. Students need to learn to be critical readers of *all* information, but the seemingly anonymous nature of many websites requires students to be active in seeking out, identifying, and evaluating the sources of the digital information they are reading.

Students also need teaching to efficiently use search engines to find information and evaluate the results of their searches. In a study at the University of Maryland, a team of researchers found that children (ages seven through eleven) in their sample group showed an inability to construct queries requiring more than one search step (http://www.cs.umd.edu/hcil/trs/2009-04/2009-04.pdf). This limitation created frustration for students involved in the search process because they couldn't find exactly what they were looking for. The study also showed that when students *did* successfully execute a search, they focused primarily on the first few items on the results page and ignored the rest of the information. The first two lessons in Umbrella 7 offer techniques for searching effectively and evaluating which search results seem relevant and worthy of further investigation. We hope this umbrella will get you started in establishing critical reading within a digital environment and inspire you and your students to learn more about navigating this challenging, yet rewarding, world of information.

Figure 6-2: Minilessons on reading in digital environments help students learn how to search for information online and to stay focused while reading it.

Chapter 7

Writing About Reading Minilessons: The Reading-Writing Connection

THROUGH DRAWING/WRITING ABOUT READING, students reflect on their understanding of a text. For example, a story might have a captivating character or characters or a humorous sequence of events. A nonfiction text might have interesting information or call for an opinion. Two kinds of writing about reading are highly effective with sixth-grade students.

▶ **Shared Writing.** In shared writing (see Figure 7-1) you offer the highest level of support to the students. You act as scribe while the students participate fully in the composition of the text. You help shape the text, but the students supply the language and context.

Jack learned that if he saved money for a present, he shouldn't spend it on himself. Jack might tell his mom about how he spent the money he saved. Jack also learned that he shouldn't steal. He will tell his mom about taking the necklace from the store. He will explain that he returned it and sold his bike because he knew he did something wrong and he wanted to make things right.

Figure 7-1: In shared writing, the teacher acts as scribe.

▶ **Independent Writing.** After you have introduced and modeled different forms of writing about reading, sixth graders begin trying these different ways independently (see Figure 7-2). Occasionally, it may be helpful to teach students how to use graphic organizers to bring structure to their writing about both fiction and nonfiction books (see Umbrella 4: Using Graphic Organizers to Share Thinking About Books in the Writing About Reading section). Sixth graders also enjoy writing independently about their reading in a weekly letter to you (see Figure 7-6). Keep good examples of different writing on hand (possibly in a scrapbook) for students to use as models.

Figure 7-2: The independent writing in response to reading minilessons will reflect students' thinking about their reading.

> Dion thought his mom's rules cramped his style and were little kid rules. But he followed the rules to protect his sister from danger. He took her home right away and made her stay away from the windows. When Dion broke the rule and got close to the window himself, he heard loud pops and glass shattering. He was terrified, but he was OK. He realized that Mom's rules were for him, too.

In most Literary Analysis lessons, you will find a suggestion for extending the learning using shared or independent writing. In whatever way students write, they are exposed to different ways of thinking about their reading. You can expect sixth graders to accurately spell a significant number of high-frequency words as well as words with patterns that you have introduced in phonics and word study lessons; however, they will try many others using their growing vocabulary and knowledge about the way words work. You want them to move beyond "safe" words they know and try new vocabulary, using tools to achieve standard spelling. You will notice that in Umbrella 3: Writing Letters to Share Thinking About Texts, we have provided a lesson for students to evaluate the qualities of a good dialogue letter. In this lesson, students learn to proofread and evaluate the use of standard conventions as one aspect of writing quality letters.

The students' independent writing about reading will be in a reader's notebook. The first two umbrellas in Section Four provide inquiry-based lessons for exploring the reader's notebook and establish routines for writing about reading. Some of these routines include keeping lists of books read and books "to be read," maintaining a section of minilesson notes, and tallying the types of writing about reading that have been attempted and completed. This section also includes inquiry-based lessons to help students learn different genres and forms for responding to their reading in independent writing.

The minilessons in Umbrella 5: Introducing Different Genres and Forms for Responding to Reading provide examples of how to use a particular genre or form to explore an aspect of literary analysis. For example, in RML2, students participate in analyzing an example of a written sketch in which the writer examines a biographical subject's traits. The extensions provided for the minilessons in this umbrella suggest other literary genres to which students can respond with one of the writing genres or forms. For example, the extension to RML2 suggests students use what they learned about writing a sketch about the subject of a biography to analyzing the traits of fictional characters. You can find a comprehensive list of different genres and forms for sixth grade in the Writing About Reading section of *The Literacy Continuum* (Fountas and Pinnell 2017b).

Like Management minilessons, the lessons in the Writing About Reading umbrellas need not be taught consecutively within the umbrella; instead, they can be paired with the Literary Analysis lessons that support the concept students are being asked to write about. For example, if you have just completed Literary Analysis minilessons about plot (Umbrella 27: Understanding Plot), you might decide it would be an appropriate time to teach students how write a summary of a fiction book. After writing a few summaries as a whole class through shared writing and teaching the summary lesson in Writing About Reading (WAR.U5.RML4), students will be able to write a sophisticated summary independently. Through this gradual release of responsibility, students learn how to transition to writing about their reading independently as they learn how to use each section of the notebook. A reader's notebook is an important tool to support student independence and response to books. It becomes a rich collection of thinking across the years.

For English language learners, a reader's notebook is a safe place to practice a new language. It eventually becomes a record of their progress not only in content and literary knowledge but in acquiring a new language. However, they may do as much drawing as writing depending on where they are in acquiring English. Drawing is key because it provides a way to rehearse

ELL CONNECTION

Figure 7-3: Occasionally ask students to reflect on their understanding of a text by writing independently about their reading.

ideas. Use this opportunity to ask students to talk about what they have drawn, and then help them compose labels for their artwork so they begin to attach meaning to the English words. In some cases, you might choose to pull together small groups of students and engage them in interactive writing, in which the teacher and students compose together and share the pen. This might be particularly helpful with English language learners who might still be learning English letter and sound correlations. Students who struggle with spelling and phonics can also benefit from interactive writing in small groups.

Eventually, the students will do more writing, but you can support the writing by providing a chance for them to rehearse their sentences before writing them and encouraging students to borrow language from the texts they are writing about. The writing in a reader's notebook is a product they can read because they have written it. It is theirs. They can read and reread it to themselves and to others, thereby developing their confidence in the language.

Using a Reader's Notebook in Sixth Grade

A reader's notebook is a place where students can collect their thinking about books. They draw and write to tell about themselves and respond to books and to keep a record of their reading lives. A reader's notebook includes

> a section for students to list the title, author, and genre of the books they have read and write a one-word response to show their reaction to the book.

> a section for helping students choose and recommend books, including a place to list books to read in the future,

Figure 7-4: Students write to share their thinking about reading in a reader's notebook.

- a section that supports genre studies, including space to write working definitions of the genres, noticings about the genres' characteristics, and book examples.

- a section to write or glue in reading minilesson principles to refer to as needed (see Figure 7-5),

- a section for students to respond to books they have read or listened to, and

- a glossary of literary terms useful for clarification or when writing about reading.

Grade 6
Section Three: Strategies and Skills
Umbrella 7 Reading Minilesson Principles (RML1–RML6)

Reading in Digital Environments

Search efficiently and effectively for information on the internet.

Evaluate whether you have found the information you need.

Stay focused while reading on the internet.

Evaluate the credibility of the source of the information you read on the internet.

Evaluate whether a website presents one perspective or multiple perspectives.

Notice when bloggers or website authors link to other sources to provide evidence for an argument.

Figure 7-5: At the end of each umbrella, download the umbrella's principles, like the sample shown here. Students can glue the principles in the reader's notebook to refer to as needed. Encourage students to make notes or sketches to help remember the principles. To download the principles, go to **resources.fountasand pinnell.com**.

With places for students to make a record of their reading and respond to books in a variety of ways using different kinds of writing (including charts, webs, short writes, and letters), a reader's notebook thus represents a rich record of progress. To the student, the notebook represents a year's work to reflect on with pride and share with family. Students keep their notebooks in their personal boxes, along with their bags of book choices for independent reading time. We provide a series of minilessons in Section Four: Writing About Reading for teaching students how to use a reader's notebook. As described previously, reading minilessons in the Writing About Reading section focus on writing in response to reading.

If you do not have access to the preprinted *Reader's Notebook: Advanced* (Fountas and Pinnell 2011), simply give each student a plain notebook (bound if possible). Glue in sections and insert tabs yourself to make a neat, professional notebook that can be cherished.

Writing Letters About Reading: Moving from Talk to Writing

In sixth grade, we continue the routine of having students write a weekly letter about their reading in the past week. In most cases, they address these letters to you, the teacher, although occasionally they may write to other readers in the classroom or school. Letter writing is an authentic way to transition from oral conversation to written conversation about books. Students have had rich experiences talking about books during interactive read-aloud, guided reading, book clubs, and reading conferences. Writing letters in a reader's notebook allows them to continue this dialogue in writing and provides an opportunity to increase the depth of reader response.

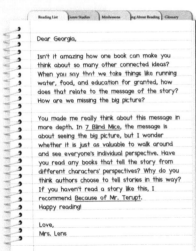

Figure 7-6: Weekly letters about reading allow you and your students to participate in a written dialogue to share thinking about the books the class has read together or books the students have read on their own.

By using the Writing About Reading section of *The Literacy Continuum* (Fountas and Pinnell 2017b) and carefully analyzing students' letters, you can systematically assess students' responses to the texts they are reading independently. The *Fountas & Pinnell Prompting Guide, Part 2, for Comprehension: Thinking, Talking, and Writing* (2009b) is a useful resource for choosing the language to prompt the thinking you want to see in a student's response. A weekly letter from you offers the opportunity to respond in a timely way to address students individually, differentiating instruction by asking specific questions or making comments targeted at the strengths and needs of each student's individual processing system.

Letters about reading also provide you with the opportunity to model your own thinking about reading. This reader-to-reader dialogue helps students learn more about what readers do when they actively respond to a text. The depth of their oral discussions will increase as students experience writing letters over time. Just as the discussions in your classroom set the stage for readers to begin writing letters, the writing of letters about reading will in turn enrich the discussions in your classroom.

Umbrella 3: Writing Letters to Share Thinking About Texts, in Section Four, provides minilessons for getting dialogue letters started in your classroom. Through inquiry-based lessons, students learn the routines involved in writing a weekly letter and the qualities of a strong response. They learn to identify the different types of thinking they might include in a letter and how to integrate evidence to support their thinking.

We recommend that you teach these minilessons over a period of time instead of one right after another. For example, after you teach RML1, revisit the lesson as necessary over the next couple of weeks to familiarize students with the routines of writing and responding in a weekly letter. After students have had ample opportunity to experience dialogue letters, teach RML2, which is an inquiry lesson about the qualities of a strong dialogue letter. The more experience students have with writing and responding to letters about reading, the richer the discussion will be about the characteristics of a strong letter. The discussions will then inform students' evaluation of their own letters about reading. RML2 can be revisited as students develop a repertoire for literary analysis concepts and increase the level of sophistication of their letter writing. Once students are comfortable with the format of a friendly dialogue letter, introduce RML3 to teach how to write a formal letter in response to a newspaper or magazine article. When you teach these minilessons over time, you give students the opportunity to gain experience writing letters about their reading before introducing another new principle.

Managing Letters About Reading

Before introducing dialogue letters, think about how you will manage to read and respond to your students in a timely way. Some teachers assign groups of students to submit their letters on particular days of the week as shown in Figure 7-7. Many teachers find it more manageable to respond to five or six letters a day versus responding to the whole class at once. As the students write letters about reading, collect samples of quality letters that you might be able to share as examples in subsequent years to launch the writing of letters in your classroom.

We recommend that students work on their weekly letters during independent reading time. They can write their letters all at one time or over the course of two or three days. Monitor how long students are spending on writing versus reading to make sure they are dedicating enough time to both. However you choose to organize and manage this system, you will want to make sure it is feasible for both you and your students. It is critical that you are able to respond to the letters in a timely manner because students will quickly move on to new books and ask new questions about their reading.

You will find several other suggestions for helping students write thoughtful letters in Chapter 27 of *Teaching for Comprehending and Fluency* (Fountas and Pinnell 2006).

Figure 7-7: To make reading and responding to students' letters manageable, set up a schedule so that only a few letters are due each day.

Letters Due

Monday	Tuesday	Wednesday	Thursday
Tyler	Aiden	Gabriella	Nevaeh
Evan	Madison	Mason	Owen
Ava	Chloe	Liam	Jaxon
Keyarie	Abdul	Nohjee	Kylie
Hasan	Mairelisa	Isaac	Mohamed
Leighana	Carter	Grady	Harper
	Luke		

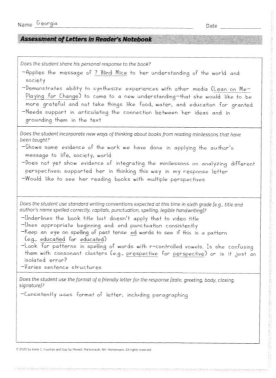

Name Georgia   Date

Assessment of Letters in Reader's Notebook

Does the student share his personal response to the book?
—Applies the message of 7 Blind Mice to her understanding of the world and society
—Demonstrates ability to synthesize experiences with other media (Lean on Me—Playing for Change) to come to a new understanding—that she would like to be more grateful and not take things like food, water, and education for granted
—Needs support in articulating the connection between her ideas and in grounding them in the text

Does the student incorporate new ways of thinking about books from reading minilessons that have been taught?
—Shows some evidence of the work we have done in applying the author's message to life, society, world
—Does not yet show evidence of integrating the minilessons on analyzing different perspectives; supported her in thinking this way in my response letter
—Would like to see her reading books with multiple perspectives

Does the student use standard writing conventions expected at this time in sixth grade (e.g., title and author's name spelled correctly, capitals, punctuation, spelling, legible handwriting)?
—Underlines the book title but doesn't apply that to video title
—Uses appropriate beginning and end punctuation consistently
—Keep an eye on spelling of past tense ed words to see if this is a pattern (e.g., educated for educated)
—Look for patterns in spelling of words with r-controlled vowels. Is she confusing them with consonant clusters (e.g., prespective for perspective) or is it just an isolated error?
—Varies sentence structures

Does the student use the format of a friendly letter for the response (date, greeting, body, closing, signature)?
—Consistently uses format of letter, including paragraphing

Figure 7-8: Use questions such as these to evaluate students' letters about their reading. To download the questions, visit **resources.fountasandpinnell.com.**

Chapter 8 Putting Minilessons into Action: Assessing and Planning

As NOTED IN CHAPTER 2, the minilessons in this book are examples of teaching that address the specific bullets that list the behaviors and understandings to notice, teach for, and support in *The Literacy Continuum* (Fountas and Pinnell 2017b) for sixth grade. We have drawn from the sections on Interactive Read-Aloud, Shared and Performance Reading, Guided Reading, Writing About Reading, Technological Communication, and Oral and Visual Communication to provide a comprehensive vision of what students need to become aware of, understand, and apply to their own literacy learning. With such a range of important goals, how do you decide what to teach and when?

Deciding Which Reading Minilessons to Teach

To decide which reading minilessons to teach, first look at the students in front of you. Teach within what Vygotsky (1978) called the "zone of proximal development"—the zone between what the students can do independently and what they can do with the support of a more expert other. Teach on the cutting edge of students' competencies. Select topics for minilessons that address the needs of the majority of students in your class.

Think about what will be helpful to most readers based on your observations of their reading and writing behaviors. Here are some suggestions and tools to help you think about the students in your classroom:

▶ **Use *The Literacy Continuum*** (Fountas and Pinnell 2017b) to assess your students and observe how they are thinking, talking, and writing/drawing about books. Think about what they can already do, almost do, and not yet do to select the emphasis for your teaching. Look at the Selecting Goals pages in each section to guide your observations.

▶ **Use the Interactive Read-Aloud and Literature Discussion section.** Scan the Selecting Goals in this section and think about the ways you have noticed students thinking and talking about books.

▶ **Use the Writing About Reading section** to analyze how students are responding to texts in their drawing and writing. This analysis will help you determine possible next steps. Talking and writing about reading provides concrete evidence of students' thinking.

▶ **Use the Oral and Visual Communication continuum** to help you think about some of the routines your students might need for better communication between peers. You will find essential listening and speaking competencies to observe and teach.

▶ **Use the Technological Communication section** to help you assess your students' technological skills and plan teaching that will help them improve their computer literacy and their ability to read digital texts.

▶ **Look for patterns in your anecdotal records.** Review the anecdotal notes you take during reading conferences, shared and performance reading, guided reading, and book clubs to notice trends in students' responses and thinking. Use *The Literacy Continuum* to help you analyze the records and determine strengths and areas for growth across the classroom. Your observations will reveal what students know and what they need to learn next as they build knowledge over time. Each goal becomes a possible topic for a minilesson.

▶ **Consult district and state standards as a resource.** Analyze the skills and areas of knowledge specified in your local and state standards. Align these standards with the minilessons suggested in this text to determine which might be applicable within your frameworks (see fountasandpinnell.com/resourcelibrary for an alignment of *The Literacy Continuum* with Common Core Standards).

▶ **Use the Assessment section after each umbrella.** Take time to assess student learning after the completion of each umbrella. Use the guiding questions on the last page of each umbrella to determine strengths and next steps for your students. This analysis can help you determine what minilessons to reteach if needed and what umbrella to teach next.

A Suggested Sequence

The suggested sequence of umbrellas, Minilessons Across the Year, shown in Figure 8-2 (also downloadable from the online resources for record keeping), is intended to help you establish a community of independent readers and writers early in the year and work toward more sophisticated concepts across the year. Learning in minilessons is applied in many different situations and so is reinforced daily across the curriculum. Minilessons in this sequence are timed so they occur after students have had sufficient opportunities to build some explicit understandings as well as a great deal of implicit knowledge of aspects of written texts through interactive read-aloud and shared and performance reading texts. In the community of readers, they have acted on texts through talk, writing, and extension through writing and art. These experiences have prepared them to fully engage in the reading minilesson and move from this shared experience to the application of the concepts in their independent reading.

The sequence of umbrellas in Minilessons Across the Year follows the suggested sequence of text sets in *Fountas & Pinnell Classroom™ Interactive Read-Aloud Collection* (Fountas and Pinnell 2020). If you are using this collection, you are invited to follow this sequence of texts. If you are not using it, the first page of each umbrella describes the types of books students will need to have read before you teach the minilessons. The text sets are grouped together by theme, topic, author, and genre, not by skill or concept. Thus, in many minilessons, you will use books from several different text sets, and you will see the same books used in more than one umbrella.

We have selected the most concrete and instructive examples from the recommended books. The umbrellas draw examples from text sets that have been read and enjoyed previously. In most cases, the minilessons draw on text sets that have been introduced within the same month or at least in close proximity to the umbrella. However, in some cases, minilessons taught later, for example in month eight, might draw on texts introduced earlier in the year. Most of the time, students will have no problem recalling the events of these early books because you have read and discussed them thoroughly as a class, and sometimes students have responded to them through writing or art. However, in some cases, you might want to quickly reread a book or a portion of it before teaching the umbrella so it is fresh in the students' minds.

If you are new to these minilessons, you may want to follow the suggested sequence, but remember to use the lessons flexibly to meet the needs of the students you teach:

▶ Omit lessons that you think are not necessary for your students (based on assessment and your experiences with them in interactive read-aloud).

- Repeat some lessons that you think need more time and instructional attention (based on observation of students across reading contexts).

- Repeat some lessons using different examples for a particularly rich experience.

- Move lessons around to be consistent with the curriculum that is adopted in your school or district.

The minilessons are here for your selection according to the instructional needs of your class, so do not be concerned if you do not use them all within the year. Record or check the minilessons you have taught so that you can reflect on the work of the semester and year. You can do this simply by downloading the minilessons record form (see Figure 8-1) from online resources (resources.fountasandpinnell.com).

Figure 8-1: Download this record-keeping form to record the minilessons that you have taught and to make notes for future reference.

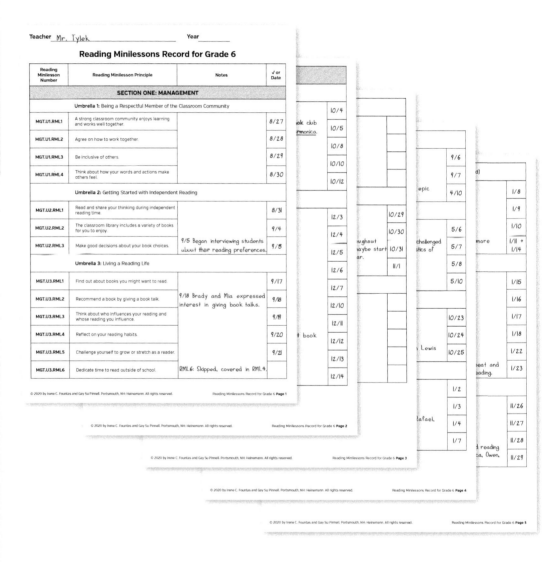

MINILESSONS ACROSS THE YEAR

Month	Recommended Umbrellas	Approximate Time
Month 1	**MGT U1:** Being a Respectful Member of the Classroom Community	**1 week**
	MGT U2: Getting Started with Independent Reading	**1 week**
	LA U6: Understanding Fiction and Nonfiction Genres (RML1–RML2)	**2 days**
	WAR U1: Introducing a Reader's Notebook	**1 week**
	LA U1: Getting Started with Book Clubs	**1 week**
Month 2	**MGT U3:** Living a Reading Life	**1.5 weeks**
	WAR U2: Using a Reader's Notebook	**1 week**
	LA U13: Understanding Memoir	**0.5 week**
	WAR U3: Writing Letters to Share Thinking About Texts (RML1)	**1 day**
	LA U8: Thinking About Themes and the Author's Message	**0.5 week**
	WAR U3: Writing Letters to Share Thinking About Texts (RML2)	**1 day**
	SAS U1: Solving Multisyllable Words	**0.5 week**
	LA U4: Reading Graphic Texts	**1 week**
	LA U2: Learning Conversational Moves in Book Club	**2 weeks**
	SAS U6: Monitoring Comprehension of Difficult Texts	**1 week**
Month 3	**LA U11:** Studying Illustrators and Analyzing an Illustrator's Craft *Note: We recommended teaching the first lesson in this umbrella as part of an illustrator study. The first minilesson can be repeated each time an illustrator is studied. If you are using the* Fountas & Pinnell Classroom™ Interactive Read-Aloud Collection, *the first illustrator study is S. D. Nelson.*	**1 week**
	LA U3: Studying Authors and Their Processes (RML1) *Note: We recommend teaching this minilesson as part of an author study. The lesson can be repeated each time an author is studied. If you are using the* Fountas & Pinnell Classroom™ Interactive Read-Aloud Collection, *the first author study is S. D. Nelson.*	**1 day**
	LA U29: Understanding Characters' Feelings, Motivations, and Intentions	**0.5 week**
	LA U30: Understanding Round and Flat Characters	**0.5 week**

KEY

MGT	Section One	Management Minilessons
LA	Section Two	Literary Analysis Minilessons
SAS	Section Three	Strategies and Skills Minilessons
WAR	Section Four	Writing About Reading Minilessons

Figure 8-2: Use this chart as a guideline for planning your year with minilessons.

Month	Recommended Umbrellas	Approximate Time
Month 4	**SAS U4:** Maintaining Fluency	**1 week**
	LA U32: Analyzing Perspective and Point of View	**1 week**
	WAR U8: Responding Creatively to Reading (RML1)	**1 day**
	LA U14: Studying Biography	**1.5 weeks**
	SAS U5: Summarizing (RML1)	**1 day**
	WAR U8: Responding Creatively to Reading (RML2)	**1 day**
	WAR U4: Using Graphic Organizers to Share Thinking About Books (RML1)	**1 day**
	WAR U5: Introducing Different Genres and Forms for Responding to Reading (RML1–RML2)	**2 days**
Month 5	**LA U27:** Understanding Plot	**1.5 weeks**
	SAS U5: Summarizing (RML2)	**1 day**
	WAR U5: Introducing Different Genres and Forms for Responding to Reading (RML3–RML4)	**2 days**
	LA U21: Understanding Realistic Fiction	**0.5 week**
	LA U9: Reading Like a Writer: Analyzing the Writer's Craft	**1.5 weeks**
	WAR U4: Using Graphic Organizers to Share Thinking About Books (RML2)	**1 day**
Month 6	**SAS U7:** Reading in Digital Environments	**1.5 weeks**
	LA U12: Noticing Book and Print Features	**1 week**
	WAR U5: Introducing Different Genres and Forms for Responding to Reading (RML5)	**1 day**
	SAS U3: Understanding Connectives	**1 week**
	LA U17: Thinking About the Topic of Expository Nonfiction	**1 week**
	LA U16: Noticing How Nonfiction Authors Choose to Organize Information	**1 week**

Month	Recommended Umbrellas	Approximate Time
	LA U20: Using Text Features to Gain Information	0.5 week
	WAR U4: Using Graphic Organizers to Share Thinking About Books (RML3–RML4)	2 days
	LA U19: Learning Information from Illustrations and Graphics	0.5 week
	SAS U5: Summarizing (RML3)	1 day
Month 7	**SAS U2:** Deriving Word Meanings	1 week
	LA U24: Studying Epic Tales	1 week
	LA U11: Studying Illustrators and Analyzing Illustrator's Craft (RML1)	1 day
	Note: We recommend teaching this minilesson as part of an illustration study. The lesson can be repeated each time an illustrator is studied. If you are using the Fountas & Pinnell Classroom™ Interactive Read-Aloud Collection, *the second illustrator study is K. Y. Craft.*	
	LA U25: Understanding Myths	0.5 week
	LA U6: Understanding Fiction and Nonfiction Genres (RML3)	1 day
	WAR U4: Using Graphic Organizers to Share Thinking About Books (RML5)	1 day
Month 8	**LA U23:** Studying Modern Fantasy	1.5 weeks
	LA U28: Exploring Conflict in Fiction Texts	1 week
	WAR U7: Writing Literary Essays	1 week
	LA U3: Studying Authors and Their Processes (RML2–RML4)	0.5 week
	LA U7: Exploring Different Kinds of Poetry	1 week
	LA U10: Understanding the Craft of Poetry	1.5 weeks
	WAR U5: Introducing Different Genres and Forms for Responding to Reading (RML6)	1 day
Month 9	**WAR U8:** Responding Creatively to Reading (RML3)	1 day
	LA U15: Exploring Persuasive Texts	1.5 weeks
	LA U5: Thinking Critically About Texts	1 week
	WAR U6: Writing About Reading to Persuade	2 days

Month	Recommended Umbrellas	Approximate Time
Month 10	**WAR U3:** Writing Letters to Share Thinking About Texts (RML3)	1 day
	LA U18: Reading and Evaluating Multiple Sources	1 week
	LA U22: Exploring Historical Fiction	1 week
	LA U26: Thinking About the Setting in Fiction Books	1 week
	LA U31: Thinking Critically About Characters	0.5 week
	LA U11: Studying Illustrators and Analyzing an Illustrator's Craft (RML1)	1 day

Note: If you are using the Fountas & Pinnell Classroom™ Interactive Read-Aloud Collection, *the last illustrator study is Melissa Sweet.*

*Note: Minilessons Across the Year offers general guidance as to the time of year you might teach a particular umbrella and is aligned with the *Fountas & Pinnell Classroom™ Interactive Read-Aloud Collection* sequence. However, because there are 230 reading minilessons in *The Reading Minilessons Book, Grade 6*, it would not be possible to teach every one of these lessons in a normal 180-day school year. You will need to make choices about which minilessons will benefit your students. The minilessons are designed for you to pick and choose what your students need at a particular point in time based on your careful observation of students' reading behaviors.

Chapter 9

Reading Minilessons Within a Multitext Approach to Literacy Learning

THIS COLLECTION OF 230 LESSONS for sixth grade is embedded within an integrated set of instructional approaches that build an awareness of classroom routines, literary characteristics, strategies and skills, and ways of writing about texts. In Figure 9-8, this comprehensive, multitext approach is represented, along with the central role of minilessons. Note that students' processing systems are built across instructional contexts so that students can read increasingly complex texts independently. *The Literacy Quick Guide: A Reference Tool for Responsive Literacy Teaching* (Fountas and Pinnell 2018) provides concise descriptions of these instructional contexts. In this chapter, we will look at how the reading minilessons fit within this multitext approach and provide a balance between implicit and explicit teaching that allows for authentic response and promotes the enjoyment of books.

Throughout this chapter we describe how to build the shared literary knowledge of your classroom community, embedding implicit and explicit teaching with your use of intentional conversation and specific points of instructional value to set a foundation for explicit teaching in reading minilessons. All of the teaching in minilessons is reinforced in shared and performance reading, guided reading, and book clubs, with all pathways leading to the goal of effective independent reading.

Let's look at the range of research-based instructional contexts that constitute an effective literacy design.

Interactive Read-Aloud

Interactive read-aloud provides the highest level of teacher support for students as they experience a complex, grade-appropriate text. In this instructional context, you carefully select sets of high-quality student literature, fiction and nonfiction, and read them aloud to students. We use the word *interactive* because talk is a salient characteristic of this instructional context. You do the reading but pause to invite student discussion in pairs, in triads, or as a whole group at selected points. After the reading, students engage in a lively discussion. Finally, you invite students to revisit specific points in the text for deeper learning and may provide further opportunities for responding to the text through writing, drama, movement, or art.

We recommend that you read aloud from high-quality, organized text sets that you use across the year. A text set contains several titles that are related in some conceptual way, such as the following categories:

▶ Author   ▶ Topic

▶ Illustrator   ▶ Theme or big idea

▶ Genre   ▶ Format (such as graphic texts)

ELL CONNECTION

When you use books organized in text sets, you can support students in making connections across a related group of texts and in engaging in deeper thinking about texts. All students benefit from the use of preselected sets, but these connected texts are particularly supportive for English language learners. Text sets allow students to develop vocabulary around a particular theme, genre, or topic. This shared collection of familiar texts and the shared vocabulary developed through the talk provide essential background knowledge that all students will be able to apply during subsequent reading minilessons.

Figure 9-1: Interactive read-aloud in a sixth-grade class

The key to success with reading minilessons is providing the intentional instruction in interactive read-aloud that will, first, enable the students to enjoy and come to love books and, second, build a foundation of shared understandings about texts within a community of readers and writers.

If you are using *Fountas & Pinnell Classroom™* (Fountas and Pinnell 2020), you will notice that we have used examples from the *Interactive Read-Aloud Collection* as the mentor texts in the minilessons. If you do not have the texts from *Fountas & Pinnell Classroom™*, select read-aloud texts with the same characteristics (described at the beginning of each umbrella) to read well ahead of the minilessons and then use the lessons as organized and presented in this book. Simply substitute the particular texts you selected. You can draw on any texts you have already read and discussed with your students as long as the genre is appropriate for the set of minilessons and the ideas can be connected. For example, if you are going to teach a set of minilessons about characters, pull examples from fiction stories and include engaging characters. If you are reading rich literature in various genres to your students, the chances are high that many of the types of reading behaviors or understandings you are teaching for in reading minilessons can be applied to those texts.

At the beginning of each umbrella (set of related minilessons), you will find a section titled Before Teaching Minilessons that offers guidance in the use of interactive read-aloud as a prelude to teaching the explicit minilessons in the umbrella. It is important to note that the texts in a text set can be used for several different umbrellas. In general, text sets are connected with each other in particular ways so students can think about concepts across texts and notice literary characteristics during read-aloud lessons. But the texts have multiple uses. When you have finished reading the books in a set, you will have provided students with a rich, connected set of literacy

Figure 9-2: Examples of preselected text sets from *Fountas & Pinnell Classroom™ Interactive Read-Aloud Collection*

Books We Have Shared

<u>Chachaji's Cup</u> by Uma Krishnaswami

<u>Wings</u> by Christopher Myers

<u>It Doesn't Have to Be This Way</u>
by Luis J. Rodriguez

<u>Eagle Song</u> by Joseph Bruchac

<u>Rosa</u> by Nikki Giovanni

<u>Merlin and the Dragons</u> by Jane Yolen

<u>Kitchen Knight: A Tale of King Arthur</u>
by Margaret Hodges

<u>Ida B. Wells: Let the Truth Be Told</u>
by Walter Dean Myers

<u>Separate Is Never Equal: Sylvia Mendez & Her Family's Fight for Desegregation</u>
by Duncan Tonatiuh

<u>The Search for Delicious</u> by Natalie Babbit

Figure 9-3: Keep a list of books that you have shared with your students as a record of shared literary knowledge.

experiences that include both explicitly taught and implicitly understood concepts. Then, you have a rich resource from which you can select examples to use as mentor texts in minilessons. We have selected examples across sets. Rich literary texts can be used for multiple types of lessons, so you will see many of the same familiar texts referenced throughout the reading minilessons. Each time a text is used for a different focus, students have a chance to view it with new eyes and see it differently. Usually, texts are not reread in entirety during a minilesson. They are already known because of the rich and deep experiences in your classroom. The result is shared literary knowledge for the class. In minilessons, they are revisited briefly with a particular focus. It is most powerful to select examples from texts that students have heard in their *recent* experience. But, you can always revisit favorites that you read at the very beginning of the year. In fact, reading many picture books at the beginning of the year will quickly build students' repertoire of shared texts, providing you with a variety of choices for mentor texts for your minilessons. When texts have been enjoyed and loved in interactive read-aloud, students know them deeply and can remember them over time. It is helpful to keep an ongoing list of books read during interactive read-aloud so you and your students can refer to them throughout the year (see Figure 9-3). Some of the books in the *Interactive Read-Aloud Collection* are novels, and you are apt to include novels in text sets you assemble yourself as well. This is appropriate for readers in sixth grade. It is important, however, to remember the power of shorter picture books to expose students to a wide variety of genres, authors, and themes. When you continue to read aloud age-appropriate picture books while working through a longer novel, you expose your students to different authors and genres while developing some of the deeper understandings a novel can offer. It is also important to note that you can use familiar novels as mentor texts in your minilesson examples in the same way that you use picture books.

Here are some steps to follow for incorporating your own texts into the minilessons:

1. Identify a group of read-aloud texts that will be valuable resources for use in the particular minilesson. (These texts may be from the same text set, but usually they are drawn from several different sets. The key is their value in teaching routines, engaging in literary analysis, building particular strategies and skills, or writing about reading.)

2. The mentor texts you select will usually be some that you have already read to and discussed with the students, but if not, read and discuss them with the goal of enjoyment and understanding. The emphasis in interactive read-aloud is not on the minilesson principle but on enjoying and deeply understanding the text, appreciating the illustrations and design, and constructing an understanding of the deeper messages of the text.

3. Teach the reading minilesson as designed, substituting the texts you have chosen and read to the students.

Interactive read-aloud will greatly benefit your English language learners. In *Fountas & Pinnell Classroom*™ (Fountas and Pinnell 2020), we have selected the texts with English language learners in mind and recommend that you do the same if you are selecting texts from your existing resources. In addition to expanding both listening and speaking vocabularies, interactive read-aloud provides constant exposure to English language syntax. Stories read aloud provide "ear print" for the students. Hearing grammatical structures of English over and over helps English language learners form an implicit knowledge of the rules. Here are some other considerations for your English language learners:

 **ELL CONNECTION**

▶ Increase the frequency of your interactive read-alouds.

▶ Choose books that have familiar themes and concepts and take into account the cultural backgrounds of all the students in your classroom.

▶ Be sure that students can see themselves as well as the diversity of the world in a good portion of the texts you read.

▶ Reread texts that your English language learners enjoy. Rereading texts that students especially enjoy will help them acquire and make use of language that goes beyond their current understanding.

▶ Choose texts that are simple and have high picture support. This will allow you to later revisit concrete examples from these texts during reading minilessons.

▶ Seat English language learners in places where they can easily see, hear, and participate in the text.

▶ Preview the text with English language learners by holding a small-group discussion before reading the book to the entire class. As they hear it the second time, they will understand more and will have had the experience of talking. This will encourage the students to participate more actively during the discussion.

When you provide a rich and supportive experience through interactive read-aloud, you prepare English language learners for a successful experience in reading minilessons. They will bring the vocabulary and background knowledge developed in interactive read-aloud to the exploration of the reading minilesson principle. These multiple layers of support will pave the road to successful independent reading.

Shared and Performance Reading

ELL CONNECTION

In the early grades, shared reading of big books and enlarged texts plays a vital role in helping students understand how to find and use information from print—directional movement, one-to-one correspondence, words and letters, and the whole act of reading and understanding a story or nonfiction text. As readers become more proficient, shared reading and performance reading (see Figure 9-4) continue to offer opportunities for more advanced reading work than students can do independently. In fact, a form of shared reading can be used at every grade level and is especially supportive to English language learners, who can benefit greatly from working with a group of peers.

For students in grade 6 and above, you can use the level of support that shared reading affords to develop readers' competencies in word analysis, vocabulary, fluency, and comprehension. You'll want to provide regular opportunities for shared and performance reading not only of fiction and nonfiction books but of poems, readers' theater scripts, plays, speeches, and primary source documents as well. Select a page or pages from a text and use a document camera to enlarge it so that students can see the features you are asking them to discuss. If you have a class set of novels, distribute them to focus on a particular section or chapter as a shared reading experience. Of course, you would want to choose a section that would be meaningful on its own without having to have the context of the entire novel.

Like the books read aloud, the texts you select for shared and performance reading should offer students the opportunity to discuss characters, events, concepts, and ideas. Read the text to the students and then invite them to read all or a portion of it in unison. Having students reread the text several times until they know it well, gives you the option of revisiting it for different purposes; for example, to locate content words, practice fluency, or use inflection to convey the author's meaning. If you want, you can then extend the meaning through writing, art, or drama.

Here are some steps to follow for incorporating shared and performance reading as part of your classroom activities:

1. Display an enlarged text or provide individual copies if available. The text may be one that the students have previously read.

2. Engage students in a shared reading of the text. Plan to reread it several times. (Use your own judgment. Sometimes two or three readings are

sufficient.) Remember, the focus at this point is on understanding and enjoying the enlarged text, not on teaching a specific principle.

3. Revisit the text to do some specific teaching toward any of the systems of strategic actions listed in *The Literacy Continuum* (Fountas and Pinnell 2017b). If the text you've selected is a choral reading, script, poem, or speech, encourage students to perform it, using their voices and inflection to convey the writer's meaning.

4. If you plan to use a shared reading text in a reading minilesson, implement the lesson as designed using the texts you have used in teaching.

On the occasions that you use a shared reading text in a minilesson, students will have had opportunities to notice print and how it works and to practice fluent reading. They will have located individual words and noticed the use of bold and italicized words. They will have learned how to use the meaning, language, and print together to process the text fluently and may have used performance techniques to amplify the writer's intent. In addition, here, too, they will have noticed characteristics of the genre, the characters, and the message anchors.

Shared and performance reading can also be important in reinforcing students' ability to apply understandings from the minilesson. You can revisit the texts to remind students of the minilesson principle and invite them to notice text characteristics or engage strategic actions to process them. When you work across texts, you help students apply understandings in many contexts.

Figure 9-4: Performance reading (readers' theater) in a sixth-grade class

Shared and performance reading provide a supportive environment for English language learners to both hear and produce English language structures and patterns. Familiar shared reading texts often have repeated or rhythmic text, which is easy to learn. Using shared reading texts to teach Strategies and Skills minilessons can be particularly supportive for English language learners because they have had the opportunity to develop familiarity with the meaning, the vocabulary, and the language structures of the text. They can focus on exploring the minilesson principle because they are not working so hard to read and understand the text. Shared reading gives them the background and familiarity with text that makes it possible to easily learn the minilesson principle.

Shared reading is a context that is particularly supportive to English language learners because of the enjoyable repetition and opportunity to "practice" English syntax with the support of the group. Shared reading can be done in a whole-group or small-group setting. Following are some suggestions you can use to support English language learners:

▶ Use enlarged texts, projected texts, or, if available, an individual copy of the text for every student.

▶ Select texts with easy-to-say refrains, often involving rhyme and repeating patterns.

▶ Reread the text as much as needed to help students become confident in joining in.

▶ Use some texts that lend themselves to inserting students' names or adding repetitive verses.

Guided Reading

Guided reading is small-group instruction using an appropriately selected leveled text that is at students' instructional level. This means that the text is more complex than the students can process independently, so it offers appropriate challenge.

Supportive and precise instruction with the text enables the students to read it with proficiency, and in the process they develop in-the-head strategic actions that they can apply to the reading of other texts. Guided reading involves several steps:

1. Assess students' strengths through the analysis of oral reading behaviors as well as the assessment of comprehension—thinking within, beyond, and about the text. This knowledge enables you to determine an appropriate reading level for instruction.

2. Bring together a small group of students who are close enough to the same level that it makes sense to teach them together. (Ongoing assessment takes place in the form of running records or reading records

so that the information can guide the emphasis in lessons and groups may be changed and reformed as needed.)

3. Based on assessment, select a text that is at students' instructional level and offers opportunities for new learning.

4. Introduce the text to the students in a way that will support reading and engage them with the text.

5. Have students read the text individually. (In sixth grade, this means reading silently. You may choose to hear several students read softly to you so you can check on their processing.) Support reading through quick interactions that use precise language to support effective processing.

6. Invite students to engage in an open-ended discussion of the text and use some guiding questions or prompts to help them extend their thinking.

7. Based on previous assessment and observation during reading, select a teaching point.

8. Engage students in quick word work that helps them flexibly apply principles for solving words that have been selected based on information gained from the analysis of oral reading behaviors and reinforcement of principles explored in phonics minilessons (see *The Fountas & Pinnell Comprehensive Phonics, Spelling, and Word Study Guide* [2017a] and *Fountas & Pinnell Word Study Lessons, Grade 6* [2021]).

9. As an option, you may have students engage in writing about the book to extend their understanding, but it is not necessary—or desirable—to write about every book.

Guided reading texts are not usually used as examples in minilessons because they are not texts that are shared by the entire class. However, on occasion, you might find a guided reading book that perfectly illustrates a minilesson

Figure 9-5: Guided reading in a sixth-grade class

principle. In this case, you will want to introduce the book to the entire class as an interactive read-aloud before using it as a mentor text. You can also take the opportunity to reinforce the minilesson principle across the guided reading lesson at one or more points:

▶ In the introduction to the text, refer to a reading minilesson principle as one of the ways that you support readers before reading a new text.

▶ In your interactions with students during the reading of the text, remind them of the principle from the reading minilesson.

▶ In the discussion after the text, reinforce the minilesson principle when appropriate.

▶ In the teaching point, reinforce the minilesson principle.

In small-group guided reading lessons, students explore aspects of written texts that are similar to the understandings they discuss in interactive read-aloud and shared and performance reading. They evaluate the authenticity of characters, analyze character change, talk about the significance of the setting, talk about the problem in the story and the ending, and discuss the theme or message of the story. They talk about information they learned and questions they have, they notice genre characteristics, and they develop phonics knowledge and word-solving strategies. So, guided reading also gives readers the opportunity to apply what they have learned in reading minilessons.

 ELL CONNECTION

When you support readers in applying the minilesson principle within a guided reading lesson, you give them another opportunity to talk about text with this new thinking in mind. It is particularly helpful to English language learners to have the opportunity to try out this new thinking in a small, safe setting. Guided reading can provide the opportunity to talk about the minilesson principle before the class comes back together to share. Often, students feel more confident about sharing their new thinking with the whole group because they have had this opportunity to practice talking about a book in the small-group setting.

Book Clubs

For a book club meeting, bring together a small group of students who have chosen the same book to read and discuss with their classmates. The book can be one that you have read to the group or one that the students can either read independently or listen to and understand from an audio recording.

The implementation of book clubs follows these steps:

1. Preselect about four books that offer opportunities for deep discussion. These books may be related in some way (for example, they might be by the same author or feature stories around a theme). Or, they might just be a group of titles that will give students good choices.

2. Give a book talk about each of the books to introduce them to students. A book talk is a short "commercial" for the book.

3. Have students read and prepare for the book club discussion. (If the student cannot read the book, prepare an audio version that can be used during independent reading time.) Each reader marks a place or places that he wants to discuss with a sticky note.

4. Convene the group and facilitate the discussion.

5. Have students self-evaluate the discussion.

Book clubs provide students the opportunity for deep, enjoyable talk with their classmates about books. Minilessons in two umbrellas are devoted to teaching the routines of book clubs. Literary Analysis Umbrella 1: Getting Started with Book Clubs focuses on the routines for getting started and takes students through the process of choosing books, marking pages they want to discuss, and participating in the discussion in meaningful ways. Umbrella 2: Learning Conversational Moves in Book Club teaches students how to enter a conversation, invite others to participate, build on other people's ideas, and change the focus when necessary.

A discussion among four or five diverse sixth-grade students can go in many directions, and you want to hear all of their ideas! *Prompting Guide, Part 2, for Comprehension: Thinking, Talking, and Writing* (Fountas and Pinnell 2009b) is a helpful tool. The section on book discussions contains precise teacher language for getting a discussion started, asking for thinking, affirming thinking, agreeing and disagreeing, changing thinking, clarifying thinking, extending thinking, focusing on the big ideas, making connections, paraphrasing, questioning and hypothesizing, redirecting, seeking evidence, sharing thinking, and summarizing.

Figure 9-6: Book club in a sixth-grade class

Before teaching several of the book club minilessons, we suggest holding a fishbowl observation of a book club discussion. To do this, prepare a small book group ahead of time and help them mark pages in the book they want to discuss. Have the small group sit in a circle with the remaining students sitting outside the circle to observe. Lead the conversation as needed, having book club members talk about their thinking for a few minutes. Encourage them to invite others in the group to talk, ask each other questions, and agree or disagree with one another in a respectful way. In some cases, you will ask students to observe through a particular lens. In others, they will be asked to make general observations. In either case, the prepared group models what a book club meeting should look like. The minilessons in the book club umbrellas offer suggestions for how to conduct these fishbowl observations prior to teaching the lesson.

ELL CONNECTION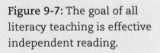

Book clubs offer English language learners the unique opportunity to enter into conversations about books with other students. If they have listened to an audio recording many times, they are gaining more and more exposure to language. The language and content of the book lifts the conversation and gives them something to talk about. They learn the conventions of discourse, which become familiar because they do it many times. They can hear others talk and respond with social language, such as "I agree with _____ because _____."

Independent Reading

In independent reading, students have the opportunity to apply all they have learned in minilessons. To support independent reading, assemble a well-organized classroom library with a range of engaging fiction and nonfiction books. Although you will take into account the levels students

Figure 9-7: The goal of all literacy teaching is effective independent reading.

can read independently to assure a range of options, we do *not* suggest that you arrange the books by level. It is not productive and can be destructive for the students to choose books by "level." Instead, create tubs or baskets by author, topic, genre, and so forth. There are minilessons in Section One: Management to help you teach sixth graders how to choose books for their own reading (see MGT.U2.RML3). Consider the following as you prepare students to work independently.

▶ **Personal Book Boxes.** A personal book box is where students keep their materials (e.g., reader's notebook, writer's notebook, writing folder, books to read) all together and organized. A magazine holder or cereal box works well. Students can label the boxes with their names and decorate them. Keep these boxes in a central place so that students can retrieve them during independent reading time.

▶ **Classroom Library.** The classroom library is filled with baskets or tubs of books that sixth-grade students will love. Books are organized by topic, theme, genre, series, or author. Management minilesson MGT.U2.RML2 provides guidance for how to organize and introduce your classroom library. Have students help you organize the books so that they share some ownership of the library. In some minilessons, there is a direction to guide students to read from a particular basket in the classroom library so that they have the opportunity to apply the reading minilesson to books that include the characteristics addressed in the minilesson. For example, you might have them read from a basket of fantasy books or a basket of poetry books.

Becoming independent as a reader is an essential life skill for all students. English language learners need daily opportunities to use their systems of strategic actions on text that is accessible, meaningful, and interesting to them. Here are some suggestions for helping English language learners during independent reading:

 **ELL CONNECTION**

▶ Make sure your classroom library has a good selection of books at a range of levels. If possible, provide books in the first language of your students as well as books with familiar settings and themes.

▶ During individual conferences, help students prepare—and sometimes rehearse—something that they can share with others about the text during group share. When possible, ask them to think about the minilesson principle.

▶ Provide opportunities for English language learners to share with partners before being asked to share with the whole group.

Combining Implicit and Explicit Teaching for Independent Reading

You are about to embark on a highly productive year of literacy lessons. We have prepared these lessons as tools for your use as you help students engage with texts, making daily shifts in learning. When students participate in a classroom that provides a multitext approach to literacy learning, they are exposed to textual elements in a variety of instructional contexts. As described in Figure 9-8, all of these instructional contexts involve embedding literary and print concepts into authentic and meaningful experiences with text. A powerful combination of many concepts is implicitly understood as students engage with books, but the explicit teaching brings them to conscious awareness and supports students' ability to articulate the concepts using academic language.

Figure 9-8: Text experiences are supported and developed by implicit and explicit teaching in all instructional contexts, including interactive read-aloud, shared reading, guided reading, book clubs, and independent reading conferences. Reading minilessons provide explicit teaching that makes learning visible and is reinforced in the other contexts.

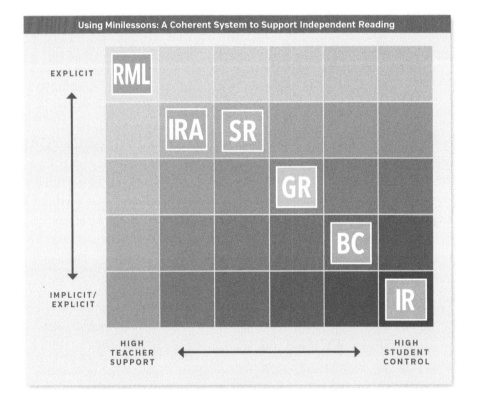

In interactive read-aloud, students are invited to respond to text as they turn and talk and participate in lively discussions after a text is read. You will be able to support your students in thinking within, beyond, and about the text because you will have used *The Literacy Continuum* (Fountas and Pinnell 2017b) to identify when you will pause and invite these conversations and how you will ask questions and model comments to support the behaviors you have selected. In response, your students will experience and articulate deeper thinking about texts.

In shared and performance reading, students learn from both implicit and explicit teaching. For example, when they work on performing a reader's theater script, they read and discuss the text several times, enjoying the story and discussing aspects of the text that support their thinking within, beyond, and about the text. As they prepare to perform the script, the teacher might provide explicit teaching for fluency (e.g., interpreting a character's dialogue using appropriate intonation and stress). The embedded, implicit teaching, as well as some of the more explicit teaching that students experience in shared and performance reading, lays the groundwork for the explicit teaching that takes place in reading minilessons. Reading minilessons become the bridge from these shared and interactive whole-group reading experiences to independent reading.

Guided reading and book clubs scaffold the reading process through a combination of implicit and explicit teaching that helps students apply the reading minilesson principles across a variety of instructional-level texts. The group share reinforces the whole process. Reading minilessons do not function in the absence of these other instructional contexts; rather, they all work in concert to build processing systems for students to grow in their ability to independently read increasingly complex texts over time.

The minilessons in this book serve as a guide to a meaningful, systematic approach to joyful literacy learning across multiple reading contexts. Students acquire a complex range of understandings. Whole-class minilessons form the "glue" that connects all of this learning, makes it explicit, and turns it over to the students to apply to their own independent reading and writing. You will find that the talk and learning in those shared experiences will bring your class together as a community with a shared knowledge base. We know that you and your students will enjoy the rich experiences as you engage together in thinking, talking, and responding to a treasure chest of beautiful books. Students deserve these rich opportunities—every child, every day.

Works Cited

Clay, Marie. 2015 [1991]. *Becoming Literate: The Construction of Inner Control*. Auckland, NZ: Global Education Systems.

Fountas, Irene C., and Gay Su Pinnell. 2006. *Teaching for Comprehending and Fluency: Thinking, Talking, and Writing About Reading, K–8*. Portsmouth, NH: Heinemann.

———. 2009a. *Fountas & Pinnell Prompting Guide, Part 1, for Oral Reading and Early Writing*. Portsmouth, NH: Heinemann.

———. 2009b. *Fountas & Pinnell Prompting Guide, Part 2, for Comprehension: Thinking, Talking, and Writing*. Portsmouth, NH: Heinemann.

———. 2011. *Reader's Notebook: Advanced*. Portsmouth, NH: Heinemann.

———. 2012a. *Fountas & Pinnell Genre Prompting Guide for Fiction*. Portsmouth, NH: Heinemann.

———. 2012b. *Fountas & Pinnell Genre Prompting Guide for Nonfiction, Poetry, and Test Taking*. Portsmouth, NH: Heinemann.

———. 2012c. *Genre Study: Teaching with Fiction and Nonfiction Books*. Portsmouth, NH: Heinemann.

———. 2017a. *The Fountas & Pinnell Comprehensive Phonics, Spelling, and Word Study Guide*. Portsmouth, NH: Heinemann.

———. 2017b. *The Fountas & Pinnell Literacy Continuum: A Tool for Assessment, Planning, and Teaching*. Portsmouth, NH: Heinemann.

———. 2017c. *Guided Reading: Responsive Teaching Across the Grades*. Portsmouth, NH: Heinemann.

———. 2018. *The Literacy Quick Guide: A Reference Tool for Responsive Literacy Teaching*. Portsmouth, NH: Heinemann.

———. 2020. *Fountas & Pinnell Classroom™*. Portsmouth, NH: Heinemann.

———. 2021. *Fountas & Pinnell Word Study Lessons, Grade 6*. Portsmouth, NH: Heinemann.

Bodeen, Stephanie. *Babu's Song*. 2008. New York: Lee & Low.

Vygotsky, Lev. 1978. *Mind in Society: The Development of Higher Psychological Processes*. Cambridge, MA: Harvard University Press.

Management minilessons focus on routines for thinking and talking about reading and working together in the classroom. These lessons allow you to teach effectively and efficiently. They are directed toward the creation of an orderly, busy classroom in which students know what is expected as well as how to behave responsibly and respectfully within a community of learners. Most of the minilessons at the beginning of the school year will focus on management.

1 Management

Minilessons in This Umbrella

RML1 A strong classroom community enjoys learning and works well together.

RML2 Agree on how to work together.

RML3 Be inclusive of others.

RML4 Think about how your words and actions make others feel.

Before Teaching Umbrella 1 Minilessons

The purpose of this umbrella is to help students identify as members of a community of readers and writers who work and learn together. You can support this concept by creating an inviting and well-organized classroom in which students can take ownership of their space and materials and by giving students plenty of opportunities to choose, read, and talk about books.

Read books about positive relationships, inclusivity, handling emotions, fitting in, empathy, and conflict resolution to help students understand what it means to be part of a caring and considerate community. The minilessons in this umbrella use books from the following *Fountas & Pinnell Classroom™ Interactive Read-Aloud Collection* text sets, but you can use other books closely related to your students' experiences and interests.

Handling Emotions/Positive Relationships

The Banana-Leaf Ball: How Play Can Change the World by Katie Smith Milway

It Doesn't Have to Be This Way: A Barrio Story by Luis J. Rodríguez

Kindness and Compassion

Wings by Christopher Myers

Chachaji's Cup by Uma Krishnaswami

Babu's Song by Stephanie Stuve-Bodeen

Handling Emotions/ Positive Relationships

Kindness and Compassion

Section 1: Management

Reading Minilesson Principle

A strong classroom community enjoys learning and works well together.

Being a Respectful Member of the Classroom Community

You Will Need

- classroom set up with areas to support students in reading and writing activities
- chart paper and markers

Academic Language / Important Vocabulary

- community
- respectful
- organized
- inclusion

Continuum Connection

- Actively participate in conversation during whole- and small-group discussion (p. 341)

Goal

Learn what makes a strong classroom community of students who enjoy learning and who work well together.

Rationale

To create a healthy and positive classroom community, all students need to take responsibility for treating each other with respect and doing what they can to support each other. In addition to social and emotional responsibility, students also need to care for the surroundings, the materials, and other physical aspects of the communal space.

Assess Learning

Observe students when they work and learn together and notice if there is evidence of new learning based on the goal of this minilesson.

- ▶ Do students understand their individual roles in fostering a positive classroom community?
- ▶ Do they treat each other and the classroom with respect?
- ▶ Do they understand and use the terms *community, respectful, organized,* and *inclusion*?

Minilesson

To help students think about the minilesson principle, engage them in a discussion about what responsibilities the members of a community have in creating a positive place for working and learning together. Here is an example.

> We are all part of this classroom community. What is a classroom community?
>
> For each of us to learn and do our best work together, we need to build a strong community. Think about what you can do to make everyone feel good about being part of the classroom community. What are your ideas?

- ▶ Use the following prompts as needed to support the conversation:
  - *How can the members of a classroom community make everyone feel part of the community?*
  - *How can the members of a classroom community support each other in their learning?*
- ▶ After time for discussion, ask students to share their thinking. Make a student-generated list of how each student can support the work of the community.
- ▶ Record responses on the chart.

Have a Try

Invite the students to talk in small groups about being a member of the classroom community.

> What is something you can do to support a strong classroom community?

▶ After time for discussion, ask students to share.

Summarize and Apply

Summarize the learning by reviewing the chart.

▶ Write the principle at the top.

> Keep the items on the chart in mind as you go through the day. Later, we will meet to share. Be ready to talk about something you did to make our classroom community strong.

Share

Following independent reading time, gather students together in the meeting area.

> Who would like to share what you did to help build a strong community?

Extend the Lesson (Optional)

After assessing students' understanding, you might decide to extend the learning.

▶ Have regular whole-class meetings to discuss how well the class is working as a learning community and to allow students to voice concerns or suggest ways to improve.

A strong classroom community enjoys learning and works well together.

- Treat others with respect.
- Make everyone feel welcome and included.
- Listen to what others have to say.
- Share ideas honestly and respectfully.
- Ask others for help and give help to others.
- Work well independently or with your group.

community

Being a Respectful Member of the Classroom Community

You Will Need

- chart paper and markers

Academic Language / Important Vocabulary

- classroom community
- agreement
- classroom norms

Continuum Connection

- Listen respectfully and responsibly (p. 341)
- Speak at an appropriate volume (p. 341)
- Use respectful turn-taking conventions (p. 341)

Goal

Create norms and agreements for a classroom community to follow.

Rationale

When students understand that a community works well together and that they can create a classroom agreement to establish norms, they learn to take ownership of their classroom and behaviors so that a positive classroom environment can be maintained.

Assess Learning

Observe students when they construct and follow a classroom agreement and notice if there is evidence of new learning based on the goal of this minilesson.

- Do students contribute ideas about learning and working well together?
- Do they exhibit the behaviors the class has agreed upon?
- Do they understand the terms *classroom community, agreement,* and *classroom norms?*

Minilesson

To help students think about the minilesson principle, engage them in discussing and creating a community agreement or a set of norms for working together. Here is an example.

> We have talked about what the members of a strong classroom community can do to make everyone feel good as part of the community. When community members agree on ways to work together well, they create a set of classroom norms, or expectations, for the way each person should behave. Norms are expectations for how each person will behave.
>
> What are the norms we can agree upon to make it possible for everyone to enjoy working and learning together? Let's make a list.

- As needed, support the conversation with prompts such as the following:
  - *When you are reading or writing, how can you do your best work?*
  - *How can you make the classroom a place where everyone can learn?*
  - *How can you participate positively when you are working in a group?*
  - *How should you show caring for the resources and materials in the classroom?*
- After time for discussion, record students' ideas on chart paper.

  > This chart will remind us of how we have agreed to work and learn together.

Have a Try

Invite the students to talk with a partner about the community agreement.

> Do you have any additional ideas for the chart? Turn and talk to your partner about that. You can also talk about why the ideas we have written on the chart are important.

> ▶ After time for discussion, ask a few students to share ideas. Discuss whether any new items should be added to the classroom agreement.

Summarize and Apply

Summarize the learning and remind students to think about the community agreement.

> Today we made a community agreement. Why is this important for our classroom?

> Today, take a moment to think about our agreement and how it will help you as a reader and writer. What things will you do to follow each part of the agreement? After you have thought about these things, come up and sign the agreement at the bottom. Be ready to share your thinking when we come back together.

Share

Following independent reading time, gather students together in the meeting area to discuss the classroom agreement.

> Take a look at our list of classroom norms. What do you think? Is there anything we should change or add?

Extend the Lesson (Optional)

After assessing students' understanding, you might decide to extend the learning.

> ▶ Keep the norms posted in the classroom and have new discussions from time to time to evaluate whether any changes should be made.

> ▶ Recognize when students solve problems independently and provide positive reinforcement for their efforts.

Classroom Norms

- Use an appropriate voice level.
- Focus on your work.
- Take turns talking and listen carefully.
- Help each other feel safe taking risks.
- Be respectful of what others say.
- Help each other learn.
- Take care of the classroom and materials.
- Try to solve problems independently:
  - Conflict? Talk to the person or compromise.
  - Help with directions? Reread them, think about past assignments, or ask another student.
  - Finish work early? Review your work, read, finish other work, study for a test.

Ava Liam *Nam*   *Idris*   Pazie MAZ
Harper NICHOLAS stef *PIA*   Hamish Sydney
TAMI GRETA *Kim*   Hali *Massimo*
TOMMIE Nya Cora AMELIA oliver
Jackie *Mark*   Anna Hugo

RML 3
MGT.U1.RML3

Reading Minilesson Principle
Be inclusive of others.

Being a Respectful Member of the Classroom Community

You Will Need

- several fiction books that have examples of getting to know one another and being inclusive, such as the following:
  - *The Banana-Leaf Ball* by Katie Smith Milway, from Text Set: Handling Emotions/ Positive Relationships
  - *Chachaji's Cup* by Uma Krishnaswami and *Wings* by Christopher Myers, from Text Set: Kindness and Compassion
- chart paper and markers
- sticky notes

Academic Language / Important Vocabulary

- classroom community
- conversation
- unique
- diverse
- inclusive

Continuum Connection

- Learn from vicarious experiences with characters in stories (p. 81)
- Respect the age, gender, position, and cultural traditions of the speaker (p. 341)

Goal

Value the unique identities of others and use language and take actions that make others feel included.

Rationale

When students learn words and actions to get to know one another, invite others to join in, value the unique identities of others, and embrace diversity, they create a rich, interesting, and safe environment in which all classroom community members feel valued.

Assess Learning

Observe students as they interact with classmates and notice if there is evidence of new learning based on the goal of this minilesson.

- ▶ Do students use words and actions to get to know someone?
- ▶ Are they taking steps to include others?
- ▶ Do they understand the terms *classroom community, conversation, unique, diverse,* and *inclusive*?

Minilesson

To help students think about the minilesson principle, engage them in a discussion about getting to know one another and inclusion. Here is an example.

▶ Revisit pages 15 and 24–25 from *The Banana-Leaf Ball*.

Remember in *The Banana-Leaf Ball* when the boys first meet the coach and each other? Think about what they did as I revisit a few parts from the book.

▶ Revisit pages 4 and 11 from *Chachaji's Cup*.

Remember how Neel invited Daniel over to his house and Neel's great-uncle, Chachaji, would share their family customs and stories?

▶ Revisit pages 5, 9, 16, 17, 26, and 37 from *Wings*.

Think about the ways the narrator and Ikarus felt excluded because of the ways they were different. Also think about how they became friends.

All of these stories have examples of getting to know someone or being inclusive. Turn and talk in threes about some different ways you can get to know someone and what you can do to be inclusive.

▶ After time for discussion, ask students to share ideas. Begin a list on chart paper about ways to get to know other people and ways to be inclusive.

Have a Try

Invite the students to talk with a partner about being inclusive.

> Why is it important to take steps to get to know others and to be inclusive? Turn and talk about that.

▶ After time for discussion, briefly discuss new ideas. Add responses to the chart.

Summarize and Apply

Summarize the learning and remind students to think about ways they can include others.

> Think about the different ideas posted on the chart and try to use these ideas in the classroom or around the school.

▶ Write the principle at the top of the chart.

> When you read today, notice examples of how characters get to know each other, when they are inclusive, or when they make someone feel left out. Place a sticky note on the page with the example. Bring the book when we meet so you can share.

Be inclusive of others.

Get to know someone	Be inclusive
• Help a new person get to know the classroom and school.	• What do you think about that?
• Talk about favorite books.	• What is your opinion?
• Share information about yourself.	• Can I help you with that?
• Look for common interests.	• Would you like to come with us?
• See if you can help with anything.	• Do you want to sit with me/us?
• Ask questions:	• Do you want to join our game?
• Who is in your family?	• Do you have any suggestions?
• What do you like to do when you're not at school?	
• What is your favorite music, movie, sport, food?	
• What pets do you have?	

Share

Following independent reading time, gather students in the meeting area.

> Did you find any examples of characters who got to know each other, who included others, or who did not include others? Share the examples that you noticed.

Extend the Lesson (Optional)

After assessing students' understanding, you might decide to extend the learning.

▶ Have students create graphic organizers, modeled after a character web, as a way of sharing information about themselves so that students can get to know them better.

▶ **Writing About Reading** Have students write about a character who made another character feel included or excluded. Encourage them to also write about how they felt when they read that part of the book.

Reading Minilesson Principle
Think about how your words and actions make others feel.

Being a Respectful
Member of the Classroom
Community

You Will Need

- several familiar fiction books that encourage thinking about empathy, such as the following:
  - *Babu's Song* by Stephanie Stuve-Bodeen, from Text Set: Kindness and Compassion
  - *It Doesn't Have to Be This Way* by Luis J. Rodríguez, from Text Set: Handling Emotions/Positive Relationships
  - *Chachaji's Cup* by Uma Krishnaswami, from Text Set: Kindness and Compassion
- chart paper and markers
- sticky notes

Academic Language / Important Vocabulary

- classroom community
- empathy

Continuum Connection

- Learn from vicarious experiences with characters in stories (p. 81)

Goal

Show empathy toward others.

Rationale

When students reflect on how their words and actions affect classmates, they develop empathy and concern for others, which contributes to a positive learning environment.

Assess Learning

Observe students as they discuss empathy and interact with others. Notice evidence of new learning based on the goal of this minilesson.

- ▶ Do students talk about how someone's words or actions make another person feel?
- ▶ Are they able to infer how their own words and actions make others feel?
- ▶ Do they understand the terms *classroom community* and *empathy*?

Minilesson

To help students think about the minilesson principle, use familiar texts with examples of empathy to help them think about how words and actions make others feel. Here is an example.

- ▶ Revisit page 1 from *Babu's Song*.

    Think about how Bernadi is feeling. How do you know? Turn and talk about that.

- ▶ As students share ideas, create a two-column chart. On the left side, write things that characters say and do. On the right side, write how those words or actions make other characters feel.

- ▶ Revisit pages 3 and 14, pausing after each to ask students to notice empathy and add ideas to the chart.

- ▶ Revisit page 10 and then page 25 from *It Doesn't Have to Be This Way*.

    What did you notice about how Monchi feels?

- ▶ Add examples to the chart.

- ▶ Revisit pages 20–21 from *Chachaji's Cup* and repeat the activity.

    Trying to understand how others feel is called empathy.

Have a Try

Invite the students to talk with a partner about empathy.

> Think of a time when someone's words or actions made you feel good or feel bad. Turn and talk to your partner about that.

▶ Make sure the discussions don't name individuals in a negative way. Keep them general. After students turn and talk, ask a couple of pairs to share.

Summarize and Apply

Summarize the learning and remind students to think about how their words and actions affect others.

> Think about the examples on the chart and how you can use words and actions to make others feel good.

▶ Write the minilesson principle at the top of the chart paper.

> When you read today, notice examples of characters who show empathy toward others, or notice when one character understands how another character feels. Place a sticky note on any pages with examples. Bring the book when we meet so you can share.

Think about how your words and actions make others feel.

Title	What Someone Says or Does	How That Makes Someone Feel
Babu's Song	The boys let Bernardi play soccer with them.	He feels included.
	Babu makes Bernardi a music box.	Bernardi feels loved and cared for.
It Doesn't Have To Be This Way	Clever offers Monchi a chance to join a gang.	Monchi feels included. He thinks he has no other options.
	Dreamer is injured and in the hospital.	Monchi feels responsible and guilty.
Chachaji's Cup	Neel glues the pieces of Chachaji's broken cup back together.	Chachaji feels grateful.

Share

Following independent reading time, gather students together in the meeting area to discuss examples of empathy.

> Did you find any examples of characters who used words or actions to make others feel good or bad? Share what you noticed.

Extend the Lesson (Optional)

After assessing students' understanding, you might decide to extend the learning.

▶ Have students write about examples from their own lives of how the words or actions of others made them feel, what others could have said or done to show more empathy, or about times when they were empathetic toward another person. Reassure students that they should share only what they are comfortable sharing.

▶ Notice when students practice empathy in the classroom and point out the specific examples to show how it helps build a strong community of learners, readers, and writers.

Assessment

After you have taught the minilessons in this umbrella, observe students as they learn and interact with others in the classroom.

▶ What evidence do you have of new understandings related to being respectful members of the classroom community?

- Are students developing skills to work and learn together as a community?
- How well do they take care of the classroom and the materials they use?
- Do they try to get to know one another?
- Do they participate in making and honoring classroom agreements?
- Can they find ways to solve problems on their own?
- Are they inclusive of others?
- Do they think about how their words and actions make others feel?
- Do they use terms such as *community, respectful, organized, agreement, problem, solution, inclusive, and unique* when they talk about the classroom community?

▶ What other minilessons might you teach to help students grow and function as members of a community of readers and writers?

- Are students able to find books to read and books to recommend to others?
- Are they able to share their thinking with others during turn and talk or during a book club meeting?

Use your observations to determine the next umbrella you will teach. You may also consult Minilessons Across the Year (pp. 61–64) for guidance.

Reader's Notebook

When this umbrella is complete, provide a copy of the minilesson principles (see resources.fountasandpinnell.com) for students to glue in the reader's notebook (in the Minilessons section if using *Reader's Notebook: Advanced* [Fountas and Pinnell 2011]), so they can refer to the information as needed.

Minilessons in This Umbrella

RML1 Read and share your thinking during independent reading time.

RML2 The classroom library includes a variety of books for you to enjoy.

RML3 Make good decisions about your book choices.

Reader's Notebook

Before Teaching Umbrella 2 Minilessons

The purpose of the minilessons in this umbrella is to help students learn about what to do during the time set aside for independent reading and writing. Students learn that reading, writing, and discussion are all important aspects of independent reading time, explore how the classroom library system makes finding books easier, and learn how to make good decisions about their book choices. Before teaching the minilessons in this umbrella, decide whether you will organize the library ahead of time or whether you will engage students in the process of categorizing the books. Give students plenty of opportunities to choose, read, and talk about books. Also, decide where students will do their reading and writing during independent reading time. Here are some suggestions for preparing for introducing independent reading time:

- Organize (or have students help you organize) books in the classroom library into baskets in a way that allows students to see the front covers and that provides easy access for browsing.

- In each basket, display high-quality, diverse, and interesting books that offer a range of difficulty levels and are grouped by category.

- Label (or have students label) baskets with the topic, author, illustrator, series, genre, or theme.

- Give each student a personal book box for keeping books and other literacy materials.

Section 1: Management

Reading Minilesson Principle

Read and share your thinking during independent reading time.

Getting Started with Independent Reading

You Will Need

- chart paper and markers
- a reader's notebook for each student

Academic Language / Important Vocabulary

- independent reading
- turn and talk
- reader's notebook

Continuum Connection

- Give reasons/evidence (either text-based or from personal experience) to support thinking (pp. 79, 84)
- Engage actively in conversational routines: e.g., turn and talk (p. 341)

Goal

Read independently and share thinking through talking and writing about reading.

Rationale

When students understand the expectations for independent reading time, they spend this time reading silently, allowing them to do their best thinking about their reading. When they share their thinking about books, they develop identities as readers and deepen their understanding and appreciation of texts. They also strengthen their interpersonal and communication skills.

Assess Learning

Observe students during independent reading time and notice if there is evidence of new learning based on the goal of this minilesson.

- Do students understand what to do during independent reading time?
- Do they understand and use the terms *independent reading*, *turn and talk*, and *reader's notebook*?

Minilesson

To help students think about the minilesson principle, engage them in a discussion about how to work during independent reading time and ways to share thinking about books. Here is an example.

> When you read a book, what are some of the things you think about?

- Record students' responses on chart paper.

> To do your best thinking while you read, what should it be like in the classroom?

> During independent reading time, you will read silently so everyone can do their best thinking. Sometimes you will share your thinking by talking about your reading with your classmates and me.

- Write the heading *Turn and Talk* on the chart.

> What are some guidelines for when you turn and talk with a partner?

- Record responses under the heading. If students mention looking at their partner, take into consideration that some may not be comfortable with establishing or able to establish eye contact because of cultural conventions or for other reasons.

> Another way to share your thinking is by writing about your reading.

- Write the heading *Write About Reading* on the chart.

> One place to write about your reading is in your reader's notebook.

Have a Try

Invite the students to talk with a partner about their reading.

> Turn and talk to your partner about the book you are reading now or the last book you read. Look at what we wrote on the chart under Turn and Talk, and remember to do these things.

▶ After time for discussion, invite several pairs to evaluate their discussion, using the chart for guidance.

Summarize and Apply

Summarize the learning and remind students to read and share their thinking during independent reading time.

> Independent reading time will be part of almost every day. What will you do when it's time for independent reading?
>
> How can you share your thinking about your reading?

▶ Write the principle at the top of the chart.

> During independent reading time today, remember to read a book silently. When we come back together, you will have the opportunity to talk about your reading. Sometimes, you will also write about your reading in a reader's notebook.

Share

Following independent reading time, gather students together in the meeting area to talk about the books they read.

> Turn and talk to a partner about the book you read today. Look at the chart if you need ideas for sharing.

Extend the Lesson (Optional)

After assessing students' understanding, you might decide to extend the learning.

▶ If you are using *Reader's Notebook: Advanced* (Fountas and Pinnell 2011), refer students to the Guidelines for Readers' Workshop on the inside front cover.

▶ **Writing About Reading** Teach the minilessons in Section Four: Writing About Reading to formally introduce the reader's notebook and familiarize students with different ways of writing about reading.

Read and share your thinking during independent reading time.

Think About Your Reading

- Characters
- Setting
- Author's message
- Author's writing style
- Something that surprised you
- Something interesting you learned
- Predictions about what might happen next
- Opinion about the book
- The theme(s) of the book

Share Your Thinking

Turn and Talk
- Look at your partner.
- Listen carefully.
- Ask questions to clarify.
- Give reasons and evidence for your thinking.

Write About Reading

Reader's Notebook

Section 1: Management

Reading Minilesson Principle
The classroom library includes a variety of books for you to enjoy.

You Will Need

- an organized, inviting classroom library
- several books from your classroom library for each group (see Have a Try)
- chart paper and markers
- sticky notes

Academic Language / Important Vocabulary

- classroom library
- organized
- topic
- genre
- theme
- series

Goal

Understand the classroom library is organized by author, illustrator, genre, series, theme, and topic to make finding books easier.

Rationale

When you teach students how the classroom library is organized, they are better able to find and select books that they will enjoy reading. As an alternative to the process suggested in this lesson, you could have your students work with you to sort books, create categories, and label the baskets.

Assess Learning

Observe students when they select books from the classroom library and notice if there is evidence of new learning based on the goal of this minilesson.

- ▶ Can students explain how and why the classroom library is organized?
- ▶ Do they use their understanding of the organization of the classroom library to choose books to read?
- ▶ Do they understand and use the terms *classroom library*, *organized*, *topic*, *genre*, *theme*, and *series*?

Minilesson

To help students think about the minilesson principle, have them gather in the classroom library and engage them in a discussion about the organization of the books. Here is an example.

> Take a look around. What do you notice about how the books in our classroom library are organized?

- ▶ Help students notice the specific ways the books are organized by asking questions such as the ones below. Alter the questions to reflect the specific categories of books available in your own classroom library, but try to include all the ways the books are organized (e.g., author, illustrator, genre, series, theme, topic).

  - *Where would I find books by Lois Lowry?*
  - *What kind of books are in this basket?*
  - *Where would I look if I wanted to find the next book in the Wollstonecraft Detective Agency series?*
  - *Where should I look for books about inspiration and creativity?*
  - *Where can I find myths?*

- ▶ Record each category of books that students notice (and an example of that category) on the chart paper.

Have a Try

Invite the students to talk with a partner about how to organize books in the classroom library.

▶ Put students into small groups, and give each group a small stack of books. Each book should clearly correspond with a basket in your classroom library.

Talk in your group about where you think each of your books should go. Then write your decision on a sticky note and stick the note on the front cover.

▶ After time for discussion, invite groups to share and explain their decisions.

Summarize and Apply

Summarize the learning and remind students to use the organization of the classroom library to help them find and select books.

What did you notice today about our classroom library?

▶ Write the principle at the top of the chart.

When it's time for independent reading, think about what kind of book you'd like to read. Maybe you would like to read a book about a certain topic or a book by your favorite author. Use what you now know about our classroom library to help you find the kind of book that you want to read.

Share

Following independent reading time, gather students together in the meeting area to talk about the books they chose.

What book did you choose today? Where did you find it?

How did the way our classroom library is organized help you find a book?

Extend the Lesson (Optional)

After assessing students' understanding, you might decide to extend the learning.

▶ Give regular book talks about books you are adding to your classroom library or that you want to highlight.

▶ **Writing About Reading** Teach Umbrella 1: Introducing a Reader's Notebook in Section Four: Writing About Reading so students can begin recording books they have read and books they want to read.

The classroom library includes a variety of books for you to enjoy.

Author	Illustrator	Genre
Lois Lowry	K. Y. Craft	Myths

Series	Theme	Topic
Wollstonecraft Detective Agency	Inspiration and Creativity	Astronomy

RML 3
MGT.U2.RML3

Reading Minilesson Principle
Make good decisions about your book choices.

Getting Started with Independent Reading

You Will Need

▶ chart paper and markers

Academic Language / Important Vocabulary

▶ choice
▶ decision
▶ independent reading
▶ recommendation
▶ genre
▶ abandon

Continuum Connection

▶ Express tastes and preferences in reading and support choices with descriptions and examples of literary elements: e.g., genre, setting, plot, theme, character, style, and language (pp. 593, 605, 617)

Goal

Choose books for independent reading.

Rationale

When you teach students to be aware of the ways they choose books and to make good decisions about their reading, they spend more time reading books they enjoy. They also become more independent and confident, and they develop their interests and identities as readers. They are more likely to love reading and to become lifelong readers.

Assess Learning

Observe students when they choose books and talk about books they have chosen. Notice if there is evidence of new learning based on the goal of this minilesson.

▶ Do students choose books that interest them and that are about right for the ability they have at this time?

▶ Can they explain why they chose a particular book?

▶ Do they vary their book choices in terms of genre, topic, and difficulty level?

▶ Do they understand the terms *choice, decision, independent reading, recommendation, genre,* and *abandon*?

Minilesson

To help students think about the minilesson principle, engage them in a discussion about how to choose books. Here is an example.

> Sometimes it can be hard to choose just the right book to read. One way I choose books is to ask friends for recommendations. What are some ways you choose books to read?

▶ Record responses on chart paper.

> These are all great ways to choose books. Something else to think about is whether a book is the right difficulty level for you—not too easy and not too challenging. How do you know when you have picked a book that is just right for you?

> Sometimes you might choose to read a book that is easy or one that is a little challenging. Why might you sometimes want to read an easy book?

> When might you choose a book that is challenging?

> Sometimes you might choose an easy book because you want to relax or you love the topic or series. Other times, you might choose a challenging book because it is about something you really want to learn about or because it was highly recommended to you. It is a good idea to choose a book with some challenges, but not so many that you can't enjoy it.

Have a Try

Invite the students to talk with a partner about choosing books.

> Turn and talk to your partner about what you think about when choosing a book.

▶ After students turn and talk, ask a few students to share their responses. Add responses to the chart.

> Now turn and talk about whether the book you chose most recently was a good choice for you. Be sure to explain why or why not.

▶ Invite a few students to share their thinking.

Summarize and Apply

Summarize the learning and remind students to make good decisions about book choices.

> What did you learn today about choosing books?

> It's important to choose books you think you'll enjoy. It's also a good idea to sometimes choose books that are different from the books you normally read or that may be a little challenging for you. Sometimes you may surprise yourself by loving a book that is different from what you usually read! However, sometimes you might start a book and find that it is not a good choice for you. If that happens, you can abandon it after you've given it a good try.

▶ Write the principle at the top of the chart.

> If you choose a new book to read today, try to choose one that you think you'll enjoy and that is right for you as a reader. Be ready to share why you chose your book when we come back together.

Share

Following independent reading time, gather students in small groups to discuss their reading choices.

> Talk in your group about why you chose the book you are reading.

Extend the Lesson (Optional)

After assessing students' understanding, you might decide to extend the learning.

▶ **Writing About Reading** Have students keep a list in a reader's notebook of books they have read and assess whether each book was a good choice for them (see WAR.U1.RML2).

Make good decisions about your book choices.

Ways to Choose Books

- Recommendations from other readers
- Good reviews
- Favorite author or illustrator
- Won awards
- Part of a favorite series
- Interesting title
- Appealing front cover
- Description on the back cover sounds interesting
- Favorite genre
- Loved the movie version
- About right for you as a reader

Assessment

After you have taught the minilessons in this umbrella, observe students as they use classroom spaces and materials. Use *The Literacy Continuum* (Fountas and Pinnell 2017) to observe students' reading and writing behaviors.

▶ What evidence do you have of new understandings related to independent reading?

- Are students able to find and select books?

- Are they making good decisions about book choices?

- Do they read silently during independent reading time?

- Do they share their thinking about books both orally and in writing?

- Do they use terms such as *independent reading, turn and talk, reader's notebook*, and *classroom library*?

▶ What other minilessons might you teach to help students grow and function as readers and as members of the classroom community?

- Do students treat each other respectfully and inclusively?

- How do they show they are living a reading life?

Use your observations to determine the next umbrella you will teach. You may also consult Minilessons Across the Year (pp. 61–64) for guidance.

Reader's Notebook

When this umbrella is complete, provide a copy of the minilesson principles (see resources.fountasandpinnell.com) for students to glue in the reader's notebook (in the Minilessons section if using *Reader's Notebook: Advanced* [Fountas and Pinnell 2011]), so they can refer to the information as needed.

Minilessons in This Umbrella

RML1	Find out about books you might want to read.
RML2	Recommend a book by giving a book talk.
RML3	Think about who influences your reading and whose reading you influence.
RML4	Reflect on your reading habits.
RML5	Challenge yourself to grow or stretch as a reader.
RML6	Dedicate time to read outside of school.

Before Teaching Umbrella 3 Minilessons

The importance of literacy instruction extends far beyond the classroom. It is not enough simply to teach students the skills to comprehend what they read. Students who love reading, dedicate time to reading, and think of themselves as readers have the greatest chance of success in school and beyond. The purpose of this umbrella is to help students develop lifelong reading habits. The minilessons guide students to dedicate time to reading both in school and outside of school, to reflect on their reading habits, and to develop their identities and preferences as readers. Before teaching this umbrella, provide students with several opportunities to choose, read, enjoy, share, and talk about books. For RML2, use the following book from the *Fountas & Pinnell Classroom™ Independent Reading Collection* or select a book that your students will find engaging.

Independent Reading Collection

   The Thing About Jellyfish by Ali Benjamin

RML1
MGT.U3.RML1

Reading Minilesson Principle
Find out about books you might want to read.

Living a Reading Life

You Will Need

▶ chart paper and markers

Academic Language / Important Vocabulary

▶ recommendation
▶ review
▶ book talk

Continuum Connection

▶ Express tastes and preferences in reading and support choices with descriptions and examples of literary elements: e.g., genre, setting, plot, theme, character, style, and language (pp. 593, 605, 617)

Goal

Find books using different resources both inside and outside of the classroom.

Rationale

When students learn about the many resources for finding books, they expand the book choices that they have available to them. They are therefore more likely to find books that they enjoy reading.

Assess Learning

Observe students when they talk about how they find out about books and notice if there is evidence of new learning based on the goal of this minilesson.

▶ Do students find out about books in a variety of ways?

▶ Do they talk about the different ways they find out about books?

▶ Do they use terms such as *recommendation*, *review*, and *book talk*?

Minilesson

To help students think about the minilesson principle, discuss different ways to find out about books. Here is an example.

> There are many different ways to find out about books. How did you find out about the book you are reading now, or the last book you read?

▶ Record responses on chart paper.

> What are some other methods that you use to find out about books that you might like to read?

▶ Add responses to the chart. If necessary, ask questions such as the following to prompt students to name ways to find out about books:

- *What are some places in our school where you can find out about books?*
- *Whom can you ask for book recommendations?*
- *What are some places outside of school where you can find out about books?*

Have a Try

Invite the students to talk with a partner about ways to find out about books.

> Which of these ways to find out about books have you already tried, and which would you like to try in the future? Turn and talk to your partner about this. If you know of any other ways to find out about books, share them with your partner as well.

▶ After students turn and talk, invite a few students to share their thinking. Add any new ideas to the list.

Summarize and Apply

Summarize the learning and encourage students to take advantage of the different ways to find out about books.

> Today you thought about different ways to find out about books you might want to read.

▶ Write the principle at the top of the chart.

> When you read today, take a moment to think about your favorite way to find out about new books to read. Be ready to talk about it when we come back together.

Share

Following independent reading time, gather students together in the meeting area to talk about ways to find out about books.

> Turn and talk to your partner about your favorite way to find out about books to read.

> What are you going to do next time you need a new book to read? Is anybody going to try something new?

Extend the Lesson (Optional)

After assessing students' understanding, you might decide to extend the learning.

▶ Use a section of the classroom library to feature books recommended by you or by particular students. Each recommended book should have a notecard explaining why it is recommended and the signature of the person who recommended it.

▶ Guide students in using various websites (e.g., Goodreads) for finding new books to read.

Find out about books you might want to read.

- classroom, school, or public library
- book talks by teacher or classmates
- librarian's recommendations
- recommendations from friends or family members
- bookstores (special displays and recommendations from booksellers)
- lists of books that have won awards
- book reviews in magazines or online
- websites about books
- online reading communities
- online bookstores
- blogs
- online videos
- authors' websites

RML 2
MGT.U3.RML2

Reading Minilesson Principle
Recommend a book by giving a book talk.

Living a Reading Life

You Will Need

- a book that is likely to be of interest to your students but that they have not read, such as *The Thing About Jellyfish* by Ali Benjamin, from *Independent Reading Collection*
- chart paper and markers
- sticky notes

Academic Language / Important Vocabulary

- book talk
- recommend

Continuum Connection

- Evaluate aspects of a text that add to enjoyment: e.g., humorous character or surprising information (p. 593, 605)
- Express personal opinions about aspects of the text that make it engaging or interesting and provide examples and evidence from the text to justify (p. 617)
- Communicate interest in and enthusiasm about a topic (p. 342)
- Present information in ways that engage listeners' attention (p. 342)
- Speak with appropriate volume for audience size and location (p. 342)
- Speak with confidence and in a relaxed manner (p. 342)

Goal

Recommend a book by presenting a book talk confidently and enthusiastically.

Rationale

Book talks give students the opportunity to share their enthusiasm for certain books with other readers. When students learn how to give a good book talk, they learn public speaking skills and develop their identities as readers. Book talks also offer listeners a valuable opportunity for finding out about books to read.

Assess Learning

Observe students when they give book talks and notice if there is evidence of new learning based on the goal of this minilesson.

- Do students give engaging and effective book talks?
- Do they use the terms *book talk* and *recommend*?

Minilesson

To help students think about the minilesson principle, provide a model book talk and then discuss the characteristics that made it effective. Here is an example.

- Prior to the lesson, make note of a few important ideas about the book on a notecard and place sticky notes on a few pages to share in the book talk. The example below uses *The Thing About Jellyfish* by Ali Benjamin.

  > After her best friend drowns, Suzy convinces herself that the true cause of her friend's death was a sting by an extremely rare jellyfish. She hatches a plan to prove her theory—a plan that involves traveling to the other side of the world on her own. *The Thing About Jellyfish* by Ali Benjamin is beautifully written and thought provoking. Even though it is fiction, it also provides a lot of accurate and very interesting information about jellyfish. If you're looking for a moving story that will pull you in and even teach you a thing or two about science, this is the book for you!

  > What did you notice about my book talk?

- As needed, prompt the conversation with questions such as the following:
  - *How did I interest you in reading the book?*
  - *What do you think I did to prepare for the book talk?*
  - *Where did I look and what did I do while I was giving the book talk?*

- Record students' responses on chart paper. If students mention looking at the audience, take into consideration that some may not be comfortable with establishing or able to establish eye contact because of cultural conventions or for other reasons.

Have a Try

Invite the students to talk with a partner about book talks.

> Why might you want to listen to someone giving a book talk? How can listening to book talks help you? Turn and talk to your partner about what you think.

▶ After time for discussion, invite a few students to share their thinking.

Summarize and Apply

Summarize the learning and remind students to use the techniques they learned for giving a good book talk.

> What did you learn today about how to give a good book talk?

▶ Write the principle at the top of the chart.

> Today, choose a book that you've read and enjoyed and that you think your classmates might enjoy reading. Prepare to give a book talk about that book. When we come back together, you will present your book talk to a small group.

Recommend a book by giving a book talk.

- Get people excited to read the book by giving a good introduction.
- Tell the title and author of the book.
- Write important words or phrases on a notecard or sticky note.
- Mark pages that you want to talk about.
- Practice your book talk.
- Hold the book so everyone can see it.
- Stand up straight and look at the audience.
- Be enthusiastic.
- Speak clearly and loudly.
- Tell why people should read the book.
- Keep it short.

Share

Following independent reading time, gather students in small groups to present their book talks.

▶ Have students present a book talk to their groups.

▶ After students have presented, bring the whole class back together.

> What worked well for you when you gave your book talk?

> What will you do differently next time?

Extend the Lesson (Optional)

After assessing students' understanding, you might decide to extend the learning.

▶ **Writing About Reading** Tell students that they can write the titles of books they hear about in book talks on the Books to Read page in a reader's notebook (see WAR.U2.RML1).

▶ Give book talks frequently to keep students' interest in reading high: at the beginning of readers' workshop, when you introduce a new book to the classroom library, or when you want to highlight a particular book.

RML 3

MGT.U3.RML3

Reading Minilesson Principle
Think about who influences your reading and whose reading you influence.

Goal

Notice and identify the people or reading communities that influence reading choices.

Rationale

When students think about how they influence and are influenced by other readers, they begin to understand the importance of being part of a reading community. Students who develop reading relationships with other people are more likely to enjoy reading, to be confident about talking about their reading, and to become lifelong readers.

Assess Learning

Observe students when they talk about their reading influences and notice if there is evidence of new learning based on the goal of this minilesson.

▶ Can students identify other readers who influence them and whom they influence?

▶ Can they explain how they are influenced by and influence other readers?

▶ Do they understand and use the term *influence*?

Minilesson

To help students think about the minilesson principle, engage them in a discussion about reading influences. Here is an example, but use your own personal story.

> I just finished reading a wonderful book that my mother recommended to me. My mother and I have similar taste in books. We frequently discuss our reading and recommend books to each other. My mother is one of the people who influences my reading, or has an effect on what I choose to read. Who influences your reading?
>
> How does that person influence your reading?

▶ Use students' responses to create on chart paper a list of influential people and a list of the ways readers can influence other readers.

Have a Try

Invite the students to talk with a partner about whose reading they influence.

> Now take a moment to think about whose reading you influence and how. Then turn and talk to your partner about how you influence the reading of other people.

▶ After time for discussion, ask a few students to share their thinking. Add new ideas to the chart.

Summarize and Apply

Summarize the learning and remind students to think about their relationships with other readers.

▶ Write the principle at the top of the chart.

> Why do you think it's important to influence and be influenced by other readers? How does this help you as a reader?

> After you read today, take five or ten minutes to write about how you influence and are influenced by other readers. Be sure to give specific examples. Be ready to share your thinking when we come back together.

Share

Following independent reading time, gather students together in the meeting area to talk about their reading influences.

> Who would like to share something you wrote showing how you influence or are influenced by other readers?

Extend the Lesson (Optional)

After assessing students' understanding, you might decide to extend the learning.

▶ When you hold individual reading conferences, ask students who or what influenced a decision to read a particular book.

▶ **Writing About Reading** Encourage students to exchange letters about their reading with influential friends, family members, or classmates.

Think about who influences your reading and whose reading you influence.

WHO?	HOW?
• Friends	• Book recommendations
• Parents	• Loan books to each other
• Siblings	• Talk about what you are reading
• Grandparents	• Participate in book clubs
• Cousins	• Read or watch book reviews online
• Aunts and uncles	• Write book reviews or post comments about books online
• Teachers	
• School librarian	
• Neighbors	
• Online reading communities	
• Book bloggers	

Section 1: Management

Reading Minilesson Principle
Reflect on your reading habits.

Living a Reading Life

You Will Need

▶ chart paper and markers

**Academic Language /
Important Vocabulary**

▶ reflect
▶ reading habits

**Continuum
Connection**

▶ Express tastes and preferences
in reading and support choices
with descriptions and examples
of literary elements: e.g., genre,
setting, plot, theme, character,
style, and language (pp. 593,
605, 617)

▶ Express preferences with specific
references to characteristics of
fiction and nonfiction genres
(pp. 605, 617)

Goal

Reflect on reading habits, including text selection, commitment, engagement level, etc.

Rationale

When students reflect on their reading habits, they get to know themselves as readers. They develop their identities as readers and identify potential areas for growth. They become more engaged readers and are more likely to become lifelong readers.

Assess Learning

Observe students when they reflect on their reading habits and notice if there is evidence of new learning based on the goal of this minilesson.

▶ Do students reflect on their reading habits (e.g., text selection, commitment, engagement level)?

▶ Can they identify areas where they might change or strengthen their reading habits?

▶ Do they understand and use the terms *reflect* and *reading habits*?

Minilesson

To help students think about the minilesson principle, engage them in a discussion about how to reflect on their reading habits. Here is an example.

> We've been discussing how to find interesting new books to read and how other people influence your reading choices. When you thought about these things, you were reflecting on your reading. What does it mean to reflect on something?

> When you reflect on something, you think seriously and carefully about it. Take a moment to reflect on yourself as a reader. Would you say that you are generally successful at choosing books to read? Why or why not?

▶ Invite a few volunteers to share. Then use a few more questions such as the following to prompt students' reflections:

  • *Do you read across a variety of genres? Why or why not?*

  • *Do you stay committed when you choose a book to read, or do you abandon books easily? If you often abandon books, why do you think that is?*

  • *Are you excited or bored by most of the things you read? If you are often bored, why do you think that is?*

▶ Write each question that you discuss on chart paper.

Have a Try

Invite the students to reflect on their reading habits with a partner.

> Do you regularly talk to other people about your reading? If so, how does that help you as a reader? If not, why not? Turn and talk to your partner about this.

▶ After time for discussion, invite a few students to share.

Summarize and Apply

Summarize the learning and remind students to reflect on their reading habits.

> What are some of the things you can think about when you reflect on your reading habits?

> Why is it important to reflect on your reading habits?

▶ Write the principle at the top of the chart.

> After you read today, take a few minutes to reflect on and write about your reading habits. You might choose to write about one of the questions on our list, or you can reflect on a different aspect of your reading life. Be ready to share your thinking when we come back together.

Share

Following independent reading time, gather students together in the meeting area to share their reflections on their reading habits.

> How did you reflect on your reading habits today? What did you think and write about?

Extend the Lesson (Optional)

After assessing students' understanding, you might decide to extend the learning.

▶ **Writing About Reading** Have students keep a list in a reader's notebook of the books they have read (see WAR.U1.RML2). Encourage them to briefly reflect on one or two of their reading choices (e.g., how they chose the book, their reaction to it, whether it was a good choice).

Reflect on your reading habits.

- Are you generally successful at choosing books to read?
- Do you read across a variety of genres?
- Are you committed to your reading?
- Do the books you read excite you?
- How much time do you dedicate to reading?
- Do you regularly talk to others about your reading?

Reading Minilesson Principle

Challenge yourself to grow or stretch as a reader.

You Will Need

▶ chart paper and markers

Academic Language / Important Vocabulary

▶ reading plan
▶ goal
▶ challenge

Goal

Make reading plans to stretch and grow as a reader.

Rationale

When students make plans for their reading, they are more likely to maintain their reading habits and develop their competencies and identities as readers. Examples of reading plans include reading more books, spending more time reading outside of school, reading more challenging books, and reading different genres of books.

Assess Learning

Observe students when they set, work toward, and discuss their reading plans and notice if there is evidence of new learning based on the goal of this minilesson.

▶ Do students make personalized reading plans that are challenging but realistic?

▶ Do they stay committed to their reading plans? If not, do they reflect on the reasons and adjust their reading plans as appropriate?

▶ Do they use the terms *reading plan*, *goal*, and *challenge*?

Minilesson

To help students think about the minilesson principle, engage them in a discussion about reading plans. Here is an example.

> Sometimes I find it hard to decide what to read next. One thing that helps me is to keep a list of the books that I plan to read in the future. When I finish a book on my list, I cross it off and choose another. Do any of you keep a list of books like that? What book are you planning on reading next?

> Making a list of the books you want to read is an example of a reading plan. Reading plans help you reach your reading goals. A reading goal might be to read more. To reach that goal, you might plan to read at least one book every week or an hour every day. You might have a few reading goals and plans or just one, but try not to have so many that you can't accomplish them. Reading goals and plans help you grow as a reader. In what other ways can you challenge yourself to grow as a reader?

▶ Record students' responses on chart paper. Use questions such as the following to prompt the conversation as needed:

- *What reading plan could you make if you wanted to read more outside of school?*

- *If you only read fantasy books, how could you challenge yourself to read other kinds of books?*

- *If the books you read are too easy for you, and you get bored while reading them, what reading plan might you make?*

Have a Try

Invite the students to talk with a partner about their reading plans.

> Turn and talk to your partner about one type of book that you'd like to read more of this year.

▶ After time for discussion, invite a few students to share.

Summarize and Apply

Summarize the learning and remind students to always have a plan for challenging themselves as readers.

> How can having a reading plan help you grow as a reader?

▶ Write the principle at the top of the chart.

> After you read today, take five or ten minutes to think about how you are going to challenge yourself to grow or stretch as a reader this year. What reading plans would help you reach your reading goal? Write down at least one way that you are going to challenge yourself this year.

Share

Following independent reading time, gather students together in the meeting area to discuss their reading plans.

> Who made a reading plan for yourself that you would like to share?

Extend the Lesson (Optional)

After assessing students' understanding, you might decide to extend the learning.

▶ Consider using the Reading Requirements page in *Reader's Notebook: Advanced* (Fountas and Pinnell 2011) as a way for students to set goals for reading different kinds of books.

▶ At the end of the school year, encourage students to set goals for summer reading.

Challenge yourself to grow or stretch as a reader.

Examples of Reading Plans

• Read <u>Gathering Blue</u> by Lois Lowry next.

• Read one book every week.

• Read for at least an hour every evening.

• Read books that are more challenging.

• Read ten books about science this year.

• Read more poetry books.

Section 1: Management

Reading Minilesson Principle
Dedicate time to read outside of school.

Living a Reading Life

You Will Need

▸ chart paper and markers

Academic Language / Important Vocabulary

▸ dedicate

Goal

Find more time to read outside of school.

Rationale

Students who spend time reading outside of school on a regular basis do better in school and are more likely to love reading and become lifelong readers. Many people, adults and children alike, find it challenging to find time to read, and this minilesson offers suggestions for carving out more reading time.

Assess Learning

Observe students when they talk about their reading habits and notice if there is evidence of new learning based on the goal of this minilesson.

▸ Do students report that they read outside of school on a regular basis?

▸ Do they understand the word *dedicate*?

Minilesson

To help students think about the minilesson principle, engage them in a discussion about reading outside of school. Here is an example.

> When you read books that you choose, you are in charge of yourself as a reader. You are independent. You are making personal choices, and you'll be doing this all your life. Your choices are not only about the books you read; you also choose where and when you will read. Do you have a special place outside of school where you like to read? Why do you like that place?

> I like to read every night before going to bed. When do you like to read?

▸ Record students' responses on chart paper.

> Sometimes it is challenging to find enough time to read all the books you want to read.

> One way that I've found more time to read is to bring a book with me everywhere I go. Sometimes I read when I'm on the bus, when I'm waiting for a movie to begin, or when I'm in the waiting room at the doctor's office. If you always have a book with you, you can spend a few minutes reading whenever you have a little bit of spare time. Does anyone else have any tips for finding more time to read?

Have a Try

Invite the students to talk with a partner about their reading habits.

> Turn and talk to your partner about whether it is easy or challenging to dedicate time to read outside of school. Be sure to explain the reasons why.

▶ After students turn and talk, invite several students to share. If some students express obstacles to reading, collectively brainstorm ways to overcome them.

Summarize and Apply

Summarize the learning and remind students to dedicate time to reading outside of school.

▶ Write the principle at the top of the chart.

> We talked about when and where you like to read and about ways to find more time to read. What are some of the ways we talked about?

> Today, take five or ten minutes to think and write about your reading time outside of school. You might write about your favorite time and place to read. You may also write about ways that you could find more time to read.

Share

Following independent reading time, gather students together in the meeting area to discuss their plans for reading outside of school.

> What ideas do you have for how you could find more time to read outside of school?

Extend the Lesson (Optional)

After assessing students' understanding, you might decide to extend the learning.

▶ Regularly invite students to talk about the books they read outside of school.

▶ During individual reading conferences with students, discuss their reading habits and, if applicable, make a plan for overcoming obstacles to reading outside of school.

Dedicate time to read outside of school.

Where?	When?
• "in my bedroom" – Andrew	• "before bedtime" – Malik
• "on the bus" – Ella	• "first thing in the morning" – Jazmin
• "in my backyard" – Jacob	• "after school" – Landen
• "at my grandma's" – Brooklyn	

Assessment

After you have taught the minilessons in this umbrella, observe students as they talk about their reading. Use *The Literacy Continuum* (Fountas and Pinnell 2017) to guide the observation of students' reading and writing behaviors.

▶ What evidence do you have of new understandings related to living a reading life?

- Do students actively seek out new books they might want to read?
- Do they recommend books to classmates, sometimes in a book talk?
- Do they think about who influences their reading and whose reading they influence?
- Do they reflect on their reading habits?
- Do they make reading plans that help them grow and stretch as readers?
- Do they view themselves as readers?
- Do they regularly spend time reading outside of school?
- Do they use terms such as *recommend, review, book talk, influence, reading plan,* and *challenge*?

▶ What other minilessons might you teach to maintain and grow independent reading habits?

- Do students know how to find books that interest them in your classroom library?

Use your observations to determine the next umbrella you will teach. You may also consult Minilessons Across the Year (pp. 61–64) for guidance.

Reader's Notebook

When this umbrella is complete, provide a copy of the minilesson principles (see resources.fountasandpinnell.com) for students to glue in the reader's notebook (in the Minilessons section if using *Reader's Notebook: Advanced* [Fountas and Pinnell 2011]), so they can refer to the information as needed.

Literary Analysis

Literary Analysis minilessons support students' growing awareness of the elements of literature and the writer's and illustrator's craft. The minilessons help students learn how to think analytically about texts and to identify the characteristics of fiction and nonfiction genres. The books that you read during interactive read-aloud can serve as mentor texts when applying the principles of literary analysis.

Minilessons in This Umbrella

RML1 Choose a book you would like to read and talk about.

RML2 Mark places you want to talk about.

RML3 Talk about your thinking in book clubs.

RML4 Ask questions to clarify understanding.

RML5 Give directions to help everyone get to a specific place in the book quickly.

Before Teaching Umbrella 1 Minilessons

The minilessons in this umbrella are designed to help you introduce and teach procedures and routines to establish book clubs in your classroom. Book clubs (pp. 74–76) are meetings with about six students of varying reading abilities who come together to discuss a common text. The meeting is facilitated by the teacher. The goal is for students to share their thinking with each other and build a richer meaning than one reader could gain alone. You may want to conduct a fishbowl lesson to demonstrate how a book club discussion works, either before selected minilessons as a model or afterward as a reflection. This umbrella will take students through the first set in the *Book Clubs Collection*. Based on RML1, students will choose a book club book. Then, after each lesson, you can meet with a different book club. The minilessons in this umbrella use the following books from the *Fountas and Pinnell Classroom™ Book Clubs Collection* and *Interactive Read-Aloud Collection* text sets; however, you can use other book sets from your classroom. Refer to the *Book Clubs Collection* cards for book summaries to use for book talks and additional discussion ideas.

Book Clubs Collection

Compassion and Caring for Others

  Iqbal by Francesco D'Adamo

  Half a Man by Michael Morpurgo

  Kids at Work: Lewis Hine and the Crusade Against Child Labor
    by Russell Freedman

  The Harmonica by Tony Johnston

Interactive Read-Aloud Collection

Kindness and Compassion

  Chachaji's Cup by Uma Krishnaswami

**Book Clubs
Compassion and
Caring for Others**

**Interactive Read-Aloud
Kindness and
Compassion**

Section 2: Literary Analysis

Reading Minilesson Principle
Choose a book you would like to read and talk about.

Getting Started with Book Clubs

You Will Need

- prepared book talks for four books students have not read or heard, such as the following from the *Book Clubs Collection* Text Set: Compassion and Caring for Others:
  - *Iqbal* by Francesco D'Adamo
  - *Half a Man* by Michael Morpurgo
  - *Kids at Work* by Russell Freedman
  - *The Harmonica* by Tony Johnston
- chart paper and markers
- sticky notes
- a slip of paper for each student that has the four book club titles written on it
- To download the following online resource, visit **resources.fountasandpinnell.com**: Book Talks

Academic Language / Important Vocabulary

- book club
- title
- author
- illustrator
- choice
- preference

Continuum Connection

- Form and express opinions about a text and support with rationale and evidence (pp. 79, 84)

Goal

Make a good book choice for book club meetings.

Rationale

When students make their own choices about what to read, they are more engaged and motivated to read. This contributes to a positive book club experience and increases the possibility of a lifelong love of reading.

Assess Learning

Observe students when they choose books for book club meetings and notice if there is evidence of new learning based on the goal of this minilesson.

- ▶ Are students able to identify information that will help them select a book they want to read?
- ▶ Do they express and reflect on the reasons they choose particular books to read?
- ▶ Do they use the terms *book club, title, author, illustrator, choice,* and *preference*?

Minilesson

To help students think about the minilesson principle, demonstrate the process of choosing a book for book club and help students reflect on that process. Here is an example.

> Think about your interest in each of these four books as I tell you a little about them.

- ▶ Show the cover of *Iqbal* and offer a short book talk.

> Imagine being taken from your family as a small child and forced to work twelve hours a day, seven days a week to pay off a family debt. Now imagine what it would be like to rebel against your master, putting your own life in danger to help save other enslaved children like you. Read to learn how a brave Pakistani boy named Iqbal did just this and what it cost him.

- ▶ Turn through a few pages.

> What are some reasons why this fictionalized book about Iqbal Masih might be enjoyable to read?

- ▶ Continue giving short book talks for the other three books (use your own book talks or the prepared book talks in online resources).

> You have now listened to a book talk about four different books. Think about your preferences.

Have a Try

Invite the students to talk with a partner about which book interests them.

> Turn and talk to a partner about your first and second choices.

▶ After time for discussion, ask students to share their thinking.

Summarize and Apply

Summarize the learning for students.

> We talked about different reasons you might choose a book for your book club meeting.

> During reading today, fill out the sheet of paper to show your preferences for a book club book. Number the books in the order you want to read them. Number one will be your first choice. Be sure to put your name on the paper.

▶ While students are reading, collect the numbered sheets of paper and create four book clubs. Make a chart to show when each club will meet.

Book Club Groups

Monday	Tuesday
Ainsley	Liana
Tessa	Emma
Noah	Lucas
Colby	Saha
Jayden	Brayden
Daniela	Huy

Wednesday	Thursday
Naveh	Mai
Elliot	Satchiko
Janea	Quinn
Sami	Santiago
Ian	Juliette
Jaxon	Tomma

Share

Following independent reading time, gather students in the meeting area.

> This chart shows which group you will be in for the first book club of the year. It also shows when your book club will meet. Turn and talk to a partner about what you think you will enjoy about the book you will read.

Extend the Lesson (Optional)

After assessing students' understanding, you might decide to extend the learning.

▶ After the first round of book club meetings, use the same set of books for a second round, asking students to choose a different book this time. Use the opportunity to explain that not everyone will get to read their first choice every time.

RML2
LA.U1.RML2

Reading Minilesson Principle
Mark places you want to talk about.

Getting Started with Book Clubs

You Will Need

- a familiar book, such as the following:
  - *Chachaji's Cup* by Uma Krishnaswami, from *Interactive Read-Aloud Collection* Text Set: Kindness and Compassion
- chart paper and markers
- sticky notes prepared with page numbers and a few words indicating discussion topics, placed on corresponding pages in *Chachaji's Cup*
- document camera (optional)
- sticky notes
- set of book club books

Academic Language / Important Vocabulary

- book club
- sticky notes

Continuum Connection

- Form and express opinions about a text and support with rationale and evidence (pp. 79, 84)

Goal

Identify the important information to discuss in preparation for a book club.

Rationale

When students learn to note parts of a book they want to discuss, they think critically about the book and develop a process for preparing for a discussion.

Assess Learning

Observe students when they discuss characters and notice if there is evidence of new learning based on the goal of this minilesson.

▶ Are students able to identify and mark relevant pages in a book to prepare for a book club meeting?

▶ Do they understand the terms *book club* and *sticky notes*?

Minilesson

To help students think about the minilesson principle, use a familiar book to model how to mark pages for a book club meeting. Here is an example.

▶ Show the cover of *Chachaji's Cup* with the sticky notes showing.

> While I was reading the book, I thought of some things I could talk about in a book club meeting.

▶ Show page 3 with the first sticky note.

> On page 3, I placed a sticky note to remember to talk about the fact that this family's daily teatime shows their connection as a family. It shows character relationships. The note helps me remember the page and the information that interests me.

▶ Place the sticky note on the top of the chart. On the bottom of the chart, write *character relationships* to show that this is the information that the sticky note is helping you remember.

> What do you notice about the information I included on the sticky note?

▶ Guide the conversation so students notice to include the page number in case the note falls off and to include just a few words to remind them of what they want to discuss.

▶ Continue discussing the other sticky notes in the book, placing them on the chart.

> Looking over these sticky notes, what are some things that you might think about marking to discuss?

▶ Add students' ideas to the list at the bottom of the chart.

120 ■ *The Reading Minilessons Book, Grade 6*

Have a Try

Invite the students to talk with a partner about using sticky notes to prepare for book club meetings.

> Turn and talk about what other kinds of information a sticky note can help you remember in a book.

▸ After time for discussion, ask students to share ideas. Add new ideas to the chart list.

Summarize and Apply

Summarize the learning and remind students to use sticky notes to prepare for book club discussions.

> What did you learn about preparing for a book club discussion?

▸ Add the principle to the top of the chart.

> When you read today, use a few sticky notes to prepare for your book club meeting. Remember to add the page number in case the sticky note falls off the page. Write just a few words on the note, like the examples you see on the chart. Bring the book when we all meet so you can share.

▸ Meet with one of the book club groups.

Share

Following independent reading time, gather students in pairs.

> Share the pages that you marked with a sticky note. Tell your partner why you wanted to remember that page.

Extend the Lesson (Optional)

After assessing students' understanding, you might decide to extend the learning.

▸ As an alternative to using sticky notes, teach the students how to use a Thinkmark. Students may fill in a Thinkmark for books they read and want to talk about in a book club or a conference. (Visit resources.fountasandpinnell.com to download a Thinkmark.)

Mark places you want to talk about.

Page 3 Daily teatime	Page 7 Special cup/title?	Page 8 Time spent together	Page 10 Illustration of Chachaji's story

Ideas for What to Mark for Discussion

- character relationships
- connection to title
- insight into characters
- details in illustrations
- word choice or language
- interesting parts
- character traits
- character change
- symbolism
- questions
- author's message or theme
- turning point
- author's craft
- confusing parts

Reading Minilesson Principle
Talk about your thinking in book clubs.

Getting Started with Book Clubs

You Will Need

- students' book club books
- one fiction and one nonfiction book that you are reading
- chart paper and markers

Academic Language / Important Vocabulary

- author
- illustrator
- book club
- discussion

Continuum Connection

- Form and express opinions about a text and support with rationale and evidence (pp. 79, 84)
- Identify and discuss interesting, surprising, and important information in a text (p. 84)

Goal

Brainstorm different ways of talking about books during book club.

Rationale

When students learn to share ideas in a book club, it expands comprehension, creates enthusiasm for reading, and contributes to a rich conversation. You may wish to have one group of students model how to hold a book club by staging a fishbowl discussion (p. 76).

Assess Learning

Observe students when they meet for book club and notice if there is evidence of new learning based on the goal of this minilesson.

- ▶ Are students expressing opinions about books?
- ▶ Are they trying out new ways to talk about books?
- ▶ Do they use the terms *author, illustrator, book club,* and *discussion*?

Minilesson

To help students think about the minilesson principle, help them think about what they might want to talk about in book club. Here is an example.

- ▶ Show a fiction book and a nonfiction book that you are reading yourself.

  I am reading these two books. One is a fiction book, and the other is a nonfiction book. I'm really enjoying the plot and subplots in the fiction book, and I'm impressed with the expertise and life experience of the author of the nonfiction book. If I meet with other friends who are reading these books, these are things I might like to talk about.

- ▶ Begin a list on chart paper with ideas about what to talk about in book club. Add the ideas you shared.

  Think about the book you have been reading for your book club. What are some of the things you find interesting to talk about in book club?

- ▶ As students share ideas, add them to the list using generalized language that could be applied to any book, though some items may be more appropriate for fiction or nonfiction books. Prompt the conversation as needed.

Have a Try

Invite the students to talk with a partner about book club discussion ideas.

> Turn and talk about the book you are reading for your book club. What would you like to talk about with members of your book club?

▶ After time for discussion, ask students to share. Add new ideas to the chart.

Summarize and Apply

Summarize the learning and remind students to think about what they might talk about in book club meetings.

> Today you talked about a range of topics you might discuss in book club meetings.

> As you read your book club book today, think about what you would like to talk about and whether there is anything else to add to the chart. I will be meeting with one book club, and those students will be sharing about their book during our class meeting.

▶ Meet with one of the book club groups.

Share

Following independent reading time, gather students in the meeting area. Have the book club members you met with share the things they discussed in their book club. Then invite the class to talk about new ideas.

> Is there anything that you want to add to the chart based on what the book club members shared with you?

Extend the Lesson (Optional)

After assessing students' understanding, you might decide to extend the learning.

▶ **Writing About Reading** Have students glue a list of items they can reflect on into a reader's notebook as a reference for thinking and writing about books. (Visit resources.fountasandpinnell.com for a copy of the list of discussion items from this lesson or make a copy of the list your class created.)

Talk about your thinking in book clubs.

- plot, subplots, multiple plots
- meaning of the title
- characters' dialogue, behaviors, or thoughts
- setting (believability, accuracy)
- topic
- illustrations or photographs
- something interesting, humorous, confusing, exciting, or surprising
- genre

- symbolism, figurative language, sensory details
- predictions
- social issues
- messages or themes
- author's point of view/perspective/purpose
- organizational structure
- representation and stereotypes
- author's or illustrator's craft

Section 2: Literary Analysis

Reading Minilesson Principle
Ask questions to clarify understanding.

Getting Started with Book Clubs

You Will Need

- four students who are prepared to share questions they might raise in a book club meeting
- the book club selection that students will be sharing, such as the following:
  - *The Harmonica* by Tony Johnston, from the *Book Clubs Collection* Text Set: Compassion and Caring for Others
- students' book club selections
- sticky notes
- chart paper and markers

Academic Language / Important Vocabulary

- book club
- questions
- phrase
- clarify

Continuum Connection

- Monitor own understanding of others' comments and ask for clarification and elaboration (p. 341)

Goal

Ask genuine questions to clarify understandings about the book and about one another's thinking.

Rationale

When students learn to ask questions to clarify understanding, they learn how to engage in rich conversations about books and learn to converse with each other to understand what others are thinking.

Assess Learning

Observe students during book club meetings and notice if there is evidence of new learning based on the goal of this minilesson.

- ▸ Are students asking relevant, thoughtful questions during book club meetings?
- ▸ Do they understand the terms *book club, questions, phrase,* and *clarify*?

Minilesson

To help students think about the minilesson principle, engage them in a discussion about how to ask genuine questions to clarify the understanding and interpretation of a book. Here is an example.

▸ Gather students in the meeting area so they can all view the chart.

> Today, several book club members are going to share the questions they prepared for their book club selection, *The Harmonica*.

▸ Have the book club members read their questions aloud one at a time, and as they do, add the sticky note with the question across the top of the chart.

> What do you notice about the book club members' questions?

> These are some questions that your classmates had when they read *The Harmonica*. Sometimes there is something in a book that doesn't quite make sense, or you want to know more about something. You can ask questions like these in a book club meeting. The questions help you think together about the book's meaning. Let's look at how these questions were formed.

▸ Guide students to notice that they, too, can start questions in a similar way. Make a list on the chart of question or wondering starters.

> When someone asks a question to understand the book better, you can respond. What are some ways that you might start a response to questions that start like the ones in our list?

▸ Guide students to come up with response frames that they can refer to in their next book club meetings. Record on the chart.

Have a Try

Invite the students to talk in small groups about questions they could ask during book club meetings.

> In your small group, practice asking a question or wondering about something in the book club book you are reading. Some of you can ask a question and some of you can practice responding.

▶ After time for discussion, ask students to share what they shared with their partners. Write additional responses on the chart.

Summarize and Apply

Summarize the learning and remind students to think about questions they want to ask during book club meetings.

▶ Write the principle at the top of the chart.

> If you are reading your book club selection today and you get confused or wonder about something, write it on a sticky note to bring to your book club meeting. If you are meeting with me today for book club, bring any questions you have about the book so we can talk about them and you can understand the book better.

▶ Meet with one of the book club groups.

Share

Following independent reading time, gather students in the meeting area. Ask the students who met in book club to talk about whether they had any questions answered in book club today.

> Why is your book club meeting a good place to talk about real questions you might have about what you read?

▶ Guide the conversation so students understand the value of getting multiple perspectives.

Extend the Lesson (Optional)

After assessing students' understanding, you might decide to extend the learning.

▶ Introduce higher-level questions as students become more proficient with asking questions during book club. If you have *Fountas & Pinnell Prompting Guide, Part 2, for Comprehension: Thinking, Talking, and Writing* (Fountas and Pinnell 2009), refer to Section IV: Prompts for Book Discussions.

Ask questions to clarify understanding.

Why did the writer choose to start the book the way she did?	Is anyone else confused about why the parents and kids were sent to different concentration camps?	Why do you think the Nazi soldiers were able to dehumanize so many people, yet treated this young musician differently?

Questions/Wonderings	Possible Responses
Why did the writer ____?	Maybe the author ____.
What I wonder is ____?	One possibility is ____.
I'm confused about ____.	Could it be that ____?
Why do you think ____?	My explanation is that ____.
What does that mean ____?	One explanation might be ____.

RML 5
LA.U1.RML5

Reading Minilesson Principle
Give directions to help everyone get to a specific place in the book quickly.

You Will Need

- any book club book
- document camera (optional)
- chart paper and markers
- students' book club books

Academic Language / Important Vocabulary

- directions
- exact place
- line
- paragraph
- caption
- panel

Goal

Understand how to give directions for everyone to locate the same section of a text.

Rationale

When students learn to use precise language to ensure that everyone can locate the same section of a text, everyone can stay together and be a participating member of the book club.

Assess Learning

Observe students when they talk about books to notice evidence of new learning based on the goal of this minilesson.

- ▶ Can students follow and use specific language to identify sections of a text?
- ▶ Do they use the terms *directions, exact place, line, paragraph, caption,* and *panel*?

Minilesson

To help students think about the minilesson principle, help them practice using exact language to ensure they can locate a specific place in a book quickly. Here is an example.

- ▶ Show a page from any book club book, or project it using a document camera.

    If I want to talk about this specific page, what words can I use to direct you to the exact place?

- ▶ Start a list on chart paper.

    What words can I use to help you locate an exact place on a page?

- ▶ As needed, guide the conversation to include a variety of specific ways to describe a place in a book (e.g., words, paragraphs, lines, captions, graphic panels, sidebars), using a different book if needed for examples. Ask students to talk about words they could use to help others locate that place or feature. Add ideas to the chart.

Have a Try

Invite the students to talk with a partner about ways to help others find an exact place in a book.

▶ Have students sit with book club groups and book club books. Each person in the group should have a copy of the same book.

> Practice using directions to help each other find a specific place in your book.

▶ After time for discussion, ask students to share the words or phrases they used. Add new ideas to the chart.

Summarize and Apply

Summarize the learning and remind students to think about how to be sure that everyone is in a specific place during book club meetings.

> Using exact language helps everyone get to a specific place in a book.

▶ Add the principle to the top of the chart.

> During book club, use exact words to make sure everyone is at the specific place in the book. While some of you are reading or writing, I will meet with a book club and they will be able to try this out. Then they will share what they noticed when we all meet.

▶ Meet with a book club group.

Share

Following independent reading time, gather students in the meeting area. Ask the group that met in book club to share.

> What are examples of words and phrases you used to make sure everyone was in a specific place when you talked about the book?

▶ Add new ideas to the chart.

Extend the Lesson (Optional)

After assessing students' understanding, you might decide to extend the learning.

▶ **Writing About Reading** Have students use Ways to Have a Good Book Discussion on the inside back cover of *Reader's Notebook: Advanced* (Fountas and Pinnell 2011) to reflect on their book club meetings.

> **Give directions to help everyone get to a specific place in the book quickly.**
>
> • page 16
>
> • the fourth line from the bottom
>
> • the second sentence on page 12
>
> • the last word in the first sentence
>
> • the fifth paragraph
>
> • the caption on page 19
>
> • the sidebar on page 32
>
> • the third panel on the top row

Assessment

After you have taught the minilessons in this umbrella, observe students as they talk and write about their reading across instructional contexts: interactive read-aloud, independent reading, guided reading, shared reading, and book club. Use *The Literacy Continuum* (Fountas and Pinnell 2017) to observe students' reading and writing behaviors.

▶ What evidence do you have of new understandings related to the way students engage with book clubs?

- Are students able to choose an appropriate book for book club and explain why they chose it?

- Do they mark the pages and make a note about what they want to talk about?

- Can they articulate their thinking in book clubs?

- Are they asking questions to clarify understanding?

- Do they use clear directions to make sure everyone is at the same place in the book they are discussing?

- Do they understand terms such as *book club, preference, clarify,* and *discussion*?

▶ In what other ways, beyond the scope of this umbrella, are students talking about books?

- Are students showing an interest in specific authors or illustrators?

- Do they notice elements of an author's craft?

Use your observations to determine the next umbrella you will teach. You may also consult Minilessons Across the Year (pp. 61–64) for guidance.

Link to Writing

After teaching the minilessons in this umbrella, help students link the new learning to their own writing:

▶ Encourage students to write book reviews and recommendations that can be displayed in the classroom and used by others when choosing books.

Reader's Notebook

When this umbrella is complete, provide a copy of the minilesson principles (see resources.fountasandpinnell.com) for students to glue in the reader's notebook (in the Minilessons section if using *Reader's Notebook: Advanced* [Fountas and Pinnell 2011]), so they can refer to the information as needed.

Minilessons in This Umbrella

RML1	Be a strong listener and a strong speaker.
RML2	Recognize appropriate times to take a turn.
RML3	Monitor your participation and encourage others to participate.
RML4	Start the discussion in different ways.
RML5	Invite each other to provide evidence.
RML6	Value and encourage diverse perspectives.
RML7	Add on to the important ideas to extend the thinking of the group.
RML8	Focus on the big ideas in the discussion.
RML9	Change the topic and refocus the discussion as needed.
RML10	Reflect on and evaluate your book club discussion.

Before Teaching Umbrella 2 Minilessons

Once students have begun to participate in book club meetings, you can teach these minilessons to help them learn conversational moves that will improve the quality of the discussions. During book club meetings, the teacher plays a key role in facilitating the group to assure new levels of understanding, so even if students are taught to start the discussion, you are still part of the group to lift the conversation as needed. You might want to take students through one set of book club meetings (see Umbrella 1: Getting Started with Book Clubs) prior to teaching these minilessons so that they have a basic understanding of how a book club meeting goes.

Several lessons suggest doing a fishbowl observation (see p. 76) right before teaching the minilesson, in which one book club group is prepared ahead of time and then sits in a circle while the remaining students sit in an outer circle to observe. Lead the conversation as needed, having book club members talk about their thinking for a few minutes. Encourage them to invite others in the group to talk, ask each other questions, support their thinking with evidence, and agree or disagree with each other in a respectful way.

For additional prompts and to learn more, please see *Fountas & Pinnell Prompting Guide, Part 2, for Comprehension: Thinking, Talking, and Writing* (Fountas and Pinnell 2009), Section IV: Prompts for Book Discussions (pp. 61–78). This umbrella reflects some of the language from that section.

Section 2: Literary Analysis

Reading Minilesson Principle
Be a strong listener and a strong speaker.

Learning Conversational
Moves in Book Club

You Will Need

- chart paper and markers
- students' book club books

Academic Language / Important Vocabulary

- book club
- listener
- speaker

Continuum Connection

- Actively participate in conversation by listening and looking at the person speaking (p. 341)
- Refrain from speaking over others (p. 341)
- Use conventions of respectful conversation (p. 341)
- Listen to and speak to a partner about a given idea, and make a connection to the partner's idea (p. 341)

Goal

Understand the verbal and nonverbal ways to demonstrate committed listening and strong, clear speaking skills.

Rationale

When students think about what it means to be a strong listener and a strong speaker during a book club meeting, they learn to attend to their interactions with other classmates and notice what messages their body language is sending. They learn more about the text through balanced, rich discussions. These understandings and actions lay the foundation for becoming a good communicator and an engaged member of the class.

Assess Learning

Observe students when they communicate with classmates and notice if there is evidence of new learning based on the goal of this minilesson.

- Do students show characteristics of being a strong speaker and a strong listener during book club meetings?
- Do they use the terms *book club, listener,* and *speaker*?

Minilesson

To help students think about the minilesson principle, help them notice the kind of behaviors they might demonstrate as strong listeners and speakers. Take into consideration that some students are not comfortable with establishing or able to establish eye contact because of cultural conventions or for other reasons. Here is an example.

- Before teaching this lesson, make sure students have had a recent book club experience to reflect on, whether it is a fishbowl demonstration (p. 76) or their own book club meeting.

  To be an active member of a book club, it is important to be a strong listener and a strong speaker.

- Ask students to reflect on what they noticed about the conversations during the fishbowl demonstration.

  What does it look (sound) like to be a strong listener?

- Prompt students' thinking by asking about where their eyes are looking, how their bodies are positioned, or how they might respond when they are the listener. Record students' responses on chart paper.

  What does it look (sound) like to be a strong speaker?

- Prompt students' thinking by asking about what they are doing and how their voices sound when they are the speaker. Record responses on the chart.

Have a Try

Invite the students to talk in a small group and demonstrate what it means to be a strong listener and speaker.

> Talk in your group about the book you are reading. When you listen, show what it looks like and sounds like to be a strong listener. When you speak, show what it looks and sounds like to be a strong speaker. Take turns being the speaker in the group while the others listen.

▶ After time for discussion, ask students to share what they noticed. Add new ideas to the chart.

Summarize and Apply

Summarize the learning and remind students to be a strong listener and a strong speaker during book club meetings.

> You learned some ways to be a strong listener and a strong speaker during your book club meeting.

▶ Add the principle to the top of the chart.

> Today I will meet with one book club group. Later when we all meet to share, I will ask the book club members to share what they noticed about listening and speaking.

Share

Following independent reading time, gather students in the meeting area. Ask the group that met in book club to share.

> What did you notice about listening and speaking when you met in book club today?

▶ After book club members respond, ask the whole group to reflect.

> Why is it important to be a good listener and speaker?

Extend the Lesson (Optional)

After assessing students' understanding, you might decide to extend the learning.

▶ For additional practice getting started with book clubs or on asking clarifying questions, please see Umbrella 1: Getting Started with Book Clubs in this section.

▶ If you have *Fountas & Pinnell Prompting Guide, Part 2, for Comprehension: Thinking, Talking, and Writing* (Fountas and Pinnell 2009), refer to the prompts that support strong listening and speaking in Section IV: Prompts for Book Discussions.

Be a strong listener and a strong speaker.

	Looks Like	Sounds Like
Strong Listener	• Makes eye contact with the speaker • Body is turned toward the speaker • Might nod at the speaker	• Responds to ideas before changing the subject • Does not talk over the speaker • "Can you say that in a different way?" • "I see why you might say that, but did you think about _____?" • "So, you mean _____."
Strong Speaker	• Takes turns • Makes eye contact with everyone in the group • Might nod or gesture to someone in the group	• Uses appropriate volume • Asks questions • Adds on to comment • Has a confident and enthusiastic voice

RML2
LA.U2.RML2

Reading Minilesson Principle
Recognize appropriate times to take a turn.

Learning Conversational Moves in Book Club

You Will Need

- chart paper and markers
- students' book club books

Academic Language / Important Vocabulary

- book club
- lull
- respect
- appropriate

Continuum Connection

- Demonstrate balance in conversation by taking turns (p. 341)
- Refrain from speaking over others (p. 341)
- Enter a conversation appropriately (p. 341)
- Use conventions of respectful conversation (p. 341)
- Understand the role of nonverbal language and use it effectively (p. 341)

Goal

Use verbal and nonverbal cues to know when to enter a discussion.

Rationale

When students learn how to take turns speaking during book club discussions by looking for verbal and nonverbal cues, they can share their ideas, comment on and extend one another's thoughts, and learn more about the text they are reading. This skill extends beyond book clubs to other conversations and discussions inside and outside of the classroom.

Assess Learning

Observe students when they converse with classmates and notice if there is evidence of new learning based on the goal of this minilesson.

- ▶ Can students recognize appropriate times to speak during a discussion?
- ▶ Do they invite others to share their thinking?
- ▶ Do they use nonverbal cues to signal that they have something to say?
- ▶ Do they understand the terms *book club, lull, respect,* and *appropriate*?

Minilesson

To help students think about taking turns in a book club discussion, engage them in discussion about how to look for verbal and nonverbal cues in deciding when it is appropriate to take a turn. Here is an example.

- ▶ Before teaching this lesson, be sure that students have had a recent book club experience to reflect on, whether it is a fishbowl demonstration (p. 76) or their own book club meeting.

  Think about the book club discussions you have seen or participated in. What did you notice about how everyone took turns speaking? Turn and talk about that.

- ▶ As needed, provide several prompts to encourage the conversation.
  - *What did people do when they had something to add to the conversation?*
  - *How did you know when it was your turn to speak?*
  - *Did you, or anyone else, say something to encourage others to take a turn sharing?*
- ▶ After time for discussion, bring the group back together and ask students to share their thinking about how to know when it is an appropriate time to speak. Make a list of responses on chart paper.

Have a Try

Invite the students to talk in a small group about identifying when it is time to take a turn speaking.

> Talk in your group about a book you are currently reading. Take turns sharing and adding on to what your classmates have said.

▶ After time for discussion, ask students to share what they noticed about taking turns. Add new ideas to the chart.

> Why is it important for you to know how to respectfully take turns in a conversation?

Summarize and Apply

Summarize the learning and remind students to think about book club discussions.

> What did you learn about taking turns speaking during a discussion?

▶ Add the principle to the top of the chart.

> Today I will meet with one book club group. Later when we come together to share, I will ask them to talk about what they observed about taking turns in a discussion.

Share

Following independent reading time, gather students in the meeting area. Ask the group that met in book club to share.

> What are some examples of how you took turns talking?

> What did you remember to do when you wanted to add to the conversation?

Extend the Lesson (Optional)

After assessing students' understanding, you might decide to extend the learning.

▶ Knowing when to enter a conversation is useful in many contexts, not just book club meetings. Remind students to use the same techniques when they speak in other settings.

Recognize appropriate times to take a turn.

- Wait for a natural break, pause, or lull in the conversation.
- Notice the speaker's eyes and look for a clue that she is finished speaking.
- Notice if the speaker is looking around for someone to add to the conversation.
- Notice if a speaker nods or gestures in a way that indicates it is an appropriate time to speak.
- Lean in or gesture to show you have something to say.

Reading Minilesson Principle
Monitor your participation and encourage others to participate.

Learning Conversational Moves in Book Club

You Will Need

- chart paper and markers

Academic Language / Important Vocabulary

- book club
- participation
- monitor
- encourage

Continuum Connection

- Use conventional techniques that encourage others to talk: e.g., "What do you think?" "Do you agree? Why or why not?" (p. 341)

- Evaluate one's own part in a group discussion as well as the effectiveness of the group (p. 341)

- Facilitate a group discussion by ensuring that everyone has a chance to speak (p. 341)

Goal

Monitor your own participation and learn language for encouraging others to participate.

Rationale

When students are aware of their own level of participation in a book club discussion, they are better prepared to adjust their behavior to either add more to the conversation or contribute less, inviting others to share their own thinking.

Assess Learning

Observe students when they are participating in a book club discussion and notice if there is evidence of new learning based on the goal of this minilesson.

- Do students participate in the discussion in a balanced way?
- Can they evaluate whether they are talking too much or too little?
- Do they use the terms *book club, participation, monitor,* and *encourage*?

Minilesson

To help students think about the minilesson principle, engage them in a discussion about how to self-monitor their participation in a book club meeting. Here is an example.

- Before teaching this lesson, be sure that students have had a recent book club experience to reflect on, whether it is a fishbowl demonstration or their own book club meeting.

    What does it mean to monitor your participation in a book club discussion? It means to check how you are taking part in the group. Turn and talk to a partner about what questions you can ask yourself to monitor your participation.

- After time for discussion, invite students to share. Prompt the conversation as needed. Record student ideas on the chart for questions under the heading *Ask Yourself*.

    Now think about how you can invite others to talk during a book club meeting. What are some ways you could encourage someone to participate?

- Make a list of questions under the heading *Invite Others to Talk* on the chart.

    Look back at the questions on the chart. Why is it important to check your participation and include others during a book club discussion?

- Prompt the conversation as needed.

Have a Try

Invite the students to talk with a small group about how they can invite others to participate.

> Turn and talk about any other questions you might ask yourself and language you might use to monitor your participation during book clubs.

▶ After a short time for discussion, ask students to share. Add new ideas to the chart.

Summarize and Apply

Summarize the learning and remind students to monitor themselves and to invite others to talk during book club discussions.

> What did you learn about monitoring yourself during book club discussions?

▶ Add the principle to the top of the chart. Ask a volunteer to read the questions on the chart.

> Use the chart when you meet with your book club. Members of the book club who meet with me
> today will talk about their book club when we have our class meeting.

Share

Following independent reading time, gather students in the meeting area. Have the book club members you met with share with the whole group.

> How well did you monitor your participation and support the participation of other book club members?

Extend the Lesson (Optional)

After assessing students' understanding, you might decide to extend the learning.

▶ If you have *Fountas & Pinnell Prompting Guide, Part 2, for Comprehension: Thinking, Talking, and Writing* (Fountas and Pinnell 2009), refer to the prompts that support participation in Section IV: Prompts for Book Discussions.

Monitor your participation and encourage others to participate.

Ask Yourself	Invite Others to Talk
• Am I talking too much?	• What do you think?
• Am I talking too little?	• Do you agree? Why or why not?
• Has everyone shared?	• Did anyone else notice that?
• Have I encouraged others to add on?	• Does anyone want to add to that?
	• Can you say more about that?

Section 2: Literary Analysis

Reading Minilesson Principle
Start the discussion in different ways.

Learning Conversational Moves in Book Club

You Will Need

▸ chart paper and markers

Academic Language / Important Vocabulary

▸ book club

▸ discussion

Continuum Connection

▸ Use conventional techniques that encourage others to talk: e.g., "What do you think?" "Do you agree? Why or why not?" (p. 341)

▸ Demonstrate effectiveness as a group leader (p. 341)

Goal

Learn language to initiate a book club discussion.

Rationale

When students identify and use different types of ways to begin a book club discussion, they learn to start in an efficient way so that time is spent on valuable discussion and rich conversation.

Assess Learning

Observe students in book club discussions to notice evidence of new learning based on the goal of this minilesson.

▸ Do students understand that it is important to start a book club discussion right away?

▸ Can students use a variety of language to get a book club started?

▸ Do they use the terms *book club* and *discussion*?

Minilesson

To help students think about taking turns in a book club discussion, engage them in conversation on how to start a book club discussion. Here is an example.

▸ Before teaching this lesson, be sure that students have had a recent book club experience to reflect on, whether it is a fishbowl demonstration (p. 76) or their own book club meeting.

> Think about the book club discussions you have seen or participated in. What did you notice about how the conversation about the book started? Turn and talk about that.

▸ As needed, provide several prompts to encourage the conversation.

- *Why is it important to get a book club discussion started right away?*

- *What are some different ways you could get a book club discussion started?*

▸ After time for discussion, ask students to share their thinking about ways to start a discussion about a book. Make a list of responses on chart paper.

Have a Try

Invite the students to talk with a partner about book club discussions.

> Look back at the chart. Turn and talk about any other ways you can start a book club discussion.

▶ After time for discussion, ask students to share. Add new ideas to chart.

Summarize and Apply

Summarize the learning and remind students to think about how to get a book club discussion started.

> Why is it important to have some different ways to start a book club discussion?

▶ Add the principle to the top of the chart.

> Look back at the chart when you have your book club discussion today and use one of the ways on the list to get the conversation started. Today I will meet with one book club. When we have our class meeting, they will share the way they started the conversation.

> ### Start the discussion in different ways.
>
> - Who wants to get us started?
> - What does this book make you wonder about?
> - What is important about this story (or book)?
> - Let's think together about _____ .
> - What are your first thoughts about this book?
> - What surprised you as you read?
> - Does this book (character, plot, setting) remind you of anything else you've read?

Share

Following independent reading time, gather students in the meeting area. Ask the group that met in book club to share.

> Talk about how you started your book club discussion. How well did it work?

▶ Add new ideas to the chart. After book club members have responded, ask the class to reflect on book club discussions and provide any new ideas for the chart.

Extend the Lesson (Optional)

After assessing students' understanding, you might decide to extend the learning.

▶ If you have *Fountas & Pinnell Prompting Guide, Part 2, for Comprehension: Thinking, Talking, and Writing* (Fountas and Pinnell 2009), refer to the prompts on pages 69 and 70 in Section IV: Prompts for Book Discussions.

Reading Minilesson Principle
Invite each other to provide evidence.

You Will Need

- chart paper and markers
- students' book club books

Academic Language / Important Vocabulary

- book club
- clarify
- evidence

Continuum Connection

- Use evidence from the text to support statements about it (pp. 79, 84)

Goal

Develop language to give evidence and to invite others to provide evidence for their thinking.

Rationale

When students learn to provide evidence for their thinking, they learn to clarify their thinking, clear up potential misconceptions, develop more sophisticated conversation skills, monitor their understanding, and share new insights with classmates.

Assess Learning

Observe students during book club meetings to notice evidence of new learning based on the goal of this minilesson.

- Do students know when more information is needed and how to ask for it?
- Do they use the terms *book club, clarify,* and *evidence?*

Minilesson

To help students think about the minilesson principle, engage them in a discussion using evidence from the text during book club meetings. Here is an example.

- Right before teaching this minilesson, conduct a fishbowl observation (p. 76) of a book club meeting. Ask students to focus on how the group members provide evidence for their thinking or ask each other for evidence for their opinions. (You may want to prepare the book club members being observed beforehand with some of the language from the chart, and you can also model this language.) Ask students to record their observations. Once the observation is complete, engage students in a reflective discussion.

  What did you notice about some of the ways group members gave evidence to support their thinking and invited each other to add evidence?

- As students share ideas, generalize their thinking to create two lists, one labeled *Give Evidence* and one labeled *Ask for Evidence.* Add responses to the appropriate section. Prompt the conversation as needed. For example:

  - *Why is it important to provide evidence from the book for your thinking during book club?*
  - *How can you make sure you are specific with your evidence?*

- Conclude by offering a reason that evidence is important.

  Sometimes you want to be sure that you understand the point that a book club member is making. If so, you can ask for evidence from the book.

Have a Try

Invite the students to talk about how they might give evidence or ask for evidence during book club.

▶ Have students sit with one or more members of their current book clubs. Each person in the group should have a copy of the same book.

Practice giving evidence or asking for evidence about your book club book.

▶ After a brief time for practice, ask students to share the types of things they said to give or ask for evidence. Add new ideas to the chart.

Summarize and Apply

Summarize the learning and remind students to think about how to give or ask for evidence during book club meetings.

Today you learned about giving evidence for your thinking and asking for it from others.

▶ Add the principle to the top of the chart.

Think about using the chart when you have book club discussions. Today, I will meet with one book club. Later, when we have our class meeting, the book club members will share how they provided evidence in their discussion.

Share

Following independent reading time, gather students in the meeting area. Ask the group that met in book club to share.

In what ways did you give evidence or ask for evidence?

▶ Add new ideas to the chart. After the group members have shared, ask others in the class to reflect on providing evidence during book club meetings.

Why is it important to share evidence for your thinking and to ask others to share evidence for their thinking?

Extend the Lesson (Optional)

After assessing students' understanding, you might decide to extend the learning.

▶ If you have *Fountas & Pinnell Prompting Guide, Part 2, for Comprehension: Thinking, Talking, and Writing* (Fountas and Pinnell 2009), refer to Section IV: Prompts for Book Discussions.

Invite each other to provide evidence.

Give Evidence	Ask for Evidence
• An example of that is on page _____ .	• What makes you think that?
• I think _____ because _____ .	• Can you provide some details?
• On page _____ , paragraph _____ , the writer says _____ , so_____ .	• How do you know that?
• One place I noticed this is on page _____ .	• What part of the story led you to that conclusion?
• I used this quote because_____ .	• Help me understand why you thought that.

Learning Conversational Moves in Book Club

You Will Need

▶ chart paper and markers

Academic Language / Important Vocabulary

▶ book club

▶ diverse

▶ perspective

Continuum Connection

▶ Use conventions of respectful conversation (p. 341)

▶ Listen and respond to a partner by agreeing, disagreeing, or adding on, and explain reasons (p. 341)

Goal

Learn to share different perspectives, agree and disagree respectfully, and validate other people's opinions.

Rationale

When students share new and different ideas about a text, they are expanding and deepening their classmates' understandings of the text and working to ensure that a book club discussion is a safe place for everyone to share ideas.

Assess Learning

Observe students during book club discussions to notice evidence of new learning based on the goal of this minilesson.

▶ Do students show that they value perspectives that differ from their own by respectfully responding to their classmates?

▶ Are they sharing a variety of ideas during book club meetings?

▶ Do they use the terms *book club, diverse,* and *perspective*?

Minilesson

To help students think about the minilesson principle, engage them in a discussion about how to encourage and value diverse opinions. Here is an example.

▶ Right before teaching this lesson, conduct a fishbowl observation (p. 76) of one book club group discussing their book. Ask students to notice ways they show that they are valuing each other's opinions. Prepare students in the book club with some of the language from the chart.

Think about a time during a book club discussion when people had different, or diverse, ideas about aspects of the book. Why is it important to hear a variety of ideas, or diverse perspectives?

▶ Prompt the conversation as needed.

Now think about respectful language you can use when you hear an idea that is different from yours or when you disagree with an idea. Also think about ways you can invite others to share ideas that might be different from yours. Turn and talk about that.

▶ After time for discussion, ask volunteers to suggest ways to discuss diverse ideas. Create two lists on chart paper, one for ways to respond to diverse ideas and one for ways to ask for diverse ideas.

Have a Try

Invite the students to talk about what they can say to share or encourage diverse perspectives during book club meetings.

> Think about a book we have recently read aloud together in class. Have a conversation about the book and practice sharing opinions using words that show you are listening. You can look to the chart for ideas if you wish.

▶ After time for a brief discussion, ask students to share about the experience. Add new ideas to the chart.

Summarize and Apply

Summarize the learning and remind students to think about how to share and ask for diverse perspectives.

> Today you learned how to respond to classmates who have new or different ideas. You also learned how to ask your classmates to share different ideas.

▶ Add the principle to the top of the chart.

> Use the chart when you meet with your book club. Today I will meet with one book club. When we have our class meeting, they will share their thinking about the book club discussion.

Share

Following independent reading time, gather students in the meeting area. Ask the group that met in book club to share.

> Think about your book club meeting. In what ways did you respond to your classmates' ideas? How did you show that you value their ideas? How did you invite others to share their perspective? Talk about that.

Extend the Lesson (Optional)

After assessing students' understanding, you might decide to extend the learning.

▶ If you have *Fountas & Pinnell Prompting Guide, Part 2, for Comprehension: Thinking, Talking, and Writing* (Fountas and Pinnell 2009), refer to Section IV: Prompts for Book Discussions.

Value and encourage diverse perspectives.

Respond Respectfully	Invite Others to Share Different Ideas
• I agree with what you are saying because _____. • I disagree with what you are saying because _____. • That seems possible because _____. • That's interesting. I hadn't thought of that. • That makes sense to me, but _____. • That helps me understand this in a different way. • I understand, but I looked at this a different way.	• Does anyone see it another way? • What is everyone else thinking? • Is there another way to think about that?

Reading Minilesson Principle
Add on to the important ideas to extend the thinking of the group.

You Will Need

▸ chart paper and markers

Academic Language / Important Vocabulary

▸ book club
▸ focus
▸ extend
▸ restate

Continuum Connection

▸ Listen and respond to a partner by agreeing, disagreeing, or adding on, and explain reasons (p. 341)

▸ Sustain a discussion by staying on the main topic and requesting or signaling a change of topic (p. 341)

Goal

Add on to important ideas to build a deeper understanding.

Rationale

When students learn how to add on to an important idea and invite others to extend their thinking, they gain a deeper understanding of the text. Some teachers use hand signals for students to indicate when they plan to add on to a topic versus changing the subject. This lesson is designed to move students past using hand signals and to recognize language they can use to have an extended discussion on one idea.

Assess Learning

Observe students in book club discussions to notice evidence of new learning based on the goal of this minilesson.

▸ Can students identify the important ideas in a discussion?

▸ Can they determine how to appropriately refocus or add on?

▸ Do they use the terms *book club, focus, extend,* and *restate*?

Minilesson

To help students think about the minilesson principle, engage them in a discussion about how to focus on main ideas and add on. Here is an example.

▸ Right before you plan to teach this minilesson, have your students participate in a fishbowl observation (p. 76) of a book club group. You can prepare the book club members ahead of time by teaching them some of the language from the chart and by modeling it yourself. Ask students to record some of the things the book club members say to stay focused and add on to an important idea. After they have conducted this fishbowl, engage them in reflective discussion about how to add on to an idea to extend the group's thinking.

> What did you notice about some of the ways group members added on to each other's ideas?

▸ Support the conversation as needed. Some suggested prompts are below.

  • *What are some other ways you might add on to a conversation?*

  • *Did you notice the book club members inviting each other to add on to the conversation?*

  • *What were some of the ways they invited each other to add on to an idea?*

▸ Write the headings *Add On* and *Invite Others to Add On* and record responses in the appropriate category.

> When an idea has been fully discussed, then it is time to move on.

Have a Try

Invite the students to talk with a partner about book club discussions.

> Look back at the chart. Turn and talk about any other ways you add on to a discussion or invite others in.

▶ After time for discussion, ask students to share. Add new ideas to chart.

Summarize and Apply

Summarize the learning and remind students to think about how to focus, add on to, and restate ideas during book club meetings.

> Why is it important to add on to the conversation in a respectful way?

▶ Add the principle to the top of the chart.

> Use the chart when you meet with your book club. Today I will meet with one book club. When we have our class meeting, they will share what they learned about their book club discussion.

Share

Following independent reading time, gather students in the meeting area. Ask the group that met in book club to share.

> Share what you noticed about your book club discussion. How did group members add on to or restate what others said?

▶ Add new ideas to the chart. After book club members have responded, ask the class to reflect on book club discussions and provide any new ideas for the chart.

Extend the Lesson (Optional)

After assessing students' understanding, you might decide to extend the learning.

▶ If you have *Fountas & Pinnell Prompting Guide, Part 2, for Comprehension: Thinking, Talking, and Writing* (Fountas and Pinnell 2009), refer to Section IV: Prompts for Book Discussions.

Add on to the important ideas to extend the thinking of the group.

Add On +	Invite Others to Add On
• I would like to add that _____.	• Say more about that.
• Building on what _____ said, I think _____.	• Does anyone else want to add to that?
• To add on, _____.	• What else does that make you think of?
• I also think _____.	• Say more about what you mean about _____.
• Now I'm thinking _____.	• Did anyone else notice that?
• You made me think _____.	• What do others think about that?
• I'm changing my thinking because you _____.	• Can anyone add on to _____'s comment/idea?
• And this part of the text makes me think _____.	• Let's reread that paragraph to notice more.

Reading Minilesson Principle
Focus on the big ideas in the discussion.

You Will Need

▶ chart paper and markers

Academic Language / Important Vocabulary

▶ book club

▶ focus

▶ big idea

Continuum Connection

▶ Demonstrate effectiveness as group leader (p. 341)

▶ Recall, restate, or paraphrase information, big ideas, or points made by others (p. 341)

Goal

Learn language to help the group identify, summarize, and focus on the big ideas in the discussion.

Rationale

When students learn how to focus on the big ideas in a book club discussion, they gain a deeper understanding of the text and are able to guide their conversations to focus on the themes, messages, and big ideas from books in their discussions.

Assess Learning

Observe students in book club discussions to notice evidence of new learning based on the goal of this minilesson.

▶ Can students identify the big ideas in a discussion?

▶ Are they able to focus on the big ideas?

▶ Do they use the terms *book club, focus,* and *big idea*?

Minilesson

To help students think about the minilesson principle, engage them in a discussion about how to focus on the big ideas in a book club discussion. Here is an example.

▶ Right before you plan to teach this minilesson, have your students participate in a fishbowl observation (p. 76) of a book club group. You can prepare the book club members ahead of time by teaching them some of the language from the chart and by modeling it yourself. Ask students to record some of the things the book club members say to identify, summarize, and stay focused on the big ideas. After they have conducted this fishbowl, engage them in reflective discussion about how to focus on the big ideas in a book club discussion.

> What did you notice about some of the ways group members identified the big ideas, summarized the big ideas, and stayed focused on the big ideas during their book club discussion?

▶ Support the conversation as needed. Some suggested prompts are below.

- *What are some ways you can identify the big ideas in a fiction or nonfiction book?*

- *How do you summarize the big ideas from a book in just a few words?*

- *Why is it important to focus on big ideas in a book club discussion, and how do you do that?*

▶ Write the headings *Focus on the Big Ideas* and *Encourage Others to Focus on the Big Ideas* and record responses in the appropriate category.

> When you feel that an idea has been fully discussed, then it is time to move on.

Have a Try

Invite the students to talk with a partner about book club discussions.

> Look back at the chart. Turn and talk about any other ways you identify the big ideas, summarize the big ideas, and stay focused on the big ideas.

> ▶ After time for discussion, ask students to share. Add new ideas to the chart.

Summarize and Apply

Summarize the learning and remind students to think about how to identify the big ideas, summarize the big ideas, and stay focused on the big ideas during book club meetings.

> Why is it important to focus on the big ideas in a book club discussion?

> ▶ Add the principle to the top of the chart.

> Use the chart when you meet with your book club. Today I will meet with one book club. When we have our class meeting, they will share what they learned about their book club discussion.

Share

Following independent reading time, gather students in the meeting area. Ask the group that met in book club to share.

> Share what you noticed about your book club discussion. How did group members focus on the big ideas?

> ▶ Add new ideas to the chart. After book club members have responded, ask the class to reflect on book club discussions and provide any new ideas for the chart.

Extend the Lesson (Optional)

After assessing students' understanding, you might decide to extend the learning.

> ▶ If you have *Fountas & Pinnell Prompting Guide, Part 2, for Comprehension: Thinking, Talking, and Writing* (Fountas and Pinnell 2009), refer to pages 68 and 78 in Section IV: Prompts for Book Discussions.

Focus on the big ideas in the discussion.

Focus on the Big Ideas	Encourage Others to Focus on the Big Ideas
• I think the writer is really trying to say_____.	• What are the big ideas you took from this book?
• The writer says _____, but really means _____.	• What were the writer's messages?
• Some of the important ideas to remember here are_____.	• What lessons does this book teach you about the real world?
• So this can all be summarized to mean_____.	• What was that all about?
	• How would you describe_____ in just a few sentences?
	• Where are we now with this idea?

Reading Minilesson Principle
Change the topic and refocus the discussion as needed.

Learning Conversational
Moves in Book Club

You Will Need

▶ chart paper and markers

Academic Language / Important Vocabulary

▶ book club

▶ refocus

▶ discussion

Continuum Connection

▶ Suggest new lines of discussion when appropriate (p. 341)

▶ Demonstrate effectiveness as a group leader (p. 341)

▶ Sustain a discussion by staying on the main topic and requesting or signaling a change of topic (p. 341)

Goal

Learn language to change or refocus a discussion and identify when it is appropriate to use it.

Rationale

When students learn to change or refocus a book club discussion, they learn to keeep a conversation moving forward. Students may eventually start the discussion, but that doesn't mean you aren't part of the group to observe and lift the conversation as needed. The teacher plays a key role in facilitating the group to ensure new levels of understanding.

Assess Learning

Observe students when they are in book club meetings and notice if there is evidence of new learning based on the goal of this minilesson.

▶ Do students recognize when the discussion needs to be changed or refocused and use appropriate language to do so?

▶ Do they use the terms *book club, refocus,* and *discussion*?

Minilesson

To help students think about the minilesson principle, engage them in a discussion about noticing when a book club discussion needs to change or be refocused. Here is an example.

▶ Right before you plan to teach this minilesson, have students participate in a fishbowl observation (p. 76) of a book club group. Prepare the members ahead of time by teaching them some of the language from the chart. Ask students to record some of the things the book club members say to change and refocus the discussion. After they have conducted this fishbowl, engage them in reflective discussion.

> Some ways to get the conversation in a book club meeting started might be to ask, who wants to get us started? Or, what do you think would be important to talk about today? But what about when you want to move the discussion in a new direction? What are some ways you noticed the book club group members doing that?

▶ As needed, provide prompts to support the conversation.

• *What might you say to the group to respectfully change the topic?*

• *If a conversation gets off course, what could you say to bring the conversation back to the topic?*

▶ After time for discussion, have students share ideas. On chart paper, make a list of ideas for changing and refocusing the discussion.

Have a Try

Invite the students to talk with a partner about book club discussions.

> When you feel that an idea has been fully discussed, then it is time to move on. Turn and talk about what else you could say to change or refocus a discussion during a book club meeting.

▶ After a brief time for discussion, ask students to share ideas. Add to chart.

Summarize and Apply

Summarize the learning and remind students to think about ways to start, change, or refocus the conversation during book club meetings.

> Why is it important to talk about more than one idea during a book club discussion?

▶ Add the principle to the top of the chart.

> Use the chart when you meet with your book club. Today I will meet with one book club. When we meet together later, they will share their thinking about their discussion.

Change the topic and refocus the discussion as needed.

Change the Topic	Refocus the Discussion
• If everyone is finished with that idea, I'd like to change the topic.	• Another way to say that is _____.
• Let's think together about _____.	• I'd like to return to our discussion of _____.
• Who has another idea they want us to think about?	• Where are we now with this idea?
• What else would be important for us to talk about?	• We were talking about _____.
• Take us to another part of the story you want us to think about.	• We're getting far away from the book.

Share

Following independent reading time, gather students in the meeting area. Ask the group that met in book club to share.

> How did your book club discussion go? What did you do to have a good discussion?

▶ Add new ideas to the chart. After book club members have responded, ask the class to reflect on book club discussions.

> Why is it important to notice when a book club conversation needs to change or be refocused?

Extend the Lesson (Optional)

After assessing students' understanding, you might decide to extend the learning.

▶ If you have *Fountas & Pinnell Prompting Guide, Part 2, for Comprehension: Thinking, Talking, and Writing* (Fountas and Pinnell 2009), refer to Section IV: Prompts for Book Discussions.

Section 2: Literary Analysis

RML10
LA.U2.RML10

Reflect on and evaluate your book club discussion.

Learning Conversational Moves in Book Club

You Will Need

- chart paper and markers
- charts from previous minilessons in this umbrella

Academic Language / Important Vocabulary

- book club
- reflect
- assess
- evaluate

Continuum Connection

- Evaluate one's own part in a group discussion as well as the effectiveness of the group (p. 341)

Goal

Develop guidelines to self-assess book club meetings.

Rationale

When students reflect on a book club meeting, they begin to consider how their preparation and participation help the group better understand the text. Their evaluation process improves their self-assessment skills and increases their ownership and engagement of their work.

Assess Learning

Observe students during book club meetings to notice evidence of new learning based on the goal of this minilesson.

- ▶ Do students reflect on their participation so that they can identify what went well and what they can improve upon?
- ▶ Do they use the terms *book club, reflect, assess,* and *evaluate*?

Minilesson

To help students think about the minilesson principle, engage them in a reflection of a recent book club discussion. Here is an example.

- ▶ Before teaching this lesson, all students should have participated in at least one book club meeting. Post the charts from the previous minilessons in this umbrella.

    Here are the charts we made about ways to have a good book club meeting.

- ▶ Ask students to quickly review the charts.

    At the end of a book club meeting, you can reflect on what went well for you and your peers and what things you would like to work on so that your next book club meeting is even better.

    Let's create a list of what you can do to ensure a good book club meeting.

- ▶ Ask students for suggestions. As they respond, generalize their thinking and write statements on the chart paper. Prompt the conversation as needed.

    After your next meeting, you can use the list to evaluate how well your meeting went.

Have a Try

Invite the students to talk with a partner about ways to reflect on and evaluate a book club discussion.

> Turn and talk with a partner about something on the list that went well in your last book club meeting. What made it go well?

▶ After time for discussion, ask students to share ideas. Add to chart.

Summarize and Apply

Summarize the learning and remind students to reflect after book club meetings.

> Today you created a list to help you think about your book club meetings.

▶ Add the principle to the top of the chart.

> Think about the things on this list after your next book club meeting. Think about what went well and decide on something that you can make better the next time.

▶ Meet with a book club while the other students engage in independent reading.

Share

Following independent reading time, gather students in the meeting area. Ask the group that met in book club to share.

> What went well in your book club discussion?

> What is something you would like to improve for next time?

> How did the checklist help you evaluate your book club meeting?

Extend the Lesson (Optional)

After assessing students' understanding, you might decide to extend the learning.

▶ Have students write in a reader's notebook a way to improve their next book club discussion and what steps they might take to do that.

Reflect on and evaluate your book club discussion.

- ☐ We came prepared with pages marked and ideas to talk about.
- ☐ We took turns talking.
- ☐ We added on to each other's ideas.
- ☐ We invited others to participate.
- ☐ We stayed on topic.
- ☐ We supported our ideas with evidence from the text or personal experience.
- ☐ We respected everyone's ideas, including those we didn't agree with.
- ☐ We asked questions when we wanted to know more or didn't understand something.

Section 2: Literary Analysis

Assessment

After you have taught the minilessons in this umbrella, observe students as they listen and speak about their reading across instructional contexts: interactive read-aloud, independent reading, guided reading, shared reading, and book club. Use *The Literacy Continuum* (Fountas and Pinnell 2017) to observe students' reading and writing behaviors.

▶ What evidence do you have of new understandings related to the way students engage with book clubs?

  • Are students effectively using conversation skills and effective language in book club discussions?

  • Do they know when to continue addressing one topic or when to move the discussion in a new direction?

  • Do they demonstrate that they value everyone's ideas and opinions?

  • Are they monitoring their own participation and encouraging others to share?

  • Do they use terms such as *book club, listener, speaker, respect, discussion,* and *reflect*?

▶ In what other ways, beyond the scope of this umbrella, are students talking or writing about books?

  • Are students talking about the characters in fiction books (e.g., their feelings and motivations, their perspective)?

  • Do they write in response to what they have read?

Use your observations to determine the next umbrella you will teach. You may also consult Minilessons Across the Year (pp. 61–64) for guidance.

Link to Writing

After teaching the minilessons in this umbrella, help students link the new learning to their own writing:

▶ Encourage students to write in a reader's notebook about ways in which a book club discussion has enhanced and deepened their understanding of a book.

Reader's Notebook

When this umbrella is complete, provide a copy of the minilesson principles (see resources.fountasandpinnell.com) for students to glue in the reader's notebook (in the Minilessons section if using *Reader's Notebook: Advanced* [Fountas and Pinnell 2011]), so they can refer to the information as needed.

Minilessons in This Umbrella

RML1 Study authors to learn about their craft.

RML2 Hypothesize the author's reasons for choosing a topic or idea.

RML3 Authors engage in research for their writing.

RML4 Authors often have their own unique style.

Before Teaching Umbrella 3 Minilessons

During an author study (see pp. 42–43), students learn that authors repeatedly make decisions as part of the authoring process. Author study supports students in noticing and appreciating elements of an author's craft and also the kind of research an author engages in to create an authentic and accurate book. Teach one or more of these lessons throughout the year as you conduct an author study or as students think about the decisions authors make in creating their books.

The first step in studying authors is to collect a set of mentor texts for students to read and enjoy. Use the following books from the *Fountas & Pinnell Classroom™ Interactive Read-Aloud Collection* text sets; however, you can use books by a single author or authors that your students have read.

Author/Illustrator Study: S. D. Nelson

Black Elk's Vision

Digging a Hole to Heaven

Red Cloud

Leadership

Sitting Bull by S. D. Nelson

Animal Adaptations

Glow by W. H. Beck

Neighborhood Sharks by Katherine Roy

Human Inventiveness

Iqbal and His Ingenious Idea by Elizabeth Suneby

Chef Roy Choi and the Street Food Remix by Jacqueline Briggs Martin and June Jo Lee

Illustrator Study: K. Y. Craft

Cupid and Psyche by M. Charlotte Craft

King Midas and the Golden Touch by Charlotte Craft

Memoir/Autobiography

Drawing from Memory by Allen Say

Perseverance

Silent Days, Silent Dreams by Allen Say

As you read aloud and enjoy these texts together, help students

- look across texts to learn about authors and their craft, and
- think about the research an author needs to do in order to make a book authentic.

Author/Illustrator Study: S. D. Nelson

Leadership

Animal Adaptations

Human Inventiveness

Illustrator Study: K. Y. Craft

Memoir/Autobiography

Perseverance

Section 2: Literary Analysis

RML1

LA.U3.RML1

Reading Minilesson Principle
Study authors to learn about their craft.

Studying Authors and Their Processes

You Will Need

- multiple books by the same author, such as the following by S. D. Nelson:
  - *Black Elk's Vision* and *Digging a Hole to Heaven*, from Text Set: Author/Illustrator Study: S. D. Nelson
  - *Sitting Bull* from Text Set: Leadership
  - *Red Cloud* from Text Set: Author/Illustrator Study: S. D. Nelson
- chart paper and markers
- large sticky notes

Academic Language / Important Vocabulary

- author
- style
- characteristics
- craft

Continuum Connection

- Connect texts by a range of categories: e.g., content, theme, message, genre, author/illustrator, character, setting, special forms, text structure, or organization (pp. 79, 84)
- Analyze texts to determine aspects of a writer's style: e.g., use of language, choice of setting, plot, characters, themes, and ideas (p. 82)
- Recognize some authors by the style of their illustrations, their topics, characters they use, or typical plots (p. 82)
- Recognize some authors by the topics they choose or the style of their illustrations (p. 86)

Goal

Understand that an author usually writes several books and that there are often recognizable characteristics across the books.

Rationale

When students analyze the characteristics of an author's work, they begin to appreciate that writing is a process of decision making and that artistry is involved. Recognizing an author's patterns or style can heighten anticipation, enjoyment, and depth of understanding because familiarity has been established. Note that this lesson format can be used for future author studies.

Assess Learning

Observe students when they talk about authors and notice if there is evidence of new learning based on the goal of this minilesson.

- Do students recognize similar characteristics across books by the same author?
- Are they able to ascertain whether characteristics *always* or *often* occur in books by the same author?
- Do they use the terms *author, characteristics, style,* and *craft*?

Minilesson

To help students think about the minilesson principle, engage them in noticing characteristics of an author's style. Here is an example.

- Show the covers of at least two books by an author, such as *Black Elk's Vision* and *Digging a Hole to Heaven* by S. D. Nelson.

    Think about these books you have been reading by S. D. Nelson. What are some things you have noticed about his writing?

    Which of these ideas are *always* true of S. D. Nelson's books and which of these ideas are *often* true?

- On chart paper, write the author's name at the top, with *Noticings* underneath. Create separate columns for *Always* and *Often* and record the students' ideas in the appropriate column on the chart. (You might want to write the ideas on sticky notes so that they can be moved from column to column as students read more books and learn more about the author.)

- Read or show pages from *Sitting Bull* to prompt the conversation, and make additions to the chart.

    Each characteristic that you notice in S. D. Nelson's writing is a decision that he made.

Have a Try

Invite the students to talk with a partner about another of S. D. Nelson's books.

▶ Show the cover and a few pages of *Red Cloud*.

   Turn and talk about S. D. Nelson's writing in this book. Do you notice any of the characteristics on the chart? Is there anything else that should be added?

▶ After time for discussion, ask a few students to share. Add new ideas to the chart.

Summarize and Apply

Summarize the learning and remind students to think about the characteristics of an author's writing as they read.

   Today you learned that if you think closely about several books by the same author you begin to notice the decisions the author has made and the characteristics of that author's writing. This is called the author's craft.

   When you read today, choose a book by S. D. Nelson or choose a book by a different author if you have read at least one other book by that author. Place a sticky note on any pages you want to remember that show characteristics of the author's craft. Bring the book when we meet so you can share.

Share

Following independent reading time, gather students in the meeting area to talk about books by the same author.

   Did anyone read a book by S. D. Nelson or by a different author who is familiar to you? Share what you noticed.

Extend the Lesson (Optional)

After assessing students' understanding, you might decide to extend the learning.

▶ Use this same lesson format to conduct an illustrator study.

S. D. Nelson
Noticings:

Always	Often
• Writes about people struggling in hard times or who have been treated poorly	• Writes about the conflict between the Lakota and Wasichu
• Includes messages of hope for the future	• Writes biographies from the point of view of the subject
• Writes historical fiction or biographies	• Is both the author and illustrator
• Writes about a setting in the United States, set in the past	
• Illustrates his own books	

Section 2: Literary Analysis

RML 2

LA.U3.RML2

Reading Minilesson Principle

Hypothesize the author's reasons for choosing a topic or idea.

Studying Authors and Their Processes

You Will Need

- several familiar fiction texts that provide information or clues about where authors get ideas for writing, such as the following:
  - *Glow* by W. H. Beck, from Text Set: Animal Adaptations
  - *Digging a Hole to Heaven* by S. D. Nelson, from Text Set: Author/Illustrator Study: S. D. Nelson
  - *Neighborhood Sharks* by Katherine Roy, from Text Set: Animal Adaptations
- chart paper and markers
- document camera (optional)

Academic Language / Important Vocabulary

- hypothesize
- author
- dedication page
- author's note
- author's page

Continuum Connection

- Infer a writer's purpose in writing a fiction text (p. 79)
- Hypothesize the writer's reasons for choosing a topic and infer how the writer feels about a topic (p. 85)

Goal

Use different parts of the book (e.g., dedication, author's note, biographical information) to hypothesize why the author chose the idea or topic of the text.

Rationale

When students find out where an author gets ideas for books, they begin to think about topics or ideas they might write about using experiences from their own lives.

Assess Learning

Observe students when they talk about where authors get ideas for writing and notice if there is evidence of new learning based on the goal of this minilesson.

- ▶ Are students noticing different ways authors get writing ideas?
- ▶ Do they use academic vocabulary, such as *hypothesize, author, dedication page, author's note,* and *author's page*?

Minilesson

To help students think about the minilesson principle, engage them in discovering how authors get ideas for books. Here is an example.

- ▶ Show the cover of *Glow.*

    Where do you think W. H. Beck got her ideas for writing this book?

    Where are some places we could look in the book to find out about this?

    Where else could you look to find out how the author chose the topic?

- ▶ Guide students to think about places to look to find out more about an author. Then show (or project) and read the author's bio on the inside back flap and the dedication page.

    What information did you learn about W. H. Beck?

    How do you see this information about W. H. Beck being used in this book?

- ▶ As students share ideas, create a chart. Ask them for ideas about other places to find out more about the author and add to chart.

- ▶ Show the cover of *Digging a Hole to Heaven* and read the first paragraph of the acknowledgments on page 63.

    Where did S. D. Nelson get his idea to write this book about coal miners trapped in a mine?

    Where could you look to find out more?

- ▶ Add responses to the chart.

Have a Try

Invite the students to talk with a partner about where another author got her ideas for writing.

> Turn and talk about where Katherine Roy got her idea for writing *Neighborhood Sharks*.

▶ After time for discussion, ask students to share their thinking. Read or project the dedication page and author's note if needed. Add to chart.

Summarize and Apply

Summarize the learning and remind students to think about where authors get ideas.

> What did you learn about authors today?

▶ Add the principle to the chart.

> When you read today, look for places where you might find additional information about where the author found ideas for the book you are reading. You also can hypothesize, or make an informed guess, based on what you know about the book or author, or you can do online research to learn more. Bring the book when we meet so you can share.

Share

Following independent reading time, gather students in the meeting area in pairs.

> Did anyone find information or hypothesize about where an author got an idea for writing? Turn and talk about why you think the author wrote the book. Does this impact your understanding of the book or what you are thinking about the story or topic?

Extend the Lesson (Optional)

After assessing students' understanding, you might decide to extend the learning.

▶ Encourage students to use ideas from their own lives as they write stories.

▶ Talk about how knowing where an author gets ideas for writing helps in appreciating the book (e.g., develops empathy for characters, the story feels more authentic, the story becomes more engaging).

Hypothesize the author's reasons for choosing a topic or idea.

Author and Title	Where can you find out about how the author chose the topic or idea?	Where did the author find ideas to write about?
W. H. Beck GLOW	• inside back flap • dedication page • other books • author website • author interviews	• nature • books and information from work as librarian and teacher • her parents
S. D. Nelson DIGGING A HOLE TO HEAVEN	• acknowledgments • author website • author interviews	• author's own twin boys • field observations • research done for other books • teaching experiences
Katherine Roy NEIGHBORHOOD SHARKS	• author's note • online resources • author website	• interest in science, history, and adventure • grew up near the area she writes about • care and interest in protecting sharks

RML3

LA.U3.RML3

Reading Minilesson Principle
Authors engage in research for their writing.

Studying Authors and Their Processes

You Will Need

- several familiar historical fiction or nonfiction books, such as the following:
  - *Neighborhood Sharks* by Katherine Roy, from Text Set: Animal Adaptations
  - *Chef Roy Choi and the Street Food Remix* by Jacqueline Briggs Martin and June Jo Lee and *Iqbal and His Ingenious Idea* by Elizabeth Suneby, from Text Set: Human Inventiveness
- document camera (optional)
- chart paper and markers
- sticky notes

Academic Language / Important Vocabulary

- author
- research
- source
- accurate
- authentic

Continuum Connection

- Notice and evaluate the accuracy of the text, citing evidence for opinions (p. 86)

Goal

Understand that authors engage in research for their writing.

Rationale

When you teach students to think about what an author needs to research before writing a book, they learn to evaluate the authenticity and accuracy of the writing. They understand that research is an essential part of writing a book.

Assess Learning

Observe students when they discuss the research authors do and notice if there is evidence of new learning based on the goal of this minilesson.

▶ Can students locate information in a book that shows how authors have researched a topic?

▶ Do they think critically about how an author gains expertise on a topic?

▶ Do they use the terms *author, research, source, accurate,* and *authentic*?

Minilesson

To help students think about the minilesson principle, engage them in discovering how authors conduct research prior to writing. Here is an example.

▶ Show the cover of *Neighborhood Sharks.*

> What types of things do you think Katherine Roy had to learn about before writing this book about sharks living around California's Farallon Islands?

▶ Record their examples on a chart.

> Sometimes books provide information about the research the author conducted to learn about the topic.

▶ Read and show (or project) the inside back flap, the author's note, sources, and acknowledgments.

> What are some sources that the author used to do research?

> What other places do you think she might have looked to learn more about the sharks?

▶ Record responses.

▶ Repeat with *Chef Roy Choi and the Street Food Remix* (using the authors' notes, bibliography, resources, and author biographies). Record responses.

> Looking at the sources an author uses to research a topic before writing helps you determine whether the book is accurate and authentic.

Have a Try

Invite the students to talk with a partner about an author's research.

▶ Read and show (or project) the acknowledgments, the author bio, and the About Clean Cookstoves note from *Iqbal and His Ingenious Idea*.

> Think about the information Elizabeth Suneby had to find through research before writing this book. What sources did she use? Turn and talk about that.

▶ After students turn and talk, ask a few students to share ideas. Add to the chart.

Summarize and Apply

Summarize the learning and remind students to think about the research that authors conduct before writing.

> What do authors do before writing about a topic?

▶ Write the principle at the top of the chart.

> When you read today, look outside the main part of the book to see if there is information that tells about the research conducted by the author. Use sticky notes to mark pages you want to remember and bring the book when we meet so you can share.

Share

Following independent reading time, gather students in pairs to talk about an author's research.

> Share with your partner what you learned about an author's research. Talk about what the author needed to learn before writing and the different sources used by the author.

Extend the Lesson (Optional)

After assessing students' understanding, you might decide to extend the learning.

▶ Students may find it less obvious that an author needs to do research to write a fiction story. When you read a fiction book during interactive read-aloud, discuss with students what the author needed to know in order to make the story believable.

▶ **Writing About Reading** Help students engage in research about a nonfiction topic before writing about it.

Authors engage in research for their writing.

Author and Title	What did the author need to learn about to write this book?	Resources the Author Used
Katherine Roy Neighborhood Sharks	Sharks, specifically those living around the Farallon Islands in California	• books, journals • films • online resources • Farallon Island scientists • California Academy of Sciences and other marine organizations
Jacqueline Briggs Martin and June Jo Lee Chef Roy Choi and the Street Food Remix	Roy Choi Korean food and street trucks	• books, articles • videos, interviews • personal experiences eating diverse food • experiences eating at Roy Choi's food trucks and restaurants
Elizabeth Suneby Iqbal and His Ingenious Idea	Bangladesh and the cooking methods used there Clean cooking and the environment	• Global Alliance for Clean Cookstoves • Solar Cookers International • books, websites

Reading Minilesson Principle
Authors often have their own unique style.

Studying Authors and Their Processes

You Will Need

▸ several sets of books by the same authors, such as the following:

- *Black Elk's Vision* and *Digging a Hole to Heaven* by S. D. Nelson, from Text Set: Author/Illustrator Study: S. D. Nelson

- *Cupid and Psyche* and *King Midas and the Golden Touch* by Charlotte Craft, from Text Set: Illustrator Study: K. Y. Craft

- *Drawing from Memory* by Allen Say, from Text Set: Memoir/Autobiography

- *Silent Days, Silent Dreams* by Allen Say, from Text Set: Perseverance

▸ chart paper and markers

▸ sticky notes

Academic Language / Important Vocabulary

▸ author
▸ theme
▸ setting
▸ characteristics
▸ topic
▸ style

Continuum Connection

▸ Analyze texts to determine aspects of a writer's style: e.g., use of language, choice of setting, plot, characters, themes, and ideas (p. 82)

▸ Recognize some authors by the topics they choose or the style of their illustrations (p. 86)

Goal

Compare authors and their unique styles (e.g., the use of recurring themes/topics; craft moves; choices of settings and characters, etc.).

Rationale

When you teach students to see patterns across texts written by the same author, they learn to think in depth about an author's style, interests, values, and ideas, as well as anticipate similarities as they read books by the same author. Before teaching this umbrella, it would be helpful to teach Umbrella 8: Thinking About Themes and the Author's Message, found in this section.

Assess Learning

Observe students when they talk about authors and notice if there is evidence of new learning based on the goal of this minilesson.

▸ Can students discuss similarities across books by the same author?

▸ Do they understand that authors can be identified by individual style?

▸ Do they use the terms *author, setting, topic, theme, characteristics,* and *style*?

Minilesson

To help students think about the minilesson principle, engage them in thinking about similarities across texts by the same author. Here is an example.

▸ Ahead of time, gather two books by S. D. Nelson. Cover the author's name on one of the books, such as *Black Elk's Vision*, with a sticky note and display the cover.

▸ Show the cover of the book with the covered author's name. Read and show the illustrations from several pages.

> Based on what you have noticed in other books, who wrote this book? How do you know?

▸ Reveal the author's name. Show the other book by S. D. Nelson.

> The similarities help you notice books by S. D. Nelson. What are some of the characteristics you notice in these books by S. D. Nelson?

▸ Guide the conversation so that students notice the similarities in types of settings, topics, and themes. Fill in a chart with students' responses.

▸ Repeat the activity with two books by another author, such as Charlotte Craft.

Have a Try

Invite the students to talk with a partner about the style of an author.

▶ Show the covers and a few pages from two books by Allen Say.

Turn and talk about Allen Say. What are the characteristics of his writing style?

▶ After students turn and talk, add responses to the chart.

Summarize and Apply

Summarize the learning and remind students to notice the style of the author when they read.

Today you looked at multiple books by the same author and recognized that you can identify an author by noticing similarities in settings, topics, and themes.

▶ Add the principle to the top of the chart.

When you read today, you might choose a book by an author you have read before. If you do, use a sticky note to note similarities between the books. Bring the book when we meet so you can share.

Share

Following independent reading time, gather students in the meeting area to talk about an author's style.

Did anyone read a book by an author you have read before? How is it helpful to think about things that are similar across books by the same author? Share your thoughts.

Extend the Lesson (Optional)

After assessing students' understanding, you might decide to extend the learning.

▶ **Writing About Reading** Have students use a grid to compare books by the same author (see resources.fountasandpinnell.com) and then write about their noticings in a reader's notebook.

Authors often have their own unique style.

	S. D. Nelson	Charlotte Craft	Allen Say
Settings	United States in the past	Ancient Greece	Japan, United States in the past
Topics	people who have faced hardships or who have been treated poorly (historical fiction or biography)	mythology	real people, artists
Themes	struggling in hard times, hope for the future	life lessons, such as about love, kindness, and greed	working hard, perseverance

Assessment

After you have taught the minilessons in this umbrella, observe students as they talk and write about their reading across instructional contexts: interactive read-aloud, independent reading, guided reading, shared reading, and book club. Use *The Literacy Continuum* (Fountas and Pinnell 2017) to observe students' reading and writing behaviors.

- What evidence do you have of new understandings related to authors and their work?
- Do students understand that studying an author will help them learn about the author's craft?
- Are they thinking about how an author came up with a topic or idea?
- Do they understand and think about the ways authors do research before writing?
- Are they aware that authors often write about similar settings, topics, or themes in their books?
- Are they using terms such as *characteristics, style, craft, author's note, author's page, dedication page, research, authentic, theme, topic,* and *setting*?

▶ In what other ways, beyond the scope of this umbrella, are students thinking about authors and illustrators?

- Are they noticing and talking about the illustrator's craft?

Use your observations to determine the next umbrella you will teach. You may also consult Minilessons Across the Year (pp. 61–64) for guidance.

Link to Writing

After teaching the minilessons in this umbrella, help students link the new learning to their own writing:

▶ Students can write books in the style of an author they enjoy.

▶ Students can include an author bio, author's note, or dedication page in their own writing that shares information about their craft.

Reader's Notebook

When this umbrella is complete, provide a copy of the minilesson principles (see resources.fountasandpinnell.com) for students to glue in the reader's notebook (in the Minilessons section if using *Reader's Notebook: Advanced* [Fountas and Pinnell 2011]), so they can refer to the information as needed.

Minilessons in This Umbrella

RML1 Study the illustrations closely to understand what is happening in the text.

RML2 Notice the text features the author/illustrator uses to help you follow the action.

RML3 Notice the text features the author/illustrator uses to create narration, sound, and dialogue.

RML4 Notice how the author/illustrator uses color and lines to show setting, mood, and motion.

Before Teaching Umbrella 4 Minilessons

Though not a genre, graphic texts are a popular text format. They can be fiction or nonfiction. Studying graphic texts with students prepares them to read and understand graphic texts independently. When reading fiction graphic texts together, encourage students to pay close attention to the illustrations because they carry much of the action. Introduce the various features of graphic texts. For example, panels in graphic texts function like paragraphs and are read left to right and top to bottom. They hold the pictures and the speech and thought bubbles (also called balloons), and they carry the narrative. Gutters are the spaces between the panels, which sometimes show time passing. Often, the reader must infer action between panels. Other text features in graphic texts are narrative boxes and sound words, both of which help the reader understand the text.

Before introducing this umbrella, create a basket of graphic texts in a variety of genres for use during independent reading. You may choose to use the texts from the *Fountas & Pinnell Classroom™ Guided Reading Collection* listed below, but also collect other graphic texts from your own library that engage students' intellectual curiosity and emotions, making sure the texts have content, themes, and ideas that are appropriate for your students' cognitive development, emotional maturity, and life experience.

Guided Reading Collection

Rebound by Patrick Jones

The Jewel Heist by Teri Eastman

Lights, Camera, Action: How to Make a Video by Margie Sigman

On the Edge by Sean Petrie

As you read aloud and enjoy these texts together, help students

- notice that the illustrations carry most of the action,

- read the text and study the text features for meaning, and

- notice an author/illustrator's color and line choices.

Guided Reading

Section 2: Literary Analysis

Reading Minilesson Principle
Study the illustrations closely to understand what is happening in the text.

You Will Need

- one or two graphic texts students are reading, such as the following from *Guided Reading Collection*:
  - *Rebound* by Patrick Jones
  - *The Jewel Heist* by Teri Eastman
- document camera (optional)
- chart paper and markers
- sticky notes

Academic Language / Important Vocabulary

- graphic text
- action

Continuum Connection

- Follow a complex plot with multiple events, episodes, or problems (p. 81)
- Notice how illustrations and graphics go together with the text in a meaningful way (p. 83)
- Understand that graphics provide important information (p. 87)

Goal

Study the illustrations closely to understand what is happening in the text.

Rationale

Graphic texts have both illustrations and printed text, and illustrations carry a good deal of the information. Students must learn to follow the story and infer character feelings and traits from the illustrations. This will ensure they understand what they are reading.

Assess Learning

Observe students when they read graphic texts. Notice if there is evidence of new learning based on the goal of this minilesson.

- ▸ Can students describe what they see in the illustrations?
- ▸ Do they use the illustrations to understand the story?
- ▸ Are they using language such as *graphic text* and *action*?

Minilesson

To help students understand the minilesson principle, engage them in a discussion about the role of the illustrations in a graphic text. Use a document camera, if available, to support viewing the illustrations. Here is an example.

- ▸ Show the cover of *Rebound*. Read and show pages 5–8.

  Rebound is an example of a graphic text. How is this book different from other kinds of books that you have read?

  There are more illustrations than words. Look at the illustrations on this page while I read it to you. What do you see in the illustrations? What do they help you understand?

  How do the illustrations help you know what the phrase "dirty player" means?

- ▸ Record noticings about how the illustrations help a reader to understand the story.
- ▸ Read parts of pages 3, 5, 11, and 16–22.

  What does the author want you to think about on these pages? What is the author's message?

- ▸ Record noticings about how the illustrations help a reader to understand the theme.

  In a graphic text, you look at both the words and the illustrations, but the illustrations carry at least as much—often more—information as the words.

Have a Try

Invite the students to talk with a partner about some illustrations from *The Jewel Heist*.

- Have students study the illustrations on pages 6 and 11–12.

  Turn and talk to your partner. What do the illustrations show? How do they help you understand this part of the text?

- After time to turn and talk, ask a few students to share. Record responses on the chart.

Summarize and Apply

Summarize the learning and remind students to study the illustrations in a graphic text.

  Take a look at the chart we created. What do you need to do to understand a graphic text?

- Write the principle at the top of the chart.

  When you read today, you might choose a graphic text. If you do, mark with a sticky note an illustration that helps you understand what is happening in the book. Bring the book when we meet so you can share.

Share

Following independent reading time, gather students in the meeting area to talk about their reading.

  Tell us what you learned from the illustrations on a page in your book.

- Display the students' pages on a document camera, if possible, so that everyone can see.

Extend the Lesson (Optional)

After assessing students' understanding, you might decide to extend the learning.

- Encourage students to use illustrations to determine the theme of a graphic text.

- **Writing About Reading** Encourage students to write in a reader's notebook about how the illustrations in a graphic text helped them to understand what was happening in the story.

Graphic Text	What do you see in the illustrations?	What does that help you understand in the story?
REBOUND	• Coach tells Titus to go in the game • "24 is a dirty player" • Basketball court • A "dirty player" is someone who doesn't play by the rules/does things they shouldn't in order to win • Circle with Titus' surprised face	• Action • Problem • Setting • Meaning of a word or phrase • Character's Feelings • Author's Message
Jewel Heist	• The contents of her pockets • Fingerprints • Crime lab team takes fingerprints	• Elaborates on details in the story

Study the illustrations closely to understand what is happening in the text.

Section 2: Literary Analysis

RML1 LA.U4.RML1

Reading Minilesson Principle
Notice the text features the author/illustrator uses to help you follow the action.

You Will Need

- one or two graphic texts students are reading, such as the following from *Guided Reading Collection*:
  - *Rebound* by Patrick Jones
  - *Lights, Camera, Action* by Margie Sigman
- document camera (optional)
- chart paper and markers

Academic Language / Important Vocabulary

- panels
- gutters
- illustrations

Continuum Connection

- Notice how illustrations and graphics go together with the text in a meaningful way (p. 83)
- Understand that graphics and text are carefully placed in a nonfiction text so that ideas are communicated clearly (p. 87)

Goal

Notice and understand the function of the panels, gutters, and pictures in a graphic text and the author/illustrator's craft in creating them.

Rationale

Studying the function of panels and gutters within graphic texts, and how an author/illustrator uses these text features, allows students to successfully read graphic texts and appreciate the author/illustrator's craft.

Assess Learning

Observe students when they read graphic texts. Notice if there is evidence of new learning based on the goal of this minilesson.

- Do students read all the panels to follow the action in a story?
- Can they talk about how the panels and gutters help them understand a story?
- Are they using language such as *panels, gutters,* and *illustrations*?

Minilesson

To help students understand more about the minilesson principle, use familiar texts to engage them in a discussion about the text features in a graphic text. Use a document camera, if available, so that everyone can see the books. Here is an example.

- Show the cover of *Rebound*. Display a few pages, stopping and reading page 5.

  How do the features of the illustration help you read this graphic text?

- Read page 11, pointing to the panels and gutters as you read.

  These boxes are called panels. The blank spaces between the boxes are called gutters.

  Why is having this blank space here important?

- Record noticings on a chart. As necessary, prompt students to expand upon their thinking about how the author and illustrator show what is happening in the story.

  - *Why did the author and illustrator use panels?*
  - *What did they include in the panels?*
  - *In what order should you read the panels?*

- Continue to record noticings on the chart.

Have a Try

Invite the students to talk with a partner about a procedural/realistic fiction text, such as *Lights, Camera, Action*.

▶ Show page 11, reviewing what is happening on these pages.

> Turn and talk to your partner. What do the illustrations on these pages help you to understand?

▶ After time to turn and talk, ask a few students to share. Record responses on the chart.

Summarize and Apply

Summarize the learning and remind students to use the panels and gutters to understand the action of the text.

▶ Review the chart and write the principle at the top.

> When you read today, you might choose to read a graphic text. As you read, notice how the panels and gutters help you understand what is happening in the story. Bring the book when we meet today so you can share.

Share

Following independent reading time, gather students in the meeting area to talk about their reading.

> Who read a graphic text today? Talk about how you used the panels and gutters to help you follow the action of the story.

▶ Display students' pages on a document camera, if possible, so that everyone can see.

Extend the Lesson (Optional)

After assessing students' understanding, you might decide to extend the learning.

▶ If you have not already displayed graphic texts in the classroom library, enlist several students to create a display.

▶ Use this lesson as a model for teaching students to use text features to gather information in other kinds of graphic texts, such as graphic text biographies.

▶ **Writing About Reading** Encourage students to create a response to a book in a reader's notebook using a few panels and gutters to show their thinking.

Notice the text features the author/illustrator uses to help you follow the action.

Panels

- Help the reader follow the action
- Read left to right and top to bottom
- Different sizes show the importance of the action.
- Contain speech bubbles
- Contain thought bubbles
- Panels within panels change the reader's focus.
- Provide information about the topic

Gutters

- Blank spaces between panels
- Separate each panel for clarity
- Often show that time has passed
- Help the reader understand the information/procedure the author is teaching

Reading Minilesson Principle
Notice the text features the author/illustrator uses to create narration, sound, and dialogue.

Reading Graphic Texts

You Will Need

- one or two graphic texts students are reading, such as the following from *Guided Reading Collection*:
  - *Rebound* by Patrick Jones
  - *On the Edge* by Sean Petrie
- document camera (optional)
- chart paper and markers
- sticky notes

Academic Language / Important Vocabulary

- speech bubbles
- thought bubbles
- narrative boxes
- onomatopoeia

Continuum Connection

- Notice how illustrations and graphics go together with the text in a meaningful way (p. 83)

Goal

Notice and understand the use of speech and thought bubbles, lettering, and sound words to create narration, sound, and dialogue in a graphic text.

Rationale

Teaching students to notice and use text features in a graphic text (e.g., speech and thought bubbles, lettering, narrative boxes, and sound words)—and to understand how they create narration, sound, and dialogue—helps them create a story in the mind and supports them in understanding.

Assess Learning

Observe students when they read graphic texts. Notice if there is evidence of new learning based on the goal of this minilesson.

- ▶ Do students use and understand the features authors and illustrators use in graphic texts to show the action in the story?
- ▶ Are they using language such as *speech bubbles, thought bubbles, narrative boxes,* and *onomatopoeia*?

Minilesson

To demonstrate the minilesson principle, use a familiar graphic text to engage them in a discussion about text features that show narration, sound, and dialogue. Use a document camera, if available. Here is an example.

- ▶ Read aloud and display page 3 from *Rebound*.

    Look at the speech bubble on this page. What do you notice about it?

    Now look at the thought bubbles. How are they similar to speech bubbles? How are they different?

- ▶ Record noticings on chart paper. Then display page 7.

    What do you notice about the print on this page?

    What does the word *swish* help you understand?

    Swish is an example of onomatopoeia. *Swish* makes the sound it represents.

- ▶ Record noticings on a chart. Then display page 4.

    What do you notice about the referee's words?

    They are in bold print and they are in all capital letters. Why?

- ▶ Record noticings on the chart.

Have a Try

Invite the students to talk with a partner about more text features in *On the Edge*.

▸ Display page 2 from *On the Edge*.

> Turn and talk to your partner about what you notice at the top of the first panel and why it is there.

▸ After time to turn and talk about the narrative box, ask a few students to share. Record responses on the chart.

Summarize and Apply

Summarize the learning and remind students to notice text features when they read graphic texts.

> Take a look at the chart we created. What can you say about the features authors and illustrators use in graphic texts?

▸ Review the chart and write the principle at the top.

> If you choose a graphic text to read today, mark with a sticky note one or two features that the author or illustrator used to create narration, sound, and/or dialogue. Bring the book when we meet so you can share.

Share

Following independent reading time, gather students in the meeting area to talk about their graphic texts.

> What text features did you notice in your reading? How did they help you understand that part of the story?

▸ Ask a few students to share with the class, and add to the chart as necessary.

Extend the Lesson (Optional)

After assessing students' understanding, you might decide to extend the learning.

▸ **Writing About Reading** Ask students to create a response in a reader's notebook using narrative boxes, speech and thought bubbles, lettering, and sound words to share their thinking.

Notice the text features the author/illustrator uses to create narration, sound, and dialogue.

Speech and Thought Bubbles	Onomatopoeia (Sound Words)	Lettering	Narrative Boxes
Speech Bubbles • Tell what characters are saying • Point to the character who is talking (Play smart, Titus!) Thought Bubbles • Tell what characters are thinking • Point to the character who is thinking (Come on, Coach!)	• Tell sounds • Various sizes tell how loud or soft the sound would be *SWISHH!*	• ALL CAPITAL LETTERS draw your attention • **BOLD** letters can mean yelling FOUL! BACK TO THE BENCH!	• Introduce characters or set the scene • Written in third person • Act like a narrator in a play Summer had just begun . . .

RML4

LA.U4.RML4

Notice how the author/illustrator uses color and lines to show setting, mood, and motion.

Reading Graphic Texts

You Will Need

- one or two graphic texts students are reading, such as the following from *Guided Reading Collection*:
  - *The Jewel Heist* by Teri Eastman
  - *Rebound* by Patrick Jones
- document camera (optional)
- chart paper and markers
- sticky notes

Academic Language / Important Vocabulary

- illustrator
- illustration
- mood

Continuum Connection

- Notice how illustrations and graphics go together with the text in a meaningful way (p. 83)
- Notice and infer how illustrations contribute to mood in a fiction text (p. 83)
- Interpret some illustrations with symbolic characteristics: e.g., use of color or symbols (p. 83)

Goal

Notice how the author/illustrator uses color and lines to show setting, mood, and motion.

Rationale

Encouraging students to notice and understand how illustrators use and make decisions about color and lines in graphic texts supports them in gaining deeper meaning from their reading and in developing an understanding of the illustrator's craft.

Assess Learning

Observe students when they read graphic texts. Notice if there is evidence of new learning based on the goal of this minilesson.

- Are students able to discuss why an illustrator makes certain color choices?
- Can they talk about how an illustrator uses lines in illustrations?
- Do they use academic language, such as *illustrator*, *illustration*, and *mood* when they talk about graphic texts?

Minilesson

To help students think about the minilesson principle, use a familiar graphic text to engage them in a discussion about an illustrator's use of color and lines. Here is an example.

- Display pages 2 and 6–9 from *The Jewel Heist*.

  What do you notice about the illustrator's use of color on these pages?

  What does the color show you?

  The illustrator used different colors to show the setting—the time of day and the place.

- Record noticings on a chart.

  Look again at page 9. What do you see near Tamra Cho's brush as she dusts for fingerprints?

  Why do you think the illustrator used those lines?

  The illustrator used lines to show the motion of the brush sweeping back and forth.

- Record noticings on the chart.
- Repeat, noticing the way color indicates mood on page 21 of *Rebound*.

Have a Try

Invite the students to talk about lines in *Rebound*, looking at pages 6–11.

> Turn and talk to your partner about how the illustrator used lines on these pages.

▶ After time to turn and talk, ask a few students to share. Record responses on the chart.

Summarize and Apply

Summarize the learning and remind students to notice how authors/illustrators use color and lines in graphic texts.

▶ Review the chart and write the principle at the top.

> When you read today, you might choose a graphic text to read. If you do, notice the author/illustrator's use of color and lines to show setting, mood, and motion. Bring the book when we meet so you can share.

Share

Following independent reading time, gather students in the meeting area to talk about graphic texts.

> What did you notice about color and lines in the book you read today? What did you learn from them?

Extend the Lesson (Optional)

After assessing students' understanding, you might decide to extend the learning.

▶ Continue collecting and offering graphic texts to students for independent reading. Add to the chart as necessary.

▶ **Writing About Reading** Ask students to write a letter in a reader's notebook about how the author/illustrator used color and lines in a graphic text to show setting, mood, or motion.

Notice how the author/illustrator uses color and lines to show setting, mood, and motion.		
		Color and Lines Show
Color	Lighter colors for daytime and dark greens, purples, blues, and black for nighttime Darker colors indoors versus brighter colors outdoors	Orange and yellow background indicate the intensity of Titus' thinking Blue and white background reflects a change in Titus' thinking to something more positive	Setting Mood
Lines	Lines near fingerprint dusting brush	Star-like figure around the high five Lines around shoulders White lines around the basketball Lines around elbow, shoulder, arms, and basketball Lightning bolt around the thought bubbles	Motion Mood Sound Character's emotions

Section 2: Literary Analysis

Assessment

After you have taught the minilessons in this umbrella, observe students as they talk and write about their reading across instructional contexts: interactive read-aloud, independent reading, guided reading, shared reading, and book club. Use *The Literacy Continuum* (Fountas and Pinnell 2017) to guide the observation of students' reading and writing behaviors.

▶ What evidence do you have of new understandings related to graphic texts?

  • Do students understand that the illustrations carry much of the meaning?

  • Do they read panels and text left to right and top to bottom?

  • Do they understand and use text features to support their understanding of the text (e.g., panels, gutters, narrative boxes, speech bubbles, thought bubbles, sound words)?

  • Do they understand how authors/illustrators use text features to create narration, sound, and dialogue?

  • Do they notice and discuss an illustrator's decisions around color and lines?

  • Are they using vocabulary such as *graphic texts*, *illustrations*, *panels*, *gutters*, *narrative boxes*, *speech bubbles*, *thought bubbles*, and *onomatopoeia*?

▶ In what other ways, beyond the scope of this umbrella, are students talking about the decisions authors and illustrators make?

  • Do students notice the craft decisions that authors and illustrators make?

Use your observations to determine the next umbrella you will teach. You may also consult Minilessons Across the Year (pp. 61–64) for guidance.

Link to Writing

After teaching the minilessons in this umbrella, help students link the new learning to their own writing:

▶ Provide students with time to work on writing their own graphic texts. Encourage them to include text features.

Reader's Notebook

When this umbrella is complete, provide a copy of the minilesson principles (see resources.fountasandpinnell.com) for students to glue in the reader's notebook (in the Minilessons section if using *Reader's Notebook: Advanced* [Fountas and Pinnell 2011]), so they can refer to the information as needed.

Minilessons in This Umbrella

RML1   Critique books for representation and omission.

RML2   Evaluate how different groups of people are represented in illustrations and graphics.

RML3   Evaluate how characters or biographical subjects are portrayed in books.

RML4   Think about how a story is affected by an author's choice of characters (e.g., gender, race/culture, socioeconomic status).

RML5   Critique the quality of fiction and nonfiction books.

Before Teaching Umbrella 5 Minilessons

All students, regardless of background, benefit from exposure to a broad range of literature that represents the heterogeneous world in which we live so that they can learn in a culturally relevant environment.

   The first minilesson provides a framework for critiquing the classroom library (or other book collection) to ensure that books represent people from many backgrounds. It is also important to include books that show people as they exist today, rather than older stereotypical representations or just a narrow segment of a particular population. Use the books listed below from the *Fountas & Pinnell Classroom ™ Interactive Read-Aloud Collection* or suitable books from your classroom library.

Activists/Change Makers

Walking in the City with Jane
  by Susan Hughes

Gordon Parks
  by Carole Boston Weatherford

Ballots for Belva
  by Sudipta Bardhan-Quallen

Equality

Mama Africa! by Kathryn Erskine

Nelson Mandela by Kadir Nelson

Human Inventiveness

Chef Roy Choi and the Street Food Remix by Jacqueline Briggs Martin and June Jo Lee

Leadership

Sitting Bull by S. D. Nelson

Countering Stereotypes

Africa Is Not a Country
  by Margy Burns Knight and Mark Melnicove

A Shelter in Our Car
  by Monica Gunning

The Whispering Cloth
  by Pegi Deitz Shea

Kindness and Compassion

Chachaji's Cup by Uma Krishnaswami

Life on Earth

Living Fossils by Caroline Arnold

As you read aloud and enjoy these texts together, help students think and talk about the people who are represented in books they read.

Activists/Change Makers

Equality

Human Inventiveness

Leadership

Countering Stereotypes

Kindness and Compassion

Life on Earth

Section 2: Literary Analysis

Thinking Critically
About Texts

You Will Need

- one set of books that shows diversity in representation, such as books in the text sets Activists/Change Makers and Equality
- chart paper and markers
- sticky notes
- classroom library books, divided into random sets (one per group)

Academic Language / Important Vocabulary

- critique
- representation
- diversity
- race
- gender
- socioeconomic

Continuum Connection

- Share opinions about a written text and/or about illustrations and give rationales and examples (pp. 593, 605)

Goal

Evaluate the diversity of representation in sets of books.

Rationale

When students learn to critique whether books are culturally responsive and diverse, they learn to value and embrace reading about a wide range of people that resemble the heterogeneous world in which we live, as well as to see themselves represented and valued in the classroom through literature.

Assess Learning

Observe students when they critique sets of books and notice if there is evidence of new learning based on the goal of this minilesson.

- ▶ Can students ask relevant questions to determine whether a body of literature is diverse and culturally relevant?
- ▶ Do they understand the terms *critique, representation, diversity, race, gender,* and *socioeconomic*?

Minilesson

To help students think about the minilesson principle, engage them in thinking about how to critique sets of books for representation. Here is an example.

> Think about the world we live in and all of the different types of people and their backgrounds. Today let's think about whether the books we have in the classroom reflect that diversity. In other words, who is represented in and who is missing from our books?

- ▶ Display the books from Text Set: Activists/Change Makers and Text Set: Equality.

  > One question we might ask about a collection of books is whether people from different races are represented.

  > What other kinds of people are represented? Turn and talk about that.

- ▶ After time for discussion, ask students to share ideas, and begin a list on chart paper. Guide the conversation to support their thinking. Introduce academic vocabulary that defines their thinking as appropriate (e.g., if students say *rich or poor*, introduce the term *socioeconomic*).

  > Take a look at the different kinds of people we have listed. Are there kinds of people you don't see in books but would like to read about?

  > Why is it important that we have a diverse range of books available to read?

Have a Try

Invite the students to critique a set of books.

▶ Have students sit in groups, each with a set of books randomly selected from the classroom library.

Take a look at the chart. With your group, critique the set of books. Talk about whether the books represent a wide range of people. Ask yourselves who is represented and who is missing. Place a sticky note on books with notes about your findings.

▶ After time for discussion, have groups share their noticings. Add any new diversities to the chart.

Summarize and Apply

Summarize the learning and remind students to think critically about representation in books.

What did you learn to do today?

▶ Write the principle on the top of chart.

When you read today, think about the people who are represented in the book you are reading. Also think about any books you have read recently that were about different types of people from the one you are reading now. Bring the book when we meet so you can share.

Share

Following independent reading time, gather students in the meeting area in a circle to talk about books.

▶ Ask each student to briefly describe the main character(s) or subject(s) in the book. After all students have shared, ask them to talk about the kinds of people in the books and the kinds of people who are not in the books.

Extend the Lesson (Optional)

After assessing students' understanding, you might decide to extend the learning.

▶ Have students meet with the librarian to talk about the library collection and how the librarian goes about choosing which books to purchase for the library.

▶ Ask students to research books about people who are not represented in the school or classroom library and compile a list of titles that would be worthwhile purchases for the school. Ask them to also consider funding sources (e.g., present the list at PTA/PTO meeting, hold a fundraising event).

Critique books for representation and omission.

What to Look for in a Set of Books

- [ ] different races
- [ ] main characters of different genders
- [ ] roles that are not stereotypical
- [ ] different socioeconomic backgrounds
- [ ] people with disabilities
- [ ] a variety of cultures
- [ ] various countries
- [ ] diverse religions
- [ ] different backgrounds interacting
- [ ] different ages and generations
- [ ] languages other than English
- [ ] different types of families

RML 2
LA.U5.RML2

Thinking Critically About Texts

You Will Need

- several books that show illustrations of diverse people, such as the following:
  - *Nelson Mandela* by Kadir Nelson from Text Set: Equality
  - *Africa Is Not a Country* by Margy Burns Knight and Mark Melnicove, from Text Set: Countering Stereotypes
  - *Sitting Bull* by S. D. Nelson, from Text Set: Leadership
  - *Chef Roy Choi and the Street Food Remix* by Jacqueline Briggs Martin and June Jo Lee, from Text Set: Human Inventiveness
- document camera (optional)
- books or online resources that show modern photographs of people (optional)
- chart paper and markers
- sticky notes
- basket of books with illustrations of people

Academic Language / Important Vocabulary

- diversity
- representation
- depicted
- stereotype

Continuum Connection

- Critique the text in terms of bias, stereotypes, prejudice, misrepresentation, sexism, racism (p. 91)
- Share opinions about a written text and/or about illustrations and give rationales and examples (pp. 593, 605)

Goal

Evaluate how different groups of people are represented in illustrations and graphics.

Rationale

When students think critically about the way people are represented in illustrations, they not only see themselves accurately and feel valued, but they also experience realistic depictions of people outside their community in order to develop empathy and a broader worldview.

Assess Learning

Observe students as they discuss illustrations in the books they read and notice if there is evidence of new learning based on the goal of this minilesson.

▶ Do students think and talk about the way people are depicted in illustrations?

▶ Are they using language such as *diversity, depicted, representation,* and *stereotype*?

Minilesson

To help students think about the minilesson principle, engage them in a discussion about the way people are depicted in illustrations. Here is an example.

▶ If possible, project pages so that students can see illustrations in detail, or provide time before the lesson for students to look closely at illustrations. You may be able to gather contemporary photographs from books or online sources that show young people from various countries in Africa, especially those who live in cities, so that the diversity within the culture is evident.

> Think about the way people are depicted, or shown, in illustrations. Sometimes they are accurate, and sometimes they show stereotypes.

▶ Show several illustrations of people from *Nelson Mandela* and *Africa Is Not a Country* and if available, contemporary photographs of children from different countries in Africa.

> Turn and talk about the illustrations in these books and how they show people from different countries in Africa, compared to the way people really look.

▶ After discussion, ask students to share, and add a few of their comments to the chart. Support the conversation as needed:

- *What do you notice about the illustrations and the way people are depicted?*
- *What message do the illustrations send when they are depicted accurately? What message is sent when they show stereotypes?*

▶ Add to chart. Repeat with *Sitting Bull* and *Chef Roy Choi.*

Have a Try

Invite the students to talk in small groups about the ways people are represented in books.

▶ Provide each group with one or two books that show illustrations of people. Try to include a diversity of people in the books so that the follow-up conversation will be rich and diverse.

> In your group, talk about the ways the people are depicted in the illustrations. Do you think the illustrations are accurate, or do they show stereotypes? Is there a range in the way people look that is realistic, or do they all look the same?

▶ After time for discussion, ask students to share their thinking.

Summarize and Apply

Summarize the learning and remind students to evaluate the ways people are depicted in illustrations.

> Today you learned that you can evaluate how different groups of people are represented in illustrations and graphics.

▶ Write the principle at the top of the chart.

> If you read a book today with illustrations of people, notice how they are shown in the illustrations. Place a sticky note on any pages you want to remember. Bring the book when we meet so you can share your noticings.

Share

Following independent reading time, gather students in the meeting area.

> What did you notice about the way people are depicted in illustrations? Show an example that supports your thinking.

Extend the Lesson (Optional)

After assessing students' understanding, you might decide to extend the learning.

▶ Have students compare the illustrations in an older book to the illustrations in a contemporary book on a similar topic and talk about how awareness of the importance to accurately depict people has changed the way books are illustrated.

▶ Encourage students to consider the background, style, and intentions of the author and illustrator as they critique the illustrations in books.

Evaluate how different groups of people are represented in illustrations and graphics.

Title	Representation of People in Illustrations
Nelson Mandela	• realistic • unique features • diverse/accurate skin tones and clothing
Africa Is Not a Country	• diverse representation (for example, people from Egypt are drawn differently than people from Ghana) • clothing styles appropriate for different places
Sitting Bull	• not realistic; very stereotypical • illustrations intended to honor Native American traditional art
Chef Roy Choi	• highly stereotypical and cartoon-like • illustrations intended to reflect the diverse street culture that Roy Choi wanted to cook for

Reading Minilesson Principle

Evaluate how characters or biographical subjects are portrayed in books.

Thinking Critically About Texts

You Will Need

- several books with a variety of human characters, such as the following:
  - *A Shelter in Our Car* by Monica Gunning, from Text Set: Countering Stereotypes
  - *Ballots for Belva* by Sudipta Bardhan-Quallen, from Text Set: Activists/Change Makers
  - *Nelson Mandela* by Kadir Nelson, from Text Set: Equality
- chart paper and markers
- sticky notes
- basket of biographies and fiction books with human characters

Academic Language / Important Vocabulary

- represented
- portrayed
- authentic
- stereotypes

Continuum Connection

- Critique the text in terms of bias, stereotypes, prejudice, misrepresentation, sexism, racism (p. 91)
- Share opinions about a written text and/or about illustrations and give rationales and examples (pp. 593, 605)

Goal

Evaluate the way characters or people in biographies are portrayed in books, including critiquing for stereotyping and overgeneralizations of different groups of people.

Rationale

When students think critically about how characters or people in biographies are portrayed in books, they begin to notice the perpetuation of stereotypes and will begin to understand how an author can accurately and respectfully portray people of different races, cultures, genders, and abilities.

Assess Learning

Observe students when they talk about characters and/or people in biographies and notice if there is evidence of new learning based on the goal of this minilesson.

- ▶ Do students discuss how characters and biographical subjects are portrayed in the books they read?
- ▶ Do they notice whether characters and biographical subjects are portrayed in a stereotypical way?
- ▶ Are they using language such as *represented, portrayed, authentic,* and *stereotypes*?

Minilesson

To help students think about the minilesson principle, engage them in a thoughtful discussion about evaluating how characters and biographical subjects are portrayed. Here is an example.

- ▶ Revisit a few pages from *A Shelter in Our Car*.

  Think about Zettie. How would you describe her?

- ▶ Guide the conversation to help students focus on her country of origin and socioeconomic background.

  How is Zettie portrayed?

  Does she seem like an authentic person, or is she portrayed as a stereotype? Turn and talk about that.

- ▶ After time for discussion, discuss the way Zettie is portrayed and write a description on chart paper.

- ▶ Repeat the activity with *Ballots for Belva*, focusing on her gender and age.

  What are some questions you might ask yourself when you evaluate how characters and people in biographies are portrayed in books?

- ▶ Guide the conversation and make a list of questions on a separate chart.

Have a Try

Invite the students to evaluate the way a character or biographical subject is portrayed in a story.

▶ Revisit several pages from *Nelson Mandela*.

Think about the way this biography of Nelson Mandela portrays him. Take a look at the questions on the chart and talk with a partner about the way he is portrayed.

▶ After time for discussion, ask students to share their thinking. Guide the conversation as needed. Add to the chart.

Summarize and Apply

Summarize the learning and remind students to think about how characters or biographical subjects are portrayed in books.

You talked about some ways you can evaluate how characters and biographical subjects are portrayed in books.

▶ Write the principle on the first chart.

When you read today, evaluate the characters in a fiction book or the people in a biography. Mark any pages you want to remember with a sticky note and bring the book when we meet so you can share.

Share

Following independent reading time, gather students in the meeting area in groups of two or three to talk about how they evaluated characters or people in biographies.

Talk with your group about what you noticed in the way characters or people in biographies are portrayed in the book you are reading.

Extend the Lesson (Optional)

After assessing students' understanding, you might decide to extend the learning.

▶ Have students critique texts for stereotypes and misrepresentations. If appropriate for your class, you might provide books that have these negative attributes to small groups so students can think critically about the impact the misrepresentations have on the reader. Guide students to understand that stereotypical characters are often simple and one-dimensional. When characters are rounder and more complex, they are less likely to seem like a stereotype of a certain group.

Evaluate how characters or biographical subjects are portrayed in books.

Title	How Characters Are Portrayed
	• Zettie and her mom are portrayed as unique people with distinct personalities. • The characters are living in poverty but they are not stereotypes.
	• Despite the time period, Belva was not constrained by gender or age. • Belva's unique personality shows through.
	• Nelson is represented as his true self, not a stereotype. • The topic of discrimination is described accurately.

Questions to Ask About How Characters Are Portrayed

Do characters or people in biographies reflect diverse groups fairly and accurately?

Do characters or people represented in biographies show diversity within a group?

Do characters or biographical subjects show a variety of characteristics or are they just stereotypes?

RML4
LA.U5.RML4

Reading Minilesson Principle
Think about how a story is affected by an author's choice of characters (e.g., gender, race/culture, socioeconomic status).

Thinking Critically About Texts

You Will Need

- several familiar fiction texts with diverse characters, such as the following:
  - *A Shelter in Our Car* by Monica Gunning, from Text Set: Countering Stereotypes
  - *Chachaji's Cup* by Uma Krishnaswami, from Text Set: Kindness and Compassion
  - *The Whispering Cloth* by Pegi Deitz Shea, from Text Set: Countering Stereotypes
- chart paper and markers
- sticky notes

Academic Language / Important Vocabulary

- impact
- gender
- race
- culture
- socioeconomic status

Continuum Connection

- Share opinions about a written text and/or about illustrations and give rationales and example (pp. 593, 605)

Goal

Notice how the author's choice of a character's gender, race, etc., influences a story.

Rationale

When students think about how culture, race, gender, location, historical time period, political environment, and/or socioeconomic status impacts a story, they develop empathy for people and an awareness of inequalities, unfairness, and misrepresentation of people now and in the past.

Assess Learning

Observe students as they discuss characters and notice if there is evidence of new learning based on the goal of this minilesson.

- ▶ Do students notice how a character's race, gender, or socioeconomic status impacts a story?
- ▶ Can they talk about how the story would be different if the character's race, gender, or socioeconomic status were different?
- ▶ Are they using language such as *impact, gender, race, culture,* and *socioeconomic status*?

Minilesson

To help students think about the minilesson principle, engage them in a discussion about how a character's gender, race /culture, or socioeconomic status affects the story. Here is an example.

- ▶ Show the cover of *A Shelter in Our Car*.

  Authors make very specific choices about how they describe characters in their stories—their ages, whether they are male or female, where they are from, how rich or poor they are. What are the choices the author of *A Shelter in Our Car* made about the characters in this story?

  In what ways do the types of characters chosen by the author have an impact on the story?

  How would the story be different if the characters were in a different socioeconomic position, were a different gender, or were not immigrants?

- ▶ Record responses on the chart.
- ▶ Continue the conversation with *Chachaji's Cup*.

  In what ways do race, culture, country of origin, age, gender, and socioeconomic status affect the story?

  How does thinking about this help you understand the characters better?

Have a Try

Invite the students to talk about how the gender, race/culture, or socioeconomic status of a character impacts a story.

▶ Show the cover of *The Whispering Cloth*.

What are the choices the author made about the characters? How do those factors impact this story? Turn and talk about that.

▶ Invite a few students to share. Record responses on the chart.

Summarize and Apply

Summarize the learning and remind students to think about the ways that an author's character choices do or do not impact a story.

What have you noticed today about characters?

▶ Review the chart and write the principle at the top.

When you read today, think about how the choice of the characters' gender, race, culture, or socioeconomic status impacts the story. Bring the book when we meet so you can share your noticings.

Share

Following independent reading time, gather students in small groups.

Share how the story is influenced by the characters' race, culture, gender, or socioeconomic background. How does this help you to better understand the characters and the story?

Extend the Lesson (Optional)

After assessing students' understanding, you might decide to extend the learning.

▶ **Writing About Reading** Have students write in a reader's notebook about how a character's race, culture, gender, or socioeconomic status influences, or does not influence, a story they are reading.

Think about how a story is affected by an author's choice of characters (e.g., gender, race/culture, socioeconomic status).

Title	Choices	What impact does the character choice have on the story?
A Shelter in Our Car	Socioeconomic status	If the characters were wealthy, this story would not have happened.
	Race/culture/gender/country of origin	The characters could be from anywhere.
Machado's Cup	Age	It's important to see the relationship between an older person and a younger person.
	Culture/country of origin/gender	The characters could be from anywhere.
Whispering Cloth	Country of origin/culture/political environment/gender/age	The plot is about the treatment of Hmong refugees and the traditions older women pass down to younger women. Other cultures pass on traditions, too.

Section 2: Literary Analysis

Reading Minilesson Principle
Critique the quality of fiction and nonfiction books.

Thinking Critically
About Texts

You Will Need

- one familiar fiction book and one familiar nonfiction book, such as the following:
  - *A Shelter in Our Car* by Monica Gunning, from Text Set: Countering Stereotypes
  - *Living Fossils* by Caroline Arnold, from Text Set: Life on Earth
- chart paper and markers
- document camera (optional)
- sticky notes
- classroom library books, randomly selected, in sets of one fiction and one nonfiction book

Academic Language / Important Vocabulary

- critique
- quality

Continuum Connection

- Think critically about the quality of a text and how well it exemplifies its genre, and share opinions (pp. 593, 605, 617)
- Critique a text in the way that expresses the student's own opinions and impressions (as opposed to merely summarizing) (p. 616)

Goal

Critique the quality of fiction and nonfiction books and provide evidence for an opinion.

Rationale

When students learn to critique the quality of books, they learn to value their own opinions and support their opinions with text examples as well as learn to apply critical thinking skills when reading and self-selecting literature.

Assess Learning

Observe students when they critique books and notice if there is evidence of new learning based on the goal of this minilesson.

- ▶ Are students able to analyze books and notice different factors affecting the book's quality?
- ▶ Do they understand the terms *critique* and *quality*?

Minilesson

To help students think about the minilesson principle, engage them in thinking about how to critique books for quality. Here is an example.

- ▶ Have students take a close look at *A Shelter in Our Car* and *Living Fossils*.

  Think about a fiction book, *A Shelter in Our Car*, and a nonfiction book, *Living Fossils: Clues to the Past*. As I revisit a few pages of text and illustrations, think about how you would rate these books for quality.

- ▶ Revisit several pages and illustrations.

  What is your overall opinion of these books?

- ▶ As students share thoughts, ask them to provide specific examples to support their opinions.

  What are some general things that are helpful to consider when evaluating the quality of a fiction book and a nonfiction book? Turn and talk about that.

- ▶ After time for discussion, ask students to share ideas and begin a generalized list on chart paper. As needed, support the conversation by revisiting additional pages from the fiction and nonfiction books, or use additional books as needed to generate a useful list.

Have a Try

Invite the students to critique a fiction and nonfiction book.

▶ Have students sit in groups, each with a fiction and nonfiction book randomly selected from the classroom library.

> With your group, critique the fiction and nonfiction book, using the list of ideas we generated. Talk about the overall quality of each book and think about how you would rate it. Support your opinions with specific examples. You can place a sticky note on a book with notes about your findings.

▶ After time for discussion, have a few groups share their noticings. Add any new ideas to the chart.

Summarize and Apply

Summarize the learning and remind students to think critically about the quality of books when they read.

> Today you generated a list of things to think about when critiquing the quality of books.

▶ Write the principle at the top of chart.

> When you read today, think critically about the book you are reading. Look back at the list we made and mark any pages with sticky notes that have examples to support your opinion. Bring the book when we meet so you can share.

Share

Following independent reading time, gather students in groups of three to share their critique of the book they are reading.

> In your group, talk about how you would rate the quality of the book you are reading. Provide examples from the book to support your critique.

Extend the Lesson (Optional)

After assessing students' understanding, you might decide to extend the learning.

▶ **Writing About Reading** Encourage students to use a reader's notebook to critique the quality of the books they read. Have them use examples from the book to support their opinion.

Critique the quality of fiction and nonfiction books.

What to Think About When Critiquing Quality

- design
- organization
- plot construction
- development of characters
- believable setting
- words that show instead of tell
- figurative language
- accurately represented subjects of biographies
- clear, understandable layout
- effectiveness of illustrations or photographs
- interesting topic
- applicable facts
- appropriate text boxes, captions, sidebars
- author's purpose met

Assessment

After you have taught the minilessons in this umbrella, observe students as they talk and write about their reading across instructional contexts: interactive read-aloud, independent reading, guided reading, shared reading, and book club. Use *The Literacy Continuum* (Fountas and Pinnell 2017) to observe students' reading and writing behaviors.

▶ What evidence do you have of new understandings related to the way people are represented in texts?

- Are students able to critique books for fair representation of people?
- Can they evaluate how different groups of people are represented in illustrations and graphics?
- Are they able to analyze how characters are portrayed in books?
- Do they think about how the story is affected by an author's choice of gender, race/culture, or socioeconomic status of a character?
- Are they able to critique fiction and nonfiction books for quality?
- Are they using the terms *critique, representation, diversity, race, gender, socioeconomic, evaluate, portrayed,* and *quality*?

▶ In what other ways, beyond the scope of this umbrella, are students thinking about representation?

- Are students beginning to self-select books that show a broader diversity of people, including people from backgrounds that are both similar to and different from their own?

Use your observations to determine the next umbrella you will teach. You may also consult Minilessons Across the Year (pp. 61–64) for guidance.

Link to Writing

After teaching the minilessons in this umbrella, help students link the new learning to their own writing:

▶ Encourage students to write about what they notice about representation as they read books, including both positive and negative examples.

Reader's Notebook

When this umbrella is complete, provide a copy of the minilesson principles (see resources.fountasandpinnell.com) for students to glue in the reader's notebook (in the Minilessons section if using *Reader's Notebook: Advanced* [Fountas and Pinnell 2011]), so they can refer to the information as needed.

Minilessons in This Umbrella

RML1   There are different genres of nonfiction books.

RML2   There are different genres of fiction books.

RML3   There are several types of traditional literature.

Before Teaching Umbrella 6 Minilessons

Before teaching the minilessons in this umbrella, read and discuss fiction and nonfiction books from a range of genres. Make a Books We Have Shared chart (see p. 68) and add to it as you read books together.

The minilessons in this umbrella support students in understanding that there are different genres of books (see p. 40) and that each one has specific characteristics. We recommend teaching the first two minilessons early in the year to provide students with a framework for thinking about fiction and nonfiction texts. The third minilesson should ideally be taught later in the year, when students have had exposure to several different types of traditional literature and have a deeper understanding of the genre. For RML3 use the following suggested books from the *Fountas & Pinnell Classroom™ Interactive Read-Aloud Collection* or choose appropriate books from your classroom library.

Genre Study: Epic Tales

  The Last Quest of Gilgamesh by Ludmila Zeman

Illustrator Study: K. Y. Craft

  Cinderella by K. Y. Craft

  King Midas and the Golden Touch by Charlotte Craft

As you read aloud and enjoy books together, help students notice and discuss defining characteristics of various types of fiction and nonfiction.

Genre Study: Epic Tales

Illustrator Study: K. Y. Craft

Section 2: Literary Analysis

RML1

LA.U6.RML1

Reading Minilesson Principle
There are different genres of nonfiction books.

You Will Need

- eleven notecards, each printed with one of the following labels: *Nonfiction, Told Like a Story, Not Told Like a Story, Biographical Texts, Procedural/How-to Texts, Narrative Nonfiction, Expository Texts, Persuasive Texts, Biography, Autobiography, Memoir*
- chart paper and markers
- glue stick or tape

Academic Language / Important Vocabulary

- genre
- nonfiction
- biographical
- narrative nonfiction
- expository
- procedural

Continuum Connection

- Notice and understand the characteristics of some specific nonfiction genres: e.g., expository, narrative, procedural and persuasive texts, biography, autobiography, memoir, hybrid text (p. 84)

Goal

Understand that there are different genres of nonfiction texts (e.g., biography, autobiography, informational, memoir, and narrative nonfiction).

Rationale

Studying the characteristics of different nonfiction genres—e.g., narrative nonfiction, expository, and procedural—helps students know what to expect when reading and increases their comprehension.

Assess Learning

Observe students when they read and talk about nonfiction books and notice if there is evidence of new learning based on the goal of this minilesson.

- Can students name different nonfiction genres and describe their basic characteristics?
- Do they use academic vocabulary, such as *genre, nonfiction, biographical, narrative nonfiction, expository,* and *procedural*?

Minilesson

To help students think about the minilesson principle, engage them in discussing and categorizing the different genres of nonfiction. Here is an example.

- Attach the card that says *Nonfiction* to the top of a sheet of chart paper.

    All books are either nonfiction or fiction, but these big categories can be broken down into smaller genres, or types, of books. For example, nonfiction books can be categorized according to whether they are told like a story or not told like a story.

- Place the cards that say *Told Like a Story* and *Not Told Like a Story* underneath *Nonfiction*. Draw connecting lines. Then show the card that says *Biographical Texts*.

    What are biographical texts?

    Biographical texts are books that give information about someone's life. Are biographical texts usually told like a story or not told like a story?

- Place the card underneath *Told Like a Story*. Then show the card labeled *Procedural/How-to Texts*.

    Procedural texts give directions for how to do something. Where should I put this card on the chart? What makes you think that?

- Place the card. Then continue in a similar manner with the cards labeled *Narrative Nonfiction, Expository Texts,* and *Persuasive Texts*.

Have a Try

Invite the students to talk with a partner about biographical texts.

▶ Show the *Biography*, *Autobiography*, and *Memoir* cards.

Turn and talk to your partner about biographies, autobiographies, and memoirs. Decide where they should go on our chart.

▶ After students turn and talk, invite a few pairs to share their thinking, and add the cards to the chart.

Summarize and Apply

Summarize the learning and remind students to notice different genres of nonfiction books.

What does our chart show?

▶ Write the principle at the top of the chart.

Choose a nonfiction book to read today, or continue reading one that you have started. Think about which genre of nonfiction it is. Be ready to share your thinking when we come back together.

Share

Following independent reading time, gather students together in the meeting area to talk about nonfiction books.

What genre of nonfiction did you read? How could you tell which genre it was?

Extend the Lesson (Optional)

After assessing students' understanding, you might decide to extend the learning.

▶ Point out the genre chart on the orange tab in *Reader's Notebook: Advanced* (Fountas and Pinnell 2011).

▶ Have students use the categories to organize the classroom library (see MGT.U2.RML2).

There are different genres of nonfiction books.

Nonfiction

Told Like a Story | Not Told Like a Story

Biographical Texts | Narrative Nonfiction | Expository Texts | Procedural/How-to Texts | Persuasive Texts

Biography

Autobiography

Memoir

RML 2
LA.U6.RML2

Reading Minilesson Principle
There are different genres of fiction books.

Understanding Fiction and Nonfiction Genres

You Will Need

▸ seven notecards, each printed with one of the following labels: *Fiction, Fantasy, Realism, Realistic Fiction, Historical Fiction, Modern Fantasy, Traditional Literature*

▸ chart paper and markers

▸ glue stick or tape

Academic Language / Important Vocabulary

▸ genre

▸ fiction

▸ fantasy

▸ realism

▸ realistic fiction

▸ historical fiction

Continuum Connection

▸ Understand that there are different types of fiction and nonfiction texts and that they have different characteristics (p. 79)

▸ Notice and understand the characteristics of some specific fiction genres: e.g., realistic fiction, historical fiction, folktale, fairy tale, fractured fairy tale, fable, myth, legend, epic, ballad, fantasy including science fiction, hybrid text (p. 79)

Goal

Understand that there are different genres of fiction texts (e.g., realistic fiction, historical fiction, traditional literature, and fantasy) that fall within the broader categories of realism or fantasy.

Rationale

Studying the characteristics of fiction genres (e.g., realistic, historical, traditional, and fantasy) helps students know what to expect when reading and increases their comprehension. They understand how the text "works."

Assess Learning

Observe students when they read and talk about books and notice if there is evidence of new learning based on the goal of this minilesson.

▸ Can students name different fiction genres and describe their basic characteristics?

▸ Do they use academic vocabulary, such as *genre, fiction, fantasy, realism, realistic fiction*, and *historical fiction*?

Minilesson

To help students think about the minilesson principle, engage them in discussing and categorizing different genres of fiction. Here is an example.

▸ Attach the card that says *Fiction* to the top of a sheet of chart paper.

> You've been thinking about the different genres of nonfiction books. Fiction can also be broken down into smaller genres of books. Some fiction stories are fantasy, and some are realism. What do you think is the difference between fantasy and realism?

▸ Attach the *Fantasy* and *Realism* cards underneath *Fiction* and draw connecting lines.

> The categories fantasy and realism can be broken down even further.

▸ Show the card that says *Realistic Fiction*.

> Where would realistic fiction books go on our chart? Are they realism or fantasy? How do you know?

▸ Add the card to the chart, and then continue in a similar manner with the cards labeled *Historical Fiction* and *Modern Fantasy*.

Have a Try

Invite the students to talk with a partner about traditional literature.

▶ Show the *Traditional Literature* card.

> Traditional literature includes genres like folktales, fairy tales, myths, legends, and fables. Turn and talk to your partner about where traditional literature should go on our chart. Is traditional literature realism or fantasy? Why?

▶ After time for discussion, invite a few students to share their thinking. Add the card to the chart.

Summarize and Apply

Summarize the learning and remind students to notice different genres of fiction books.

> What does our chart show?

▶ Write the principle at the top of the chart.

> Choose a fiction book to read today, or continue reading one you have already started. Notice which genre of fiction it is. Be ready to share your thinking when we come back together.

Share

Following independent reading time, gather students together in the meeting area to talk about fiction books.

> Which genre of fiction is your book? How could you tell?

Extend the Lesson (Optional)

After assessing students' understanding, you might decide to extend the learning.

▶ Point out the genre chart on the orange tab in *Reader's Notebook: Advanced* (Fountas and Pinnell 2011).

▶ There are different forms of modern fantasy, including animal fantasy, low fantasy, high fantasy, and science fiction. Teach LA.U23.RML3 to help students explore the different types of modern fantasy.

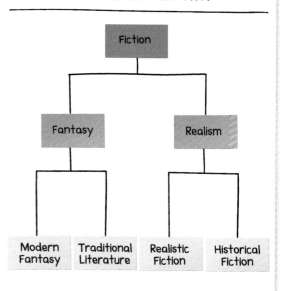

There are different genres of fiction books.

- Fiction
  - Fantasy
    - Modern Fantasy
    - Traditional Literature
  - Realism
    - Realistic Fiction
    - Historical Fiction

Section 2: Literary Analysis

Reading Minilesson Principle
There are several types of traditional literature.

Understanding Fiction and Nonfiction Genres

You Will Need

- at least two or three familiar books that represent different types of traditional literature, such as the following:
  - *Cinderella* by K. Y. Craft and *King Midas and the Golden Touch* by Charlotte Craft, from Text Set: Illustrator Study: K. Y. Craft
  - *The Last Quest of Gilgamesh* by Ludmila Zeman, from Text Set: Genre Study: Epic Tales
- chart paper and markers

Academic Language / Important Vocabulary

- traditional literature
- folktale
- myth
- epic
- fairy tale
- fable

Continuum Connection

- Understand that there are different types of fiction and nonfiction texts and that they have different characteristics (p. 79)
- Notice and understand the characteristics of some specific fiction genres: e.g., realistic fiction, historical fiction, folktale, fairy tale, fractured fairy tale, fable, myth, legend, epic, ballad, fantasy including science fiction, hybrid text (p. 79)
- Identify elements of traditional literature and fantasy: e.g., the supernatural; imaginary and otherworldly creatures; gods and goddesses; talking animals, toys, and dolls; heroic characters; technology or scientific advances; time travel; aliens or outer space (p. 79)

Goal

Understand that there are different types of traditional literature (e.g., folktales, fairy tales, legends, and fables).

Rationale

Studying the characteristics of traditional literature helps students know what to expect when reading and increases comprehension.

Assess Learning

Observe students when they read and talk about traditional literature and notice if there is evidence of new learning based on the goal of this minilesson.

- ▶ Can students describe the basic characteristics of different types of traditional literature?
- ▶ Do they use academic vocabulary, such as *traditional literature*, *folktale*, *myth*, *epic*, *fairy tale*, and *fable*?

Minilesson

To help students think about the minilesson principle, use familiar examples of traditional literature to provide an inquiry-based lesson about different types of traditional literature. Here is an example.

- ▶ Show the cover of *Cinderella*.

  Cinderella is a kind of traditional literature called a fairy tale. What do you know about fairy tales? What characteristics of this story tell you that it is a fairy tale?

- ▶ Record students' responses on chart paper. Then show the cover of *King Midas and the Golden Touch*.

  This book is a type of traditional literature called a myth. How are myths different from fairy tales? What are the characteristics of myths?

- ▶ Record students' responses on the chart. Then hold up *The Last Quest of Gilgamesh*.

  This book is an epic, which is another kind of traditional literature. Talk about the characteristics of an epic.

- ▶ Record responses on the chart.

  Folktales are another type of traditional literature. You are probably familiar with folktales like "The Three Little Pigs," "Little Red Riding Hood," and "Goldilocks and the Three Bears." What are some characteristics of folktales?

- ▶ Record students' responses.

Have a Try

Invite the students to talk with a partner about fables.

> Fables are also a type of traditional literature. You are probably familiar with "The Boy Who Cried Wolf" and "The Tortoise and the Hare," which are both fables. Turn and talk to your partner about the characteristics of fables.

▶ After time for discussion, invite several pairs to share their thinking. Record responses on the chart.

Summarize and Apply

Summarize the learning and remind students to read different kinds of traditional literature.

> What did you notice about traditional literature today?

▶ Write the principle at the top of the chart.

> When you read today, you may want to read a traditional literature story. If you do, think about the type of traditional literature it is. Be ready to share your thinking when we come back together.

Share

Following independent reading time, gather students together in the meeting area to talk about their reading.

> Who read traditional literature today?

> What kind of traditional literature is the book you read? How do you know?

Extend the Lesson (Optional)

After assessing students' understanding, you might decide to extend the learning.

▶ Introduce students to different types of folktales (beast tales, cumulative tales, trickster tales, etc.).

There are several types of traditional literature.

Type of Traditional Literature	Example(s)	Characteristics
Fairy tale	CINDERELLA	• Characters with magical abilities • Good and bad characters • Good wins over evil
Myth	KING MIDAS GOLDEN TOUCH	• Explains something (beginning of the world, something in nature, human behavior) • Often involves gods and goddesses
Epic		• Long story about the actions of a single hero • Often involves a quest
Folktale	"The Three Little Pigs," "Little Red Riding Hood," and "Goldilocks and the Three Bears"	• Stories about ordinary people (or sometimes animals) • Handed down over many years • Simple plot and characters
Fable	"The Boy Who Cried Wolf" "The Tortoise and the Hare"	• Very short • Teaches a moral or lesson • Animals who talk and act like people

Assessment

After you have taught the minilessons in this umbrella, observe students as they talk and write about their reading across instructional contexts: interactive read-aloud, independent reading, guided reading, shared reading, and book club. Use *The Literacy Continuum* (Fountas and Pinnell 2017) to observe students' reading and writing behaviors.

▶ What evidence do you have of new understandings related to fiction and nonfiction genres?

- Are students able to describe the characteristics of specific nonfiction genres, such as biography, autobiography, memoir, expository, and narrative nonfiction?

- Are they able to describe the characteristics of specific fiction genres, such as realistic fiction, historical fiction, science fiction, and fantasy?

- Can they describe the characteristics of specific traditional literature genres, such as fairy tales, fables, and folktales?

- Do they use academic language, such as *fiction, nonfiction, realism,* and *fantasy*?

▶ In what other ways, beyond the scope of this umbrella, are students talking about fiction and nonfiction?

- Are students thinking about theme and author's message?

- Are they analyzing writer's and illustrator's craft?

Use your observations to determine the next umbrella you will teach. You may also consult Minilessons Across the Year (pp. 61–64) for guidance.

Link to Writing

After teaching the minilessons in this umbrella, help students link the new learning to their own writing:

▶ Give students numerous opportunities to write their own texts in various genres. Before they write a text in a particular genre, review the characteristics of that genre and remind students to implement them in their own writing.

Reader's Notebook

When this umbrella is complete, provide a copy of the minilesson principles (see resources.fountasandpinnell.com) for students to glue in the reader's notebook (in the Minilessons section if using *Reader's Notebook: Advanced* [Fountas and Pinnell 2011]), so they can refer to the information as needed.

Minilessons in This Umbrella

RML1   A lyrical poem is a songlike poem that has rhythm and sometimes rhyme.

RML2   A free verse poem doesn't have to rhyme or have rhythm.

RML3   Haiku is an ancient Japanese form of non-rhyming poetry that creates a picture and often conveys emotion.

RML4   A narrative poem tells a story and usually has rhyme and/or rhythm.

Poetry

Countering Stereotypes

Before Teaching Umbrella 7 Minilessons

"Poetry is compact writing characterized by imagination and artistry and imbued with intense meaning" (*Genre Study: Teaching with Fiction and Nonfiction Books*, Fountas and Pinnell 2012, 19). Studying poetry helps students understand the role poetry plays in their lives as readers. Looking closely at and discussing the characteristics of different kinds of poems prepares students to understand the range of emotions poetry can make one feel. However, before students study poems or identify characteristics of certain types of poetry, they need to have the experience of enjoying individual poems. As you and your students read poetry together, take time to appreciate the sound of each poem's language and the meaning or feeling each poet conveys.

Select poems that your students will enjoy and that represent characteristics of different kinds of poetry (e.g., lyrical, free verse, haiku, narrative). Choose some poems that have rhythm, rhyme, or descriptive or figurative language. Use the following books from the *Fountas & Pinnell Classroom™ Interactive Read-Aloud Collection* or choose poetry texts from your own library or online to support students in studying poetry.

Poetry

> *Neighborhood Odes: A Poetry Collection* by Gary Soto
>
> *The Flag of Childhood: Poems from the Middle East* selected by Naomi Shihab Nye
>
> *The Death of the Hat: A Brief History of Poetry in 50 Objects* selected by Paul B. Janeczko

Countering Stereotypes

> *Wabi Sabi* by Mark Reibstein

As you read aloud and enjoy these poems together, help students

- enjoy each poem,
- think and talk about the meaning of each poem, and
- notice and generalize the characteristics of poetry.

Reading Minilesson Principle
A lyrical poem is a songlike poem that has rhythm and sometimes rhyme.

Exploring Different Kinds of Poetry

You Will Need

- several familiar, lyrical poems, such as the following:
  - "City Trees," "I Wandered Lonely as a Cloud," and "My Shadow" from *The Death of the Hat* selected by Paul B. Janeczko, from Text Set: Poetry
- chart paper and markers
- document camera (optional)
- two sticky notes, one that says *Rhythm* and one that says *Rhyme*
- sticky notes
- basket of poetry books

Academic Language / Important Vocabulary

- lyrical
- stanza
- rhyme scheme
- alliteration
- consonance
- assonance

Continuum Connection

- Recognize and understand some of the specific types of poetry when they appear in nonfiction: e.g., lyrical poetry, free verse, limerick, haiku, narrative poetry, ballad, epic/saga, concrete poetry (p. 85)

Goal

Recognize and understand the characteristics of lyrical poetry.

Rationale

Once students have read, enjoyed, and talked about poems, they can begin to understand the characteristics of different kinds of poems. This minilesson will help them know what to expect when reading lyrical poetry.

Assess Learning

Observe students when they read and discuss poetry. Notice if there is evidence of new learning based on the goal of this minilesson.

- Are students able to describe the characteristics of a lyrical poem?
- Do they use the words *lyrical, stanza, rhyme scheme, alliteration, consonance,* and *assonance*?

Minilesson

To help students think about the minilesson principle, engage them in noticing the characteristics of poems they have enjoyed and discussed. Here is an example.

- Project or display a lyrical poem, such as "City Trees" by Edna St. Vincent Millay from *The Death of the Hat*. Read it aloud, emphasizing the rhythmic qualities.

  What do you notice about how the lines of the poem sound? What do they make you feel like doing?

- Lead students to notice the regular rhythm of the poem. Record what students notice about the language on chart paper, leaving room for a label at the top.

  The word for language that has a beat is *rhythm*. How does a poet create rhythm?

- Have a student place the sticky note for *Rhythm* on the chart.

  Does the poem make you feel a certain way? What word describes your feeling?

- Project or display "I Wandered Lonely as a Cloud" by William Wordsworth from the same book. Read it aloud, emphasizing the rhyme.

  What do you notice about how some of the words in this poem sound?

- Record responses on chart paper, leaving room for a label. Have a student place the sticky note for *Rhyme* on the chart.

  Poems like the ones you just heard could easily be set to music. They have songlike qualities. These are lyrical poems.

Have a Try

Invite the students to talk with a partner about the qualities of lyrical poetry.

▸ Ask a student to read aloud "My Shadow" by Robert Louis Stevenson from *The Death of the Hat*.

> Turn and talk to your partner. What do you notice about the lines and words in this poem?

▸ After time for discussion, ask a few students to share their thinking. Record responses on the chart.

Summarize and Apply

Summarize the learning and remind students to notice rhythm and rhyme in lyrical poems.

> Today you read some lyrical poems. Let's describe a lyrical poem. Who can start?

▸ Invite responses and write the principle at the top of the chart.

> Today, read and enjoy poems from this basket.
> Notice if any poem you read has rhythm or rhyme. If it does, mark it with a sticky note and bring it to share when we meet.

Share

Following independent reading time, gather students together in groups of three or four to discuss the poems they read.

> Is the poem you read today a lyrical poem? How can you tell that it is or isn't?

Extend the Lesson (Optional)

After assessing students' understanding, you might decide to extend the learning.

▸ Give students time to rehearse and then read a lyrical poem as a choral reading. Have them decide whether to read the poem all together in unison or divide the lines among small groups of readers.

▸ **Writing About Reading** Have students respond to a lyrical poem in a reader's notebook. They could illustrate the poem or write about how it made them feel.

A lyrical poem is a songlike poem that has rhythm and sometimes rhyme.

Rhythm	Rhyme
• Has a beat • Sounds like a song • May be fast or slow • Line breaks and punctuation affect rhythm • Repeated words may start each line within the same stanza • May suggest a feeling (for example, suspense, excitement, peacefulness)	• Two-line rhyme (couplet) • Same pattern of rhyme in each stanza (rhyme scheme) • Repeated sounds (alliteration, consonance, assonance)

Section 2: Literary Analysis

RML2
LA.U7.RML2

Reading Minilesson Principle
A free verse poem doesn't have to rhyme or have rhythm.

Exploring Different Kinds of Poetry

You Will Need

- several familiar, free verse poems such as the following from Text Set: Poetry:
  - "Ode to the Sprinkler" from *Neighborhood Odes* by Gary Soto
  - "The Land Across the Valley" from *The Flag of Childhood* selected by Naomi Shihab Nye
  - "The Death of the Hat" from *The Death of the Hat* selected by Paul B. Janeczko
- chart paper prepared to make a word web (oval in center, spokes)
- markers
- sticky notes
- basket of poetry books

Academic Language / Important Vocabulary

- free verse
- rhythm
- rhyme
- characteristic

Continuum Connection

- Recognize and understand some of the specific types of poetry when they appear in nonfiction: e.g., lyrical poetry, free verse, limerick, haiku, narrative poetry, ballad, epic/saga, concrete poetry (p. 85)

Goal

Recognize and understand the characteristics of free verse poetry.

Rationale

Once students have read, enjoyed, and talked about poems, they can begin to understand the characteristics of different kinds of poems. This minilesson will help them understand that free verse poems do not have to have rhyme or rhythm, but they can have either or both. They also often exhibit a variety of poetic techniques.

Assess Learning

Observe students when they read and discuss poetry. Notice if there is evidence of new learning based on the goal of this minilesson.

- ▶ Can students describe what they notice about the poems they read?
- ▶ Do they talk about free verse poems not needing to have rhyme or rhythm?
- ▶ Do they use the words *free verse, rhythm, rhyme,* and *characteristic*?

Minilesson

To help students think about the minilesson principle, use familiar free verse poems to engage them in noticing the characteristics. Choose poems the students already have enjoyed and discussed for meaning. Here is an example.

- ▶ Read a free verse poem, such as "Ode to the Sprinkler" from *Neighborhood Odes*.

    What do you notice about this poem? Is it similar to or different from other poems you have read? How?

- ▶ Record noticings around the center oval on the chart.
- ▶ Repeat this process with "The Land Across the Valley" from *The Flag of Childhood*.

    What are you noticing about these poems, especially as compared with other poems you have read?

    These poems don't have to have the "usual" characteristics of poetry, such as rhythm and rhyme, though they might. These poems are free of any poetic "have-to's," so they are called free verse.

- ▶ Write *Free Verse* inside the oval.

Have a Try

Invite the students to talk with a partner about a free verse poem.

▶ Ask a student to read aloud "The Death of the Hat" from *The Death of the Hat*.

Turn and talk to your partner. Is this a free verse poem, or another type of poem? How do you know?

Summarize and Apply

Summarize the learning and remind students to think about how free verse poems differ from other types of poetry.

Look at the chart we made today. What can we write to describe free verse poems?

▶ Write the principle at the top of the chart.

Today, read and enjoy poems from this basket. Decide if any of the poems you read are free verse. If you read a free verse poem, mark it with a sticky note and bring it to share when we meet.

A free verse poem doesn't have to rhyme or have rhythm.

- May tell a story
- Does not have to rhyme
- Does not always have a regular beat (rhythm)
- Free Verse
- Uses figurative language
- Can be short or long
- Poets make their own rules

Share

Following independent reading time, gather students together in groups of three or four to discuss the poems they read.

Did you read a free verse poem today? How did you know it was a free verse poem?

Extend the Lesson (Optional)

After assessing students' understanding, you might decide to extend the learning.

▶ As students become more confident in noticing how an author uses poetic techniques in free verse poems, you might decide to introduce concrete poems, which are shaped to show what the poem is about.

▶ Encourage students to write and illustrate free verse poems.

▶ **Writing About Reading** Ask students to describe in a reader's notebook their opinion of a free verse poem they read.

RML 3
LA.U7.RML3

Reading Minilesson Principle
Haiku is an ancient Japanese form of non-rhyming poetry that creates a picture and often conveys emotion.

Exploring Different Kinds of Poetry

You Will Need

- select haiku from a variety of sources, such as the following from *Wabi Sabi* by Mark Reibstein, from Text Set: Countering Stereotypes:
  - page 2, "The cat's tail twitching"
  - page 10, "Even in cities"
  - page 16, "Alive and dying"
  - page 21, "The sun's last rays stretched"
- document camera (optional)
- chart paper and markers
- collection of poetry books and poems, including haiku

Academic Language / Important Vocabulary

- haiku
- non-rhyming
- emotions

Continuum Connection

- Recognize and understand some of the specific types of poetry when they appear in nonfiction: e.g., lyrical poetry, free verse, limerick, haiku, narrative poetry, ballad, epic/saga, concrete poetry (p. 85)

Goal

Recognize and understand the characteristics of haiku.

Rationale

When you study haiku with students, it broadens their understanding of different kinds of poems, teaches them to create a picture in their mind when reading poems, and gives them the opportunity to discuss the emotions conveyed by haiku, all of which support them in understanding more about reading poetry.

Assess Learning

Observe students when they read and discuss poetry. Notice if there is evidence of new learning based on the goal of this minilesson.

- ▶ Can students recognize haiku?
- ▶ Are they able to describe the characteristics of haiku?
- ▶ Do they use the words *haiku, non-rhyming,* and *emotions*?

Minilesson

To help students think about the minilesson principle, engage them in listening to and noticing the characteristics of haiku. Here is an example.

- ▶ Read several haiku, such as examples from *Wabi Sabi* or the one on the chart.

  What do you notice is the same about these poems?

  What do you notice about the topics of these poems?

  Think about the syllables in each line. What do you notice?

  What do you think the author is trying to get you to think about?

- ▶ Record responses on chart paper.

  These poems are an ancient Japanese form of poetry called haiku. Sometimes, however, haiku have nontraditional syllable counts because many of them are translated from another language.

Have a Try

Invite the students to talk with a partner about another haiku from *Wabi Sabi*.

▶ Choose another haiku to read aloud.

Turn and talk to your partner. Is this a haiku? How do you know?

Summarize and Apply

Summarize the learning and remind students to notice the characteristics of haiku.

Today you learned about a form of poetry called haiku.

▶ Write the principle at the top of the chart.

Today, read and enjoy poems from the basket. Think about whether the poem is a haiku or another type of poetry. Be prepared to talk about the poem when we meet.

Share

Following independent reading time, gather students together in groups in the meeting area to talk about poems.

Did anyone read a haiku? Read it aloud for us.

How did you know it was a haiku?

If you didn't read a haiku, tell us about the poem you did read.

Extend the Lesson (Optional)

After assessing students' understanding, you might decide to extend the learning.

▶ Encourage students to continue reading, writing, and illustrating haiku. Often watercolor paints convey just the right mood of a haiku.

▶ **Writing About Reading** Ask students to respond to a haiku in a reader's notebook.

Haiku is an ancient Japanese form of non-rhyming poetry that creates a picture and often conveys emotion.

Rain falls softly down
    slipping off the ends of leaves
        moistening the ground.

- Short
- No rhyme or rhythm
- About something in nature
- Creates a picture in your mind
- 5 syllables in the first and last lines
- 7 syllables in the middle line

Section 2: Literary Analysis

Reading Minilesson Principle

A narrative poem tells a story and usually has rhyme and/or rhythm.

Exploring Different Kinds of Poetry

You Will Need

- in advance, choose two narrative poems from your own library or online sources, such as the following:
- "The Walrus and the Carpenter" by Lewis Carroll
- "Casey at the Bat" by Ernest Lawrence Thayer
- chart paper prepared to make a word web (oval in center, spokes)
- markers
- examples of narrative poems

Academic Language / Important Vocabulary

- narrative
- rhyme
- rhythm
- tone
- episode

Continuum Connection

- Recognize and understand some of the specific types of poetry when they appear in nonfiction: e.g., lyrical poetry, free verse, limerick, haiku, narrative poetry, ballad, epic/saga, concrete poetry (p. 85)

Goal

Recognize and understand the characteristics of narrative poetry.

Rationale

Once students have read, enjoyed, and talked about poems, they can begin to understand the characteristics of different kinds of poems, such as narrative poetry, which tells a story in poetic form. They can think about an author's choice to recount an event as a poem, and how the rhythm or rhyme conveys tone.

Assess Learning

Observe students when they read and discuss poetry. Notice if there is evidence of new learning based on the goal of this minilesson.

- ▸ Can students identify the characteristics of a narrative poem?
- ▸ Can they discuss an author's choice to tell a story in poetic form? The tone the author is trying to convey?
- ▸ Do they use the words *narrative, rhyme, rhythm, tone,* and *episode*?

Minilesson

To help students think about the minilesson principle, use a narrative poem to engage students in noticing the characteristics. Choose a poem students already have enjoyed and discussed for meaning. Here is an example.

- ▸ Read aloud a narrative poem, such as "The Walrus and the Carpenter."

    What do you notice about this poem?

    What story does the poem tell?

    Why do you think the writer chose to tell the story in poetic form?

    What tone does the poet convey?

- ▸ Record noticings around the center oval on the chart.

    This is a narrative poem, which is a story told in the format of a poem.

- ▸ Write *Narrative Poem* inside the oval.

Have a Try

Invite the students to talk with a partner about a narrative poem, such as "Casey at the Bat."

▶ Read the poem aloud.

> Turn and talk to your partner. How is this poem like a story? Why do you think the author chose to tell the story as a poem instead of as a short story or a book?

Summarize and Apply

Summarize the learning and remind students to notice the characteristics of narrative poetry.

> Today you learned about narrative poetry, a kind of poem that tells a story.

▶ Write the principle at the top of the chart.

> Today, read and enjoy narrative poems from this basket. Think about what the poet is trying to say and notice the characteristics of the poems you read. Be prepared to share your noticings when we come back together.

Share

Following independent reading time, gather students together in groups of three or four to discuss the narrative poems they read.

> What characteristics did you notice in the narrative poem you read? What story is the author trying to tell?

Extend the Lesson (Optional)

After assessing students' understanding, you might decide to extend the learning.

▶ Have students prepare and perform a narrative poem (e.g., "Paul Revere's Ride" by Henry Wadsworth Longfellow, "Annabel Lee" by Edgar Allan Poe). They could read it chorally in unison or divide the lines among several small groups of readers.

▶ Encourage students to compare a narrative poem to a book about the same topic or event.

▶ **Writing About Reading** Ask students to respond in a reader's notebook to a narrative poem.

A narrative poem tells a story and usually has rhyme and/or rhythm.

Narrative Poem: Tells a story, sometimes a long tale; Can be fantasy; Has rhyme and rhythm; Uses repetition; Tells about an important event or heroic deeds; May have dialogue; Can be funny or serious

Section 2: Literary Analysis

Assessment

After you have taught the minilessons in this umbrella, observe students as they talk and write about their reading across instructional contexts: interactive read-aloud, independent reading, guided reading, shared reading, and book club. Use *The Literacy Continuum* (Fountas and Pinnell 2017) to observe students' reading and writing behaviors.

▶ What evidence do you have of new understandings related to different kinds of poetry?

- Do students understand and discuss different kinds of poetry—lyrical, free verse, haiku, and narrative?

- Can they talk about the characteristics of each different kind of poetry?

- Do they use vocabulary words such as *rhythm, rhyme, free verse, haiku,* and *narrative*?

▶ In what other ways, beyond the scope of this umbrella, are students talking about the poetry they read?

- Are students discussing why a poet chose certain words?

- Are they able to compare and contrast two different types of poems?

Use your observations to determine the next umbrella you will teach. You may also consult Minilessons Across the Year (pp. 61–64) for guidance.

Link to Writing

After teaching the minilessons in this umbrella, help students link the new learning to their own writing:

▶ When students write their own poetry, encourage them to try out different forms. They could try writing a poem about the same topic using a different form of poetry. Have them choose which type of poem fits best with the topic of their poem.

Reader's Notebook

When this umbrella is complete, provide a copy of the minilesson principles (see resources.fountasandpinnell.com) for students to glue in the reader's notebook (in the Minilessons section if using *Reader's Notebook: Advanced* [Fountas and Pinnell 2011]), so they can refer to the information as needed.

Minilessons in This Umbrella

RML1   The author gives a message related to the theme of the book.

RML2   Think about what the writer's message means to you, to society, or to the world.

RML3   Books often have themes that address human challenges and social issues.

Before Teaching Umbrella 8 Minilessons

These minilessons are designed to help students think about and discuss the relationship between the theme and the author's message in fiction and nonfiction books. Theme and message are related, but there is a difference. Theme is the big, universal idea or larger aspect of human existence explored in a literary work (e.g., courage, kindness), often expressed in one word or a few words. The message is a specific aspect of the theme—a directive or specific understanding for the reader. The message in a book that explores the theme of courage might be "You can conquer fears by facing them." If the theme is kindness, the message might be "Treat others as you would like to be treated."

To prepare for these minilessons, read and discuss a variety of engaging fiction and nonfiction books with clear and diverse themes and messages. Use the following texts from the *Fountas & Pinnell Classroom™ Interactive Read-Aloud Collection* text sets or choose books from your classroom library.

Kindness and Compassion

Babu's Song by Stephanie Stuve-Bodeen

Handling Emotions/Positive Relationships

Bird by Zetta Elliott

The Banana-Leaf Ball: How Play Can Change the World by Katie Smith Milway

Inspiration/Creativity

My Name Is Gabito: The Life of Gabriel García Márquez by Monica Brown

Piano Starts Here: The Young Art Tatum by Robert Andrew Parker

Illustration Study: Mood

An Angel for Solomon Singer by Cynthia Rylant

As you read aloud and enjoy these texts together, help students

- infer and discuss the author's message(s),
- think about the big ideas explored in each book,
- think about and discuss the author's treatment of human challenges and social issues, and
- think about how to apply the lessons in each book to their own lives.

Kindness and Compassion

Handling Emotions/ Positive Relationships

Inspiration/Creativity

Illustration Study: Mood

Reading Minilesson Principle

The author gives a message related to the theme of the book.

Thinking About Themes
and the Author's Message

You Will Need

- two or three familiar fiction or nonfiction books, each with a clear theme and message, such as the following:
  - *Piano Starts Here* by Robert Andrew Parker and *My Name Is Gabito* by Monica Brown, from Text Set: Inspiration/ Creativity
  - *The Banana-Leaf Ball* by Katie Smith Milway, from Text Set: Handling Emotions/ Positive Relationships
- chart paper and markers

Academic Language / Important Vocabulary

- theme
- message
- author

Continuum Connection

- Notice that a book may have more than one message or big (main) idea (p. 80)
- Infer the messages in a work of fiction (p. 80)
- Understand that there can be different interpretations of the meaning of a text (p. 80)
- Infer the larger (main) ideas or messages in a nonfiction text (p. 86)
- Understand that a nonfiction text can have more than one message or big (main) idea (p. 86)

Goal

Infer the major messages and themes of books.

Rationale

A theme is a big, universal idea or concept explored in a book. The author's message is a specific aspect of the theme and what the author wants the reader to learn from reading the book. Understanding the author's message offers a vicarious learning opportunity for students.

Assess Learning

Observe students when they read and talk about books and notice if there is evidence of new learning based on the goal of this minilesson.

> Can students infer the author's message and the theme in both fiction and nonfiction books?

> Do they use academic vocabulary, such as *theme*, *message*, and *author*?

Minilesson

To help students think about the minilesson principle, use familiar books to discuss theme and author's message. Here is an example.

> Show *Piano Starts Here* and read the title.

> What do you think the author wants you to learn?

> Record students' responses on chart paper.

> Beyond writing a good book, some authors want you to learn or understand an important idea. This is the author's message. Different readers may have different ideas about what the author's message is. Does anyone else have any other ideas about what the author's message in this book is?

> Record responses.

> In addition to having a message, most books also have a theme. A theme is a big idea—for example, friendship, love, or imagination. The theme and the author's message are related, but they are not the same. The theme is a big idea that the author wants you to think about, while the message is a specific lesson about the big idea. Look at the messages on the chart. What do they suggest the theme could be?

> Record responses on the chart. Emphasize that a book can have more than one theme.

> Continue in a similar manner with *My Name Is Gabito*. Ask students to identify the author's message and the theme, and record them on the chart.

Have a Try

Invite the students to talk with a partner about the messages and themes in *The Banana-Leaf Ball*.

▶ Show the cover of *The Banana-Leaf Ball*.

> Turn and talk to your partner about this book. What theme, or big idea, does the author want you to think about? What is her message, or the specific lesson that she wants you to learn?

▶ After time for discussion, invite a few students to share their ideas. Record responses on the chart.

Summarize and Apply

Summarize the learning and remind students to think about the author's message and theme when they read.

> Both fiction and nonfiction books can have themes and messages. Remember that a book can have more than one message or theme and that different readers can have different opinions about the message or theme.

▶ Write the principle at the top of the chart.

> When you read today, think about the author's message and the theme. What big ideas does the author want you to think about or learn? Be ready to share your thinking about the author's message and theme when we come back together.

Share

Following independent reading time, gather students together in the meeting area to talk about their books' themes and messages.

> Turn and talk to your partner about the theme and the author's message in the book you read today.

Extend the Lesson (Optional)

After assessing students' understanding, you might decide to extend the learning.

▶ **Writing About Reading** Have students write about and reflect on the theme and/or author's message of a book in a reader's notebook.

The author gives a message related to the theme of the book.

Book	Message	Theme
	• Persistence and creativity can overcome obstacles. • Family and community support can inspire talented young people to develop their art.	• Persistence • Creativity • Overcoming obstacles • Family • Community
gabíto	• The world is full of magic—if only you allow yourself to see it. • Storytellers have tremendous power.	• Imagination • Creativity
BANANA-LEAF BALL	• Play can change the world. • Playing sports can help people overcome their differences. • Sport and play can help build peaceful communities.	• The power of play • Cooperation • Overcoming differences • Building communities

Reading Minilesson Principle
Think about what the writer's message means to you, to society, or to the world.

Thinking About Themes and the Author's Message

You Will Need

- two familiar books with clear messages, such as the following:
  - *Piano Starts Here* by Robert Andrew Parker, from Text Set: Inspiration/Creativity
  - *The Banana-Leaf Ball* by Katie Smith Milway, from Text Set: Handling Emotions/Positive Relationships
- chart from RML1 (optional)
- chart paper and markers

Academic Language / Important Vocabulary

- message
- author
- society

Continuum Connection

- Understand that the messages or big ideas in fiction texts can be applied to their own lives or to other people and society (p. 80)
- Notice and infer importance of ideas relevant to their world (p. 80)
- Notice and understand themes that are close to their own experiences and also themes that are beyond them (p. 80)
- Infer the significance of nonfiction content for their own lives (p. 86)

Goal

Understand that the messages or big ideas can be applied to their own lives or to other people and society.

Rationale

When you teach students to think about how an author's message can be applied in real life, they understand the power of the written word. They learn that something they write might someday influence how other people think and act.

Assess Learning

Observe students when they read and talk about books and notice if there is evidence of new learning based on the goal of this minilesson.

- ▶ Can students identify the author's message in fiction and nonfiction books?
- ▶ Can they explain how an author's message can be applied to their own lives, to society, or to the world?
- ▶ Do they use the terms *message, author,* and *society*?

Minilesson

To help students think about the minilesson principle, engage them in a discussion about author's message. Here is an example.

- ▶ Show the cover of *Piano Starts Here*. (Display the chart from RML1 if you have it.)

    Even though Art Tatum lived a long time ago and had a life very different from yours, you can still learn important lessons from this book. And, you can use these lessons in your own life. You noticed that one of the author's messages is "Family and community support can inspire talented young people to develop their art." What does this message mean to you? How could you learn from this message and apply it to your own life?

- ▶ Allow time for partners to turn and talk briefly before asking a couple of volunteers to share their thinking.

    You can also think about what an author's message means to society. A society is a group of people who live together in a community. For example, all the people in our town, state, country, or even the world are members of a society. How could our society use this message? What could members of our society do based on the message in *Piano Starts Here*?

- ▶ Record students' responses on chart paper.

Have a Try

Invite the students to talk with a partner about the author's messages in another book.

▶ Show the cover of *The Banana-Leaf Ball*.

> You noticed that two of the author's messages in this book are "Playing sports can help people overcome their differences" and "Sport and play can help build peaceful communities." Turn and talk to your partner about how one or both of these messages could be applied to real life. Think about your own life, society, and the world.

▶ After students turn and talk, invite several students to share their thinking. Record responses on the chart.

Summarize and Apply

Summarize the learning and remind students to think about the author's message when they read.

> Today you thought about what the author's message means to you and how the message could be applied to your own life, to society, or to the world.

▶ Write the principle at the top of the chart.

> When you read today, think about the author's message. Then think about what the message means to you, how you could use it in your own life, or how society could use it. Be ready to share your thinking when we come back together.

Share

Following independent reading time, gather students together in the meeting area to talk about their reading.

> What is the author's message in the book you read today?

> How could this message be applied to your own life, to society, or to the world?

Extend the Lesson (Optional)

After assessing students' understanding, you might decide to extend the learning.

▶ **Writing About Reading** Have students write in a reader's notebook about how the author's message in a book could be applied to their own lives, to society, or to the world.

Think about what the writer's message means to you, to society, or to the world.

"Family and community support can inspire talented young people to develop their art."	• I can encourage my friends and siblings to work on their artistic projects. • Schools and community organizations can offer art and music classes. • The government should provide more funding for art programs.
"Playing sports can help people overcome their differences." "Sport and play can help build peaceful communities."	• I can invite someone I don't know to play ball with me. • Organizations can start sports teams that bring together children who wouldn't normally play together. • Countries can organize international sports matches (like the Olympics or the World Cup).

Section 2: Literary Analysis

RML3
LA.U8.RML3

Reading Minilesson Principle
Books often have themes that address human challenges and social issues.

Thinking About Themes and the Author's Message

You Will Need

- two or three familiar books that explore human challenges or social issues, such as the following:
  - *Babu's Song* by Stephanie Stuve-Bodeen, from Text Set: Kindness and Compassion
  - *Bird* by Zetta Elliott, from Text Set: Handling Emotions/ Positive Relationships
  - *An Angel for Solomon Singer* by Cynthia Rylant, from Text Set: Illustration Study: Mood
- chart paper and markers

Academic Language / Important Vocabulary

- theme
- human challenge
- social issue

Continuum Connection

- Notice and understand themes reflecting important human challenges and social issues (p. 80)
- Think across texts to derive larger messages, themes, or ideas (p. 80)
- Infer the larger (main) ideas in a nonfiction text (p. 86)

Goal

Notice and understand themes reflecting important human challenges and social issues.

Rationale

When students notice and think about themes reflecting human challenges and social issues, they learn about important ideas and values (e.g., equality, compassion, justice) and think about how to apply them to their lives. They are more likely to become engaged, active, and compassionate members of society.

Assess Learning

- Do students notice and discuss themes that address human challenges and social issues?
- Do they use vocabulary such as *theme*, *human challenge*, and *social issue*?

Minilesson

To help students think about the minilesson principle, use familiar books to engage them in a discussion about theme. Here is an example.

- Show the cover of *Babu's Song* and read the title.

  What problems do the characters in this story face?

  What do you think is the theme, or big idea, of this story?

  What makes you think that?

- Record all reasonable responses on chart paper.
- Show the cover of *Bird*.

  What problems does the boy in this book struggle with?

  What do you think is the theme of this story? What big ideas does the author want you to think about?

- Record responses on the chart.

Have a Try

Invite the students to talk with a partner about the theme of *An Angel for Solomon Singer*.

▶ Show the cover of *An Angel for Solomon Singer* and review the book as needed.

> Turn and talk to your partner about what you think is the theme of this story.

▶ After time for discussion, invite several pairs to share their ideas. Record responses on the chart.

Summarize and Apply

Summarize the learning and remind students to notice themes addressing human challenges and social issues.

> What do you notice about the themes of the three books we looked at today?

> All of these books have themes that address human challenges and social issues. Human challenges and social issues are problems or challenges that affect people, particularly problems having to do with living together in a society.

▶ Write the principle at the top of the chart.

> When you read today, think about the theme or themes of your book. If your book has themes addressing human challenges or social issues, bring it to share when we come back together.

Share

Following independent reading time, gather students together in the meeting area to talk about themes.

> Who read a book with themes that address human challenges or social issues?

> What challenge or social issue do the characters or people in your book face?

> What do you think is the theme of your book?

Extend the Lesson (Optional)

After assessing students' understanding, you might decide to extend the learning.

▶ **Writing About Reading** Have students write in a reader's notebook about a book with a theme that addresses human challenges or social issues.

Books often have themes that address human challenges and social issues.

	• Overcoming adversity • Poverty • Compassion • Family
	• Overcoming adversity • Grief • Family
	• Loneliness • Overcoming adversity • Helping others • Empathy

Section 2: Literary Analysis

Assessment

After you have taught the minilessons in this umbrella, observe students as they talk and write about their reading across instructional contexts: interactive read-aloud, independent reading, guided reading, shared reading, and book club. Use *The Literacy Continuum* (Fountas and Pinnell 2017) to observe students' reading and writing behaviors.

- ▶ What evidence do you have of new understandings related to theme and author's message?
  - Can students infer the author's message(s) and the theme(s) in both fiction and nonfiction books?
  - Do they talk about ways to apply an author's message to real life?
  - How well do they notice and discuss themes related to human challenges and social issues?
  - Do they use academic language, such as *theme* and *message*?
- ▶ In what other ways, beyond the scope of this umbrella, are students talking about books?
  - Do students notice that different characters have different points of view and perspectives?
  - Are they noticing different genres of fiction and nonfiction?

Use your observations to determine the next umbrella you will teach. You may also consult Minilessons Across the Year (pp. 61–64) for guidance.

Link to Writing

After teaching the minilessons in this umbrella, help students link the new learning to their own writing:

- ▶ When students write their own fiction and nonfiction texts, remind them to think about the theme(s) and message(s) they want to communicate and how they want to convey them.
- ▶ Have students choose a theme represented in two or more of the books they have read and write about how they see that theme in their own lives.

Reader's Notebook

When this umbrella is complete, provide a copy of the minilesson principles (see resources.fountasandpinnell.com) for students to glue in the reader's notebook (in the Minilessons section if using *Reader's Notebook: Advanced* [Fountas and Pinnell 2011]), so they can refer to the information as needed.

Minilessons in This Umbrella

RML1 Writers use similes and metaphors to compare one thing to another.

RML2 Writers use personification to give human qualities to something that is not human.

RML3 Writers use idioms to add interest.

RML4 Writers choose specific language to fit the setting.

RML5 Writers choose precise words to create a mood.

RML6 Writers choose specific words to communicate the tone of the book.

RML7 Writers use language in surprising ways to create humor or interest.

RML8 Writers use symbolism to communicate a message.

Before Teaching Umbrella 9 Minilessons

The lessons in this umbrella do not need to be taught consecutively but can be taught when you observe a need. Use the following books from the *Fountas & Pinnell Classroom™ Interactive Read-Aloud Collection* or choose books with rich language.

Handling Emotions/Positive Relationships

Bird by Zetta Elliott

It Doesn't Have to Be This Way: A Barrio Story by Luis J. Rodríguez

Kindness and Compassion

Chachaji's Cup by Uma Krishnaswami

Nubs: The True Story of a Mutt, a Marine, and a Miracle by Brian Dennis, Kirby Larson, and Mary Nethery

Problem Solving/Giving Back

The Red Bicycle: The Extraordinary Story of One Ordinary Bicycle by Jude Isabella

Exploring Identity

Border Crossing by Maria Colleen Cruz

Garvey's Choice by Nikki Grimes

Author/Illustrator Study: S. D. Nelson

Digging a Hole to Heaven by S. D. Nelson

Crazy Horse's Vision by Joseph Bruchac

Perseverance

The Herd Boy by Niki Daly

Illustration Study: Mood

Teacup by Rebecca Young

Life on Earth

Rotten! Vultures, Beetles, Slime, and Nature's Other Decomposers by Anita Sanchez

Once students have enjoyed the texts as readers, have them look at the texts as writers, noting elements of the writer's craft.

Handling Emotions/Positive Relationships

Kindness and Compassion

Problem Solving/Giving Back

Exploring Identity

Author/Illustrator Study: S. D. Nelson

Perseverance

Illustration Study: Mood

Life on Earth

Section 2: Literary Analysis

RML1

LA.U9.RML1

Reading Minilesson Principle

Writers use similes and metaphors to compare one thing to another.

Reading Like a Writer: Analyzing the Writer's Craft

You Will Need

- familiar texts or poems with similes and metaphors, such as the following:
  - *Bird* by Zetta Elliott, from Text Set: Handling Emotions/ Positive Relationships
  - *Border Crossing* by Maria Colleen Cruz, from Text Set: Exploring Identity
  - *Chachaji's Cup* by Uma Krishnaswami, from Text Set: Kindness and Compassion
- chart paper and markers
- document camera (optional)
- three sticky notes labeled *simile*, one sticky note labeled *metaphor*
- sticky notes
- basket of familiar texts that have metaphors or similes

Academic Language / Important Vocabulary

- simile
- metaphor
- compare
- comparison

Continuum Connection

- Notice and understand how the author uses idioms and literary language, including metaphor, simile, symbolism, and personification (p. 82)

Goal

Notice and understand how the author uses similes and metaphors.

Rationale

Writers use metaphors and similes to make abstract ideas more concrete and to prompt readers to use their imagination to create lasting images. Students can think about how they might use figurative language in their own writing.

Assess Learning

Observe students when they talk about the writer's craft. Notice if there is evidence of new learning based on the goal of this minilesson.

▶ Do students notice similes and metaphors in books they hear read aloud or read independently?

▶ Can they describe what the simile or metaphor means?

▶ Do they use the terms *simile*, *metaphor*, *compare*, and *comparison*?

Minilesson

To help students think about the minilesson principle, use familiar texts to discuss similes and metaphors. If a document camera is available, consider projecting the pages to provide visual support. Here is an example.

▶ Hold up *Bird* and read the page that begins "Marcus stopped drawing."

What does the author mean by "he would snarl like a fierce pit bull"?

▶ Record responses on the chart. Read the page that begins "After the funeral."

What does the author tell you about the bird by writing "When it flies, the cardinal looks like a fiery spark blowing through the trees"?

▶ Record responses on the chart.

The author compares the bird to something you know—a spark. When an author compares two things using the word *like* or *as*, it is called a simile.

▶ Have a volunteer underline the word *like* in each example. Have another volunteer add two of the sticky notes labeled *simile* to the chart.

When you read the word *like* or *as*, think about the simile, or what things the author is comparing.

▶ Repeat this process using page 29 from *Border Crossing*.

Have a Try

Invite the students to talk about how writers compare one thing to another.

▶ Hold up *Chachaji's Cup* and read page 23.

> How does the author describe Chachaji?

> When a writer makes a direct comparison by saying that one thing *is* or *was* something else, it is called a metaphor. Why does the author do that?

▶ Record responses on the chart. Have a volunteer underline *was* and place the sticky note labeled *metaphor*.

Summarize and Apply

Summarize the learning and remind students to notice how writers use similes and metaphors.

> How do writers use similes and metaphors?

▶ Write the principle at the top of the chart.

> You may choose a book from this basket to read today. As you are reading, notice whether the author uses any metaphors or similes. Mark the page with a sticky note and bring the book when we meet so you can share.

Writers use similes and metaphors to compare one thing to another.

Book	Comparison	What the Comparison Describes	
Bird	"snarl <u>like</u> a fierce pit bull"	• the ferocious, powerful way he speaks	simile
	"the cardinal looks <u>like</u> a fiery spark"	• the brightness and speed of the cardinal	simile
Border Crossing / CAUTION	"my thoughts flew around <u>like</u> butterflies"	• her scattered thinking	simile
Chachaji's Cup	"Chachaji <u>was</u> a small brown ghost"	• Chachaji, small and very sick	metaphor

Share

Following independent reading time, gather students together in the meeting area to talk about figurative language.

> Tell us about a simile or metaphor you found in your reading. What did it help you to understand?

Extend the Lesson (Optional)

After assessing students' understanding, you might decide to extend the learning.

▶ Have students help you collect examples of metaphors and similes on a large poster to display so that students can be inspired to use language in creative and evocative ways when they do their own writing.

▶ **Writing About Reading** Invite students to fill in a chart similar to the one in this minilesson (see resources.fountasandpinnell.com) to record metaphors or similes and their meanings from books such as *Rotten!* by Anita Sanchez (Text Set: Life on Earth) or *A Different Pond* by Bao Phi (Text Set: Exploring Identity). Students can glue the chart into a reader's notebook.

Reading Minilesson Principle
Writers use personification to give human qualities to something that is not human.

Reading Like a Writer:
Analyzing the Writer's Craft

You Will Need

- several familiar texts with personification, such as the following:

  - *Digging a Hole to Heaven* by S. D. Nelson, from Text Set: Author/Illustrator Study: S. D. Nelson

  - *Bird* by Zetta Elliott, from Text Set: Handling Emotions/ Positive Relationships

  - *Chachaji's Cup* by Uma Krishnaswami, from Text Set: Kindness and Compassion

- chart paper and markers

- sticky notes

Academic Language / Important Vocabulary

- personification

Continuum Connection

- Notice and understand how the author uses idioms and literary language, including metaphor, simile, symbolism, and personification [p. 82]

Goal

Notice and understand how the author uses personification.

Rationale

Personification brings nonhuman things to life and helps a reader connect with an object. This creates a clear image in readers' minds and leads to a deeper understanding of their reading. Students may then experiment with using personification in their own writing.

Assess Learning

Observe students when they discuss the writer's craft. Notice if there is evidence of new learning based on the goal of this minilesson.

- ▶ Do students recognize personification in their reading?
- ▶ Can they describe what and how something is being personified?
- ▶ Do they understand and use the word *personification*?

Minilesson

To help students think about the minilesson principle, use familiar texts to engage them in noticing and understanding personification. Here is an example.

- ▶ Hold up *Digging a Hole to Heaven* and read page 3.

  What do you notice about the way the author describes the timbers? What do the timbers do?

- ▶ Record the action of the timbers on chart paper.
- ▶ Repeat this process with page 8.

  What do you notice about how the shadows are described?

- ▶ Record the actions attributed to the shadows. Then draw attention to the chart.

  Are these things that the timbers and shadows can really do?

  When an author writes about an object that does something that only a human can do, it is called personification. Notice that the word *person* is in *personification*. What does the personification show in these books?

- ▶ Repeat this with *Bird*, reading the page that begins "In the wintertime."

Have a Try

Invite the students to talk with a partner about why writers use personification.

▶ Read pages 3 and 4 of *Chachaji's Cup*.

Turn and talk to your partner. Where does the author use personification? How does this help you understand the story?

▶ Invite a few students to share. Record responses on the chart.

Summarize and Apply

Summarize the learning and remind students to notice how writers use personification.

▶ Review the chart and write the principle at the top.

Writers use personification to make their writing interesting and to help readers understand the story even better. Today when you read, be on the lookout for personification. If you find an example, mark it with a sticky note and bring the book back when we meet so you can share.

Writers use personification to give human qualities to something that is not human.		
Book	**Human Quality**	**What the Personification Shows**
DIGGING A HOLE TO HEAVEN	• Timbers "groaned" • Shadows "danced wildly"	• Shows how stressed the timbers were by the weight • Describes how the shadows were moving
Bird	• Blue jays "playing tag"	• Describes the birds having fun like kids
Chachaji's Cup	• Flavors "sing" and "dance"	• Helps you smell and taste the bold flavors

Share

Following independent reading time, gather students together in the meeting area to talk about personification.

Who marked a page in your reading that shows personification?

What is the human action the author used? How did it help you understand that part of the story?

Extend the Lesson (Optional)

After assessing students' understanding, you might decide to extend the learning.

▶ Ask students to critique an author's use of personification. Does it add interest to the writing?

▶ **Writing About Reading** When students write letters about books they have read, encourage them to share examples of personification they have found and describe whether they were effective.

Reading Minilesson Principle
Writers use idioms to add interest.

Reading Like a Writer: Analyzing the Writer's Craft

You Will Need

- two or three familiar texts with idioms, such as the following:
  - *Border Crossing* by Maria Colleen Cruz, from Text Set: Exploring Identity
  - *Bird* by Zetta Elliott, from Text Set: Handling Emotions/ Positive Relationships
- chart paper and markers
- sticky notes

Academic Language / Important Vocabulary

- idiom

Continuum Connection

- Notice and understand how the author uses idioms and literary language, including metaphor, simile, symbolism, and personification (p. 82)

Goal

Notice and understand that writers use idioms to add interest to their writing.

Rationale

Writers use idioms to add interest and sometimes humor to their writing. Idioms create a clear image in readers' minds, which leads to a deeper understanding of their reading. Students may then experiment with using idioms in their own writing.

Assess Learning

Observe students when they discuss the writer's craft. Notice if there is evidence of new learning based on the goal of this minilesson.

- ▶ Do students recognize idioms in their reading?
- ▶ Can they talk about what an idiom means?
- ▶ Do they understand and use the word *idiom*?

Minilesson

To help students think about the minilesson principle, use familiar texts to engage them in a discussion of idioms. Here is an example.

> Have you ever heard someone say, "That job is a piece of cake"?
>
> It doesn't mean a task is *actually* a piece of cake, but it's a fun way to say a task is easy, maybe even enjoyable! An expression or saying that means something different from its literal meaning is called an idiom.

- ▶ Hold up *Border Crossing* and read page 12.

  > What do you know about the phrase "the wrong side of the tracks"?
  >
  > This is an idiom used to describe an area that is considered poor or dangerous.

- ▶ Record the idiom and its meaning.

  > Why do you think the author used the word *literally* before the idiom?

- ▶ Repeat this process with *Bird*, reading the page that begins "Mama and Papa named me."

Have a Try

Invite the students to talk with a partner about why writers use idioms.

> ▷ In *Bird*, read the page that begins "I like to draw."
>
> > Turn and talk to your partner. What is the idiom? How does it help you understand the story?
>
> ▷ Invite a few students to share. Record responses on the chart.

Summarize and Apply

Summarize the learning and remind students to notice how writers use idioms.

> ▷ Review the chart and write the principle at the top.
>
> > Writers use idioms to make their writing interesting and to help readers understand the story even better. Today when you read, be on the lookout for idioms. If you find an example, mark it with a sticky note and bring the book back when we meet so you can share.

Share

Following independent reading time, gather students together in the meeting area to talk about their reading.

> > Who found an example of an idiom?
>
> > Read it aloud. How did it help you understand that part of the story?

Extend the Lesson (Optional)

After assessing students' understanding, you might decide to extend the learning.

> ▷ Idioms can challenge students whose native language is not English. Take time to explain the meaning of idioms that are encountered in the classroom.
>
> ▷ **Writing About Reading** Have students respond to an author's use of an idiom, sharing their thinking about whether the idiom is effective.

Writers use idioms to add interest.

Title	Idiom	Meaning
Border Crossing — CAUTION	• "the wrong side of the tracks"	• An area that is considered poor or dangerous
Bird	• "I keep him on his toes."	• Stay active and ready for anything
	• "do it with your eyes closed"	• Able to do something easily

Section 2: Literary Analysis

RML4

LA.U9.RML4

Writers choose specific language to fit the setting.

Reading Like a Writer: Analyzing the Writer's Craft

You Will Need

- two or three familiar fiction books, such as the following:
  - *It Doesn't Have to Be This Way* by Luis J. Rodríguez, from Text Set: Handling Emotions/Positive Relationships
  - *Bird* by Zetta Elliott, from Text Set: Handling Emotions/Positive Relationships
- chart paper and markers

Academic Language / Important Vocabulary

- author
- language
- setting
- specific
- grammar
- dialect

Continuum Connection

- Notice a writer's use of some words from languages other than English [p. 82]
- Notice a writer's use of regional or historical vocabulary or features of dialect included for literary effect [p. 82]
- Notice a writer's intentional use of language that violates conventional grammar to provide authentic dialogue to achieve the writer's voice [p. 82]

Goal

Notice how a writer chooses language to fit the setting.

Rationale

Writers often shape their language to fit the setting by using unconventional grammar, dialects, and words from other languages. These choices make the setting seem more authentic. When students notice language choices, they become more aware of the myriad decisions that writers must make when writing a book, and they are more likely to make similar decisions in their own writing.

Assess Learning

Observe students when they talk about the setting of a book. Notice if there is evidence of new learning based on the goal of this minilesson.

- Can students explain how a writer's language choices fit the setting?
- Do they use academic vocabulary, such as *author, language, setting, specific, grammar,* and *dialect*?

Minilesson

To help students think about the minilesson principle, guide them in noticing how writers choose specific language to fit the setting. Here is an example.

- Read the full title of *It Doesn't Have to Be This Way: A Barrio Story*.

  What is the setting for this book?

  What does the word *barrio* mean?

  What does the writer's use of the word *barrio* help you to know about the neighborhood?

- Review other examples on pages 15 (*placa*), 21 (*oralé pues, primo*), and 27 (*m'ijo*).

  Why do you think the writer chose these words to use in the book?

- Record the words and student responses on chart paper.

- Read pages 13 and 19.

  How is this language different from the language that you usually read in books?

- If necessary, help students notice the unconventional grammar, "jumped in." Repeat this with page 21, "babysittin'."

Have a Try

Invite the students to talk with a partner about the language used in *Bird*.

> Show the cover of *Bird* and read portions of the pages that begin "Once I told Uncle Son," "Marcus used to go up," and "Marcus was real good."

> > What do you notice about the words the writer used? What do they tell you? Turn and talk to your partner.

> After students turn and talk, invite a volunteer to share. Record responses on the chart.

Summarize and Apply

Summarize the learning and remind students to notice how writers choose specific language to fit the setting.

> > What did you notice today about the language writers use?

> Write the principle at the top of the chart.

> > When you read today, notice if the author of your book used language to fit the setting—for example, by using non-English words, unconventional grammar, or dialects. A dialect is a particular style of speech—certain word choices and pronunciations—that is specific to people in a region or community. Bring your book to share when we come back together.

Share

Following independent reading time, gather students together to talk about their reading.

> > Did anyone find an example of an author choosing language to fit the setting?

> > How did the author of your book shape the language to fit the setting?

Extend the Lesson (Optional)

After assessing students' understanding, you might decide to extend the learning.

> Use the structure of this minilesson to discuss how writers of historical fiction use the language of the times in dialogue to create authenticity. Refer to examples in *Memphis, Martin, and the Mountaintop* by Alice Faye Duncan, from Text Set: Civic Engagement; *As Fast As Words Could Fly* by Pamela M. Tuck, from Text Set: Equality; *The Memory Coat* by Elvira Woodruff and *The Turtle Ship* by Helena Ku Rhee, from Text Set: Perseverance; and *What You Know First* by Patricia MacLachlan, from Text Set: Illustration Study: Mood.

Writers choose specific language to fit the setting.

Book	Setting	Language Choices
	a Spanish-speaking neighborhood	Spanish words help you imagine the neighborhood: • barrio • primo • placa • m'ijo • oralé pues
		Unconventional grammar helps you hear how the characters speak: • "jumped in" • "babysittin'"
	an inner city	Dialect helps you imagine the characters and setting: • "everybody got their somethin'" • "Sure can't find no peace" • "our 'hood was his museum"

RML 5
LA.U9.RML5

Reading Minilesson Principle
Writers choose precise words to create a mood.

**Reading Like a Writer:
Analyzing the Writer's Craft**

You Will Need

- three or four familiar fiction books, such as the following:
  - *Bird* by Zetta Elliott, from Text Set: Handling Emotions/ Positive Relationships
  - *Crazy Horse's Vision* by Joseph Bruchac, from Text Set: Author/Illustrator Study: S. D. Nelson
- chart paper and markers
- document camera (optional)
- sticky notes

Academic Language / Important Vocabulary

- mood
- feeling

Continuum Connection

- Notice language that conveys an emotional atmosphere (mood) in a text, affecting how the reader feels: e.g., tension, sadness, whimsicality, joy (p. 82)
- Infer the mood by noticing aspects of a text, such as word choice (p. 82)

Goal

Notice how a writer's word choices create the mood.

Rationale

Writers choose words to create a mood or feeling in their writing, which helps readers connect to the characters and the plot. When you support students in noticing these language choices, you engage them in their reading and make books more enjoyable. You also help them think about what they can learn from writers to enhance their own writing.

Assess Learning

Observe students when they talk about the writer's craft. Notice if there is evidence of new learning based on the goal of this minilesson.

- ▶ Can students identify when an author uses language to help the reader experience a feeling?
- ▶ Do they point out a writer's use of language to create mood during individual reading conferences, book clubs, or small-group guided reading?
- ▶ Do they understand how the words *mood* and *feeling* are used in this lesson?

Minilesson

To help students think about the minilesson principle, help them notice the author's use of language to create a mood. If a document camera is available, consider projecting the pages to provide visual support. Here is an example.

- ▶ From *Bird* show and read the first page of print.

   What feeling do you get from reading this page?

   What are some of the words that make you feel that way?

- ▶ Record words on chart paper.

   The feeling that you get when you read is called mood.

- ▶ Repeat this process with the page that begins "In the wintertime" and the last six lines on the page that begins "Granddad passed."

   Which words create the mood?

   How would the mood be different if the author had described the sunset as "the setting sun" instead of a "pink and silver blanket"?

Have a Try

Invite the students to talk with a partner about the words writers choose to create a mood.

▶ Show *Crazy Horse's Vision*. Read the page beginning "Two summers later."

> Turn and talk to your partner. What mood does the writer create? What words create the mood?

▶ Ask a couple of students to share. Record the language that creates the mood.

Summarize and Apply

Summarize the learning and remind students to notice how writers choose words to create a mood.

> How do writers create a mood in their writing?

▶ Write the principle at the top of the chart.

> As you read today, be on the lookout for words the author uses to create a mood. Use a sticky note to mark the pages. Bring your book when we come back together so you can share.

Writers choose precise words to create a mood.		
Title	**Mood**	**Author's Words**
	• depressing • hopeless	• "rusty rail" • "shivering in the winter wind" • "sudden gust of wind"
Bird	• sad • discouraged • lonely • hopeless	• "wintertime" • "fragile" • "You can't fix a broken soul."
	• peace • warmth • hope	• "a pink and silver blanket . . . about to cover the world" • "calm and still" • "smiled"
Crazy Horse's Vision	• fear • danger	• "hooves sounded like thunder"

Share

Following independent reading time, gather students together in small groups to talk about the mood of the stories they read.

> If you marked a page that helped you notice language that creates a mood, share that with your group. Talk about the mood that the author's words created?

▶ Choose a few students to share with the class.

Extend the Lesson (Optional)

After assessing students' understanding, you might decide to extend the learning.

▶ Many of the words authors use to create a mood describe the setting. During interactive read-aloud, talk with students about how the setting impacts the mood of a story.

▶ **Writing About Reading** Have students critique an author's choice of language in establishing a mood or describe how an author uses language to change the mood of a book in a letter, a short write, or another form of writing.

RML 6

LA.U9.RML6

Writers choose specific words to communicate the tone of the book.

Reading Like a Writer: Analyzing the Writer's Craft

You Will Need

- three or four familiar fiction books, such as the following:
  - *Rotten!* by Anita Sanchez, from Text Set: Life on Earth
  - *The Herd Boy* by Niki Daly, from Text Set: Perseverance
  - *It Doesn't Have to Be This Way* by Luis J. Rodríguez, from Text Set: Handling Emotions/Positive Relationships
- chart paper and markers
- document camera (optional)
- sticky notes

Academic Language / Important Vocabulary

- mood
- attitude
- feeling
- tone

Continuum Connection

- Notice language that expresses the author's attitude or feelings toward a subject reflected in the style of writing (tone): e.g., lighthearted, ironic, earnest, affectionate, formal (p. 82)
- Infer the writer's tone in a fiction text by noticing the language (p. 82)

Goal

Notice how writers choose words that express their feelings or attitude toward a subject (tone).

Rationale

Tone is an author's attitude toward or feeling about a subject. The tone is revealed in part through the author's carefully chosen language. When you support students in noticing language that shows the writer's tone, you deepen their understanding. You also help them think about how to learn from writers to support their own craft.

Assess Learning

Observe students when they talk about the writer's craft. Notice if there is evidence of new learning based on the goal of this minilesson.

- ▶ Can students identify language that reveals the author's tone?
- ▶ Do they understand how the words *mood, attitude, feeling,* and *tone* are used in this lesson?

Minilesson

To help students think about the minilesson principle, help them notice a writer's use of language that creates tone. If a document camera is available, consider projecting the pages to provide visual support. Here is an example.

- ▶ Review the first and last paragraphs from the first page of *Rotten!*

   How do you think the author feels about the topic of the book? What makes you think that?

- ▶ Record words, phrases, or sentences that show the author's tone on the chart paper.

   An author's feeling or attitude toward a topic or subject is called tone.

   How would you describe the tone of this book?

- ▶ From *The Herd Boy,* show and read page 23 and the author's note.

   How do you think the author feels about the possibility of achieving something if you come from humble beginnings?

   What are some of the words that make you think that?

   What words could you use to describe his tone?

- ▶ Record students' responses on the chart.

Have a Try

Invite the students to talk with a partner about the words writers choose to create a tone.

- ▶ Show *It Doesn't Have to Be This Way* and read page 31.

    Turn and talk to your partner. What is the writer's tone? How does he reveal it?

- ▶ Ask a couple of students to share. Record the language that creates the tone.

Summarize and Apply

Summarize the learning and remind students to notice how writers choose words to create a tone.

    How do writers communicate the tone in their writing?

- ▶ Write the principle at the top of the chart.

    As you read today, be on the lookout for words the author uses to communicate the tone. Use a sticky note to mark pages that show the tone. Bring your book when we come back together so you can share.

Share

Following independent reading time, gather students together in small groups to talk about the author's tone.

    If you marked a page that helped you notice the tone in a story, share that with your group. What feeling or attitude did it help you understand that the author had toward their subject?

- ▶ Choose a few students to share with the class.

Extend the Lesson (Optional)

After assessing students' understanding, you might decide to extend the learning.

- ▶ During interactive read-aloud, talk with students about the tone of the author's writing. Notice how the tone impacts the mood of a story.

- ▶ Discuss how the illustrations need to fit the tone. For example, readers might be confused if heavy, dark drawings illustrate a piece of writing that has a lighthearted and irreverent tone.

Writers choose specific words to communicate the tone of the book.

Title	Author's Words	Author's Tone
RUMBLY	• "Rot is everywhere!" • "even between your teeth" • "After decomposition comes new life."	• irreverent • humorous • serious • respectful
The Herd Boy	• "'Ah, a boy who looks after his herd will make a very fine leader. Sala Kahle, Mr. President.'" • "Many great men come from humble beginnings."	• wise • hopeful • encouraging
It Doesn't Have To Be This Way	• "'We can make good things happen, m'ijo, if we all work together.'"	• supportive • loving • inclusive

Reading Minilesson Principle
Writers use language in surprising ways to create humor or interest.

Reading Like a Writer: Analyzing the Writer's Craft

You Will Need

- two or three familiar fiction texts that use language to create humor or interest such as the following:
  - *Nubs* by Brian Dennis, Kirby Larson, and Mary Nethery, from Text Set: Kindness and Compassion
  - *Rotten!* by Anita Sanchez, from Text Set: Life on Earth
  - *Garvey's Choice* by Nikki Grimes, from Text Set: Exploring Identity
- chart paper and markers
- sticky notes

Academic Language / Important Vocabulary

- humor
- humorous
- sarcasm
- oxymoron
- contradiction

Continuum Connection

- Notice a writer's use of contradiction: e.g., paradox, figurative language, malaprop, oxymoron ["a silent roar"] (p. 82)
- Notice that words have special qualities, such as musical or pleasing sound, dramatic impact, or humor (p. 82)

Goal

Notice how writers use contradiction and other techniques to create humor or interest.

Rationale

When you teach students to notice how a writer uses language—such as sarcasm, oxymorons, or contradiction—to create humor or interest, you help them to notice writers' choices, stories become more enjoyable, and they learn to create humor through language use in their own writing.

Assess Learning

Observe students when they talk about the writer's craft. Notice if there is evidence of new learning based on the goal of this minilesson.

- ▶ Can students talk about the way a writer used language to make a story humorous or interesting?
- ▶ Do they understand and use the words *humor, humorous, sarcasm, oxymoron,* and *contradiction*?

Minilesson

To help students think about the minilesson principle, discuss familiar books that bring in an element of humor or interest through the use of language. Here is an example.

- ▶ Show *Nubs* and read the page that begins "When Nubs stepped off."

  What do you notice that is funny about this page?

  The word *pawparazzi* is a word the authors made up. Why do you think they did that?

- ▶ Record responses on a chart.
- ▶ Show *Rotten!* and read page 16.

  How did the author use language in a humorous or interesting way?

  "Delicious and disgusting" is an oxymoron—two or more words used together that have opposite meanings.

- ▶ Discuss the use of contradiction on page 8 ("delicious droppings") and page 21 ("banquet of death").

  What does the author mean by this phrase?

  Why is the phrase humorous or interesting to read?

- ▶ Record responses on the chart.

Have a Try

Invite the students to notice with a partner how writers use language to create humor or interest.

▸ Repeat the inquiry with *Garvey's Choice*, reading page 7.

> Turn and talk to your partner about the questions Garvey's parents ask.

> They are being sarcastic—the literal answers to the questions are not what they intend; instead, they are using humor to prove a point and argue with each other.

▸ Ask a couple of students to share. Record responses.

Summarize and Apply

Summarize the learning and remind students to notice how writers use language to create humor or interest.

> What does the chart show you?

▸ Write the principle at the top of the chart.

> When you read today, notice places in your book where the author uses language to create humor or interest and mark them with a sticky note. Bring the book when we meet so you can share.

Share

Following independent reading time, gather students together in the meeting area to talk about the use of language to create humor.

> Who noticed an author's use of language to create humor or interest today?

Extend the Lesson (Optional)

After assessing students' understanding, you might decide to extend the learning.

▸ Take time during interactive read-aloud for students to respond to and critique a writer's use of humor.

Writers use language in surprising ways to create humor or interest.		
Title	Humorous or Interesting Part	How does the author use language to make it humorous or interesting?
	Nubs, the dog, posed for the "pawparazzi"	• Made-up word (combines paparazzi and paw)
	"deliciously disgusting" "delicious droppings" "banquet of death"	• Oxymorons • Contradiction
	"Garvey likes to read. When was that not a good thing?" "But reading doesn't build muscles, does it?"	• Sarcasm (asking questions for which the speakers don't expect an answer)

Section 2: Literary Analysis

Reading Minilesson Principle
Writers use symbolism to communicate a message.

You Will Need

- three or four familiar books with strong use of symbols, such as the following:
  - *Chachaji's Cup* by Uma Krishnaswami, from Text Set: Kindness and Compassion
  - *Teacup* by Rebecca Young, from Text Set: Illustration Study: Mood
  - *The Red Bicycle* by Jude Isabella, from Text Set: Problem Solving/Giving Back
- document camera (optional)
- chart paper and markers

Academic Language / Important Vocabulary

- symbol
- theme
- reflect
- indicate

Continuum Connection

- Recognize and understand symbolism in a text and illustrations (p. 80)

Goal

Notice how writers use symbolism to communicate a message.

Rationale

Writers use symbols to support and emphasize the theme of a story and to communicate a message in a way that is more engaging and meaningful than words alone. When you encourage students to notice how and why symbols are used, you help them appreciate the writer's craft and gain a better understanding of the text. They also learn possibilities for their own writing.

Assess Learning

Observe students when they talk about the writer's craft. Notice if there is evidence of new learning based on the goal of this minilesson.

- ▶ Do students recognize writers' use of symbols?
- ▶ Can they discuss the meaning of a symbol and how its use emphasizes or enhances the story?
- ▶ Can they use the words *symbol, theme, reflect,* and *indicate*?

Minilesson

To help students think about the minilesson principle, help them notice a writer's use of symbols. Here is an example.

- ▶ Show *Chachaji's Cup*.

  You could say that this book is about a cup, but what is the book really about?

  What does the cup have to do with the message that the writer wants you to know?

- ▶ Record responses on the chart paper.

  Why do you think the author decided to focus on the teacup?

  When an author uses an object to represent an idea, that object is called a symbol.

- ▶ Repeat this process with the book *Teacup*. After discussion, point out that the two authors used the same symbol but for two different reasons.

Have a Try

Invite the students to notice with a partner how writers use symbols to communicate a message.

▶ Show *The Red Bicycle*.

Turn and talk to your partner. What symbol does the author use in this book? Why? What does it mean?

▶ Ask a couple of students to share. Record responses.

Summarize and Apply

Summarize the learning and remind students to notice how writers use symbols.

What did you learn about how writers use symbols?

▶ Write the principle at the top of the chart.

When you read today, notice whether the writer uses a symbol in the book. If you notice a symbol, think about what it means and why the author chose to use it. Bring the book when we come back together so you can share.

Writers use symbolism to communicate a message.

Title	Symbol	Meaning/Message
Chachaji's Cup	(cup)	• perseverance • remembering the past
	(cup)	• courage • facing change
The Red Bicycle	(bicycle)	• making a difference

Share

Following independent reading time, gather students together in the meeting area to talk about the symbols in the books they read.

Who found a symbol in your reading today? Why do you think the author chose to use that object as a symbol?

Extend the Lesson (Optional)

After assessing students' understanding, you might decide to extend the learning.

▶ As you read aloud or as students read independently, help them notice how authors use symbols to communicate a message. Add examples to the chart.

▶ **Writing About Reading** Have students write about how a writer uses symbolism to communicate a message. Choose an appropriate form of writing, such as a letter about reading or a short write.

Section 2: Literary Analysis

Assessment

After you have taught the minilessons in this umbrella, observe students as they talk and write about their reading across instructional contexts: interactive read-aloud, independent reading, guided reading, shared reading, and book club. Use *The Literacy Continuum* (Fountas and Pinnell 2017) to guide the observation of students' reading and writing behaviors.

▶ What evidence do you have of new understandings related to analyzing the writer's craft?

- Are students able to discuss why a writer uses similes, metaphors, or personification in a piece of writing?
- Can they discuss how authors use idioms to create interest?
- Do they understand the importance of word choice to convey mood and tone?
- Are they able to talk about how writers create humor?
- Can they share examples of symbols used to communicate a message?
- Do they use vocabulary such as *language, simile, metaphor, idiom, compare, personification, mood, tone, humor* and *symbol*?

▶ In what other ways, beyond the scope of this umbrella, are students talking about the writer's craft?

- Do students talk about the decisions that writers of various genres must make?

Use your observations to determine the next umbrella you will teach. You may also consult Minilessons Across the Year (pp. 61–64) for guidance.

Link to Writing

After teaching the minilessons in this umbrella, help students link the new learning to their own writing:

▶ As students do their own writing, encourage them to model their writing after an author whose work they admire. Have them analyze how the author conveys mood, tone, or humor so that they can apply the same techniques to their own writing.

Reader's Notebook

When this umbrella is complete, provide a copy of the minilesson principles (see resources.fountasandpinnell.com) for students to glue in a reader's notebook (in the Minilessons section if using *Reader's Notebook: Advanced* [Fountas and Pinnell 2011]), so they can refer to the information as needed.

Inspiration/Creativity

Poetry

Minilessons in This Umbrella

RML1	Poets use line breaks and white space to show you how to read the poem.
RML2	Poets use imagery to make you see, hear, and feel things.
RML3	Poets use repetition to draw your attention or create rhythm.
RML4	Poets use alliteration and assonance to create rhythm and make the poem interesting.
RML5	Poets use onomatopoeia to help you make an image with sound.
RML6	Poets use stressed and unstressed syllables to develop rhythm and help you read the poem.

Before Teaching Umbrella 10 Minilessons

In *Genre Study: Teaching with Fiction and Nonfiction Books*, prose and poetry are described not as genres but as "broad, overarching categories of the language of writing that can appear in *any genre*. . . . Poetry is compact writing characterized by imagination and artistry and imbued with intense meaning" (Fountas and Pinnell 2012, 19). Studying the craft of poetry allows students to understand the characteristics of poetry and to think about applying the craft to their own writing.

Before beginning this umbrella, give students the opportunity to hear, read, and enjoy poems that represent a variety of forms (e.g., lyrical, free verse, haiku, limerick) and topics, tell stories, convey information, explore emotions and ideas, and play with sound, language, space, and imagery. Use the following books from the *Fountas & Pinnell Classroom™ Interactive-Read-Aloud Collection* text sets listed below or choose poetry texts from your own library.

Inspiration/Creativity

World Make Way: New Poems Inspired by Art from The Metropolitan Museum of Art edited by Lee Bennett Hopkins

Poetry

Out of Wonder: Poems Celebrating Poets by Kwame Alexander

Neighborhood Odes: A Poetry Collection by Gary Soto

The Flag of Childhood: Poems from the Middle East selected by Naomi Shihab Nye

The Death of the Hat: A Brief History of Poetry in 50 Objects selected by Paul B. Janeczko

Bravo! Poems About Amazing Hispanics edited by Margarita Engle

As you read aloud and enjoy these texts together, help students notice and discuss characteristics of poetry, such as line breaks, white space, imagery, repetition, alliteration, assonance, onomatopoeia, and stressed and unstressed syllables.

Section 2: Literary Analysis

RML1
LA.U10.RML1

Reading Minilesson Principle
Poets use line breaks and white space to show you how to read the poem.

You Will Need

- two familiar poems with multiple stanzas, such as the following from Text Set: Inspiration/Creativity:
  - "Walking to Temple" by Janet Wong and "Paint Me" by Marilyn Singer from *World Make Way* edited by Lee Bennett Hopkins
- chart paper and markers
- document camera (optional)

Academic Language / Important Vocabulary

- poet
- poem
- line break
- white space

Continuum Connection

- Notice and understand some elements of poetry: e.g., figurative language, rhyme, repetition, onomatopoeia, layout/line breaks (shape), imagery, alliteration, assonance (p. 80)

- Notice and understand some elements of poetry when they appear in nonfiction: e.g., figurative language, rhyme, repetition, onomatopoeia, layout/ line breaks (shape), imagery, alliteration, assonance (p. 85)

Goal

Learn how to read the line breaks and white space of a poem.

Rationale

Poets intentionally use line breaks and white space to construct the rhythm of a poem and to group ideas thematically. When you teach students to notice this, they are better able to think about the structure and meaning of the poems they read.

Assess Learning

Observe students when they read and talk about poetry and notice if there is evidence of new learning based on the goal of this minilesson.

▶ Do students understand how a poet uses line breaks and white space?

▶ Do they use vocabulary such as *poet, poem, line break,* and *white space* when talking about poetry?

Minilesson

To help students think about the minilesson principle, use a familiar poem to help them notice the effects of line breaks and white space. Project the poem, if possible, so that all students can see it. Here is an example.

▶ Display the poem "Walking to Temple" from *World Make Way* so all students can see it.

▶ Read the poem aloud, emphasizing the line breaks.

> What do you notice about how I read these lines? How did I know when to pause?
>
> How would I read these sentences differently if this were a paragraph instead of a poem?
>
> When you're reading a paragraph, you pause when you reach the end of a sentence. When you're reading a poem, pause slightly when you reach the end of a line. The end of a line in a poem is called a line break. Poets choose where to put the line breaks. How do you think poets decide where to put line breaks?
>
> How do line breaks help you when you read poetry?

▶ Point to the space between the two stanzas of the poem.

> When I was reading aloud the poem, what did I do when I got to this part?
>
> This is called white space. White space is a place in a poem where there are no words. Why do you think the poet put white space here?
>
> How will the white space help you read the poem?

Have a Try

Invite the students to talk with a partner about line breaks and white space in a poem.

▶ Display another familiar poem, such as "Paint Me" from *World Make Way*.

> Read this poem aloud with your partner. Remember to pay attention to the line breaks and white space. After you read it, turn and talk about how and why the poet used line breaks and white space.

▶ After students read and discuss the poem in pairs, ask a few students to share their thinking with the class.

Summarize and Apply

Summarize the learning and remind students to pay attention to line breaks and white space when they read poetry.

> Why do poets use line breaks?

> Why do poets use white space?

▶ Record students' responses on chart paper. Write the principle at the top of the chart.

> If you read poetry today, pay attention to how the poet uses line breaks and white space. Bring one poem that you would like to share when we come back together.

Share

Following independent reading time, gather students together in the meeting area to talk about poetry.

> Who would like to share a poem that you read today? What did you notice about the poem?

Extend the Lesson (Optional)

After assessing students' understanding, you might decide to extend the learning.

▶ Use familiar poems for small groups of students or the whole class to read together as shared or performance reading (pp. 70–72).

▶ Encourage students to think about how to effectively use line breaks and white space when they write their own poems.

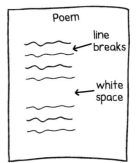

Poets use line breaks and white space to show you how to read the poem.

Line breaks...
  group certain words together
  tell you to pause slightly
  make the poem sound a certain way

White space...
  separates different parts of the poem
  tells you to pause a little longer

Section 2: Literary Analysis

RML2
LA.U10.RML2

Reading Minilesson Principle
Poets use imagery to make you see, hear, and feel things.

Understanding the Craft of Poetry

You Will Need

- two or three familiar poems that contain imagery, such as the following from Text Set: Poetry:
  - "(Loving) the World and Everything in It" by Marjory Wentworth from *Out of Wonder* edited by Kwame Alexander
  - "Ode to El Molcajete" and "Ode to Mi Gato" from *Neighborhood Odes* by Gary Soto
- document camera (optional)
- chart paper and markers
- sticky notes

Academic Language / Important Vocabulary

- poet
- poem
- poetry
- imagery

Continuum Connection

- Notice and understand some elements of poetry: e.g., figurative language, rhyme, repetition, onomatopoeia, layout/line breaks (shape), imagery, alliteration, assonance (p. 80)
- Notice and understand some elements of poetry when they appear in nonfiction: e.g., figurative language, rhyme, repetition, onomatopoeia, layout/line breaks (shape), imagery, alliteration, assonance (p. 85)

Goal

Notice and understand how poets use imagery to appeal to the senses—sight, sound, touch, smell, taste.

Rationale

When you teach students to recognize imagery in poetry, they are better able to understand and connect with the poem's meaning.

Assess Learning

Observe students when they read and talk about poetry and notice if there is evidence of new learning based on the goal of this minilesson.

- ▶ Do students notice imagery in poems?
- ▶ Do they understand and talk about how the use of imagery impacts the meaning of the poem?
- ▶ Do they use vocabulary such as *poet*, *poem*, *poetry*, and *imagery*?

Minilesson

To help students think about the minilesson principle, use familiar poems to engage them in noticing imagery in poetry. Project the poems, if possible, so all students can see them. Here is an example.

> As I read a poem to you, close your eyes, listen carefully, and use the words to make a picture in your mind.

- ▶ Read the poem "(Loving) the World and Everything in It" from *Out of Wonder*.

  > What did you see in your mind? What did you hear?

  > What did you imagine feeling with your body?

- ▶ Display the poem.

  > How did the poet help you use your senses?

- ▶ Record responses on chart paper.

  > Now close your eyes again and listen carefully as I read another poem.

- ▶ Read "Ode to El Molcajete" from *Neighborhood Odes*.

  > What did you see in your mind while I read this poem?

  > What sounds did you imagine hearing? What could you imagine tasting?

- ▶ Display the poem.

  > How did the poet help you use your senses?

- ▶ Record responses on the chart.

Have a Try

Invite the students to talk with a partner about the imagery in a poem.

▶ Display "Ode to Mi Gato" from *Neighborhood Odes* and read it aloud.

> What did you imagine seeing, hearing, or feeling while I read this poem? What did the poet do to create images in your mind? Turn and talk to your partner to share your thinking.

▶ After students turn and talk, ask a few students to share. Record responses on the chart.

Summarize and Apply

Summarize the learning and remind students to notice and think about imagery in poetry.

> Poets use certain words and phrases that help you see, hear, smell, taste, or feel the touch of things in your mind. This is called imagery. The decisions the poet makes about using imagery are elements of the poet's craft.

▶ Write the principle at the top of the chart.

> If you read poetry today, notice if the poet uses imagery to help you see, hear, or feel things. If you find an example of imagery, mark it with a sticky note and bring your book to share when we come back together.

Share

Following independent reading time, gather students together in the meeting area to share examples of imagery.

> Who found an example of imagery in a poem today?

> Read aloud the example you found. What did you imagine while you read the poem? How did the imagery help you better understand or enjoy the poem?

Extend the Lesson (Optional)

After assessing students' understanding, you might decide to extend the learning.

▶ Help students think about creating imagery by showing a particular image (e.g., a city scene) or by playing a sound (e.g., a police siren). Have students write phrases that could help readers imagine the image or sound.

Poets use imagery to make you see, hear, and feel things.

Poem	Imagery	How did the poet create imagery?
"(Loving) the World and Everything in It"	• Feel the grass • Hear the birds sing • See the girl flying	• Described walking on the damp, morning grass • Used the words symphony and perfect note • As she imagined flying, so did the reader.
"Ode to El Molcajete"	• See the tomatoes • Feel the abuela's tears run down her face • Smell the chilies • Feel and taste the spicy chilies	• Compared the juice of tomatoes to blood • Described tears in different ways • Made the fumes visible, rising up to the ceiling • Compared his tongue to things that are red or hot
"Ode to Mi Gato"	• See the color of the cat • Feel the sun • Hear and see the cat food	• Compared the cat to milk • Described the sun like a warm hand • Used words like rattles, bag, brown nuggets, and raining

RML 3
LA.U10.RML3

Reading Minilesson Principle
Poets use repetition to draw your attention or create rhythm.

Understanding the Craft of Poetry

You Will Need

- two familiar poems that use repetition, such as the following from Text Set: Poetry:
  - "I Have No Address" by Hamza El Din from *The Flag of Childhood* selected by Naomi Shihab Nye
  - "Things" by Eloise Greenfield from *The Death of the Hat* selected by Paul B. Janeczko
- document camera (optional)
- chart paper and markers

Academic Language / Important Vocabulary

- refrain
- repetition

Continuum Connection

- Notice and understand some elements of poetry: e.g., figurative language, rhyme, repetition, onomatopoeia, layout/line breaks (shape), imagery, alliteration, assonance (p. 80)
- Notice and understand some elements of poetry when they appear in nonfiction: e.g., figurative language, rhyme, repetition, onomatopoeia, layout/line breaks (shape), imagery, alliteration, assonance (p. 85)

Goal

Notice and understand a poet's use of repetition.

Rationale

Repetition in poetry emphasizes certain ideas and makes a poem memorable. When you teach students to notice repetition in poetry, they are better able to understand and appreciate the language and meaning of poetry. They also think about the decisions poets make when writing poetry, which helps them when writing their own poems.

Assess Learning

Observe students when they read and discuss poetry and notice if there is evidence of new learning based on the goal of this minilesson.

- ▶ Do students notice when a poet uses repetition?
- ▶ Do they understand how repetition impacts the meaning and enjoyment of a poem?
- ▶ Do they use vocabulary such as *refrain* and *repetition*?

Minilesson

To help students think about the minilesson principle, use familiar poems to help them notice and think about repetition in poetry. Here is an example.

- ▶ Display "I Have No Address" from *The Flag of Childhood* so all students can see it.

  As I read this poem aloud, listen carefully and notice how the poet uses words.

- ▶ Read the poem aloud, emphasizing the repeated refrain.

  What do you notice about how this poem sounds? What phrase do you hear repeated?

  A repeated word, group of words, line, or group of lines repeated at a specific moment in a poem is called a refrain.

- ▶ Read the poem again.

  What does the repetition of the refrain help you to think about or understand?

- ▶ Record students' responses on chart paper.

  The words *peace, love,* and *humanity* are used in the first stanza. Notice how the second and fourth stanzas repeat similar kinds of words. Turn and talk to your partner about this kind of repetition. What do you think all of these words have in common?

- ▶ After students turn and talk, record responses on chart paper.

Have a Try

Invite the students to talk with a partner about repetition in a poem.

▶ Display the poem "Things" from *The Death of the Hat* and read it aloud, emphasizing its repetition.

> Turn and talk to your partner about what you notice about this poem. Why do you think the author chose to use repetition?

▶ After students turn and talk, invite several pairs to share their thinking. Record their responses on the chart.

Summarize and Apply

Summarize the learning and remind students to notice repetition when they read poetry.

> What did you notice about the poems we read aloud today?

▶ Write the principle at the top of the chart.

> If you read poetry today, notice if the author uses repetition of a word, refrain, or similar kind of words. If you read a poem that has repetition, bring it to share when we come back together.

Share

Following independent reading time, gather students together in the meeting area to talk about repetition in poetry.

> Who read a poem with an interesting use of repetition today?

> Read aloud the poem. How did the repetition help you to understand the poem or better enjoy it?

Extend the Lesson (Optional)

After assessing students' understanding, you might decide to extend the learning.

▶ Read and discuss more poems with repetition.

▶ **Writing About Reading** Have students write in a reader's notebook about how an author uses repetition in a poem. They may include a few words or phrases from the poem as an example. Encourage them to discuss how the repetition adds to the appeal or meaning of the poem.

Poets use repetition to draw your attention or create rhythm.

Poem	Repetition	Effects
"I Have No Address"	• A phrase • Similar types of words (things that people have in common no matter where they are from or live)	• Emphasizes the message that people are connected by common experiences and feelings • Creates rhythm
"Things"	• Refrain at end of stanza • Repetition of similar kinds of words in first three lines of each stanza (past-tense verbs)	• For emphasis (refrain at the end of the 1st and 2nd stanzas contrasts with the refrain in the 3rd stanza) • Creates rhythm

Reading Minilesson Principle

Poets use alliteration and assonance to create rhythm and make the poem interesting.

Understanding the Craft of Poetry

You Will Need

- three or four familiar poems that contain alliteration and/or assonance, such as the following:
  - "Cat Watching a Spider" by Julie Fogliano and "Night-Shining White" by Elaine Magliaro from *World Make Way* edited by Lee Bennett Hopkins, from Text Set: Inspiration/Creativity
  - "The Magic of Words" by José Martí from *Bravo!* edited by Margarita Engle, from Text Set: Poetry
- document camera (optional)
- chart paper and markers

Academic Language / Important Vocabulary

- repetition
- vowel
- consonant
- alliteration
- assonance

Continuum Connection

- Notice and understand some elements of poetry: e.g., figurative language, rhyme, repetition, onomatopoeia, layout/line breaks (shape), imagery, alliteration, assonance (p. 80)
- Notice and understand some elements of poetry when they appear in nonfiction: e.g., figurative language, rhyme, repetition, onomatopoeia, layout/line breaks (shape), imagery, alliteration, assonance (p. 85)

Goal

Notice when poets use alliteration and assonance.

Rationale

Alliteration and assonance lend coherence to poems and make them enjoyable for the reader or listener. Teaching students to notice alliteration and assonance is likely to deepen their appreciation of poetry. It also encourages them to think about the decisions poets make when writing poetry, which helps them when writing their own poems.

Assess Learning

Observe students when they read and talk about poetry and notice if there is evidence of new learning based on the goal of this minilesson.

- ▶ Can students notice and define alliteration and assonance in poetry?
- ▶ Do they use vocabulary such as *repetition, vowel, consonant, alliteration,* and *assonance?*

Minilesson

To help students think about the minilesson principle, use familiar poems to help them notice alliteration and assonance in poetry. Project the poems, if possible, so all students can see them. Here is an example.

▶ Display "Cat Watching a Spider" from *World Make Way*. Read the poem aloud, emphasizing the alliteration.

What do you notice about the words in the first two lines of this poem?

They repeat the /s/ sound. This is called alliteration. Alliteration is when two or more words close together start with the same consonant sound. Where else do you see or hear alliteration in this poem?

Why do you think the poet chose to use alliteration?

▶ Display "Night-Shining White" from *World Make Way* and read it aloud.

Who can find an example of alliteration in this poem?

▶ Write the definition of *alliteration* and examples of alliteration on chart paper. Ask a student to highlight the repeated consonants.

▶ Continue to display "Night-Shining White" and reread the last stanza aloud.

What do you notice about the words *night-shining* and *white?*

A repeated vowel sound in words close together is called assonance. Why do you think the poet chose to use assonance?

▶ Write the definition of *assonance* and the example on the chart. Ask a student to highlight the repeated vowel sound.

Have a Try

Invite the students to talk with a partner about alliteration and assonance in a poem.

▶ Display "The Magic of Words" from *Bravo!* and read it aloud.

> With your partner, see if you can find any examples of repeated sounds in this poem. If you find any, talk about whether they are alliteration or assonance.

▶ After students turn and talk, invite a few pairs to share their thinking. Record examples on the chart.

Summarize and Apply

Summarize the learning and remind students to notice alliteration and assonance when they read poetry.

> What did you notice about the poems we read today?

> You noticed that the poets repeated certain sounds in different words. You learned that this repetition of sounds is called alliteration and assonance. What's the difference between alliteration and assonance?

> Why do you think poets sometimes use alliteration and assonance?

▶ Write the principle at the top of the chart.

> If you read poetry today, notice if the poet uses alliteration or assonance. If you find any examples, bring them to share when we come back together.

Share

Following independent reading time, gather students together in the meeting area to share examples of alliteration and assonance.

> Did anyone find any examples of alliteration or assonance in poetry today?

> Please share the examples you found.

Extend the Lesson (Optional)

After assessing students' understanding, you might decide to extend the learning.

▶ Encourage students to use alliteration and assonance in their own poetry. You might consider giving them writing prompts that challenge them to focus on alliteration or assonance.

Poets use alliteration and assonance to create rhythm and make the poem interesting.

Alliteration	The repetition of consonant sounds at the beginning of words

"Cat Watching a Spider"	"Night-Shining White"
• so, silent, certain, spider • can, cause • watchful, wondering • prowl, prance	• best, breed • flashing, fire • stands, stiff

Assonance	The repetition of vowel sounds

"Night-Shining White"	"The Magic of Words"
• night, shining, white	• exiles, telling, gentle, elephants, enchanted

Reading Minilesson Principle

Poets use onomatopoeia to help you make an image with sound.

Understanding the Craft of Poetry

You Will Need

- three or four familiar poems that contain onomatopoeia, such as the following:
  - "Mouse's Nest" by John Clare from *The Death of a Hat* selected by Paul B. Janeczko, from Text Set: Poetry
  - "Studio" by Marilyn Nelson from *World Make Way* edited by Lee Bennett Hopkins, from Text Set: Inspiration/Creativity
  - "Ode to the Sprinkler" from *Neighborhood Odes* by Gary Soto, from Text Set: Poetry
- document camera (optional)
- chart paper and markers

Academic Language / Important Vocabulary

- poem
- poet
- poetry
- onomatopoeia

Continuum Connection

- Notice and understand some elements of poetry: e.g., figurative language, rhyme, repetition, onomatopoeia, layout/line breaks (shape), imagery, alliteration, assonance (p. 80)
- Notice and understand some elements of poetry when they appear in nonfiction: e.g., figurative language, rhyme, repetition, onomatopoeia, layout/ line breaks (shape), imagery, alliteration, assonance (p. 85)

Goal

Notice when and why poets use onomatopoeia.

Rationale

Poets use onomatopoeia to help the reader use sounds to create an image in the mind and to make poems more enjoyable. Teaching students to notice onomatopoeia is likely to deepen their appreciation of poetry. It also encourages them to think about the decisions poets make (craft decisions), which helps them when writing their own poems.

Assess Learning

Observe students when they read and talk about poetry and notice if there is evidence of new learning based on the goal of this minilesson.

- ▶ Do students notice onomatopoeia in poetry?
- ▶ Can they explain why a poet might use onomatopoeia?
- ▶ Do they use vocabulary such as *poem*, *poet*, *poetry*, and *onomatopoeia*?

Minilesson

To help students think about the minilesson principle, use familiar poems to help them discuss onomatopoeia in poetry. Here is an example.

> I'm going to read you a few lines from a poem called "Mouse's Nest." As I read, I want you to close your eyes, listen carefully, and use the words to make a picture in your mind.

▶ Read the two sentences beginning "Then the mouse" aloud, emphasizing the onomatopoetic words.

> That poem makes an image in your mind with sounds. What do you hear?

> Which words in the poem help you to hear those sounds?

> The words *craking* and *squeaked* describe the sounds the mice make and also really sound like the mice! This is onomatopoeia. Onomatopoeia is when a word imitates the sound an object or animal makes. Say the word slowly aloud with me: /on / uh / mat /uh / PEE /uh.

▶ Repeat this process with the first stanza of "Studio" from *World Make Way*, emphasizing the heartbeat quality of the last line.

▶ Write the definition of *onomatopoeia* and examples of onomatopoeia from the poems on chart paper.

Have a Try

Invite the students to talk with a partner about onomatopoeia in a poem.

▶ Display "Ode to a Sprinkler" from *Neighborhood Odes* and read it aloud.

With your partner, find examples of onomatopoeia in this poem. Why do you think the author chose to use those words?

▶ After students turn and talk, invite a few pairs to share their thinking. Record examples on the chart.

Summarize and Apply

Summarize the learning and remind students to notice onomatopoeia when they read poetry.

Poets sometimes use words that imitate the sound of the thing they refer to. What is that called?

Why do you think poets sometimes use onomatopoeia?

▶ Write the principle at the top of the chart.

If you read poetry today, notice if the poet uses onomatopoeia. If you find any examples, bring them to share when we come back together.

Share

Following independent reading time, gather students together in the meeting area to share examples of onomatopoeia.

Did anyone find any examples of onomatopoeia in poetry today?

Please share the examples you found. How did they help you understand or enjoy the poem?

Extend the Lesson (Optional)

After assessing students' understanding, you might decide to extend the learning.

▶ Encourage students to use onomatopoeia in their own poetry. You might consider giving them writing prompts that challenge students to focus on onomatopoeia (e.g., write a poem about or a description of school dismissal time, a construction site, or a glass shattering on a tile floor).

▶ **Writing About Reading** Have students write in their reader's notebook about examples of onomatopoeia, what they add to the poem, and how the poem would be different without onomatopoeia.

Poets use onomatopoeia to help you make an image with sound.

Definition	Examples
When a word imitates the sound an object or animal makes.	craking squeaked
	Make Art, Make Art, Make Art
	slicing dripping pounding buzz

Reading Minilesson Principle
Poets use stressed and unstressed syllables to develop rhythm and help you read the poem.

Understanding the Craft of Poetry

You Will Need

▶ chart paper prepared with a poem from the public domain (or a projected poem), such as the following:

   • "Stopping by Woods on a Snowy Evening" by Robert Frost

▶ markers

▶ document camera (optional)

Academic Language / Important Vocabulary

▶ rhythm

▶ stressed syllable

▶ unstressed syllable

▶ stanza

▶ meter

Continuum Connection

▶ Notice a writer's use of poetic language and sound devices: e.g., rhythm, rhyme, repetition, refrain, onomatopoeia, alliteration, assonance (p 82)

Goal

Notice and understand a poet's use of stressed and unstressed syllables to create rhythm.

Rationale

All speech has a rhythm formed by stressed and unstressed syllables. Poets intentionally use stressed and unstressed syllables to develop a rhythm or melodious quality in a poem that is called meter. When you teach students to notice the stressed and unstressed syllables in a poem, they are better able to read poetry and think about its structure.

Assess Learning

Observe students when they read and talk about poetry and notice if there is evidence of new learning based on the goal of this minilesson.

▶ Do students understand how poets create meter?

▶ Do they use vocabulary such as *rhythm, stressed syllable, unstressed syllable, stanza,* and *meter* when talking about poetry?

Minilesson

To help students think about the minilesson principle, use a familiar poem to help them notice stressed and unstressed syllables. Here is an example.

▶ Display the poem "Stopping by Woods on a Snowy Evening" by Robert Frost.

▶ Read the poem aloud, giving more stress to the words that are underlined on the chart. Acknowledge the pattern of stressed and unstressed syllables, but read the poem naturally rather than in an excessively sing-song way.

> What did you notice about how I read the words in this poem? Did I read all of them the same way?

> I read some words by giving a little more emphasis, or stress, to the whole word or to one of the syllables. How would these lines sound different if all the syllables were given the same stress? Let's try that by reading the first two lines.

> How did that sound?

> Poets put together words in patterns of stressed and unstressed syllables to create rhythm. In this poem, each line has eight syllables and every other syllable is stressed, resulting in a rhythm called meter. Why do you think poets pay attention to the meter in their poems?

▶ To emphasize the meter of this poem, read a couple of lines with the stress on different syllables (e.g., "Whose woods *these* are *I* think *I* know"). Talk about how the meter reflects the way one would read the poem in a natural voice.

Have a Try

Invite the students to talk with a partner about stressed and unstressed syllables in the last stanza of the displayed poem.

> Read the last stanza of the poem aloud with your partner. After you read it, turn and talk about how the rhythm affects your experience with the poem.

▶ After students read and discuss the poem in pairs, ask several students to share their thinking.

Summarize and Apply

Summarize the learning and remind students to pay attention to stressed and unstressed syllables when they read poetry.

> Why do poets use stressed and unstressed syllables?

▶ Write the principle at the top of the chart.

> If you read poetry today, pay attention to how the poet uses stressed and unstressed syllables—the meter of the poem. Bring one poem that you would like to share when we come back together.

Share

Following independent reading time, gather students together in the meeting area to talk about poetry.

> Who would like to share a poem that you read today? Read the poem aloud and we will all clap the meter.

Extend the Lesson (Optional)

After assessing students' understanding, you might decide to extend the learning.

▶ Have pairs or small groups of students work together on presenting a choral reading of "Stopping by Woods on a Snowy Evening" or another poem.

▶ Continue to notice and discuss how poets use stressed and unstressed syllables to develop rhythm. Consider introducing terms such as *verse*, *foot*, and *iambic pentameter.*

▶ **Writing About Reading** Ask students to write in a reader's notebook about how rhythm created by stressed and unstressed syllables added to the mood or feeling of a poem they enjoyed.

Poets use stressed and unstressed syllables to develop rhythm and help you read the poem.

"Stopping by Woods on a Snowy Evening"
by Robert Frost

Whose woods these are I think I know.
His house is in the village though;
He will not see me stopping here
To watch his woods fill up with snow.

My little horse must think it queer
To stop without a farmhouse near
Between the woods and frozen lake
The darkest evening of the year.

He gives his harness bells a shake
To ask if there is some mistake.
The only other sound's the sweep
Of easy wind and downy flake.

The woods are lovely, dark, and deep.
But I have promises to keep,
And miles to go before I sleep,
And miles to go before I sleep.

Section 2: Literary Analysis

Assessment

After you have taught the minilessons in this umbrella, observe students as they talk and write about their reading across instructional contexts: interactive read-aloud, independent reading, guided reading, shared reading, and book club, as well as their poetry writing in writers' workshop. Use *The Literacy Continuum* (Fountas and Pinnell 2017) to guide the observation of students' reading and writing behaviors across instructional contexts.

▶ What evidence do you have of new understandings related to the craft of poetry?

- Do students pay attention to line breaks and white space in poems?
- Do they notice and enjoy the imagery and repetition in poems?
- Do they understand why poets use alliteration, assonance, and onomatopoeia?
- Do they appreciate how poets create rhythm in their poems?
- Do they use academic language, such as *poetry, poet, poem, line break, white space, imagery, repetition, alliteration, assonance, onomatopoeia,* and *syllable*?

▶ In what other ways, beyond the scope of this umbrella, are students talking about author's craft?

- Do students write about an author's craft in their letters about reading?
- Have they noticed and discussed an illustrator's craft?

Use your observations to determine the next umbrella you will teach. You may also consult Minilessons Across the Year (pp. 61–64) for guidance.

Link to Writing

After teaching the minilessons in this umbrella, help students link the new learning to their own writing:

▶ Invite students to write a poem about a topic that describes an idea or emotion, tells a story, or gives information. Alternatively, they may want to write a poem that is a response to or inspired by another poem. Remind them of the craft decisions poets make.

Reader's Notebook

When this umbrella is complete, provide a copy of the minilesson principles (see resources.fountasandpinnell.com) for students to glue in the reader's notebook (in the Minilessons section if using *Reader's Notebook: Advanced* [Fountas and Pinnell 2011]), so they can refer to the information as needed.

Minilessons in This Umbrella

RML1 Study illustrators to learn about their craft.

RML2 Illustrators create art to show the mood.

RML3 Illustrators use perspective in their art to communicate an idea or a feeling.

RML4 Illustrators use symbols or color to reflect the theme of the book.

Before Teaching Umbrella 11 Minilessons

Read and discuss books with strong illustration support that engage students' intellectual curiosity and emotions. The minilessons in this umbrella use the following books from the *Fountas & Pinnell Classroom™ Interactive Read-Aloud Collection* text sets; however, you can use books that have strong illustration support and are based on the experiences and interests of the students in your class.

Author/Illustrator Study: S. D. Nelson

Digging a Hole to Heaven: Coal Miner Boys by S. D. Nelson

Black Elk's Vision: A Lakota Story by S. D. Nelson

Red Cloud: A Lakota Story of War and Surrender by S. D. Nelson

Crazy Horse's Vision by Joseph Bruchac

Illustration Study: Mood

Teacup by Rebecca Young

An Angel for Solomon Singer by Cynthia Rylant

Handling Emotions/Positive Relationships

A Stone for Sascha by Aaron Becker

Kindness and Compassion

Wings by Christopher Myers

Inspiration/Creativity

My Name Is Gabito: The Life of Gabriel García Márquez by Monica Brown

As you read aloud and enjoy these texts together, help students look closely at the illustrations so that they can understand and appreciate the many decisions an illustrator makes about how to support the text.

Author/Illustrator Study: S. D. Nelson

Illustration Study: Mood

Handling Emotions/Positive Relationships

Kindness and Compassion

Inspiration/Creativity

Section 2: Literary Analysis

RML1
LA.U11.RML1

Reading Minilesson Principle
Study illustrators to learn about their craft.

Studying Illustrators and Analyzing an Illustrator's Craft

Goal

Understand that an illustrator illustrates several books and that there are often recognizable characteristics across the books.

Rationale

By studying the characteristics of an illustrator's work, students begin to appreciate that illustrating books is a process of making decisions that involves meaning (of the text) and artistry. Students learn that illustrators have individual styles that they can learn to recognize, much as they recognize the style of individual authors. Note that this lesson format can be used to study an author, illustrator, or author/illustrator.

Assess Learning

Observe students when they talk about an illustrator's craft and notice if there is evidence of new learning based on the goal of this minilesson.

- Do students recognize similar characteristics among different books with the same illustrator?
- Do they understand the terms *illustrator, perspective, distance, angle, craft,* and *authentic*?

Minilesson

To help students think about the minilesson principle, use familiar books to engage them in a discussion of an illustrator's craft. Here is an example.

> Let's look closely at illustrations by S. D. Nelson and talk about them. What do you notice?

- As the conversation progresses, read the illustrator's note from *Crazy Horse's Vision* and then show several other books illustrated by S. D. Nelson, such as *Red Cloud*, *Digging a Hole to Heaven*, and *Black Elk's Vision*.

> Think about what you *always* notice in S. D. Nelson's illustrations and what you *often* notice in his illustrations.

- The following prompts can be used to support the discussion:
  - *How do the illustrations add to the meaning of the story?*
  - *How does the illustrator use color?*
  - *What does the perspective of the illustration help you to understand about the story or characters?*
  - *How do the illustrations make the characters and backgrounds seem real and authentic?*
- On chart paper, create a noticings chart. Label one column *Always* and the other column *Often*. Add student responses to the chart.

Have a Try

Invite the students to talk in groups about an illustrator.

▶ Provide each group with a book by S. D. Nelson.

Talk about what you notice about S. D. Nelson's illustrations. How do they help you understand more about the story?

▶ After time for discussion, ask students to share. Add to chart.

Summarize and Apply

Summarize the learning and remind students to think about an illustrator's craft.

Today you learned that when you read many books that are illustrated by the same person, you begin to notice decisions the illustrator makes. When an illustrator chooses an art style, that is part of the illustrator's craft.

When you read today, select a book illustrated by S. D. Nelson or by another illustrator you enjoy. As you read, think about the decisions the illustrator had to make. Mark any pages you want to remember with a sticky note. Bring the book when we meet so you can share.

Share

Following independent reading time, gather students in the meeting area to discuss an illustrator's work. If you have access to a projector, project the illustrations that students share.

Who would like to share what you noticed about an illustrator's craft? Share any illustrations that show what you are thinking.

Extend the Lesson (Optional)

After assessing students' understanding, you might decide to extend the learning.

▶ During interactive read-aloud, stop at an illustration. Ask students to talk about the decisions the illustrator had to make for that illustration (e.g., what exactly to show in the illustration, how to portray a character, what colors to use).

▶ Encourage students to draw in the style of S. D. Nelson. As they study his illustrations closely, they may make additional observations. Add them to the chart.

S. D. Nelson
Noticings:

Always	Often
• Authentic background details reflect the time period and place.	• Two-dimensional figures with indistinct facial expressions
• Background colors and shapes create sound and energy.	• Lines to show movement
• Clothing and outside/inside scenes reflect the time period.	• Color of the sky indicates day, night, or a dream.
• Illustration style suits the topic of each particular book.	• Texture/geometric shapes within the illustrations
	• Maps
	• Use of acrylic paints, ink, watercolors, colored pencils
	• Combination of illustrations and black and white photos

Section 2: Literary Analysis

Reading Minilesson Principle
Illustrators create art to show the mood.

Studying Illustrators and Analyzing an Illustrator's Craft

You Will Need

- several familiar fiction books that show clear examples of illustrations that support the mood of the story, such as the following:
  - *Teacup* by Rebecca Young and *An Angel for Solomon Singer* by Cynthia Rylant, from Text Set: Illustration Study: Mood
  - *My Name Is Gabito* by Monica Brown, from Text Set: Inspiration/Creativity
- chart paper and markers
- sticky notes
- document camera (optional)

Academic Language / Important Vocabulary

- illustrations
- physical space
- texture
- mood

Continuum Connection

- Notice and infer how illustrations contribute to mood in a fiction text (p. 83)

Goal

Understand that illustrators create and change the mood using different techniques.

Rationale

Illustrators use color, size, and physical space to create and change the mood of a story. When students notice these techniques, they can better understand the mood that the author and illustrator want to convey.

Assess Learning

Observe students when they talk about illustrations and notice if there is evidence of new learning based on the goal of this minilesson.

- ▶ Are students able to identify examples of an illustrator's use of color, size, and physical space to create or change the mood of a story?
- ▶ Do they use the terms *illustrations, physical space, texture,* and *mood*?

Minilesson

To help students think about the minilesson principle, provide an interactive lesson about the impact an illustrator has on mood. If you have access to a projector, project the illustrations. Here is an example.

- ▶ Ensure that your students understand what is meant by *mood*.

  Illustrators think very carefully about their artistic choices and how they support and expand upon the writing. The illustrator thinks about the mood of the text—how the author wants readers to feel. When an illustrator uses a certain color, shows objects in a certain size, or uses a technique to create a feeling, she creates a mood.

  Think about the illustrations on a few pages from *Teacup*.

- ▶ From *Teacup*, show and read pages 3–4 and discuss how the colors show a mood.

  How do you feel when you look at the illustration? That feeling is the mood of the illustration.

  How did the illustrator create that mood?

- ▶ Record students' responses about the illustrations and mood on chart paper.
- ▶ Show and read pages 5–6 and discuss the change in mood.

  What mood did the illustrator create here? How?

  Has the mood changed? What signals a change?

- ▶ As time allows, repeat this process with *An Angel for Solomon Singer*, showing and reading pages 7–8 and 19–20.

Have a Try

Invite the students to talk with a partner about how illustrators show mood.

▶ From *My Name Is Gabito*, show and read the three pages beginning with "Can you imagine?"

> Turn and talk about how these illustrations create or change the mood of the book.

Summarize and Apply

Summarize the learning and remind students to think about mood in illustrations when they read fiction stories.

> Look at the chart. What is one reason illustrators create art?

▶ Add the principle to the top of the chart.

> When you read today, notice illustrations that create or change the mood. Place a sticky note on those pages. Bring the book when we meet so you can share.

		Illustrators create art to show the mood.	
Title	**Mood**	**Description of the Illustration**
	• calm ⬇ • stormy • fierce	• white and pink water • dolphins • shades of blue getting darker
An Angel for Solomon Singer	• lack of clarity, loneliness ⬇ • feeling of belonging	• background and city unclear • background and city come into focus
gabito	• big ideas • endless opportunity	• rainbows of color

Share

Following independent reading time, gather students in small groups to talk about mood in illustrations.

> With your group, talk about any illustrations you found that created or changed the mood.

▶ After time for discussion, ask a few students to share. If you have access to a projector, project the illustrations that students share.

Extend the Lesson (Optional)

After assessing students' understanding, you might decide to extend the learning.

▶ Use the format of this minilesson to discuss a similar but different concept: tone (an author's attitude or feeling toward a subject). Use examples from familiar texts such as the following:

- *A Stone for Sascha* by Aaron Becker and *It Doesn't Have to Be This Way* by Luis J. Rodriguez, from Text Set: Handling Emotions/Positive Relationships
- *Teacup* by Rebecca Young, from Text Set: Illustration Study: Mood
- *The Red Bicycle* by Jude Isabella, from Text Set: Problem Solving/Giving Back

Reading Minilesson Principle

Illustrators use perspective in their art to communicate an idea or a feeling.

Studying Illustrators and Analyzing an Illustrator's Craft

You Will Need

- several familiar fiction books, such as the following:

  - *Teacup* by Rebecca Young and *An Angel for Solomon Singer* by Cynthia Rylant, from Text Set: Illustration Study: Mood

  - *Wings* by Christopher Myers, from Text Set: Kindness and Compassion

- chart paper and markers
- sticky notes
- document camera (optional)

Academic Language / Important Vocabulary

- perspective
- communicate
- zoom
- close-up
- distance

Continuum Connection

- Understand that there can be different interpretations of the meaning of an illustration (p. 83)

- Notice how illustrations and graphics go together with the text in a meaningful way (p. 83)

- Notice how illustrations and graphics help to communicate the writer's message (p. 87)

Goal

Understand that illustrators use perspective to communicate an idea or feeling.

Rationale

Helping students notice perspective in illustrations teaches them to consider what an illustrator might be bringing to their attention at that point in the story. Illustrators might zoom in on a central image or place an image in the distance to create a feeling of space. Illustrators make decisions about the position of images to evoke certain feelings in a reader.

Assess Learning

Observe students when they talk about perspective in illustrations and notice if there is evidence of new learning based on the goal of this minilesson.

- ▶ Are students able to identify when an illustrator uses perspective to communicate an idea or a feeling (e.g., illustrations that are zoomed in on, far away, or have distance between them)?

- ▶ Do they use language such as *perspective, communicate, zoom, close-up,* and *distance*?

Minilesson

To help students think about the minilesson principle, engage them in a discussion about perspective in illustrations. If you have access to a projector, you can project the illustrations. Here is an example.

- ▶ From *Teacup*, show pages 3–4, 5–6, 7–8, and 9–10.

  Notice how the illustrator made the boy and the boat small and the surroundings large. I wonder why he decided to illustrate the pages from that perspective? What do you think about that? Does it give you a certain feeling?

- ▶ On chart paper, record student responses in two columns, one for the illustration perspective example and one for the idea or feeling it supports.

- ▶ Show pages 13–14.

  What do you notice about this illustration from *Teacup*?

  Why did the illustrator choose this perspective?

- ▶ Record student responses on the chart.

- ▶ Repeat this process with *An Angel for Solomon Singer*, showing and reading pages 1–2, 3–4, 9–10, and 13–14.

  Why does the illustrator show the reflection of Solomon Singer in the tea kettle, the window, the puddle, and the spoon? What feeling do you get from looking at these illustrations?

Have a Try

Invite the students to talk in groups of three about perspective in illustrations.

▶ Show and read pages 15–16 and 31–32 from *Wings*.

Talk in your group about the feeling or idea that the illustrator creates. How does he do that?

▶ Prompt the conversation so students discuss perspective. After time for discussion, record student responses.

Summarize and Apply

Summarize the learning and remind students to think about perspective in illustrations when they read fiction stories.

Look back at the chart. What can you say about how illustrators use perspective?

▶ Add the principle to the top of the chart.

When you read today, notice if the illustrator uses perspective in the illustrations to communicate a feeling or idea. Mark any pages that you would like to share with a sticky note. Bring the book when we meet.

Share

Following independent reading time, gather students in the meeting area to discuss perspective in illustrations.

Did anyone notice an example of an illustrator's use of perspective to show a feeling or an idea? Share what you noticed.

▶ As a few volunteers share, you might choose to project the illustrations so students can see the details.

Extend the Lesson (Optional)

After assessing students' understanding, you might decide to extend the learning.

▶ Encourage students to think about how they could use perspective effectively to show a scene when they illustrate a story.

▶ **Writing About Reading** Encourage students to choose an illustration from a book and write in a reader's notebook about how the perspective influences the feeling or idea conveyed by the illustration.

Illustrators use perspective in their art to communicate an idea or a feeling.

Title	Perspective of the Illustration	Idea or Feeling
	Boat and boy are very small, and the sea and surroundings loom large.	• loneliness • isolation • overwhelmed
An Angel for Solomon Singer	Reflection of Solomon Singer in tea kettle, window, puddle, and spoon	• loneliness • solitude • reflection
WINGS	Kids are above Ikarus Jackson, who is at the bottom of the picture. Kids are above Ikarus Jackson, laughing.	• scared • embarrassed • overwhelmed by the crowd

Section 2: Literary Analysis

Illustrators use symbols or color to reflect the theme of the book.

Studying Illustrators and Analyzing an Illustrator's Craft

You Will Need

- several familiar fiction books, such as the following:
  - *Wings* by Christopher Myers, from Text Set: Kindness and Compassion
  - *A Stone for Sascha* by Aaron Becker, from Text Set: Handling Emotions/Positive Relationships
  - *Teacup* by Rebecca Young, from Text Set: Illustration Study: Mood
- chart paper and markers
- sticky notes
- document camera (optional)

Academic Language / Important Vocabulary

- symbols
- theme
- color
- reflect

Continuum Connection

- Interpret some illustrations with symbolic characteristics: e.g., use of color or symbols (p 83)

Goal

Understand that illustrators use symbols or color to reflect the theme of a book.

Rationale

Illustrators make deliberate choices about color and use of symbols to support and emphasize the theme of a story. Theme is the big idea of a story and can often be expressed in one or a few words (see Umbrella 8: Thinking About Themes and the Author's Message). When you teach students to notice these choices, they read more closely and find books more enjoyable.

Assess Learning

Observe students when they talk about an illustrator's use of color or symbols to reflect theme and notice if there is evidence of new learning based on the goal of this minilesson.

- ▶ Do students recognize an illustrator's use of symbols or color to reflect or highlight the theme of a book?
- ▶ Do they use the terms *symbols, theme, color,* and *reflect*?

Minilesson

To help students think about the minilesson principle, use familiar books to engage them in a discussion about how illustrators use symbols or color in illustrations. If you have access to a projector, project the illustrations. Here is an example.

- ▶ From *Wings*, show a few pages of Ikarus, the fly boy, with wings.

  What is the theme of *Wings*? Remember that the theme is the big idea that the book is really about. Sometimes a book has more than one theme.

  Why are the wings an important symbol in this book?

- ▶ On chart paper, record students' responses.

  Now think about the theme and the illustrations in another book, *A Stone for Sascha*.

- ▶ Show and read a few pages emphasizing the color yellow.

  What do you notice about the illustrator's use of color on these pages?

  How has Aaron Becker used color to help you understand the theme of this book?

Have a Try

Invite the students to talk with a partner about color and symbols in illustrations.

▶ Show the cover and the illustrations in *Teacup* showing the teacup and the dirt the boy takes care of on his journey.

  What is the theme of this book?

  How does the illustrator show the theme in the art? Do you think the symbols are a good representation of the theme? Turn and talk to a partner about that.

▶ After time for discussion, ask students to share. Record responses.

Summarize and Apply

Summarize the learning and remind students to think about how illustrators use color and symbols to reflect the theme of a book.

  How do illustrators reflect the theme of the book in their illustrations?

▶ Add the principle to the top of the chart.

  When you read today, choose a book with illustrations. Notice symbols or colors the illustrator uses to reflect the theme of the book. Place a sticky note on any pages you want to remember. Bring the book when we meet so you can share.

Share

Following independent reading time, gather students in small groups to talk about the relationship of the illustrations and the theme.

  Who would like to share a use of color or symbols you noticed in an illustration?

▶ Ask a few volunteers to share. You may want to project the illustrations to help students notice details.

Extend the Lesson (Optional)

After assessing students' understanding, you might decide to extend the learning.

▶ **Writing About Reading** Encourage students to use a reader's notebook to write about examples they find of illustrators using color or symbols to reflect theme.

Illustrators use symbols or color to reflect the theme of the book.

Book	Color or Symbol	Theme
WINGS	• Wings on Ikarus, the fly boy	• Kindness • Individuality
Stone Sasúa	• The color yellow is used throughout the book	• Importance of the past • Loyalty • Hope • Connection
	• Teacup • Dirt	• Importance of the past • The search for something new

Section 2: Literary Analysis

Assessment

After you have taught the minilessons in this umbrella, observe students as they talk and write about illustrations across instructional contexts: interactive read-aloud, independent reading, guided reading, shared reading, and book club. Use *The Literacy Continuum* (Fountas and Pinnell 2017) to guide the observation of students' reading and writing behaviors.

- ▶ What evidence do you have of new understandings related to studying illustrations?
  - Do students notice and discuss an illustrator's style after reading several books by that illustrator?
  - Do they notice how illustrators create or change mood?
  - Are they able to discuss how illustrators make decisions about using perspective, symbols, or color?
  - Do they use vocabulary such as *illustrations, perspective, details, symbols, meaning,* and *mood*?
- ▶ In what other ways, beyond the scope of this umbrella, are students demonstrating an understanding of illustrations?
  - Do students look at illustrations in expository texts to get more information about the topic?
  - Do they use other graphics and text features to gain knowledge?

Use your observations to determine the next umbrella you will teach. You may also consult Minilessons Across the Year (pp. 61–64) for guidance.

Link to Writing

After teaching the minilessons in this umbrella, help students link the new learning to their own writing:

- ▶ When students illustrate their own stories, encourage them to experiment with some of the illustration techniques they have learned about (e.g., create or change the mood, use perspective to communicate an idea or feeling, support a theme).

Reader's Notebook

When this umbrella is complete, provide a copy of the minilesson principles (see resources.fountasandpinnell.com) for students to glue in the reader's notebook (in the Minilessons section if using *Reader's Notebook: Advanced* [Fountas and Pinnell 2011]), so they can refer to the information as needed.

Minilessons in This Umbrella

RML1 Authors honor/thank people and give information about themselves in parts outside of the main text.

RML2 Authors/illustrators use a note or afterword to give important information.

RML3 Authors include prologues and epilogues to tell about something that happened before and after the main story.

RML4 Authors provide resources outside the main text to help you understand more about the story or topic.

RML5 The design (book jacket, cover, title page, endpapers) often adds to or enhances the meaning or appeal of the book.

Before Teaching Umbrella 12 Minilessons

The minilessons in this umbrella help students understand the peritext—the text resources outside the body of the text—and how those resources provide further information about the book and/or the author. Read and discuss engaging fiction and nonfiction books that have peritext resources (e.g., dedication, acknowledgments, author's note) from the following *Fountas & Pinnell Classroom™ Interactive Read-Aloud Collection, Independent Reading Collection,* and *Guided Reading Collection* or from your classroom library.

Interactive Read-Aloud Collection

Human Inventiveness

Marvelous Mattie: How Margaret E. Knight Became an Inventor by Emily Arnold McCully

Chef Roy Choi and the Street Food Remix by Jacqueline Briggs Martin and June Jo Lee

Take a Picture of Me, James VanDerZee! by Andrea J. Loney

Life on Earth

Living Fossils: Clues to the Past by Caroline Arnold

Grand Canyon by Jason Chin

Genre Study: Biography (Pioneers)

Tiny Stitches: The Life of Medical Pioneer Vivien Thomas by Gwendolyn Hooks

Independent Reading Collection

A Tangle of Knots by Lisa Graff

Wolf Hollow by Lauren Wolk

Guided Reading Collection

The Frozen Zoo by Tina Kafka

As you read aloud and enjoy these texts together, help students notice and discuss peritext resources.

Interactive Read-Aloud
Human Inventiveness

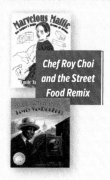

Life on Earth

Genre Study:
Biography (Pioneers)

Independent Reading

Guided Reading

Section 2: Literary Analysis

Reading Minilesson Principle
Authors honor/thank people and give information about themselves in parts outside of the main text.

Noticing Book and Print Features

You Will Need

- at least two familiar books that contain a dedication, acknowledgments, and/or author information, such as the following:
  - *Chef Roy Choi and the Street Food Remix* by Jacqueline Briggs Martin and June Jo Lee, from Text Set: Human Inventiveness
  - *Grand Canyon* by Jason Chin, from Text Set: Life on Earth
- chart paper and markers

Academic Language / Important Vocabulary

- author
- dedication
- acknowledgments
- author's page

Continuum Connection

- Notice and use and understand the purpose of some text resources outside the body (peritext): e.g., dedication, acknowledgments, author's note, illustrator's note, endpapers, foreword, prologue, pronunciation guide, footnote, epilogue, appendix, endnote, references (pp. 83, 87)

Goal

Notice, use, and understand the purpose of the dedication, acknowledgments, and author's page.

Rationale

When you teach students to notice and read peritext resources (e.g., dedication, acknowledgments, author's page), they understand that behind every book is a real person who was helped, inspired, and influenced by other people. Depending on the specific resource, they may gain insight into the author's creative process, who or what inspired the author to write the book, and/or who helped the author write the book.

Assess Learning

Observe students when they read and talk about books and notice if there is evidence of new learning based on the goal of this minilesson.

- Do students understand the purpose of peritext resources, such as the dedication, acknowledgments, and author's page?
- Do they use academic vocabulary, such as *author, dedication, acknowledgments,* and *author's page?*

Minilesson

To help students think about the minilesson principle, use familiar books to engage them in noticing and understanding the purpose of peritext resources. Here is an example.

- Show the cover of *Chef Roy Choi and the Street Food Remix.* Read the title and the authors' and illustrator's names. Turn to the copyright page and point to the dedications. Read them aloud.

  What is this part of the book called?

  Why do you think there are three dedications in this book? Who are J.B.M., J.J.L, and M.O.?

  What do you notice about the dedications? Why do you think they chose these people?

- Show the cover of *Grand Canyon* and read the title aloud. Then turn to the acknowledgments at the end of the book and read them aloud.

  What are acknowledgments?

  Whom does the author of this book thank and why?

- Read the dedications and acknowledgments in one or two other books. Ask students what they notice about them, and then ask them to describe what each is and why each was included in the book. Record responses on chart paper.

Have a Try

Invite the students to talk with a partner about the author information in *Grand Canyon*.

▶ Turn to the author information on the back flap of *Grand Canyon* and read it aloud.

> Turn and talk to your partner about this part of the book. What kind of information is given on the back flap?

▶ After time for discussion, ask a few students to share their thinking. Help students come up with a definition of and purpose for *author's page* and add it to the chart.

Summarize and Apply

Summarize the learning and remind students to read peritext resources.

> We looked at some parts of books that are outside the main body of the text. What did you notice about these parts?

▶ Write the principle at the top of the chart.

> When you read today, notice if your book has a dedication, acknowledgments, or an author's page. If so, be sure to read it. Be ready to share what you learned about the author when we come back together.

Share

Following independent reading time, gather students together in the meeting area to talk about their reading.

> Turn and talk to your partner about what you learned from the dedication, acknowledgments, or author's page in the book you read today.

Extend the Lesson (Optional)

After assessing students' understanding, you might decide to extend the learning.

▶ When students write their own books, encourage them to include a dedication, acknowledgments, and/or an author's page.

Authors honor/thank people and give information about themselves in parts outside of the main text.

	What	Why
Dedication	A message usually at the beginning of a book in which the author (and sometimes the illustrator) honors someone	To honor the person or people who inspired the author or whom the author has strong feelings for, like good friends or family members
Acknowledgments	A message thanking people for their help with the book	To thank people who helped the author (helped with research, provided photographs, or read the first draft)
Author's Page	A page or section that gives biographical information about the author	To give information about the author (where the author lives, hobbies, reason for writing the book)

Section 2: Literary Analysis

Reading Minilesson Principle
Authors/illustrators use a note or afterword to give important information.

Noticing Book and Print Features

You Will Need

- two or three familiar books that contain an author's and/or illustrator's note or an afterword, such as the following:
  - *Grand Canyon* by Jason Chin, from Text Set: Life on Earth
  - *Chef Roy Choi and the Street Food Remix* by Jacqueline Briggs Martin and June Jo Lee and *Take a Picture of Me, James VanDerZee!* by Andrea J. Loney, from Text Set: Human Inventiveness
- chart paper and markers

Academic Language / Important Vocabulary

- author's note
- illustrator's note
- afterword

Continuum Connection

- Notice and use and understand the purpose of some text resources outside the body (peritext): e.g., dedication, acknowledgments, author's note, illustrator's note, endpapers, foreword, prologue, pronunciation guide, footnote, epilogue, appendix, endnote, references (pp. 83, 87)

Goal

Notice and understand that authors and illustrators often give important information in the author's or illustrator's note.

Rationale

An author's or illustrator's note may reveal the inspiration for writing or illustrating a book or offer important contextual information. An afterword might give further information about the topic. When students read and think about the author's or illustrator's note or the afterword, they gain a fuller understanding of the book and of the process and purpose behind the creation of the book.

Assess Learning

Observe students when they read and talk about books and notice if there is evidence of new learning based on the goal of this minilesson.

- ▶ Do students understand the purpose of an author's/illustrator's note and an afterword?
- ▶ Do they use academic language, such as *author's note*, *illustrator's note*, and *afterword*?

Minilesson

To help students think about the minilesson principle, use familiar books to engage students in noticing and understanding the purpose of an author's/illustrator's note and an afterword. Here is an example.

- ▶ Show the cover of *Grand Canyon* and read the title.

  The author of this book wrote a special page at the end of the book that I'd like to share with you.

- ▶ Turn to "A Note from the Author" near the end of the book and read it aloud.

  What do you notice about the author's note? Why do you think he included it in his book?

- ▶ Record students' responses, generalizing them as necessary, on chart paper.

- ▶ Show the cover of *Chef Roy Choi and the Street Food Remix* and read the title. Then read parts of the authors' and the illustrator's notes.

  What did you learn from the authors' and illustrator's notes in this book?

- ▶ Record students' responses on the chart.

Have a Try

Invite the students to talk with a partner about the afterword in *Take a Picture of Me, James VanDerZee!*

▶ Show the cover of *Take a Picture of Me, James VanDerZee!* Turn to the afterword.

> At the end of this book there is a special section called an afterword. Why do you think it has that name?

▶ Read aloud the first paragraph or two of the afterword.

> Turn and talk to your partner about what you noticed about and learned from the afterword.

▶ After time for discussion, invite a few pairs to share their thinking. Record their responses on the chart.

Summarize and Apply

Summarize the learning and remind students to read author's or illustrator's notes and afterwords.

> An afterword is similar to an author's note. Sometimes it is written by the author, but usually it is written by someone other than the author.

> When you read today, notice if your book has an author's note, illustrator's note, or afterword. If so, be sure to read it. Be ready to share what you learned from it when we come back together.

Share

Following independent reading time, gather students together in the meeting area to talk about their reading.

> Who read an author's note, an illustrator's note, or an afterword today?

> What did you learn from it?

Extend the Lesson (Optional)

After assessing students' understanding, you might decide to extend the learning.

▶ Encourage students to include an author's note, illustrator's note, and/or afterword when they write and illustrate their own books.

Author's Note

Illustrator's Note

Afterword

- What inspired the author/illustrator to write/illustrate the book
- More information about the topic of the book
- What the author wants you to understand (author's message)
- Why the topic of the book is important
- How the author/illustrator wrote/illustrated the book

Section 2: Literary Analysis

Authors include prologues and epilogues to tell about something that happened before and after the main story.

Noticing Book and Print Features

You Will Need

- two or three familiar fiction books that have a prologue and/or an epilogue, such as the following:
  - *A Tangle of Knots* by Lisa Graff and *Wolf Hollow* by Lauren Wolk, from *Independent Reading Collection*
- chart paper prepared with two rows labeled *Prologue* and *Epilogue* and two columns labeled *Where* and *What*
- markers

Academic Language / Important Vocabulary

- fiction
- author
- prologue
- epilogue

Continuum Connection

- Notice and use and understand the purpose of some text resources outside the body (peritext): e.g., dedication, acknowledgments, author's note, illustrator's note, endpapers, foreword, prologue, pronunciation guide, footnote, epilogue, appendix, endnote, references (pp. 83, 87)

Goal

Notice and understand the purpose of a prologue and epilogue.

Rationale

When students read a prologue or an epilogue, they gain a fuller understanding of the characters and plot of a story. A prologue may set the context for the rest of the story. A prologue or an epilogue may also help show how the characters have changed or developed over a long period of time.

Assess Learning

Observe students when they read and talk about fiction books and notice if there is evidence of new learning based on the goal of this minilesson.

- ▶ Do students read prologues and epilogues?
- ▶ Can they explain the purpose of prologues and epilogues?
- ▶ Do they use academic vocabulary, such as *fiction*, *author*, *prologue*, and *epilogue*?

Minilesson

To help students think about the minilesson principle, use familiar fiction books to discuss prologues and epilogues. Here is an example.

> Where in a book would you find a prologue?

- ▶ If no one knows, show the prologue in *A Tangle of Knots*.
- ▶ Read the first few paragraphs of the prologue.

> What does the prologue in this book tell you?
>
> What is the purpose of a prologue?

- ▶ Record students' responses on chart paper.
- ▶ Then turn to page 223 and read the beginning of the epilogue.

> If a prologue is at the beginning of a book, where do you think you would find an epilogue?
>
> What happens in the epilogue of this book?
>
> What is the purpose of an epilogue?

- ▶ Add students' responses to the chart.

Have a Try

Invite the students to talk with a partner about the prologue in *Wolf Hollow*.

- Read the prologue on pages 1–2 of *Wolf Hollow* but do not display it or identify it as the prologue.

    Is what I just read a prologue or an epilogue? What makes you think that? Turn and talk to your partner about what you think.

- After time for discussion, invite a few students to share their thinking.

Summarize and Apply

Summarize the learning and remind students to read prologues and epilogues.

    Where do authors include prologues and epilogues? Why?

- Write the principle at the top of the chart.

    If you read a fiction book today, notice if your book has a prologue or an epilogue. If so, be sure to read it when you get to it. Be ready to share your thinking about the prologue or epilogue when we come back together.

Share

Following independent reading time, gather students together in the meeting area to talk about their reading.

    Who read a prologue or an epilogue today?

    How did the prologue or epilogue add to your understanding or enjoyment of the story?

Extend the Lesson (Optional)

After assessing students' understanding, you might decide to extend the learning.

- Explain that *prologue* comes from Greek words that mean "speech before" and *epilogue* comes from Greek words that mean "words attached." Often in nonfiction, the terms *foreword* and *afterword* are used instead.

- Encourage students to include a prologue and/or epilogue when they write their own stories.

- **Writing About Reading** Ask students to imagine what happened before or after a story they have read and write their own prologue or epilogue for it.

Authors include prologues and epilogues to tell about something that happened before and after the main story.

	Where	What
Prologue	Before the story	• May tell about something that happened before the main story • May introduce the story or give background information about it
Epilogue	After the story	• Tells about something that happened after the main story

Reading Minilesson Principle

Authors provide resources outside the main text to help you understand more about the story or topic.

You Will Need

- a few familiar books that contain footnotes, a glossary, an appendix, and/or a pronunciation guide, such as the following:
  - *Grand Canyon* by Jason Chin, from Text Set: Life on Earth
  - *The Frozen Zoo* by Tina Kafka, from *Guided Reading Collection*
  - *Tiny Stitches* by Gwendolyn Hooks, from Text Set: Genre Study: Biography (Pioneers)
- chart paper and markers
- four sticky notes prepared with labels: *Appendix, Footnotes¹, Glossary, Pronunciation Guide*
- document camera (optional)

Academic Language / Important Vocabulary

- footnotes
- appendix
- glossary
- pronunciation guide

Continuum Connection

- Notice and use and understand the purpose of some other text resources: e.g., glossary (pp. 83, 87)
- Notice and use and understand the purpose of some text resources outside the body (peritext): e.g., dedication, acknowledgments, author's note, illustrator's note, endpapers, foreword, prologue, pronunciation guide, footnote, epilogue, appendix, endnote, references (pp. 83, 87)

Goal

Notice, use, and understand the purpose of text resources.

Rationale

When students notice and read footnotes and appendixes, they learn more about the topic of the book. When they know how to use a glossary and pronunciation guide, they are better equipped to determine the meaning and pronunciation of unfamiliar words while reading independently.

Assess Learning

Observe students when they read and talk about books and notice if there is evidence of new learning based on the goal of this minilesson.

- ▶ Are students able to use and explain the purpose of text resources?
- ▶ Do they use academic vocabulary, such as *footnotes, glossary, appendix,* and *pronunciation guide*?

Minilesson

To help students think about the minilesson principle, use familiar books to discuss how to use footnotes, a glossary, an appendix, and a pronunciation guide. Here is an example.

- ▶ Turn to the appendix (the white pages) at the back of *Grand Canyon*. Point to and read several of the headings and the paragraph underneath the first heading.

  What do you notice about this section of the book?

  What is the purpose of this part of the book?

- ▶ Record students' responses on chart paper.

  A section like this at the end of a nonfiction book is called an appendix.

- ▶ Add the *Appendix* sticky note to the chart.

- ▶ Display page 2 of *The Frozen Zoo*. Point to and read aloud the sentence in the second paragraph that begins with "Poaching, pollution, habitat destruction, and climate change."

  What do you notice at the end of this sentence?

  Why do you think there's a small number 1 here? What does this mean?

- ▶ Point to the footnote and read it aloud.

  This small text at the bottom of the page is called a footnote. Why do you think it's called that?

  What is the purpose of this footnote?

▶ Record students' responses on chart paper. Add the *Footnotes*[1] sticky note to the chart.

> Sometimes authors use footnotes to tell where they found a piece of information, to give more information about something in the body of the text, or to define difficult words.

Have a Try

Invite the students to talk with a partner about the glossary and pronunciation guide in *Tiny Stitches*.

▶ Turn to the Glossary of Medical Terms in *Tiny Stitches*. Read the heading and the first few entries.

> This page combines a glossary and a pronunciation guide. Turn and talk to your partner about the information provided on this page.

▶ After students turn and talk, invite a few pairs to share their thinking. Record their responses on the chart and add the remaining sticky notes.

Authors provide resources outside the main text to help you understand more about the story or topic.

Appendix Facts about . . .	• A section at the end of a nonfiction book • Gives additional information
Footnotes [1] [1] This is what a footnote looks like.	• May give additional information or define difficult words • May tell where the author found a piece of information • Are numbered
Glossary **atrium** – one of the two collecting chambers that transfer blood to the ventricles	• Gives the definition of important or difficult words in the book
Pronunciation Guide (EH-tree-uhm)	• Tells how to pronounce challenging words

Summarize and Apply

Summarize the learning and remind students to use text resources.

▶ Write the principle at the top of the chart.

> When you read today, notice if your book has an appendix, footnotes, a glossary, or a pronunciation guide. Bring your book to share when we come back together.

Share

Following independent reading time, gather students together in the meeting area to talk about text resources.

> Who read a book that has an appendix, footnotes, a glossary, or a pronunciation guide?

> How did it help you understand more about the story or topic?

Extend the Lesson (Optional)

After assessing students' understanding, you might decide to extend the learning.

▶ If students notice other resources in nonfiction books (e.g., table of contents, index, or sidebars), teach minilessons in Umbrella 20: Using Text Features to Gain Information.

▶ **Writing About Reading** Have students create a glossary and/or pronunciation guide for a book that does not already have one.

Reading Minilesson Principle
The design (book jacket, cover, title page, endpapers) often adds to or enhances the meaning or appeal of the book.

You Will Need

▶ a few familiar books that have a book jacket, cover, title page, and/or endpapers, such as the following:

- *Marvelous Mattie* by Emily Arnold McCully, from Text Set: Human Inventiveness

- *Grand Canyon* by Jason Chin, from Text Set: Life on Earth

▶ chart paper and markers

Academic Language / Important Vocabulary

▶ design

▶ book jacket

▶ cover

▶ title page

▶ endpapers

Continuum Connection

▶ Notice and understand other features of the peritext that have symbolic or cultural significance or add to aesthetic enjoyment (p. 83)

▶ Notice and understand other features of the peritext that have symbolic value, add to aesthetic enjoyment, or add meaning (p. 87)

▶ Appreciate artistry in text design: e.g., book jacket, cover, end pages, title page (peritext) (pp. 83, 87)

Goal

Understand and appreciate that the design of the peritext often adds to the meaning or appeal of the text and sometimes has cultural or symbolic significance.

Rationale

The book jacket, cover, title pages, and endpapers are part of the art of the book and add to or enhance its meaning. When you encourage students to notice the design of these features and to think about how they relate to the meaning of the book, they develop an appreciation for the thought and care that went into creating the book.

Assess Learning

Observe students when they read and talk about books and notice if there is evidence of new learning based on the goal of this minilesson.

▶ Can students explain how the design of the book jacket, cover, title pages, and/or endpapers adds to or enhances the meaning of a book?

▶ Do they use academic language, such as *design*, *book jacket*, *cover*, *title page*, and *endpapers*?

Minilesson

To help students think about the minilesson principle, use familiar books to talk about the design of the peritext. Here is an example.

▶ Show the cover of *Marvelous Mattie* and read the title and subtitle.

What do you see in the illustration on the front cover?

What does the cover illustration help you understand about Margaret Knight?

▶ Record students' responses on chart paper. Then turn to the title page.

What does the illustration on the title page show?

What does this help you understand about Margaret Knight?

▶ Record responses on the chart.

▶ Show the cover of *Grand Canyon* and read the title. Then display the front and back flaps.

What do you notice about the design of the book jacket?

How does this design relate to the meaning of the book?

▶ Record responses.

Have a Try

Invite the students to talk with a partner about the endpapers in *Grand Canyon*.

▶ Turn to the endpapers in *Grand Canyon*.

How does the design of the endpapers add to the meaning of the book? Turn and talk to your partner about what you think.

▶ After students turn and talk, invite a few pairs to share their thinking. Record their responses on the chart.

Summarize and Apply

Summarize the learning and remind students to notice the design of the peritext when they read.

What does the chart show about the design of some of the book parts?

▶ Write the principle at the top of the chart.

When you read today, look at the design of parts of your book outside the main text, such as the cover and title page. If you are reading a hardcover book, look to see if there are endpapers or a book jacket. Think about how their design adds to the meaning of your book. Bring your book to share when we come back together.

The design (book jacket, cover, title page, endpapers) often adds to or enhances the meaning or appeal of the book.

	Book Part	The Design	Why Important
Marvelous Mattie	Front cover	• Shows some of Margaret Knight's sketches	• The subject started her career by sketching her ideas for inventions as a young girl.
	Title page	• Shows the subject, as a young girl, making one of her inventions.	• The subject started making her own inventions when she was still a child.
GRAND CANYON	Book jacket	• Illustrations of animals	• Shows some animals that live in the Grand Canyon
	Endpapers	• Cross section of the Grand Canyon	• Helps you understand that the Grand Canyon is made up of many different layers and sections

Share

Following independent reading time, gather students together in the meeting area to share what they noticed about the design of the peritext in their book.

Turn and talk to your partner about how the design of the book jacket, cover, title page, or endpapers adds to or relates to the meaning of your book.

Extend the Lesson (Optional)

After assessing students' understanding, you might decide to extend the learning.

▶ You may want to teach a lesson on asking students to evaluate the layout and design of a book. Use prompts such as these: *Is the book easy to follow? Does the design add to the meaning and appeal of the book?*

Assessment

After you have taught the minilessons in this umbrella, observe students as they talk and write about their reading across instructional contexts: interactive read-aloud, independent reading, guided reading, shared reading, and book club. Use *The Literacy Continuum* (Fountas and Pinnell 2017) to observe students' reading and writing behaviors.

▶ What evidence do you have of new understandings related to book and print features?

  • Do students read and understand the purpose of peritext resources (dedication, acknowledgments, author's/illustrator's note, afterword, prologue, epilogue, footnotes, glossary)?

  • Do they notice the design of the book jacket, the cover, the title page, and/or the endpapers? Can they explain how they add to the meaning of the book?

  • Do they use academic language related to text resources, such as *dedication, acknowledgments, author's note,* and *glossary*?

▶ In what other ways, beyond the scope of this umbrella, are students talking about books?

  • Are students noticing and using text features, such as headings, sidebars, and indexes?

  • Are they noticing the different ways nonfiction books are organized?

Use your observations to determine the next umbrella you will teach. You may also consult Minilessons Across the Year (pp. 61–64) for guidance.

Link to Writing

After teaching the minilessons in this umbrella, help students link the new learning to their own writing:

▶ Encourage students to create text resources when they write their own books.

Reader's Notebook

When this umbrella is complete, provide a copy of the minilesson principles (see resources.fountasandpinnell.com) for students to glue in the reader's notebook (in the Minilessons section if using *Reader's Notebook: Advanced* [Fountas and Pinnell 2011]), so they can refer to the information as needed.

Minilessons in This Umbrella

RML1 Memoirists tell a brief, often intense, memory of a time, place, person, or event in their lives.

RML2 Memoirists often write a series of vignettes to tell their story.

RML3 Memoirists choose to tell about a memory that is important to them and also shows something significant to others.

Before Teaching Umbrella 13 Minilessons

Before teaching the minilessons in this umbrella, students should be familiar with memoir as a genre, be able to recognize texts as memoir, and be able to name some characteristics of the genre.

Choose texts that focus on an important time, place, person, or event and have a reflective element in which the writer learns something about himself and the reader learns a larger message. Use the following books from the *Fountas & Pinnell Classroom™ Interactive Read-Aloud Collection* text sets or use memoirs that you have on hand.

Memoir/Autobiography

Under the Royal Palms: A Childhood in Cuba by Alma Flor Ada

Where Fireflies Dance by Lucha Corpi

Drawing from Memory by Allen Say

As you read aloud and enjoy these texts together, help students

- discuss how the time, place, person, or event shared is a memory of something that occurred in the writer's life,

- notice the use of vignettes, and

- recognize the larger message.

RML1

LA.U13.RML1

Reading Minilesson Principle
Memoirists tell a brief, often intense, memory of a time, place, person, or event in their lives.

Understanding Memoir

You Will Need

- familiar memoirs, such as the following from Text Set: Memoir/Autobiography:
  - *Under the Royal Palms* by Alma Flor Ada
  - *Where Fireflies Dance* by Lucha Corpi
  - *Drawing from Memory* by Allen Say
- chart paper and makers
- basket of memoirs

Academic Language / Important Vocabulary

- memoir
- perspective
- vignettes
- reflection

Continuum Connection

- Understand memoir or personal narrative as a brief, often intense, memory of or reflection on a person, time or event (p. 299)
- Understand that a memoir is an account of a memory or set of memories written by the person who experienced it (p. 84)

Goal

Understand that a memoir is an account of a memory or set of memories written by the person who experienced it.

Rationale

When students think about the personal memories of a time, place, person, or event that authors choose to write about in their memoirs, they consider the choices authors make and develop a deeper understanding of the genre.

Assess Learning

Observe students when they read and discuss memoirs. Notice if there is evidence of new learning based on the goal of this minilesson.

- ▶ Do students understand that a memoir is an account of a memory written by the person who experienced it?
- ▶ Can they talk about why the author may have chosen to write about that memory?
- ▶ Do they use the terms *memoir, perspective, vignettes,* and *reflection* when talking about memoir?

Minilesson

To help students think about the minilesson principle, engage them in a discussion of memoir using familiar texts. Here is an example.

- ▶ Show the covers of *Under the Royal Palms* and *Where Fireflies Dance.* Invite students to turn and discuss the books.

  Think about the stories each writer shares in these memoirs.

  What do you think inspired each memoir? How do you know?

  What types of things inspire writers to write memoirs?

- ▶ After time for discussion, invite a few students to share. Record the broad categories on the chart and some examples from the memoirs.

  Do memoirists write about just any memories? What is it about the memories that inspires writing about them?

- ▶ Guide students to understand that memoirists write about the times, places, people, and events that were intense or memorable and, therefore, stand out in their minds.

Have a Try

Invite the students to talk with a partner about *Drawing from Memory*.

> Turn and talk to a partner about what you think inspired Allen Say to write *Drawing from Memory*.

▶ After time for discussion, ask a few students to share.

Summarize and Apply

Summarize the learning and remind students to think about what inspires writers to write their memoirs.

> What does the chart show about what writers tell in their memoirs?

▶ Review the chart and write the principle at the top.

> When you read today, you can choose a memoir from this basket. If you do, think about the particular time, place, person, or event that inspired the writer to tell their story. Why do you think the author chose to write about that? Bring the book when we meet so you can share.

Memoirists tell a brief, often intense, memory of a time, place, person, or event in their lives.

Time
- Post-war Cuba
- Childhood
- Post-war Japan

Place
- Small town in Cuba
- Small town in Mexico
- Tokyo

Memoir

Person
- Ballet teacher
- Parent
- Other family member
- Sensei/art teacher

Important Events
- Sneaking into a haunted house
- Loss of a family member
- Working as an apprentice cartoonist

Share

Following independent reading time, gather students in the meeting area to talk about memoirs.

> Who read a memoir today? What part of the writer's life was it about?

> Did anyone read a biography or autobiography? How is it the same as or different from a memoir?

Extend the Lesson (Optional)

After assessing students' understanding, you might decide to extend the learning.

▶ Discuss with students the similarities and differences between memoir and autobiography. Help them notice that both are biographical texts in which the story of a real person's life is written and narrated by that person. An autobiography is usually told in chronological sequence (but may be in another order). In memoir, the writer takes a reflective stance in looking back on a particular memory in a briefer, more intense way. Memoir is usually written in the first person.

▶ **Writing About Reading** Encourage students to create lists in a reader's notebook of important people, places, or events that might inspire them to write their own memoir. Have them include details of the memory that most interests them.

Reading Minilesson Principle

Memoirists often write a series of vignettes to tell their story.

Goal

Notice and understand that memoirs are often composed of a series of vignettes.

Rationale

When students think about a writer's decision to tell their story in vignettes, they begin to notice how individual stories weave together to tell a larger story and impart a message.

Assess Learning

Observe students when they discuss memoir. Notice if there is evidence of new learning based on the goal of this minilesson.

▸ Do students discuss a writer's choice to tell their story in vignettes?

▸ Are they able to connect vignettes to the larger story and message of a memoir?

▸ Can they use the language *vignettes* and *reflection*?

Minilesson

To help students think about the minilesson principle, engage them in noticing how a familiar memoir is written in vignettes and what the impact of that choice on the larger story is. Here is an example.

▸ Review the structure of *Under the Royal Palms* by showing the table of contents and reading a few sentences from the beginnings of two or three chapters.

> What do you notice about the chapters in *Under the Royal Palms*?

> Instead of writing events in order, one after the other, she wrote a series of vignettes—short, intense accounts within a larger story. Each chapter is like a little story from Alma Flor Ada's life.

> Turn and talk to a partner. What are some of the vignettes about?

▸ After they turn and talk, ask a few students to share. Chart responses.

> Turn and talk to your partner again. Not all authors use vignettes. It is the author's choice to use them. Why do authors choose to use vignettes in their writing?

▸ After they turn and talk, ask a few students to share. Record responses on the chart.

Have a Try

Invite the students to talk with a partner about memoirs.

> As needed, review *Where Fireflies Dance*.

> Turn and talk to a partner about how the structures of *Where Fireflies Dance* and *Under the Royal Palms* are different.

> Students should note that *Where Fireflies Dance* is told in chronological order and *Under the Royal Palms* is told in a series of vignettes.

Summarize and Apply

Summarize the learning and remind students to notice when a writer uses vignettes to write a memoir.

> What did you learn today?

> Review the chart and write the minilesson principle at the top.

> You can choose a memoir from the basket to read today. If you do, think about how the writer is telling the story. What do you learn about the writer? Are there any vignettes?

Share

Following independent reading time, gather students together in the meeting area to talk about memoirs.

> Did anyone read a memoir today that used vignettes? Were the stories connected to tell a larger story or message? What did you learn about the writer?

Extend the Lesson (Optional)

After assessing students' understanding, you might decide to extend the learning.

> Encourage students to think about and discuss how a memoir compares to another text written by or about the same person.

> **Writing About Reading** Encourage students to write in a reader's notebook about a writer's choice of using vignettes. What do they think about that choice? Why?

Memoirists often write a series of vignettes to tell their story.

	Vignettes from the Memoir	Why Authors Use Vignettes
UNDER THE ROYAL PALMS	• Counting bats • Uncle's devastating and tragic death • Getting lost in a dense field of flowers • Friendship with ballet teacher	• Share a memory that taught an important life lesson • Give the opportunity to reflect deeply on past events • Describe an important person in their life • Allow writer to be more descriptive • Highlight a unique part of a writer's life • Tell about an important place

Section 2: Literary Analysis

Reading Minilesson Principle

Memoirists choose to tell about a memory that is important to them and also shows something significant to others.

Understanding Memoir

You Will Need

- familiar memoirs that teach a larger message, such as the following from Text Set: Memoir/Autobiography:
  - *Where Fireflies Dance* by Lucha Corpi
  - *Drawing from Memory* by Allen Say
  - *Under the Royal Palms* by Alma Flor Ada
- chart paper and markers

Academic Language / Important Vocabulary

- reflection
- message
- insight

Continuum Connection

- Understand that a memoir has significance in the writer's life and usually shows something significant to others [p. 299]

Goal

Understand that memoirists usually have a larger message that they are communicating through their stories.

Rationale

When students notice a writer's larger message in a memoir, they gain a deeper understanding of the writer, the significance of the story, and life in general.

Assess Learning

Observe students when they read and discuss memoirs. Notice if there is evidence of new learning based on the goal of this minilesson.

- Can students recognize a writer's personal insight about an event, time, or person they have written about?
- Do they discuss the larger message or reflection of a memoir in whole- or small-group discussion?
- Do they use the terms *reflection, message,* or *insight* in conversation or in writing?

Minilesson

To help students think about the minilesson principle, engage them in a discussion of the larger meaning of familiar memoirs. Here is an example.

> When a writer chooses to write a memoir, she often does so because she has reflected on a moment in her life and realizes that she learned something about herself in that moment that she wants to share. This is called insight.

- Hold up *Where Fireflies Dance.*

  > Turn and talk to a partner. What did Lucha Corpi learn about herself in this book?

- Record responses on a chart.

  > What can you learn from Lucha Corpi? What do you think she wants you to know?

- Add responses to the chart.

  > Lucha Corpi thought that her memory was important not only to her but also important enough to share with others.

- Repeat this process with *Drawing from Memory* by Allen Say.

Have a Try

Invite the students to talk with a partner about a familiar memoir.

▷ Show the cover of *Under the Royal Palms*.

Turn and talk to your partner. What did Alma Flor Ada learn about herself in this memoir? What is a larger message she wants to share?

▷ After students turn and talk, ask a few pairs to share their thinking.

Summarize and Apply

Summarize the learning and remind students to think about the larger message of a memoir.

How do writers choose the memories to tell about in their memoirs?

▷ Review the chart and write the principle at the top.

If you read a memoir today, think about what the writer learned about himself and what you can learn from the writer's memory.

Share

Following independent reading time, gather students together to talk about memoirs.

If you read a memoir today, what do you think is significant about the memory the writer shares?

▷ Ask a few students to share.

Extend the Lesson (Optional)

After assessing students' understanding, you might decide to extend the learning.

▷ Take time during interactive read aloud to talk about the larger message of the story. As students talk and write about memoirs they are reading, encourage them to write about larger messages and what the writer learned.

▷ **Writing About Reading** As students demonstrate they can talk about the larger message in a memoir, you may suggest they fill in a graphic organizer similar to the chart in this lesson with information from the memoirs they have read (visit resources.fountasandpinnell.com).

Memoirists choose to tell about a memory that is important to them and also shows something significant to others.		
Title	**What the Writer Learned**	**Larger Message of the Memoir**
Where Fireflies Dance	Writing stories is what she was born to do.	There's nothing more important than fulfilling your destiny.
Drawing from Memory	Sensei shaped him as an artist and a person.	Seek out people who believe in you and your dreams.
Under the Royal Palms	Growing up in Cuba shaped her into the person she is today.	True wealth is not from material things. It's the journey that matters, not the finish line.

Assessment

After you have taught the minilessons in this umbrella, observe students as they talk and write about their reading across instructional contexts: interactive read-aloud, independent reading, guided reading, shared reading, and book club. Use *The Literacy Continuum* (Fountas and Pinnell 2017) to guide the observation of students' reading and writing behaviors across instructional contexts.

▶ What evidence do you have of new understandings related to the understanding of memoir?

- Can they identify why the event, time, place, or person is important to the writer?
- Do they notice the use of vignettes?
- Can they understand and articulate the larger message?
- Do they use language such as *memoir, perspective, reflection, message, vignettes,* and *insight*?

▶ In what other ways, beyond the scope of this umbrella, are students talking about memoir?

- Are students writing about memoir?
- Have students expressed an interest in reading other kinds of books that tell a person's story, such as autobiography, biography, or historical fiction?
- Do they show interest in the writer's craft?

Use your observations to determine the next umbrella you will teach. You may also consult Minilessons Across the Year (pp. 61–64) for guidance.

Link to Writing

After teaching the minilessons in this umbrella, help students link the new learning to their own writing:

▶ When students write a memoir, remind them to write about an event, time, or place that is important to them as the writer and that also shows something significant to others. They may consider using vignettes to tell their story.

Reader's Notebook

When this umbrella is complete, provide a copy of the minilesson principles (see resources.fountasandpinnell.com) for students to glue in the reader's notebook (in the Minilessons section if using *Reader's Notebook: Advanced* [Fountas and Pinnell 2011]), so they can refer to the information as needed.

Minilessons in This Umbrella

RML1 Biographies are alike in many ways.

RML2 The definition of biography is what is always true about it.

RML3 Biographers choose their subjects for a variety of reasons.

RML4 Biographers include details about the societal, cultural, and personal influences on a subject's life.

RML5 Biographers choose to include facts that reveal something important about the subject's personality traits and motivations.

RML6 Sometimes biographers include imagined scenes but base them on facts.

RML7 Think about the author's stance toward the subject of the biography.

RML8 Think about how the subject's accomplishments have influenced life today.

Genre Study: Biography (Pioneers)

Before Teaching Umbrella 14 Minilessons

During a genre study (pp. 39–42), students learn what to expect when reading in the genre, expand comprehension skills, notice distinguishing characteristics, and develop tools to navigate a variety of texts. Select books that are clear examples of biography, such as the following books from the *Fountas & Pinnell Classroom™ Interactive Read-Aloud Collection.*

Genre Study: Biography (Pioneers)

Talkin' About Bessie: The Story of Aviator Elizabeth Coleman by Nikki Grimes

When the Beat Was Born: DJ Kool Herc and the Creation of Hip Hop by Laban Carrick Hill

Schomburg: The Man Who Built a Library by Carole Boston Weatherford

Life in the Ocean: The Story of Oceanographer Sylvia Earle by Claire A. Nivola

Tiny Stitches: The Life of Medical Pioneer Vivien Thomas by Gwendolyn Hooks

Activists/Change Makers

Ballots for Belva: The True Story of a Woman's Race for the Presidency by Sudipta Bardhan-Quallen

Gordon Parks: How the Photographer Captured Black and White America by Carole Boston Weatherford

On Our Way to Oyster Bay: Mother Jones and Her March for Children's Rights by Monica Kulling

Walking in the City with Jane: A Story of Jane Jacobs by Susan Hughes

Activists/Change Makers

As you read aloud and enjoy these texts together, help students notice things that are *always* and *often* true about biographies.

Section 2: Literary Analysis

Studying Biography

You Will Need

- a variety of familiar biographies, such as those in Text Set: Genre Study: Biography (Pioneers)
- chart paper and markers
- basket of biographies

Academic Language / Important Vocabulary

- biography
- genre
- characteristics
- subject

Continuum Connection

- Notice and understand the characteristics of some specific nonfiction genres: e.g., expository, narrative, procedural and persuasive texts, biography, autobiography, memoir, hybrid texts (p. 84)

Goal

Notice and understand the characteristics of biography as a genre.

Rationale

When you teach students the characteristics of biographies, they will know what to expect when reading a story written by one person about another person's life.

Assess Learning

Observe students when they talk about biographies and notice if there is evidence of new learning based on the goal of this minilesson.

- ▶ Do students talk about the characteristics of biographies?
- ▶ Do they realize that characteristics either *always* or *often* occur in biographies?
- ▶ Are they using the terms *biography, genre, characteristics,* and *subject*?

Minilesson

To help students think about the minilesson principle, guide them to recognize the characteristics of biographies. Here is an example.

- ▶ Show the covers of multiple familiar biographies.

  In what ways are all these books alike?

- ▶ Record responses. For each suggestion, prompt the students to think about whether the similarities occur *always* or *often* in the books. Create separate columns on the chart for each category.

- ▶ Select a few of the biographies to discuss in greater detail by revisiting a few pages of text and illustrations.

  What else do you notice?

  Where should we add that information to the chart?

- ▶ Continue recording responses. The following prompts may be used as needed:
  - *What do you notice about the subject's accomplishments?*
  - *What types of things does the author focus on?*
  - *Why do you think the author chose this person to write about?*
  - *What do you think the author's attitude or feeling toward the subject is?*

Have a Try

Invite the students to talk with group about the characteristics of the books.

▶ Provide each group with a biography.

> As you look through this book with your group, think about the things on the chart and see how many can be found in the book. Look for anything new to add to the chart.

▶ After time for discussion, ask if students found anything new that can be added to the chart.

Summarize and Apply

Summarize the learning by explaining that all the books they discussed are biographies. Remind them to think about what *always* or *often* occurs in biographies when they read one.

▶ Review the chart.

> Today choose a biography from the basket unless you are already reading one from the library. As you read, look at the chart to see which items from the chart you can find in the biography you are reading. Bring the book when we meet so you can share.

Share

Following independent reading time, gather students in the meeting area to talk about biographies.

> What did you notice about the biography you read or started to read today?

Extend the Lesson (Optional)

After assessing students' understanding, you might decide to extend the learning.

▶ Have students record the titles of biographies they read on the Reading List page of a reader's notebook (see WAR.U1.RML2).

▶ Teach a minilesson similar to this one to study autobiographies.

▶ Introduce students to the Genre Thinkmark for biography (to download this resource, see resources.fountasandpinnell.com). A Genre Thinkmark is a tool that guides students to notice certain characteristics of a genre in their reading. They can quickly note page numbers so they can share the information with classmates.

Biography

Noticings:

Always	Often
• The author tells about a person's accomplishments and challenges.	• The author tells about a person's life in the order it happened.
• The author chooses facts to include about the person's life.	• The author includes some imagined scenes and made-up dialogue but bases them on facts.
• The author tells about the important things a person did or why the person is interesting.	• The author includes quotes by the person.
• The author gives an important message.	• The author includes additional information at the beginning or end of the book (like a timeline).
• The author includes the setting and the people who influenced the person's life.	• The author includes photographs and illustrations.
	• Biographies are told like a story.

Section 2: Literary Analysis

Reading Minilesson Principle
The definition of biography is what is always true about it.

Studying Biography

You Will Need

- several familiar biographies, such as the following from Text Set: Genre Study: Biography (Pioneers):
  - *Life in the Ocean* by Claire A. Nivola
  - *When the Beat Was Born* by Laban Carrick Hill
- biography noticings chart from RML1
- chart paper and markers
- basket of biographies

Academic Language / Important Vocabulary

- biography
- definition
- subject

Continuum Connection

- Understand that a biography is the story of a person's life written by someone else (p. 84)

Goal

Construct a working definition for biography.

Rationale

When you teach students to construct a working definition of biography, they need to analyze examples of the genre and summarize the characteristics. Then they will know what to expect when they read in the genre. They will be able to revise and expand their understandings as they have new experiences with biographies.

Assess Learning

Observe students when they discuss biographies and notice if there is evidence of new learning based on the goal of this minilesson.

- ▶ Do students cooperate to create a working definition of a biography?
- ▶ Are they talking about the definition of a biography and able to tell what is true of all biographies?
- ▶ Do they use the terms *biography, definition,* and *subject*?

Minilesson

To help students think about the minilesson principle, help them construct a working definition of biography. Here is an example.

- ▶ Discuss the characteristics of biography by revisiting the biography noticings chart.

  What do you know about biographies?

  The definition of biography tells what is *always* true about books in this genre.

- ▶ On chart paper, write the words *A biography is,* leaving space for constructing a working definition.

  How could this sentence be finished in a way that describes all biographies? Think about the noticings chart. Turn and talk about that.

- ▶ After time for discussion, ask students to share. Use the ideas to construct a working definition and add it to the chart.

- ▶ Show the cover of *Life in the Ocean* and show a few pages.

  Think about *Life in the Ocean*. Does it fit the definition of a biography?

  Give an example of what makes it a biography.

- ▶ As students share, ask for text examples to show that it fits the definition.

  As you learn more about the genre of biography, you can revise the definition.

Have a Try

Invite the students to talk with a partner about the definition of biography.

▶ Show the cover of *When the Beat Was Born* and revisit a few pages.

Turn and talk about whether *When the Beat Was Born* fits the definition of biography.

▶ Ask a few volunteers to share their thinking. Have them point out examples from the book to show that it fits the definition.

Summarize and Apply

Summarize the learning and remind students to think about what is always true about biographies.

Today we created a definition of biography.

Choose a biography from the basket to read, unless you are already reading one from the library. Think about whether it fits the definition. Bring the book when we meet so you can share.

Share

Following independent reading time, gather students in pairs to talk about their reading.

With a partner, explain how the book fits the definition of biography.

Extend the Lesson (Optional)

After assessing students' understanding, you might decide to extend the learning.

▶ Have students do research to evaluate the accuracy and quality of the biographies they read.

Biography

A biography is a story about a person written by someone else.

RML3
LA.U14.RML3

Reading Minilesson Principle
Biographers choose their subjects for a variety of reasons.

Studying Biography

You Will Need

▸ several familiar biographies, such as the following:

  • *Ballots for Belva* by Sudipta Bardhan-Quallen and *Gordon Parks* by Carole Boston Weatherford, from Text Set: Activists/Change Makers

  • *Talkin' About Bessie* by Nikki Grimes, from Text Set: Genre Study: Biography (Pioneers)

▸ chart paper and markers

▸ basket of biographies

Academic Language / Important Vocabulary

▸ biography

▸ subject

▸ accomplished

▸ obstacles

▸ message

Continuum Connection

▸ Infer the importance of a subject's accomplishments (biography) (p. 84)

▸ Infer the purpose of a writer of a biography, autobiography, or memoir (pp. 590, 602)

▸ Talk about why the subject of a biography is important or sets an example for others (pp. 593, 605)

Goal

Understand that biographers choose their subjects for a variety of reasons.

Rationale

Teaching students to think about why a biographer chooses to write about a subject makes them aware of the decisions a biographer makes and gives a clue to the purpose and message of the biography.

Assess Learning

Observe students when they talk about biographies and notice if there is evidence of new learning based on the goal of this minilesson.

▸ Do students understand that a biographer chooses a particular subject to write about?

▸ Are they discussing why a biographer chose the subject?

▸ Do they use the terms *biography, subject, accomplished, obstacles,* and *message*?

Minilesson

To help students think about the minilesson principle, engage them in a discussion about the reasons a biographer chooses to write about a particular subject. Here is an example.

▸ Show the cover of *Ballots for Belva* and share a few entries from the timeline at the back of the book.

> Why do you think the biographer decided to write about Belva Lockwood?

▸ On chart paper, write a sentence that makes a generalization based on the students' responses that includes one reason the biographer might have decided to write about the subject.

▸ The sentences created in class may look different than the sample chart because they will be based on your students' noticings. The important thing is that students are thinking about the reasons why an author chooses a subject.

> Now think about the subject of a different biography, *Gordon Parks*.

▸ Show the cover and read About Gordon Parks at the back of the book.

> What do you think about Gordon Park's accomplishments and why the biographer might have written a book about him?

▸ Add to the chart.

Have a Try

Invite the students to talk with a partner about why a biographer chooses to write about a particular subject.

▶ Show the cover of *Talkin' About Bessie*.

> Think about Bessie Coleman and the obstacles she had to overcome. Why was her life important to write about?

▶ After time for discussion, ask a few volunteers to share. Summarize their thinking on the chart.

Summarize and Apply

Summarize the learning and remind students to think about the reasons biographers choose a particular subject.

> A biographer chooses a subject for different reasons. Often, it is because the subject's life sends a message, she has accomplished something important, or she has overcome obstacles.

▶ Add the principle to the chart.

> Choose a biography to read from the basket, unless you are already reading one from the library. Think about the subject's life and why the biographer might have decided to write about that person. Bring the book when we meet so you can share.

Share

Following independent reading time, gather students in small groups to talk about biographies.

> Share with your group the reasons you think the biographer decided to write about the subject of the biography you read.

Extend the Lesson (Optional)

After assessing students' understanding, you might decide to extend the learning.

▶ Have students continue the discussion about the reasons biographers choose their subject with other books, such as *Walking in the City with Jane: The Story of Jane Jacobs* from Text Set: Activists/Change Makers, about a person who accomplished something important by becoming one of the first and greatest urban activists.

Biographers choose their subjects for a variety of reasons.

Title	Why the Biographer Chose the Subject
	Important Message Belva Lockwood's life showed that you can fight for what you believe in and inspire future generations to do the same.
	Important Accomplishment Gordon Parks persevered despite obstacles and used a camera to show the unfairness of segregation.
	Overcame Obstacles Bessie Coleman succeeded despite poverty, segregation/racism, and gender discrimination.

RML 4
LA.U14.RML4

Reading Minilesson Principle
Biographers include details about the societal, cultural, and personal influences on a subject's life.

Studying Biography

You Will Need

- several familiar biographies that have details about the time in which the subject lived and the people who influenced the subject, such as the following:
  - *Talkin' About Bessie* by Nikki Grimes and *Tiny Stitches* by Gwendolyn Hooks, from Text Set: Genre Study: Biography (Pioneers)
- chart paper and markers
- sticky notes
- basket of biographies

Academic Language / Important Vocabulary

- biography
- subject
- time period
- society
- culture
- influenced

Continuum Connection

- Understand that biographies are often set in the past (p. 84)
- Infer the impact of the setting on the subject of a biography and the motives or reasons for the subject's decisions (pp. 590, 602)
- Infer the significance of the setting in a biographical text (p. 614)

Goal

Understand why biographers include details about the society and culture of the time in which the subject lived.

Rationale

When students learn to think about the details related to society, culture, and other people that a biographer chooses to include, they learn to consider how the time period and personal experiences affected the subject and the subject's accomplishments.

Assess Learning

Observe students when they talk about biographies and notice if there is evidence of new learning based on the goal of this minilesson.

- Do students recognize the time period in which the subject of a biography lived and its impact on the subject?
- Do they understand the impact of society and culture on the subject of a biography?
- Do they use the terms *biography, subject, time period, society, culture,* and *influenced*?

Minilesson

To help students think about the minilesson principle, engage them in a discussion about the way society, culture, and other people influence the subject of a biography. Here is an example.

- Revisit the introduction page from *Talkin' About Bessie.*

  What information does the author provide that shows the time period and political climate that had an impact on Bessie Coleman's life?

  Why do you think it is important that the author includes information about the world in which she lived?

- As students offer suggestions, record their thinking on the chart.
- Revisit the Susan Coleman page.

  Why does the author include details about Bessie's mother making sure her children learned to read and write?

- Record student responses.

Assessment

After you have taught the minilessons in this umbrella, observe students as they talk and write about biographies across instructional contexts: interactive read-aloud, independent reading, guided reading, shared reading, and book club. Use *The Literacy Continuum* (Fountas and Pinnell 2017) to observe students' reading and writing behaviors.

▶ What evidence do you have of new understandings related to biographies?

- Can students articulate the ways biographies are alike and create a definition of a biography?
- Are they talking about the reasons a biographer chooses a subject to write about?
- Do they understand that biographers choose the details to show what led the subject to become so accomplished?
- How well do they understand the author's attitude or feeling toward the subject?
- Can they identify the ways that a subject's accomplishments have influenced life today?
- Do they use vocabulary terms such as *biography, biographer, subject, stance, influence,* and *accomplishments*?

▶ In what other ways, beyond the scope of this umbrella, are students showing an interest in nonfiction genres?

- Are students reading other types of nonfiction?

Use your observations to determine the next umbrella you will teach. You may also consult Minilessons Across the Year (pp. 61–64) for guidance.

Read and Revise

After completing the steps in the genre study process, help students read and revise their definition of the genre based on their new understandings.

▶ **Before:** A biography is a story about a person written by someone else.

▶ **After:** A biography is the story of an interesting and often influential person and is written by someone else.

Reader's Notebook

When this umbrella is complete, provide a copy of the minilesson principles (see resources.fountasandpinnell.com) for students to glue in the reader's notebook (in the Minilessons section if using *Reader's Notebook: Advanced* [Fountas and Pinnell 2011]), so they can refer to the information as needed.

Reading Minilesson Principle

Think about how the subject's accomplishments have influenced life today.

Studying Biography

You Will Need

▸ several familiar biographies, such as the following:

- *Walking in the City with Jane* by Susan Hughes and *On Our Way to Oyster Bay* by Monica Kulling, from Text Set: Activists/Change Makers

- *Tiny Stitches* by Gwendolyn Hooks, from Text Set: Genre Study: Biography (Pioneers)

▸ chart paper and markers

▸ basket of biographies

▸ sticky notes

Academic Language / Important Vocabulary

▸ biography

▸ biographer

▸ subject

▸ accomplishments

▸ influenced

Continuum Connection

▸ Infer the importance of a subject's accomplishments (biography) (p. 84)

Goal

Infer ways the subject's accomplishments might have influenced life today.

Rationale

When students learn to infer the influence that a biography subject has had on life today, they think about how biographers choose their subjects and consider why biographies are written about certain people.

Assess Learning

Observe students when they talk about a subject's accomplishments and notice if there is evidence of new learning based on the goal of this minilesson.

▸ Can students identify the accomplishments of the subject of a biography?

▸ Are students able to infer the way that a subject's accomplishments have influenced life today?

▸ Do they understand the terms *biography, biographer, subject, accomplishments,* and *influenced*?

Minilesson

To help students think about the minilesson principle, engage them in a discussion about a subject's influence. Here is an example.

▸ Show the cover of *Walking in the City with Jane*.

> Think about this biography of Jane Jacobs. Why do you think the biographer chose Jane for a subject?

▸ Revisit a few parts of the book that show the impact she has had on life today.

> What are Jane Jacob's accomplishments?

> How has she influenced life today?

▸ Ask students to help you craft a statement of how Jane's influence is felt today for the chart.

▸ Show the cover of *On Our Way to Oyster Bay*.

> Now think about this biography of Mother Jones. Why do you think the biographer wrote a book about her?

▸ Revisit a few parts of the book that show her influence.

> What are the accomplishments of Mother Jones and how has she influenced life today?

▸ Add students' responses to the chart.

Have a Try

Invite the students to talk in small groups about a biographer's stance toward the subject of a biography.

▶ Show the cover of *Life in the Ocean* and read the last sentence on page 15. Revisit parts of the author's note as needed.

> Turn and talk about the biographer's stance toward Sylvia Earle.

▶ After time for discussion, ask a few volunteers to share. Add to the chart.

Summarize and Apply

Summarize the learning and remind students to think about an author's stance toward the subject of a biography.

> You thought about authors' attitudes or feelings toward the subjects of their biographies, which is called their stance.

▶ Add the principle to the top of the chart.

> Today when you read, choose a biography from the basket unless you are already reading one. Think about the author's stance toward the subject of the biography. Bring the book when we meet so you can share.

Share

Following independent reading time, gather students in partners.

> What did you notice about the biographer's stance toward the subject of the biography you read? Turn and talk about that.

▶ After time for discussion, ask a few volunteers to tell what their partner shared.

Extend the Lesson (Optional)

After assessing students' understanding, you might decide to extend the learning.

▶ Provide opportunities for students to think about an author's stance toward a topic or subject as you read other nonfiction books.

Think about the author's stance toward the subject of the biography.

Title and Subject	Biographer's Stance
Belva Lockwood	**Admiration** Belva Lockwood showed that determination and courage can lead to accomplishing goals.
Arturo Schomburg	**Gratitude** The author is a scholar and appreciates the way Schomburg expanded the historical record for African Americans and corrected errors in existing records.
Sylvia Earle	**Respect** The author seems to want to follow in Earle's footsteps to educate others about ocean life and the concerns about damage that is being done to the underwater world.

Section 2: Literary Analysis

Studying Biography

You Will Need

▶ several familiar biographies, such as the following:

  • *Ballots for Belva* by Sudipta Bardham-Quallen, from Text Set: Activists/Change Makers

  • *Schomburg* by Carole Boston Weatherford and *Life in the Ocean* by Claire A. Nivola, from Text Set: Genre Study: Biography (Pioneers)

▶ chart paper and markers

▶ sticky notes

▶ basket of biographies

Academic Language / Important Vocabulary

▶ biography

▶ biographer

▶ subject

▶ stance

Continuum Connection

▶ Infer a writer's stance (position, argument, or thesis) toward a topic or the subject of a biography (p. 85)

Goal

Infer the author's stance toward the subject of the biography.

Rationale

When students learn to think about a biographer's attitude or feeling toward a subject, they are better able to critique the biography, including what is and is not included about a subject's life. They also better understand the message a biographer wants to send by choosing to write about a particular subject's life.

Assess Learning

Observe students when they talk about biographies and notice if there is evidence of new learning based on the goal of this minilesson.

▶ Are students thinking and talking about a biographer's attitude or feeling toward the subject of the biography?

▶ Do they use the terms *biography, biographer, subject* and *stance*?

Minilesson

To help students think about the minilesson principle, engage them in a discussion about a biographer's stance toward the subject of a biography. Here is an example.

▶ Show the cover of *Ballots for Belva*. Read the first paragraph of the author's note at the back of the book.

  Think about the author's attitude, or feeling, toward Belva Lockwood. This is called the author's stance.

▶ Read the first paragraph on the first page, the last page of the book, and the end of the author's note, starting with "Throughout her life."

  Turn and talk about the biographer's stance toward Belva Lockwood.

▶ After time for discussion, ask volunteers to share their thinking. Begin a chart with their thoughts about the biographer's stance.

▶ Show the cover of *Schomburg*. Read the first dedication and then read the epitaph and show the illustration on the last page.

  What stance does the biographer have toward Arturo Schomburg?

▶ Guide the conversation and add student responses to the chart.

Have a Try

Invite the students to talk with a partner about a biographer's decisions.

▶ Read the third paragraph on the Susan Coleman page of *Talkin' About Bessie*.

Turn and talk about this scene. Have a conversation about how you would fill in the chart for this book.

▶ After time for discussion, ask several volunteers to share their thinking. Then read the first sentence of the book that explains that the form is fictional, but the story is based on fact. Add to chart.

Summarize and Apply

Summarize the learning and remind students to think about a biographer's decisions when they read biographies.

What does the chart show you about scenes that biographers include in their biographies?

▶ Add the principle to the top of the chart.

Today when you read, choose a biography from the basket unless you are already reading one from the library. Think about the scenes that the biographer includes. Place a sticky note on any pages you want to remember. Bring the book when we meet so you can share.

Share

Following independent reading time, gather students in the meeting area to talk about biographies.

What are some decisions the biographer made about what to include in the biography you read today?

Extend the Lesson (Optional)

After assessing students' understanding, you might decide to extend the learning.

▶ When you read a biography during interactive read-aloud, discuss with students the decisions a biographer makes about whether to use fictionalized dialogue and, if so, when to use it and how to create it.

Sometimes biographers include imagined scenes but base them on facts.

Title and Subject	Scene	Importance	Imagined?	Based on Facts?
Mother Jones	Aidan and Gussie meet Mother Jones. Aidan says, "She looks like someone's granny!" (p. 3)	Mother Jones encountered and influenced many people, including children, as she marched from Philadelphia to Washington, DC.	Yes The author says that the children are fictionalized.	Yes Mother Jones gave speeches on her protest march and was surrounded by many children.
Bessie Coleman	Susan Coleman describes the details of how Bessie read, including which words she struggled with and how she paused to lick her lips between verses.	Bessie was very serious about reading and learning, so her persistence and efforts at an early age show her developing personality.	Yes The author does not know exactly what Susan Coleman experienced.	Yes The author states that the story is fictional but based on facts.

Reading Minilesson Principle
Sometimes biographers include imagined scenes but base them on facts.

You Will Need

- several familiar biographies, such as the following:
  - *On Our Way to Oyster Bay* by Monica Kulling, from Text Set: Activists/Change Makers
  - *Talkin' About Bessie* by Nikki Grimes, from Text Set: Genre Study: Biography (Pioneers)
- chart paper prepared ahead of time with headings (*Title and Subject, Scene, Importance, Imagined?* and *Based on Facts?*) and scenes filled in
- markers
- sticky notes
- basket of biographies

Academic Language / Important Vocabulary

- biography
- fictionalized biographies
- subject
- imagined
- facts
- authentic

Continuum Connection

- Think critically about how a writer does (or does not) make a topic interesting and engaging, and share opinions (pp. 593, 605)

Goal

Analyze the craft decisions the biographer makes in writing a biography.

Rationale

It is important for students to understand that some scenes in biographies are imagined and that authors use them to convey information about the subject or to make the writing more interesting. When you teach students to think critically about the way a biographer sometimes uses imagined scenes in a biography, they understand the choices the biographer makes and deepen their thinking about an author's craft.

Assess Learning

Observe students when they talk about a biographer's decisions to include imagined scenes and notice if there is evidence of new learning based on the goal of this minilesson.

- ▶ Can students identify scenes that are imagined?
- ▶ Are students aware that a biographer makes decisions about what to include when writing a biography?
- ▶ Do they understand the terms *biography, fictionalized biographies, subject, imagined, facts,* and *authentic*?

Minilesson

To help students think about the minilesson principle, help them recognize the imagined scenes a biographer includes. Here is an example.

- ▶ Revisit page 3 of *On Our Way to Oyster Bay*.

  Why is this scene important to include in the book?

- ▶ As students share their thinking, begin filling in the chart with their responses.

  Do you think Mother Jones really met these two children, Aidan and Gussie, and that Aidan said these exact words to Gussie? Why or why not?

  Thinking about the choices a biographer makes, why do you think she made the decision to include this scene?

- ▶ Continue adding to chart.
- ▶ Revisit the author's note at the end, reading the first paragraph under the heading Who Was Mother Jones?

  Why is it important that imagined scenes in a fictionalized biography are based on fact?

Have a Try

Invite the students to talk with a partner about how a biographer shows the personality traits and motivations of a subject.

▶ Show the cover of *When the Beat Was Born*. Revisit a few pages.

Turn and talk about the facts the biographer includes and what they reveal about DJ Kool Herc's personality traits and motivations.

▶ After time for discussion, ask students to share their thinking. Add to chart.

Summarize and Apply

Summarize the learning and remind students to think about what the facts in a biography show about the subject's personality traits and motivations.

Biographers carefully choose the information they include in a biography to show what the subject is or was like.

▶ Add the principle to the chart.

Choose a biography to read today unless you are already reading one from the library. Think about facts that the biographer includes and what those facts show about the subject. Mark pages with sticky notes that you want to remember. Bring the book when we meet so you can share.

Share

Following independent reading time, gather students in the meeting area to talk about biographies.

Share one or two facts that show something about the subject's personality traits and motivations.

Extend the Lesson (Optional)

After assessing students' understanding, you might decide to extend the learning.

▶ If you have access to two or more biographies of the same person, have students compare the facts that each biographer included. Discuss the similarities and differences and the reasons that the biographers chose the facts that they did.

Biographers choose to include facts that reveal something important about the subject's personality traits and motivations.		
Title and Subject	**What is the subject like?**	**How does the biographer show this?**
Vivien Thomas	Confident	believed he was worthy of equal pay and stood up for it
	Overcame adversity	refused to let prejudice interfere with his work
	Willing to go against societal norms	disregarded those who thought he shouldn't be involved with medical research
	Persistent	researched and patiently experimented until he got procedure right
DJ Kool Herc	Dedicated	life-long love of music in which he immersed himself
	Outgoing	able to get the crowds excited and to participate in music and dance
	Creative	tried new things, mixing sounds in different ways
	Innovative	made a new kind of music

Reading Minilesson Principle
Biographers choose to include facts that reveal something important about the subject's personality traits and motivations.

You Will Need

- several familiar biographies, such as the following from Text Set: Genre Study: Biography (Pioneers):
  - *Tiny Stitches* by Gwendolyn Hooks
  - *When the Beat Was Born* by Laban Carrick Hill
- chart paper and markers
- basket of biographies
- sticky notes

Academic Language / Important Vocabulary

- biography
- biographer
- subject
- reveal
- personality traits
- motivations

Continuum Connection

- Notice that a biography is built around significant events, problems to overcome, and the subject's decisions (pp. 591, 603, 615)

Goal

Infer a subject's personality traits and motivations from the facts and details the biographer includes about the subject's life.

Rationale

When you teach students to think about what the facts in a biography reveal about a subject, they begin to think about the decisions a biographer makes about how to portray the subject.

Assess Learning

Observe students when they talk about biographies and notice if there is evidence of new learning based on the goal of this minilesson.

- Can students identify facts in a biography that reveal something about the subject?
- Are they talking about the decisions a biographer makes about which facts to include about the subject?
- Do they understand the terms *biography, biographer, subject, reveal, personality traits,* and *motivations*?

Minilesson

To help students think about the minilesson principle, engage them in a discussion about what the facts reveal about the subject of a biography. Here is an example.

- Show the cover of *Tiny Stitches* and revisit a few pages.

  How would you describe Vivien Thomas?

  What examples does the biographer include that show you what Vivien Thomas was like?

  What do these facts show you about his personality traits and motivations?

- As students share their thinking, begin recording their responses to link personality traits and motivations with examples from the book. As needed, prompt the conversation so they use the terms *personality traits* and *motivations*.

- Revisit a few more pages as needed to help students think of text examples. Continue adding to the chart as students share their thinking.

Have a Try

Invite the students to talk with a partner about the significance of the details in a biography.

▶ Revisit a few pages of *Tiny Stitches* that show the time period and personal influences on Vivien Thomas, such as pages 5–7.

Think about the details that the author includes about the time period, economic and racial climate, and personal influences that affected the life of Vivien Thomas. Turn and talk about why they are important in a book about his life.

▶ After time for discussion, ask students to share. Add to the chart.

Summarize and Apply

Summarize the learning and remind students to notice the details the author includes in a biography when they read one.

Today we talked about why a biographer includes details about the time period and others who influenced a subject in a biography.

▶ Add the principle to the chart.

Choose a biography to read, unless you are already reading one. Think about facts that the biographer included and why they are important. Mark pages with sticky notes that give a clue. Bring the book when we meet so you can share.

Share

Following independent reading time, gather students in pairs to talk about biographies.

Talk to your partner about what influenced the subject to become accomplished enough to be the subject of a biography.

Extend the Lesson (Optional)

After assessing students' understanding, you might decide to extend the learning.

▶ Encourage students to think about the influences on subjects of other biographies and why it was important for the author to include that information. For example, discuss Arturo Schomburg's quest for information about Africa and the African diaspora in *Schomburg: The Man Who Built a Library* by Carole Boston Weatherford, from Text Set: Genre Study: Biography: Pioneers.

Biographers include details about the societal, cultural, and personal influences on a subject's life.

Title and Subject	Societal/ Cultural Influences	Personal Influences	How the Subject Was Influenced
Bessie Coleman	Segregation Gender discrimination	Susan Coleman	Where Bessie grew up, there were few job opportunities beyond manual labor. Bessie wanted to do more. Knowing how to read and write helped her achieve her goals.
Vivien Thomas	The Depression Lack of opportunity for people of color	Dr. Blalock	Vivien lost his job during the Depression. He then applied to Vanderbilt University Medical School, which changed the course of his life. Dr. Blalock recognized Vivien's gifts and hired him for a job, allowing him to conduct experiments even without a medical degree.

Section 2: Literary Analysis

Minilessons in This Umbrella

Countering Stereotypes

RML1   Notice the author's stance on a topic.

RML2   Notice the difference between fact and opinion.

RML3   Authors use evidence to support an argument.

RML4   Notice how authors use counterarguments and evidence against those counterarguments.

Life on Earth

RML5   Notice the techniques authors use to persuade you.

RML6   Consider an author's qualifications and sources when you read a persuasive text.

RML7   Notice the differences between persuasive texts in digital and print formats.

Problem Solving/ Giving Back

Before Teaching Umbrella 15 Minilessons

Students should be familiar with recognizing an author's opinion or message (see LA.U8.RML1) before you begin this umbrella. Read and discuss high-quality, engaging nonfiction books that present a variety of topics and viewpoints. Explore and discuss the notes and resources found at the end of nonfiction books. Focus on persuasive texts, most of which are nonfiction. Consider collecting and reading shorter persuasive texts, such as news articles and essays. Use the following books from the *Fountas & Pinnell Classroom™ Interactive Read-Aloud Collection* or choose books from your classroom library.

Countering Stereotypes

Stormy Seas: Stories of Young Boat Refugees by Mary Beth Leatherdale

Life on Earth

Rotten! Vultures, Beetles, Slime, and Nature's Other Decomposers by Anita Sanchez

Buried Sunlight: How Fossil Fuels Have Changed the Earth by Molly Bang and Penny Chisholm

Problem Solving/Giving Back

The Mangrove Tree: Planting Trees to Feed Families by Susan L. Roth and Cindy Trumbore

As you read aloud and enjoy these texts together, help students

- notice the author's stance on a topic,
- discuss evaluating evidence, including the difference between fact and opinion,
- notice how authors use counterarguments and other techniques to persuade you,
- understand the author's qualifications to write on the topic, and
- notice the differences between persuasive texts in digital and print formats.

Section 2: Literary Analysis

Reading Minilesson Principle
Notice the author's stance on a topic.

You Will Need

- a collection of familiar persuasive texts, such as the following:
  - *Stormy Seas* by Mary Beth Leatherdale, from Text Set: Countering Stereotypes
  - *Rotten!* by Anita Sanchez and *Buried Sunlight* by Molly Bang and Penny Chisholm, from Text Set: Life on Earth
- chart paper and markers

Academic Language / Important Vocabulary

- author's stance
- persuade

Continuum Connection

- Infer a writer's stance (position, argument, or thesis) toward a topic or subject of a biography (p. 85)

Goal

Infer a writer's stance (position, argument, or thesis) toward a topic.

Rationale

When students learn to notice an author's stance in a persuasive text (book or article), they can draw conclusions about the author's purpose and consider their own new beliefs or actions.

Assess Learning

Observe students when they read and discuss persuasive texts. Notice if there is evidence of new learning based on the goal of this minilesson.

- ▶ Are students able to identify what an author is trying to persuade readers to believe or do?
- ▶ Can they discuss the author's stance on the topic?
- ▶ Do they understand and use the terms *author's stance* and *persuade*?

Minilesson

To help students think about the minilesson principle, use familiar persuasive texts to engage them in noticing an author's stance on a topic. Here is an example.

- ▶ Read page *v* from *Stormy Seas*.

   What do you think the author wants to persuade you to think or do about boat refugees?

- ▶ Record responses on chart paper.

   The attitude an author has toward a topic is called the author's stance. What is the author's stance on boat refugees?

   How does she convey that idea?

   The author introduced the struggle of boat refugees so that you would understand the problem. Then she described their perseverance and stated that each of us plays a role in the circumstances refugees face. The author wants you to feel accountable for the problem so that you do something to help the refugees. You can tell what the author's stance is in a persuasive text by what the author wants you to think or do.

- ▶ Record responses on the chart.
- ▶ Repeat this process with page 1 of *Rotten!*

Have a Try

Invite the students to talk with a partner about the author's stance in another persuasive text.

▶ Hold up *Buried Sunlight* and, as necessary, read pages 1, 24–26, 29, and 31.

> Turn and talk to your partner. What do the authors want you to believe or do? What is the authors' stance on the topic?

▶ Invite a few students to share with the class. Record responses on the chart.

Summarize and Apply

Summarize the learning and remind students to notice an author's stance when they read a persuasive text.

> Look at the chart. What did you notice about these nonfiction persuasive texts?

▶ Review the chart and write the principle at the top.

> Choose a nonfiction book to read today. Notice whether or not it is a persuasive text. If it is, be ready to share what you think the author is persuading you to believe or do and what the author's stance is on the topic when we come back together.

Share

Following independent reading time, gather students together in the meeting area to talk about their reading.

> Who read a persuasive book today? What did the author try to persuade you to believe or do? What was the author's stance on the topic?

Extend the Lesson (Optional)

After assessing students' understanding, you might decide to extend the learning.

▶ Introduce your students to Genre Thinkmarks for persuasive texts (visit resources.fountasandpinnell.com to download this resource). A Genre Thinkmark is a tool that guides readers to note certain elements of a genre in their reading. Once students can identify persuasive texts, they can use this resource to note points the author is making as well as supporting details.

▶ Discuss with students the authors' use of second person in *Buried Sunlight*. Ask them whether they think the technique is effective in persuading them to reduce their use of fossil fuels.

Notice the author's stance on a topic.

Title	What the Author Wants You to Believe or Do	Author's Stance
Stormy Seas	• Understand that everyone has a part in the terrible circumstances refugees face • Become more informed about refugees	• Empathetic to refugees because of the conditions they face • Feels strongly people can help ease the situation for refugees
Rot	• Understand that even though rot is gross, it is necessary for life	• Appreciates the importance of rot
Buried Sunlight	• Find sources of energy other than fossil fuels	• Believe in the importance of using different sources of energy

RML2

Reading Minilesson Principle
Notice the difference between fact and opinion.

Exploring Persuasive Texts

You Will Need

- a collection of familiar persuasive texts, such as the following:
  - *Stormy Seas* by Mary Beth Leatherdale, from Text Set: Countering Stereotypes
  - *Rotten!* by Anita Sanchez and *Buried Sunlight* by Molly Bang and Penny Chisholm, from Text Set: Life on Earth
- chart paper and markers
- sticky notes
- basket of persuasive texts

Academic Language / Important Vocabulary

- fact
- opinion
- persuasive

Continuum Connection

- Distinguish fact from opinion (p. 86)
- Follow arguments in a persuasive text (p. 86)

Goal

Notice the difference between fact and opinion.

Rationale

When you teach students to evaluate evidence in a persuasive text as either fact or opinion, they can decide if the author's argument is believable to them.

Assess Learning

Observe students when they read and discuss persuasive texts. Notice if there is evidence of new learning based on the goal of this minilesson.

- ❯ Can students identify an author's argument?
- ❯ Are they able to sort the evidence as fact or opinion?
- ❯ Do they understand and use the terms *fact, opinion,* and *persuasive*?

Minilesson

To help students think about the minilesson principle, use familiar persuasive texts to engage them in noticing the difference between fact and opinion. Here is an example.

- ❯ Show *Stormy Seas*. Read pages *iv*, 9, and 16.

  What information does the author give on these pages?

- ❯ Record responses on a chart in separate columns. Sort into facts and opinion but do not label the columns or discuss how you are sorting yet.

  What do you notice about the information in the middle column? The last column?

  Information that can be proved to be true is called a fact .

- ❯ Label the middle column *Facts*.

  An opinion is what someone believes. Opinions cannot be proved true or false. You may agree with an opinion, but that does not make it true.

- ❯ Label the last column *Author's Opinion*.

- ❯ Repeat the sorting process with pages 13 and 18 of *Rotten!*

  Why do authors of persuasive texts include both facts and opinions?

Have a Try

Invite the students to notice and sort the facts and opinions in *Buried Sunlight*.

▶ Read pages 21, 25, and 26.

> What do the authors share here? Are these facts or opinions?

▶ Record responses.

Summarize and Apply

Summarize the learning and remind students to differentiate facts and opinions when they read persuasive texts.

> Why is it important to notice which are the facts and which are the opinions when you read a persuasive text?

▶ Write the principle at the top of the chart.

> If you read a persuasive text from the basket today, notice the facts and opinions the author provides. Be ready to share when we come back together.

Share

Following independent reading time, gather students together in the meeting area to talk about their reading.

> Who read a persuasive text? What facts and opinions did the author share? Was the author's writing persuasive?

Extend the Lesson (Optional)

After assessing students' understanding, you might decide to extend the learning.

▶ As you read persuasive texts, discuss whether the author provides facts that persuade the reader. Consider having students research some of the facts to confirm that they are true.

▶ **Writing About Reading** After reading a persuasive text, have students write in a reader's notebook how an author used facts and opinions to persuade readers.

Notice the difference between fact and opinion.

Title	Facts	Author's Opinion
Stormy Seas	• 65 million of the 7 billion people on Earth do not live in a peaceful, prosperous place. • Cuba, Argentina, Uruguay, Paraguay, and other countries refused to provide refuge to St. Louis passengers. • Malaysia and Thailand also refused refugees.	• Many countries are or have been hostile to refugees and migrants.
	• Vultures are scavengers. • The scent of blood in the water lures sharks. • Sharks eat carcasses of dead whales.	• Dead animals smell nasty. • A bite from a great white is everyone's nightmare.
Buried Sunlight	• Scientists can measure the CO_2 in the air. • Arctic ice and glaciers are melting. • Seas are warming.	• Changes in the future will probably be more severe.

Section 2: Literary Analysis

RML 3
LA.U15.RML3

Reading Minilesson Principle
Authors use evidence to support an argument.

Exploring Persuasive Texts

You Will Need

- a few familiar persuasive texts, such as the following from Text Set: Life on Earth:
  - *Buried Sunlight* by Molly Bang and Penny Chisholm
  - *Rotten!* by Anita Sanchez
- chart from RML1 (optional)
- chart paper and markers
- sticky notes
- basket of persuasive texts

Academic Language / Important Vocabulary

- persuade
- argument
- evidence

Continuum Connection

- Evaluate the way the writer of an argument supports statements with evidence (p. 86)
- Follow arguments in a persuasive text (p. 86)

Goal

Identify the evidence authors use to support an argument.

Rationale

To persuade readers, an author presents an argument and supports it with evidence. When you teach students to read texts with a critical eye, they recognize the author's argument and the supporting evidence. From there, they can evaluate the effectiveness of the argument and form their own opinions.

Assess Learning

Observe students when they read and discuss persuasive texts. Notice if there is evidence of new learning based on the goal of this minilesson.

- Can students identify what an author wants them to believe or do?
- Are they able to find the evidence for the author's argument?
- Do they understand and use the terms *persuade, argument,* and *evidence*?

Minilesson

To help students think about the minilesson principle, use a familiar persuasive text to engage them in noticing how the author uses evidence to support an argument. Here is an example.

- Show *Buried Sunlight* or refer to the chart from RML1.

  What do the authors want you to think about?

  Their argument is that if we don't do something about fossil fuel use, Earth will change in ways worse than we can predict.

- Record the argument at the top of the chart, leaving room to write the principle later.

  For an argument to be successful, it should be supported with evidence. What evidence does the author give to support the argument?

- Review a few key pages with the students. Record findings in a logical order on the chart.

Have a Try

Invite the students to talk with a partner about how the author used evidence to support her argument in *Rotten!*

> Turn and talk to your partner. The author states, "Rot can be gross, yet it is necessary." How does the author use evidence to support this argument?

▶ Invite a few students to share with the class.

Summarize and Apply

Summarize the learning and remind students to notice how authors use evidence to support an argument when they read.

> What should you look for when you read a book that presents an argument?

▶ Write the principle at the top of the chart.

> If you choose to read a persuasive text from the basket, notice how the author supports the argument. Use sticky notes to mark the evidence the author uses to support the argument. Be ready to share when we come back together.

Share

Following independent reading time, gather students together in the meeting area to talk about persuasive texts.

> What is the author's argument? Share the evidence the author used to support the argument.

Extend the Lesson (Optional)

After assessing students' understanding, you might decide to extend the learning.

▶ Read aloud or have students read independently other persuasive texts (editorials are a good example). Ask students to evaluate whether the writer provided convincing evidence to support the argument.

▶ **Writing About Reading** After reading a persuasive text, have students write in a reader's notebook about the author's argument and the evidence (or lack thereof) the author provides to support the argument.

Authors use evidence to support an argument.

Argument: If we don't do something to stop the warming of Earth, changes could be more severe.

Burning fossil fuels puts more carbon dioxide into the air.

⬇

Too much carbon dioxide traps heat and warms our land and seas.

⬇

The warming causes changes to the earth, the sea, the weather.

⬇

These changes are happening more quickly than they ever have.

Section 2: Literary Analysis

Reading Minilesson Principle
Notice how authors use counterarguments and evidence against those counterarguments.

You Will Need

- a few familiar persuasive texts, such as the following from Text Set: Life on Earth:
  - *Buried Sunlight* by Molly Bang and Penny Chisholm
  - *Rotten!* by Anita Sanchez
- chart paper prepared with the argument from RML3
- highlighters
- sticky notes

Academic Language / Important Vocabulary

- argument
- counterargument

Continuum Connection

- Notice counterarguments and evidence against those counterarguments in a text (p. 84)

Goal

Notice a writer's use of counterarguments and evidence against those counterarguments.

Rationale

Sometimes to persuade readers, an author presents a counterargument and then provides evidence against that counterargument to support her stance. When you teach students to notice both sides of an argument when they read a persuasive text, you support them in becoming more thoughtful and critical readers and forming their own opinions.

Assess Learning

Observe students when they read and discuss persuasive texts. Notice if there is evidence of new learning based on the goal of this minilesson.

- ▶ Are students able to identify a counterargument and the evidence against it?
- ▶ Can they explain how a counterargument supports a writer's argument?
- ▶ Do they understand and use the terms *argument* and *counterargument*?

Minilesson

To help students think about the minilesson principle, use a familiar persuasive text to engage them in noticing how the author uses counterargument and evidence against the counterargument. Here is an example.

- ▶ Show *Buried Sunlight* and review the argument (from RML3). Refer to the prepared chart.

  Here is the authors' argument in *Buried Sunlight*. What is some of the evidence the authors used to support the argument?

- ▶ Read pages 27–28 ("Some people still ask").

  What do you notice about what the authors wrote on these pages?

  The authors wrote about some views that do not support their argument. In fact, they are the opposite of the argument. These opposite views are called counterarguments. What are the counterarguments that the authors give?

- ▶ Record them on the other side of the chart.

  Why would an author include ideas that do not support the argument?

- ▶ After time for discussion, ask several students to share their thinking.

  Authors anticipate what the audience might be thinking and address those thoughts in their writing. This can strengthen an author's argument.

Have a Try

Invite the students to repeat the minilesson process with a partner using pages 7, 9, and 10–11 from *Rotten!*

▶ After time for discussion, invite a few pairs to share with the class.

Summarize and Apply

Summarize the learning and remind students to think about how authors use evidence to support an argument.

> Take a look at the chart. What did you discover about persuasive texts today?

▶ Write the principle at the top of the chart.

> Choose a nonfiction book to read today. Notice if it is a persuasive text. If it is, notice if the author uses a counterargument, and mark it with a sticky note. Then mark the evidence the author uses against the counterargument. Be ready to share when we come back together.

Share

Following independent reading time, gather students together in the meeting area to talk with a partner about persuasive texts.

> If you read a persuasive text today, did you notice a counterargument? Did the author provide evidence against the counterargument?

Extend the Lesson (Optional)

After assessing students' understanding, you might decide to extend the learning.

▶ Provide students with short, persuasive articles to read. Ask them to evaluate and highlight the argument, counterargument, and evidence against the counterargument. Then ask students to share in pairs or with the whole class.

▶ When students conduct persuasive writing, remind them to consider a counterargument and to provide evidence against the counterargument as a way to persuade a reader.

Notice how authors use counterarguments and evidence against those counterarguments.

Argument	Counterarguments
If we don't do something to stop the warming of Earth, changes could be severe.	Earth has changed many times over many years. Earth has been a lot colder than it is now. Earth has been a lot hotter than it is now.

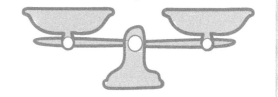

Reading Minilesson Principle
Notice the techniques authors use to persuade you.

Exploring Persuasive Texts

You Will Need

- several familiar persuasive texts, such as the following:
  - *Stormy Seas* by Mary Beth Leatherdale, from Text Set: Countering Stereotypes
  - *Buried Sunlight* by Molly Bang and Penny Chisholm, from Text Set: Life on Earth
- chart paper and markers
- basket of familiar persuasive texts, letters, speeches, or simple editorials
- sticky notes in different colors

Academic Language / Important Vocabulary

- persuade
- persuasion
- techniques

Continuum Connection

- Recognize a writer's use of the techniques for persuasion in a persuasive text (p. 86)

Goal

Recognize a writer's use of the techniques for persuasion.

Rationale

When students read critically, they notice the techniques authors use in a persuasive text, learn about the craft of writing—which they may apply to their own persuasive writing—and are able to discuss the strength of an author's argument and evidence.

Assess Learning

Observe students when they read and discuss persuasive texts. Notice if there is evidence of new learning based on the goal of this minilesson.

- ▶ Can students identify techniques an author uses to persuade?
- ▶ Do they understand terms such as *persuade*, *persuasion*, and *techniques*?

Minilesson

To help students think about the minilesson principle, use familiar persuasive texts to engage them in noticing how authors persuade the reader. Here is an example:

- ▶ Show *Stormy Seas*.

  In this book, the author wants to persuade you that the experiences of refugees are important for us all to understand.

- ▶ Show and read the quotation from Ruth about going back to Germany (on the bottom of page 1).

  How is the author trying to persuade you with these sentences? What do you notice about these sentences?

- ▶ Write the minilesson principle at the top of the chart and record responses.

- ▶ Write *Oral History/Direct Quote* on a sticky note and attach it to the chart.

- ▶ Read the first two sentences of the last paragraph on page v ("At first glance").

  What do you notice about these sentences? To whom are they addressed?

  The author uses first-person point of view (*we*) to make you part of the problem and the solution.

- ▶ Continue by pointing out the facts on the bottom of page 9 and reading some of the strong words on page *v*.

Have a Try

Invite the students to talk with a partner about how authors try to persuade their readers in *Buried Sunlight*.

▶ Read the first sentence on page 1.

> Turn and talk to your partner. What do you notice about the language the authors use? How do the authors try to persuade you that humans need to find ways to protect Earth from climate change?

▶ Continue with pages 9 ("You gobble"), 23 ("So this"), and 33 ("Will you humans"). Label the techniques as before.

Summarize and Apply

Summarize the learning and remind students to notice how authors try to persuade readers.

▶ Review the chart.

> Choose a persuasive text from this basket to read today. When you notice something the author does to try to persuade you, mark it with a sticky note so you can share when we come back together.

Share

Following independent reading time, gather students in the meeting area to talk about persuasive texts.

> What persuasive techniques did you notice?

▶ Add new techniques to the chart.

Extend the Lesson (Optional)

After assessing students' understanding, you might decide to extend the learning.

▶ Discuss other techniques an author might use to persuade (personal experience, repetition, comparison, or addressing oppositions).

▶ **Writing About Reading** Have students write in a reader's notebook about a technique a writer uses to persuade and whether that technique is effective.

Notice the techniques authors use to persuade you.

Stormy Seas		Buried Sunlight	
What the Author Does	Technique	What the Authors Do	Technique
Uses quotations from real people	Oral History/ Direct Quote	Write from the point of view of the sun: "I am your sun"	Use first-person point of view.
Uses we to make readers feel involved	Uses first-person point of view	Write as if the sun is speaking to the readers: "YOU gobble up the plants!"	Speak directly to you
Tells what happened to the 937 passengers aboard the St. Louis	Provides Facts	Tell the effects of burning fossil fuels	Provide Facts
Uses words like traumatic, precarious, treacherous, horrific	Persuasive Language	Ask questions directly to the readers: "Will you humans keep burning more and more fossil fuels every year...?"	Persuasive Language

Reading Minilesson Principle

Consider an author's qualifications and sources when you read a persuasive text.

Exploring Persuasive Texts

You Will Need

- several familiar persuasive texts, such as the following:
  - *Stormy Seas* by Mary Beth Leatherdale, from Text Set: Countering Stereotypes
  - *Rotten!* by Anita Sanchez, from Text Set: Life on Earth
  - *The Mangrove Tree* by Susan L. Roth and Cindy Trumbore, from Text Set: Problem Solving/Giving Back
- chart paper and markers
- basket of persuasive texts

Academic Language / Important Vocabulary

- biographical
- persuade
- qualified
- evaluate
- sources

Continuum Connection

- Critically examine the quality or accuracy of the text, citing evidence for opinions (p. 86)

Goal

Evaluate an author's qualifications and sources when you read a persuasive text.

Rationale

When students apply critical thinking and research skills to their reading they can evaluate a writer's claims and begin to draw their own conclusions from persuasive texts.

Assess Learning

Observe students when they talk about persuasive texts. Notice if there is evidence of new learning based on the goal of this minilesson.

- Are students able to identify ways to check an author's qualifications and sources?
- Can they explain why evaluating qualifications and sources is important?
- Do they use language such as *biographical*, *persuade*, *qualified*, *evaluate*, and *sources*?

Minilesson

To help students understand how to evaluate an author's qualifications and sources when reading a persuasive text, use familiar texts in which the author tries to persuade the reader. Here is an example.

- Read the acknowledgments at the end of *Stormy Seas*.

    Why do you think the author included these acknowledgments in her book?

    How does this help you to know the author is able, or qualified, to persuade you?

    The author listed the experts that she consulted to make sure the facts in her book are correct.

- Record responses on chart paper.
- Read elements like the dedication, acknowledgments, sources, and additional sources (print and digital) in other persuasive texts such as *Rotten!* and *The Mangrove Tree*.

Have a Try

Invite the students to consider with a partner how to evaluate an author's qualifications and sources.

▶ Have students list where outside of the book they can look to determine whether an author is qualified to persuade readers of a certain belief or action.

▶ Record responses on the chart.

Summarize and Apply

Summarize the learning and remind students to think about how readers consider an author's qualifications and sources.

> For you to be convinced by an author's writing, what do you need to do?

▶ Review the chart and write the principle at the top.

> Choose a persuasive text from the basket to read today. As you read, look for the author's qualifications for writing the persuasive text. Be ready to share your thoughts with the class.

Share

Following independent reading time, gather students in the meeting area to talk about persuasive texts.

> How do you know the author is qualified to write persuasively about the topic of the book you read today?

Extend the Lesson (Optional)

After assessing students' understanding, you might decide to extend the learning.

▶ Provide time for students to research online some of the claims in *Buried Sunlight* by Molly Bang and Penny Chisholm, from Text Set: Life on Earth, as a way to confirm the authors' claims.

▶ **Writing About Reading** Have students write in a reader's notebook about a persuasive text they have read, including how they know the author is qualified to write the text.

Consider an author's qualifications and sources when you read a persuasive text.

Where can you look to check an author's qualifications and sources?	How does this help you to know an author is qualified to persuade you?
• Acknowledgments and Dedication	• Describes how the author gathered information • Lists other researchers or organizations that reviewed the author's work/the facts the author used
• Author's Note • Afterword	• Provides additional details about the topic of the book as well as information about what the reader can do to take action
• Interviews • Nonfiction books • Websites • Videos/Television/Radio news reports	• You know where the information originated. • You can read more to check if the author is correct.

Reading Minilesson Principle
Notice the differences between persuasive texts in digital and print formats.

You Will Need

▸ a familiar persuasive text, such as *Buried Sunlight* by Molly Bang and Penny Chisholm, from Text Set: Life on Earth

▸ a persuasive electronic text on a similar topic (e.g., https://www.ducksters.com/science/environment/solar_power.php) to project or print out copies for each student, preserving the screen attributes

▸ a premade chart with the principle at the top and two columns labeled *Print Format* and *Digital Format*

▸ markers

▸ a prepared list of hyperlinks to persuasive texts (preview all digital texts prior to the lesson to ensure the links work, are grade appropriate, and adhere to your school's digital content policy)

▸ computers or tablets

Academic Language / Important Vocabulary

▸ digital format   ▸ hyperlink
▸ print format   ▸ bibliography

Continuum Connection

▸ Examine and think critically about the different strategies used by the media (TV, movies, news, video, multimedia blogs) and other content providers to engage and influence (p. 356)

▸ Notice and understand the characteristics of some specific nonfiction genres: e.g., expository, narrative, procedural and persuasive texts, biography, autobiography, memoir, hybrid text (p. 84)

Goal

Notice the difference between persuasive texts in digital and print formats.

Rationale

When you teach students to notice the differences between digital- and print-format persuasive texts, they begin to understand the volume and variability of information provided online and can think critically as they navigate digital texts.

Assess Learning

Observe students when they talk about persuasive texts in print and digital format. Notice if there is evidence of new learning based on the goal of this minilesson.

▸ Are students able to identify ways persuasive texts differ in print and digital formats?

▸ Are they critically evaluating links and new information when reading digital texts?

▸ Do they use terms such as *digital format, print format, hyperlink,* and *bibliography*?

Minilesson

To help students notice the difference between persuasive texts in digital and print format, choose familiar print texts and digital examples on the same topic that will be meaningful to them. Here is an example.

▸ Show *Buried Sunlight* and a digital text on a similar topic, such as the example about solar energy.

   Both the book and the website are about solar energy. What do you notice about how information is presented in the book? How is it presented online?

▸ Record responses on chart paper.

   What aspects of the book and the article do you find persuasive? Turn and talk about that.

▸ After a brief time for partners to talk, lead a discussion about reading persuasive texts in print format versus digital format.

▸ Record responses on the chart. As necessary, prompt the conversation by asking:

   • *How do hyperlinks affect your reading? Do they help or hinder?*

   • *What effect do ads have on your reading experience?*

   • *What role do readers' comments play?*

   • *How are the fonts and layouts of the two formats of texts different and the same?*

   • *What impact do photos have? What about videos?*

Have a Try

Invite the students to apply the new thinking about print and digital texts with a partner.

▶ Demonstrate clicking on a hyperlink from the example digital text that you have checked prior to class.

> Turn and talk to your partner. How does this hyperlink impact your reading and understanding of the topic?

▶ After time for discussion, ask a few students to share.

Summarize and Apply

Summarize the learning and remind students to think about how print and digital texts differ.

> Today you discussed the differences between persuasive texts in digital and print format.

▶ Review the chart.

> When you read today, read a persuasive article in digital format. Notice how the digital format is different from a print text. Jot down what you notice on a sticky note. Bring that with you when we come back together to share.

Share

Following independent reading time, gather students in the meeting area to talk with a partner about print and digital texts.

> What did you notice about the persuasive text you read in digital format? How might it have been different in print format?

Extend the Lesson (Optional)

After assessing students' understanding, you might decide to extend the learning.

▶ Teach a minilesson on noticing when bloggers or website authors link to other sources to provide evidence for an argument (see SAS.U7.RML6).

▶ Provide time for students to write persuasive texts and "publish" them in digital format. Encourage them to think about font, format, graphics, and photos as they plan how to persuade the reader.

▶ Utilize the text *Argument in the Real World: Teaching Adolescents to Read and Write Digital Texts* by Kristen Hawley Turner and Troy Hicks (Heinemann 2017) to support students in understanding more about reading and writing digital texts.

Notice the differences between persuasive texts in digital and print formats.

Print Format	Digital Format
No hyperlinks	Hyperlinks
No ads	Information surrounded by ads
Turn the pages to read information	Scroll through the article
Limited by space on the page	Not limited by space
No reader comments	Can have reader comments
Sources listed in the back of the book	Sources not always listed
Can't be updated quickly	Information can be updated quickly
More design and art	Not much art
Can have photos	Can have photos and videos

Assessment

After you have taught the minilessons in this umbrella, observe students as they talk and write about their reading across instructional contexts: interactive read-aloud, independent reading, guided reading, shared reading, and book club. Use *The Literacy Continuum* (Fountas and Pinnell 2017) to guide the observation of students' reading and writing behaviors.

▶ What evidence do you have of new understandings related to persuasive texts?

- Can students discuss an author's stance on a topic?
- Do they recognize evidence, facts, opinion, counterarguments, and other techniques of persuasion?
- Are they evaluating an author's qualifications and sources?
- Can they discuss the differences between persuasive texts in digital and print formats?
- Do they use vocabulary such as *persuade, evaluate, qualified, argument, opinion,* and *evidence*?

▶ In what other ways, beyond the scope of this umbrella, are students talking about persuasive texts?

- Are students writing about persuasive texts?
- Do they read and evaluate multiple sources on the same topic?

Use your observations to determine the next umbrella you will teach. You may also consult Minilessons Across the Year (pp. 61–64) for guidance.

Link to Writing

After teaching the minilessons in this umbrella, help students link the new learning to their own writing:

▶ Ask students to take a stance on a topic, provide evidence to support an argument, include facts and opinions, and cite sources as a way to build their credibility. Students may use Analyzing Persuasive Writing to create an outline for their writing (visit resources.fountasandpinnell.com).

Reader's Notebook

When this umbrella is complete, provide a copy of the minilesson principles (see resources.fountasandpinnell.com) for students to glue in the reader's notebook (in the Minilessons section if using *Reader's Notebook: Advanced* [Fountas and Pinnell 2011]), so they can refer to the information as needed.

Minilessons in This Umbrella

RML1   Nonfiction authors tell information in chronological order or temporal order.

RML2   Nonfiction authors organize information into categories and subcategories.

RML3   Nonfiction authors organize information by comparing and contrasting two things.

RML4   Nonfiction authors organize information using cause and effect.

RML5   Nonfiction authors organize information by explaining the problem and solution.

RML6   Nonfiction authors organize information in several ways within the same book.

RML7   Think critically about the way a writer has organized information.

Before Teaching Umbrella 16 Minilessons

Read and discuss a variety of high-quality, engaging nonfiction books in which the authors have organized information in a variety of ways (e.g., sequence, cause and effect, problem and solution). Use the following texts from the *Fountas & Pinnell Classroom™ Interactive Read-Aloud Collection* or choose nonfiction books that have a clear organization from the classroom library.

Life on Earth

Buried Sunlight: How Fossil Fuels Have Changed the Earth by Molly Bang and Penny Chisholm

Mountains by Seymour Simon

Scientists at Work

Scaly Spotted Feathered Frilled: How Do We Know What Dinosaurs Really Looked Like? by Catherine Thimmesh

Neo Leo: The Ageless Ideas of Leonardo da Vinci by Gene Barretta

Human Inventiveness

Chef Roy Choi and the Street Food Remix by Jacqueline Briggs Martin and June Jo Lee

Take a Picture of Me, James VanDerZee! by Andrea J. Loney

As you read aloud and enjoy these texts together, help students notice the different ways that authors organize information and the signal words that indicate the organization.

Life on Earth

Scientists at Work

Human Inventiveness

Section 2: Literary Analysis

Reading Minilesson Principle
Nonfiction authors tell information in chronological order or temporal order.

You Will Need

- two or three familiar nonfiction books that include information organized in chronological or temporal order, such as the following:
  - *Take a Picture of Me, James VanDerZee!* by Andrea J. Loney, from Text Set: Human Inventiveness
  - *Buried Sunlight* by Molly Bang and Penny Chisholm, from Text Set: Life on Earth
- chart paper and markers

Academic Language / Important Vocabulary

- nonfiction
- author
- organize
- information
- chronological
- temporal

Continuum Connection

- Recognize and use a writer's use of underlying text structures: e.g., description, cause and effect, sequence (chronological, temporal), compare and contrast, problem and solution, question and answer, combination (p. 85)

- Understand that a writer can tell about something that usually happens in the same order (temporal sequence) and something that happens in time order (chronological order) (p. 85)

Goal

Notice nonfiction authors' use of chronological and temporal sequence.

Rationale

When students are aware of chronological order, they better understand how a series of events unfolds over time as well as the relationships between the events. When they notice temporal sequence, they understand that certain processes always follow the same sequence of steps.

Assess Learning

Observe students when they read and talk about nonfiction books and notice if there is evidence of new learning based on the goal of this minilesson.

- ▸ Do students notice chronological and temporal sequences in nonfiction books?
- ▸ Do they use academic vocabulary, such as *nonfiction, author, organize, information, chronological,* and *temporal*?

Minilesson

To help students think about the minilesson principle, use familiar nonfiction books to engage them in noticing chronological order and temporal order. Here is an example.

- ▸ Read pages 5–7 from *Take a Picture of Me, James VanDerZee!*

    What do you notice about how the author organized the information in this book?

    The author told what happened in James VanDerZee's life in the order that it happened. This is called chronological order.

- ▸ Record an example of chronological order on the chart paper.

    Which words helped you figure out that the information is in chronological order?

- ▸ Record students' responses on chart paper.
- ▸ Read pages 8–10 from *Buried Sunlight*.

    What do you notice about how the information on these pages is organized?

- ▸ Record students' responses on a separate chart.

    These pages tell about a process that happens in the same order all the time. This is called temporal order. How is temporal order different from chronological order?

- ▸ Help students understand the difference between temporal and chronological sequence. Write a definition of each and add them to the first chart.

Have a Try

Invite the students to talk with a partner about how the information is organized in another part of *Buried Sunlight*.

▶ Read aloud pages 13–15 of *Buried Sunlight*.

> Turn and talk to your partner about how the authors organized the information on these pages. How do you know?

▶ After students turn and talk, invite a few pairs to share their thinking.

Summarize and Apply

Summarize the learning and remind students to notice how nonfiction books are organized.

> What does the first chart show about how authors sometimes organize information in nonfiction books?

▶ Write the principle at the top of the first chart.

> If you read a nonfiction book today, notice how the author organized the information. If you find an example of chronological order or temporal order in your book, bring it to share when we come back together.

Share

Following independent reading time, gather students together in the meeting area to talk about the organization of nonfiction books.

> Did anyone find an example of chronological order or temporal order in a nonfiction book today?

> How could you tell what order the information was in?

Extend the Lesson (Optional)

After assessing students' understanding, you might decide to extend the learning.

▶ Make available a list of words that indicate chronological or temporal order for students to use as a resource when writing (see resources.fountasandpinnell.com). Also add words to the chart as students encounter them.

▶ **Writing About Reading** Have students make a timeline of the events in a book that is organized in chronological order. If they read a book that describes a continuous sequence (such as a life cycle), have them make a cycle diagram.

Nonfiction authors tell information in chronological order or temporal order.

Order of Events	A man came to the VanDerZee home with a camera → He took the family's picture → He returned with a photograph.	Plants catch the sunlight → They use the sun's energy to build chains of carbon. → They photosynthesize and release O2 into the air...
Type of Order	Chronological	Temporal
Definition	Describes a series of events in the order they happened	Describes the sequence in which something always/usually occurs (such as the steps in a process)

Signal Words for Chronological and Temporal Order

one day

later

after months of

until

then

cycle

step 1, 2, 3

Reading Minilesson Principle
Nonfiction authors organize information into categories and subcategories.

Noticing How Nonfiction Authors Choose to Organize Information

You Will Need

▸ two familiar nonfiction books that have information organized into categories and subcategories, such as the following:

  • *Mountains* by Seymour Simon, from Text Set: Life on Earth

  • *Scaly Spotted Feathered Frilled* by Catherine Thimmesh, from Text Set: Scientists at Work

▸ chart paper and markers

Academic Language / Important Vocabulary

▸ nonfiction
▸ author
▸ organize
▸ information
▸ category
▸ subcategory

Continuum Connection

▸ Notice a nonfiction writer's use of categories and subcategories to organize an informational text (expository) (p. 85)

▸ Notice a writer's use of organizational tools: e.g., title, table of contents, chapter title, heading, subheading, sidebar (p. 85)

Goal

Notice when nonfiction authors organize information into categories and subcategories.

Rationale

When students notice the organization of information into categories and subcategories, they are able to recognize relationships and make connections between different details. They are also better able to find information in nonfiction books and organize their own nonfiction texts.

Assess Learning

Observe students when they read and talk about nonfiction books and notice if there is evidence of new learning based on the goal of this minilesson.

  ▸ Do students understand the relationship of categories and subcategories?

  ▸ Do they use academic vocabulary, such as *nonfiction, author, organize, information, category,* and *subcategory*?

Minilesson

To help students think about the minilesson principle, use familiar nonfiction books to engage them in noticing categories and subcategories of information. Here is an example.

  ▸ Show the cover of *Mountains* and read the title. Then read pages 3–4.

    What is the information in this section of the book about?

  ▸ Read aloud pages 9–17.

    What is the information in this part of the book about?

    The information on these pages is about how mountains are formed. Let's now take a closer look at how the author organized this information..

  ▸ Reread the second paragraph on page 11, page 13, and the first paragraph on page 15. After reading each section, ask what each part is about.

  ▸ If necessary, help students understand that each page or paragraph discusses how a different type of mountain is formed.

    What do you notice about how the information in this book is organized?

    The information is organized into categories of information. Some of the categories can be divided into smaller categories, called subcategories.

  ▸ With students' input, make a chart showing how the information in this book is divided into categories and subcategories.

Have a Try

Invite the students to talk with a partner about how the information is organized in *Scaly Spotted Feathered Frilled*.

▶ Show the cover of *Scaly Spotted Feathered Frilled*. Read the headings on pages 11, 16, and 22.

> Turn and talk to your partner about how the author of this book organized her information.

▶ After students turn and talk, invite a few students to share their thinking.

Summarize and Apply

Summarize the learning and remind students to notice how nonfiction books are organized.

> What did you notice today about how nonfiction authors sometimes organize information?

▶ Write the principle at the top of the chart.

> If you read a nonfiction book today, notice how the author organized the information. If the information in your book is organized into categories and subcategories, bring it to share when we come back together.

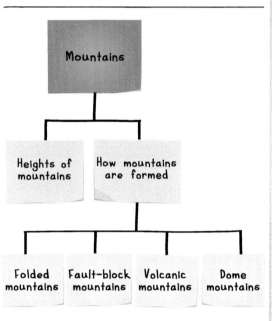

Nonfiction authors organize information into categories and subcategories.

Mountains

- Heights of mountains
- How mountains are formed
  - Folded mountains
  - Fault-block mountains
  - Volcanic mountains
  - Dome mountains

Share

Following independent reading time, gather students together in the meeting area to talk about categories and subcategories.

> Did anyone read a nonfiction book that is organized into categories?
> Are any of those categories divided into subcategories?

Extend the Lesson (Optional)

After assessing students' understanding, you might decide to extend the learning.

▶ Teach a minilesson to show how a table of contents reflects the structure of a book (categories, subcategories).

▶ **Writing About Reading** Have students make or fill in a graphic organizer similar to this lesson's chart (visit resources.fountasandpinnell.com to download a graphic organizer) to show categories and subcategories.

RML 3
LA.U16.RML3

Reading Minilesson Principle
Nonfiction authors organize information by comparing and contrasting two things.

Noticing How Nonfiction Authors Choose to Organize Information

You Will Need

- two familiar nonfiction books that contain examples of comparison and contrast, such as the following from Text Set: Scientists at Work:
  - *Scaly Spotted Feathered Frilled* by Catherine Thimmesh
  - *Neo Leo* by Gene Barretta
- chart paper and markers

Academic Language / Important Vocabulary

- nonfiction
- author
- organize
- information
- compare
- contrast

Continuum Connection

- Recognize and use a writer's use of underlying text structures: e.g., description, cause and effect, sequence (chronological, temporal), compare and contrast, problem and solution, question and answer, combination (p. 85)

Goal

Notice when nonfiction authors organize information using a compare-and-contrast structure.

Rationale

When you teach students to recognize compare-and-contrast text structures, they are better able to acquire and understand information about how two things are alike or different. They also understand that nonfiction writers must make decisions about how best to present information.

Assess Learning

Observe students when they read and talk about nonfiction books and notice if there is evidence of new learning based on the goal of this minilesson.

- ▶ Do students notice compare-and-contrast structures in nonfiction books?
- ▶ Do they recognize words that signal a compare-and-contrast text structure?
- ▶ Do they use academic vocabulary, such as *nonfiction, author, organize, information, compare,* and *contrast*?

Minilesson

To help students think about the minilesson principle, use familiar nonfiction books to engage them in noticing compare-and-contrast text structures. Here is an example.

- ▶ Show the cover of *Scaly Spotted Feathered Frilled* and read the title. Read aloud the first two captions on page 20 and display the illustrations.

   What do you notice about how the author organized the information about the two *Triceratops* illustrations?

   The author compared and contrasted the two images. What did you learn about how the two images are different?

- ▶ Use students' responses to make a chart contrasting the two images.

   What word did the author use to signal that the two images were going to be compared and contrasted?

   The author used the word *differences*. What other words do writers sometimes use when they are comparing and contrasting two things?

- ▶ Record signal words on a separate chart.

Have a Try

Invite the students to talk with a partner about how the information is organized in *Neo Leo*.

▶ Show the cover of *Neo Leo* and read the title. Read pages 4–9.

> Turn and talk to your partner about how the information in this book is organized.

▶ After students turn and talk, invite a few students to share their thinking.

Summarize and Apply

Summarize the learning and remind students to notice how nonfiction books are organized.

> What did you notice today about how nonfiction authors sometimes organize information?

▶ Write the principle at the top of the first chart.

> If you read a nonfiction book today, notice how the author organized the information. Bring your book to share when we come back together.

Share

Following independent reading time, gather students together in the meeting area to talk about nonfiction text structures.

> Did anyone find an example of a compare-and-contrast text structure today?

> What did the author of your book compare and contrast?

Extend the Lesson (Optional)

After assessing students' understanding, you might decide to extend the learning.

▶ Make available a list of words that indicate comparisons and contrasts for students to use as a resource when writing (see resources.fountasandpinnell.com).

▶ **Writing About Reading** Have students make or fill in a Venn diagram (visit resources.fountasandpinnell.com) to show how a nonfiction author compares and contrasts two things. They can glue the diagram into a reader's notebook.

Nonfiction authors organize information by comparing and contrasting two things.

Knight's Triceratops	Hallett's Triceratops
• Smoother skin	• Scaly skin with repeating patterns
• No triangular bones on the frill	• Triangular bones on the frill
• Less active	• Reflects warm-blooded dinosaur theory (highly active)
• Front leg is straight under the body	• Front leg is slightly splayed out

Signal Words for Comparing and Contrasting

differences

both

but

compared to

on the other hand

RML4
LA.U16.RML4

Reading Minilesson Principle
Nonfiction authors organize information using cause and effect.

Noticing How Nonfiction Authors Choose to Organize Information

You Will Need

- two familiar nonfiction books that contain examples of cause and effect, such as the following from Text Set: Life on Earth:
  - *Buried Sunlight* by Molly Bang and Penny Chisholm
  - *Mountains* by Seymour Simon
- chart paper and markers

Academic Language / Important Vocabulary

- nonfiction
- author
- organize
- information
- cause
- effect

Continuum Connection

- Recognize and use a writer's use of underlying text structures: e.g., description, cause and effect, sequence (chronological, temporal), compare and contrast, problem and solution, question and answer, combination (p. 85)

Goal

Notice when nonfiction authors organize information using cause and effect.

Rationale

When you teach students to recognize cause-and-effect text structures, they are better able to understand causal relationships. They also understand that nonfiction writers must make decisions about how best to present information.

Assess Learning

Observe students when they read and talk about nonfiction books and notice if there is evidence of new learning based on the goal of this minilesson.

- ▶ Do students notice cause-and-effect structures in nonfiction books?
- ▶ Do they recognize words that signal a cause-and-effect relationship?
- ▶ Do they use academic vocabulary, such as *nonfiction, author, organize, information, cause,* and *effect*?

Minilesson

To help students think about the minilesson principle, use familiar nonfiction books to engage them in noticing cause-and-effect text structures. Here is an example.

- ▶ Show the cover of *Buried Sunlight* and read the title. Read pages 22–26.

  What are the effects of burning fossil fuels?

- ▶ Record students' responses on chart paper.

  What could you say about how the authors organized information in this part of the book?

  The authors organized information using cause and effect. They described a cause—people burning fossil fuels—and the effects of that cause. A cause is something that makes something else happen, and an effect is something that happens as a result of the cause.

- ▶ Reread pages 25–26.

  Which words on these pages signal that the authors are describing a cause and its effects?

  What are some other words an author might use to show a cause or an effect?

- ▶ List the words on a separate piece of chart paper.

Have a Try

Invite the students to talk with a partner about how the information is organized in *Mountains*.

▶ Show the cover of *Mountains*. Read the title and then the first paragraph of page 11.

> What causes folded mountain chains to form? Turn and talk about this with your partner.

▶ After time for discussion, invite a few pairs to share their thinking. Record their responses on the chart.

Summarize and Apply

Summarize the learning and remind students to notice how nonfiction books are organized.

> What did you notice today about how nonfiction authors sometimes organize information?

▶ Write the principle at the top of the chart.

> If you read a nonfiction book today, notice how the author organized the information in your book. Bring your book to share when we come back together.

Share

Following independent reading time, gather students together in the meeting area to talk about nonfiction books.

> Did anyone find an example of information that is organized using cause and effect? What is the cause and what is the effect or effects?

Extend the Lesson (Optional)

After assessing students' understanding, you might decide to extend the learning.

▶ Help students understand that something can be both a cause and an effect (if X causes Y, which then causes Z, then Y is both an effect and then a cause).

▶ Make available a list of words that indicate cause and effect for students to use as a resource when writing (see resources.fountasandpinnell.com).

Nonfiction authors organize information using cause and effect.

Cause	Effect
(Something that makes something else happen)	(Something that happens because of a cause)
People burn fossil fuels. →	• Carbon dioxide traps heat in Earth's atmosphere. • Earth warms up.
Buried Sunlight	• The warming causes storms, droughts, and floods.
Pressure pushes sideways against the rocks in Earth's crust. →	• The rocks twist and bend. • Folded mountain chains form.
Mountains	

Signal Words for Cause and Effect

causes

changes

because

so

therefore

as a result

RML 5
LA.U16.RML5

Reading Minilesson Principle
Nonfiction authors organize information by explaining the problem and solution.

Noticing How Nonfiction Authors Choose to Organize Information

You Will Need

- two familiar nonfiction books that contain examples of problem-and-solution text structure, such as the following:
  - *Chef Roy Choi and the Street Food Remix* by Jacqueline Briggs Martin and June Jo Lee, from Text Set: Human Inventiveness
  - *Scaly Spotted Feathered Frilled* by Catherine Thimmesh, from Text Set: Scientists at Work
- chart paper and markers

Academic Language / Important Vocabulary

- nonfiction
- author
- organize
- information
- problem
- solution

Continuum Connection

- Recognize and use a writer's use of underlying text structures: e.g., description, cause and effect, sequence (chronological, temporal), compare and contrast, problem and solution, question and answer, combination (p. 85)

Goal

Notice when nonfiction authors organize information by explaining the problem and solution.

Rationale

When you teach students to recognize problem-and-solution text structures, they are better able to acquire and understand information pertaining to problems and solutions. They also understand that nonfiction writers must make decisions about how best to present information.

Assess Learning

Observe students when they read and talk about nonfiction books and notice if there is evidence of new learning based on the goal of this minilesson.

- ▶ Do students notice problem-and-solution structures in nonfiction books?
- ▶ Do they use academic vocabulary, such as *nonfiction, author, organize, information, problem,* and *solution?*

Minilesson

To help students think about the minilesson principle, use familiar nonfiction books to engage them in noticing problem-and-solution structures. Here is an example.

- ▶ Show the cover of *Chef Roy Choi and the Street Food Remix* and read the title. Then read pages 7–8.

  What problem did Roy have?

- ▶ Read page 9.

  What was the solution to this problem?

- ▶ Continue in a similar manner with page 10 (problem) and page 11 (solution).
- ▶ Write the problems and solutions on chart paper.

  How did the authors organize information in this part of the book?

  The authors organized information by explaining problems and solutions.

  What words might authors use to let you know that they are writing about a problem and a solution?

- ▶ List the words on a separate piece of chart paper.

Have a Try

Invite the students to talk with a partner about how the information is organized in *Scaly Spotted Feathered Frilled*.

▶ Show the cover of *Scaly Spotted Feathered Frilled* and read the title. Read pages 42–46.

Think about how the author organized information in this section by explaining a problem and its solution. What is the problem, and what is the solution or solutions? Turn and talk to your partner about this.

▶ After students turn and talk, invite a few students to share their thinking. Record responses on the chart.

Summarize and Apply

Summarize the learning and remind students to notice how nonfiction books are organized.

What did you notice today about how nonfiction authors sometimes organize information?

▶ Write the principle at the top of the first chart.

If you read a nonfiction book today, notice how the author organized the information. Bring your book to share when we come back together.

Share

Following independent reading time, gather students together in the meeting area to talk about nonfiction books.

Did anyone find an example of problem-and-solution organization? What was the problem and what was the solution?

Extend the Lesson (Optional)

After assessing students' understanding, you might decide to extend the learning.

▶ Make available a list of words that indicate problem and solution for students to use as a resource when writing (see resources.fountasandpinnell.com). Add signal words to the chart as students encounter them.

▶ Have students write their own nonfiction texts that are organized using a problem-and-solution text structure.

Nonfiction authors organize information by explaining the problem and solution.

	PROBLEM	SOLUTION
Chef Roy Choi	Roy felt like he didn't fit in, and he didn't know what to do with his life.	Roy decided to become a chef.
	Roy couldn't keep up at work, and he lost his job.	Roy opened a taco truck with his friends.
Scaly Spotted Feathered Frilled	It is difficult for paleoartists to determine the true colors of dinosaurs.	• Choose colors that are grounded in nature or based on modern analogs. • Use a special microscope to see pigment-carrying structures.

Signal Words

problem

solution

solve

fix

Section 2: Literary Analysis

RML 6
LA.U16.RML6

Reading Minilesson Principle
Nonfiction authors organize information in several ways within the same book.

Noticing How Nonfiction Authors Choose to Organize Information

You Will Need

- two or three familiar nonfiction books that contain multiple text structures, such as the following:
  - *Scaly Spotted Feathered Frilled* by Catherine Thimmesh, from Text Set: Scientists at Work
  - *Buried Sunlight* by Molly Bang and Penny Chisholm, from Text Set: Life on Earth
  - *Chef Roy Choi and the Street Food Remix* by Jacqueline Briggs Martin and June Jo Lee, from Text Set: Human Inventiveness
- chart paper and markers

Academic Language / Important Vocabulary

- organize
- information
- chronological order
- temporal order
- compare and contrast
- cause and effect

Continuum Connection

- Recognize and use a writer's use of underlying text structures: e.g., description, cause and effect, sequence (chronological order, temporal order), compare and contrast, problem and solution, question and answer, combination (p. 85)

Goal

Understand that sometimes nonfiction authors use several different organizational structures within the same book.

Rationale

When students notice that nonfiction authors sometimes use several different organizational structures within the same book, they understand that nonfiction writers are constantly making decisions about how best to organize information and that different types of information are suited to different structures.

Assess Learning

Observe students when they read and talk about nonfiction books and notice if there is evidence of new learning based on the goal of this minilesson.

- ▶ Can students identify multiple organizational structures within a single nonfiction book?
- ▶ Do they use academic vocabulary, such as *organize, information, chronological order, temporal order, compare and contrast,* and *cause and effect*?

Minilesson

To help students think about the minilesson principle, use familiar nonfiction books to engage them in noticing the variety of organizational structures writers use. Here is an example.

- ▶ Show the cover of *Scaly Spotted Feathered Frilled*.

  We have been talking about different ways that authors organize information in nonfiction books. What did you notice about how the author of *Scaly Spotted Feathered Frilled* organized her information?

- ▶ Record students' responses on chart paper. If necessary, revisit the specific pages that you discussed during previous minilessons (categories and subcategories: pp. 11, 16, and 22; compare and contrast: p. 20; problem and solution: pp. 42–46) and ask students to notice how the information on these pages is organized.

- ▶ Show the cover of *Buried Sunlight*.

  What did you notice about how the authors of this book organized information?

- ▶ Record students' responses on the chart. Revisit pages 8–10, 13–15, and 22–26 if necessary.

Have a Try

Invite the students to talk with a partner about how the information is organized in *Chef Roy Choi and the Street Food Remix*.

▶ Show the cover of *Chef Roy Choi and the Street Food Remix*.

> You noticed that the authors of this book organized information in one part of this book by explaining problems and their solutions. What's another way that the authors of this book organized information? Turn and talk to your partner about what you think.

▶ After time for discussion, invite a few students to share their thinking. Add responses to the chart.

Summarize and Apply

Summarize the learning and remind students to notice how nonfiction books are organized.

> What did you notice today about how nonfiction authors organize information in their books?

▶ Write the principle at the top of the chart.

> If you read a nonfiction book today, notice all the different ways the author organized the information. Be ready to share your thinking when we come back together.

Share

Following independent reading time, gather students together in the meeting area to talk about the organization of nonfiction books.

> Who read a nonfiction book today?

> In what ways is the information in your book organized?

Extend the Lesson (Optional)

After assessing students' understanding, you might decide to extend the learning.

▶ During interactive read-aloud, point out the nonfiction text structures with which students are familiar as you notice them.

▶ Provide a chart of nonfiction text structures and signal words to use as a reference (see resources.fountasandpinnell.com).

Nonfiction authors organize information in several ways within the same book.

Scaly Spotted Feathered Frilled	• Categories and subcategories • Compare and contrast • Problem and solution
Buried Sunlight	• Temporal order • Chronological order • Cause and effect
Chef Roy Choi	• Problem and solution • Chronological order

Section 2: Literary Analysis

Reading Minilesson Principle

Think critically about the way a writer has organized information.

Noticing How Nonfiction Authors Choose to Organize Information

You Will Need

- two of the nonfiction books discussed in earlier minilessons in this umbrella, such as the following:
  - *Neo Leo* by Gene Barretta, from Text Set: Scientists at Work
  - *Take a Picture of Me, James VanDerZee!* by Andrea J. Loney, from Text Set: Human Inventiveness
- chart paper and markers

Academic Language / Important Vocabulary

- organize
- information
- critically
- purpose
- logically

Continuum Connection

- Think critically about the way a writer has organized information (clear presentation, logic, appropriate to purpose) (p. 85)
- Understand that a nonfiction text can be expository or narrative in structure and that the writer selects the structure for a specific purpose (p. 85)

Goal

Think critically about the way a writer has organized information.

Rationale

When you teach students to think critically about the way a writer has organized information, they understand that writers choose a particular organizational structure for a specific purpose, and they learn to express and justify their opinions about whether the organization of a text is successful.

Assess Learning

Observe students when they read and talk about nonfiction books and notice if there is evidence of new learning based on the goal of this minilesson.

- ▶ Do students think critically about the way writers have organized information?
- ▶ Do they express their opinions about the success of a text's organization and support those opinions with evidence?
- ▶ Do they use academic vocabulary, such as *organize, information, critically, purpose,* and *logically*?

Minilesson

To help students think about the minilesson principle, engage them in evaluating the organization of a familiar nonfiction book. Here is an example.

- ▶ Show the cover of *Neo Leo* and briefly review some pages to remind students of its contents.

  Do you think the information in this book is clearly presented and logically organized? What makes you think that?

  When we discussed the organization of this book, you noticed that the author organized his information by comparing and contrasting modern inventions with the ideas of Leonardo da Vinci hundreds of years earlier. What do you think the author wants you to understand from reading this book?

  Why do you think Gene Barretta chose to use a compare-and-contrast text structure for his book?

  Do you think that compare-and-contrast organization was a good choice for this book? Why or why not?

Have a Try

Invite the students to talk with a partner about the organization of *Take a Picture of Me, James VanDerZee!*

▶ Show the cover of *Take a Picture of Me, James VanDerZee!*

You noticed that the information in this book is organized in chronological order. What do you think of the way the author organized the information? Is the information organized in a clear and logical way? Is it appropriate for the author's purpose? Turn and talk to your partner about what you think.

▶ After time for discussion, invite a few students to share their thinking.

Summarize and Apply

Summarize the learning and remind students to think critically about how nonfiction books are organized.

Today you thought critically about, or evaluated, the way a couple of authors organized information. What questions can you ask to evaluate the organization of a nonfiction book?

▶ Write students' responses on chart paper. Write the principle at the top of the chart.

If you read a nonfiction book today, think critically about the way the author organized information. Ask yourself the questions on the chart. Be ready to share your thinking when we come back together.

Share

Following independent reading time, gather students together in the meeting area to talk about the organization of nonfiction books.

Who read a nonfiction book today?

What do you think of the way the author organized the information in your book?

Extend the Lesson (Optional)

After assessing students' understanding, you might decide to extend the learning.

▶ **Writing About Reading** When students write reviews of nonfiction books, encourage them to include an evaluation of the book's organization.

Think critically about the way a writer has organized information.

- What is the author's purpose?
- How has the author organized the information?
- Why did the author organize information in that way?
- Is the way the information is organized appropriate for the author's purpose?
- Is the information clearly presented?
- Is the information logically organized?

Section 2: Literary Analysis

Assessment

After you have taught the minilessons in this umbrella, observe students as they talk and write about their reading across instructional contexts: interactive read-aloud, independent reading, guided reading, shared reading, and book club. Use *The Literacy Continuum* (Fountas and Pinnell 2017) to observe students' reading and writing behaviors.

▶ What evidence do you have of new understandings related to organizational structures in nonfiction?

▶ Are students able to identify organizational structures (e.g., chronological, temporal, categories and subcategories, compare and contrast, cause and effect, problem and solution)?

▶ Do they understand that writers can organize information in multiple ways within the same text?

▶ Do they think critically about the ways writers organize information?

▶ Do they use academic language, such as *nonfiction, author, organize, information, chronological, temporal, category, compare, contrast, cause,* and *effect*?

▶ In what other ways, beyond the scope of this umbrella, are students talking about nonfiction?

  • Have they noticed that there are different genres of nonfiction?

  • Are they using text features to find and gain information?

Use your observations to determine the next umbrella you will teach. You may also consult Minilessons Across the Year (pp. 61–64) for guidance.

Link to Writing

After teaching the minilessons in this umbrella, help students link the new learning to their own writing:

▶ Give students various opportunities to write their own nonfiction texts throughout the school year. Remind them of the different ways to organize nonfiction and discuss how to choose the most appropriate organizational structure for the topic.

Reader's Notebook

When this umbrella is complete, provide a copy of the minilesson principles (see resources.fountasandpinnell.com) for students to glue in the reader's notebook (in the Minilessons section if using *Reader's Notebook: Advanced* [Fountas and Pinnell 2011]), so they can refer to the information as needed.

Life on Earth

Minilessons in This Umbrella

RML1   Evaluate the significance of a topic.

RML2   Think critically about how the author explains the topic.

RML3   Notice the author's perspective on a topic and how it impacts his voice and choice of language.

RML4   Evaluate how the design features help you understand the topic.

Before Teaching Umbrella 17 Minilessons

Before teaching the minilessons in this umbrella, read and discuss a variety of engaging, high-quality expository nonfiction books that focus on a single topic. Use the following texts from the *Fountas & Pinnell Classroom™ Interactive Read-Aloud Collection* or choose appropriate nonfiction books from your classroom library.

Life on Earth

Living Fossils: Clues to the Past by Caroline Arnold

Mountains by Seymour Simon

Grand Canyon by Jason Chin

Buried Sunlight: How Fossil Fuels Have Changed the Earth by Molly Bang and Penny Chisholm

Rotten! Vultures, Beetles, Slime, and Nature's Other Decomposers by Anita Sanchez

As you read aloud and enjoy these texts together, help students

- think about why the topic of each book is important,

- evaluate the writing and design features of each book, and

- notice the author's perspective on the topic.

Section 2: Literary Analysis

Thinking About the Topic of Expository Nonfiction

You Will Need

- two or three familiar expository nonfiction books, such as the following from Text Set: Life on Earth:
  - *Living Fossils* by Caroline Arnold
  - *Buried Sunlight* by Molly Bang and Penny Chisholm
  - *Grand Canyon* by Jason Chin
- chart paper prepared with four columns, the first column filled in with book titles
- markers
- three sticky notes labeled *Yes*

Academic Language / Important Vocabulary

- expository nonfiction
- topic
- significant
- significance

Continuum Connection

- Infer the importance of a topic of a nonfiction text (p. 85)

Goal

Evaluate the significance of a nonfiction topic.

Rationale

When students evaluate the significance of the topic of an expository nonfiction book, they develop a better understanding of the author's message and of the importance of the content of the book for the world and/or their own lives.

Assess Learning

Observe students when they read and talk about expository nonfiction books and notice if there is evidence of new learning based on the goal of this minilesson.

▶ Can students explain why the topic of an expository nonfiction book is significant?

▶ Do they use academic vocabulary, such as *expository nonfiction, topic, significant, and significance*?

Minilesson

To help students think about the minilesson principle, use familiar expository nonfiction books to talk about evaluating the significance of a topic. Here is an example.

▶ Show the cover of *Living Fossils*.

What is the topic of this book?

▶ Write the topic in the second column on the prepared chart paper. Then read page 6.

Why would a writer write about this topic?

▶ Record students' responses in the next column on the chart.

▶ Show the cover of *Buried Sunlight*.

What is the topic of this book?

Why would a writer choose to write about fossil fuels?

▶ Record responses in the middle two columns on the chart.

What can you say about why the writers chose to write about these topics?

You could say that these writers chose to write their books because the topics are important, or significant. It is important for people to learn about these topics.

▶ Label the last column and place (or have a student place) two of the labeled sticky notes.

Have a Try

Invite the students to talk with a partner about the significance of a third topic.

▶ Show the cover of *Grand Canyon*.

What is this book about?

Turn to a partner and talk about whether the Grand Canyon is a significant topic and, if so, why.

▶ After time for discussion, invite several students to share their thinking. Record responses on the chart and place the final sticky note. If students disagree on the significance of the topic, ask them for evidence to support their thinking.

Summarize and Apply

Summarize the learning and remind students to evaluate the significance of topics.

▶ Write the principle at the top of the chart.

Why is it important to evaluate the significance of the topic of a nonfiction book?

If you read an expository nonfiction book today, think about whether the topic of your book is significant and why. Be ready to share your thinking when we come back together.

Share

Following independent reading time, gather students together in the meeting area to talk about the significance of the topics of nonfiction books.

Did anyone read an expository nonfiction book today?

What is the topic of your book?

Why is that topic significant?

Extend the Lesson (Optional)

After assessing students' understanding, you might decide to extend the learning.

▶ **Writing About Reading** Have students write an evaluation of the topic of an expository nonfiction book in a reader's notebook.

Evaluate the significance of a topic.

Title	Topic	Why write about the topic?	Is the topic significant?
Living Fossils	Living fossils	Scientists learn about the prehistoric world from them.	Yes
Buried Sunlight	Fossil fuels	Our dependence on them is causing serious damage to the environment.	Yes
Grand Canyon	Grand Canyon	It's important for people to learn about and protect the thousands of species of plants and animals that live in the Grand Canyon.	Yes

<table>
<tr>
<td>

RML2

LA.U17.RML2

</td>
<td>

Reading Minilesson Principle
Think critically about how the author explains the topic.

</td>
</tr>
</table>

Thinking About the Topic of Expository Nonfiction

You Will Need

- two familiar expository nonfiction books, such as the following from Text Set: Life on Earth:
  - *Buried Sunlight* by Molly Bang and Penny Chisholm
  - *Rotten!* by Anita Sanchez
- chart paper and markers

Academic Language / Important Vocabulary

- expository nonfiction
- topic
- author
- critically

Continuum Connection

- Think critically about the quality of a nonfiction text: e.g., quality of writing, contribution of illustration and other graphic design, accuracy (p. 84)

Goal

Critique how the author explains the topic in terms of quality of writing, organization, and clarity.

Rationale

When you teach students to think critically about how the author explains the topic, they become more aware of the various choices that authors must make and they learn to express and justify their opinions about the quality of expository nonfiction books.

Assess Learning

Observe students when they read and talk about expository nonfiction books and notice if there is evidence of new learning based on the goal of this minilesson.

- Do students critique expository nonfiction books in terms of writing, organization, and clarity?
- Do they support their opinions with evidence?
- Do they use vocabulary such as *expository nonfiction, topic, author,* and *critically*?

Minilesson

To help students think about the minilesson principle, use familiar expository nonfiction books to talk about critiquing expository nonfiction. Here is an example.

- Show the cover of *Buried Sunlight*. Reread the last few pages of the book.

  Do you think the authors of this book do a good job explaining the topic of fossil fuels? Why or why not?

- As needed, prompt the discussion with further questions, such as the following, about the quality of the book's writing, organization, and clarity:
  - *What do you think of the writing in this book? Is the language easy to understand? Is it written in an interesting way?*
  - *Is the information logically organized? Is the organizational structure clear?*
  - *Do the authors explain scientific concepts in a clear way? How do they make it easy for you to understand difficult concepts?*
  - *Do the authors provide enough evidence to support their ideas?*
  - *Do the authors make it easy to understand why the topic is important? If so, how?*
- Encourage students to support their responses with evidence from the text.

Have a Try

Invite the students to talk with a partner about *Rotten!*

▶ Show the cover of *Rotten!* and review the contents briefly.

> Turn and talk to your partner about how well the author of this book explains the topic.

▶ After students turn and talk, invite several students to share their thinking.

Summarize and Apply

Summarize the learning and remind students to think critically about how nonfiction authors explain topics.

> Today you thought critically about how the authors of two expository nonfiction books explain their topics. What are some of the questions you can ask yourself to think critically about how well an author explains a topic?

▶ Record students' responses on chart paper. Write the principle at the top.

> If you read an expository nonfiction book today, remember to think critically about how the author explains the topic.

Share

Following independent reading time, gather students together in the meeting area to talk about how well an author explains a topic.

> Who read an expository nonfiction book today?

> What do you think of the way the author of your book explains the topic?

Extend the Lesson (Optional)

After assessing students' understanding, you might decide to extend the learning.

▶ **Writing About Reading** Have students write book reviews of expository nonfiction books. Encourage them to respond to some of the questions discussed in this lesson in their reviews.

Think critically about how the author explains the topic.

Writing
- What do you think of the writing in this book?
- Is the writing interesting?
- Is the language easy to understand?

Organization
- Is the information logically organized?
- Is the organizational structure clear?

Clarity
- Does the author explain concepts in a clear way?
- Does the author provide evidence to support his or her ideas?
- Does the author clearly show or explain why the topic is important?

Section 2: Literary Analysis

RML 3

LA.U17.RML3

Reading Minilesson Principle

Notice the author's perspective on a topic and how it impacts his voice and choice of language.

Thinking About the Topic of Expository Nonfiction

You Will Need

- two or three familiar expository nonfiction books, such as the following:
  - *Living Fossils* by Caroline Arnold and *Mountains* by Seymour Simon, from Text Set: Life on Earth
- information about the authors of the books you have chosen (e.g., from the author's website)
- document camera (optional)
- chart paper and markers

Academic Language / Important Vocabulary

- expository nonfiction
- topic
- author
- perspective
- voice

Continuum Connection

- Notice language that expresses the author's attitude or feelings toward a subject reflected in the style of writing (tone): e.g., lighthearted, ironic, earnest, affectionate, formal (p. 86)

Goal

Notice the author's perspective on a topic and how it impacts voice and choice of language.

Rationale

Nonfiction writers view their topic through a particular lens—for example, that of a scientist, historian, or hobbyist. This lens influences how they choose to write about the topic, including their voice and their choice of language. When students recognize this, they think more analytically about the content of the nonfiction books they read.

Assess Learning

Observe students when they read and talk about expository nonfiction books and notice if there is evidence of new learning based on the goal of this minilesson.

- ▸ Can students explain how an author's perspective impacts the writing voice and choice of language?
- ▸ Do they use academic vocabulary, such as *expository nonfiction*, *topic*, *author*, *perspective*, and *voice*?

Minilesson

To help students think about the minilesson principle, use familiar expository nonfiction books to engage students in a discussion about author's perspective. Here is an example.

- ▸ Show the cover of *Living Fossils*. Display (project, if possible) information about the author (e.g., from her personal website). Read aloud some of the information.

  > What do you learn about what inspires Caroline Arnold to write books?

  > All authors have a perspective on the topics they write about. A perspective is the angle or viewpoint from which they are looking at the topic. For example, they might look at the topic as a scientist, a historian, or a nature lover. Caroline Arnold is a nature lover and a traveler. An author's perspective can influence how she writes about the topic.

- ▸ Read aloud the first three sentences on page 14 of the book.

  > An author's voice is her unique way of writing. An author's personality comes through in her voice. How would you describe Caroline Arnold's voice in this book? What can you tell about her personality?

  > What do you notice about Caroline Arnold's language choices?

  > How does the author's perspective—as a nature lover—influence her writing?

- ▸ Record students' responses on chart paper.

Have a Try

Invite the students to talk with a partner about *Mountains*.

▶ Show the cover of *Mountains*. Display information about the author and read it aloud.

> It says on Seymour Simon's website that he used to be a middle-school science teacher. As I read from the book, think about how his past as a science teacher influences his writing.

▶ Read pages 2–5.

> Turn and talk to your partner about how the author's perspective on the topic impacts his voice and language choices.

▶ After time for discussion, invite several students to share their thinking. Record responses on the chart.

Summarize and Apply

Summarize the learning and remind students to notice how an author's perspective on a topic influences the author's voice and choice of language.

> What did you notice about author's perspective today?

▶ Write the principle at the top of the chart.

> If you read an expository nonfiction book today, think about the author's perspective on the topic. You may want to read the author page or the author's website to find out about this. Bring your book to share when we meet.

Share

Following independent reading time, gather students together in the meeting area to talk about the effect of the author's perspective on the writing.

> Who read an expository nonfiction book today?

> What is the author's perspective on the topic, and how does it affect his or her writing?

Extend the Lesson (Optional)

After assessing students' understanding, you might decide to extend the learning.

▶ Help students develop their own authorial voice. Remind them that expository nonfiction writing does not need to be dry and strictly factual—rather, their writing should reveal their personality and their interest in the topic.

Notice the author's perspective on a topic and how it impacts his voice and choice of language.

Title	Author's Perspective	Voice	Language Choices
Living Fossils	Nature lover	Excited and fascinated by the natural world	Descriptive and poetic ("iridescent wings flash in the sun")
Mountains	Middle-school science teacher	Factual, to the point; explains things clearly and simply; serious	Provides a lot of facts and figures; not very descriptive

Section 2: Literary Analysis

Reading Minilesson Principle
Evaluate how the design features help you understand the topic.

You Will Need

- two or three familiar expository nonfiction books, such as the following from Text Set: Life on Earth:
  - *Buried Sunlight* by Molly Bang and Penny Chisholm
  - *Grand Canyon* by Jason Chin
- chart paper and markers
- document camera (optional)
- sticky notes

Academic Language / Important Vocabulary

- expository nonfiction
- topic
- design features
- evaluate

Continuum Connection

- Think critically about the quality of a nonfiction text: e.g., quality of writing, contribution of illustration and other graphic design, accuracy (p. 84)

Goal

Evaluate how the design features help you understand the topic.

Rationale

When you teach students to evaluate the design features in an expository nonfiction book, they learn that design features are not just for looks. Instead, they enhance or extend information about the topic. Students become more aware of the various choices that go into the development of a book, and they learn to express and justify their opinions about the quality of nonfiction books.

Assess Learning

Observe students when they read and talk about expository nonfiction books and notice if there is evidence of new learning based on the goal of this minilesson.

- ▶ Can students evaluate how the design features in an expository nonfiction book help them understand the topic?
- ▶ Do they use academic vocabulary, such as *expository nonfiction, topic, design features,* and *evaluate*?

Minilesson

To help students think about the minilesson principle, use familiar expository nonfiction books to guide them in evaluating design features. Here is an example.

- ▶ Show the cover of *Buried Sunlight*.

  As I show you several pages from this book, think about how the design features help you better understand the topic. Design features are illustrations and other graphics. They also include organizational features, the page layout, and the size and style of the print.

- ▶ Display several pages from the book, using a document camera if possible.

  What did you notice about the design features in this book? Are they effective, or successful, at helping you understand fossil fuels? Why or why not?

- ▶ As needed, prompt the discussion with further questions, such as the following:
  - *Do the graphics add meaning to the text?*
  - *Do they help you understand difficult concepts?*
  - *Is the print easy to read?*
  - *Is there a good balance between print and graphics?*
  - *Are the organizational features useful and clear?*
- ▶ Encourage students to support their responses with evidence from the text.
- ▶ Record each question that you discuss on chart paper.

Have a Try

Invite the students to talk with a partner about the design features in *Grand Canyon*.

▶ Show the cover of *Grand Canyon* and then display several pages from it, using a document camera if possible.

> Turn and talk to your partner about how effective the design features are in helping you understand the topic. Think about the questions on our chart.

▶ After students turn and talk, invite several pairs to share their thinking.

Summarize and Apply

Summarize the learning and remind students to evaluate design features in nonfiction books.

> Today you evaluated how the design features in a couple of expository nonfiction books help you understand the topic.

▶ Write the principle at the top of the chart.

> If you read an expository nonfiction book today, remember to evaluate the effectiveness of the design features in helping you understand the topic. If there is a page that you think has a very clear and useful design, mark it with a sticky note and bring it with you when we come back together.

Share

Following independent reading time, gather students together in the meeting area to talk about their reading.

> Who read an expository nonfiction book today?

> How well did the design features in your book help you understand the topic?

Extend the Lesson (Optional)

After assessing students' understanding, you might decide to extend the learning.

▶ **Writing About Reading** When students write book reviews of expository nonfiction books, encourage them to include an evaluation of the design features.

Evaluate how the design features help you understand the topic.

- Are the graphics of high quality?
- Do the graphics add meaning to the text?
- Does other art (such as border decorations) enhance the meaning?
- Do the graphics help you understand difficult concepts?
- Is the print easy to read?
- Is there a good balance between print and graphics?
- Are the organizational features useful and clear?

Section 2: Literary Analysis

Assessment

After you have taught the minilessons in this umbrella, observe students as they talk and write about their reading across instructional contexts: interactive read-aloud, independent reading, guided reading, shared reading, and book club. Use *The Literacy Continuum* (Fountas and Pinnell 2017) to observe students' reading and writing behaviors.

▶ What evidence do you have of new understandings related to thinking about the topic of expository nonfiction?

- Can students evaluate the significance of a topic?

- Do they think critically about the writing and design features in expository nonfiction books?

- Can they explain how an author's perspective impacts the choice of language and the voice?

- Do they use vocabulary such as *expository nonfiction*, *topic*, *perspective*, *voice*, and *evaluate*?

▶ In what other ways, beyond the scope of this umbrella, are students talking about nonfiction?

- Are students noticing other genres of nonfiction (e.g., memoir, biography)?

- Are they noticing how nonfiction authors organize information?

- Are they using text features to gain information?

Use your observations to determine the next umbrella you will teach. You may also consult Minilessons Across the Year (pp. 61–64) for guidance.

Link to Writing

After teaching the minilessons in this umbrella, help students link the new learning to their own writing:

▶ Give students numerous opportunities throughout the school year to write their own expository nonfiction texts. Remind them to think about why the topic they are writing about is important and to consider how their own perspectives on a topic may influence their writing. Encourage them to include design features that will help readers better understand the topic.

Reader's Notebook

When this umbrella is complete, provide a copy of the minilesson principles (see resources.fountasandpinnell.com) for students to glue in the reader's notebook (in the Minilessons section if using *Reader's Notebook: Advanced* [Fountas and Pinnell 2011]), so they can refer to the information as needed.

Minilessons in This Umbrella

RML1   Read multiple sources of information about a topic.

RML2   Use multiple sources to answer a bigger question.

RML3   Read primary and secondary sources for information on a topic.

RML4   Evaluate multiple sources for bias.

RML5   Evaluate the accuracy of information presented across sources.

Before Teaching Umbrella 18 Minilessons

The minilessons in this umbrella teach students how to synthesize information from multiple sources in order to arrive at a deeper understanding of a theme or topic. Before teaching these minilessons, read aloud and discuss engaging informational texts about a variety of high-interest topics with your students. Use the following texts from the *Fountas & Pinnell Classroom™ Interactive Read-Aloud Collection* or choose nonfiction books from your classroom library.

Animal Adaptations

The Most Amazing Creature in the Sea by Brenda Z. Guiberson

Glow: Animals with Their Own Night-Lights by W. H. Beck

Exploding Ants: Amazing Facts About How Animals Adapt by Joanne Settel

Scientists at Work

Scaly Spotted Feathered Frilled: How Do We Know What Dinosaurs Really Looked Like? by Catherine Thimmesh

Human Inventiveness

The Dinosaurs of Waterhouse Hawkins by Barbara Kerley

Countering Stereotypes

Stormy Seas: Stories of Young Boat Refugees by Mary Beth Leatherdale

Leadership

Sitting Bull: Lakota Warrior and Defender of His People by S. D. Nelson

As you read aloud and enjoy these texts together, help students

* discuss information and big ideas in each text,
* synthesize information from multiple sources, and
* evaluate sources for bias and accuracy.

Animal Adaptations

Scientists at Work

Human Inventiveness

Countering Stereotypes

Leadership

Section 2: Literary Analysis

RML1
LA.U18.RML1

Reading Minilesson Principle
Read multiple sources of information about a topic.

Reading and Evaluating Multiple Sources

You Will Need

- three sources of information about a single topic, such as the following:
  - *The Dinosaurs of Waterhouse Hawkins* by Barbara Kerley, from Text Set: Human Inventiveness
  - *Scaly Spotted Feathered Frilled* by Catherine Thimmesh, from Text Set: Scientists at Work
  - a website about Waterhouse Hawkins
- chart paper and markers

Academic Language / Important Vocabulary

- source
- multiple
- information
- topic
- nonfiction

Continuum Connection

- Think across texts to construct knowledge of a topic (p. 85)
- Notice and understand multiple points of view on the same topic (p. 86)
- Notice and evaluate the accuracy of the information presented in the text and across texts (p. 86)

Goal

Think across nonfiction texts to construct knowledge of a topic and to confirm accuracy of texts.

Rationale

When you teach students to read multiple sources of information about a topic, they learn more about the topic and develop their ability to synthesize information and judge its accuracy across sources. They learn that every resource is an incomplete source of information, and they begin to read nonfiction with a more critical eye.

Assess Learning

Observe students when they read and talk about nonfiction books and notice if there is evidence of new learning based on the goal of this minilesson.

- ▷ Can students explain why it is important to read multiple sources of information?
- ▷ Can they explain how each source they read added to or confirmed their understanding about the topic?
- ▷ Do they understand and use terms such as *source*, *multiple*, *information*, *topic*, and *nonfiction*?

Minilesson

To help students think about the minilesson principle, engage them in a discussion about considering multiple sources of information. Here is an example.

- ▶ Show the cover of *The Dinosaurs of Waterhouse Hawkins* and read the title. Then read pages 5–7.

  What did you learn about the dinosaurs of Waterhouse Hawkins from these pages?

- ▶ Record students' responses on chart paper.

  Listen carefully as I read from another book about dinosaurs. Think about how the information is the same or different.

- ▶ Read pages 11–12 of *Scaly Spotted Feathered Frilled*.

  What did you notice about the information in this book? How is it similar to the information in the other book? What new information did you learn?

- ▶ Record responses on the chart.

Have a Try

Invite the students to talk with a partner about how another source adds to or contradicts their knowledge of Waterhouse Hawkins.

▶ Display another source, such as a website, about Waterhouse Hawkins. Read aloud a section that relates to the information you read aloud in the two books.

> Turn and talk to your partner about how this source adds to or contradicts your learning about the dinosaurs of Waterhouse Hawkins.

▶ After students turn and talk, invite a few students to share their thinking. Record responses on the chart.

Summarize and Apply

Summarize the learning and remind students to read multiple sources of information.

> How can you gain a more complete understanding of a topic?

▶ Write the principle at the top of the chart.

> Choose a nonfiction book to read today, or continue reading one that you have already started. Where can you look for more information about the topic? Ask me for help if you need it.

Share

Following independent reading time, gather students together in the meeting area to talk about reading multiple sources on the same topic.

> Who read multiple sources of information about a topic today?

> How did reading multiple sources add to or confirm your understanding?

Extend the Lesson (Optional)

After assessing students' understanding, you might decide to extend the learning.

▶ Help students compare and contrast two sources of information about a topic. Discuss why the authors may have made different choices about what information to include or how to present it.

▶ Point out that the purpose of a bibliography is to show the sources that the author used to find and verify the information used in the book.

Read multiple sources of information about a topic.	
Source 1:	• Scientists thought that if they studied dinosaur fossils and compared them to living animals, they could learn what dinosaurs looked like. • Waterhouse Hawkins based his model of the iguanodon on the modern iguana. He made it look like a giant iguana.
Source 2:	• Waterhouse Hawkins' model of an iguanodon was a "very large, modified" iguana. • His dinosaurs weren't very accurate. • However, he got some things right. (The iguanodon did stand on straight legs.)
Source 3: Website about Waterhouse Hawkins	• Waterhouse Hawkins' dinosaurs were inaccurate compared to modern-day interpretations, but they represented the latest scientific knowledge at the time. • His dinosaur sculptures are still on display in Crystal Palace Park in London, England.

Section 2: Literary Analysis

Reading Minilesson Principle
Use multiple sources to answer a bigger question.

Reading and Evaluating Multiple Sources

You Will Need

- three nonfiction sources centered around a single topic or theme, such as the following from Text Set: Animal Adaptations:
  - *The Most Amazing Creature in the Sea* by Brenda Z. Guiberson
  - *Glow* by W. H. Beck
  - *Exploding Ants* by Joanne Settel
- chart paper prepared with a research question about the sources listed above (e.g., *How do animals adapt to their environment?*)
- several other research questions and a collection of relevant sources for each one (see Summarize and Apply)
- markers

Academic Language / Important Vocabulary

- multiple
- source
- nonfiction

Continuum Connection

- Think across texts to compare and expand understanding of content and ideas from academic disciplines: e.g., social responsibility, environment, climate, history, social and geological history, cultural groups (p. 85)

Goal

Use multiple sources of information to answer a research question.

Rationale

To respond to a research question whose answer is more than a simple response, students must understand that they need to read more than one source. They learn to read nonfiction purposefully. They also develop the understanding that different nonfiction writers may approach the same theme or topic from different angles and that reading multiple sources allows them to gain a more complete understanding of the theme or topic.

Assess Learning

Observe students when they read and talk about nonfiction books and notice if there is evidence of new learning based on the goal of this minilesson.

- ▶ Do students read multiple sources to answer a research question?
- ▶ Can they explain how each source helps them answer the question?
- ▶ Do they use academic vocabulary, such as *multiple, source,* and *nonfiction*?

Minilesson

To help students think about the minilesson principle, use familiar nonfiction books to engage them in thinking about how to use multiple sources to answer a bigger question. Here is an example.

> Sometimes you want to answer a big question, perhaps when you are writing a research paper. Think about the question on the chart as I reread a couple of pages from *The Most Amazing Creature in the Sea.*

- ▶ Read pages 3–4 of *The Most Amazing Creature in the Sea.*

  > How does this book help you answer the question?

- ▶ Record students' responses on chart paper.

  > How thoroughly does this information answer the question about animal adaptation?

  > This source has some information, but it feels incomplete. Let's look in another source.

- ▶ Show the cover of *Glow* and read the title. Read pages 14–15.

  > What does this book help you understand about how animals adapt?

- ▶ Record responses on the chart.

  > Even though these two books are about different kinds of animals, both contribute to the answer to our question.

Have a Try

Invite the students to talk with a partner about *Exploding Ants*.

▶ Read page 8 of *Exploding Ants*.

Turn and talk to your partner about how this source helps you answer our big question.

▶ After students turn and talk, invite a few pairs to share their thinking. Record responses on the chart.

What can we conclude about how animals adapt to their environment?

▶ After time for discussion, invite several students to share their thinking. Combine their responses to create an agreed-upon class answer to write on the chart.

Summarize and Apply

Summarize the learning for students.

How can using multiple sources help you answer a bigger question?

▶ Display a sheet of chart paper that lists several bigger questions. For example: *What inspires people to make the world better? How can one person change the world? What rights and responsibilities do we have as citizens? What are the qualities of an effective leader?* Provide resources to support each question.

When you read today, think about one of these questions and read multiple sources to help you answer it. You can also come up with your own question and find your own sources.

Share

Following independent reading time, gather students together in the meeting area to talk about what they learned about a topic from multiple sources.

What question did you think about today? How did reading multiple sources help you answer it?

Extend the Lesson (Optional)

After assessing students' understanding, you might decide to extend the learning.

▶ Have students write a research paper or an informational article. Have them define a research question. Then walk them through finding relevant sources, reading the sources and taking notes, organizing the information, and writing and editing.

Use multiple sources to answer a bigger question.

Big Question: How do animals adapt to their environment?

 The leatherback sea turtle can both breathe air and stay underwater for a long time. Its thick skin allows it to eat jellyfish without being poisoned by their toxins.

 Some sea creatures use bioluminescence (the ability to glow) to defend against predators or to attract prey.

 A swallowtail butterfly larva disguises itself as a bird dropping to avoid being eaten.

Answer: Animals develop physical characteristics and behaviors that allow them to survive.

Section 2: Literary Analysis

Reading Minilesson Principle
Read primary and secondary sources for information on a topic.

Reading and Evaluating Multiple Sources

You Will Need

- two familiar nonfiction books that contain examples of primary sources (e.g., photographs, journal entries, letters), such as the following:
  - *Stormy Seas* by Mary Beth Leatherdale, from Text Set: Countering Stereotypes
  - *Sitting Bull* by S. D. Nelson, from Text Set: Leadership
- chart paper and markers

Academic Language / Important Vocabulary

- primary source
- secondary source
- information
- topic

Continuum Connection

- Notice the writer's use of primary and secondary sources as integral parts of a text (p. 85)
- Draw information from secondary sources and other sources that may be in a nonfiction text (p. 84)

Goal

Understand and learn about a topic from primary and secondary sources.

Rationale

Understanding the difference between primary and secondary sources helps students realize that the study of history reflects *interpretations* of past events and that those interpretations are constructed through the study and analysis of primary sources.

Assess Learning

Observe students when they read and talk about nonfiction books and notice if there is evidence of new learning based on the goal of this minilesson.

- ▶ Can students explain what primary and secondary sources are?
- ▶ Do they use academic vocabulary, such as *primary source, secondary source, information,* and *topic*?

Minilesson

To help students think about the minilesson principle, use familiar nonfiction books to discuss primary and secondary sources. Here is an example.

- ▶ Show the cover of *Stormy Seas* and read the title. Show the print on the bottom of page 16 and read a few sentences.

  What do you notice about this part of the book?

  These are Phu's own words from an interview with the author. The transcript of an interview is an example of a primary source. What is a primary source?

  A primary source is something written or recorded by someone who was directly involved in or witnessed an event.

- ▶ Read and display page 17. Ask students to identify primary sources on the page.

  Photographs are also primary sources. So are newspaper articles from the time of the event, especially if they have quotes from interviews, eyewitness accounts, and photos. What else is a primary source?

- ▶ Record students' responses on chart paper. If needed, offer a few more examples.

  All the parts of this book that were written by the author, Mary Beth Leatherdale, are secondary sources. What do you think a secondary source is?

  A secondary source is written by someone who was not directly involved in the event but is telling about it based on several primary and secondary sources. What are some examples of secondary sources?

- ▶ Record responses on the chart.

Have a Try

Invite the students to talk with a partner about *Sitting Bull*.

▶ Show the cover of *Sitting Bull* and read the title. Then read pages 34–35.

> Turn and talk to your partner about the primary and secondary sources on this page. What's a primary source, and what's a secondary source? How can you tell?

▶ After students turn and talk, invite a few students to share their thinking.

Summarize and Apply

Summarize the learning and remind students to read both primary and secondary sources.

▶ Write the principle at the top of the chart.

> Why is it important to read both primary and secondary sources when you research a topic?

> Choose a nonfiction book to read today, or continue one you have already started. Notice if your book includes any primary sources or whether it is a secondary source. Bring your book to share when we come back together.

Share

Following independent reading time, gather students together in the meeting area to talk about primary and secondary sources.

> Who found an example of a primary source in the book you read today?

> What did the primary source help you understand about the topic?

Extend the Lesson (Optional)

After assessing students' understanding, you might decide to extend the learning.

▶ Discuss the benefits and drawbacks of both primary and secondary sources.

▶ When students write informational texts about historical events, encourage them to refer to both primary and secondary sources. Help them find relevant, appropriate sources of each type. The Library of Congress website is a good resource for primary sources.

Read primary and secondary sources for information on a topic.

PRIMARY SOURCE	SECONDARY SOURCE
Written or recorded by someone who witnessed an event	Written by someone who did <u>not</u> witness the event
Examples: • Interviews • Photographs • Newspaper articles (from the time the event happened) • Journal entries • Letters • Videos • Speeches • Memoirs/ autobiographies • Films of real events	Examples: • History books • Textbooks • Movies
Example: "I was very afraid when I had to leave my country to escape the war."	Example: "Many Vietnamese people left their country to escape the war."

Section 2: Literary Analysis

RML4
LA.U18.RML4

Reading Minilesson Principle
Evaluate multiple sources for bias.

You Will Need

- two or three news articles (not editorials/opinion pieces) about the same event or topic from different sources; there should be clear differences in how the articles approach the subject, and at least one of them should contain obvious indications of bias
- chart paper and markers
- document camera (optional)

Academic Language / Important Vocabulary

- bias
- sources
- evaluate
- prejudice

Continuum Connection

- Notice and understand multiple points of view on the same topic (p. 86)
- Recognize bias and be able to identify evidence of it (p. 86)
- Assess the objectivity with which a nonfiction topic is presented (p. 86)

Goal

Notice and evaluate multiple sources for bias.

Rationale

Teaching students how to recognize bias helps them understand that works of nonfiction, although based in fact, are not necessarily entirely objective and are influenced by the writer's background and attitudes. This underscores the importance of reading multiple sources in order to gain a more complete understanding of a topic, event, or issue.

Assess Learning

Observe students when they read and talk about nonfiction and notice if there is evidence of new learning based on the goal of this minilesson.

- ▶ Do students understand what bias is and why it is important to be aware of bias?
- ▶ Do they use academic vocabulary, such as *bias, sources, evaluate,* and *prejudice*?

Minilesson

To help students think about the minilesson principle, use news articles to provide an inquiry-based lesson about bias. Here is an example.

- ▶ Using a document camera or enlarged printouts, display side by side two of the articles you chose before class.

   I'm going to read aloud two news articles about the same topic. As I read them, think about how they are different.

   How do you think each author feels about the topic? How can you tell?

- ▶ Draw students' attention to specific examples of bias and ask them what they notice, using the following prompts as needed:
  - *What details are in one article but not in the other?*
  - *What do the headlines reveal about the authors' feelings?*
  - *What do you notice about the words each author uses to describe _____? Are they positive or negative?*
  - *What do you notice about the photos included with the articles?*

- ▶ Help students conclude that nonfiction texts can contain elements of bias.

   Bias is an attitude or prejudice in favor of or against one thing, person, group, or idea, often considered to be unfair. Even though news articles aren't supposed to include the writer's opinion, they still often contain clues about how the writer feels about the topic.

Have a Try

Invite the students to talk with a partner about how to evaluate sources for bias.

> Think about the discussion we just had. Turn and talk to your partner about some questions you can ask yourself to determine if there is bias in a source.

▶ After time for discussion, invite a few pairs to share their thinking. Use their responses to create a list of questions to guide students in evaluating sources for bias. Write the principle at the top of the chart.

Summarize and Apply

Summarize the learning and remind students to evaluate sources for bias.

> Why do you think it is important to be aware of bias when you read about a topic?

> If you read a nonfiction book or article today, notice if the author seems to have an attitude or prejudice for or against someone or something. Make a note of any evidence of bias that you find, and be ready to share your thinking when we come back together.

Share

Following independent reading time, gather students together in the meeting area to talk about examples of bias.

> Did anyone find any examples of bias today?

> What examples did you find? What do those examples show about how the author feels about the topic?

Extend the Lesson (Optional)

After assessing students' understanding, you might decide to extend the learning.

▶ Discuss pairs of words with positive versus negative connotations (e.g., *unique/strange, confident/conceited, satisfied/smug*). Help students notice when word choice reveals clues about a writer's attitude toward a person or topic.

Evaluate multiple sources for bias.

Checking for Bias

- Are certain details included or left out?

- Does the headline or title contain clues about how the writer feels about the topic?

- Does the author's choice of words reveal an attitude toward the topic? (For example, "They <u>took</u> the diamond" vs. "They <u>stole</u> the diamond.")

- What do you notice about the photographs? Do they show a person in a positive or negative way?

RML 5

LA.U18.RML5

Reading Minilesson Principle
Evaluate the accuracy of information presented across sources.

Reading and Evaluating Multiple Sources

Goal

Notice and evaluate the accuracy of the information presented across sources.

Rationale

Students who learn to evaluate the accuracy of information presented across sources read with a critical eye. They understand that although nonfiction texts are based in fact, they are not necessarily perfect sources of information. This insight underscores the importance of reading multiple sources of information to learn about a topic.

Assess Learning

Observe students when they read and talk about nonfiction books and notice if there is evidence of new learning based on the goal of this minilesson.

> ▶ Do students evaluate the accuracy of information presented across sources?

> ▶ Do they use academic vocabulary, such as *nonfiction, information, sources,* and *accuracy*?

Minilesson

To help students think about the minilesson principle, model using multiple sources to evaluate the accuracy of a familiar nonfiction book. Here is an example.

> ▶ Show the cover of *Exploding Ants*. Read aloud the final paragraph on page 17.

> > I was surprised to read that the Aboriginal people in Australia eat honey ants like candy! I wonder if that's really true.

> ▶ Display another reliable source of information about honey ants. Explain how you know it is a good source of information.

> > This website says that some groups of Aboriginal people in Australia eat honey ants and that they are considered a sweet, tasty treat. I think this information is probably accurate because the same information is in multiple sources.

> > What do you notice about my thinking?

> > I evaluated the accuracy of some of the information in this book. When you evaluate the accuracy of information, you think about whether it's correct. You can use other books or websites to check.

Have a Try

Invite the students to talk with a partner about how to evaluate the accuracy of information.

▶ Display a source, such as a website, that provides information about the credentials of Joanne Settel, the author of *Exploding Ants*. Read it aloud.

> Turn and talk to your partner about how using a source like this could help you evaluate the accuracy of the information in this book.

▶ After time for discussion, invite a few students to share their thinking.

Summarize and Apply

Summarize the learning and remind students to evaluate the accuracy of information presented across sources.

> How can you use multiple sources to evaluate the accuracy of information in a nonfiction book?

▶ Record students' responses and write the principle at the top of the chart.

> Why is it important to evaluate the accuracy of the information in the books you read?

> If you read a nonfiction book today, you may want to look for other sources to help you verify that the information in your book is accurate. Be ready to share your opinion about the accuracy of your book when we come back together.

Share

Following independent reading time, gather students together in the meeting area to talk about evaluating the accuracy of nonfiction books.

> Did anyone use other sources to help you evaluate the accuracy of the information in a nonfiction book today?

> What is your opinion about the accuracy of the book you read?

Extend the Lesson (Optional)

After assessing students' understanding, you might decide to extend the learning.

▶ Discuss how to determine if a website is a reliable source of information. Explain that web addresses that end in .edu or .gov are usually good resources.

▶ **Writing About Reading** When students write book reviews of nonfiction books, encourage them to evaluate the accuracy of the information in the book.

> ### Evaluate the accuracy of information presented across sources.
>
> - Read other books or websites about the topic.
>
> - Compare the information in the book to the information in other sources.
>
> - Check the credentials of the author.
>
> - Check the research the author has done on the topic.

Assessment

After you have taught the minilessons in this umbrella, observe students as they talk and write about their reading across instructional contexts: interactive read-aloud, independent reading, guided reading, shared reading, and book club. Use *The Literacy Continuum* (Fountas and Pinnell 2017) to observe students' reading and writing behaviors.

> ▶ What evidence do you have of new understandings related to reading and evaluating multiple sources?
>
> - Do students understand why it is important to read multiple sources of information about a topic?
> - Do they read both primary and secondary sources, and can they differentiate between them?
> - How well are they able to evaluate sources for bias and accuracy?
> - Do they use terms such as *source, information, topic, bias,* and *evaluate*?
>
> ▶ In what other ways, beyond the scope of this umbrella, are students talking about nonfiction books?
>
> - Are they noticing different organizational structures in nonfiction?
> - Are they using text features to gain information?

Use your observations to determine the next umbrella you will teach. You may also consult Minilessons Across the Year (pp. 61–64) for guidance.

Link to Writing

After teaching the minilessons in this umbrella, help students link the new learning to their own writing:

> ▶ Remind students to read multiple sources when they conduct research for writing their own informational texts. Encourage them to include both primary and secondary sources in their research, and remind them to evaluate the sources they use for accuracy and bias.

Reader's Notebook

When this umbrella is complete, provide a copy of the minilesson principles (see resources.fountasandpinnell.com) for students to glue in the reader's notebook (in the Minilessons section if using *Reader's Notebook: Advanced* [Fountas and Pinnell 2011]), so they can refer to the information as needed.

Minilessons in This Umbrella

RML1 Authors use graphics to help you understand bigger ideas.

RML2 Authors use infographics to show information in a clear and interesting way.

RML3 The graphics and print are carefully placed in a nonfiction text to communicate ideas clearly.

Before Teaching Umbrella 19 Minilessons

Read and discuss high-quality, engaging nonfiction picture books that include a variety of graphics, such as illustrations, photographs, maps, diagrams, and infographics. Use the following books from the *Fountas & Pinnell Classroom™ Interactive Read-Aloud Collection* and *Guided Reading Collection* or choose nonfiction books with clear, interesting graphics from your classroom library.

Animal Adaptations

Scientists at Work

Guided Reading

Interactive Read-Aloud Collection

Life on Earth

Living Fossils: Clues to the Past by Caroline Arnold

Buried Sunlight: How Fossil Fuels Have Changed the Earth by Molly Bang and Penny Chisholm

Grand Canyon by Jason Chin

Animal Adaptations

Glow: Animals with Their Own Night-Lights by W. H. Beck

Scientists at Work

Neo Leo: The Ageless Ideas of Leonardo da Vinci by Gene Barretta

Guided Reading Collection

E-sports: The Fastest-Growing Sport in the World by Carmen Morais

As you read aloud and enjoy these texts together, help students

- notice and discuss graphics, and
- understand information and ideas conveyed through graphics.

Section 2: Literary Analysis

RML1

LA.U19.RML1

Reading Minilesson Principle
Authors use graphics to help you understand bigger ideas.

Learning Information from Illustrations and Graphics

You Will Need

- two or three familiar nonfiction books that contain graphics that help communicate bigger ideas and messages, such as the following:
  - *Neo Leo* by Gene Barretta, from Text Set: Scientists at Work
  - *Buried Sunlight* by Molly Bang and Penny Chisholm and *Grand Canyon* by Jason Chin, from Text Set: Life on Earth
- chart paper and markers

Academic Language / Important Vocabulary

- illustration
- graphic
- diagram
- nonfiction
- author

Continuum Connection

- Notice how illustrations and graphics help to communicate the writer's message [p. 87]

Goal

Understand that authors use graphics to help you understand bigger ideas.

Rationale

Nonfiction authors use graphics–such as illustrations, photographs, diagrams, charts, and maps–to convey information visually. These graphics enhance the information in the text and often help to communicate a big idea. When students understand how to acquire information from graphics in nonfiction books, they are better able to understand the author's big ideas or central messages.

Assess Learning

Observe students when they read and talk about nonfiction books and notice if there is evidence of new learning based on the goal of this minilesson.

- ▶ Can students explain how a graphic helps communicate a bigger idea?
- ▶ Do they use academic vocabulary, such as *illustration, graphic, diagram, nonfiction,* and *author*?

Minilesson

To help students think about the minilesson principle, use familiar nonfiction books to engage them in a discussion about graphics. Here is an example.

- ▶ Show the cover of *Neo Leo* and read the title. Turn to and read aloud pages 5–6.

  What does the illustration on the left show?

  What does the illustration on the right show?

- ▶ Record students' responses on chart paper.

  Why do you think the author included an illustration of the Wright Brothers' aircraft as well as an illustration of Leonardo da Vinci's design for an aircraft? What big idea is he trying to illustrate?

- ▶ Record students' responses on the chart.

- ▶ Show the cover of *Buried Sunlight* and read the title. Display and read pages 19–20. Read the labels on the diagram.

  What do you notice about the graphic on these pages? What kind of graphic is it?

  This is a diagram. A diagram shows the parts of something or how something works. What does this diagram show?

  What big idea does the diagram help you understand?

- ▶ Record students' responses on the chart.

Have a Try

Invite the students to talk with a partner about *Grand Canyon*.

▶ Show page 4 of *Grand Canyon*. Point to and read the labels on the "Ecological Communities in Grand Canyon" diagram.

> What kind of graphic is this? What big idea does it help you understand? Turn and talk to your partner about the graphic.

▶ After time for discussion, invite a few students to share their thinking. Record responses on the chart.

Summarize and Apply

Summarize the learning and remind students to notice and think about graphics in nonfiction books.

> Why do nonfiction authors include graphics in their books?

> Nonfiction authors often include graphics to help you understand bigger ideas.

▶ Write the principle at the top of the chart.

> If you read a nonfiction book today, remember to notice, read, and think about the graphics. If you find an example of a graphic that helps you understand a bigger idea, bring your book to share when we come back together.

Share

Following independent reading time, gather students together in the meeting area to talk about their reading.

> Who found an example of a graphic that helped you understand a bigger idea?

> What kind of graphic is it? What bigger idea did it help you understand?

Extend the Lesson (Optional)

After assessing students' understanding, you might decide to extend the learning.

▶ When you read a nonfiction book with an interesting graphic during interactive read-aloud, discuss how it helps communicate a bigger idea.

Authors use graphics to help you understand bigger ideas.

Book	Type of Graphic	What does it show?	Big Idea
Neo Leo	Illustrations	The Wright Brothers' aircraft da Vinci's design for an aircraft	Leonardo da Vinci's ideas foreshadowed many modern inventions.
Buried Sunlight	Diagram	Fossil fuels underneath the surface of Earth How fossil fuels are retrieved and used	Fossil fuels contribute to an increase of carbon dioxide in Earth's atmosphere.
GRAND CANYON	Diagram	The different ecological communities in the Grand Canyon and their elevations	The Grand Canyon is home to many different ecosystems.

Reading Minilesson Principle

Authors use infographics to show information in a clear and interesting way.

Learning Information from Illustrations and Graphics

You Will Need

- two or three nonfiction books that contain infographics, such as the following:
  - *E-sports* by Carmen Morais, from *Guided Reading Collection*
  - *Buried Sunlight* by Molly Bang and Penny Chisholm, from Text Set: Life on Earth
- chart paper and markers
- document camera (optional)

Academic Language / Important Vocabulary

- infographic
- information
- nonfiction
- graphic
- author

Continuum Connection

- Understand that graphics provide important information (p. 87)
- Recognize and use information in a variety of graphics: e.g., photo and/ or drawing with label or caption, diagram, cutaway, map with legend and scale (p. 87)

Goal

Understand that authors use infographics to show patterns and trends.

Rationale

In today's digital age, infographics are used more and more frequently to convey complex information in a clear and interesting way, both online and in print publications. When you teach students how to read infographics, they are better prepared to acquire information from the many infographics that they will inevitably encounter.

Assess Learning

Observe students when they read and talk about infographics and notice if there is evidence of new learning based on the goal of this minilesson.

> ▶ Do students notice and read infographics?
>
> ▶ Can they explain what they learned from an infographic?
>
> ▶ Do they use academic vocabulary, such as *infographic, information, nonfiction, graphic,* and *author*?

Minilesson

To help students think about the minilesson principle, help them notice the important information in infographics. Here is an example.

> ▶ Display the infographic from page 5 of *E-sports*.
>
>> What do you notice about this graphic?
>
> ▶ Read the text aloud, pointing to each text element as you read it.
>
>> What do you notice about how I read this graphic?
>>
>> What information does this graphic provide?
>>
>> This is a kind of graphic called an infographic. How do the parts of the word help you know what it means?
>>
>> The word *infographic* is a combination of the words *information* and *graphic*. An infographic is a graphic that usually shows more than one kind of information plus print that you can put together to learn about an idea.
>
> ▶ With students' input, label the different parts of the infographic.

Have a Try

Invite the students to talk with a partner about another infographic.

▶ Display the infographic from pages 29–30 of *Buried Sunlight*.

Think about this infographic with your partner. Turn and talk about what you notice about the infographic and what you learned from it.

▶ After students turn and talk, invite a few pairs to share their thinking. Ask how they read the infographic, what they noticed about how the infographic displays information, and what they learned from it.

Summarize and Apply

Summarize the learning and remind students to read and think about infographics.

Why do you think nonfiction authors sometimes use infographics? Why are they helpful?

▶ Write the principle at the top of the chart.

If you read a nonfiction book today, notice if it has any infographics. If so, be sure to look closely at them and think about the information they provide. If you find an example of an infographic, bring it to share when we come back together.

Share

Following independent reading time, gather students together in the meeting area to talk about their reading.

Who found an example of an infographic today?

How did the infographic help you learn more about the topic of the book?

Extend the Lesson (Optional)

After assessing students' understanding, you might decide to extend the learning.

▶ Infographics are easily found on the internet. Find infographics that are engaging and appropriate for your class and use them as models for students to work in pairs or small groups to make infographics to use in their own nonfiction writing.

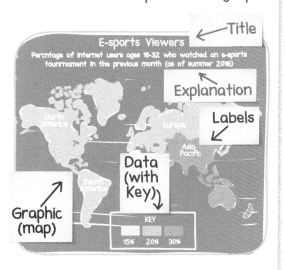

Authors use infographics to show information in a clear and interesting way.

Information + Graphic = Infographic

Title

E-sports Viewers

Percentage of internet users ages 18-32 who watched an e-sports tournament in the previous month (as of summer 2016)

Explanation

Labels

Data (with Key)

Graphic (map)

KEY

15%   20%   30%

RML3
LA.U19.RML3

Reading Minilesson Principle
The graphics and print are carefully placed in a nonfiction text to communicate ideas clearly.

Learning Information from Illustrations and Graphics

You Will Need

- two or three familiar nonfiction books that have pages with multiple graphics and print elements, such as the following:
  - *Living Fossils* by Caroline Arnold and *Grand Canyon* by Jason Chin, from Text Set: Life on Earth
  - *Glow* by W. H. Beck, from Text Set: Animal Adaptations
- chart paper and markers

Academic Language / Important Vocabulary

- graphics
- print
- nonfiction
- placed
- communicate

Continuum Connection

- Understand that graphics and text are carefully placed in a nonfiction text so that ideas are communicated clearly (p. 87)

Goal

Understand that graphics and print are carefully placed in a nonfiction text so that ideas are communicated clearly.

Rationale

When students think about how the graphics and print are placed in nonfiction books, they understand that the graphics and print work together to communicate ideas. They also understand that the people who create books (e.g., editors, designers) need to make decisions about how best to place the graphics and print.

Assess Learning

Observe students when they read and talk about nonfiction books and notice if there is evidence of new learning based on the goal of this minilesson.

- Can students infer why the graphics and print were placed on the page in a certain way?
- Do they use vocabulary such as *graphics, print, nonfiction, placed,* and *communicate*?

Minilesson

To help students think about the minilesson principle, engage them in a discussion about the placement of graphics and print. Here is an example.

- Show the cover of *Living Fossils* and read the title. Display and read aloud pages 4–5.

  What do you notice about how the graphics and print are arranged on these pages? What order are the photographs placed in, and why?

- Show the cover of *Grand Canyon* and read the title. Display pages 37–38. Point to and read the headings and captions.

  What do you notice about how the graphics and print are placed on these pages?

  Why do you think they are placed in this way?

Have a Try

Invite the students to talk with a partner about the placement of graphics and print in *Glow*.

▸ Show the cover of *Glow* and read the title. Then read and display pages 18–19.

> Turn and talk to your partner about what you notice about how the graphics and print are placed on these pages. Why do you think they are placed in this way?

▸ After time for discussion, invite a few pairs to share their thinking.

Summarize and Apply

Summarize the learning and remind students to notice the placement of graphics and print in nonfiction books.

> What did you notice today about the placement of the graphics and print in nonfiction books?

▸ Record students' responses on chart paper, and write the principle at the top of the chart.

> If you read a nonfiction book today, notice how the graphics and print are placed on the pages and think about why they might be placed that way. If you find a page that has the graphics and print placed in an interesting way, bring your example to share when we come back together.

Share

Following independent reading time, gather students together in the meeting area to talk about their reading.

> Did anyone find an example in a nonfiction book that has the graphics and print placed in an interesting way? Share a page layout with a partner.

> Why do you think the graphics and print are placed in that way?

Extend the Lesson (Optional)

After assessing students' understanding, you might decide to extend the learning.

▸ When students write their own nonfiction texts, encourage them to think about how best to place the print and graphics on a page. Teach them how to place graphics and print in interesting ways using word-processing or page-layout software.

The graphics and print are carefully placed in a nonfiction text to communicate ideas clearly.

- Graphics are usually placed near the print that they relate to.

- The graphics may be placed in a certain order to indicate a sequence.

Saguaro Cactus

Section 2: Literary Analysis

Assessment

After you have taught the minilessons in this umbrella, observe students as they talk and write about their reading across instructional contexts: interactive read-aloud, independent reading, guided reading, shared reading, and book club. Use *The Literacy Continuum* (Fountas and Pinnell 2017) to observe students' reading and writing behaviors.

▶ What evidence do you have of new understandings related to learning information from illustrations and graphics?

- Do students talk about what they learned from graphics in nonfiction books?
- Can they explain how a particular graphic communicates a bigger idea?
- Do they know how to read infographics?
- Can they infer why the graphics and print are placed a certain way on a page?
- Do they use academic language, such as *illustration, photograph, graphic, author, illustrator, diagram,* and *infographic*?

▶ In what other ways, beyond the scope of this umbrella, are students talking about nonfiction?

- Are students noticing different ways that nonfiction authors organize information?
- Are they using text features to find and gain information?

Use your observations to determine the next umbrella you will teach. You may also consult Minilessons Across the Year (pp. 61–64) for guidance.

Link to Writing

After teaching the minilessons in this umbrella, help students link the new learning to their own writing:

▶ Give students numerous opportunities to write their own nonfiction texts. Let them decide whether to include illustrations, photographs, infographics, or other types of graphics, and help them find or create relevant images. Remind them to use graphics that help the reader understand bigger ideas and to think about how to place the images on the page.

Reader's Notebook

When this umbrella is complete, provide a copy of the minilesson principles (see resources.fountasandpinnell.com) for students to glue in the reader's notebook (in the Minilessons section if using *Reader's Notebook: Advanced* [Fountas and Pinnell 2011]), so they can refer to the information as needed.

Minilessons in This Umbrella

RML1 Authors use headings and subheadings to help you understand the category of information.

RML2 Authors and illustrators use sidebars and timelines to emphasize or give additional information.

RML3 Authors include a table of contents and an index to help you find information.

Before Teaching Umbrella 20 Minilessons

Before teaching this umbrella, you might find it helpful to teach Umbrella 16: Noticing How Nonfiction Authors Choose to Organize Information. Additionally, be sure to read aloud and discuss a number of engaging, high-quality nonfiction books that include a variety of text and organizational features, such as headings, subheadings, sidebars, timelines, tables of contents, and indexes. Use the suggested examples from the *Fountas & Pinnell Classroom™ Interactive Read-Aloud Collection* or choose nonfiction books from your classroom library that have text and organizational features.

Animal Adaptations

Exploding Ants: Amazing Facts About How Animals Adapt by Joanne Settel

Life on Earth

Rotten! Vultures, Beetles, Slime, and Nature's Other Decomposers by Anita Sanchez

Living Fossils: Clues to the Past by Caroline Arnold

As you read aloud and enjoy these texts together, help students

- discuss the main idea of each page or section, and

- notice and use text features and organizational tools, such as headings and subheadings, sidebars, timelines, tables of contents, and indexes.

Animal Adaptations

Life on Earth

RML1
LA.U20.RML1

Reading Minilesson Principle
Authors use headings and subheadings to help you understand the category of information.

Using Text Features to Gain Information

You Will Need

- two familiar nonfiction books that have headings, including at least one that has subheadings, such as the following:
  - *Exploding Ants* by Joanne Settel, from Text Set: Animal Adaptations
  - *Rotten!* by Anita Sanchez, from Text Set: Life on Earth
- chart paper and markers
- document camera (optional)

Academic Language / Important Vocabulary

- nonfiction
- heading
- subheading
- category
- subcategory
- information

Continuum Connection

- Use headings and subheadings to search for and use information (p. 85)
- Notice and use and understand the purpose of some organizational tools: e.g., title, table of contents, chapter title, heading, subheading (p. 85)

Goal

Notice, use, and understand the purpose of headings and subheadings.

Rationale

When students notice and read headings and subheadings, they know what the upcoming section will be about and are better prepared for the information they will encounter because they can call on related information they already know. Using the organization of the headings and subheadings will help them locate information more quickly.

Assess Learning

Observe students when they read and talk about nonfiction books and notice if there is evidence of new learning based on the goal of this minilesson.

- ▸ Can students describe the purpose of and physical differences between headings, subheadings, and body text (font size, color, capital letters, etc.)?
- ▸ Can they use headings and subheadings to predict what a page or section will be about?
- ▸ Do they use academic language, such as *nonfiction, heading, subheading, category, subcategory,* and *information*?

Minilesson

To help students think about the minilesson principle, use familiar nonfiction texts to help students notice and discuss headings and subheadings. Project the pages, if possible, so that everyone can see them. Here is an example.

> Display pages 8–9 of *Exploding Ants*. Point to the heading ("fooled ya"). How is the print at the top of page 8 different from the rest of the print on these pages?
>
> The large print at the top of the page is the heading.

- ▸ Read the heading aloud and then the body text on pages 8–9.

  > Why did the author use a heading? What does the heading tell you?

- ▸ Point to the subheadings ("a disgusting disguise" and "fatal flashes") and read them aloud.

  > What do you notice about this print?
  >
  > These are subheadings. Why did the author use subheadings?
  >
  > How are subheadings different from headings?

Have a Try

Invite the students to talk with a partner about the headings in *Rotten!*

▶ Show the cover of *Rotten!* and pages 14–15.

> Turn and talk to your partner about what you think the information on these pages will be about and how you know.

▶ After time for discussion, invite a few students to share their thinking.

Summarize and Apply

Summarize the learning and remind students to read headings and subheadings.

▶ Ask students to summarize what they have learned about headings and subheadings. Make a chart summarizing their observations. Write the principle at the top.

> If you read a nonfiction book today, notice if it has headings and subheadings. If so, remember to read them and think about the information you'll find in the section.

Share

Following independent reading time, gather students together in the meeting area to talk about text features in nonfiction books.

> Who read a nonfiction book with headings and subheadings today?

> Show us a sample and describe how you used the heading or subheading while reading.

Extend the Lesson (Optional)

After assessing students' understanding, you might decide to extend the learning.

▶ **Writing About Reading** Have students create headings (and possibly subheadings) for a nonfiction book that does not have them.

Authors use headings and subheadings to help you understand the category of information.

	Purpose	Appearance
Headings	• to help you find information in the book • to indicate what category of information is on the page or in the section • to show the organization of the information	• bigger than the main print on the page • may be a different color • may have capital letters • located at the top of a page or section
Subheadings	• to indicate what the paragraph or short section is about • to show how a category of information is divided into subcategories	• smaller than the heading • look different from the main print (might be bigger, bold, italics, etc.)

Fooled Ya
A Disgusting Disguise

RML2
LA.U20.RML2

Reading Minilesson Principle
Authors and illustrators use sidebars and timelines to emphasize or give additional information.

Using Text Features to Gain Information

You Will Need

- one or two familiar nonfiction books that have sidebars and/or timelines, such as the following from Text Set: Life on Earth:
  - *Living Fossils* by Caroline Arnold
  - *Rotten!* by Anita Sanchez
- chart paper and markers
- document camera (optional)

Academic Language / Important Vocabulary

- author
- illustrator
- nonfiction
- body
- sidebar
- timeline
- information

Continuum Connection

- Gain new understandings from searching for and using information found in text body, sidebars, and graphics (p. 87)

Goal

Gain new understandings from sidebars and timelines and understand how they relate to the information in the body of the text.

Rationale

When students know how to look for, read, and think about the additional information provided in sidebars and timelines, they gain a fuller understanding of the topic of the book.

Assess Learning

Observe students when they read and talk about nonfiction books and notice if there is evidence of new learning based on the goal of this minilesson.

- ▶ Can students explain how the information in a sidebar or timeline relates to the information in the text body?
- ▶ Do they use academic vocabulary, such as *author, illustrator, nonfiction, body, sidebar, timeline,* and *information*?

Minilesson

To help students think about the minilesson principle, engage them in a discussion about the purpose of sidebars and timelines. Project the pages, if possible, so that everyone can see them. Here is an example.

- ▶ Show the cover of *Living Fossils* and read the title. Then display page 10. Read the body text and then the sidebar.

  How does this part of the page look different from the rest of the page?

  Does anyone know what this text feature is called?

  This is a sidebar. How does the information in the sidebar relate to the information on the main part of the page? The main part is called the body of the text.

  On this page, the author uses sidebars to give some extra information about horseshoe crabs: how they survive. Sometimes, a writer might also use a sidebar to highlight or emphasize information that is in the body of the text.

- ▶ Display pages 28–29. Read a few of the entries on the timeline.

  What is this text feature called?

  What does this timeline tell you about?

  What is the purpose of a timeline?

Have a Try

Invite the students to talk with a partner about the sidebars in *Rotten!*

▶ Display page 56 from *Rotten!* Read the text body followed by the sidebar.

> Why do you think the author put this information in a sidebar instead of in the body of the page? Turn and talk to your partner about what you think.

▶ After students turn and talk, invite a few students to share their thinking.

Summarize and Apply

Summarize the learning and remind students to read sidebars and timelines.

> Why do nonfiction authors use sidebars and timelines?

▶ Record students' responses on chart paper and write the principle at the top.

> When you read today, remember to read every part of the page, including the sidebars or timelines if your book has them. Think about how the information in the sidebars or timelines relates to the information in the rest of the book. Be ready to share your thinking when we come back together.

Share

Following independent reading time, gather students together in the meeting area to talk about text features in nonfiction books.

> Who read a book that has sidebars or timelines?

> What did the information in the sidebars or timelines have to do with the rest of the book?

Extend the Lesson (Optional)

After assessing students' understanding, you might decide to extend the learning.

▶ Encourage students to include sidebars and timelines when they write their own nonfiction books.

▶ **Writing About Reading** Have students make a timeline of the events described in a nonfiction book.

Authors and illustrators use sidebars and timelines to emphasize or give additional information.

Authors use sidebars and timelines to—

- give extra information about the topic.

- give more details about something discussed in the body of the text.

Sidebar
• Gives more information
• Emphasizes information

- share information that is not important enough to be included in the main text but is still interesting.

- highlight or emphasize information.

Timeline

I billion years ago	500 million years ago	Now

Reading Minilesson Principle

Authors include a table of contents and an index to help you find information.

Using Text Features to Gain Information

You Will Need

- two familiar nonfiction books that have a table of contents and/or an index, such as the following:
  - *Exploding Ants* by Joanne Settel, from Text Set: Animal Adaptations
  - *Rotten!* by Anita Sanchez, from Text Set: Life on Earth
- chart paper and markers
- document camera (optional)

Academic Language / Important Vocabulary

- nonfiction
- topic
- subtopic
- information
- index
- table of contents

Continuum Connection

- Notice and use and understand the purpose of some other text resources: e.g., glossary, index (p. 87)

Goal

Notice, use, and, understand the purpose of the table of contents and the index.

Rationale

When students know how to use a table of contents and an index, they are able to find information about a specific topic in a nonfiction book.

Assess Learning

Observe students when they read and talk about nonfiction books and notice if there is evidence of new learning based on the goal of this minilesson.

▶ Can students explain the similarities and differences between a table of contents and an index?

▶ Do they use academic vocabulary, such as *nonfiction, topic, subtopic, information, index,* and *table of contents*?

Minilesson

To help students think about the minilesson principle, use familiar nonfiction texts to discuss the information in tables of contents and indexes. Project the pages, if possible, so that everyone can see them. Here is an example.

▶ Show the cover of *Exploding Ants* and read the title. Then display the table of contents.

▶ Guide students to talk about a table of contents: its purpose, its organization, its use. Then display the index and guide students in a similar discussion.

▶ Point to the entry for *birds*.

> What do you notice about the words underneath *birds*? What do they have to do with birds?

> This index lists both topics and subtopics. *Birds* is a topic that is discussed in this book. This topic is divided into smaller subtopics, like cuckoo birds and the feeding of young birds. What do you notice about the order of the topics and subtopics in the index?

> The topics are listed in alphabetical order. The subtopics under each topic are also in alphabetical order. How is an index different from a table of contents?

Have a Try

Invite the students to talk with a partner about the index in *Rotten!*

▶ Show the cover of *Rotten!* and read the title. Then display the index.

> What page would you go to if you wanted to read about how a rotting tree smells? Look carefully at the index, and then turn and talk to your partner about what you think.

▶ After students turn and talk, invite a few pairs to share their thinking. If necessary, guide students to look under the *smell and smelling* entry for the *rotting tree* subentry.

Summarize and Apply

Summarize the learning and remind students to use tables of contents and indexes.

▶ Have students summarize what they know about tables of contents and indexes. Use their responses to make a Venn diagram that shows the similarities and differences between them. Write the principle at the top.

> If you read a nonfiction book today, notice if it has a table of contents or an index. If so, use it to find information in your book. Be ready to share how you used the table of contents or index when we come back together.

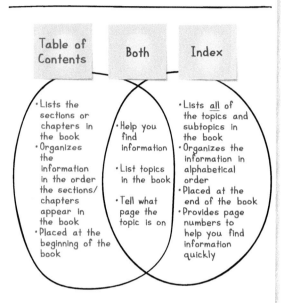

Authors include a table of contents and an index to help you find information.

Table of Contents
- Lists the sections or chapters in the book
- Organizes the information in the order the sections/chapters appear in the book
- Placed at the beginning of the book

Both
- Help you find information
- List topics in the book
- Tell what page the topic is on

Index
- Lists <u>all</u> of the topics and subtopics in the book
- Organizes the information in alphabetical order
- Placed at the end of the book
- Provides page numbers to help you find information quickly

Share

Following independent reading time, gather students together in the meeting area to talk about text features in nonfiction books.

> Who read a nonfiction book that has a table of contents or an index?

> How did you use the table of contents or index? How did it help you?

Extend the Lesson (Optional)

After assessing students' understanding, you might decide to extend the learning.

▶ Teach students how to use a bibliography to evaluate the accuracy and quality of a text. The bibliography in *Rotten!* can be used as an example.

Section 2: Literary Analysis

Assessment

After you have taught the minilessons in this umbrella, observe students as they talk and write about their reading across instructional contexts: interactive read-aloud, independent reading, guided reading, shared reading, and book club. Use *The Literacy Continuum* (Fountas and Pinnell 2017) to guide the observation of students' reading and writing behaviors.

▶ What evidence do you have of new understandings related to students' use of text features to gain information?

- Can students describe the purpose and appearance of headings and subheadings?

- Can they explain what sidebars and timelines are used for?

- Are they able to use a table of contents and an index to find information?

- Do they use academic language, such as *nonfiction, heading, subheading, information, sidebar, timeline, table of contents,* and *index*?

▶ In what other ways, beyond the scope of this umbrella, are students talking about nonfiction books?

- Have they noticed that there are different types of nonfiction books (e.g., biography, persuasive)?

- Are they noticing different ways nonfiction books are organized?

Use your observations to determine the next umbrella you will teach. You may also consult Minilessons Across the Year (pp. 61–64) for guidance.

Link to Writing

After teaching the minilessons in this umbrella, help students link the new learning to their own writing:

▶ Encourage students to use headings and subheadings in their own writing. Suggest that they include extra information about the topic in sidebars and/ or timelines. Encourage them to include a table of contents and/or an index to help readers find information.

Reader's Notebook

When this umbrella is complete, provide a copy of the minilesson principles (see resources.fountasandpinnell.com) for students to glue in the reader's notebook (in the Minilessons section if using *Reader's Notebook: Advanced* [Fountas and Pinnell 2011]), so they can refer to the information as needed.

Minilessons in This Umbrella

RML1   Notice how realistic fiction writers make the plot and characters seem real.

RML2   Evaluate whether the plot and story outcome are believable.

RML3   Evaluate whether the author accurately portrays current social issues.

Before Teaching Umbrella 21 Minilessons

Before teaching the minilessons in this umbrella, students should be familiar with realistic fiction as a genre and be able to recognize texts as realistic fiction and name some characteristics of the genre.

While reading realistic fiction as a class, notice and read any author's notes included in the books in order to gain a richer understanding of the stories.

Use the following books from the *Fountas & Pinnell Classroom™ Interactive Read-Aloud Collection* text sets or choose other realistic fiction texts with which your students are familiar.

Exploring Identity

A Different Pond by Bao Phi

Garvey's Choice by Nikki Grimes

Flying Lessons & Other Stories edited by Ellen Oh

Border Crossing by Maria Colleen Cruz

Handling Emotions/Positive Relationships

The Banana-Leaf Ball: How Play Can Change the World by Katie Smith Milway

Eagle Song by Joseph Bruchac

Perseverance

Stepping Stones: A Refugee Family's Journey by Margriet Ruurs

As you read aloud and enjoy these texts together, help students

- identify what makes them realistic fiction,
- think about what makes the plot and story outcome believable,
- recognize ways a writer makes the plot and characters seem real, and
- evaluate how social issues are portrayed.

Exploring Identity

Handling Emotions/ Positive Relationships

Perseverance

Section 2: Literary Analysis

RML1

LA.U21.RML1

Reading Minilesson Principle

Notice how realistic fiction writers make the plot and characters seem real.

Understanding Realistic Fiction

Goal

Notice how realistic fiction writers make the plot and characters seem real.

Rationale

When you teach students to notice how realistic fiction writers make the plot and characters seem real, it helps them to understand the text better, make authentic personal connections, analyze the writer's craft, and learn how to add believable plot and character details to their own writing.

Assess Learning

Observe students when they talk about realistic fiction. Notice if there is evidence of new learning based on the goal of this minilesson.

- Can students explain how an author makes the plot and characters seem real?
- Do they recognize which details make a plot or character seem real?
- Do they understand and use the terms *realistic fiction, character, plot,* and *dialogue*?

Minilesson

To help students think about the minilesson principle, use familiar realistic fiction texts and invite them to notice how authors make the plot and characters seem real. Here is an example.

- Show *A Different Pond*.

    Here's a book you've read before. What type of book is it?

- Make sure students understand that *A Different Pond* is realistic fiction.

    The most important characteristic of realistic fiction is that you, the reader, have to be convinced that everything in the book could exist in real life. How does the author of *A Different Pond* do that? Think about activities that the boy and his father do, for example.

    The author has the characters do things that real people would do. That makes the story seem real.

    What else does the author do to make the book seem real? Think about how the dialogue sounds or how the characters are feeling.

- Record responses on chart paper.

- Guide students to consider the reality of the characters' actions and dialogue as well as the characters' feelings and the story's events.

Have a Try

Invite the students to notice how realistic fiction writers make the plot and characters seem real.

▶ Show *Flying Lessons & Other Stories*.

> Turn and talk to your partner about Merci and her father in the short story "Sol Painting, Inc." What does the author do to make the characters and the plot seem real?

▶ Have a few students share. Add responses to the chart.

Summarize and Apply

Summarize the learning and remind students to think about how realistic fiction authors make characters and the plot seem real.

▶ Review the chart and write the principle at the top.

> When you read today, choose a realistic fiction story if you are not already reading one. As you read, think about what the author does to make the characters and the plot seem real. Be ready to share your noticings when we come back together.

Notice how realistic fiction writers make the plot and characters seem real.

What Makes Realistic Fiction Seem Real		
The characters do things that real people would do.	• The boy helps his father by starting a fire and catching fish for dinner. • The boy asks about his father's brother.	• Merci argues with her mother about her grades.
The dialogue sounds natural.	• "Can I help?" • "Sure."	• "You think they'll need a painter soon?"
The characters' feelings seem real.	• The boy misses his parents when they are at work.	• Merci is angry the girls aren't punished for messing up the paint job.
The story events seem real.	• The boy and his father go fishing early in the morning. • The family eats the fish for dinner.	• Merci's father takes a job to pay her school tuition. He must swallow his pride so that her chances of going to that school aren't ruined.

Share

Following independent reading time, gather students in small groups to talk about realistic fiction books.

> Talk in your groups about how the author made the characters and the plot seem real.

▶ Invite a few students to share after their small-group discussions.

Extend the Lesson (Optional)

After assessing students' understanding, you might decide to extend the learning.

▶ Ask students to notice other ways writers make characters and plots seem real, such as by showing characters' feelings and thoughts, by describing a realistic setting, or by incorporating realistic themes.

▶ **Writing About Reading** Have students fill in a grid similar to the chart in this lesson (visit resources.fountasandpinnell.com) to analyze how an author makes a realistic fiction book seem real. They can glue the grid into a reader's notebook.

RML2
LA.U21.RML2

Evaluate whether the plot and story outcome are believable.

Understanding Realistic Fiction

You Will Need

- two or three realistic fiction books, such as the following:
  - *Border Crossing* by Maria Colleen Cruz, from Text Set: Exploring Identity
  - *The Banana-Leaf Ball* by Katie Smith Milway, from Text Set: Handling Emotions/ Positive Relationships
  - *Stepping Stones* by Margriet Ruurs, from Text Set: Perseverance
- chart paper and markers

Academic Language / Important Vocabulary

- realistic fiction
- events
- plot
- dialogue
- ending
- believable
- evaluate

Continuum Connection

- Evaluate the logic and believability of the plot and its resolution [p. 81]

Goal

Evaluate the believability of a realistic fiction text.

Rationale

A key characteristic of realistic fiction is that, even though parts are imagined by the author, the story has to be believable. When you teach students to read realistic fiction with this awareness, looking to see that each part of the story seems real, you teach them to read critically.

Assess Learning

Observe students when they talk about realistic fiction. Notice if there is evidence of new learning based on the goal of this minilesson.

- ▶ Can students decide whether the elements of a realistic fiction story are believable or not?
- ▶ Are they thinking critically about realistic fiction stories?
- ▶ Can they use important language, such as *realistic fiction, events, plot, dialogue, ending, believable,* and *evaluate*?

Minilesson

To help students think about the minilesson principle, use familiar realistic fiction texts to help them consider the believability of the plot and story outcome. Here is an example.

- ▶ Hold up *Border Crossing*.

  This book is realistic fiction. What happens in the story that you think could happen in real life?

- ▶ Record responses on a chart.

  Are there also parts of the plot that are harder to believe could actually happen in real life? Why do you think that?

- ▶ Record responses on the chart.

  Do you believe the story outcome—the ending—could happen in real life? Why do you think that?

- ▶ Record responses on the chart.

  Why do you think the story outcome in a realistic fiction book should seem believable?

- ▶ Repeat this process for another realistic fiction text, such as *The Banana-Leaf Ball*.

Section 2: Literary Analysis

Have a Try

Invite the students to talk with a partner about the plot and story outcome of *Stepping Stones*.

> Turn and talk to a partner about the parts of *Stepping Stones* that you find believable and the parts that you find less believable.

▶ After they turn and talk, ask a few students to share. Record responses on the chart.

Summarize and Apply

Summarize the learning and remind students to evaluate the believability of the plot and story outcomes in a realistic fiction text.

> A realistic fiction story has characters, a plot, a setting, and an outcome that could be real, but you may not always find the elements believable. You can think about—or evaluate—whether parts of the story are believable.

▶ Write the principle at the top of the chart.

> Choose a realistic fiction book to read today. As you read, think about whether the plot and story outcome are believable. Be ready to share when we meet.

Title	What seems believable?	What seems harder to believe?
Border Crossing CAUTION	• Cesi wants to learn more about her father and his family. • She learns she has two families, one in California and one in Mexico.	• That a twelve-year-old could cross the border without being questioned • The coincidence that the stranger who helps Cesi is actually a relative
The Banana-Leaf Ball	• The family flees their country to escape the war. • Deo makes new friends through soccer.	• That a young boy could survive separation from his family during a war and travel alone to a refugee camp
STEPPING STONES	• The family leaves their home country because of a war. • People in their new country help them.	• That the family could actually walk to safety

Evaluate whether the plot and story outcome are believable.

Share

Following independent reading time, gather students together in the meeting area to talk about realistic fiction.

> Were the plot and its outcome believable in the realistic fiction book you read today? What makes you say that?

Extend the Lesson (Optional)

After assessing students' understanding, you might decide to extend the learning.

▶ If a plot or story outcome seems hard to believe, encourage students to look for notes or resources in the book that support the believability of the plot, such as in *A Different Pond* and *Stepping Stones*.

▶ Extend the discussion about the believability of realistic fiction so that students think about whether that lack of believability affects the quality of the story. Do they like the story any less if some parts are not believable?

▶ **Writing About Reading** Have students write in a reader's notebook an evaluation of whether a realistic fiction story is believable.

RML 3

LA.U21.RML3

Reading Minilesson Principle

Evaluate whether the author accurately portrays current social issues.

Understanding Realistic Fiction

You Will Need

- two or three familiar realistic fiction texts, such as the following:
  - *Garvey's Choice* by Nikki Grimes, from Text Set: Exploring Identity
  - *The Banana-Leaf Ball* by Katie Smith Milway and *Eagle Song* by Joseph Bruchac, from Text Set: Handling Emotions/ Positive Relationships
- chart paper and markers

Academic Language / Important Vocabulary

- realistic fiction
- author
- portrays
- social issue
- accurate

Continuum Connection

- Critique a fiction text in terms of authenticity of characters, accurate portrayal of current or past issues, voice, tone, accuracy of setting (p. 79)

Goal

Evaluate whether an author accurately portrays current social issues.

Rationale

When you teach students to exercise critical thinking skills to evaluate a story's portrayal of current social issues, they learn to make connections between their reading and the world around them.

Assess Learning

Observe students when they read and talk about realistic fiction. Notice if there is evidence of new learning based on the goal of this minilesson.

- ▶ Can students identify social issues in realistic fiction texts?
- ▶ Can they evaluate whether the social issues are accurately portrayed?
- ▶ Are they using language such as *realistic fiction, author, portrays, social issue,* and *accurate*?

Minilesson

To help students think about the minilesson principle, use familiar realistic fiction texts to evaluate whether the author accurately portrays current social issues.

- ▶ Show *Garvey's Choice* and review a few pages to remind students of the story.

  This is a realistic fiction book. What are some of the issues Garvey deals with? What happens to him?

  Bullying is an example of a social issue—a problem that affects a lot of people and that people want to solve.

  Do you think the author portrays, or shows, bullying in an accurate way? Could what happens to Garvey happen in real life? What makes the issue seem real or not?

- ▶ Record responses on a chart.
- ▶ Repeat this process for the book *The Banana-Leaf Ball*.

  The effect of war on families such as Deo's is another example of a social issue.

Have a Try

Invite the students to talk with a partner about the portrayal of a social issue in *Eagle Song*.

> Turn and talk to a partner. What social issue does the author portray in this book? How does the author write about it? Is this portrayal realistic?

▶ After students turn and talk, ask a few students to share, and record their responses on the chart.

Summarize and Apply

Summarize the learning and remind students to evaluate how social issues are portrayed in realistic fiction.

> Today you thought about how authors portray current social issues and whether the portrayals are accurate.

▶ Review the chart and write the principle at the top.

> Today, choose a realistic fiction book to read, or continue reading one you have started. Notice if the author writes about a social issue. Think about what makes the portrayal accurate. Be prepared to share when we come back together.

Evaluate whether the author accurately portrays current social issues.		
Title	Social Issue	Is the issue portrayed accurately?
GARVEY'S CHOICE	Bullying	Yes — • Bullying sometimes happens to kids. • Learning to love yourself and appreciate your talents helps cope with it.
	War	Yes — • War can force families apart. • Refugee camps try to help people fleeing their country.
EAGLE SONG	Racism	Yes — • Prejudice happens when people don't understand one another. • Learning about your own culture and sharing that with others helps overcome prejudices.
	Prejudice	

Share

Following independent reading time, gather students together to share as a group.

> Who noticed a social issue in a realistic fiction story today? Tell us what it was. Did the author accurately portray it?

Extend the Lesson (Optional)

After assessing students' understanding, you might decide to extend the learning.

▶ Continue to identify and discuss social issues in the realistic fiction books students read. Encourage students to conduct research to learn more about the social issues they identify that interest them.

▶ **Writing About Reading** Ask students to use a realistic fiction book they read and enjoyed to create a web with a social issue at the center and notes about the issue radiating out from the center. Ask them to write a short paragraph explaining why they thought the issue was or was not portrayed accurately.

Section 2: Literary Analysis

Assessment

After you have taught the minilessons in this umbrella, observe students as they talk and write about their reading across instructional contexts: interactive read-aloud, independent reading, guided reading, shared reading, and book club. Use *The Literacy Continuum* (Fountas and Pinnell 2017) to guide the observation of students' reading and writing behaviors.

▶ What evidence do you have of new understandings related to realistic fiction?

  • Are students able to identify realistic fiction texts?

  • Can they explain how the characters, plot, and outcome are realistic?

  • Do they notice how writers make the plot and characters seem real?

  • Do they identify parts of the story that may not be as believable as other parts of the story, and can they explain their thinking?

  • Do they use terms such as *realistic fiction, character, plot, outcome, believable, evaluate,* and *dialogue*?

▶ In what other ways, beyond the scope of this umbrella, are students talking about realistic fiction?

  • Do students show an interest in the writer's craft?

  • Are they able to summarize a fiction text?

Use your observations to determine the next umbrella you will teach. You may also consult Minilessons Across the Year (pp. 61–64) for guidance.

Link to Writing

After teaching the minilessons in this umbrella, help students link the new learning to their own writing:

▶ When students write a realistic fiction story, remind them that the characters, plot, and setting must seem like they could occur in real life. Ask them to consider the details that will make their story seem real.

Reader's Notebook

When this umbrella is complete, provide a copy of the minilesson principles (see resources.fountasandpinnell.com) for students to glue in the reader's notebook (in the Minilessons section if using *Reader's Notebook: Advanced* [Fountas and Pinnell 2011]), so they can refer to the information as needed.

Minilessons in This Umbrella

RML1 Historical fiction is always imagined but may be based on real people, places, or events.

RML2 The setting is important to the story in historical fiction.

RML3 Evaluate whether the author accurately portrays past social issues.

RML4 Historical fiction writers use the past to give a message that can be applied today.

Before Teaching Umbrella 22 Minilessons

Before teaching the minilessons in this umbrella, students should be familiar with historical fiction as a genre and be able to recognize texts as historical fiction and name some characteristics of the genre.

While reading historical fiction aloud, notice and read any author's notes included in the books to give students a richer understanding of the stories. Use the following books from the *Fountas & Pinnell Classroom™ Interactive Read-Aloud Collection* text sets or choose other historical fiction texts with which your students are familiar.

Perseverance

The Memory Coat by Elvira Woodruff

The Turtle Ship by Helena Ku Rhee

Civic Engagement

Memphis, Martin, and the Mountaintop: The Sanitation Strike of 1968 by Alice Faye Duncan

Equality

As Fast As Words Could Fly by Pamela M. Tuck

Illustration Study: Mood

What You Know First by Patricia MacLachlan

As you read aloud and enjoy these texts together, help students

* think about whether characters, settings, or problems are based on actual historic events,

* evaluate the accuracy of the author's portrayal of past social issues, and

* make connections between an author's message and their own lives.

Perseverance

Civic Engagement

Equality

Illustration Study: Mood

Section 2: Literary Analysis

Reading Minilesson Principle

Historical fiction is always imagined but may be based on real people, places, or events.

Exploring Historical Fiction

You Will Need

- several familiar historical fiction books, such as the following:
  - *The Turtle Ship* by Helena Ku Rhee and *The Memory Coat* by Elvira Woodruff, from Text Set: Perseverance
  - *Memphis, Martin, and the Mountaintop* by Alice Faye Duncan, from Text Set: Civic Engagement
- chart paper and markers
- basket of historical fiction books

Academic Language / Important Vocabulary

- historical fiction
- characters
- setting
- imagined

Continuum Connection

- Notice and understand the characteristics of some specific fiction genres: e.g., realistic fiction, historical fiction, folktale, fairy tale, fractured fairy tale, fable, myth, legend, epic, ballad, fantasy including science fiction, hybrid text (p. 79)

Goal

Understand that historical fiction is always imagined but may be based on real people, places, or events.

Rationale

When students recognize that historical fiction stories are always imagined but that they may be based on real people, places or events, they understand that the author is recreating a period of history but not everything in the story actually happened. Knowing which parts are based in reality and which parts are imagined by the author will help them evaluate the authenticity of historical fiction books they read.

Assess Learning

Observe students when they read and talk about historical fiction stories. Notice if there is evidence of new learning based on the goal of this minilesson.

- ▶ Do students recognize that historical fiction stories are imagined but that they may be based on real people, places, or events?
- ▶ Can they distinguish between the imagined and the real people, places, and events?
- ▶ Do they use language such as *historical fiction*, *characters*, *setting*, and *imagined*?

Minilesson

To help students think about the minilesson principle, use familiar historical fiction stories to engage them in a discussion of what is imagined and what is real. Here is an example.

- ▶ Show the cover of *The Turtle Ship* and then review a few pages to remind students of the story. Then read the author's note.

    What do you notice about the author's note?

    Which parts of *The Turtle Ship* are imagined and which parts are based on real people or real events?

    What is real about the setting?

- ▶ Record responses on a chart.

    Think about another historical fiction book, *The Memory Coat*.

- ▶ From the section called Historic Notes at the end of the book, read the first paragraphs of Life in Russia and Ellis Island.

    What is real and what is imagined about the characters, setting, and events?

- ▶ Add responses to the chart.

    Why do authors base historical fiction stories on real characters, places, and events?

Have a Try

Invite the students to talk with a partner about whether a historical fiction book is based on real people, places, or events.

▶ Show *Memphis, Martin, and the Mountaintop* and read the first page of text.

Turn and talk with a partner about which parts of this historical fiction book are based on real people, places, or events. What evidence do you have for that?

▶ Ask students to share their thinking and add responses to the chart. Show the timeline and other notes from the author at the end of the book if the students don't refer to these themselves.

Summarize and Apply

Summarize the learning and remind students to think about whether a historical fiction book they read is based on real people, places, or events.

Look at the chart. What did you learn today about historical fiction stories?

▶ Add the principle to the top of the chart.

Additional information included in an author's note, on the back of the book, or on the book jacket will help you know which parts are real and which parts are imagined.

You may want to choose a historical fiction book from this basket today. If you do, think about whether the people, places, or events are real or imagined. Bring the book with you when we meet so you can share.

Share

Following independent reading time, gather students in the meeting area to talk about historical fiction.

Who read a historical fiction book today?

Tell about a part that is based on real people, places, or events.

Extend the Lesson (Optional)

After assessing students' understanding, you might decide to extend the learning.

▶ Have students conduct research on a real person, place, or event they have read about. Ask them to share what they learned with the class.

Historical fiction is always imagined but may be based on real people, places, or events.

Title	Real People	Real Place	Real Event
THE TURTLE SHIP	• Admiral Yi Sun-Sin	• Korea	• During the Joseon Dynasty, the Turtle Ship was used for battle by Korea's royal navy
The Memory Coat	• Russian-Jewish immigrants	• Russia • Ellis Island	• Immigration to the US through Ellis Island
MEMPHIS, MARTIN, AND THE MOUNTAINTOP	• Sanitation workers • Mayor Henry Loeb • Martin Luther King Jr.	• Memphis, TN	• Sanitation Strike of 1968

Reading Minilesson Principle
The setting is important to the story in historical fiction.

You Will Need

- several familiar historical fiction books, such as the following:
  - *Memphis, Martin, and the Mountaintop* by Alice Faye Duncan, from Text Set: Civic Engagement
  - *What You Know First* by Patricia MacLachlan, from Text Set: Illustration Study: Mood
  - *The Memory Coat* by Elvira Woodruff, from Text Set: Perseverance
- chart paper and markers

Academic Language / Important Vocabulary

- historical fiction
- setting
- plot
- characters

Continuum Connection

- Infer the importance of the setting to the plot of the story in realistic and historical fiction and fantasy (p. 80)

Goal

Infer the importance of the setting to the plot of the story in historical fiction.

Rationale

When students understand the importance of setting in historical fiction stories, they gain a deeper understanding of the time period. They also develop an awareness of the author's craft: choices that writers make to create a sense of authenticity and to drive the plot.

Assess Learning

Observe students when they read and talk about historical fiction books. Notice if there is evidence of new learning based on the goal of this minilesson.

- ▶ Do students understand the importance of setting in historical fiction books?
- ▶ Do they use academic language, such as *historical fiction, setting, plot,* and *characters*?

Minilesson

To help students think about the minilesson principle, use familiar historical fiction stories to demonstrate how they can think about the setting and its importance to the plot. Here is an example.

- ▶ From *Memphis, Martin, and the Mountaintop,* show and read the page titled Memphis—1968.

  Describe the setting (place and time) in this historical fiction book.

- ▶ Record responses on a chart.

  Why do you think the author has the story take place in Memphis, Tennessee, at this time?

- ▶ As students share ideas, engage them in a conversation about the importance of setting in historical fiction. The following prompts may be helpful:
  - *How does the setting affect the plot?*
  - *How does the setting affect what the characters do and say?*
  - *Could the events in this story occur in a different time and place?*

- ▶ Continue the discussion about setting. Add responses to the chart.

  Now think about the setting in another familiar historical fiction book, *What You Know First.* What do you know about the setting?

  Why is it important that this story takes place in a prairie farmhouse during the Great Depression?

Have a Try

Invite the students to talk with a partner about the setting in a historical fiction book.

▶ Show *The Memory Coat.*

> Turn and talk with a partner about the setting in this historical fiction book. Where does the beginning of the book take place? How does the setting impact the plot?

▶ After time for discussion, ask a few students to share. Add to the chart.

Summarize and Apply

Summarize the learning and remind students to think about how setting impacts plot in historical fiction.

> What does the chart show about the setting in historical fiction stories?

▶ Review the chart and add the principle to the top.

> If you read a historical fiction book today, think about how the setting is important to the plot. Bring the book with you when we meet so you can share.

Share

Following independent reading time, gather students in the meeting area to talk about historical fiction.

> Did anyone read a historical fiction book today?

> Tell about the setting. Why was it important to the plot?

Extend the Lesson (Optional)

After assessing students' understanding, you might decide to extend the learning.

▶ Have students work with partners to conduct research about the setting of historical fiction books they read. Invite students to share their findings with the class.

▶ **Writing About Reading** Have students write in a reader's notebook about the setting of a historical fiction book and how the setting is related to the plot. Encourage them to write about how the plot would be different if the setting were different.

The setting is important to the story in historical fiction.

Title	Setting	Why is it important to the plot?
MEMPHIS, MARTIN, AND THE MOUNTAINTOP	• Memphis, Tennessee • During the civil rights movement and the Sanitation Strike of 1968	• The city was completely focused on these events. • Lorraine's father was a sanitation worker in Memphis. • Lorraine joined a protest to fight for equal rights.
WHAT YOU KNOW FIRST	• Prairie farmhouse • During the Great Depression	• The main character often thinks about and misses her home after the family has to sell the farm.
The Memory Coat	• Pogroms in Jewish towns throughout Russia	• This is the reason Rachel's family flees Russia and emigrates to the United States.

Reading Minilesson Principle
Evaluate whether the author accurately portrays past social issues.

You Will Need

- several familiar historical fiction books, such as the following:
  - *The Memory Coat* by Elvira Woodruff, from Text Set: Perseverance
  - *As Fast As Words Could Fly* by Pamela M. Tuck, from Text Set: Equality
- chart paper prepared with four columns and the headings and first column filled in
- markers

Academic Language / Important Vocabulary

- historical fiction
- accurate
- portray
- social issues

Continuum Connection

- Critique a fiction text in terms of authenticity of characters, accurate portrayal of current or past issues, voice, tone, accuracy of setting (p. 79)

Goal

Evaluate whether a historical fiction author accurately portrays past social issues.

Rationale

When you teach students to exercise critical thinking skills to evaluate an author's portrayal of past social issues, they learn to utilize and expand those skills. You may also want to discuss how students can use other resources to check the text for accuracy.

Assess Learning

Observe students when they read and talk about historical fiction books. Notice if there is evidence of new learning based on the goal of this minilesson.

- ▶ Can students evaluate whether social issues are accurately portrayed?
- ▶ Do they use terms such as *historical fiction, accurate, portray,* and *social issues*?

Minilesson

To help students think about the minilesson principle, use familiar historical fiction texts to evaluate whether the author accurately portrays past social issues. Here is an example.

- ▶ Show *The Memory Coat.*

  This is a historical fiction book. What are some of the issues Rachel faces? What happens to her and her family?

  Discrimination because of a person's religion is an example of a social issue—a problem—that a lot of people think about and want to solve. Do you think the author portrays, or shows, discrimination against Jewish people during that time in history accurately?

  What about their emigration from Russia? How could you evaluate whether the author presents these issues in a way that is true to how they actually happened?

- ▶ Record responses on the prepared chart.
- ▶ Show the sections titled Author's Note and Historic Notes at the end of the book and read short excerpts of both.

  What do these facts tell you about how the social issues in the book are presented?

  What actually happened? Is this different from or the same as what happens in the story?

  Do you think that the author accurately portrays these social issues?

- ▶ Record responses on the chart.

Have a Try

Invite the students to talk with a partner about the portrayal of a past social issue in another historical fiction text.

▶ Show a few pages of *As Fast As Words Could Fly* and then read paragraphs two and four from the page titled Author's Note.

> Turn and talk with a partner. What past social issue does the author portray in this book? How does the author write about it? Is this portrayal accurate? Why do you think that?

▶ After time for discussion, ask students to share. Add to the chart.

Summarize and Apply

Summarize the learning and remind students to evaluate how past social issues are portrayed in historical fiction.

> What do you understand about how writers of historical fiction portray past social issues?

▶ Review the chart and add the principle to the top.

> If you are reading a historical fiction book today, notice if the author writes about a past social issue. Think about what makes the portrayal accurate. Be prepared to share when we come back together.

Share

Following independent reading time, gather students together to talk about historical fiction.

> Who noticed a past social issue in a historical fiction story today? Tell us what it was. Did the author accurately portray it? How do you know that?

Extend the Lesson (Optional)

After assessing students' understanding, you might decide to extend the learning.

▶ Continue to identify and discuss past social issues in the historical fiction books students read. Encourage students to conduct research to learn more about the past social issues they identify that interest them.

▶ **Writing About Reading** Ask students to compare and contrast how two different historical fiction texts portray the same social issue of the past.

Evaluate whether the author accurately portrays past social issues.

Title	How is the social issue portrayed in the book?	What actually happened during this time in history?	How do you check for accuracy?
	• Cossacks killed Jewish people in Rachel's town. • Rachel and her family were afraid they would not be allowed entrance to the US.	• Pogroms (mass killings) occurred in Jewish towns across Russia. • Emigrants faced many difficulties at Ellis Island. Many were deported to their home countries.	• Author's Note • Historic Notes
As Fast As Words Could Fly	• Mason faced prejudice as one of the first African Americans to attend Belvoir High School. • He persevered and succeeded despite the prejudice.	• Racial segregation of schools ended in 1954. • Moses Teel Jr. used his typing talents to overcome the challenges of attending a previously all-white school.	• Author's Note

RML4
LA.U22.RML4

Reading Minilesson Principle
Historical fiction writers use the past to give a message that can be applied today.

You Will Need

- several familiar historical fiction books, such as the following:
  - *Memphis, Martin, and the Mountaintop* by Alice Faye Duncan, from Text Set: Civic Engagement
  - *As Fast As Words Could Fly* by Pamela M. Tuck, from Text Set: Equality
  - *The Memory Coat* by Elvira Woodruff, from Text Set: Perseverance
- chart paper and markers

Academic Language / Important Vocabulary

- historical fiction
- message
- apply

Continuum Connection

- Understand that the messages or big ideas in fiction texts can be applied to their own lives or to other people and society (p. 80)

Goal

Understand that the messages in historical fiction can be applied to their own lives, to other people's lives, or to society today.

Rationale

When you teach students to notice and think about the message in historical fiction books, they understand that events that happened in the past affect how we live our lives in the present. You may want to teach LA.U8.RML1 before this lesson to ensure students understand how to notice the author's message.

Assess Learning

Observe students when they read and talk about historical fiction books. Notice if there is evidence of new learning based on the goal of this minilesson.

- ▶ Are students able to identify the author's message(s) in historical fiction books?
- ▶ Can they explain how these messages are applied to their own lives?
- ▶ Do they use language such as *historical fiction*, *message*, and *apply*?

Minilesson

To help students think about the minilesson principle, guide students to infer the author's message and think about how the message applies to life today. Here is an example.

- ▶ Show *Memphis, Martin, and the Mountaintop*.

  What message about this time in history do you think the author is trying to share with you? Turn and talk about that.

- ▶ After time for discussion, ask students to share their thinking. Use students' responses to create a chart.

  Do you think this message applies to your own life today? How?

- ▶ Add to the chart.
- ▶ Repeat this process with *As Fast As Words Could Fly*.

Have a Try

Invite the students to talk with a partner about the message in another historical fiction story.

▶ Show *The Memory Coat*.

Turn and talk with a partner. What do you think the author's message is about this time in history? Does it apply to your life today?

▶ After time for discussion, ask students to share. Add to the chart.

Summarize and Apply

Summarize the learning and remind students to think about how the message in a historical fiction book might be applied to their own lives.

What does the chart show you about historical fiction?

▶ Add the principle to the top of the chart.

As you read historical fiction, notice the author's message and how it relates to the time period and your own life. If you read historical fiction today, bring the book with you when we meet so you can share.

Share

Following independent reading time, gather students together in the meeting area to talk about their reading.

Who read a historical fiction book today? What is the message? How does it apply to life today? Share your thinking.

Extend the Lesson (Optional)

After assessing students' understanding, you might decide to extend the learning.

▶ As students read more historical fiction books, have them notice any recurring themes or messages. Continue to have them think about how these messages might apply to life today.

▶ Encourage discussion about why authors choose to write historical fiction.

▶ **Writing About Reading** Have students write in a reader's notebook about the message in a historical fiction book and the supporting details that help them recognize that message.

Historical fiction writers use the past to give a message that can be applied today.		
Title	Author's Message, Related to a Time in History	How the Message Applies Today
MEMPHIS, MARTIN, AND THE MOUNTAINTOP	• Even after a riot and Dr. Martin Luther King Jr.'s assassination, the sanitation workers persevered in their fight for equal rights.	• There can be a cost to fighting for what you believe. • All workers deserve equal rights.
As Fast As Words Could Fly	• It took hard work and determination for African Americans to overcome segregation.	• Change is not easy. • Don't give up in the face of challenges. • Use your talents and gifts to overcome struggles.
The Memory Coat	• Immigrants faced hardships in order to find a better life for their families.	• Remembering your culture and heritage connects you to your community. • Value and accept people of all cultures and backgrounds.

Assessment

After you have taught the minilessons in this umbrella, observe students as they talk and write about their reading across instructional contexts: interactive read-aloud, independent reading, guided reading, shared reading, and book club. Use *The Literacy Continuum* (Fountas and Pinnell 2017) to observe students' reading and writing behaviors.

> ▶ What evidence do you have of new understandings related to historical fiction?
>
> > • Do they understand that historical fiction is always imagined, but that it can be based on real people, places, or events?
> >
> > • How well do they understand the importance of the setting to the story?
> >
> > • Can they evaluate whether the author accurately portrays past social issues?
> >
> > • Can students identify the author's message and how it can be applied to their own lives?
> >
> > • Do they use language such as *historical fiction, message, portray, social issues, setting,* and *imagined*?
>
> ▶ In what other ways, beyond the scope of this umbrella, are students talking about historical fiction?
>
> > • Do students notice the impact of setting in other types of fiction?
> >
> > • Can they recognize elements of an illustrator's craft?

Use your observations to determine the next umbrella you will teach. You may also consult Minilessons Across the Year (pp. 61–64) for guidance.

Link to Writing

After teaching the minilessons in this umbrella, help students link the new learning to their own writing:

> ▶ When students write a historical fiction story, remind them that the characters, plot, and setting are imagined, but some part of the story must be based on real people, places, or events. Ask them to consider the setting they choose and how it is important to the story.

Reader's Notebook

When this umbrella is complete, provide a copy of the minilesson principles (see resources.fountasandpinnell.com) for students to glue in the reader's notebook (in the Minilessons section if using *Reader's Notebook: Advanced* [Fountas and Pinnell 2011]), so they can refer to the information as needed.

Minilessons in This Umbrella

RML1   Modern fantasy stories are alike in many ways.

RML2   The definition of modern fantasy is what is always true about it.

RML3   There are different types of modern fantasy.

RML4   Fantasy stories often take place in unusual settings.

RML5   The characters in modern fantasy often represent the symbolic struggle of good and evil.

RML6   Modern fantasy stories have a magical element.

RML7   Modern fantasy stories often reveal a lesson or something true about the world.

Before Teaching Umbrella 23 Minilessons

Prior to teaching this series of minilessons as part of a genre study (pp. 39–42), students should have read and discussed a variety of fantasy books. While this umbrella focuses only on modern fantasy, students should also be experienced with traditional literature. Modern fantasy includes animal fantasy, low fantasy, high fantasy, and science fiction. Traditional literature includes folktales, fairy tales, fables, legends, epics, ballads, and myths. Use the following books from the *Fountas & Pinnell Classroom™ Interactive Read-Aloud Collection* and *Independent Reading Collection* (see conferring cards for details about individual *Independent Reading* books) or choose fantasy stories from your own library. Also encourage students to share knowledge from modern fantasy books they have read at home.

Interactive Read-Aloud Collection

Genre Study: Modern Fantasy

The Book of Three by Lloyd Alexander

The Search for Delicious by Natalie Babbitt

Journey by Aaron Becker

A Wizard of Earthsea by Ursula K. LeGuin

Kindness and Compassion

Wings by Christopher Myers

Countering Stereotypes

Wabi Sabi by Mark Reibstein

Independent Reading Collection

Above World by Jenn Reese

As you read aloud and enjoy these texts together, help students

- discuss what is unique about fantasy literature, and
- notice which elements always and often occur in fantasy stories.

Interactive Read-Aloud
**Genre Study:
Modern Fantasy**

**Kindness and
Compassion**

Countering Stereotypes

Independent Reading

Reading Minilesson Principle

Modern fantasy stories are alike in many ways.

You Will Need

- a variety of familiar modern fantasy stories, such as those in Text Set: Genre Study: Modern Fantasy
- chart paper and markers
- basket of modern fantasy stories
- sticky notes

Academic Language / Important Vocabulary

- modern fantasy
- genre
- characteristics
- magical
- imagined

Continuum Connection

- Notice and understand the characteristics of some specific fiction genres: e.g., realistic fiction, historical fiction, folktale, fairy tale, fractured fairy tale, fable, myth, legend, epic, ballad, fantasy including science fiction, hybrid text (p. 79)

Goal

Notice and understand the characteristics of modern fantasy.

Rationale

When you teach students the characteristics of modern fantasy, they will recognize that fantasy stories could not happen in real life and often have magic, good versus evil, and life lessons, and they will know what to expect when reading fantasy stories.

Assess Learning

Observe students when they read and discuss fantasy stories and notice if there is evidence of new learning based on the goal of this minilesson.

- ▶ Can students describe the characteristics of fantasies?
- ▶ Do they use the terms *modern fantasy, genre, characteristics, magical,* and *imagined*?

Minilesson

To help students think about the minilesson principle, engage them in thinking about the characteristics of fantasy stories. Here is an example.

- ▶ Show the covers of multiple fantasy books that are familiar to students.

    Turn and talk about how these modern fantasy stories are alike. Notice whether the ways they are alike happen *always* or *often* in modern fantasy stories. One thing to think about is how modern fantasy is similar to or different from traditional literature (for example, folktales, fairy tales). When were these stories created? Who wrote them?

- ▶ After time for discussion, ask students to share ideas. Record responses on chart paper. Label the sections *Always* and *Often*. (You might want to use sticky notes for responses so they can be moved around.)

- ▶ Select several fantasy books to discuss in greater detail.

    What other things do you notice about these books in the fantasy genre?

- ▶ Continue recording responses and move sticky notes to a different column if needed as the conversation develops. The following prompts may be helpful:

    - *What evidence shows that the characters are different from people in the real world?*
    - *Has time been altered? Is there anything unusual about the setting?*
    - *What do you notice about the lessons in the stories?*
    - *What do you notice about magic, technology, or science?*
    - *How has the writer convinced the reader to suspend disbelief?*

Have a Try

Invite the students to talk with a group about a modern fantasy story.

▶ Provide each group with a modern fantasy book.

    Together, look through the book and notice how it fits with the chart.

Summarize and Apply

Summarize the learning and remind students to think about the characteristics of fantasy books.

▶ Add the title *Modern Fantasy* to the chart and revisit the noticings.

    Choose a fantasy book from the basket to read today or continue reading one you have started. As you read, look for items on the chart and put a sticky note on those pages. Bring the book when we meet so you can share.

Share

Following independent reading time, gather students in pairs to talk about fantasy books.

    With a partner, talk about the fantasy book you read today. Tell your partner something that your book has in common with other fantasy books.

Extend the Lesson (Optional)

After assessing students' understanding, you might decide to extend the learning.

▶ **Writing About Reading** Have students write about the motifs they come across in fantasy stories and look for commonalities across the books.

Modern Fantasy
Noticings:

Always	Often
• Not originally passed down from generation to generation	• Characters with unusual traits (animals that behave like humans; characters who are eccentric, extraordinary, or magical)
• Original stories by known authors	
• People, events, and places that could not exist in the real world	• Universal truths or lessons about life
• Narrative structure that includes characters, plot, and setting	• Something unusual about the setting (imaginary things happening in the real world; imaginary, alternative, or parallel worlds)
• Conflict between good and evil	
• Magical elements (magical powers, objects, transformations)	• Hero on a quest or mission

Section 2: Literary Analysis

RML1
LA.U23.RML1
Umbrella 23: Studying Modern Fantasy   379

Reading Minilesson Principle

The definition of modern fantasy is what is always true about it.

You Will Need

- several familiar fantasy books, such as the following from Text Set: Genre Study: Modern Fantasy:
  - *Journey* by Aaron Becker
  - *A Wizard of Earthsea* by Ursula K. LeGuin
- noticings chart from RML1
- chart paper and markers
- basket of modern fantasy books
- sticky notes

Academic Language / Important Vocabulary

- modern fantasy
- genre
- definition
- elements

Continuum Connection

- Notice and understand the characteristics of some specific fiction genres: e.g., realistic fiction, historical fiction, folktale, fairy tale, fractured fairy tale, fable, myth, legend, epic, ballad, fantasy including science fiction, hybrid text (p. 79)

Goal

Create a working definition of modern fantasy.

Rationale

When you teach students to construct a working definition of modern fantasy, they can use these understandings to form expectations before reading stories in the genre. They will learn to revise their understandings as they gain additional experience with other books in the fantasy genre.

Assess Learning

Observe students when they read and discuss modern fantasy stories and notice if there is evidence of new learning based on the goal of this minilesson.

- ▶ Do students work together to create a working definition of a modern fantasy story?
- ▶ Do they understand the definition of modern fantasy and recognize what is always true about stories in this genre?
- ▶ Do they use the terms *modern fantasy, genre, definition,* and *elements*?

Minilesson

To help students think about the minilesson principle, engage them in creating a working definition of a modern fantasy story. Here is an example.

- ▶ Show the modern fantasy noticings chart from RML1 and discuss the characteristics.

  The definition of modern fantasy describes what is *always* true about books in this genre.

- ▶ On chart paper, write the words *Modern fantasy stories are*, leaving space for constructing a working definition.

  What would you write to finish this sentence to describe what modern fantasy stories are always like? Look at the noticings chart for ideas.

- ▶ Using students' ideas, create a working definition on chart paper. Ask a volunteer to read the definition.

- ▶ Show the cover of *Journey*.

  Think about *Journey*. Is everything in our definition true about *Journey*?

- ▶ Refer students to each part of the definition and ask for examples from the book to show that *Journey* fits the definition. As needed, revise the definition based on new understandings.

Have a Try

Invite the students to talk with a partner about a modern fantasy and whether it fits the working definition.

▶ Show the cover of *A Wizard of Earthsea*.

> Turn and talk about whether *A Wizard of Earthsea* fits the definition of a modern fantasy. What makes you think that?

▶ Ask a few students to share. Encourage them to give text examples to support their thinking. Revise the definition as needed.

Summarize and Apply

Summarize the learning and remind students to think about the definition of a modern fantasy.

> Today you created a definition of modern fantasy. When you read today, choose a modern fantasy book from the basket or continue one you are reading. Think about how the book fits the definition. Add sticky notes to pages that show examples. Bring the book when we meet so you can share.

Share

Following independent reading time, gather students in groups of three to talk about fantasy books.

> In your group, talk about the modern fantasy you read today. Share whether the story fits the definition and show any pages with sticky notes to support your thinking.

Extend the Lesson (Optional)

After assessing students' understanding, you might decide to extend the learning.

▶ Have students create a collection of modern fantasy books to display in the school library or classroom. Encourage them to think and talk about how each book fits the definition. Have them add reviews and critiques on note cards to the display.

Modern Fantasy

Modern fantasy stories are written by known authors and are about people, places, and events that cannot exist in the real world.

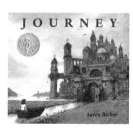

Section 2: Literary Analysis

Reading Minilesson Principle
There are different types of modern fantasy.

You Will Need

- an example of each type of modern fantasy (animal fantasy, low fantasy, high fantasy, science fiction), such as the following:
  - *Wabi Sabi* by Mark Reibstein from Text Set: Countering Stereotypes
  - *Wings* by Christopher Myers, from Text Set: Kindness and Compassion
  - *A Wizard of Earthsea* by Ursula K. LeGuin, from Text Set: Genre Study: Modern Fantasy
  - *Above World* by Jenn Reese from *Independent Reading Collection*
- chart paper prepared with four columns: *Animal Fantasy, Low Fantasy, High Fantasy, Science Fiction*
- marker
- basket of modern fantasy stories, with examples from each type of modern fantasy
- sticky notes

Academic Language / Important Vocabulary

- animal fantasy
- low fantasy
- high fantasy
- science fiction

Continuum Connection

- Notice and understand the characteristics of some specific fiction genres: e.g., realistic fiction, historical fiction, folktale, fairy tale, fractured fairy tale, fable, myth, legend, epic, ballad, fantasy including science fiction, hybrid text (p. 79)

Goal

Understand the different types of modern fantasy: animal fantasy, low and high fantasy, and science fiction.

Rationale

When students learn to categorize the different types of fantasy stories and learn how they fit into the broader category of modern fantasy, they begin to think about what all fantasy stories have in common and which characteristics are particular to each type of modern fantasy. Sometimes the lines between low and high fantasy are blurred, as when the real world exists alongside an imaginary alternative world (e.g., the Harry Potter series).

Assess Learning

Observe students when they categorize modern fantasy stories and notice if there is evidence of new learning based on the goal of this minilesson.

- ▶ Are students familiar with the characteristics of modern fantasy stories?
- ▶ Are they using the terms *animal fantasy, low fantasy, high fantasy,* and *science fiction*?

Minilesson

To help students think about the minilesson principle, use a variety of types of modern fantasy stories for them to categorize into animal fantasy, low fantasy, high fantasy, and science fiction. Here is an example.

- ▶ Display the prepared chart paper.
- ▶ Provide an example of each type of modern fantasy under each heading: *Wabi Sabi* (animal fantasy) *Wings* (low fantasy), *A Wizard of Earthsea* (high fantasy), and *Above World* (science fiction).

    Take a look at this chart and these examples of modern fantasy books. Turn and talk about the books you know and their locations on this chart.

- ▶ After time for discussion, ask volunteers to share. If no students have read the *Independent Reading* book yet, briefly give enough details to help students understand why it is placed in the science fiction category. (The technology that allows Aluna's underwater colony to breathe underwater is failing. Aluna and Hoku venture to the dangerous Above World to find a way to survive.)

    What could we write under each heading to briefly state the characteristics of each type of modern fantasy?

- ▶ Add students' ideas to the chart. Guide the conversation to ensure that students can define and differentiate between each type.

Have a Try

Invite the students to talk in groups of three about different types of modern fantasy.

> Think about modern fantasy stories you know, including ones that you have read during independent reading time, for book club meetings, or outside of school. Where would they fit on the chart? Turn and talk about that. Share the reasons for your opinion about where the titles should be placed.

▶ After time for discussion, ask students to share. As they do, add book titles to the chart.

Summarize and Apply

Summarize the learning and remind students to think about categorizing modern fantasy books.

> All the titles listed on the chart are modern fantasy. What does the chart show about modern fantasy?

▶ Add the principle to the chart.

> When you read today, you can choose a modern fantasy or continue one you are reading. Think about where it fits on the chart and why. Bring the book when we meet so you can share.

Share

Following independent reading time, gather students together to discuss modern fantasy.

> Did anyone read a modern fantasy title that isn't listed on the chart? Share the title, where you think it should be placed, and your reasons why.

▶ Add new titles to the chart.

Extend the Lesson (Optional)

After assessing students' understanding, you might decide to extend the learning.

▶ Have students record titles of fantasy books they have read in a reader's notebook. They should use *F* as the genre code for fantasy (see WAR.U1.RML2).

There are different types of modern fantasy.

Animal Fantasy (animals with human traits)	Low Fantasy (magical elements in the real world)	High Fantasy (imaginary, alternative, or parallel world)	Science Fiction (set in the future with technology or scientific advances)
Wabi Sabi	Wings	Wizard of Earthsea	Above World
Seekers: The Quest Begins	Journey (a mix of low and high fantasy)	The Book of Three	The Giver
			Freakling
Into the Wild	Teacup	The Search for Delicious	What Came from the Stars
Forest of Secrets	Bayou Magic	The Golden Compass	Daniel X Alien Hunter
Fire and Ice	Coraline (a mix of low and high fantasy)		The House of Power
Podkin One-Ear			The Gauntlet

Section 2: Literary Analysis

RML 4
LA.U23.RML4

Reading Minilesson Principle
Fantasy stories often take place in unusual settings.

Studying Modern Fantasy

You Will Need

▶ several familiar fantasy stories that have something unusual about the setting, such as the following:

- *The Book of Three* by Lloyd Alexander and *Journey* by Aaron Becker from Text Set: Genre Study: Modern Fantasy

- *Above World* by Jenn Reese, from *Independent Reading Collection*

▶ chart paper prepared with three columns and headings: *Title, Settings(s), What do you notice about the setting?*

▶ markers

▶ modern fantasies students are reading or have read

▶ sticky notes

Academic Language / Important Vocabulary

▶ modern fantasy

▶ genre

▶ setting

▶ real world

▶ imaginary world

▶ parallel world

Continuum Connection

▶ Notice science fiction and fantasy settings: e.g., alternative or secondary world, futuristic setting, alternative histories, animal kingdom, fictional planet, pseudo-medieval setting (p. 80)

Goal

Notice unusual settings in fantasy stories.

Rationale

When students understand that the setting in a fantasy story can be real or imagined, they become aware that realistic elements coincide with fantasy elements. This enables them to engage fully with the story and understand the connection between setting, characters, and plot.

Assess Learning

Observe students when they read and discuss fantasy stories and notice if there is evidence of new learning based on the goal of this minilesson.

▶ Do they notice and discuss the setting in fantasy stories?

▶ Are they able to determine which settings are real and which are imagined?

▶ Can they discuss the interconnectedness of setting with characters and plot?

▶ Do they use the terms *modern fantasy, genre, setting, real world, imaginary world*, and *parallel world*?

Minilesson

To help students think about the minilesson principle, engage them in noticing both the real and the unusual settings of familiar fantasy stories. Here is an example.

▶ Show *The Book of Three.*

> What is the setting of *The Book of Three?* What do you notice about it?

▶ Guide the conversation so that students note that it is a magical place.

▶ Begin a chart that shows what is unusual about the setting and how it influences the story.

▶ Repeat the activity with *Journey.* Continue adding to the chart.

> Modern fantasy writers create a world in which imaginary things happen in a real setting, or they create imaginary or parallel worlds that follow different rules of physics. Why must the setting in a modern fantasy make readers suspend disbelief and accept something that couldn't actually happen?

▶ You may want to use some prompts as you discuss setting, such as:

- *How does the story world differ from your own real world?*

- *How has the author altered the secondary world?*

- *Are there any clues that show time has been altered?*

Have a Try

Invite the students to talk about the setting in a modern fantasy.

▶ Have students help you fill in the chart for the setting in *Above World* (Aluna's community has always lived underwater).

Summarize and Apply

Summarize the learning and remind students to think about the unusual settings in modern fantasy stories.

> Look at the chart. What can you say about the setting in modern fantasy stories?

▶ Add the principle to the chart.

> Today, choose a modern fantasy story from the basket or continue one you have already started. Notice if all or part of the setting is unusual and what makes it unusual. Place a sticky note on any pages about setting that you want to remember. Bring the book when we meet so you can share.

Share

Following independent reading time, gather students together to discuss the settings in fantasy books.

> What did you notice about the setting in the modern fantasy you are reading?

> How did the setting affect the characters and plot?

Extend the Lesson (Optional)

After assessing students' understanding, you might decide to extend the learning.

▶ As students encounter other fantasy stories (both modern fantasy and traditional literature), bring the setting to their awareness. Have them think and talk about what is unusual about the setting and how it impacts the characters and the plot.

Fantasy stories often take place in unusual settings.

Title	Setting(s)	What do you notice about the setting?
The Book of Three	imaginary land of Prydain	Prydain is magical (a 379-year-old man lives there; Gwydion's magical mesh of grass).
Journey	both a real neighborhood/ home and an imaginary land	A magical red marker can draw a door that leads to an imaginary world.
Above World	underwater	People use special technology to live and breathe underwater.

Reading Minilesson Principle
The characters in modern fantasy often represent the symbolic struggle of good and evil.

Studying Modern Fantasy

You Will Need

- several fantasy books that have clear examples of good and evil, such as the following from Text Set: Genre Study: Modern Fantasy:
  - *The Book of Three* by Lloyd Alexander
  - *A Wizard of Earthsea* by Ursula K. LeGuin
  - *The Search for Delicious* by Natalie Babbitt
- chart paper and markers
- three sticky notes labeled *vs.*
- basket of modern fantasy stories

Academic Language / Important Vocabulary

- modern fantasy
- motif
- genre
- symbolic
- struggle
- good versus (vs.) evil

Continuum Connection

- Infer the significance of heroic or larger-than-life characters in fantasy, who represent the symbolic struggle of good and evil (p. 81)

Goal

Understand that the heroic and sometimes larger-than-life characters in fantasy represent the symbolic struggle between good and evil.

Rationale

When you teach students to notice that the struggle of good versus evil is a basic motif in modern fantasy stories, they learn to recognize characteristics of the genre and think about how it influences the characters and plot.

Assess Learning

Observe students when they read and talk about modern fantasy stories and notice if there is evidence of new learning based on the goal of this minilesson.

- ▶ Are students able to recognize symbols of good and evil in fantasy stories?
- ▶ Do they use the terms *modern fantasy, motif, genre, symbolic, struggle,* and *good versus (vs.) evil*?

Minilesson

To help students think about the minilesson principle, engage them in thinking about the struggle between good and evil in modern fantasy stories. Here is an example.

- ▶ Read a few sentences from *The Book of Three* that identify and show the struggle between good and evil, such as Taran's first sighting of the Horned King (page 15) and the final battle (pages 167–173).

  Who represents good and evil?

  Describe the struggle between good and evil.

- ▶ After time for discussion, ask students to share their thinking. Begin a chart that identifies the good and evil forces and describes their struggle.

  Now think about *A Wizard of Earthsea*. How would you describe the struggle between good and evil in this book?

- ▶ As students respond, add to the chart.

  A motif is an idea or feature that stands out. One of the basic motifs in both modern fantasy and traditional literature is the struggle between good and evil. Often, the forces can be easy to distinguish. Other times, the lines are blurred, such as when a character has an internal conflict between good and evil like Ged's conflict with his dark side in *A Wizard of Earthsea*.

Have a Try

Invite the students to talk with a partner about the struggle of good and evil in modern fantasy.

▶ Show the cover of *The Search for Delicious*. Revisit a few sections as needed.

> Turn and talk about the struggle between the forces of good and evil in *The Search for Delicious*.

▶ After time for discussion, ask students to share their thinking and add to the chart.

Summarize and Apply

Summarize the learning and remind students to think about the struggle between good and evil in modern fantasy books.

> What did you notice about modern fantasy?

▶ Add the principle to the chart.

> Today, choose a modern fantasy book from the basket or continue reading one you have already started. Think about the struggle between good and evil. Bring the book when we meet so you can share.

Share

Following independent reading time, gather students together to discuss good versus evil in fantasy books.

> Share what you noticed about the struggle of good versus evil in a modern fantasy book.

Extend the Lesson (Optional)

After assessing students' understanding, you might decide to extend the learning.

▶ Ask students to notice other characters who are not all good or all bad and write about them in a reader's notebook. Encourage them to think about how this idea applies to real life.

	The characters in modern fantasy often represent the symbolic struggle of good and evil.	
Title	Forces of Good vs. Evil	The Struggle
The Book of Three	Sons of Don, Taran vs. Arawn, Lord of Annuvin; The Horned King	Often, the forces of evil seem stronger than the forces of good. However, good wins out by having heart and using teamwork.
A Wizard of Earthsea	Ged vs. Ged's dark side (shadow)	The real struggle between good and evil takes place inside Ged himself. When his over-confidence pushes him to cast a dangerous spell, the effects are felt all through the land.
The Search for Delicious	The king, Gaylen vs. Hemlock	Hemlock represents evil. He is trying to overthrow the king by turning the people against him. In the end, good prevails over evil when Gaylen and Ardis return the water supply to the people.

RML 6
LA.U23.RML6

Reading Minilesson Principle
Modern fantasy stories have a magical element.

Studying Modern Fantasy

You Will Need

- several familiar modern fantasy stories, such as those in Text Set: Genre Study: Modern Fantasy:
  - *Journey* by Aaron Becker
  - *The Book of Three* by Lloyd Alexander
  - *The Search for Delicious* by Natalie Babbitt
  - *A Wizard of Earthsea* by Ursula K. LeGuin
- chart paper and markers
- basket of modern fantasy stories

Academic Language / Important Vocabulary

- modern fantasy
- genre
- magical
- motif

Continuum Connection

- Identify elements of traditional literature and fantasy: e.g., the supernatural; imaginary and otherworldly creatures; gods and goddesses; talking animals, toys, and dolls; heroic characters; technology or scientific advances; time travel; aliens or outer space (p. 79)

Goal

Understand that one of the recurring motifs of fantasy is the presence of magic.

Rationale

When students understand that magic is a basic motif in fantasy stories, they know what to expect from reading books in this genre and are able to recognize stories as fantasies.

Assess Learning

Observe students when they read and discuss elements of modern fantasy and notice if there is evidence of new learning based on the goal of this minilesson.

- ▶ Are students able to identify the magical element in a modern fantasy?
- ▶ Are students able to connect the relevance of magic to the overall story?
- ▶ Do they use the terms *modern fantasy, genre, magical,* and *motif*?

Minilesson

To help students think about the minilesson principle, engage them in thinking about the importance of magical elements in modern fantasy stories.

- ▶ Show several pages from *Journey* that show the girl using the marker to draw solutions to her problems. Also show the girl and the boy using both of their magic markers to make a bicycle.

  What is significant about the markers in *Journey*?

  Turn and talk about how magic is important to the story.

- ▶ After time for discussion, ask students to share ideas. Begin a chart that shows the title, the magical element, and how magic is important to the story.

- ▶ Repeat the activity with several other familiar modern fantasies, such as *The Book of Three* and *The Search for Delicious.* Continue adding to the chart.

  Magic is one of the basic fantasy motifs, found in both modern fantasy and traditional literature. It occurs in a variety of forms, such as transformations, magical objects, inanimate objects or animals that can talk, and wishes that come true with either good or evil consequences.

Have a Try

Invite the students to talk with a partner about the magic in a modern fantasy.

▸ Show the cover of *A Wizard of Earthsea*.

Think about *A Wizard of Earthsea*. Turn and talk about magical elements and how they are important to the story.

▸ After time for discussion, ask students to share. Add to chart.

Summarize and Apply

Summarize the learning and remind students to think about the magical elements in modern fantasy stories.

Today you noticed magical elements in modern fantasy stories and talked about why the magic is important in the story.

▸ Write the minilesson principle at the top of the chart paper.

When you read today, choose a modern fantasy book from the basket or continue reading one that you have already started. Notice the motif of magic in the story and why it is important. Bring the book when we meet so you can share.

Share

Following independent reading time, gather students in groups of three. Ensure that at least one group member has read a modern fantasy.

Share with your group the modern fantasy you read and the magical elements you noticed. Talk about the magic and how it is important to the story.

Extend the Lesson (Optional)

After assessing students' understanding, you might decide to extend the learning.

▸ **Writing About Reading** Have students write in a reader's notebook about the role that magic plays in a modern fantasy they have read.

Modern fantasy stories have a magical element.

Title	Magical Element	How is magic important to the story?
Journey	magic markers	• A magic red marker draws door to fantasy world. • Things drawn with the marker become real. • A friendship is formed by the girl with the magic red marker and boy with the magic purple marker.
The Book of Three	spells, ancient sword, magical creatures (oracular pig, Gurgi, Cauldron-Born), etc.	• Magic runs through the entire story. • The encounters and final battle between evil magic and good magic are essential to the story.
The Search for Delicious	magic whistle-key, magical creatures (mermaid, woldweller, dwarves), etc.	• Magic whistle-key is essential to the resolution. • Mermaid is also essential to the resolution, as Ardis helps Gaylen return free-flowing fresh water to the people, which is delicious.
A Wizard of Earthsea	spells, ancient language that has powers; magical creatures (wizards, dragons)	• Magic gets Ged into trouble, which is at the center of the plot. • Magic ties together the fantasy world.

Reading Minilesson Principle

Modern fantasy stories often reveal a lesson or something true about the world.

Studying Modern Fantasy

Goal

Understand that the messages or big ideas in fantasy stories can be applied to their own lives or to other people and society.

Rationale

When students learn to identify the messages or big ideas in modern fantasy stories, they begin to apply these lessons and universal truths to their own lives.

Assess Learning

Observe students when they read and talk about modern fantasy and notice if there is evidence of new learning based on the goal of this minilesson.

- ▶ Are students able to identify the messages or big ideas in fantasy stories?
- ▶ Can they apply a lesson or universal truth from a fantasy story to their own lives?
- ▶ Do they use the terms *modern fantasy, genre, lesson, universal truth,* and *reveal*?

Minilesson

To help students think about the minilesson principle, engage them in thinking about what lessons or truths are revealed in a modern fantasy story. Here is an example.

- ▶ Show the last few illustrations from *Wings*.

   Ikarus and the narrator are both made fun of because they are different. Think about how this plays out in the story as you turn and talk about the big idea or message from this book.

- ▶ After time for discussion, ask students to share. Encourage them to identify the lesson or universal truth that is revealed. Add the book title and information to the first two columns of a three-column chart.

   How could you apply this big idea or message to your own life?

- ▶ As students respond, add their responses to the third column.

   Now think about *The Book of Three*. What type of lesson or universal truth is revealed in this story?

   How can that idea be applied to your own life?

- ▶ Create another row on the chart and add students' responses as they relate to *The Book of Three*.

Have a Try

Invite the students to talk with a partner about the big idea or universal truth that is revealed in a modern fantasy.

▶ Show the cover of *Journey*.

What lesson or universal truth is revealed in *Journey*, and how can it be applied to your own life? Turn and talk about that.

▶ After time for discussion, add students' ideas to the chart.

Summarize and Apply

Summarize the learning and remind students to think about the big ideas in modern fantasy stories.

Modern fantasies often reveal universal truths that can be applied to your own life.

▶ Add the principle to the chart.

When you read today, choose a modern fantasy from the basket if you aren't already reading one. Think about the lessons or big ideas and mark any pages you want to remember with a sticky note. Bring the book when we meet so you can share.

Share

Following independent reading time, have students talk in pairs about modern fantasy.

Tell your partner what you noticed about the lessons or universal truths in the modern fantasy you read. Talk about how those lessons could be applied to your own lives.

Extend the Lesson (Optional)

After assessing students' understanding, you might decide to extend the learning.

▶ As students experience more modern fantasy stories, have them talk about whether multiple books have the same big idea or message. Have them compare and contrast the way that different modern fantasy authors reveal universal truths.

Modern fantasy stories often reveal a lesson or something true about the world.

Title	Lessons or Universal Truths	Connection to My Life
Wings	Don't judge others because they are different; instead, accept them for who they are.	Get to know people who might be different from you.
The Book of Three	Heroes aren't necessarily the strongest; they make mistakes, and they come in all shapes and sizes.	Try to do the right thing and help others because everyone can do something to make the world better.
Journey	Using your imagination can solve a lot of life's problems.	When faced with a problem, be creative in thinking about solutions.

Section 2: Literary Analysis

Assessment

After you have taught the minilessons in this umbrella, observe students as they talk and write about their reading across instructional contexts: interactive read-aloud, independent reading, guided reading, shared reading, and book club. Use *The Literacy Continuum* (Fountas and Pinnell 2017) to guide observation of students' reading and writing behaviors.

- What evidence do you have of new understandings related to modern fantasy?
  - Can students describe ways that modern fantasy stories are alike?
  - Can they provide a definition of the modern fantasy genre?
  - Are they able to categorize different types of modern fantasy stories?
  - Do they understand that modern fantasy stories often have unusual settings?
  - Are they recognizing recurring motifs in modern fantasy, such as the struggle between good and evil, magical elements, and universal truths?
  - Are they using academic language, such as *modern fantasy, genre, animal fantasy, low fantasy, high fantasy, science fiction,* and *motif*?
- In what other ways, beyond the scope of this umbrella, are students talking about fiction genres?
  - Are students talking about types of fiction, such as historical fiction?

Use your observations to determine the next umbrella you will teach. You may also consult Minilessons Across the Year (pp. 61–64) for guidance.

Read and Revise

After completing the steps in the genre study process, help students read and revise their definition of the genre based on their new understandings.

- **Before:** Modern fantasy stories are written by known authors and are about people, places, and events that cannot exist in the real world.
- **After:** Modern fantasy stories are original stories written by known authors. They are about people, places, and events that cannot exist in the real world. They typically have magical elements and show a struggle between good and evil.

Reader's Notebook

When this umbrella is complete, provide a copy of the minilesson principles (see resources.fountasandpinnell.com) for students to glue in the reader's notebook (in the Minilessons section if using *Reader's Notebook: Advanced* [Fountas and Pinnell 2011]), so they can refer to the information as needed.

Minilessons in This Umbrella

RML1   Epic tales are alike in many ways.

RML2   The definition of an epic tale is what is always true about it.

RML3   Epic tales have heroes who are often on a quest.

RML4   Epic tales reflect the values of the culture of origin.

RML5   Epic tales are often written as poetry or in a poetic way.

Genre Study: Epic Tales

Before Teaching Umbrella 24 Minilessons

Genre study supports students in knowing what to expect when beginning to read a text in a genre. It helps students develop an understanding of the distinguishing characteristics of a genre and gives them the tools they need to navigate a variety of texts. There are six broad steps in a genre study, described on pages 39–42.

Ensure that students are familiar with multiple epics and other types of traditional literature before beginning the genre study and select books that are clear examples. Fantasy is classified as traditional literature or modern fantasy, and epics are a type of traditional literature along with folktales, fables, fairy tales, legends, ballads, and myths. Use the following books from the *Fountas & Pinnell Classroom™ Interactive Read-Aloud Collection* or choose epics from the classroom library.

Genre Study: Epic Tales

The Adventures of Odysseus by Hugh Lupton and Daniel Morden

Prince of Fire: The Story of Diwali by Jatinder Verma

Gilgamesh the King by Ludmila Zeman

The Last Quest of Gilgamesh by Ludmila Zeman

As you read aloud and enjoy these texts together, help students

- notice similarities between them,
- notice the traits of the characters, and
- make connections to their own lives.

Section 2: Literary Analysis

RML1
LA.U24.RML1

Reading Minilesson Principle
Epic tales are alike in many ways.

Studying Epic Tales

You Will Need

- a collection of familiar epics
- chart paper with the headings *Epic Tales* and *Noticings,* and sections for *Always, Often,* and *Sometimes*
- markers

Academic Language / Important Vocabulary

- epic
- fantasy
- traditional literature
- characteristics

Continuum Connection

- Notice and understand the characteristics of some specific fiction genres: e.g., realistic fiction, historical fiction, folktale, fairy tale, fractured fairy tale, fable, myth, legend, epic, ballad, fantasy including science fiction, hybrid text (p.79)

- Identify elements of traditional literature and fantasy: e.g., the supernatural; imaginary and otherworldly creatures; gods and goddesses; talking animals, toys, and dolls; heroic characters; technology or scientific advances; time travel; aliens or outer space (p. 79)

- Notice and understand basic motifs of traditional literature and fantasy: e.g., struggle between good and evil, magic, secondary or alternative worlds, the hero's quest, special character types, fantastic or magical objects, wishes, trickery, transformations (p. 79)

Goal

Notice and understand the characteristics of epics.

Rationale

When students study epics as a genre through inquiry, they gain a deeper understanding both of individual stories and the genre as a whole. When they develop an understanding of epics, they will know what to expect when they encounter books of that genre (see pages 39–42 for more information about genre study).

Assess Learning

Observe students when they talk about epics and notice if there is evidence of new learning based on the goal of this minilesson.

- ▶ Are students able to notice similarities between multiple examples of epics?
- ▶ Can students classify characteristics by determining whether they *always, often,* or *sometimes* occur in epics?
- ▶ Do they use the terms *epic, fantasy, traditional literature,* and *characteristics?*

Minilesson

To help students develop a list of characteristics of epics, choose epics that you have read aloud to use as examples for identifying characteristics. Here is an example.

- ▶ Have students sit in small groups and provide each group with several examples of epics. Groups can rotate the books so they have an opportunity to compare several examples.

    Think about the epics you know and the examples your group has. Talk with your group about how all epics are alike.

- ▶ Provide a few minutes for conversation.

    Now think of each of the ideas your group discussed. Which ones *always* occur in epics, which occur *often,* and which occur *sometimes*?

- ▶ As students share, prompt the discussion as needed to help them identify whether characteristics occur *always, often,* or *sometimes* in epics. The following suggested prompts may be helpful:
    - *Who are epics about?*
    - *What types of things does the main character do?*
    - *What types of things happen in epics?*
    - *What types of settings do you notice?*
    - *Does that always, often, or sometimes occur in the epics you know?*

- ▶ On chart paper, create a noticings chart and add student ideas.

Have a Try

Invite the students to talk with a partner about epics.

> Think about a book you are reading. Turn and talk about whether it is an epic and why or why not. Use the chart to think about the characteristics of epics as you talk about the book.

Summarize and Apply

Summarize the learning and remind students to think about the characteristics of epics.

> An epic is a type of fantasy story that fits into the traditional literature category, along with folktales and fairy tales.

> You can choose an epic to read today. If you do, think about which of the characteristics on the chart occur in the book you read. Bring the book when we meet so you can share.

Share

Following independent reading time, gather students in the meeting area to talk about epic tales.

> Who read an epic today? Talk about which characteristics from the list you noticed in the book.

Extend the Lesson (Optional)

After assessing students' understanding, you might decide to extend the learning.

▶ Continue adding to the noticings chart as students read more examples of epics.

Epic Tales

Noticings:

Always	Often
The stories are imagined and feature characters and events that could not exist in the real world.	The hero is on a quest or journey.
Epics are long stories or a series of stories.	There is a series of tasks or tests in which the hero triumphs.
They have a hero.	The characteristics of the hero reveal what was valued at that time in the culture of origin.
They were originally told orally by storytellers for many years.	Epics are written as poetry or in a poetic way.
The moral values of the society are expressed through the epic.	Epics exaggerate the qualities of the hero.
	Epics are connected to myths.

Sometimes

There are gods and human heroes.

RML2
LA.U24.RML2

Reading Minilesson Principle
The definition of an epic tale is what is always true about it.

Studying Epic Tales

You Will Need

- a familiar epic, such as *The Adventures of Odysseus* by Hugh Lupton and Daniel Morden from Text Set: Genre Study: Epic Tales
- the epics noticings chart from RML1
- chart paper and markers
- basket of epics

Academic Language / Important Vocabulary

- epic
- genre
- definition
- characteristics

Continuum Connection

- Notice and understand the characteristics of some specific fiction genres: e.g., realistic fiction, historical fiction, folktale, fairy tale, fractured fairy tale, fable, myth, legend, epic, ballad, fantasy including science fiction, hybrid text (p.79)

Goal

Create a working definition of an epic.

Rationale

When students construct a working definition of an epic, they are able to identify and summarize the most important characteristics of the genre and will be able to recognize other books they read that fit in the genre.

Assess Learning

Observe students when they talk about epics and notice if there is evidence of new learning based on the goal of this minilesson.

- Can students identify the characteristics of an epic?
- Are they able to identify whether a book fits the definition of an epic?
- Do they use the terms *epic, genre, definition,* and *characteristics*?

Minilesson

To help students think about the minilesson principle, guide them in constructing a working definition of an epic. Here is an example.

- Show the epics noticings chart and discuss the characteristics of an epic.

    What do you know about epics?

- Ask several volunteers to read the noticings.

    Think about the ways epics are *always* alike. How does knowing how epics are *always* alike help you create a definition of an epic?

- Write *An epic tale is* on chart paper.

    Turn and talk about how you could finish this sentence to write a definition for all epics.

- After time for discussion, ask a few volunteers to share. Use the ideas to construct a working definition of an epic and write it on the chart paper.

    As you learn more about epic tales, you can revise this definition.

Have a Try

Invite the students to talk with a partner about the definition of an epic.

▶ Show the cover of a familiar epic, such as *The Adventures of Odysseus*. Revisit a few pages as needed.

> Turn and talk about whether *The Adventures of Odysseus* fits the definition you created for an epic.

▶ After time for discussion, ask students to share.

Summarize and Apply

Summarize the learning and remind students to think about the definition of an epic.

> Today you wrote a definition of an epic. As you learn more about epics, you will revise this definition.

▶ Add the principle to the chart.

> When you read today, choose an epic and think about whether it fits the definition. Bring the book when we meet so you can share.

The definition of an epic tale is what is always true about it.

An epic tale is a type of traditional literature that involves a hero.

Share

Following independent reading time, gather students in small groups.

> Share with your group the epic you read today. Did it fit the definition of an epic? Show examples from the epic.

▶ Revise the working definition if appropriate based on students' discussion.

Extend the Lesson (Optional)

After assessing students' understanding, you might decide to extend the learning.

▶ As you read other types of traditional literature during interactive read-aloud, compare and contrast another type of fantasy with what students have learned about epics. For example, talk about how characters in fables or myths are similar and/or different from the way they are in epics.

Reading Minilesson Principle
Epic tales have heroes who are often on a quest.

Studying Epic Tales

You Will Need

- several familiar epics, such as the following from Text Set: Genre Study: Epic Tales:
  - *The Last Quest of Gilgamesh* by Ludmila Zeman
  - *The Adventures of Odysseus* by Hugh Lupton and Daniel Morden
- chart paper and markers
- sticky notes

Academic Language / Important Vocabulary

- epic
- hero
- accomplishments
- quest

Continuum Connection

- Notice recurring themes and motifs in traditional literature and fantasy: e.g., struggle between good and evil, the hero's quest (p. 80)
- Notice and understand basic motifs of traditional literature and fantasy: e.g., struggle between good and evil, magic, secondary or alternative worlds, the hero's quest, special character types, fantastic or magical objects, wishes, trickery, transformations (p. 79)

Goal

Understand that epics are about heroes who are often on a quest.

Rationale

When students learn to recognize that epics often have a hero who goes on a journey or quest, they are able to identify books that fit in the genre and know what to expect when reading epics.

Assess Learning

Observe students when they read and talk about epics and notice if there is evidence of new learning based on the goal of this minilesson.

- Do students understand that epics are about heroes and their accomplishments?
- Are students aware that, often, the hero in an epic is on a quest?
- Are they using the terms *epic*, *hero*, *accomplishments*, and *quest*?

Minilesson

To help students think about the minilesson principle, use familiar epics to engage them in a discussion about heroes, their accomplishments, and their quests. Here is an example.

- Show the cover of *The Last Quest of Gilgamesh*.

  Who is the main character, and what types of things does he do?

  A hero is someone who has courage and is admired. How would Gilgamesh fit the definition of a hero, and what has he accomplished?

- If needed, revisit pages 1 and 21. As students respond, add their ideas to the chart under the heading *Hero and Accomplishments*.

  Turn and talk about what you know about a quest.

  A quest is a long and arduous journey to reach a goal. What can you say about the quest in this epic?

- After time for a brief discussion, ask students to share ideas. Prompt the conversation as needed. For example:
  - *What is the goal of Gilgamesh's journey?*
  - *Why is Gilgamesh's quest important to the epic?*

- Record responses on the chart paper under the heading *Goal of the Quest*.

Have a Try

Invite the students to talk with a partner about epics.

▶ Read and show the cover *The Adventures of Odysseus*.

> Turn and talk about whether Odysseus is a hero and what he has accomplished. If he is on a quest, what is the goal?

▶ As needed, revisit pages 9–10. After time for discussion, ask students to share ideas. Add to chart.

Summarize and Apply

Summarize the learning and remind students to think about heroes, their accomplishments, and their quests as they read epics.

> You learned that epics are about heroes, who are often on a quest, and their accomplishments.

▶ Add the principle to the chart.

> When you read today, you might choose an epic. As you read, think about who the heroes are in the story and what they accomplish. Mark any pages with sticky notes that show those things. Bring the book when we meet so you can share.

Share

Following independent reading time, gather students in small groups.

> In your group, share the epic you read today and talk about the heroes, their accomplishments, and their quests.

Extend the Lesson (Optional)

After assessing students' understanding, you might decide to extend the learning.

▶ When you read an epic during interactive read-aloud, have students think about and discuss the motivation for people to invent stories about a larger-than-life hero and the role of any secondary characters who support the hero.

Epic tales have heroes who are often on a quest.

Title	Hero and Accomplishments	Goal of the Quest
	Gilgamesh A powerful king who is loved by his people and famous for building a great wall	To find the secret of immortality
	Odysseus A great warrior and Greek king in the long Trojan War, contributing to the Greek victory and the destruction of Troy	To make his way back home to Ithaca

RML4

LA.U24.RML4

Reading Minilesson Principle
Epic tales reflect the values of the culture of origin.

Studying Epic Tales

You Will Need

▶ several familiar epics, such as the following from Text Set: Genre Study: Epic Tales:

- *Prince of Fire* by Jatinder Verma
- *Gilgamesh the King* by Ludmila Zeman
- *The Adventures of Odysseus* by Hugh Lupton and Daniel Mordon

▶ chart paper and markers

▶ sticky notes

Academic Language / Important Vocabulary

▶ epic
▶ culture
▶ values

Continuum Connection

▶ Infer and understand the moral lesson or cultural teaching in traditional literature (p. 80)

Goal

Understand that epics often reflect the values of the legend's culture of origin.

Rationale

When students learn to recognize that an epic often reflects the values of a culture, they begin to understand that epics helped people gain knowledge about their shared history in order to build a community of shared values.

Assess Learning

Observe students when they talk about and read epics and notice if there is evidence of new learning based on the goal of this minilesson.

▶ Are students able to recognize that epics often reflect the values of a culture?

▶ Do they use the terms *epic, culture,* and *values*?

Minilesson

To help students think about the minilesson principle, engage students in a discussion about the connection of epics to culture and values. Here is an example.

▶ Show the cover of *Prince of Fire*.

> Where does this story take place?
>
> What do you remember about this epic and the story of Diwali?

▶ Revisit the author's notes at the end and other pages of the story as needed.

> This story is based on the ancient epic called the *Ramayana* that tells the story of Diwali. What do you learn from it about the culture at the time of the people of India and what they valued?

▶ Record responses on the chart paper.

> Think about another book, *Gilgamesh the King*. What can you say about the setting and what was important to the people in that culture?

▶ Revisit a few pages as needed to guide students to understanding. Add notes to the chart based on the conversation.

Have a Try

Invite the students to talk with a partner about epics.

▶ Show the cover of *The Adventures of Odysseus* and revisit a few pages as needed.

> Think about the epic *The Adventures of Odysseus*. Turn and talk about the setting and what the epic reveals about what was important to the people of that time.

▶ After time for discussion, ask volunteers to share. Add to chart.

Summarize and Apply

Summarize the learning and remind students to think about how an epic often reflects the values of a culture.

> You learned that epics often show what is important to a culture. Epics enable people to learn about their history and build a shared value system. How does knowing this help you understand more about epics?

▶ Add the principle to the chart.

> If you choose to read an epic today, think about what the culture valued as you read. Place sticky notes on pages that show the values. Bring the book when we meet so you can share.

Share

Following independent reading time, gather students together to talk about their reading.

> Who would like to share your thoughts about the cultural valued of the epic you read? Talk about how that helps you understand the epic better.

Extend the Lesson (Optional)

After assessing students' understanding, you might decide to extend the learning.

▶ **Write About Reading** Have students choose one of the books discussed in this minilesson and write in a reader's notebook about the culture and values they most admire and why.

Epic tales reflect the values of the culture of origin.

Title	Setting	Culture and Values
Prince of Fire	India long ago	The legend told in this epic, the Ramayana, has been the basis for the Hindu religion. The culture and ethics of modern India can be traced back to the story. Diwali is an important yearly event in India today, and it celebrates goodness and hope.
Gilgamesh the King	Ancient Mesopotamia	The culture valued teaching a lesson and cautioned against being too proud or arrogant. The epic also shows the value placed on cooperating and working with others.
Odysseus	Ancient Greece	Strong warriors who could conquer both men and monsters were revered. Welcoming strangers was also important, as was beauty, art, honor, and truth.

RML5
LA.U24.RML5

Reading Minilesson Principle
Epic tales are often written as poetry or in a poetic way.

Studying Epic Tales

You Will Need

- a familiar poetic epic, such as the following from Text Set: Genre Study: Epic Tales:
  - *The Last Quest of Gilgamesh* by Ludmila Zeman
  - *The Adventures of Odysseus* by Hugh Lupton and Daniel Morden
- document camera (optional)
- chart paper and markers
- basket of epics
- sticky notes

Academic Language / Important Vocabulary

- epic
- poetic language

Continuum Connection

- Notice and understand the characteristics of some specific fiction genres: e.g., realistic fiction, historical fiction, folktale, fairy tale, fractured fairy tale, fable, myth, legend, epic, ballad, fantasy including science fiction, hybrid text (p.79)

Goal

Understand that epics often use poetic language.

Rationale

When students learn that epics are often told in poetic language, having originally taken the form of a poem or ballad, they understand the development of the epic and can interpret its meaning and importance.

Assess Learning

Observe students when they talk about and read epics and notice if there is evidence of new learning based on the goal of this minilesson.

- ▶ Do students recognize that the language of epics can be poetic?
- ▶ Do they use the terms *epic* and *poetic language*?

Minilesson

To help students think about the minilesson principle, engage them in a discussion of the use of poetic language in epics. Here is an example.

> Think about the type of language used in the epic *The Last Quest of Gilgamesh* as I read a page from it.

- ▶ Read and show or project page 2.

  > What do you notice about the language?

- ▶ Guide the conversation to help students notice the poetic language, rereading as needed. Write examples on the chart.

- ▶ Read and show or project the last two paragraphs on page 62 from *The Adventures of Odysseus*.

  > Often, epics are written as a poem or use poetic language.

  > What do you notice about the language in *The Adventures of Odysseus*?

- ▶ Add to chart.

Have a Try

Invite the students to talk in a small group about poetic language in epics.

▸ Provide each group with an epic.

  In your group, take a look at an epic to determine whether it uses poetry or poetic language. Discuss possible reasons why an epic is often written in poetic form.

▸ After time for discussion, ask a few volunteers to share.

Summarize and Apply

Summarize the learning and remind students to think about whether an epic is poetic.

  You learned that often epics have poetic language. Many epics were first written as poems or ballads.

▸ Add the principle to the chart.

  Today, you can choose to read an epic. Think about whether any parts of the epic use poetic language. Mark the pages with sticky notes and bring the book when we meet so you can share.

Share

Following independent reading time, gather students in the meeting area.

  Who noticed poetic language in an epic today? Tell us about that.

Extend the Lesson (Optional)

After assessing students' understanding, you might decide to extend the learning.

▸ Use an online resource or check out from the library original epics or different versions of the epics you read as a class so students can further discuss the poetic language and origins.

Epic tales are often written as poetry or in a poetic way.

"The moon cast eerie shadows. Jagged stones tore at his clothes." (p. 2)

"She reached down and lifted the mist, as though she were lifting a curtain." (p. 62)

Section 2: Literary Analysis

Assessment

After you have taught the minilessons in this umbrella, observe students as they talk and write about their reading across instructional contexts: interactive read-aloud, independent reading, guided reading, shared reading, and book club. Use *The Literacy Continuum* (Fountas and Pinnell 2017) to guide the observation of students' reading and writing behaviors.

▶ What evidence do you have of new understandings related to epics?

- Can students identify ways in which epics are alike?
- Do they participate in constructing a working definition for epics?
- Do they understand that epics are about heroes who are often on a quest?
- Do they talk about how an epic is connected to the values of a culture?
- Can they identify the poetic language in an epic?
- Are they using the terms *epics, legends, traditional literature, fantasy, characteristics, definition, heroes, quest, culture, values,* and *poetic language*?

▶ In what other ways, beyond the scope of this umbrella, are students talking about fiction books?

- Are students showing an interest in other types of fantasy?
- Do students show an interest in reading legends and ballads?

Use your observations to determine the next umbrella you will teach. You may also consult Minilessons Across the Year (pp. 61–64) for guidance.

Read and Revise

After completing the steps in the genre study process, help students read and revise their definition of the genre based on their new understandings.

▶ **Before:** An epic tale is a type of traditional literature that involves a hero.

▶ **After:** An epic tale is a long story or series of stories about a hero that has been passed down for many years. The hero sometimes has superpowers and is usually on a quest.

Reader's Notebook

When this umbrella is complete, provide a copy of the minilesson principles (see resources.fountasandpinnell.com) for students to glue in the reader's notebook (in the Minilessons section if using *Reader's Notebook: Advanced* [Fountas and Pinnell 2011]), so they can refer to the information as needed.

Minilessons in This Umbrella

RML1 Myths include gods and goddesses that take human form, are immortal, and possess supernatural powers.

RML2 Myths were written to provide an explanation for the beginning of the world, things in nature, or human behavior.

RML3 Gods and goddesses usually represent a moral belief or virtue.

Before Teaching Umbrella 25 Minilessons

Fantasy is classified as traditional literature or modern fantasy, and myths are a type of traditional literature along with folktales, fables, fairy tales, legends, ballads, and epics (see p. 40). They were at first told in the oral tradition but were written at an early time in history. It would be helpful to teach LA.U6.RML3 on types of traditional literature prior to teaching this umbrella. Ensure that students are familiar with multiple myths and other types of traditional literature. Select books that are clear examples of myths to use as mentor texts in these minilessons. You might want to collect a set of myths and conduct a genre study similar to that in Umbrella 24: Studying Epic Tales. Examples of myths can be found in the following books from the *Fountas & Pinnell Classroom™ Interactive Read-Aloud Collection* and *Independent Reading Collection*:

Interactive Read-Aloud Collection

Illustrator Study: K. Y. Craft

> *Pegasus* by Marianna Mayer
>
> *Cupid and Psyche* by M. Charlotte Craft
>
> *King Midas and the Golden Touch* by Charlotte Craft

Independent Reading Collection

> *Greek Myths* by Olivia Coolidge

As you read aloud and enjoy these texts together, help students to

- discuss what is unique about myths, and

- notice which elements *always* and *often* occur in myths.

Interactive Read-Aloud
Illustrator Study:
K. Y. Craft

Independent Reading

Section 2: Literary Analysis

Reading Minilesson Principle
Myths include gods and goddesses that take human form, are immortal, and possess supernatural powers.

Understanding Myths

You Will Need

▸ several familiar myths, such as the following from Text Set: Illustrator Study: K. Y. Craft:
- *Pegasus* by Marianna Mayer
- *Cupid and Psyche* by M. Charlotte Craft
- *King Midas and the Golden Touch* by Charlotte Craft

▸ chart paper prepared with three labeled columns: *Myth Title, Gods/Goddesses, Traits*

▸ markers

▸ basket of myths

▸ sticky notes prepared with names: Athena; Venus, Cupid, Jupiter; the man in the garden

Academic Language / Important Vocabulary

▸ myth
▸ gods
▸ goddesses
▸ immortal
▸ supernatural powers
▸ traits

Continuum Connection

▸ Identify elements of traditional literature and fantasy: e.g., the supernatural; imaginary and otherworldly creatures; gods and goddesses; talking animals, toys, and dolls; heroic characters, technology or scientific advances; time travel; aliens or outer space (p. 79)

Goal

Understand the characteristics of myths.

Rationale

When students learn that gods and goddesses who take human form, are immortal, and have supernatural powers exist in myths, they learn to pay close attention to characters; paying close attention helps them recognize which genre they are reading and know what to expect from myths.

Assess Learning

Observe students when they read and discuss myths and notice if there is evidence of new learning based on the goal of this minilesson.

▸ Are students characterizing a story with gods and goddesses as a myth?

▸ Can they discuss the qualities of gods and goddesses?

▸ Do they use the terms *myth, gods, goddesses, immortal, supernatural powers,* and *traits*?

Minilesson

To help students think about the minilesson principle, engage them in noticing and discussing the characteristics of gods and goddesses in myths. Here is an example.

▸ Show the cover of *Pegasus* and then show the illustration on page 20.

   Think about the story of *Pegasus*. Who is the character shown in the illustration, and how do you know?

▸ As needed, assist students in identifying the character as the goddess Athena, who is recognized by her owl. Place the prepared sticky note on the chart.

▸ Read the first three paragraphs on page 19.

   Look at the illustration and think about what Athena does and says. How would you describe her general characteristics?

▸ Guide the conversation as needed to help students identify the broad characteristics of mythological gods and goddesses, such as having a human form, immortality, and supernatural powers. Record responses on the chart.

   Now think about another story, *Cupid and Psyche.* Who are the gods and goddesses in this story?

   What are their traits?

▸ As needed, revisit pages 3–4 and 35–36 to help students identify the gods and goddess and their general characteristics. Add the sticky note and students' responses to the chart.

Have a Try

Invite the students to talk with a partner about the gods or goddesses in a myth.

▶ Revisit pages 8 and 26 from *King Midas and the Golden Touch*.

> Turn and talk about the god in the King Midas myth. How you would describe him?

▶ After time for discussion, ask a few volunteers to share. Fill in the last row of the chart.

Summarize and Apply

Summarize the learning and remind students to think about the gods and goddesses in myths.

> *Pegasus, Cupid and Psyche,* and *King Midas and the Golden Touch* are myths—fantasy stories that are a type of traditional literature. What did you learn about the characters in myths?

▶ Write the principle at the top of the chart.

> Today, choose a myth from the basket or continue reading one you have already started. Notice whether the story has gods or goddesses. If it does, notice the traits they have. Place a sticky note on a page that shows what the god or goddess is like. Bring the book when we meet so you can share.

Share

Following independent reading time, gather students in the meeting area to talk about myths.

> Did anyone read a story with gods or goddesses today? Tell about what you noticed.

Extend the Lesson (Optional)

After assessing students' understanding, you might decide to extend the learning.

▶ As students encounter other fantasy stories (both modern fantasy and traditional literature), discuss the characters and their traits to determine if the fantasy story is a myth.

Myths include gods and goddesses that take human form, are immortal, and possess supernatural powers.

Myth Title	Gods/Goddesses	Traits
PEGASUS	Athena	• identified by her owl • human-like form • immortal • supernatural powers (magic bridle)
	Venus Cupid Jupiter	• human forms • immortal • supernatural powers (magic arrows, immortal potion)
KING MIDAS GOLDEN TOUCH	the man in the garden	• human-like form • immortal • supernatural powers (magic wish)

Section 2: Literary Analysis

Reading Minilesson Principle
Myths were written to provide an explanation for the beginning of the world, things in nature, or human behavior.

Understanding Myths

You Will Need

- several myths, such as the following:
  - *Greek Myths* by Olivia Coolidge, from *Independent Reading Collection*
  - *King Midas and the Golden Touch* and *Cupid and Psyche* by Charlotte Craft, from Text Set: Illustrator Study: K. Y. Craft
- chart paper prepared with two columns: *Myth Title, Why was the myth written?*
- markers
- basket of myths

Academic Language / Important Vocabulary

- fantasy
- myth
- nature
- natural phenomena
- human behavior

Continuum Connection

- Notice and understand the characteristics of some specific fiction genres: e.g., realistic fiction, historical fiction, folktale, fairy tale, fractured fairy tale, fable, myth, legend, epic, ballad, fantasy including science fiction, hybrid text (p. 79)

Goal

Understand that myths were written to provide an explanation for the beginning of the world, things in nature, or human behavior.

Rationale

When students learn to recognize that myths were written to explain the beginning of the world, things in nature, or human behavior, they recognize characteristics that help them identify and understand the genre of myths.

Assess Learning

Observe students when they read and talk about myths and notice if there is evidence of new learning based on the goal of this minilesson.

- Do students understand that myths were told and then written to explain the beginning of the world, things in nature, or human behavior?
- Do they use the terms *fantasy, myth, nature, natural phenomena,* and *human behavior*?

Minilesson

To help students think about the minilesson principle, engage them in thinking about the reasons why myths were written. Here is an example.

- Show "The Origin of the Seasons" from *Greek Myths*.

  At first, myths were told orally, but they were written early in history.

  Why do you think this myth was written? The title gives you a big clue!

- Record students' responses on the chart paper.
- Repeat with "The Creation of Man" in the same book.
- Show the cover of *King Midas and the Golden Touch*.

  Why do you think this myth was written?

- Revisit the illustrations on pages 7, 24–25, and 31 if necessary. Record responses on the chart.

  What do you notice about why these myths were written?

  These myths were all written to explain something.

Have a Try

Invite the students to talk with a partner about what a myth seeks to explain.

- Show the cover of *Cupid and Psyche* and revisit a few pages as needed.

    Turn and talk about why you think the myth *Cupid and Psyche* was written. What does it explain?

- After time for discussion, add to the chart.

Summarize and Apply

Summarize the learning and remind students to think about what myths seek to explain.

    Look at the chart. The reasons these myths were written fall into several broad categories. How could you describe the reasons?

- Write the principle at the top of the chart.

    Today choose a myth from the basket or continue reading one you have already started. If you are reading a myth, think about what the myth seeks to explain. Bring the book when we meet so you can share.

Share

Following independent reading time, gather students in the meeting area to talk about myths.

    If you read a myth today, share what the myth seeks to explain.

Extend the Lesson (Optional)

After assessing students' understanding, you might decide to extend the learning.

- **Writing About Reading** As students read more myths, encourage them to think about the way that, today, science seeks to explain the beginning of the world, nature, natural phenomena, and human behavior. Have them use a reader's notebook to compare and contrast the way that myths attempted to explain those mysteries versus the way science explains them today.

Myths were written to provide an explanation for the beginning of the world, things in nature, or human behavior.

Myth Title	Why was the myth written?
"The Origin of the Seasons" "The Creation of Man"	• to explain how the seasons came to be • to explain the beginning of the world
	• to explain the danger of being greedy
	• to explain that lasting love requires trust and dedication

Reading Minilesson Principle

Gods and goddesses usually represent a moral belief or virtue.

Understanding Myths

You Will Need

- several myths with gods and goddesses who represent a moral belief or virtue, such as the following from Text Set: Illustrator Study: K. Y. Craft:
  - *Pegasus* by Marianna Mayer
  - *Cupid and Psyche* by M. Charlotte Craft
- chart paper and markers
- basket of myths
- sticky notes

Academic Language / Important Vocabulary

- traditional literature
- myth
- gods
- goddesses
- moral belief
- virtue

Continuum Connection

- Identify elements of traditional literature and fantasy: the supernatural, imaginary and otherworldly creatures; gods and goddesses; talking animals, toys, and dolls; heroic characters, technology or scientific advances; time travel; aliens or outer space (p. 79)
- Recognize and understand symbolism in a text and illustrations (p. 80)
- Infer the significance of heroic or larger-than-life characters in fantasy, who represent the struggle of good and evil (p.81)

Goal

Understand that gods and goddesses are often symbolic of the moral beliefs or virtues of the culture of origin.

Rationale

When students learn to recognize that the gods and goddesses in myths often reflect the moral beliefs or virtues of a culture, they begin to understand that myths helped people gain knowledge about their shared history in order to build a community of shared values.

Assess Learning

Observe students when they read and talk about myths and notice if there is evidence of new learning based on the goal of this minilesson.

- Can students identify the moral belief or virtue represented by the gods and goddesses in myths?
- Do they use the terms *traditional literature, myth, gods, goddesses, moral belief* and *virtue*?

Minilesson

To help students think about the minilesson principle, engage them in thinking about the moral belief or virtue represented by gods and goddesses in myths. Here is an example.

> We have talked about how in myths, gods and goddesses take human form, are immortal, and have supernatural powers. Let's talk a little deeper about what some specific gods and goddesses represent.

- Show the illustration on page 20 and read page 19 from *Pegasus*.

> Think about what Athena says and does. What moral beliefs or virtues does Athena represent?

- As needed, explain that moral belief is the way a society views right and wrong and virtue is an honorable trait.

- As students respond, begin a chart that lists the myth title, the god/goddess, and the moral belief or virtue represented by the god/goddess.

> Now think about each god and goddess in *Cupid and Psyche*: Venus, Cupid, and Jupiter. What moral beliefs or virtues do they represent? Tell your thoughts about that.

- As needed, review a few pages to help students identify the moral beliefs or virtues of each god and goddess. Add to the chart.

Have a Try

Invite the students to talk in small groups about what the gods and goddesses in a myth represent.

- ▶ Have students sit in small groups. Provide each group with a short myth.

  In your groups, take a look at the myth and think about the moral belief or virtue that its gods and goddesses represent.

- ▶ After time for discussion, ask one member from each group to share their findings.

Summarize and Apply

Summarize the learning and remind students to think about what gods and goddesses represent in myths.

  God and goddesses usually represent a moral belief or virtue that was important to the society at the time the myth was written. Many of these qualities are still valued today.

- ▶ Add the principle to the chart.

  When you read today, choose a myth from the basket if you aren't already reading one. Think about the moral belief or virtue represented by the gods and goddesses in the myth. Mark any pages you want to remember with a sticky note. Bring the book when we meet so you can share.

Share

Following independent reading time, gather students in the meeting area to talk about their reading.

  What did you notice about what the gods and goddesses represent in the myth you read? Talk about the moral beliefs or virtues you think the god or goddess embodies.

Extend the Lesson (Optional)

After assessing students' understanding, you might decide to extend the learning.

- ▶ As students experience more myths, have them notice common gods and goddesses and the way that the moral beliefs or virtues represented by those divinities are the same across multiple texts. Have them compare and contrast the way that different myths reveal the qualities of the gods and goddesses.

Gods and goddesses usually represent a moral belief or virtue.

Myth	God/Goddess	Moral Belief or Virtue Represented by God or Goddess
PEGASUS	Athena	Wisdom. Courage was an important virtue. Athena supported Bellerophon's courage.
	Venus	Love and beauty. She became angry when Psyche's beauty caused people to ignore Venus's temple.
	Cupid	Love. His relationship with Psyche shows the moral belief that real love requires commitment.
	Jupiter	The importance of rules and laws. When Cupid learned a valuable lesson, Jupiter rewarded him by making Psyche immortal so they could be together.

Assessment

After you have taught the minilessons in this umbrella, observe students as they talk and write about their reading across instructional contexts: interactive read-aloud, independent reading, guided reading, shared reading, and book club. Use *The Literacy Continuum* (Fountas and Pinnell 2017) to guide the observation of students' reading and writing behaviors.

- What evidence do you have of new understandings related to myths?
- Do students understand that myths are a type of traditional literature?
- Are students aware that myths have gods and goddesses that take human form, are immortal, and possess supernatural powers?
- Do they understand that myths were told and then written to provide an explanation for the beginning of the world, things in nature, or human behavior?
- Can they recognize the moral belief or virtue that gods and goddesses in myths represent?
- Are they using the terms *fantasy, myth, gods, goddesses, immortal, supernatural powers, nature, human behavior, moral belief,* and *virtue*?

▶ In what other ways, beyond the scope of this umbrella, are students talking about fantasy?

- Do students show an interest in modern fantasy?

Use your observations to determine the next umbrella you will teach. You may also consult Minilessons Across the Year (pp. 61–64) for guidance.

Link to Writing

After teaching the minilessons in this umbrella, help students link the new learning to their own writing:

▶ Have students begin to plan and write a myth of their own that explains creation, nature, a natural phenomenon, or human behavior.

Reader's Notebook

When this umbrella is complete, provide a copy of the minilesson principles (see resources.fountasandpinnell.com) for students to glue in the reader's notebook (in the Minilessons section if using *Reader's Notebook: Advanced* [Fountas and Pinnell 2011]), so they can refer to the information as needed.

Minilessons in This Umbrella

RML1   Writers use poetic or descriptive language to help you understand the setting.

RML2   Evaluate the significance of the setting in a story.

RML3   Evaluate the believability of the setting in fantasy books.

RML4   Evaluate the authenticity of the setting in historical and realistic fiction.

Before Teaching Umbrella 26 Minilessons

Read aloud and discuss engaging realistic fiction, historical fiction, and modern fantasy stories that take place in a variety of locations and time periods. Include books that take place in both real and imagined places. As much as possible, choose books in which the setting is central to the story. Read aloud books in which the setting is richly described with poetic or descriptive language. Use the following books from the *Fountas & Pinnell Classroom™ Interactive Read-Aloud Collection* text sets or choose books from your classroom library in which setting has an effect on the characters or plot.

Poetry

Neighborhood Odes: A Poetry Collection by Gary Soto

Activists/Change Makers

On Our Way to Oyster Bay: Mother Jones and Her March for Children's Rights by Monica Kulling

Civic Engagement

Memphis, Martin, and the Mountaintop: The Sanitation Strike of 1968 by Alice Faye Duncan

Perseverance

The Memory Coat by Elvira Woodruff

Countering Stereotypes

A Shelter in Our Car by Monica Gunning

Genre Study: Modern Fantasy

Journey by Aaron Becker

The Mysteries of Harris Burdick by Chris Van Allsburg

The Search for Delicious by Natalie Babbitt

As you read aloud and enjoy these texts together, help students

- talk about when and where the story takes place,
- notice whether the setting is real or imagined,
- notice and discuss poetic or descriptive language that describes the setting, and
- discuss the importance of the setting to the plot and characters.

Poetry

Activists/ Change Makers

Civic Engagement

Perseverance

Countering Stereotypes

Genre Study: Modern Fantasy

RML1
LA.U26.RML1

Reading Minilesson Principle
Writers use poetic or descriptive language to help you understand the setting.

Thinking About the Setting in Fiction Books

You Will Need

- several familiar fiction books that include poetic or descriptive language about the setting, such as the following:
  - *Neighborhood Odes* by Gary Soto from Text Set: Poetry
  - *On Our Way to Oyster Bay* by Monica Kulling from Text Set: Activists/Change Makers
  - *The Memory Coat* by Elvira Woodruff from Text Set: Perseverance
- chart paper and markers
- fiction books students are reading
- basket of familiar fiction books
- sticky notes

Academic Language / Important Vocabulary

- fiction
- setting
- poetic language
- descriptive language

Continuum Connection

- Notice and understand long stretches of descriptive language important to understanding setting and characters (p. 82)
- Notice when a fiction writer uses poetic or descriptive language to show the setting, appeal to the five senses, or convey human feelings such as loss, relief, or anger (p. 82)

Goal

Notice and understand the poetic or descriptive language used to show the setting.

Rationale

The setting can be an integral part of a story, so authors need to describe it in a way that the readers can visualize it. Often, authors use poetic and descriptive language to make the setting seem real. When you guide students to notice poetic and descriptive language, they develop an appreciation for and an understanding of how writers construct their settings. They can also use this knowledge in their own fiction writing.

Assess Learning

Observe students when they talk about setting and notice if there is evidence of new learning based on the goal of this minilesson.

- ▶ Are students able to visualize the setting?
- ▶ Do they use the terms *fiction, setting, poetic language,* and *descriptive language*?

Minilesson

To help students think about the minilesson principle, engage them in a discussion of an author's use of poetic and descriptive language that reveals information about the setting. Here is an example.

- ▶ Read a few pages of *Neighborhood Odes* that describe setting, such as pages 1–3.

  What is the setting?

  How does Gary Soto reveal the setting?

- ▶ Continue the conversation, reading page 12.

  What language does he use to give clues about the setting?

- ▶ On chart paper, record student responses about the setting: what it is and what language or details reveal it.

- ▶ Repeat the activity by reading page 9 from *On Our Way to Oyster Bay* and page 9 from *The Memory Coat*. Explain that *tsar* is the word for a ruler of Russia prior to the revolution in 1917.

- ▶ Add students' responses to the chart.

  Notice the kind of language that the writers use. How would you describe it?

  Writers often use poetic or descriptive language to help you understand the setting. Such language can help you "see" what is going on in the story or "feel" the heat of a summer's day.

Have a Try

Invite the students to talk with a partner about setting.

▶ Have each student bring a fiction book they are reading or have them choose one from the basket.

> Think about the language the author uses to help you imagine the setting. With your partner, look through a fiction book and find examples.

▶ After students turn and talk, invite a few students to share their thinking.

Summarize and Apply

Summarize the learning and remind students to notice poetic and descriptive language.

> What kind of language do writers use to help you understand the settings in their books?

▶ Write the principle at the top of the chart.

> If you read a fiction book today, notice if the writer uses poetic or descriptive language to help you understand the setting. If so, put a sticky note on an example and bring your book to share when we come back together.

Writers use poetic or descriptive language to help you understand the setting.

	The Setting	How do you know?
	A hot summer day in the neighborhood	"The sun is as bright as a hot dime." The neighborhood kids are barefoot, wearing T-shirts, and eating snow cones.
	A hot summer day in a field	"The days were long and hot." There were mosquitoes and blooming flowers.
	Winter in Russia a long time ago	"mittened fingers curled around a frosted twig" "a frosty afternoon" tsar's palace

Share

Following independent reading time, gather students together in the meeting area to talk about how authors describe their settings.

> Who found an example of poetic or descriptive language that describes a setting today?

> Read the language and explain how it helped you understand the setting.

Extend the Lesson (Optional)

After assessing students' understanding, you might decide to extend the learning.

▶ **Writing About Reading** Have students write in a reader's notebook an example of language an author used to help them understand a story's setting. They should explain how the language appeals to their senses.

Reading Minilesson Principle
Evaluate the significance of the setting in a story.

You Will Need

- several familiar realistic fiction or fantasy texts, such as the following:
  - *A Shelter in Our Car* by Monica Gunning, from Text Set: Countering Stereotypes
  - *Journey* by Aaron Becker, from Text Set: Genre Study: Modern Fantasy
- chart paper and markers
- realistic fiction or fantasy stories students are reading
- basket of familiar realistic fiction and fantasy stories
- sticky notes

Academic Language / Important Vocabulary

- setting
- plot
- fiction

Continuum Connection

- Infer the importance of the setting to the plot of the story in realistic and historical fiction and fantasy (p. 80)
- Evaluate the significance of the setting in the story (p. 80)

Goal

Evaluate the significance of the setting in the story.

Rationale

When you teach students to think about the importance of the setting in a story and to evaluate its significance, they understand that the setting is not an arbitrarily chosen time and place and that it has to make sense in the story. The setting contributes substantially to the plot in some stories. It's important for readers to develop an understanding of universal truths and ideas that are shaped by time and place.

Assess Learning

Observe students when they talk about setting and notice if there is evidence of new learning based on the goal of this minilesson.

- ▶ Are students able to identify the setting in a realistic fiction or fantasy story?
- ▶ Can they infer the importance of the setting to the plot?
- ▶ Are students able to evaluate the significance of the setting?
- ▶ Do they use the terms *setting, plot,* and *fiction*?

Minilesson

To help students think about the minilesson principle, engage them in thinking about and evaluating the significance of the setting in a realistic fiction or fantasy story. Here is an example.

- ▶ Revisit several pages that provide details about the setting from a familiar realistic fiction story, such as pages 7–11 of *A Shelter in Our Car.*

  Talk about where and when this story takes place.

  How does the author show you that?

- ▶ Begin a chart and add the title and setting.
- ▶ Engage the students in a conversation that guides them to discuss the significance of the setting to the plot and also to evaluate whether the setting matters. Here are some suggested prompts:
  - *Does it matter where and when the story takes place? Why do you think that?*
  - *Would the story be the same if the setting changed? Why or why not?*
- ▶ As students talk about these aspects of setting, add their ideas to the chart.
- ▶ Repeat the activity with a fantasy story, such as *Journey.*

Have a Try

Invite the students to talk with a partner about the significance of setting and evaluate whether the setting matters.

▶ Have each student bring a realistic fiction or fantasy story they are reading or have them choose one from the basket.

Think about where and when the story takes place. Turn and talk about the importance of the setting. Find specific examples from the story and tell your partner why the setting matters to the plot or why it doesn't matter.

▶ After time for discussion, ask students to share their thinking.

Some stories can happen anywhere or anytime, but other stories can happen only in a particular setting. These are things to think about as you read fiction stories.

Evaluate the significance of the setting in a story.

Title	Setting	Importance	Would the story work in a different setting?
A Shelter in Our Car	Where: a car; a large city in the United States When: over several days	• The car shows homelessness. • Large cities offer more opportunities for jobs and housing.	Maybe Most homeless people live in cities, but not all of them.
JOURNEY	Where: a girl's bedroom, an imaginary world When: not clear	• If the girl hadn't been bored in her bedroom, she wouldn't have drawn the magic door. • The imaginary settings hold the action in the story.	No

Summarize and Apply

Summarize the learning and remind students to think about setting and its significance.

What did you learn about setting?

▶ Add the principle to the chart.

If you read a fiction book today, think about the significance of the setting and whether the setting matters to the story. Mark pages you want to remember with a sticky note. Bring the book when we meet so you can share.

Share

Following independent reading time, gather students in small groups. Ensure that at least one member of each group has read a realistic fiction or fantasy story today.

Share what you noticed about the significance of the setting.

Extend the Lesson (Optional)

After assessing students' understanding, you might decide to extend the learning.

▶ You can expand on this idea by having students think about the significance of the setting in historical fiction books (see LA.U22.RML2).

Reading Minilesson Principle
Evaluate the believability of the setting in fantasy books.

Thinking About the Setting in Fiction Books

You Will Need

- several familiar fantasy books, such as the following from Text Set: Genre Study: Modern Fantasy:
  - *The Mysteries of Harris Burdick* by Chris Van Allsburg
  - *The Search for Delicious* by Natalie Babbitt
  - *Journey* by Aaron Becker
- chart paper and markers
- sticky notes

Academic Language / Important Vocabulary

- fantasy
- setting
- believable

Continuum Connection

- Notice science fiction and fantasy settings: e.g., alternative or secondary world, futuristic setting, alternative histories, animal kingdom, fictional planet, pseudo-medieval setting (p. 80)
- Evaluate the authenticity of the writer's presentation of the setting (p. 80)

Goal

Evaluate the believability of the setting in fantasy books.

Rationale

When students think about the believability of a fantasy setting, they have to think critically about the way the author has develop the setting. Whether a setting is believable relates to the parameters of the world created by the author, regardless of whether it is a realistic or fantasy setting. This lesson could also be taught in conjunction with Umbrella 23: Studying Modern Fantasy.

Assess Learning

Observe students when they discuss setting in fantasy stories and notice if there is evidence of new learning based on the goal of this minilesson.

- ▶ Do students discuss whether a setting is believable within the parameters of the story?
- ▶ Do they use the terms *fantasy, setting,* and *believable*?

Minilesson

To help students think about the minilesson principle, engage them in thinking about the believability of a fantasy setting. Here is an example.

> Look carefully at these illustrations from *The Mysteries of Harris Burdick*. Notice where each scene takes place.

- ▶ Show several of the illustrations.

> You know that for a fantasy story to be believable, the author has to convince you that impossible things can happen. You are willing to suspend disbelief because the fantasy is a good story and the author has done a good job with the setting. How does Van Allsburg convince you that the mysteries are real?

- ▶ Record their responses on chart paper.
- ▶ Repeat the activity using another modern fantasy story, such as the map and prologue in *The Search for Delicious*.

Have a Try

Invite the students to talk with a partner about the believability of a fantasy setting.

▶ Show the cover of *Journey*. As needed, revisit a few pages that show the settings.

Turn and talk about that the settings in this story. Are they believable?

▶ After students turn and talk, ask students to share ideas. Add to the chart.

Summarize and Apply

Summarize the learning and remind students to notice settings when they read fantasy stories.

Today you learned it's important that the things that happen to the characters make sense in the author's fantasy world.

▶ Add the principle to the top of the chart.

If you read a fantasy book today, notice if the setting is believable and mark any pages you want to remember. Bring the book when we come back together so you can share.

Share

Following independent reading time, gather students together in the meeting area to talk about the settings in fantasy books.

Who read a fantasy story today?

What is the setting of the book you read? Was it believable? Why or why not?

Extend the Lesson (Optional)

After assessing students' understanding, you might decide to extend the learning.

▶ **Writing About Reading** Have students write in a reader's notebook about the setting in a fantasy story. They should identify the time and place of the story and write about whether the setting is believable and why or why not.

Evaluate the believability of the setting in fantasy books.

Title	Setting	How does the writer make the setting believable?
	• a boy's bedroom • a living room • a beach	• The details—a bed, a table, water and stones—make each setting seem very real. • The illustration style is realistic.
natalie BABBITT	• four towns • woldweller's forest • the castle • the lake • the mildews	• A map shows all the places in the book. • The prologue describes the history of how the area was formed. It sounds very logical.
JOURNEY	• girl's bedroom • a forest • a castle • up in the air	• The drawings look realistic, but a person couldn't really draw her way out of danger.

Reading Minilesson Principle
Evaluate the authenticity of the setting in historical and realistic fiction.

You Will Need

- several familiar historical and realistic fiction books, such as the following:
  - *Memphis, Martin, and the Mountaintop* by Alice Faye Duncan, from Text Set: Civic Engagement
  - *A Shelter in Our Car* by Monica Gunning from Text Set: Countering Stereotypes
  - *On Our Way to Oyster Bay* by Monica Kuling, from Text Set: Activists/Change Makers
- chart paper prepared with two columns: *Historical Fiction* and *Realistic Fiction*
- markers
- six sticky notes, each labeled *Authentic*

Academic Language / Important Vocabulary

- historical fiction
- realistic fiction
- setting
- authenticity

Continuum Connection

- Evaluate the authenticity of the writer's presentation of the setting (p. 80)

Goal

Evaluate the authenticity of the setting in historical and realistic fiction.

Rationale

When students think about the authenticity of a historical or realistic fiction setting, they develop critical thinking skills and begin to evaluate the ways authors and illustrators reveal the setting. This lesson could also be taught when you teach minilessons on realistic fiction or historical fiction.

Assess Learning

Observe students when they talk about the authenticity of setting in historical and realistic fiction stories and notice if there is evidence of new learning based on the goal of this minilesson.

- ▶ Are students able to evaluate the authenticity of a setting?
- ▶ Do they use the terms *historical fiction, realistic fiction, setting,* and *authenticity*?

Minilesson

To help students think about the minilesson principle, engage them in thinking about the authenticity of a historical and realistic setting. Here is an example.

- ▶ Revisit a few pages from *Memphis, Martin, and the Mountaintop* that show setting (see chart for examples). Start with pages 1–2.

   When an author and illustrator get the setting right for the characters and events of a story, the setting is authentic. Do you think the setting on these pages is authentic?

- ▶ Place one of the labeled sticky notes next to the page numbers.

   What details did the author or the illustrator include to make the setting feel authentic?

- ▶ Record students' responses in the first column of the chart.

   This story is historical fiction, so the details have to make sense for a particular time period.

- ▶ Repeat the process for a couple of other examples in *Memphis, Martin, and the Mountaintop.*

- ▶ Repeat the process, this time using an example of realistic fiction, *A Shelter in Our Car.*

   Do you think the setting is authentic?

   What details did the author or the illustrator include to make the setting realistic and appropriate for the story?

Have a Try

Invite the students to talk with a partner about the setting of a realistic or historical fiction book.

▶ Show the cover of a realistic or historical fiction book, such as *On Our Way to Oyster Bay*. As needed, review a few pages that show the setting.

> Think about the setting in a realistic or historical fiction book. What details make the setting feel authentic? Turn and talk about that.

▶ After students turn and talk, ask several volunteers to share what they noticed about the authenticity of the setting.

Summarize and Apply

Summarize the learning and remind students to evaluate the authenticity of the settings when they read realistic and historical fiction books.

> Why is it important that the author creates an authentic setting?

▶ Add the principle to the top of the chart.

> If you read a realistic or historical fiction book today, notice the setting and evaluate its authenticity. Bring the book with you when we come together again.

Share

Following independent reading time, gather students together in the meeting area to talk about the authenticity of fictional settings.

> Who read a realistic or historical fiction book today?

> What is the setting of the book you read? What details did the author use to create an authentic setting?

Extend the Lesson (Optional)

After assessing students' understanding, you might decide to extend the learning.

▶ Have students do research to find out more about the 1968 sanitation strike in Memphis or about the lives of homeless people.

▶ **Writing About Reading** Have students write in a reader's notebook an evaluation of the setting in a realistic or historical fiction book. They should identify the time and place of the setting and describe the details used by the author or illustrator to make the setting authentic.

Evaluate the authenticity of the setting in historical and realistic fiction.

Historical Fiction	Realistic Fiction
Memphis, Martin, and the Mountaintop	A Shelter in Our Car
Pages 1-2 Authentic	**Page 4** Authentic
A sanitation strike actually happened in 1968.	A city often has flashing police lights and blaring sirens.
A sanitation strike would have animals rummaging through trash. It would stink.	People living in a car would have all their clothes in the car.
Pages 3-4 Authentic	**Pages 10-11** Authentic
January can be cold and wet with rain and clouds.	Park bathrooms probably have only cold water.
Pages 19-20 Authentic	Mr. Williams is sleeping on one of the other park benches.
Tanks really did go down the streets of Memphis, forcing all of the residents to stay inside.	**Pages 30-31** Authentic
	A motel would have a warm shower and bed with clean sheets.

Assessment

After you have taught the minilessons in this umbrella, observe students as they talk and write about their reading across instructional contexts: interactive read-aloud, independent reading, guided reading, shared reading, and book club. Use *The Literacy Continuum* (Fountas and Pinnell 2017) to observe students' reading and writing behaviors.

> ▸ What evidence do you have of new understandings related to setting?
>   - Are students able to identify where and when a story takes place?
>   - Do they use poetic or descriptive language to visualize the setting of a story?
>   - Are they talking about the significance of the setting to the characters and plot?
>   - Are they able to evaluate a text for believability and authenticity of the setting?
>   - Are they using terms such as *setting*, *poetic language*, *descriptive language*, *believable*, and *authenticity*?
>
> ▸ In what other ways, beyond the scope of this umbrella, are students talking about fiction?
>   - Do students analyze the illustrator's craft?
>   - Do they recognize the work of favorite authors?

Use your observations to determine the next umbrella you will teach. You may also consult Minilessons Across the Year (pp. 61–64) for guidance.

Link to Writing

After teaching the minilessons in this umbrella, help students link the new learning to their own writing:

> ▸ When students write their own stories, encourage them to plan the setting before they start writing. Some students may benefit from drawing the setting before writing about it. The more details students include in the drawing, the more details they can write about. Remind them to think about how the setting will influence the story's characters and action. Encourage them to use poetic or descriptive language to describe settings.

Reader's Notebook

When this umbrella is complete, provide a copy of the minilesson principles (see resources.fountasandpinnell.com) for students to glue in the reader's notebook (in the Minilessons section if using *Reader's Notebook: Advanced* [Fountas and Pinnell 2011]), so they can refer to the information as needed.

Minilessons in This Umbrella

RML1 The plot of a story usually includes a beginning, a problem, a series of events, a climax, and an ending.

RML2 Sometimes stories have more than one problem.

RML3 Writers use flashbacks or a story-within-a-story.

RML4 Writers create plots and subplots.

RML5 Writers sometimes create two or more narratives linked by common characters or a common theme.

RML6 Critique an author's selection of plot structure.

Before Teaching Umbrella 27 Minilessons

Read and discuss a variety of high-quality fiction books that vary in types of characters, setting, and plot and that include a clearly defined problem, climax, and solution. The minilessons in this umbrella use the following books from the *Fountas and Pinnell Classroom™ Interactive Read-Aloud Collection, Independent Reading Collection,* and *Book Clubs Collection;* however, you can use any fiction books you have available in the classroom that have the characteristics listed above.

Independent Read-Aloud Collection

Perseverance

The Turtle Ship by Helena Ku Rhee

Kindness and Compassion

Wings by Christopher Myers

Babu's Song by Stephanie Stuve-Bodeen

Handling Emotions/Positive Relationships

Eagle Song by Joseph Bruchac

Author/Illustrator Study: S. D. Nelson

Digging a Hole to Heaven

Exploring Identity

Border Crossing by Maria Colleen Cruz

Circle Unbroken: The Story of a Basket and Its People by Margot Theis Raven

Garvey's Choice by Nikki Grimes

Problem Solving/Giving Back

The Red Bicycle: The Extraordinary Story of One Ordinary Bicycle by Jude Isabella

Genre Study: Modern Fantasy

The Search for Delicious by Natalie Babbitt

Independent Reading Collection

The Harlem Charade by Natasha Tarpley

Book Clubs Collection

Identity

Throwing Shadows by E. L. Konigsburg

Interactive Read-Aloud
Perseverance

Kindness and Compassion

Handling Emotions/
Positive Relationships

S. D. Nelson

Exploring Identity

Problem Solving/
Giving Back

Modern Fantasy

Independent Reading

Book Clubs
Identity

Section 2: Literary Analysis

Reading Minilesson Principle
The plot of a story usually includes a beginning, a problem, a series of events, a climax, and an ending.

Understanding Plot

You Will Need

- several familiar fiction books with easily identifiable plot features, such as the following:
  - *The Turtle Ship* by Helena Ku Rhee, from Text Set: Perseverance
  - *Wings* by Christopher Myers, from Text Set: Kindness and Compassion
- chart paper prepared with a graphic organizer that includes the labels *Beginning, Problem, Event* (several), *Climax*, and *Ending*
- markers
- sticky notes
- basket of fiction books

Academic Language / Important Vocabulary

- plot
- beginning
- series of events
- climax
- ending
- narrative text structure

Continuum Connection

- Recognize and discuss aspects of narrative structure: e.g., beginning, series of events, climax (turning point) of the story, problem resolution, ending (p. 81)

Goal

Notice and understand that the plot is a sequence of events in a story, including a beginning, problem, climax, problem resolution, and ending.

Rationale

When students learn to identify the parts of a story, they learn to expect that stories have a beginning, a series of events, a climax, and an ending, and can notice these parts as they read and think deeply about them.

Assess Learning

Observe students when they read and discuss plot and notice if there is evidence of new learning based on the goal of this minilesson.

- ▶ Can students identify the beginning, series of events, climax, and ending in a fiction story?
- ▶ Are students able to chronologically summarize a story and include the important elements of plot?
- ▶ Do they use the terms *plot, beginning, series of events, climax, ending,* and *narrative text structure?*

Minilesson

To help students think about the minilesson principle, engage them in thinking about narrative text structure. Here is an example.

- ▶ Show the prepared chart paper.

  What do you notice about this organizer?

- ▶ Guide students to talk about the elements of narrative text structure.

  Think about *The Turtle Ship*. If I want to add details from this story that show each of the plot features on the organizer, what could I add? Let's start with the beginning, where the characters, setting, and problem are introduced.

- ▶ As students provide ideas, add details next to each label, either by writing directly on the chart or by using sticky notes. Make sure students understand that the problem and how the character goes about solving it is what drives the plot forward.

- ▶ Ask a volunteer to read the chart, including each label and the details from the story written next to the label.

Have a Try

Invite the students to talk with a partner about the elements of narrative text structure.

> What would you write in the organizer to show the narrative text structure of *Wings*? Turn and talk about that.

▶ After time for discussion, ask a few students to share. You can add sticky notes for this story to the chart if it will be helpful for your students.

Summarize and Apply

Summarize the learning and remind students to think about narrative text structure when they read fiction stories.

> What do you know about narrative text structure?

▶ Add the principle to the chart.

> Choose a fiction story from the basket to read or continue one that you are already reading. Notice the parts of the plot as the story unfolds. Bring the book when we meet so you can share.

Share

Following independent reading time, gather students in small groups to talk about the narrative structure of fiction books.

> In your group, share the parts of a story you noticed when you read today. Look back at the chart and see how many you can include. If you have not finished the book, you will probably not know about each part yet.

Extend the Lesson (Optional)

After assessing students' understanding, you might decide to extend the learning.

▶ You might want to use terms such as *rising action*, *falling action*, and *resolution* when you and your students discuss plot.

▶ **Writing About Reading** Have students make or fill in a graphic organizer (see resources.fountasandpinnell.com) about the plot of a story. They can glue the organizer into a reader's notebook.

The plot of a story usually includes a beginning, a problem, a series of events, a climax, and an ending.

Sun-sin wants to win a shipbuilding contest.

Problem

Gobugi's behavior impresses the King and Sun-sin wins the contest.

Sun-sin and his parents travel far to share his design idea.

Climax

Sun-sin has a new idea for a ship design.

Event

All of Sun-sin's ship designs fail.

Event

Sun-sin and Gobugi watch ships from the garden.

Event

Sun-sin became an admiral. Sun-sin and Gobugi watch ships from the garden.

Beginning

Ending

Reading Minilesson Principle
Sometimes stories have more than one problem.

Understanding Plot

You Will Need

- several familiar fiction books that have more than one problem, such as the following:
  - *Digging a Hole to Heaven* by S. D. Nelson, from Text Set: Author/Illustrator Study: S. D. Nelson
  - *Border Crossing* by Maria Colleen Cruz, from Text Set: Exploring Identity
  - *Babu's Song* by Stephanie Stuve-Bodeen, from Text Set: Kindness and Compassion
- chart paper prepared with two of the titles placed in circles, leaving room to add information
- markers
- sticky notes
- basket of fiction stories that have more than one problem

Academic Language / Important Vocabulary

- plot
- problem
- solution
- narrative text structure

Continuum Connection

- Follow a complex plot with multiple events, episodes, or problems (p. 81)
- Recognize and discuss aspects of narrative structure: e.g., beginning, series of events, climax (turning point) of the story, problem resolution, ending (p. 81)

Goal

Understand that stories can have more than one problem.

Rationale

When students understand that some stories have more than one problem, they learn how to follow the plot in more complex works of fiction and understand the connection between each problem and the overall story and solution.

Assess Learning

Observe students when they read and discuss plot and notice if there is evidence of new learning based on the goal of this minilesson.

- ▶ Are students able to identify multiple problems in a story?
- ▶ Can they discuss the relationship between the different problems?
- ▶ Do they use the terms *plot, problem, solution,* and *narrative text structure?*

Minilesson

To help students think about the minilesson principle, engage them in thinking about the problems in a fiction story. Here is an example.

▶ Show *Digging a Hole to Heaven.* Ask students to recall a problem that the characters face. Record the problem in the first web on the prepared chart paper.

> Do the characters face any other problems?

▶ Record at least one other problem on the chart. Then show the book *Border Crossing.*

> Think about another fiction story, *Border Crossing.* What is a problem in the story?

> Are there any other problems in the story?

▶ Record students' responses in the second web on the chart.

> What do you notice about these two stories?

> The characters face more than one problem in each story. Why would a writer decide to have the characters face more than one problem in a story?

Have a Try

Invite the students to talk with a partner about a story with more than one problem.

▶ Show the cover of a book with more than one problem, such as *Babu's Song*.

  Think about *Babu's Song*. Turn and talk about the problems in the story.

▶ After time for discussion, ask a few students to share their thinking.

Summarize and Apply

Summarize the learning and remind students to notice when there is more than one problem in a story.

  What does the chart show about problems in stories?

▶ Add the principle to the top of the chart.

  Today you can choose a fiction story from the basket or continue one you are already reading.
  Think about whether there is more than one problem and mark any pages with sticky notes that you want to remember. Bring the book when we meet so you can share.

Share

Following independent reading time, gather students in small groups.

  Talk about whether you noticed multiple problems and what they were. Share specific examples from the book.

Extend the Lesson (Optional)

After assessing students' understanding, you might decide to extend the learning.

▶ Have students make or fill in a graphic organizer about stories with more than one problem. They can glue the graphic organizer into a reader's notebook (visit resources.fountasandpinnell.com to download the graphic organizer).

▶ As students write their own fiction stories, have them think about whether the main character might have more than one problem and how they could weave the problems together.

Sometimes stories have more than one problem.

Problem 1: Family is very poor.

Problem 2: Tunnel collapses.

Digging a Hole to Heaven

Problem 2: Cesi has to travel alone.

Problem 3: Money is gone.

Border Crossing

Problem 1: Cesi doesn't understand her family.

Problem 4: Aunt Delfina calls Cesi's dad to pick her up.

Section 2: Literary Analysis

RML3
LA.U27.RML3

Reading Minilesson Principle
Writers use flashbacks or a story-within-a-story.

Understanding Plot

You Will Need

- several familiar fiction books that have flashbacks or a story-within-a-story, such as the following from Text Set: Exploring Identity:
  - *Border Crossing* by Maria Colleen Cruz
  - *Circle Unbroken* by Margot Theis Raven
  - *Garvey's Choice* by Nikki Grimes
- chart paper and markers
- highlighter or highlighting tape
- sticky notes

Academic Language / Important Vocabulary

- plot
- present
- flashback
- story-within-a-story

Continuum Connection

- Recognize when the writer uses literary devices such as flashback, story-within-a-story, flash-forward, or parallel plot lines to structure a text (p. 81)

Goal

Recognize when writers use literary devices, such as flashbacks and story-within-a-story, that take place apart from the main story.

Rationale

When students recognize that sometimes authors use flashbacks and a story-within-a-story, they are better able to follow the plot. They learn that the information in the flashback or story-within-a-story informs the plot and/or the characters' actions.

Assess Learning

Observe students when they read and talk about fiction stories and notice if there is evidence of new learning based on the goal of this minilesson.

- ▶ Do students understand that sometimes authors use a flashback or a story-within-a-story?
- ▶ Do they use the terms *plot, present, flashback,* and *story-within-a-story*?

Minilesson

To help students think about the minilesson principle, engage them in noticing when and why authors use flashbacks and a story-within-a-story. Here is an example.

- ▶ Read the first three paragraphs on page 19 of *Border Crossing*.

  What is happening to Cesi in this story?

- ▶ Continue reading from the last paragraph on page 19 through the end of page 21, where a flashback to a previous conversation Cesi had with her mom occurs. The action then returns to the present.

  What is happening in this part of the story?

  This part of the story takes place earlier than the main story line. It is called a flashback. What prompts Cesi to think about that previous conversation?

  Why do you think the author decided to take a break from the present time in the story to insert a flashback?

- ▶ Create a chart to show which part of the story shows the present time in the story and which part takes a break from it.

- ▶ Hold similar conversation with an example of a story-within-a-story, such as in *Circle Unbroken*.

Have a Try

Invite the students to talk with a partner about a flashback or a story-within-a-story.

▶ Revisit page 13 of *Garvey's Choice*.

Turn and talk about what is happening. What is the break from the present day in this part of *Garvey's Choice*?

▶ After time for discussion, ask students to share.

Summarize and Apply

Summarize the learning and remind students to notice when a story takes a break from the present time of the story.

How does an author fill in story details that happen in a different time or place?

▶ Add the principle to the chart.

Choose a fiction story from the basket to read or continue one that you are already reading. Notice whether there is a break from the present time of the story and mark any pages with sticky notes that show that. Bring the book when we meet so you can share.

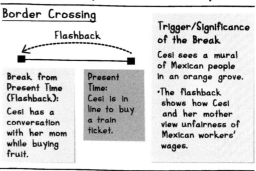

Writers use flashbacks or a story-within-a-story.

Border Crossing

Flashback

Break from Present Time (Flashback): Cesi has a conversation with her mom while buying fruit.

Present Time: Cesi is in line to buy a train ticket.

Trigger/Significance of the Break
Cesi sees a mural of Mexican people in an orange grove.
• The flashback shows how Cesi and her mother view unfairness of Mexican workers' wages.

Circle Unbroken

Present Time: Grandmother and granddaughter are weaving a basket.

Break from Present Time (Story-within-a-story): The grandmother tells a story of their shared heritage.

Trigger/Significance of the Break
Making baskets stirs up stories the grandmother knows about her grandparents.
• The story-within-a-story shows the importance of the baskets.

Share

Following independent reading time, gather students in the meeting area.

Did anyone read a book in which the author included a flashback or story-within-a-story? Share what you noticed.

Extend the Lesson (Optional)

After assessing students' understanding, you might decide to extend the learning.

▶ For additional practice with flashbacks and a story-within-a-story, use books such as *The Whispering Cloth* by Pegi Deitz Shea and *A Shelter in Our Car* by Monica Gunning from Text Set: Countering Stereotypes in *Interactive Read-Aloud Collection* and *Children of the Longhouse* by Joseph Bruchac and *Counting by 7s* by Holly Goldberg Sloan from *Independent Reading Collection*.

▶ You might want to do a similar lesson on flash-forwards or circular narratives. An example of a circular narrative is found in *The Turtle Ship* by Helena Ku Rhee from Text Set: Perseverance in *Interactive Read-Aloud Collection*.

Section 2: Literary Analysis

Reading Minilesson Principle
Writers create plots and subplots.

Understanding Plot

You Will Need

- several fiction books that include subplots, such as the following:
  - *The Harlem Charade* by Natasha Tarpley, from *Independent Reading Collection*
  - *Eagle Song* by Joseph Bruchac, from *Interactive Read-Aloud Collection* Text Set: Handling Emotions/Positive Relationships
- chart paper and markers
- fiction books students are reading
- basket of fiction books
- sticky notes

Academic Language / Important Vocabulary

- plot
- subplot

Continuum Connection

- Recognize a writer's use of plots and subplots (p. 81)

Goal

Recognize a writer's use of plots and subplots.

Rationale

When students learn to identify a main plot and subplots in a fiction story, they are better able to follow more complex, longer texts and can think deeply about how the subplot relates to the main plot.

Assess Learning

Observe students when they read and discuss fiction stories and notice if there is evidence of new learning based on the goal of this minilesson.

- ▶ Are students able to identify the plot and subplot in a fiction story?
- ▶ Do they use the terms *plot* and *subplot*?

Minilesson

To help students think about the minilesson principle, engage them in thinking about plots and subplots. Here is an example.

- ▶ Show the cover of *The Harlem Charade*. Summarize the plot for students who have not read the book (see *Independent Reading Collection* Conferring Card for additional details about the book).

  The plot of this book involves three seventh-grade students, Jin, Elvin, and Alex, who learn that some paintings have gone missing. Meanwhile, Jin's friend Rose has lost her dog and asks the others for help in finding it. Based on what I have told you about the book, what is the main plot?

- ▶ Ensure that students know the main plot centers on the missing paintings.

  Sometimes, writers include a subplot, or minor plot, that is connected to the main plot in some way but often involves a different character. What is the subplot of *The Harlem Charade*?

- ▶ Guide students to identify the subplot (finding the missing dog). As needed, clarify that a subplot has its own plot line and events.

- ▶ Show the cover of *Eagle Song*. As needed, revisit a few pages to review the main plot (Danny struggling to fit in at school and facing discrimination) and the subplots (Danny's father's distant job and accident).

  Turn and talk about the plot and subplots in *Eagle Song*.

- ▶ After time for discussion, ask students to share their thinking. Create a chart that shows the main plot and the subplots. Point out that a story can have more than one subplot.

Have a Try

Invite the students to talk in small groups about subplots.

> Based on our discussion, what is a subplot? Why would an author choose to include a subplot as part of a story? Turn and talk about that.

▶ After time for discussion, ask a few volunteers to share. Add ideas about subplots to a separate chart.

Summarize and Apply

Summarize the learning and remind students to think about plots and subplots in fiction stories.

▶ Add the principle to the second chart.

> Today choose a fiction story from the basket to read or continue one that you are already reading. Look for the main plot and notice whether the writer creates any subplots. Mark pages with sticky notes that you want to remember. Bring the book when we meet so you can share.

Share

Following independent reading time, gather students in the meeting area.

> Who would like to share a story you read that has both a plot and subplots? Tell us what you noticed.

Extend the Lesson (Optional)

After assessing students' understanding, you might decide to extend the learning.

▶ Discuss how authors use subplots as a way of slowing down the action in a story by drawing out the suspense of the main plot over the course of the book.

▶ **Writing About Reading** Have students fill in a graphic organizer about plots and subplots (see resources.fountasandpinnell.com). When it is complete, they can glue it into a reader's notebook.

Main Plot

Danny tries to find his way at a new school as he faces discrimination for being a Native American.

Subplot
Danny's father has to work far from home.

Subplot
Danny's father has an accident.

Writers create plots and subplots.

Subplots—What They Are, What They Do

- Minor plots that are often connected to the main plot

- Run parallel to the main plot line

- Can be about a different part of the main character's life or a different character

- Often add some type of understanding or believability to the main plot

- Can have a different mood from the main plot

- Add complexity to the story

Section 2: Literary Analysis

Reading Minilesson Principle
Writers sometimes create two or more narratives linked by common characters or a common theme.

You Will Need

- several familiar fiction books that include multiple narratives, such as the following:
  - *The Red Bicycle* by Jude Isabella, from Text Set: Problem Solving/Giving Back and *The Search for Delicious* by Natalie Babbitt, from Text Set: Genre Study: Modern Fantasy, from *Interactive Read-Aloud Collection*
  - *Throwing Shadows* by E. L. Konigsburg, from *Book Clubs Collection*
- chart paper and markers

Academic Language / Important Vocabulary

- narratives
- common
- theme

Continuum Connection

- Notice a writer's use of multiple narratives to reveal the plot and relationships among characters (p. 81)

Goal

Understand that writers sometimes create two or more narratives linked by common characters or a common theme.

Rationale

Narrative text structure follows a traditional sequence that includes a beginning, a problem, a series of events, a resolution of the problem, and an ending. When students learn to identify multiple narratives in a story, they think about a writer's craft and how plot structures affect them as readers.

Assess Learning

Observe students when they read and discuss fiction stories and notice if there is evidence of new learning based on the goal of this minilesson.

- ▶ Are students able to identify when a book has multiple narratives?
- ▶ Do they use the terms *narratives, common,* and *theme*?

Minilesson

To help students think about the minilesson principle, engage them in thinking about multiple narratives. Here is an example.

> Narrative structure is one way authors organize fiction texts. What are the parts of narrative structure?

- ▶ Quickly review the elements of a story with a narrative structure (beginning, problem, series of events, resolution of the problem, ending).
- ▶ Show the covers of *The Red Bicycle* and *The Search for Delicious.*

> These stories are examples of books with multiple narratives. What do you think the term *multiple narratives* means?

- ▶ As students discuss and respond, begin a chart with their descriptions of the narratives.

> A multiple narrative is a plot structure that has parallel plots connected by a common character, setting, object, or theme. Each narrative is like a story-within-a-story. Together they make up a single story because each narrative is connected to the others. What connects the narratives in each of these books?

- ▶ Show the front and back covers of *Throwing Shadows.*

> What connects these multiple narratives?

- ▶ Add to the chart.

Have a Try

Invite the students to talk with a partner about stories with multiple narratives.

> What are some reasons that a writer might choose to include multiple narratives? Turn and talk about that.

▶ After time for discussion, ask a few volunteers to share. Support a conversation about the effect that the use of multiple narratives has on them as readers. Talk about the decisions a writer makes about how to structure a story.

Summarize and Apply

Summarize the learning and remind students to think about multiple narratives in fiction stories.

▶ Review the chart and add the principle to the top.

> Choose a fiction book from the basket or continue one that you are already reading. Notice if the writer has used multiple narratives to structure the plot. Bring the book when we meet so you can share.

Share

Following independent reading time, gather students in the meeting area.

> Who would like to share a story you read that has multiple narratives? Tell us what you noticed.

Extend the Lesson (Optional)

After assessing students' understanding, you might decide to extend the learning.

▶ **Writing About Reading** Have students write in a reader's notebook about a response to a story that has multiple narratives.

Writers sometimes create two or more narratives linked by common characters or a common theme.		
Example	Description of Narratives	How are the narratives connected?
The Red Bicycle	The red bicycle is passed from one owner to the next, each of whom lives in a different place.	the red bicycle
Natalie Babbitt, *The Search for Delicious*	1. Gaylen's journey to poll the people of the kingdom 2. Hemlock's attempt to overthrow the king 3. The forgotten mermaids, dwarves, and woldweller; the missing whistle-key	same imaginary world characters are connected
e. l. konigsburg, *Throwing Shadows*	Each story is about self-awareness and the impact one person has on another.	same theme

Reading Minilesson Principle
Critique an author's selection of plot structure.

You Will Need

- examples from familiar fiction books that represent each plot structure covered in this umbrella, such as the following:
  - *The Turtle Ship* by Helena Ku Rhee, from Text Set: Perseverance
  - *Border Crossing* by Maria Colleen Cruz and *Circle Unbroken* by Margot Theis Raven, from Text Set: Exploring Identity
  - *Eagle Song* by Joseph Bruchac, from Text Set: Handling Emotions/Positive Relationships
  - *The Red Bicycle* by Jude Isabella, from Text Set: Problem Solving/Giving Back
- chart paper and markers
- sticky notes

Academic Language / Important Vocabulary

- critique
- plot structure

Continuum Connection

- Notice a writer's use of multiple narratives to reveal the plot and relationships among characters (p. 81)
- Recognize when the writer uses literary devices such as flashback, story-within-a-story, or parallel plot lines to structure the text (p. 81)

Goal

Critique an author's selection of plot structure.

Rationale

When students learn to critique the choices a writer makes regarding plot structure, they think about the writer's craft, begin to make their own choices about plot structure, and think deeply about the effect plot structure has on them as readers.

Assess Learning

Observe students when they read and discuss fiction stories and notice if there is evidence of new learning based on the goal of this minilesson.

- ▶ Are students able to critique an author's selection of plot structure?
- ▶ Do they use the terms *critique* and *plot structure*?

Minilesson

To help students think about the minilesson principle, engage them in thinking about an author's selection of plot structure. Here is an example.

- ▶ Show the cover of the books you will be using for examples of each of the plot structures you have covered so far.

  Each of these books has an example of a plot structure that we have discussed. As I list each title, tell me which type of plot structure the book has.

- ▶ As students respond, begin a chart with columns for the type of plot structure, whether the plot structure of each title was successful, and why it was or was not successful.

  Readers have personal preferences as to the type of plot structures they enjoy, and different readers have different opinions as to whether a plot structure works. Choose one of the plot structures listed on the chart and turn and talk about whether you think the plot structure works well or does not work well. In other words, did the author make a good choice about the type of plot structure to use?

- ▶ As needed, revisit a few pages of text or illustrations to refresh students' memories. Ask volunteers to briefly share their opinions, and add to the chart.

Have a Try

Invite the students to talk with a partner about the choices an author makes regarding plot structure.

> Look back at the types of plot structure listed on the chart. Turn and talk about which you prefer and why. Also talk about the impact the various types of plot structures have on you as a reader.

▶ After time for discussion, ask a few volunteers to share.

Summarize and Apply

Summarize the learning and remind students to think about plot structure as they read fiction stories.

> You critiqued some of the choices authors made about plot structure.

▶ Add the principle to the chart.

> Today choose a fiction story from the basket or continue one that you are already reading. Notice the type of plot structure in the story. Bring the book when we meet so you can share.

Share

Following independent reading time, gather students in the meeting area.

> Who would like to share your thoughts about the type of plot structure used by the author in the book you read today? Tell us what you noticed.

Extend the Lesson (Optional)

After assessing students' understanding, you might decide to extend the learning.

▶ Encourage students to use a variety of plot structures as they write their own fiction stories.

Critique an author's selection of plot structure.

Plot Structure	Title/Plot Structure Successful?	Why or Why Not?
Linear/Chronological 1st, 2nd, 3rd, 4th, 5th	The Turtle Ship — Yes	A simple story about Sun-sin's growth from a child to an adult
Flashbacks	Border Crossing — Yes	Shows Cesi's process of learning about her past
Story-within-a-Story story story	Circle Unbroken — Yes and No	The story-within-a-story is important, but takes too much time away from main story.
Plot and Subplot Plot subplot	Eagle Song — Yes	Subplot of Danny's dad helps explain the relationship of Danny and his dad.
Multiple Narratives NARRATIVE 1 NARRATIVE 2 AND NARRATIVE 3	The Red Bicycle — Yes	Interesting to see how one red bicycle was used by many

Section 2: Literary Analysis

Assessment

After you have taught the minilessons in this umbrella, observe students as they talk and write about their reading across instructional contexts: interactive read-aloud, independent reading, guided reading, shared reading, and book club. Use *The Literacy Continuum* (Fountas and Pinnell 2017) to observe students' reading and writing behaviors.

▶ What evidence do you have of new understandings related to plot?

- Do students identify the parts of narrative text structure?

- Can they recognize when a story has more than one problem?

- Do they recognize when a writer is using a flashback or a story-within-a-story?

- Can students identify the plot and any subplots?

- Can students identify when a story has two or more narratives linked by common characters or common themes?

- Are they able to critique an author's choice of plot structure?

- Are they using academic language, such as *narrative, plot, problem, beginning, events, climax, ending, flashbacks, story-within-a-story, subplot, critique,* and *plot structure*?

▶ In what other ways, beyond the scope of this umbrella, are students talking about fiction?

- Are students interested in reading different genres of fiction?

Use your observations to determine the next umbrella you will teach. You may also consult Minilessons Across the Year (pp. 61–64) for guidance.

Link to Writing

After teaching the minilessons in this umbrella, help students link the new learning to their own writing:

▶ Encourage students to use a variety of plot features as they write their own fiction stories.

Reader's Notebook

When this umbrella is complete, provide a copy of the minilesson principles (see resources.fountasandpinnell.com) for students to glue in the reader's notebook (in the Minilessons section if using *Reader's Notebook: Advanced* [Fountas and Pinnell 2011]), so they can refer to the information as needed.

Minilessons in This Umbrella

RML1 Authors write about people in conflict with nature.

RML2 Authors write about people in conflict with other people.

RML3 Authors write about people in conflict with society.

RML4 Authors write about people in conflict with themselves.

RML5 Recognize the sources of conflict within a plot.

Before Teaching Umbrella 28 Minilessons

This umbrella focuses on helping students recognize and identify sources of conflict in narrative plots and in understanding that conflict provides the foundation for a successful fiction story. Students should be reading fiction books during independent reading, or fiction books should be available, so that they have rich resources to draw from in the lessons. The minilessons in this umbrella use the following books from the *Fountas and Pinnell Classroom™ Interactive Read-Aloud Collection*; however, use any fiction books you have available in the classroom that show the main character in conflict.

Illustration Study: Mood

Teacup by Rebecca Young

Perseverance

Stepping Stones: A Refugee Family's Journey by Margriet Ruurs

The Herd Boy by Niki Daly

Hoaxes and Con Artists

Lon Po Po: A Red-Riding Hood Story from China by Ed Young

Genre Study: Epic Tales

The Adventures of Odysseus by Hugh Lupton and Daniel Morden

Gilgamesh the King by Ludmila Zeman

Kindness and Compassion

Wings by Christopher Myers

Handling Emotions/Positive Relationships

Eagle Song by Joseph Bruchac

It Doesn't Have to Be This Way: A Barrio Story by Luis J. Rodríguez

Exploring Identity

Border Crossing by Maria Colleen Cruz

Garvey's Choice by Nikki Grimes

Illustrator Study: K. Y. Craft

Cinderella

As you read aloud and enjoy these texts together, help students think about the type of conflict characters are facing.

Illustration Study: Mood

Perseverance

Hoaxes and Con Artists

Genre Study: Epic Tales

Kindness and Compassion

Handling Emotions/ Positive Relationships

Exploring Identity

K. Y. Craft

Section 2: Literary Analysis

Reading Minilesson Principle
Authors write about people in conflict with nature.

You Will Need

▶ several familiar fiction books that
have characters in conflict with
nature, such as the following:

- *Teacup* by Rebecca Young,
from Text Set: Illustration
Study: Mood

- *The Herd Boy* by Niki Daly,
from Text Set: Perseverance

- *Lon Po Po* by Ed Young, from
Text Set: Hoaxes and Con
Artists

▶ chart paper and markers

Academic Language /
Important Vocabulary

▶ plot

▶ conflict

▶ nature

Continuum
Connection

▶ Notice and understand themes
reflecting important human
challenges and social issues: e.g.,
self and self-esteem, popularity,
bullying, sportsmanship, transition
to adolescence, life cycles, survival,
interconnectedness of humans and
the environment, social awareness
and responsibility, poverty, justice,
racism, war (p. 80)

▶ Understand the problem in basic
plots: e.g., overcoming evil, poverty
and wealth, the quest, journey and
return, comedy, tragedy, villain
repents (p. 81)

Goal

Understand that authors write about people in conflict with nature (e.g., people
surviving or overcoming natural forces, such as weather, climate, natural disasters,
or geography).

Rationale

It is important for students to understand that a successful narrative plot involves
conflict, which provides tension and action. Once they understand this concept, they
can look more deeply into the story to examine what the conflict is. Conflict with
nature is a common element of storytelling.

Assess Learning

Observe students when they talk about conflict in fiction and notice if there is
evidence of new learning based on the goal of this minilesson.

▶ Are students aware that successful narrative plots involve conflict?

▶ Do they understand that writers sometimes write about people in conflict
with nature?

▶ Do they use the terms *plot, conflict,* and *nature*?

Minilesson

To help students think about the minilesson principle, use familiar texts to engage
them in thinking about conflict with nature in fiction stories. Here is an example.

▶ Show the book *Teacup*.

How would you describe the plot in this story? What does the main
character try to do?

What happens while the boy is trying to find a new home?

In a narrative plot, a problem that a character faces is called a conflict.
Conflict is the struggle between opposing forces.

▶ Make three columns on chart paper: one for the title, one for what the
characters are trying to do, and one for the conflicts. Fill in the first row
for *Teacup*.

▶ Show *The Herd Boy*.

What is Malusi trying to do throughout the book?

What conflicts does Malusi face?

▶ Record responses on the chart.

Have a Try

Invite the students to talk with a partner about conflict with nature in a fiction story.

> What happens in *Lon Po Po?* What is the conflict? Turn and talk about the conflict the children face.

▶ After time for discussion, ask students to share. Add responses to the chart.

Summarize and Apply

Summarize the learning and remind students to think about the conflict faced by the characters.

> Look at the conflicts that are listed on the chart. What do you notice is the same about them?

> Authors often write about the conflict between people and nature.

▶ Write the principle at the top of the chart.

> If you read a fiction book today, notice whether a character is in conflict with nature. Bring the book when we meet so you can share.

Authors write about people in conflict with nature.		
Title	**What are the characters trying to do?**	**What are the conflicts?**
	find a new home	• a long distance over the sea • rough seas • stormy weather • dark nights
The Herd Boy	take care of his grandfather's sheep	• a baboon • a snake • the geography of the land
	save themselves from the wolf	• a wolf

Share

Following independent reading time, gather students in the meeting area to talk about characters in conflict with nature.

> What did you notice about a character in conflict with nature?

> What evidence did the author include to help you recognize and understand the conflict?

Extend the Lesson (Optional)

After assessing students' understanding, you might decide to extend the learning.

▶ **Writing About Reading** Have students write about a character in a book they have read recently who is in conflict with nature.

Reading Minilesson Principle
Authors write about people in conflict with other people.

Exploring Conflict in Fiction Texts

You Will Need

▸ several familiar fiction books that have characters in conflict with others, such as the following:

• *Gilgamesh the King* by Ludmila Zeman, from Text Set: Epic Tales

• *Wings* by Christopher Myers, from Text Set: Kindness and Compassion

▸ chart paper and markers

Academic Language / Important Vocabulary

▸ narrative
▸ plot
▸ conflict
▸ protagonist
▸ antagonist

Continuum Connection

▸ Notice and understand themes reflecting important human challenges and social issues: e.g., self and self-esteem, popularity, bullying, sportsmanship, transition to adolescence, life cycles, survival, interconnectedness of humans and the environment, social awareness and responsibility, poverty, justice, racism, war (p. 80)

▸ Understand the problem in basic plots: e.g., overcoming evil, poverty and wealth, the quest, journey and return, comedy, tragedy, villain repents (p. 81)

Goal

Understand that authors write about people in conflict with other people (when a protagonist and antagonist collide).

Rationale

When students learn to recognize and think about the conflict between a character and other characters, they understand that a successful narrative plot must involve conflict, along with tension and action, and can comprehend the roles of the protagonist and antagonist in a fiction text.

Assess Learning

Observe students when they talk about conflict in fiction and notice if there is evidence of new learning based on the goal of this minilesson.

▸ Are students aware that successful narrative plots involve conflict?

▸ Do they understand that writers sometimes write about people in conflict with other people?

▸ Can they identify the protagonist and the antagonist in a plot?

▸ Do they use the terms *narrative, plot, conflict, protagonist,* and *antagonist*?

Minilesson

To help students think about the minilesson principle, use familiar texts to engage them in thinking about conflict between characters in a fiction text. Here is an example.

▸ Show the cover of *Gilgamesh the King*.

> In a narrative plot, conflict is the struggle between opposing forces. The main character that faces the conflict is called the *protagonist* and the character or thing that the protagonist struggles against is called the *antagonist*.

> Turn and talk about the character who is the protagonist in *Gilgamesh the King*. Also identify the antagonist.

▸ After a brief time, ask a volunteer to name the protagonist and the antagonist. Record responses on chart paper.

▸ Then ask students to describe the conflict in a sentence

> Turn and talk about the conflict in *Gilgamesh the King*. What does the character want to do and what gets in his way?

▸ After time for discussion, ask students to help you compose a sentence that describes the conflict in *Gilgamesh the King*. Write the statement on the chart in the form of "the character wants to _____ but _____."

Have a Try

Invite the students to talk with a partner about conflict between characters in a fiction text.

> Think about the protagonist, the antagonists, and the conflict in *Wings*.

▶ After time for discussion, ask students to share. Again, work with students to create a statement that describes the conflict.

Summarize and Apply

Summarize the learning and remind students to think about characters in conflict with others.

> Look at the conflicts that are listed on the chart. What similarities do you notice?

> Authors often write about the conflict between people and other people. In fantasies, characters can also be animals (usually personified) who are in conflict with other animals.

▶ Add the principle to the chart.

> If you read a fiction book today, notice if a character is in conflict with other characters. Bring the book when we meet so you can share.

Share

Following independent reading time, gather students in the meeting area to talk about people in conflict with other people.

> What did you notice about a character in conflict with other characters? What evidence did the author include to help you recognize and understand the conflict?

Extend the Lesson (Optional)

After assessing students' understanding, you might decide to extend the learning.

▶ Talk with students about other stories they have read in which the conflict is between the main character and one or more people.

▶ Encourage students to include conflict between a protagonist and other characters when they write fictional narratives.

Authors write about people in conflict with other people.

Title	Protagonist	Antagonist(s)	Conflict Statement
	Gilgamesh	Enkidu	Gilgamesh wants to build a wall to show his strength and power but must confront Enkidu to prove he is the stronger man.
WINGS	Ikarus	Others at school and in the neighborhood	Ikarus faces discrimination because he is different from other people. With the narrator's help, he is celebrated for his uniqueness.

Section 2: Literary Analysis

Reading Minilesson Principle
Authors write about people in conflict with society.

Exploring Conflict in Fiction Texts

You Will Need

- several familiar fiction books that have characters in conflict with society such as the following:
  - *Stepping Stones* by Margriet Ruurs, from Text Set: Perseverance
  - *Eagle Song* by Joseph Bruchac, from Text Set: Handling Emotions/Positive Relationships
- chart paper and markers

Academic Language / Important Vocabulary

- narrative
- plot
- conflict
- society
- protagonist

Continuum Connection

- Notice and understand themes reflecting important human challenges and social issues: e.g., self and self-esteem, popularity, bullying, sportsmanship, transition to adolescence, life cycles, survival, interconnectedness of humans and the environment, social awareness and responsibility, poverty, justice, racism, war (p. 80)
- Understand the problem in basic plots: e.g., overcoming evil, poverty and wealth, the quest, journey and return, comedy, tragedy, villain repents (p. 81)

Goal

Understand that authors write about people in conflict with society (e.g., characters struggling to overcome societal ills such as poverty, war, or racism).

Rationale

When students learn to think about a character's conflict with society, they understand that a successful narrative plot must involve conflict, along with tension and action. They can comprehend the narrative more deeply.

Assess Learning

Observe students when they talk about conflict in fiction and notice if there is evidence of new learning based on the goal of this minilesson.

- Are students aware that successful narrative plots involve conflict?
- Do they understand that writers sometimes write about people in conflict with society?
- Do they use the terms *narrative*, *plot*, *conflict*, *society*, and *protagonist*?

Minilesson

To help students think about the minilesson principle, use familiar texts to engage them in thinking about societal conflict in fiction texts. Here is an example.

- Show the cover of *Stepping Stones*.

  In a narrative plot, conflict is the struggle between opposing forces. Turn and talk about how you would describe the conflict in *Stepping Stones*. Think about what the character or characters want and what they have to do to get what they want.

- As needed, prompt the conversation to help students identify the conflict.

  What are the characters trying to do in *Stepping Stones*?

  What prevents them from doing it? What is the conflict?

  The family is struggling because of a war in their country, which means it is no longer safe to live there. War is the conflict.

- Record responses.

Have a Try

Invite the students to talk with a partner about societal conflict.

▶ Read a few pages from *Eagle Song* to help students identify the conflict Danny faces, such as pages 7–8.

> Turn and talk about the conflict faced by the protagonist, Danny.

▶ After time for discussion, ask students to share. Add responses to the chart.

Summarize and Apply

Summarize the learning and remind students to think about characters in conflict with society.

> Look at the conflicts that are listed on the chart. What do you notice about the cause of each conflict?

> Each of these conflicts is not between the main character or characters and a specific person. Rather, the conflict is a problem with society. Authors often write about the conflict between people and society.

▶ Write the principle at the top of the chart.

> If you read a fiction book today, notice if a character is in conflict with society. Bring the book when we meet so you can share.

Share

Following independent reading time, gather students in the meeting area to talk about conflict between a character and society.

> What did you notice about a character in conflict with society?

> What evidence did the author include to help you understand the conflict?

Extend the Lesson (Optional)

After assessing students' understanding, you might decide to extend the learning.

▶ Talk with students about other stories they have read in which the conflict is between the main character and society.

▶ **Writing About Reading** Have students write in a reader's notebook a response to a protagonist's struggle to overcome societal problems such as poverty, war, or discrimination.

Authors write about people in conflict with society.

Title	What is the character trying to do?	What is the conflict?
STEPPING STONES	be safe from war	war
EAGLE SONG Joseph Bruchac	become accepted in a new city	discrimination against Native Americans

Section 2: Literary Analysis

<table>
<tr>
<td>

RML4
LA.U28.RML4

</td>
<td>

Reading Minilesson Principle
Authors write about people in conflict with themselves.

</td>
</tr>
</table>

Exploring Conflict in Fiction Texts

You Will Need

- several familiar fiction books that have characters in conflict with themselves, such as the following:
  - *It Doesn't Have to Be This Way* by Luis J. Rodríguez, from Text Set: Handling Emotions/Positive Relationships
  - *Border Crossing* by Maria Colleen Cruz, from Text Set: Exploring Identity
- chart paper and markers
- sticky notes

Academic Language / Important Vocabulary

- plot
- conflict
- protagonist

Continuum Connection

- Notice and understand themes reflecting important human challenges and social issues: e.g., self and self-esteem, popularity, bullying, sportsmanship, transition to adolescence, life cycles, survival, interconnectedness of humans and the environment, social awareness and responsibility, poverty, justice, racism, war (p. 80)
- Understand the problem in basic plots: e.g., overcoming evil, poverty and wealth, the quest, journey and return, comedy, tragedy, villain repents (p. 81)

Goal

Understand that authors write about people in conflict with themselves (e.g., protagonist struggling with conflicting personal goals, actions, or identity).

Rationale

When students learn to think about characters who are in conflict with themselves, they understand that a successful narrative plot must involve conflict, along with tension and action. They began to understand internal conflict and to understand plot and characters more deeply.

Assess Learning

Observe students when they talk about conflict and notice if there is evidence of new learning based on the goal of this minilesson.

- ▶ Are students aware that successful narrative plots involve conflict?
- ▶ Do they understand that writers sometimes write about people in conflict within themselves?
- ▶ Do they use the terms *plot, conflict,* and *protagonist*?

Minilesson

To help students think about the minilesson principle, use familiar texts to engage them in thinking about internal conflicts. Here is an example.

- ▶ Read and show pages 10 and 27 from *It Doesn't Have to Be This Way*.

    In a narrative plot, conflict is the struggle between opposing forces. Turn and talk about the conflict in *It Doesn't Have to Be This Way.*

- ▶ As needed, prompt the conversation to help students identify Monchi's internal conflict.

    What does Monchi want to do?

- ▶ Record the responses on chart paper.

    What would you write in a statement that describes the conflict Monchi is experiencing?

- ▶ Work with students to compose a conflict statement and write it on the chart.

Have a Try

Invite the students to talk with a partner about a conflict that a character has with herself.

- Show the cover of *Border Crossing*.

    Turn and talk about what Cesi wants to do. How could you describe that in a conflict statement?

- After time for discussion, ask students to share. Add responses to the chart.

Summarize and Apply

Summarize the learning and remind students to think about characters in conflict with themselves.

    Look at the chart. With whom or what are the characters struggling?

    Both are struggling within themselves to change something in their lives. Authors often write about characters who experience internal conflict.

- Write the principle at the top of the chart.

    If you read a fiction book today, notice if a character is in conflict with himself or herself. Mark pages you want to remember with sticky notes. Bring the book when we meet so you can share.

Share

Following independent reading time, gather students in the meeting area to share about a character's conflict.

    Tell us about the conflict the character in your book faced. What evidence did the author include to help you recognize and understand the conflict?

Extend the Lesson (Optional)

After assessing students' understanding, you might decide to extend the learning.

- Talk with students about other stories they have read about people in conflict with themselves.

- **Writing About Reading** Have students write about the conflict a character faced in a book they have read recently. They should identify what the character was trying to do and what presented the conflict (nature, other people, society, himself).

Authors write about people in conflict with themselves.		
Title	What does the character want to do?	Conflict Statement
It Doesn't Have To Be This Way	have friends / have a good life / fix his bad decision	Monchi wants to have friends and a good life, but he makes a poor decision, feels guilty, and has to make a life choice about the person he wants to be.
Border Crossing	know more about who she is / learn about her heritage	Cesi wants to learn more about herself and her heritage, so she travels to Mexico to learn about her family's true identity.

RML5
LA.U28.RML5

Reading Minilesson Principle
Recognize the sources of conflict within a plot.

Exploring Conflict in Fiction Texts

You Will Need

- several familiar fiction books with characters who experience different types of conflict, such as the following:
  - *The Adventures of Odysseus* by Hugh Lupton and Daniel Morden, from Text Set: Genre Study: Epic Tales
  - *Cinderella* by K. Y. Craft, from Text Set: Illustrator Study: K. Y. Craft
  - *Wings* by Christopher Myers, from Text Set: Kindness and Compassion
  - *Garvey's Choice* by Nikki Grimes, from Text Set: Exploring Identity
- chart paper prepared with four columns: *Title, What does the character want? What is the conflict? Type of Conflict*
- markers
- four sticky notes: *People vs. nature, People vs. other people, People vs. society, People vs. themselves*
- sticky notes

Academic Language / Important Vocabulary

- narrative
- plot
- conflict
- versus (vs.)
- source

Continuum Connection

- Understand the problem in basic plots: e.g., overcoming evil, poverty and wealth, the quest, journey and return, comedy, tragedy, villain repents (p. 81)

Goal

Identify the source of conflict within a plot.

Rationale

When students learn to recognize the source of conflict in a fiction story, they understand that a successful narrative plot must involve conflict, and that noticing tension and action as they read will help them more fully comprehend the story. Students should be familiar with characters in conflict with nature, other people, society, and themselves before participating in this minilesson.

Assess Learning

Observe students when they talk about conflict and notice if there is evidence of new learning based on the goal of this minilesson.

- ▶ Can students recognize the sources of conflict in a plot?
- ▶ Do they use the terms *narrative, plot, conflict, versus (vs.),* and *source*?

Minilesson

To help students think about the minilesson principle, use familiar texts to engage them in thinking about the sources of conflict in fiction texts. Here is an example.

- ▶ Show the covers of four books that represent different types of conflict, such as *The Adventures of Odysseus, Cinderella, Wings,* and *Garvey's Choice.*

  In a narrative plot, conflict is the struggle between opposing forces. We can say people versus nature, people versus people, people versus society, or people versus themselves. Think about the conflict in these stories.

- ▶ Revisit several illustrations or paragraphs from each book only as necessary to help students identify the sources of conflict.

  Turn and talk in threes about the type of conflict found in each of the narrative plots.

- ▶ After time for discussion, ask volunteers help you fill in the middle two columns of the chart.

Have a Try

Invite the students to identify the types of conflict in fiction books.

> Take a look at the chart and think about the types of conflict you identified.

▶ Ask volunteers to place the prepared sticky notes in the correct rows.

Summarize and Apply

Summarize the learning and remind students to recognize the source of conflict when they read a fiction book.

> A narrative fiction story is shaped by what the character wants and the conflict(s) that stand in the way.

▶ Write the principle at the top of the chart.

> If you read a fiction book today, notice the conflict. Mark pages you want to remember with sticky notes. Bring the book when we meet so you can share.

Share

Following independent reading time, gather students in groups of three to talk about the conflict in narrative fiction.

> Turn and talk to a partner about the conflict in the book you read. What did the character want to do? What type of conflict did the character face?

Extend the Lesson (Optional)

After assessing students' understanding, you might decide to extend the learning.

▶ Take the principle from each chart and place them on a new sheet of chart paper so that students can see all four types of conflict that have been discussed. Add titles that fit each category as suggested by students.

▶ **Writing About Reading** Have students write about the conflict a character faced in a book they have read recently. They should identify what the character was trying to do and what presented the conflict (nature, other people, society, self).

Recognize the sources of conflict within a plot.

Title	What does the character want?	What is the conflict?	Type of Conflict
	to get back home	weather disasters geography disease wild animals natural forces	People vs. nature
	to go to the ball to be treated fairly	stepmother stepsisters	People vs. other people
WINGS	to be accepted and appreciated for who he is	discrimination lack of acceptance for people who are different	People vs. society
GARVEY'S CHOICE	to be accepted for who he is	guilt self-esteem loneliness lack of self-acceptance	People vs. themselves

Assessment

After you have taught the minilessons in this umbrella, observe students as they talk and write about their reading across instructional contexts: interactive read-aloud, independent reading, guided reading, shared reading, and book club. Use *The Literacy Continuum* (Fountas and Pinnell 2017) to observe students' reading and writing behaviors.

▶ What evidence do you have of new understandings related to conflict?

- Are students aware that a successful narrative plot involves conflict?

- Do they understand that authors write about people in conflict with nature, other people, society, and themselves?

- Can they recognize the sources of conflict within a plot?

- Are they using the terms *narrative, plot, conflict, protagonist, antagonist, nature,* and *society*?

▶ In what other ways, beyond the scope of this umbrella, are students talking about fiction books?

- Do students notice the setting and its impact on the plot?

- Do they think critically about the characters?

Use your observations to determine the next umbrella you will teach. You may also consult Minilessons Across the Year (pp. 61–64) for guidance.

Link to Writing

After teaching the minilessons in this umbrella, help students link the new learning to their own writing:

▶ As students write their own fiction stories, encourage them to use different sources of conflict, providing clues to slowly reveal the conflict through the use of tension and action.

Reader's Notebook

When this umbrella is complete, provide a copy of the minilesson principles (see resources.fountasandpinnell.com) for students to glue in the reader's notebook (in the Minilessons section if using *Reader's Notebook: Advanced* [Fountas and Pinnell 2011]), so they can refer to the information as needed.

Minilessons in This Umbrella

RML1 Notice what the characters think, say, and do to understand how they are feeling.

RML2 Notice what the characters say and do to understand their relationships.

RML3 Think about what characters really want.

Before Teaching Umbrella 29 Minilessons

Read and discuss books containing characters whose feelings can be observed through their words and the illustrations, as well as books with a variety of settings and diversity of characters. As always, students should be reading fiction books during independent reading, or fiction books should be available, so that they have rich examples to draw from. The minilessons in this umbrella use the following books from the *Fountas and Pinnell Classroom* ™ *Interactive Read-Aloud Collection*; however, you can use any fiction books you have available in the classroom that have the characteristics listed above.

Perseverance

The Memory Coat by Elvira Woodruff

Silent Days, Silent Dreams by Allen Say

The Turtle Ship by Helena Ku Rhee

Exploring Identity

Circle Unbroken: The Story of a Basket and Its People by Margot Theis Raven

A Different Pond by Bao Phi

Kindness and Compassion

Babu's Song by Stephanie Stuve-Bodeen

As you read aloud and enjoy these texts together, help students

• notice character thoughts, words, and actions, and

• think about how a character's thoughts, words, and actions show how the character feels about himself and others.

Perseverance

Exploring Identity

Kindness and Compassion

Section 2: Literary Analysis

Reading Minilesson Principle

Notice what the characters think, say, and do to understand how they are feeling.

Understanding Characters' Feelings, Motivations, and Intentions

You Will Need

- several familiar fiction books that have characters with clear feelings, such as the following from Text Set: Perseverance:
  - *The Memory Coat* by Elvira Woodruff
  - *Silent Days, Silent Dreams* by Allen Say
- chart paper and markers
- sticky notes

Academic Language / Important Vocabulary

- feelings
- thoughts
- words
- actions
- motivations
- intentions

Continuum Connection

- Infer a character's traits, feelings, motivations, and intentions as revealed through what they say, think, or do and what others say or think about them, and use evidence from the text to describe them (p. 81)

Goal

Infer characters' feelings as revealed through thought, dialogue and behavior.

Rationale

When students learn to infer character feelings, motivations, and intentions, they learn to relate to characters and deepen their comprehension of the text.

Assess Learning

Observe students when they talk about characters and notice if there is evidence of new learning based on the goal of this minilesson.

- ▶ Are students able to connect a character's thoughts, words, and actions with a character's feelings?
- ▶ Do they understand that something motivates a character to act? Can they infer motivations?
- ▶ Do they use evidence from the text to make inferences about a character's feelings?
- ▶ Do they use the terms *feelings, thoughts, words, actions, motivations,* and *intentions*?

Minilesson

To help students think about the minilesson principle, engage them in thinking about what helps them know how a character is feeling. Here is an example.

> Think about the character Grisha in *The Memory Coat.*

- ▶ Read pages 6–7.

  > What do you notice about how Grisha is feeling in this part of the book?

  > What details help you know how Grisha is feeling? What is motivating him to act or feel this way?

- ▶ Begin a chart and add student responses about Grisha's feelings.

  > Think about how Grisha might be feeling as I read another part of the story.

- ▶ Read page 9.

  > How is Grisha feeling now? How do you know this?

- ▶ Add responses to the chart.

Have a Try

Invite the students to talk with a partner about how they know how a character feels.

▶ Read and show the illustrations from pages 27, 28–29, and 45 in *Silent Days, Silent Dreams*.

Turn and talk about how James might be feeling during these parts of the book. What motivated him to feel that way?

▶ After time for discussion, ask students to share. Add responses to the chart.

Summarize and Apply

Summarize the learning and remind students to think about the feelings of the characters when they read fiction stories.

How can you figure out how a character is feeling?

▶ Write the principle at the top of the chart.

If you read a fiction book today, think about how a character is feeling and how the author shows you that. Mark pages you want to remember with sticky notes. Bring the book when we meet so you can share.

Share

Following independent reading time, gather students in the meeting area to talk about characters' feelings.

What did you notice about how a character is feeling in the fiction story you read? What evidence did the author include to help you understand the character's feelings?

Extend the Lesson (Optional)

After assessing students' understanding, you might decide to extend the learning.

▶ Continue to ask students to analyze how a character may be feeling by the words, thoughts, and actions of that character as well as what the words, thoughts, and actions of other characters reveal.

Notice what the characters think, say, and do to understand how they are feeling.

Title	How is the character feeling?	How do you know?
Grisha	sad	He grieved alone for his parents.
	sentimental	He refused to part with his threadbare coat because it connected him to his parents.
	content	He drew illustrations to go with Rachel's stories and spent many hours telling stories with Rachel.
	sense of belonging	
James	lonely	He drew students at the school as a way of making friends.
	angry	He ran away because the teachers took away his drawing things.
	frustrated	After his studio was trashed, he screamed and threw his work into the canal.

Section 2: Literary Analysis

Reading Minilesson Principle

Notice what the characters say and do to understand their relationships.

Understanding Characters' Feelings, Motivations, and Intentions

You Will Need

- several familiar fiction books with identifiable character relationships, such as the following:
  - *Babu's Song* by Stephanie Stuve-Bodeen, from Text Set: Kindness and Compassion
  - *A Different Pond* by Bao Phi, from Text Set: Exploring Identity
  - *The Turtle Ship* by Helena Ku Rhee, from Text Set: Perseverance
- chart paper and markers
- sticky notes

Academic Language / Important Vocabulary

- character
- relationships
- dialogue
- behavior
- inference

Continuum Connection

- Infer relationships between characters as revealed through dialogue and behavior (p. 81)

Goal

Infer relationships between characters as revealed through dialogue and behavior.

Rationale

When students learn to make inferences about how characters feel about other characters from what they say and do, they deepen their comprehension of the text and build empathy.

Assess Learning

Observe students when they talk about character relationships and notice if there is evidence of new learning based on the goal of this minilesson.

- ▶ Are students discussing the relationships characters have in fiction stories?
- ▶ Do students use text evidence showing how a character's words and actions show their relationships?
- ▶ Do they use the terms *character, relationships, dialogue, behavior,* and *inference*?

Minilesson

To help students think about the minilesson principle, engage them in thinking about character relationships. Here is an example.

> Listen to the words and notice the illustrations on these pages from *Babu's Song*. Think about how Bernardi and Babu feel about each other.

- ▶ Read pages 6, 14, 20, and 23.

> What do you notice about how the characters feel about each other?

> What evidence does the author include in the story to help you understand the relationship between Bernardi and Babu?

- ▶ As students respond, create a chart with a column for the title, a column for students' inferences about character relationships, and a column for text evidence. Add students' ideas to the chart.

> Now think about the character relationships in another book, *A Different Pond*.

- ▶ Read and show pages 2, 4, 14, 15, and 20.

> Look for clues about the relationship between the boy and his dad.

> What have you found to help you understand it?

- ▶ Add to the chart.

Have a Try

Invite the students to talk with a partner about how characters feel about each other.

▶ Read and show the first and last two pages from *The Turtle Ship*.

> In this book, the most significant relationship is between Sun-sin and his turtle. What evidence do you have about their relationship? Turn and talk about that.

▶ After time for discussion, ask students to share ideas. Add to chart.

Summarize and Apply

Summarize the learning and remind students to think about character relationships when they read fiction stories.

> How can you learn about character relationships when you read a story?

▶ Add the principle to the chart.

> If you read a fiction book today, think about the relationships between characters and how you know their feelings for one another. Mark any pages that you want to remember with sticky notes. Bring the book when we meet so you can share.

Share

Following independent reading time, gather students in the meeting area.

> Talk about the clues the author and illustrator give to reveal how the characters feel about each other. Share any pages that would be helpful to support your thinking.

Extend the Lesson (Optional)

After assessing students' understanding, you might decide to extend the learning.

▶ **Writing About Reading** Have students make or fill in a graphic organizer about character relationships (see resources.fountasandpinnell.com). They can glue the organizer into a reader's notebook to record other examples they notice as they read more fiction stories.

Notice what the characters say and do to understand their relationships.

Title	Relationships	How do you know?
Babu's Song	Babu and Bernardi care for each other deeply.	Babu hugs Bernardi and plays with him. Bernardi shares stories from his day with Babu. Babu pays for Bernardi to attend school.
A Different Pond	The father cares for his son. The boy looks up to his father as a role model and respects him.	The father is patient with his son and caring. The boy thinks his father's accent sounds like rain. The father tells stories about his childhood while they fish.
The Turtle Ship	Sun-sin and Gobugi, the turtle, are best friends.	Sun-sin and Gobugi play together. They are always together.

Section 2: Literary Analysis

Reading Minilesson Principle
Think about what characters really want.

Understanding Characters' Feelings, Motivations, and Intentions

You Will Need

- several familiar fiction books, such as the following from Text Set: Exploring Identity:
  - *Circle Unbroken* by Margot Theis Raven
  - *A Different Pond* by Bao Phi
- chart paper and markers
- sticky notes

Academic Language / Important Vocabulary

- character
- motivations
- dialogue
- behavior

Continuum Connection

- Infer a character's traits, feelings, motivations, and intentions as revealed through what they say, think, or do and what others say or think about them, and use evidence from the text to describe them (p. 81)

Goal

Infer characters' motivations as revealed through dialogue, behavior, and what others say or think about them.

Rationale

Learning to notice evidence in a story about what a character wants shows the motivation behind a character's words and actions. Often, determining character motivation enables students to fully understand the problem and solution.

Assess Learning

Observe students when they talk about character motivations and notice if there is evidence of new learning based on the goal of this minilesson.

- ▶ Are students talking about the ways that a character's words and actions indicate what is motivating him?
- ▶ Can they identify text evidence that supports their opinions about character motivations?
- ▶ Do they use the terms *character, motivations, dialogue,* and *behavior*?

Minilesson

To help students think about the minilesson principle, engage them in thinking about character motivations. Here is an example.

- ▶ Show the cover of *Circle Unbroken*.

    Think about the grandmother in this story as I read a few pages.

- ▶ Revisit pages 1–4 and 37–38 to support students' thinking. Encourage students to identify specific examples that show the grandmother's motivations.

    What do you think the grandmother really wants, or what are her motivations?

    What examples from the story help you know this?

- ▶ As needed, revisit a few more pages to prompt student thinking.
- ▶ Using students' responses, create a chart that shows the grandmother's motivations. Include a few specific examples from the story.

    Often, thinking about what a character wants, which shows the character's motivations, will help you identify the problem and solution in a story.

Have a Try

Invite the students to talk with a partner about character motivations.

▶ Revisit a few pages of the text and illustrations in *A Different Pond*, such as pages 7–8, 10, and 16.

Turn and talk about what the father in the story really wants and how knowing that helps you understand the motivation behind his words and actions.

▶ After time for discussion, ask students to share. Add ideas to the chart.

Summarize and Apply

Summarize the learning and remind students to think about what the characters really want.

You talked about what characters really want. How does this help you understand the story better?

▶ Add the principle to the chart.

As you read fiction, think about what a character really wants and how an author shows you that. If you are reading fiction today, mark pages that you want to remember with sticky notes. Bring the book when we meet so you can share.

Share

Following independent reading time, gather students in small groups. Be sure each group has at least one member who read fiction today.

Share what you noticed about what a character really wants. Show the pages that helped you know that.

Extend the Lesson (Optional)

After assessing students' understanding, you might decide to extend the learning.

▶ **Writing About Reading** Have students write in a reader's notebook about the connection between a character's motivations and the problem in the story. Encourage them to use evidence from the text to show their thinking.

Think about what characters really want.

Title and Character	What the Characters Want	What Characters Do and Say
Circle Unbroken — Grandmother	• to pass on family traditions • to make sure her granddaughter understands the family's history with slavery	• tells granddaughter the story of when their family first began making sewing baskets • begins teaching her granddaughter how to make the baskets
A Different Pond — Dad	• his son to understand his life in Vietnam • to carry on traditions of hard work and enjoying things without a lot of money	• tells stories of his life back in Vietnam when he fished with his brother • finds a way to take his son fishing early in the morning before he goes to work

Section 2: Literary Analysis

Assessment

After you have taught the minilessons in this umbrella, observe students as they talk and write about their reading across instructional contexts: interactive read-aloud, independent reading, guided reading, shared reading, and book club. Use *The Literacy Continuum* (Fountas and Pinnell 2017) to observe students' reading and writing behaviors.

▶ What evidence do you have of new understandings related to characters' feelings, motivations, and intentions?

- Are students able to understand how a character feels by noticing thoughts, words, and actions?

- Can they determine a character's relationships with other characters by noticing what the character does and says?

- Do they think about what motivates a character to feel or act?

- Are they using the terms *characters*, *feelings*, *motivations*, *intentions*, and *relationships*?

▶ In what other ways, beyond the scope of this umbrella, are students demonstrating an understanding of characters?

- Do students discuss the ways that a character's traits are revealed through what the character does, thinks, and says?

Use your observations to determine the next umbrella you will teach. You may also consult Minilessons Across the Year (pp. 61–64) for guidance.

Link to Writing

After teaching the minilessons in this umbrella, help students link the new learning to their own writing:

▶ As students write their own fiction stories, encourage them to reveal information about how a character feels, what the character wants, and what a character intends through the use of dialogue.

Reader's Notebook

When this umbrella is complete, provide a copy of the minilesson principles (see resources.fountasandpinnell.com) for students to glue in the reader's notebook (in the Minilessons section if using *Reader's Notebook: Advanced* [Fountas and Pinnell 2011]), so they can refer to the information as needed.

Minilessons in This Umbrella

RML1 Think critically about whether a character is believable and authentic.

RML2 Evaluate whether characters behave in ways consistent with the setting of the book.

RML3 Evaluate whether the writer makes you feel empathy for a character.

Before Teaching Umbrella 31 Minilessons

Read and discuss realistic fiction, historical fiction, and fantasy books with characters and settings that are complex and diverse. Discuss empathy as it relates to characters and also as it relates to the students' own lives. The minilessons in this umbrella use the following books from the *Fountas and Pinnell Classroom ™ Interactive Read-Aloud Collection*; however, you can use any fiction books you have available in the classroom that have the characteristics listed above.

Problem Solving/Giving Back

The Elephant Keeper: Caring for Orphaned Elephants in Zambia by Margriet Ruurs

The Good Garden: How One Family Went from Hunger to Having Enough by Katie Smith Milway

Kindness and Compassion

Wings by Christopher Myers

Human Inventiveness

Iqbal and His Ingenious Idea: How a Science Project Helps One Family and the Planet by Elizabeth Suneby

Perseverance

The Herd Boy by Niki Daly

The Memory Coat by Elvira Woodruff

The Turtle Ship by Helena Ku Rhee

Genre Study: Modern Fantasy

The Search for Delicious by Natalie Babbitt

As you read aloud and enjoy these texts together, help students

- think about whether characters are authentic,
- talk about how a character would behave based on the place and time period, and
- talk about whether they feel empathy for a character.

Problem Solving/ Giving Back

Kindness and Compassion

Human Inventiveness

Perseverance

Genre Study: Modern Fantasy

Section 2: Literary Analysis

Reading Minilesson Principle

Think critically about whether a character is believable and authentic.

Thinking Critically About Characters

You Will Need

- several familiar realistic fiction and fantasy stories, such as the following:
  - *The Elephant Keeper* by Margriet Ruurs, from Text Set: Problem Solving/Giving Back
  - *Wings* by Christopher Myers, from Text Set: Kindness and Compassion
  - *Iqbal and His Ingenious Idea* by Elizabeth Suneby, from Text Set: Human Inventiveness
- chart paper and markers
- two colors of sticky notes

Academic Language / Important Vocabulary

- character
- conditions
- believable
- authentic
- critically

Continuum Connection

- Think critically about the authenticity and believability of characters and their behavior, dialogue, and development (p. 81)

Goal

Think critically about the authenticity and believability of characters and their behavior and dialogue.

Rationale

When students think about the authenticity of characters, they develop critical thinking skills and begin to evaluate the ways authors develop characters. Whether a character is authentic is relative to the parameters of the world created by the author, regardless of whether it is a realistic or a fantasy setting. This lesson could also be taught as part of Umbrella 21: Understanding Realistic Fiction or Umbrella 23: Studying Modern Fantasy in this section.

Assess Learning

Observe students when they talk about character authenticity and notice if there is evidence of new learning based on the goal of this minilesson.

- ▶ Do students discuss whether a character's behavior is believable within the story?
- ▶ Are they able to analyze whether dialogue seems real?
- ▶ Do they understand the terms *character, conditions, believable, authentic,* and *critically*?

Minilesson

To help students think about the minilesson principle, engage them in thinking about the authenticity of characters. Here is an example.

- ▶ Revisit pages 1–7, 19–21, and 30 from *The Elephant Keeper.*

  How would you describe Aaron?

  Do you know any other people or characters who might act or talk like him in the same situation?

- ▶ As students share ideas, encourage them to use the terms *believable* and *authentic.*

- ▶ Create a chart with one column to show whether a character is authentic and another column for evidence from the text. Ask a few volunteers to talk about whether Aaron is authentic, and then have the volunteers write *Yes* or *No* on a sticky note and add it to the chart. In the other column, write student text examples.

- ▶ Turn through a few pages from *Wings.*

  Think about the narrator and Ikarus in *Wings.* Within the fantasy world created by the author, are the characters believable? Why or why not?

- ▶ Continue writing their examples and having students place sticky notes on the chart.

Have a Try

Invite the students to talk with a partner about whether a character is believable.

> Think about the characters in *Iqbal and His Ingenious Idea*. Is Iqbal believable and authentic? Turn and talk about that.

▶ After time for discussion, ask a few volunteers to share their thinking. Record responses on the chart.

Summarize and Apply

Summarize the learning and remind students to think about whether fiction characters are authentic.

> You talked about whether characters are authentic based on the conditions of the story.

▶ Add the principle to the chart.

> If you read a fiction book today, think about whether the characters are authentic and how the author shows you that. Bring the book when we meet so you can share.

Think critically about whether a character is believable and authentic.

Title	Are the characters believable and authentic?	Why or why not?
The Elephant Keeper	Yes	• Aaron is hard-working and spends a lot of time outdoors. • He knows to be cautious around elephants. • The dialogue is realistic.
WINGS	No Yes	• Everything seems real except Ikarus's wings. They seem out of place, even in a fantasy. • A real person can't fly. • At first, the kids at school act the way real kids would act toward a boy with wings.
IQBAL IDEA	Yes	• Iqbal goes to school and has to do a science project. • He wants to win the science fair. • His mother cooks on an open fire, typical for life in Bangladesh.

Share

Following independent reading time, gather students in small groups. Make sure at least one student in each group has read a fiction book.

> With your group, talk about what you noticed about the characters. Did the author convince you that the characters were real within the settings and other conditions of the story? What makes you think that?

Extend the Lesson (Optional)

After assessing students' understanding, you might decide to extend the learning.

▶ **Writing About Reading** Have students think critically about the authenticity of characters they read about by using a reader's notebook to write about their noticings. Encourage them to include text examples to support their thinking.

Reading Minilesson Principle

Evaluate whether characters behave in ways consistent with the setting of the book.

Thinking Critically About Characters

- several fiction stories with a variety of settings and genres, such as the following:
  - *The Herd Boy* by Niki Daly and *The Memory Coat* by Elvira Woodruff, from Text Set: Perseverance
  - *The Search for Delicious* by Natalie Babbitt, from Text Set: Genre Study: Modern Fantasy
- prepared chart with columns: *Title and Setting, Character's Behavior,* and *Is the behavior consistent with the setting?*
- markers
- fiction books students are reading
- basket of familiar fiction books

Academic Language / Important Vocabulary

- character
- behave
- consistent
- setting
- genre

Continuum Connection

- Evaluate the consistency of characters' actions within a particular setting (p. 81)

Goal

Evaluate the consistency of characters' actions within a particular setting.

Rationale

When students evaluate whether characters are speaking and behaving in ways that are consistent with the setting, they are thinking deeply about the author's craft and developing critical thinking skills.

Assess Learning

Observe students when they talk about characters and notice if there is evidence of new learning based on the goal of this minilesson.

- ▶ Are students able to evaluate whether the characters' behavior is consistent within the setting?
- ▶ Do they use the terms *character, behave, consistent, setting,* and *genre*?

Minilesson

To help students think about the minilesson principle, engage them in thinking about whether characters speak and behave in ways consistent with the setting. Here is an example.

- ▶ Revisit a few pages from *The Herd Boy*

  What is the setting of *The Herd Boy*?

  How does Malusi behave in the story?

  Do you think Malusi talks and acts like a boy who herds sheep in South Africa? Why or why not?

- ▶ As students share ideas, fill in the chart.
- ▶ Repeat the activity with a historical fiction book, such as *The Memory Coat*, and a modern fantasy book, such as *The Search for Delicious*.

  Why is it important for the characters to talk and behave in ways that are consistent with the time and place of the story?

Have a Try

Invite the students to talk with a partner about whether characters are consistent with the setting.

▶ Have students bring a fiction book they are reading or choose a familiar fiction story from the basket and sit with a partner.

Turn and talk about whether the characters speak and behave in a way that is appropriate for the setting of a fiction book. Think about the details that help you decide.

▶ After time for discussion, ask students to share ideas. Add new questions to the chart.

Summarize and Apply

Summarize the learning and remind students to think about whether characters are consistent with the setting.

When you think about whether a character's behavior is right for the setting, you evaluate whether the behavior is consistent with the setting.

▶ Add the principle to the chart.

If you read a fiction book today, evaluate the characters' behavior in relation to the setting. Bring the book when we meet so you can share.

Share

Following independent reading time, gather students in the meeting area.

Did the characters in your book behave in a way that was consistent with the setting of the story?

Extend the Lesson (Optional)

After assessing students' understanding, you might decide to extend the learning.

▶ When students write stories, remind them that the characters have to act in ways that work in the story's setting. Otherwise, readers will be confused.

▶ **Writing About Reading** Ask students to write in a reader's notebook their opinions about whether the character in a fiction book acts in a way that is consistent within the setting.

Evaluate whether characters behave in ways consistent with the setting of the book.

Title and Setting	Character's Behavior	Is the behavior consistent with the setting?
The Herd Boy / South Africa	Malusi • herds the sheep • watches insects • fights off a baboon • dreams of becoming president	Yes
Russia	Rachel and her family • realize they needed to leave Russia • sell their belongings • worry about making a good impression in America	Yes
natalie babbitt / imaginary kingdom	Gaylen • follows the king's orders as if he lives in an imaginary kingdom • speaks to the townspeople in a way that feels believable • believes in the woldweller and mermaid, which feels authentic for the fantasy setting	Yes

RML 3
LA.U31.RML3

Reading Minilesson Principle
Evaluate whether the writer makes you feel empathy for a character.

Thinking Critically About Characters

You Will Need

- several familiar fiction stories, such as the following:
  - *The Good Garden* by Katie Smith Milway, from Text Set: Problem Solving/Giving Back
  - *The Turtle Ship* by Helena Ku Rhee and *The Memory Coat* by Elvira Woodruff, from Text Set: Perseverance
- chart paper and markers
- fiction books students are reading
- basket of fiction books
- two colors of sticky notes

Academic Language / Important Vocabulary

- character
- empathy

Continuum Connection

- Assess the extent to which a writer makes readers feel empathy or identify with characters (p. 81)

Goal

Evaluate whether the writer makes the reader feel empathy for a character.

Rationale

When students feel empathy toward a character, they become more engaged in the story and thus have more motivation not only to read the story but to fully understand it. Noticing the techniques an author uses to create empathy for a character makes students aware of the author's craft.

Assess Learning

Observe students when they talk about whether they feel empathy for characters and notice if there is evidence of new learning based on the goal of this minilesson.

- ▶ Can students recognize when they feel empathy for a character?
- ▶ Do they talk about the techniques used by a writer to create empathy?
- ▶ Do they use the terms *character* and *empathy*?

Minilesson

To help students think about the minilesson principle, engage them in thinking about whether a writer makes them feel empathy for a character. Here is an example.

- ▶ Revisit pages 4–5 from *The Good Garden*.

  Think about María Luz and her family in Honduras, who don't have enough food until a teacher shows her how to garden in a different way. Do you think the author is successful in showing you what it would be like to experience the same things María Luz did? Turn and talk about that.

- ▶ Allow students time for discussion, and add the title and main character's name to the chart.

- ▶ Ask one student to share her thinking.

  Did the author make you feel empathy? Write *Yes* or *No* on a sticky note and place the sticky note on the chart next to the character's name.

- ▶ After the student places the sticky note on the chart, have a conversation about her thinking. Add an example from the story to the chart, along with her thoughts on why the author did or did not create a feeling of empathy.

- ▶ Repeat the activity with characters from other books, such as Sun-sin from *The Turtle Ship* and Grisha from *The Memory Coat*.

  Why does it matter whether you feel empathy toward a character?

Have a Try

Invite the students to talk with a partner about whether the author causes them to feel empathy for a character.

▶ Have students bring a fiction book they are reading or choose a familiar fiction story from the basket and sit with a partner.

> Turn and talk about whether the author makes you feel empathy for a character and what techniques you notice the writer using to try to make you feel empathy.

Summarize and Apply

Summarize the learning and remind students to think about whether they feel empathy for characters in fiction stories.

> You talked about whether authors caused you to feel empathy for some characters. What did you notice?

▶ Add the principle to the top of the chart.

> If you read a fiction book today, think about whether the author makes you feel empathy for any of the characters and look for examples from the story. Bring the book when we meet so you can share.

Share

Following independent reading time, gather students in the meeting area.

> Did anyone feel empathy for a character when you were reading today? Share what you noticed and tell what the author did to try to make the reader feel empathy for a character.

Extend the Lesson (Optional)

After assessing students' understanding, you might decide to extend the learning.

▶ Have students share examples of when they believe the author wanted the reader to care about a character but was not successful. Ask them to talk about how the author could have written the story in a different way that would have caused them to care more about the characters.

Evaluate whether the writer makes you feel empathy for a character.

Title and Character	Do you feel empathy?	Why or why not?
The Good Garden — María	Yes	"I could imagine overhearing my parents sounding worried about food. The way the author had the parents speak quietly, but María Luz heard anyway, added to the impact." – Ana
TURTLE SHIP — Sun-sin	No	"The story was unbelievable, and I didn't care whether Sun-sin won." – Adelina
	Yes	"Thinking about winning a contest made me feel hopeful and nervous like Sun-sin probably did. It made me want Sun-sin to win the contest." – Asher
The Memory Coat — Grisha	Yes	"Rachel's dialogue made me imagine being hugged by a family member, just like Grisha felt when wearing the coat." – Madison

Assessment

After you have taught the minilessons in this umbrella, observe students as they talk and write about their reading across instructional contexts: interactive read-aloud, independent reading, guided reading, shared reading, and book club. Use *The Literacy Continuum* (Fountas and Pinnell 2017) to observe students' reading and writing behaviors.

- ▶ What evidence do you have of new understandings related to characters?
  - Are students talking about whether a character is authentic?
  - Can they analyze whether characters behave in ways that are true to the setting?
  - Do they notice whether they feel empathy for a character?
  - Are they using the terms *character, believable, authentic, setting,* and *empathy*?
- ▶ In what other ways, beyond the scope of this umbrella, are students talking about characters?
  - Do students notice a character's traits and feelings by thinking about what text evidence reveals about a character?

Use your observations to determine the next umbrella you will teach. You may also consult Minilessons Across the Year (pp. 61–64) for guidance.

Link to Writing

After teaching the minilessons in this umbrella, help students link the new learning to their own writing:

- ▶ Encourage students to think about ways to create authentic characters and settings in their own writing.

Reader's Notebook

When this umbrella is complete, provide a copy of the minilesson principles (see resources.fountasandpinnell.com) for students to glue in the reader's notebook (in the Minilessons section if using *Reader's Notebook: Advanced* [Fountas and Pinnell 2011]), so they can refer to the information as needed.

Minilessons in This Umbrella

RML1 Writers choose the narrator and the point of view of the story.

RML2 Writers choose whether to make the third-person narrator limited or omniscient.

RML3 Sometimes writers change the narrator and the perspective of the story.

RML4 Sometimes writers show the perspective of more than one character.

Before Teaching Umbrella 32 Minilessons

The minilessons in this umbrella introduce students to some of the ways authors experiment with narrator (who is telling the story), point of view (the angle from which the reader views the story), and perspective (a character's attitude toward or way of seeing something). Before teaching these minilessons, read aloud and discuss a variety of engaging fiction books with different kinds of narrators and points of view (first, second, and third person). Include stories that clearly show the differing perspectives of characters and stories in which the narrator and/or perspective changes. Use the following books from the *Fountas & Pinnell Classroom™ Interactive Read-Aloud Collection* and *Independent Reading Collection* or choose appropriate fiction books from your classroom library.

Interactive Read-Aloud Collection

Kindness and Compassion

Nubs: The True Story of a Mutt, a Marine, and a Miracle
by Major Brian Dennis,
Kirby Larson, and Mary Nethery

Illustration Study: Mood

An Angel for Solomon Singer
by Cynthia Rylant

Exploring Identity

Flying Lessons & Other Stories
edited by Ellen Oh

A Different Pond by Bao Phi

Perseverance

The Turtle Ship by Helena Ku Rhee

Illustrator Study: K. Y. Craft

Cupid and Psyche
by M. Charlotte Craft

Independent Reading Collection

Darth Paper Strikes Back
by Tom Angleberger

As you read aloud and enjoy these texts together, help students notice and discuss

• whether the story is told from a first-, second-, or third-person point of view,

• changes in the narrator or perspective, and

• differing perspectives of different characters.

Interactive Read-Aloud
Kindness and Compassion

Illustration Study:
Mood

Exploring Identity

Perseverance

Illustrator Study:
K. Y. Craft

Independent Reading

Darth Paper
Strikes Back
by Tom
Angleberger

Section 2: Literary Analysis

Reading Minilesson Principle

Writers choose the narrator and the point of view of the story.

You Will Need

▸ two or three familiar fiction books or short stories with different kinds of narrators and points of view, such as the following:

- "Main Street" by Jacqueline Woodson and "How to Transform an Everyday, Ordinary Hoop Court into a Place of Higher Learning and You at the Podium" by Matt de la Peña in *Flying Lessons & Other Stories* edited by Ellen Oh, from Text Set: Exploring Identity

- *The Turtle Ship* by Helena Ku Rhee, from Text Set: Perseverance

▸ chart paper and markers

Academic Language / Important Vocabulary

▸ narrator
▸ first person
▸ second person
▸ third person
▸ point of view

Continuum Connection

▸ Notice the narrator of a text, identify the narrative point of view (e.g., first-person narrative, second-person narrative, omniscient third-person narrative), and talk about why the writer chose this perspective (p. 82)

Goal

Notice the narrator and point of view of the story.

Rationale

Authors choose the narrator (the person telling the story) and the point of view, or the angle from which their stories are told (first person, second person, or third person). These choices influence how the stories are told, including which details are included and omitted. Noticing the narrator and point of view helps students understand that there are multiple sides to a story and that the author must make decisions about how to tell it.

Assess Learning

Observe students when they read and talk about fiction and notice if there is evidence of new learning based on the goal of this minilesson.

▸ Can students identify the narrator and the point of view of a story?

▸ Can they differentiate between first-, second-, and third-person point of view?

▸ Do they use academic vocabulary, such as *narrator, first person, second person, third person,* and *point of view*?

Minilesson

To help students think about the minilesson principle, use familiar fiction books to help them notice the writer's choice of narrator and point of view. Here is an example.

▸ Show the cover of *Flying Lessons & Other Stories*. Turn to "Main Street" on page 123 and read the title and author's name. Then read from the second paragraph of page 126 through the end of page 127.

> Who is the narrator of this story? How can you tell?

▸ Record students' responses on chart paper.

> A girl whose nickname is Treetop is telling the story. She is the narrator. You can tell because she uses pronouns like *I, my,* and *me*. This is called first-person point of view. We see the story unfold as Treetop sees it, and we know only what she knows. The story is told from her point of view.

▸ Show *The Turtle Ship* and read the title. Then read the first page.

> Who is the narrator? How do you know?

▸ Record responses on the chart.

> This story has a third-person narrator. A third-person narrator is not involved in the story but knows what is going on. Pronouns such as *he, she,* and *they* let you know that the story is told in the third person.

Have a Try

Invite the students to talk with a partner about the narrator and the point of view in "How to Transform an Everyday, Ordinary Hoop Court into a Place of Higher Learning and You at the Podium."

▶ Turn to page 1 of *Flying Lessons & Other Stories*. Read the title, author's name, and the first page of the story.

Turn and talk to your partner about the narrator and the point of view in this story.

▶ After students turn and talk, invite a few students to share their thinking. Record responses on the chart.

This story is told by an unnamed narrator in second-person point of view. In second-person point of view, the narrator speaks directly to you, using pronouns such as *you* and *your*. This is the rarest point of view and perspective that you will find in stories.

Summarize and Apply

Summarize the learning and remind students to notice the narrator and the point of view when they read fiction.

▶ Write the principle at the top of the chart.

Why might an author choose a first-, second-, or third-person point of view? What do you think are the advantages of each one?

If you read fiction today, notice the narrator and the point of view of your story. Be ready to share what you noticed when we come back together.

Share

Following independent reading time, gather students together in the meeting area to talk about narrators and points of view.

Who read fiction today? Tell us about the narrator and the point of view from which the story was told.

Extend the Lesson (Optional)

After assessing students' understanding, you might decide to extend the learning.

▶ Have students rewrite a story (or part of a story) using a different point of view.

Writers choose the narrator and the point of view of the story.

Story	Narrator and Point of View	Evidence
"Main Street"	• A girl called Treetop • First-person point of view	• "Celeste was my new best friend" • I, me
"The Turtle Ship"	• Unnamed narrator • Third-person point of view	• "A boy named Sun-sin" • his, he, they
"How to Transform an Everyday, Ordinary Hoop Court ..."	• Unnamed narrator • Second-person point of view	• you, your, you're

Section 2: Literary Analysis

RML2
LA.U32.RML2

Reading Minilesson Principle:
Writers choose whether to make the third-person narrator limited or omniscient.

Analyzing Perspective and Point of View

You Will Need

- two or three familiar fiction books containing examples of both limited and omniscient third-person narrators, such as the following:
  - *An Angel for Solomon Singer* by Cynthia Rylant, from Text Set: Illustration Study: Mood
  - *Cupid and Psyche* by M. Charlotte Craft, from Text Set: Illustrator Study: K. Y. Craft
  - *The Turtle Ship* by Helena Ku Rhee, from Text Set: Perseverance
- chart paper and markers

Academic Language / Important Vocabulary

- narrator
- perspective
- third person
- limited
- omniscient
- point of view

Continuum Connection

- Notice the narrator of a text, identify the narrative point of view (e.g., first-person narrative, second-person narrative, omniscient third-person narrative), and talk about why the writer chose this perspective (p. 82)

Goal

Understand the difference between limited and omniscient third-person narrators.

Rationale

When writing a story with a third-person narrator, the author chooses whether to make the narrator limited (knows the inner life of one character) or omniscient (knows the inner lives of all characters). The author's choices regarding the narrator influence how the story is told, including which details are included and omitted. Noticing the type of third-person narrator helps students understand that they do not necessarily gain access to all sides of the story when they read fiction.

Assess Learning

Observe students when they read and talk about fiction books and notice if there is evidence of new learning based on the goal of this minilesson.

- ▶ Can students differentiate between limited and omniscient third-person narrators?
- ▶ Do they use academic vocabulary, such as *narrator*, *perspective*, *third person*, *limited*, *omniscient*, and *point of view*?

Minilesson

To help students think about the minilesson principle, use familiar fiction books to help students notice the difference between limited and omniscient third-person narrators. Here is an example.

- ▶ Show the cover of *An Angel for Solomon Singer*. Read the title and pages 1–6.

  What type of narrator tells this story? Whose perspective is the narrator showing? How do you know?

- ▶ Record responses on chart paper.

  This story has a third-person narrator that shows Solomon Singer's perspective. You can imagine that the third-person narrator is like a camera that follows Solomon around and records everything that he does, says, and thinks. Because the narrator is following only one character around, it is a limited third-person narrator. A limited third-person narrator knows the thoughts and feelings of only one character.

- ▶ Show the cover of *Cupid and Psyche* and read the title. Then read pages 1–7.

  Whose perspective does the narrator show? How do you know?

- ▶ Record responses on the chart.

  The third-person narrator knows everything that all the characters do and think, which means that it is an omniscient narrator. The word *omniscient* means "all-knowing."

Have a Try

Invite the students to talk with a partner about the narrator in *The Turtle Ship*.

▶ Show the cover of *The Turtle Ship*. Then read pages 10–15.

Turn and talk to your partner about the narrator in *The Turtle Ship*.

▶ After time for discussion, invite a few pairs to share their thinking. Record responses on the chart.

Summarize and Apply

Summarize the learning and remind students to notice and think about third-person narrators.

What is the difference between a limited and an omniscient third-person narrator?

▶ Help students define both types of narrators and write the definitions on a second chart. Write the principle at the top of the first chart.

If you read fiction today, think about the narrator and perspective of your story. Be ready to share your thinking when we come back together.

Share

Following independent reading time, gather students together in the meeting area to talk about the narrators in the books they read.

Who read a story with a third-person narrator today?

Is the narrator of your story limited or omniscient? How do you know?

Extend the Lesson (Optional)

After assessing students' understanding, you might decide to extend the learning.

▶ Discuss why authors might choose a limited or omniscient narrator and the advantages and disadvantages of each one.

Writers choose whether to make the third-person narrator limited or omniscient.

Story	Narrator and Point of View	Evidence
	• Third-person limited	• Refers to Solomon Singer by his name • Uses pronouns <u>he</u>, <u>him</u>
	• Third-person omniscient	• Refers to all the characters by name • Uses pronouns <u>she</u>, <u>her</u>, <u>he</u>, <u>him</u>
	• Third-person limited	• Refers to Sun-sin by his name • Uses pronouns <u>he</u>, <u>him</u>

Type of Narrator

Limited third-person narrator: Follows <u>one</u> character around and knows <u>one</u> character's thoughts and feelings

Omniscient (all-knowing) third-person narrator: Follows <u>all</u> the characters around and knows <u>all</u> their thoughts and feelings

Section 2: Literary Analysis

Reading Minilesson Principle
Sometimes writers change the narrator and the perspective of the story.

Analyzing Perspective and Point of View

Goal

Notice when a writer changes the narrator and perspective of the story.

Rationale

A character's perspective is shaped by the character's life experiences and is the lens through which he or she views the world. It is different from, though related to, point of view. When students notice a change in the narrator or perspective of a story, they understand that there are multiple sides to every story and that the author must make decisions about how to tell the story.

Assess Learning

Observe students when they read and talk about fiction books and notice if there is evidence of new learning based on the goal of this minilesson.

> ⏵ Do students notice changes in the narrator or perspective?

> ⏵ Do they use academic vocabulary, such as *narrator, perspective,* and *fiction*?

Minilesson

To help students think about the minilesson principle, use familiar fiction books to discuss changes in narrator or perspective. Here is an example.

⏵ Show the cover of *Darth Paper Strikes Back*. Then read pages 1–2.

> Who is the narrator in this part of the book?

> From what point of view is he telling the story?

> Tommy is a first-person narrator. We learn about his perspective from reading what he says about his life. His perspective is shaped by his experiences and how he views the events in the story.

⏵ Read pages 25–26.

> What do you notice about the narrator and perspective in this chapter?

⏵ Record responses on chart paper.

> Now the narrator is Sara. The chapters in this book are narrated by different characters. In Sara's chapters, we see events from her perspective.

⏵ Show the cover of *Nubs*. Read the e-mail on page 5 and the three sentences at the top of page 6.

> What do you notice about the perspective of these two excerpts?

> How do you know they are told from different perspectives?

> Most of the book is told by a third-person narrator who refers to Brian as *Brian* or *he*. The e-mails are from Brian himself. They are written in the first person, using *I, me,* and *we*.

Have a Try

Invite the students to talk with a partner about the perspectives in *Nubs*.

▶ Have students talk further about the change in perspective in *Nubs*.

Turn and talk to a partner about how the experience of reading the book would be different if the e-mails were omitted and the narration was all third-person point of view.

▶ After students turn and talk, invite a few students to share their thinking.

Summarize and Apply

Summarize the learning and remind students to notice changes in the narrator and perspective.

What did you notice about the narrator and perspective in the books we looked at today?

▶ Write the principle at the top of the chart.

If you read fiction today, think about the narrator and perspective of your story. Notice whether the narrator or perspective changes at any point in your book. Bring your book to share when we come back together.

Share

Following independent reading time, gather students together in the meeting area to talk about perspective in the books they read.

Did anyone read a story in which the narrator or perspective changes?

How did the narrator or perspective change in your story?

Extend the Lesson (Optional)

After assessing students' understanding, you might decide to extend the learning.

▶ Discuss why authors sometimes change the narrator and/or the perspective in a story.

▶ **Writing About Reading** Have students rewrite a story from a different character's perspective.

Sometimes writers change the narrator and the perspective of the story.

Title	Narrator	Whose perspective?
Darth Paper Strikes Back	• First-person narrator: different characters (Tommy, Sara, etc.)	• Sometimes Tommy's • Sometimes Sara's
Nubs	• Unnamed third-person narrator • First-person narrator	• Narrator's • Brian's

Reading Minilesson Principle

Sometimes writers show the perspective of more than one character.

Analyzing Perspective and Point of View

Goal

Notice how the writer shows different perspectives through primary and secondary characters.

Rationale

When students notice and think about the perspectives of multiple characters in a story, they gain a deeper understanding of the characters' personalities and motivations. They also develop their understanding of the bigger idea that in real life every person has his or her own perspective, or way of viewing the world. Understanding different perspectives helps students develop empathy.

Assess Learning

Observe students when they read and talk about fiction books and notice if there is evidence of new learning based on the goal of this minilesson.

▸ Can students compare the perspectives of two or more characters in a story?

▸ Do they use academic vocabulary, such as *primary character, secondary character,* and *perspective*?

Minilesson

To help students think about the minilesson principle, use familiar fiction books to help students notice different perspectives. Here is an example.

▸ Show the cover of *Flying Lessons & Other Stories*. Turn to page 123 and read the title ("Main Street") and the author's name.

Who is the main character in this story?

Treetop is the main, or primary, character in this story. Primary character is another way to say main character. Who are the other characters in this story?

The other characters in the story are called secondary characters.

▸ Read from "I had never known anyone brown" on page 128 through "*My mom said I shouldn't eat with the new one. You shouldn't either.*" on page 130.

How does Treetop react when Celeste says the word *negro*?

Does Celeste see that word in the same way as Treetop, or does she have a different perspective on the issue?

Why are their perspectives different?

▸ Record students' responses on chart paper.

Why do Treetop and her friends have different perspectives about Celeste?

▸ Record students' responses on the chart.

Have a Try

Invite the students to talk with a partner about perspective in *A Different Pond*.

▶ Show the cover of *A Different Pond* and read the title. Then read pages 5–8.

> Turn and talk to your partner about how and why the boy's perspective about money is different from his dad's perspective.

▶ After students turn and talk, invite a few pairs to share their thinking. Record their responses on the chart.

Summarize and Apply

Summarize the learning and remind students to notice differing perspectives.

> What did you notice about characters' perspectives today?

▶ Write the principle at the top of the chart.

> If you read fiction today, think about the perspectives of different characters. How do they see things differently? Be ready to share your thinking when we come back together.

Share

Following independent reading time, gather students together in the meeting area to talk about perspective in the books they read.

> Who read a fiction book today?

> What did you notice about the perspectives of the characters in your story? How were they different or similar?

Extend the Lesson (Optional)

After assessing students' understanding, you might decide to extend the learning.

▶ Regularly discuss why different characters have different perspectives. Help students build their understanding of the different factors that can influence a person's perspective (e.g., culture, religion, age, personal experiences).

▶ Help students understand that omniscient third-person narrators generally provide more insight into the perspectives of secondary characters. However, even in stories with other types of narrators, the reader still gains insight into the perspectives of secondary characters through their actions and dialogue.

Sometimes writers show the perspective of more than one character.

Title	Primary Character	Secondary Characters	Perspective
"Main Street"	Treetop says "I thought we didn't say that word anymore." Treetop is happy with her new friend.	Celeste says that she can use the word, but Treetop can't. Treetop's other friends stop being friends with Treetop.	Different— They have different skin colors and backgrounds. Different— They don't know any black people. They have heard their parents say prejudiced things about them.
	The boy doesn't understand why they have to fish for food even though his dad has two jobs.	His dad explains that "everything in America costs a lot of money."	Different— As an adult, Dad understands more about jobs and money.

Assessment

After you have taught the minilessons in this umbrella, observe students as they talk and write about their reading across instructional contexts: interactive read-aloud, independent reading, guided reading, shared reading, and book club. Use *The Literacy Continuum* (Fountas and Pinnell 2017) to observe students' reading and writing behaviors.

▶ What evidence do you have of new understandings related to perspective and point of view?

- Can students identify whether a story is told from a first- or third-person point of view?
- Can they differentiate between limited and omniscient third-person narrators?
- Do they notice when a writer changes the narrator and/or perspective of a story?
- Can they explain how two characters' perspectives differ?
- Do they use academic vocabulary, such as *narrator*, *perspective*, *omniscient*, and *point of view*?

▶ In what other ways, beyond the scope of this umbrella, are students talking about fiction books?

- Are students thinking critically about characters?
- Are they noticing the elements of plot development?

Use your observations to determine the next umbrella you will teach. You may also consult Minilessons Across the Year (pp. 61–64) for guidance.

Link to Writing

After teaching the minilessons in this umbrella, help students link the new learning to their own writing:

▶ When students write their own stories, remind them to think carefully about the narrator, point of view, and characters' perspectives before they begin writing.

▶ Have students write the same story from the point of view of two or more characters.

Reader's Notebook

When this umbrella is complete, provide a copy of the minilesson principles (see resources.fountasandpinnell.com) for students to glue in the reader's notebook (in the Minilessons section if using *Reader's Notebook: Advanced* [Fountas and Pinnell 2011]), so they can refer to the information as needed.

Section 3 | Strategies and Skills

The Strategies and Skills minilessons are designed to bring a few important strategic actions to temporary, conscious attention so that students can apply them in their independent reading. By the time students participate in these minilessons, they should have engaged these strategic actions successfully in guided reading lessons as they continue to strengthen in-the-head literacy processing systems. These lessons reinforce effective and efficient reading behaviors.

3 Strategies and Skills

Minilessons in This Umbrella

RML1 Break a multisyllable word between consonants but keep consonant digraphs and clusters together.

RML2 Break a multisyllable word after the vowel if the syllable has a long vowel sound and after the consonant if the syllable has a short vowel sound.

RML3 Break a multisyllable word between vowels.

RML4 Break a multisyllable word before the consonant and *le*.

RML5 Remove the prefix or suffix to take apart a word.

RML6 Look for a part of the word that can help.

Before Teaching Umbrella 1 Minilessons

Most of the word work you do with students will take place during small-group guided reading or a separate word study lesson. However, there are minilessons that may serve as reminders and be helpful to the whole class. They can be taught any time you see a need among your students. Before teaching these minilessons, make sure students know terms such as *syllable, multisyllable, word part, consonant*, and *vowel*. Students must also be able to recognize consonant digraphs, prefixes, and suffixes. Use the examples that are provided in these minilessons or choose multisyllable words from texts your students are reading. Use two- and three-syllable words and unknown words as examples of each principle.

Section 3: Strategies and Skills

Reading Minilesson Principle

Break a multisyllable word between consonants but keep consonant digraphs and clusters together.

Solving Multisyllable Words

You Will Need

- word cards: *compass, basketball, mushroom, garbage, subtract, gadget, distance, complete, infant, machine, suspect, plankton, hundred, athlete, capture, butterfly, hamburger, dishwasher, atmosphere, strawberry, observatory, microwave*

- chart paper and markers

Academic Language / Important Vocabulary

- consonant
- consonant digraph
- consonant cluster
- multisyllable
- syllable

Continuum Connection

- Break a word into syllables to decode manageable units: e.g., *re/mem/ber, hos/pi/tal, be/fore, de/part/ment* (p. 391)

Goal

Learn to take apart multisyllable words between consonants, keeping consonant diagraphs and consonant clusters together.

Rationale

Students need to know how to break multisyllable words apart to read new words more efficiently, to write accurately, and to know where to break multisyllable words at the end of a line when writing by hand. Multisyllable words with medial consonants are broken between two consonants (*pen/cil*), except when the consonants form a digraph. Then the word is broken after the consonant digraph (*ush/er*). When there are three medial consonants, the word is broken between a consonant and the consonant digraph or consonant cluster (*mis/trust*).

Assess Learning

Observe students when they solve unknown words. Notice if there is evidence of new learning based on the goal of this minilesson.

- Can students break apart unknown words into syllables to read them?
- Do they understand the terms *consonant, consonant digraph, consonant cluster, multisyllable,* and *syllable*?

Minilesson

To help students practice solving unknown words by breaking them apart, use examples of words that have medial consonants and medial consonant digraphs. Here is an example.

- Show the word card for *compass*. Have students tap the word and tell where to break it. Write the word on the left side of the chart and draw a slash between the two syllables (*com/pass*).

- Repeat with the word *basketball* (*bas/ket/ball*).

   What do you notice about where each word is broken?

- Show the word card for *mushroom*. Have students tap the word to note the number of syllables. Start a column on the right side of the chart. Write the word and draw a slash between the two syllables (*mush/room*).

- Continue showing the word cards, having students tap the word, and writing the words in the correct column on the chart: *garbage, subtract, gadget, distance, complete, infant, machine, suspect, plankton, hundred, athlete, capture, butterfly, hamburger,* and *dishwasher*.

   What do you notice about the words on the left? Where are they broken?

   What do you notice about how to break the words on the right?

Have a Try

Invite the students to break apart words with two or more medial consonants.

▶ Show the word card for *atmosphere*.

  Turn and talk to your partner about where you would break this word.

▶ Write (or have volunteers write) the word on the chart and draw a slash between the syllables. Repeat with *strawberry*, *observatory*, and *microwave*.

Summarize and Apply

Summarize the learning and remind students to break multisyllable words apart between two consonants and keep consonant digraphs and clusters together.

  Look at the chart. What do you notice about where to break apart words when they have two or three consonants in the middle?

▶ Write the principle at the top of the chart.

  If you come to a new word when you read today, break it apart to read it. Be prepared to share what you did when we come back together.

Share

Following independent reading time, gather students together in the meeting area to talk about how they read unknown words.

  Did anyone come to a new word while reading? What did you do?

Extend the Lesson (Optional)

After assessing students' understanding, you might decide to extend the learning.

▶ During shared writing, model how to write multisyllable words by saying them slowly, listening for the parts, and writing one part at a time.

Section 3: Strategies and Skills

RML2
SAS.U1.RML2

Reading Minilesson Principle
Break a multisyllable word after the vowel if the syllable has a long vowel sound and after the consonant if the syllable has a short vowel sound.

You Will Need

- word cards: *crater, monster, climate, program, require, contest, lever, mishap, defrost, fusion, absent, dinosaur, detective, binoculars, resist, calendar, monument*
- chart paper prepared with a strip of colored paper attached to the top, divided into three columns
- markers

Academic Language / Important Vocabulary

- long vowel sound
- short vowel sound
- multisyllable
- syllable

Continuum Connection

- Break a word into syllables to decode manageable units: e.g., *re/mem/ber, hos/pi/tal, be/fore, de/part/ment* (p. 391)

Goal

Learn to take apart words with long vowel sounds and words with short vowel sounds.

Rationale

Students learn to take words apart and write multisyllable words accurately by listening for syllable breaks. Two-syllable words are generally broken after the vowel if the first syllable has a long vowel sound (open syllable) and after the consonant if the first syllable has a short vowel sound (closed syllable).

Assess Learning

Observe students when they solve unknown words. Notice if there is evidence of new learning based on the goal of this minilesson.

- Do students listen for the vowel sound in the first syllable so they know where to break a word apart?
- Do they use the language *long vowel sound, short vowel sound, multisyllable,* and *syllable*?

Minilesson

To help students practice solving unknown words by breaking them apart, engage them in breaking apart multisyllabic words that you think will be meaningful to them. Here is an example.

- Show the word card for *crater*. Have students tap the syllables and tell where to break it. Write the word in the first column of the chart and draw a slash between the two syllables (*cra/ter*).
- Show the word card for *monster*. Have students tap the word and tell where to break it. Start a second column to the right. Write the word and draw a slash between the two syllables (*mon/ster*).
- Continue showing the word cards, having students tap the word and tell where to break it. Write the words in the correct column on the chart: *climate, program, require, contest, lever, mishap, defrost, fusion, absent,* and *dinosaur*.

  What do you notice about where the words on the left are broken?

  How are the words on the right different from the words on the left?

- Show the word card for *detective*. Have students tap the word and tell where to break it. Start a third column to the right. Write the word and draw a slash between each of the syllables (*de/tec/tive*). Continue with the word card for *binoculars* (*bin/oc/u/lars*). Note that the syllables in these words have both long and short vowel sounds in them.

  What do you notice about the words in the third column?

Have a Try

Invite the students to break apart the word *resist* with a partner. Show the word card.

> Where would you break *resist*?

▶ Write the word on the chart and draw a slash between the syllables. Repeat the process with *calendar* and *monument*.

Summarize and Apply

Summarize the learning and remind students to break a word after the vowel if the syllable has a long vowel sound and after the consonant if the syllable has a short vowel sound.

> Look at the chart. What do you notice about where the words are broken?

▶ Guide students to notice that when the first syllable has a long vowel sound, the syllable ends with the vowel. When the first syllable has a short vowel sound, the syllable ends with a consonant. These rules likewise apply when breaking apart words with more than two syllables. Write the principle at the top of the chart.

> When you read today, if you get to a new word, you may need to break the word in a couple of different places and try each vowel sound to find out which is correct. Be prepared to share what you did when we come back together.

Share

Following independent reading time, gather students together in the meeting area to talk about how they solved unknown words.

> Did anyone come to a word you didn't know? What did you do?

Extend the Lesson (Optional)

After assessing students' understanding, you might decide to extend the learning.

▶ During shared writing, model how to write multisyllable words by saying them, listening for the parts, and writing one part at a time.

Break a multisyllable word after the vowel if the syllable has a long vowel sound and after the consonant if the syllable has a short vowel sound.

cra/ter	mon/ster	de/tec/tive
cli/mate	con/test	bin/oc/u/lars
pro/gram	lev/er	mon/u/ment
re/quire	mis/hap	
de/frost	ab/sent	
fu/sion	cal/en/dar	
di/no/saur		
re/sist		

Reading Minilesson Principle
Break a multisyllable word between vowels.

Solving Multisyllable Words

You Will Need

- word cards: *riot, triumph, giant, poem, bionic, pliable, fluid, anxiety, biodegradable, hideous, evaluate, casual, gradual*
- chart paper and markers

Academic Language / Important Vocabulary

- vowel
- syllable

Continuum Connection

- Break a word into syllables to decode manageable units: e.g., *re/mem/ber, hos/pi/tal, be/fore, de/part/ment* (p. 391)

Goal

Learn to take apart a word between vowels.

Rationale

When you remind students that they may need to try more than once to find where to break apart a word and read it correctly, they are prepared to recognize that in some words vowels are broken to form syllables.

Assess Learning

Observe students when they solve unknown words. Notice if there is evidence of new learning based on the goal of this minilesson.

- Do students break unknown words into parts?
- Do they break multisyllabic words into parts between two vowel sounds if the first syllable is an open syllable (long vowel sound)?
- Are they using the terms *vowel* and *syllable*?

Minilesson

To help students think about the minilesson principle, engage them in a demonstration of breaking apart words between vowels. Here is an example.

- Show the word card for *riot*. Have students tap the word and tell where to break it. Write the word on the chart and draw a slash between the syllables (*ri/ot*).

  What do you notice about where the word is broken?

- Prompt the students to say that you broke the word apart between the two vowels and that the sound of each vowel could be heard.

- Repeat this process with the word *triumph*.

  When you get to a word you don't know, break it between the two vowels and say the short or long vowel sound of each. If that doesn't work, the two vowels make one sounds together and make a one-syllable word, for example, *rain, boat,* and *house*.

- Continue with the word cards for *giant, poem, bionic, pliable, fluid, anxiety, biodegradable,* and *hideous*. Notice that in the word *hideous*, the vowel digraph (*ou*) stays together.

Have a Try

Invite the students to break apart the word *evaluate* with a partner. Show the word card.

> Where would you break this word?

▶ Write the word on the chart and draw a slash between the syllables. Repeat the process with *casual* and *gradual*.

Summarize and Apply

Summarize the learning and remind students to break new words apart between vowels.

> Look at the chart. What do you notice about where the words are broken?

▶ Write the principle at the top of the chart.

> When you read today, if you come to a new multisyllable word, you may need to break the word between the vowels. Be ready to share when we come back together.

Share

Following independent reading time, gather students together in the meeting area to talk about word solving.

> Did anyone come to a word you didn't know? What did you do?

Extend the Lesson (Optional)

After assessing students' understanding, you might decide to extend the learning.

▶ During shared writing, model how to write multisyllable words by saying them slowly, listening for the parts, and writing one part at a time.

Break a multisyllable word between vowels.

ri/ot	anx/i/e/ty
tri/umph	bi/o/de/gra/da/ble
gi/ant	hid/e/ous
po/em	e/val/u/ate
bi/on/ic	cas/u/al
pli/a/ble	grad/u/al
flu/id	

Reading Minilesson Principle
Break a multisyllable word before the consonant and *le*.

Solving Multisyllable Words

You Will Need

- word cards: *sprinkle, trample, resemble, whistle, entitle, thistle, squabble, preamble, ventricle, straddle, chronicle, rectangle*
- chart paper and markers

Academic Language / Important Vocabulary

- consonant
- syllable

Continuum Connection

- Break a word into syllables to decode manageable units: e.g., *re/mem/ber, hos/pi/tal, be/fore, de/part/ment* (p. 391)

Goal

Learn to take apart words before the consonant and *le*.

Rationale

Students learn to take words apart and write multisyllable words accurately by listening for the syllable breaks. Students learn that in most words that end with *le*, the syllable is broken before the consonant and *le*.

Assess Learning

Observe students when they solve unknown words. Notice if there is evidence of new learning based on the goal of this minilesson.

- ▶ Do students break unknown words into parts when word solving?
- ▶ Do they know to break multisyllabic words before the consonant and *le*?
- ▶ Are they using the terms *consonant* and *syllable*?

Minilesson

To help students think about the minilesson principle, engage them in a demonstration of breaking apart words ending with a consonant and *le*. Here is an example.

- ▶ Show the word card for *sprinkle*. Have students tap the word and tell where to break it. Write the word on the chart and draw a slash between the syllables (*sprin/kle*).
- ▶ Repeat the process with *trample*.

  What do you notice about where each word is broken?

  Break the word before the consonant and *le*.

- ▶ Repeat this process with these words: *resemble, whistle, entitle, thistle, squabble, preamble,* and *ventricle*.

  When you get to a word you don't know, break it before the consonant and *le* to help you read the word.

Have a Try

Invite the students to break apart the word *straddle* with a partner. Show the word card.

> Where would you break this word?

▶ Write the word on the chart and draw a slash between the syllables. Repeat the process with *chronicle* and *rectangle*.

Summarize and Apply

Summarize the learning and remind students to break new words before the consonant and *le*.

> Look at the chart. What do you notice about where the words are broken?

▶ Write the principle at the top of the chart.

> When you read today, if you come to a new word, break it apart to help you read it. Be ready to share when we come back together.

Share

Following independent reading time, gather students together in the meeting area to talk about word solving.

> Did anyone come to a word you didn't know? What did you do?

Extend the Lesson (Optional)

After assessing students' understanding, you might decide to extend the learning.

▶ During shared writing, model how to write multisyllable words by saying them slowly, listening for the parts, and writing one part at a time.

Break a multisyllable word before the consonant and le.

sprin/kle
tram/ple
re/sem/ble
whis/tle
en/ti/tle
this/tle
squab/ble
pre/am/ble
ven/tri/cle
strad/dle
chron/i/cle
rec/tan/gle

Reading Minilesson Principle
Remove the prefix or suffix to take apart a word.

You Will Need

- chart paper with the first column filled in: *proclaim, courageous, dissatisfied, transatlantic, submarine, perishable*
- sticky notes or index cards
- markers

Academic Language / Important Vocabulary

- prefix
- suffix
- base word

Continuum Connection

- Recognize and use word parts to solve an unknown word and understand its meaning: e.g., *conference*—prefix *con-* ("with or together"), Latin root *fer* ("to bring" or "to carry"), suffix *-ence* ("state of" or "quality of") (p. 391)
- Understand and talk about the concept of a suffix (p. 389)
- Understand and discuss the concept of a prefix (p. 390)

Goal

Learn to take off the prefix or suffix to solve words.

Rationale

When you teach students to take multisyllabic words apart by removing the prefix or suffix and reading the base word, they can problem solve words more efficiently and keep their attention on meaning.

Assess Learning

Observe students when they take apart unknown words. Notice if there is evidence of new learning based on the goal of this minilesson.

- ▶ Do students break apart words between the base word and the prefix or suffix?
- ▶ Are they using the terms *prefix, suffix,* and *base word?*

Minilesson

To help students think about the minilesson principle, engage them in a demonstration of removing a prefix or suffix to identify the base word. Here is an example.

- ▶ Display the prepared chart. Use a sticky note or an index card to cover the prefix (*pro*). Read the base word (*claim*) and then reveal the prefix. Read the whole word to make sure it sounds right and looks right.

   What did you notice about what I did to read the word *proclaim?*

- ▶ Prompt the students to say that you removed the prefix, read the base word, and then added the prefix back onto the word and read the whole word. You may want to point out that a prefix or suffix can have more than one syllable. Write on the chart how you broke apart the word.

- ▶ Repeat this process with the words *courageous, dissatisfied,* and *transatlantic.*

   You can remove the suffix so you can read the base word and then the whole word.

Have a Try

Invite the students to break apart the words *submarine* and *perishable* with a partner by removing the prefix or suffix.

> Turn and talk to your partner. How would you break these words apart? Remember to reread the whole word to make sure it looks right and sounds right.

▶ Ask a student to show the break on the chart.

Summarize and Apply

Summarize the learning and remind students to solve new words by removing the prefix or suffix.

> Look at the chart. What do you notice about how the words were broken?

▶ Write the principle at the top of the chart.

> When you read today, if you come to a new word, break it into parts to help you read it. Be ready to share when we come back together.

Remove the prefix or suffix to take apart a word.	
proclaim	pro / claim
courageous	courage / ous
dissatisfied	dis / satisfied
transatlantic	trans / atlantic
submarine	sub / marine
perishable	perish / able

Share

Following independent reading time, gather students together in the meeting area to talk about word solving.

> Did anyone come to a word you didn't know? What did you do?

Extend the Lesson (Optional)

After assessing students' understanding, you might decide to extend the learning.

▶ During shared writing, model how to write multisyllable words by saying them slowly, listening for the parts, and writing one part at a time.

Reading Minilesson Principle
Look for a part of the word that can help.

Solving Multisyllable Words

You Will Need

- chart paper with the four columns filled in (see next page)
- sticky notes or index cards
- markers
- highlighter or highlighting tape

Academic Language / Important Vocabulary

- multisyllable
- unfamiliar
- known

Continuum Connection

- Recognize and use word parts to solve an unknown word and understand its meaning: e.g., *conference*—prefix *con-* ("with or together"), Latin root *fer* ("to bring" or "to carry"), suffix *-ence* ("state of" or "quality of") (p. 391)

- Recognize and use connections between or among related words that have the same word root or base word to solve unknown words: e.g., *support/supports/supported/supportive/unsupportive* (p. 391)

- Recognize and use a word's origin to solve an unknown word and understand its form and meaning (p. 391)

Goal

Search for and use familiar parts of a word to help solve the word.

Rationale

When you teach students to use what they know about words to solve them, you increase their efficiency in reading unknown words in continuous text, allowing them to improve fluency and focus on meaning.

Assess Learning

Observe students when they read unfamiliar words. Notice if there is evidence of new learning based on the goal of this minilesson.

> ▶ Do students look for parts of a word that they know to read it?
>
> ▶ Are they using the terms *multisyllable, unfamiliar,* and *known*?

Minilesson

To help students think about the minilesson principle, engage them in a demonstration of using known words parts to read unfamiliar multisyllable words. Here is an example.

> ▶ Display the prepared chart. Read the first word, *civilize*.
>
>> I'm not sure what this word is, but I see part of the word that I know how to say.
>
> ▶ Use a sticky note or an index card to cover *ize*. Say the known part of the word, *civil*, and highlight it on the chart. Reveal the rest of the word, sound it out, and then say the whole word to make sure it looks right and sounds right.
>
>> How does knowing *civil* help you read other words on this list?
>
> ▶ Repeat this process with the other words in the first column.
>
> ▶ Then repeat the process with the words *nonsense* and *constructive*.
>
>> When you come to a word you don't know, look for a part or parts of the word you do know.

Have a Try

Invite the students to work with a partner to find a part of the word *flexible* they know.

> Turn and talk to your partner. What do you know about the word *flexible*? How does knowing that help you to read the other words in that column?

▶ Ask a student to highlight the part of the word they know on the chart.

Summarize and Apply

Summarize the learning and remind students to use what they know about a word to solve unfamiliar words.

> Look at the chart. How can you read a word you don't know?

▶ Write the principle at the top of the chart.

> When you read today, if you come to an unfamiliar word, look to see if there is a part of the word that can help. Be ready to share when we come back together.

Look for a part of the word that can help.

civilize	nonsense	constructive	flexible
civilian	sensible	construction	flexibility
civilians	sensitive	unconstructive	inflexible
uncivilized	sensibility		flexed
civilization			

Share

Following independent reading time, gather students together in the meeting area to talk about word solving.

> Did anyone come to an unfamiliar word? Was there a part you did know that could help?

Extend the Lesson (Optional)

After assessing students' understanding, you might decide to extend the learning.

▶ Invite students to talk about how a word part helped them know the meaning of a word.

▶ During guided and independent reading, remind students of the ways they can read unfamiliar words.

Section 3: Strategies and Skills

Assessment

After you have taught the minilessons in this umbrella, observe students as they talk and write about their reading across instructional contexts: interactive read-aloud, independent reading, guided reading, shared reading, and book club. Use *The Literacy Continuum* (Fountas and Pinnell 2017) to observe students' reading and writing behaviors across instructional contexts.

▶ What evidence do you have of new understandings related to solving multisyllable words?

- Do students use a variety of flexible ways to take apart words?
- Can they use known parts to solve words?
- Do they remove the prefix or suffix to find the base word, or a part they do know that can help?
- Are they using language such as *syllable, base word, prefix, suffix, consonant digraph, vowel sound, unfamiliar,* and *multisyllable*?

▶ In what other ways, beyond the scope of this umbrella, do students need to strengthen their ability to process text effectively and efficiently?

- Do students need help navigating difficult texts?
- Do they read digital texts in a productive way?

Use your observations to determine the next umbrella you will teach. You may also consult Minilessons Across the Year (pp. 61–64) for guidance.

Link to Writing

After teaching the minilessons in this umbrella, help students link the new learning to their own writing:

▶ When engaging in shared writing and independent writing, refer to resources you have in the room to make connections between known words and new words.

▶ When engaging in shared writing, demonstrate how to say a word slowly, listen for the parts, and then write the word one part at a time.

Reader's Notebook

When this umbrella is complete, provide a copy of the minilesson principles (see resources.fountasandpinnell.com) for students to glue in the reader's notebook (in the Minilessons section if using *Reader's Notebook: Advanced* [Fountas and Pinnell 2011]), so they can refer to the information as needed.

Minilessons in This Umbrella

RML1 A writer provides information within the text to help you understand what a word means.

RML2 Word parts help you understand what a word means.

RML3 Greek and Latin roots help you understand what a word means.

RML4 Understand the connotative meaning of a word.

Before Teaching Umbrella 2 Minilessons

Although most of the teaching of solving words while reading happens during small-group instruction, there are some lessons that are worth presenting to the whole class. Once you teach these minilessons, you can follow them up in more detail when you meet with guided reading groups.

Use the following books from the *Fountas & Pinnell Classroom™ Interactive Read-Aloud Collection* text sets or choose other books with strong examples of context-supported vocabulary, such as books that contain words with prefixes, suffixes, Greek roots, or Latin roots and that use context clues to clarify meaning.

Memoir/Autobiography

Under the Royal Palms: A Childhood in Cuba by Alma Flor Ada

Life on Earth

Rotten! Vultures, Beetles, Slime, and Nature's Other Decomposers by Anita Sanchez

Animal Adaptations

Exploding Ants: Amazing Facts About How Animals Adapt by Joanne Settel

As you read aloud and enjoy these texts together, guide students to infer the meanings of unfamiliar words.

Memoir/Autobiography

Life on Earth

Animal Adaptations

Section 3: Strategies and Skills

Deriving Word Meanings

You Will Need

- two or three books that contain new or unfamiliar vocabulary, such as the following:
  - *Exploding Ants* by Joanne Settel, from Text Set: Animal Adaptations
  - *Rotten!* by Anita Sanchez, from Text Set: Life on Earth
- chart paper prepared with sentences from the chosen texts
- markers and highlighters

Academic Language / Important Vocabulary

- context
- synonym
- antonym
- example

Continuum Connection

- Derive the meaning of words from the context of a sentence, paragraph, or the whole text (p. 86)
- Recognize and use synonyms (words that have almost the same meaning): e.g., *mistake/error, destroy/demolish, high/tall, desperately, frantically* (p. 388)
- Recognize and use antonyms (words that have opposite meanings): e.g., *cold/hot, appear/vanish, abundant/scarce, fantasy/reality* (p. 388)

Goal

Understand that sometimes a writer tells the meaning of a word in the sentence, paragraph, or elsewhere in the book.

Rationale

Students who are able to decipher the meanings of unfamiliar words by using context clues are better able to understand the ideas in the text.

Assess Learning

Observe students when they encounter unfamiliar words while reading. Notice if there is evidence of new learning based on the goal of this minilesson.

- Can students use context to derive the meaning of an unfamiliar word?
- Are they using language such as *context, synonym, antonym,* and *example*?

Minilesson

To help students think about how to learn the meaning of new or unfamiliar words, engage them in noticing and using context clues. Here is an example.

- Display the cover of *Exploding Ants* and the prepared chart paper. Read the first example.

  What do you think the word *lure* means?

  How does the author of this book help you understand what it means?

  Sometimes authors provide explanations in the other words or sentences surrounding the word. These are called context clues.

- Highlight the words *imitate the flash patterns of other species* and *the females attack* on the chart. Write *Explanation* in the third column of the chart.

- Read the second example.

  What clues in the text help you understand what the word *mimics* means?

  Sometimes an author provides a synonym, or another word that means the same thing, to help you understand what a new word means. *Copies* and *mimics* are synonyms.

- Highlight the word *copies* and write *Synonym* in the third column.

- Read aloud the third example and help students understand that the author uses an antonym (*extra*) to illustrate the meaning of *scarce*.

Have a Try

Invite the students to talk with a partner about the meaning of another word.

▶ Show the cover of *Rotten!* Read the example sentence on the chart.

Turn and talk to your partner about how the author of this book helps you understand what the word *elements* means.

▶ After time for discussion, invite a few students to share their thinking. Highlight the clues they mention and write *Example* in the third column.

Summarize and Apply

Summarize the learning and remind students to use context clues to determine the meaning of unfamiliar words.

How do authors sometimes help you understand what unfamiliar words mean?

▶ Write the principle at the top of the chart.

If you come across a word you don't understand while you're reading today, read carefully to see if there are any context clues in the surrounding words or sentences that help you understand its meaning.

Share

Following independent reading time, gather students together in the meeting area to discuss how they figured out the meaning of an unfamiliar word.

Did anyone encounter a new word in the book you read today?

How did you figure out its meaning?

Extend the Lesson (Optional)

After assessing students' understanding, you might decide to extend the learning. During interactive read-aloud, model how to derive the meaning of a new word.

▶ Teach students how to use a similar technique for thinking about the meaning of technical words and author-created words in science fiction.

A writer provides information within the text to help you understand what a word means.

	Text	Type
	"These [female fireflies] can imitate the flash patterns of other species ... to lure in males. Then ... the females attack." (p. 9)	Explanation
exploding ants	"It could really be a ... caterpillar that copies or mimics the colors and shape of a dropping ..." (p. 8)	Synonym
	"The extra food provided by the repletes is important ... Honey ants live in ... dry desert regions ... where food is often scarce." (p.17)	Antonym
ROTTEN	"Everything in the world—a beetle, a tree, a whale—is made of atoms of elements, such as carbon, oxygen, and nitrogen." (p. 2)	Example

Reading Minilesson Principle
Word parts help you understand what a word means.

Deriving Word Meanings

You Will Need

- two or three books that contain new or unfamiliar vocabulary, such as the following:
  - *Rotten!* by Anita Sanchez, from Text Set: Life on Earth
  - *Exploding Ants* by Joanne Settel, from Text Set: Animal Adaptations
- chart paper prepared with sentences from the chosen texts
- markers

Academic Language / Important Vocabulary

- prefix
- suffix
- base word

Continuum Connection

- Understand and discuss the concept of prefixes and recognize their use in determining the meaning of some English words (p. 388)
- Understand and discuss the concept of suffixes and recognize their use in determining the meaning of some English words (p. 389)
- Recognize and use word parts to solve an unknown word and understand its meaning: e.g., *conference*—prefix *con-* ("with or together"), Latin root *fer* ("to bring" or "to carry"), suffix *-ence* ("state of" or "quality of") (p. 391)

Goal

Understand that word roots, base words, suffixes, and prefixes can be used to figure out the meaning of a word.

Rationale

When students know to look at the parts of a word (e.g., prefix, suffix, base word, word root) to solve for meaning, they can problem solve more efficiently and keep their attention on the overall meaning of a text.

Assess Learning

Observe students when they encounter unfamiliar words while reading. Notice if there is evidence of new learning based on the goal of this minilesson.

- ▶ Do students look for known word parts when they encounter unfamiliar words?
- ▶ Can they identify the base word or word root and its prefix and/or suffix?
- ▶ Are they using language such as *prefix, suffix,* and *base word*?

Minilesson

To help students think about the minilesson principle, engage them in using word parts to determine the meanings of unfamiliar words. Here is an example.

- ▶ Read the first sentence on the chart from *Rotten!* and underline the word *decomposition.*

  The author defines this word for you in the sentence, but there are other ways to figure out what this word means. Look closely at the word *decomposition.* Do you recognize any parts of the word?

- ▶ Show how the word can be broken down into the prefix (*de-*), the base word (*compose*), and the suffix (*-tion*). Note that the spelling of *compose* is changed when the suffix is added.

  Sometimes you can figure out what an unfamiliar word means by looking for parts that you do know. The prefix *de-* at the beginning of the word means "reversal" or "removal." The base word in the middle, *compose,* means "to put together the parts of something." The suffix at the end, *-tion*, means "the act or process of." By breaking the word into parts, or *decomposing* it, you can determine that *decomposition* is the process of breaking something down into its parts!

- ▶ Continue in a similar manner with the word *uncountable.*

Have a Try

Invite the students to talk with a partner about the meaning of another word.

▶ Read the final example sentence on the chart. Underline the word *motionlessly*.

> Turn and talk to your partner about what you think the word *motionlessly* means. Remember to look for parts of the word that you recognize.

▶ After time for discussion, invite a few pairs to share how they determined the meaning of the word. Record responses on the chart.

Summarize and Apply

Summarize the learning and remind students to use word parts to determine the meanings of unfamiliar words.

▶ Review the chart and write the principle at the top.

> If you come across a word you don't know as you read today, look for parts of the word that you recognize and see if you can use them to figure out what the word means.

Word parts help you understand what a word means.		
	"Decomposition is the process of breaking something down into its pieces. And as the bug, tree, or whale decomposes, all the uncountable billions of atoms ..." (p. 2)	de / compose / tion —the process of breaking something down into its pieces
		un / count / able —not able to be counted
exploding ants	"... the caterpillar also holds its body in the shape of a dropping and rests motionlessly on a leaf." (p. 8)	motion / less / ly —doing something without moving

Share

Following independent reading time, gather students together in the meeting area to discuss how they figured out the meaning of an unfamiliar word.

> Did anyone use word parts to figure out what a word means today?

Extend the Lesson (Optional)

After assessing students' understanding, you might decide to extend the learning.

▶ Support this behavior in guided or independent reading. From the *Fountas & Pinnell Prompting Guide, Part 1, for Oral Reading and Early Writing (*Fountas and Pinnell 2009), use prompts such as the following:

- *Look at the prefix.*
- *Look at the suffix.*
- *Do you see a part that might help you?*

RML 3

SAS.U2.RML3

Reading Minilesson Principle
Greek and Latin roots help you understand what a word means.

Deriving Word Meanings

You Will Need

- two or three books that contain new or unfamiliar vocabulary with Greek or Latin roots, such as the following:
  - *Exploding Ants* by Joanne Settel, from Text Set: Animal Adaptations
  - *Rotten!* by Anita Sanchez, from Text Set: Life on Earth
- chart paper prepared with sentences from the chosen texts
- markers
- highlighter or highlighting tape

Academic Language / Important Vocabulary

- root

Continuum Connection

- Understand and discuss the concept of Latin roots and recognize their use in determining the meanings of some English words (p. 389)
- Understand and discuss the concept of Greek roots and recognize their use in determining the meaning of some English words (p. 389)
- Recognize and use prefixes, suffixes, and word roots that have Greek and Latin origins to understand word meaning: e.g., incredible—*in-* ("not"), Latin *cred* ("believe") and *-ible* ("capable of"); antibiotic—*anti-* ("opposite" or "against"), Greek *bio* ("life"), and *-ic* ("related to") (p. 389)

Goal

Understand that knowledge of Greek and Latin roots can be used to figure out what a word means.

Rationale

Many words in the English language come from Greek or Latin. Exposing students to and teaching them a variety of Greek and Latin roots supports them in independently reading and understanding unfamiliar vocabulary.

Assess Learning

Observe students when they encounter unfamiliar words while reading. Notice if there is evidence of new learning based on the goal of this minilesson.

- ▶ Do students determine the meanings of unfamiliar words by using their knowledge of Greek and Latin roots?
- ▶ Do they understand this usage of the word *root*?

Minilesson

To help students think about the minilesson principle, engage them in using Greek and Latin roots to determine the meanings of unfamiliar words. Here is an example.

▶ Read the first sentence on the chart from *Exploding Ants* and highlight the word *microscopic*.

> What do you notice about the word *microscopic*? What word parts have you seen in other words?
>
> What other words have the word part *scope*?
>
> Many English words have roots that originally came from Latin or Greek. *Scope* is a word root that came from Greek and means "see." Some English words, like *microscope, telescope, stethoscope,* and *horoscope,* were created by adding prefixes to *scope.*

▶ Record notes and examples about the Greek root *scope* on the chart.

▶ Read the second example sentence, from *Rotten!,* on the chart.

> *Carnivores* contains the Latin root *carn,* which means "flesh" or "meat." What do you think the word *carnivores* means?
>
> What other words do you know that contain the root *carn*?

▶ Record responses on the chart.

Have a Try

Invite the students to talk with a partner about the meaning of another word.

▶ Read the third example sentence on the chart. Highlight the word *structure*.

   Struct is a Latin root that means "build." Turn and talk to your partner about the definition of the word *structure* and about any other words you know that contain this Latin root.

▶ After students turn and talk, invite a few students to share their thinking. Record responses on the chart.

Summarize and Apply

Summarize the learning and remind students to use Greek and Latin roots to determine the meanings of unfamiliar words.

▶ Review the chart and write the principle at the top.

   If you come across a word you don't know as you read today, look for parts of the word that you recognize and see if you can use them to figure out what the word means.

Share

Following independent reading time, gather students together in the meeting area to discuss how they solved unfamiliar words in their reading.

   Did anyone recognize a root in a word from your reading today?

   What other words have the same root?

Extend the Lesson (Optional)

After assessing students' understanding, you might decide to extend the learning.

▶ Teach additional Greek and Latin roots (download a list from resources.fountasandpinnell.com) when you lead word study lessons.

Greek and Latin roots help you understand what a word means.

	Meaning	Latin or Greek Root	Other Words
"The small, toothless, lamprey larva burrows into mud, where it feeds on microscopic organisms called plankton." (p. 27)	too small to see	scope (Greek: see)	telescope stethoscope horoscope
"Its wormy body is eaten by carnivores such as dogs." (p. 21)	meat eaters	carn (Latin: flesh, meat)	carnage carnival
". . . all the uncountable billions of atoms that made up its structure are freed . . ." (p. 2)	the way something is constructed	struct (Latin: build)	construction destructive instruction

Section 3: Strategies and Skills

Deriving Word Meanings

You Will Need

- two or three books that contain good examples of words with strong connotations, such as the following:
  - *Rotten!* by Anita Sanchez, from Text Set: Life on Earth
  - *Under the Royal Palms* by Alma Flor Ada, from Text Set: Memoir/Autobiography
- chart paper prepared with sentences from the chosen texts
- markers

Academic Language / Important Vocabulary

- connotative
- connotation

Continuum Connection

- Understand the connotative meanings of words that are essential to understanding the text (p. 86)

Goal

Understand the connotative meanings of words.

Rationale

Words have both denotative and connotative meanings. A word's denotation is its dictionary definition, while its connotation carries emotions and attitudes (e.g., *house, home; smile, smirk*). When students think about the connotative meanings of words, they are better able to infer deeper meaning and author intent.

Assess Learning

Observe students when they discuss the connotative meanings of words. Notice if there is evidence of new learning based on the goal of this minilesson.

- ▶ Do students understand how connotative meaning differs from denotative meaning?
- ▶ Can students explain the connotative meaning of a familiar word?
- ▶ Do they understand and use the terms *connotative* and *connotation*?

Minilesson

To help students think about the minilesson principle, use example sentences from familiar books to engage students in noticing connotative meaning. Here is an example.

- ▶ Show the prepared chart paper. Read the first example sentences from *Rotten!* and *Under the Royal Palms*.

   Think about the words *smelly* and *fragrant*. How are their meanings similar?

   How are their meanings different?

   Smelly and *fragrant* have similar basic meanings—they both refer to something with a strong smell. However, when you hear the word *smelly*, you probably think of something that smells bad, and when you hear the word *fragrant*, you probably think of something that smells pleasant. These words have different connotative meanings. A word's connotative meaning is the feeling or attitude that you think of when you hear it.

   What other words have a similar meaning to *smelly* or to *fragrant*?

- ▶ Ask students whether each identified word has negative or positive connotations.

Have a Try

Invite the students to talk with a partner about the connotative meaning of another word.

▶ Read the second example sentence from *Under the Royal Palms* on the chart.

> Turn and talk to your partner about the connotative meaning of the word *odd*. What do you think when you hear someone or something being described as odd? Does this seem like a positive or a negative adjective?

▶ After time for discussion, invite a few students to share their thinking. Then invite students to share other words with a similar meaning to *odd* (e.g., *strange, weird, bizarre, unique, eccentric, extraordinary*). Discuss each word's connotative meaning.

Summarize and Apply

Summarize the learning and remind students to think about the connotative meanings of words.

> When you think about the connotative meanings of words, you can get a better idea of what an author *really* means or what a character is *really* thinking or feeling.

▶ Write the principle at the top of the chart.

> When you read today, choose one word from your book that has strong negative or positive connotations. Be ready to talk about the word you chose when we come back together.

Share

Following independent reading time, gather students together in small groups to discuss the connotative meanings of words.

> Talk in your group about words that have strong negative or positive connotations. Why did the authors choose those words?

Extend the Lesson (Optional)

After assessing students' understanding, you might decide to extend the learning.

▶ Teach students how to use context clues to determine if a word is being used in a strictly literal sense or in a connotative sense.

▶ Help students use the connotative meanings of words to infer a nonfiction author's attitude toward the subject of the text.

Understand the connotative meaning of a word.

"Decomposition isn't always ugly and disgusting. And, believe it or not, it isn't always smelly." (p. 3)

Smelly – has an unpleasant smell; negative connotation

"the delightful warmth of the night, fragrant with the aroma of jasmine and gardenias." (p. 14)

Fragrant – has a pleasant smell; positive connotation

"To many in town we had always been an odd family." (p. 34)

Odd – unusual; slightly negative connotation

Section 3: Strategies and Skills

Assessment

After you have taught the minilessons in this umbrella, observe students as they talk and write about their reading across instructional contexts: interactive read-aloud, independent reading, guided reading, shared reading, and book club. Use *The Literacy Continuum* (Fountas and Pinnell 2017) to guide the observation of students' reading and writing behaviors.

▶ What evidence do you have of new understandings related to deriving word meanings?

  • Can students use context clues to derive the meanings of unfamiliar words?

  • Do they use word parts (word roots, base words, suffixes, prefixes, Greek and Latin roots) to help them determine the meanings of unfamiliar words?

  • Can they explain the connotative meaning of a familiar word?

  • Are they using academic language, such as *prefix*, *suffix*, *root*, and *connotative*?

▶ In what other ways, beyond the scope of this umbrella, are students using strategies and skills to understand what they read?

  • Do students know how to break apart words?

  • Are they able to monitor their comprehension while reading difficult texts?

Use your observations to determine the next umbrella you will teach. You may also consult Minilessons Across the Year (pp. 61–64) for guidance.

Link to Writing

After teaching the minilessons in this umbrella, help students link the new learning to their own writing:

▶ When students write independently, encourage them to think about how they can help their readers understand unfamiliar words. Remind them to pay attention to the connotative meanings of the words they use.

Reader's Notebook

When this umbrella is complete, provide a copy of the minilesson principles (see resources.fountasandpinnell.com) for students to glue in the reader's notebook (in the Minilessons section if using *Reader's Notebook: Advanced* [Fountas and Pinnell 2011]), so they can refer to the information as needed.

Minilessons in This Umbrella

RML1 Writers use connectives to add on to an idea.

RML2 Writers use connectives to show the passage of time or to sequence something.

RML3 Writers use connectives to show cause and effect.

RML4 Writers use connectives to show a different or opposite point of view.

RML5 Writers use connectives to show the connection of ideas in formal presentations.

Before Teaching Umbrella 3 Minilessons

Connectives are words and phrases that help readers understand the relationships between and among ideas. Simple connectives are *and*, *or*, and *but*. As students read more complex texts, they encounter more sophisticated connectives, many of which are rare in everyday oral language—for example, *nevertheless*, *as a result*, or *consequently*. Overlooking connectives in a text can lead to a misunderstanding of the ideas the writer is presenting. A list of connectives and phrases can be found in the appendix for grammar, usage, and mechanics in *The Literacy Continuum* (Fountas and Pinnell 2017, 642–644) and in the online resources.

Read and discuss books with a variety of connectives. The minilessons in this umbrella use the following books from the *Fountas & Pinnell Classroom™ Interactive Read-Aloud Collection* text sets; however, you can choose any books from your classroom library.

Life on Earth

Grand Canyon by Jason Chin

Rotten! Vultures, Beetles, Slime, and Nature's Other Decomposers by Anita Sanchez

Mountains by Seymour Simon

Buried Sunlight: How Fossil Fuels Have Changed the Earth by Molly Bang and Penny Chisholm

Scientists at Work

Scaly Spotted Feathered Frilled: How Do We Know What Dinosaurs Really Looked Like? by Catherine Thimmesh

As you read aloud and enjoy these texts together, help students notice how the author has used connectives to show the relationships between and among ideas.

Life on Earth

Scientists at Work

Section 3: Strategies and Skills

Understanding Connectives

- a few familiar books that use a variety of connectives to add on to ideas, such as the following:
  - *Scaly Spotted Feathered Frilled* by Catherine Thimmesh, from Text Set: Scientists at Work
  - *Grand Canyon* by Jason Chin and *Buried Sunlight* by Molly Bang and Penny Chisholm, from Text Set: Life on Earth
- chart paper prepared with example sentences from the chosen books
- a highlighter

Academic Language / Important Vocabulary

- connectives

Continuum Connection

- Understand (when listening) some sophisticated connectives (words that link ideas and clarify meaning) that are used in written texts but do not appear often in everyday oral language: e.g., *although, however, meantime, meanwhile, moreover, otherwise, therefore, though, unless, until, whenever, yet* (p. 82)
- Understand the meaning of common (simple), sophisticated, and academic connectives when listening to a nonfiction text read aloud (p. 86)

Goal

Learn connectives that are used to add on to an idea.

Rationale

When students notice connectives that writers use to add on to an idea, they think about the relationships between details and ideas and better understand the text.

Assess Learning

Observe students when they talk about connectives. Notice if there is evidence of new learning based on the goal of this minilesson.

- Do students understand the purpose of connectives?
- Can they identify connectives that add on to an idea?
- Do they use the term *connectives*?

Minilesson

To help students think about the minilesson principle, engage them in noticing connectives that writers use to add on to ideas. Here is an example.

- Read the last sentence of the italicized text on page 32 of *Scaly Spotted Feathered Frilled*. Then read the first sentence on the chart, which is the next sentence in the book.

  The author has just told you about soft structures on a dinosaur. What information does the author tell you in this sentence?

  The author adds on to the first idea by introducing additional information: dinosaurs also have bony structures. What word or phrase does she use to show how the two ideas are connected?

- Highlight the phrase *In addition to*.
- Read the second example, from page 17 of *Grand Canyon*.

  What is the main idea the author is telling you in this sentence?

  The author tells you that the condor is the largest land bird in North America.

  How does the author add specific details to support this idea?

- Highlight the word *with* and the phrase *as much as*.

  With and *as much as* are connectives because they connect ideas or details together. These words add information on to an idea.

Have a Try

Invite the students to talk with a partner about connectives that add on to an idea.

▶ Read the first two sentences on page 5 of *Buried Sunlight*. Then read the last sentence on the chart.

   Turn and talk to your partner about how the authors connect ideas in this sentence.

▶ After students turn and talk, invite a few pairs to share their thinking. Highlight *Like*.

Summarize and Apply

Summarize the learning and remind students to notice connectives when they read.

   Why do writers use connectives like the ones highlighted on the chart?

▶ Write the principle at the top of the chart.

   When you read today, notice how the author of your book uses connectives to add on to ideas. Be ready to share an example from your book when we come back together.

Share

Following independent reading time, gather students together in the meeting area to talk about connectives.

   Who would like to share an example of how the author of your book used connectives to add on to ideas?

Extend the Lesson (Optional)

After assessing students' understanding, you might decide to extend the learning.

▶ Point out connectives during interactive read-aloud. Talk with the students about how connectives help make writing smoother and more fluent in addition to linking ideas.

▶ Provide a list of connectives that are used to add on to an idea (e.g., *in fact, besides, what's more, moreover, specifically, furthermore, I also*; see also *The Literacy Continuum* pp. 642–644 and resources.fountasandpinnell.com) that students can use as a resource when they do their own writing. Add to the list as students discover new connectives in their reading.

Writers use connectives to add on to an idea.

"In addition to soft structures, there are hard, bony elements . . ." (Scaly Spotted Feathered Frilled, p. 32)

"With a 9-foot wingspan, and weighing as much as 23 pounds, the condor is the largest land bird in North America." (Grand Canyon, p. 17)

"Like dinosaurs, [fossil fuels] are ancient life that was buried deep underground." (Buried Sunlight, p. 5)

Section 3: Strategies and Skills

Reading Minilesson Principle
Writers use connectives to show the passage of time or to sequence something.

You Will Need

- a few familiar books that use a variety of connectives to show the passage of time, such as the following from Text Set: Life on Earth:
  - *Grand Canyon* by Jason Chin
  - *Mountains* by Seymour Simon
  - *Buried Sunlight* by Molly Bang and Penny Chisholm
- chart paper prepared with example sentences from the chosen books
- a highlighter

Academic Language / Important Vocabulary

- connectives
- sequence

Continuum Connection

- Understand (when listening) some sophisticated connectives (words that link ideas and clarify meaning) that are used in written texts but do not appear often in everyday oral language: e.g., *although, however, meantime, meanwhile, moreover, otherwise, therefore, though, unless, until, whenever, yet* (p. 82)
- Understand the meaning of common (simple), sophisticated, and academic connectives when listening to a nonfiction text read aloud (p. 86)

Goal

Notice how writers use connecting words to show the passage of time or to sequence something.

Rationale

When students pay attention to connectives that show the passage of time (e.g., *meanwhile, yet, finally, later*), they better understand sequences and series of events.

Assess Learning

Observe students when they talk about connectives. Notice if there is evidence of new learning based on the goal of this minilesson.

- Can students identify connectives that show the passage of time or sequence something?
- Do they use the terms *connectives* and *sequence*?

Minilesson

To help students think about the minilesson principle, engage them in noticing connectives that show the passage of time or sequence something. Here is an example.

- Read the second and third sentences on page 17 of *Grand Canyon*.

  How are the ideas in these two sentences related?

  The author first tells you about condors in the ice age and then he tells you that the population has declined over time. What words show how the ideas are related?

- Direct students' attention to the first sentence on the prepared chart and highlight *Since then*.

- Read the second sentence on the chart, from *Mountains*.

  What does this sentence tell you about when the Alps were formed?

  They were formed at the same time as the two plates were pushing against one another. Which word tells you that?

- Highlight the word *as*.

  Since then and *as* are connectives. The words *since then* show you that time has passed. The word *as* tells you when things are happening.

Have a Try

Invite the students to talk with a partner about connectives that show the passage of time or sequence something.

▶ Read the text in the middle of page 13 in *Buried Sunlight* ("Back then"). Then direct students' attention to the third sentence on the chart.

> How do the authors let you know that bacteria evolved into plants over time? Turn and talk to your partner about this.

▶ After time for discussion, invite a few students to share their thinking. Highlight *Eventually*.

Summarize and Apply

Summarize the learning and remind students to notice connectives that show the passage of time or sequence something.

> Why do writers use connectives like the highlighted words on the chart?

▶ Write the principle at the top of the chart.

> When you read today, notice how the author of your book uses connectives to show the passage of time or to sequence something. Be ready to share an example from your book when we come back together.

Share

Following independent reading time, gather students together in the meeting area to talk about connectives.

> Who would like to share an example you found of a connective that helped show the passage of time or sequence something?

Extend the Lesson (Optional)

After assessing students' understanding, you might decide to extend the learning.

▶ Provide a list of connectives that are used to show the passage of time or to sequence something (e.g., *at first, after, later, until, when, in the meantime, meanwhile, whenever, yet, finally, ultimately, as soon as, during*; see also *The Literacy Continuum* pp. 642–644 and resources.fountasandpinnell.com) that students can use as a resource when they do their own writing. Continue adding to the list as students discover new connectives in their reading.

Writers use connectives to show the passage of time or to sequence something.

"Since then, their population has declined . . ." (Grand Canyon, p. 17)

"The Alps are folded mountains that formed as the Eurasian plate pushed against the African plate." (Mountains, p. 10)

"Eventually, some of those tiny bacteria evolved into tiny green plants!" (Buried Sunlight, p. 13)

Section 3: Strategies and Skills

You Will Need

- a few familiar books that use a variety of connectives to show cause and effect, such as the following:
  - *Mountains* by Seymour Simon and *Rotten!* by Anita Sanchez, from Text Set: Life on Earth
  - *Scaly Spotted Feathered Frilled* by Catherine Thimmesh, from Text Set: Scientists at Work
- chart paper prepared with example sentences from the chosen books
- a highlighter

Academic Language / Important Vocabulary

- connectives
- cause
- effect

Continuum Connection

- Understand (when listening) some sophisticated connectives (words that link ideas and clarify meaning) that are used in written texts but do not appear often in everyday oral language: e.g., *although, however, meantime, meanwhile, moreover, otherwise, therefore, though, unless, until, whenever, yet* (p. 82)
- Understand the meaning of common (simple), sophisticated, and academic connectives when listening to a nonfiction text read aloud (p. 86)

Goal

Learn connectives that show cause and effect.

Rationale

When students notice connectives that show cause and effect, they understand that the author is explaining a cause-and-effect relationship and better understand the ideas in the text.

Assess Learning

Observe students when they talk about connectives. Notice if there is evidence of new learning based on the goal of this minilesson.

- Can students identify connectives that show cause and effect?
- Do they understand and use the terms *connectives, cause,* and *effect*?

Minilesson

To help students think about the minilesson principle, engage them in noticing connectives that show cause and effect. Here is an example.

- Show the cover of *Mountains* and display the prepared chart. Read the first example.

  Why are mountains always cold?

  The author tells you that the cause is the cold temperatures. What word connects the cause and the effect?

- Highlight the word *so.*
- Show the cover of *Rotten!* and read the second example.

  Why is there lots of good nutrition left after a cow has finished lunch? What is the cause of this?

  What word shows the relationship between cause and effect?

- Highlight the word *because.*

  The words *so* and *because* are connectives because they connect a cause to an effect.

Have a Try

Invite the students to talk with a partner about connectives that show cause and effect.

▶ Show the cover of *Scaly Spotted Feathered Frilled* and read the third example.

Why was Waterhouse's dinosaur sculpture similar to an iguana? Turn and talk to your partner about what connective the author uses to show that she's explaining a cause and an effect.

▶ After students turn and talk, invite a few pairs to share their thinking. Highlight *Since*.

Summarize and Apply

Summarize the learning and remind students to notice connectives that are used to show cause and effect.

Why do writers use connectives like *so*, *because*, and *since*?

▶ Write the principle at the top of the chart.

When you read today, notice if the author of your book uses connectives to show cause and effect. If you find an example, bring it to share when we come back together.

Share

Following independent reading time, gather students together in the meeting area to talk about connectives.

Did anyone find an example of a connective that shows cause and effect or any other words that connect ideas?

Extend the Lesson (Optional)

After assessing students' understanding, you might decide to extend the learning.

▶ Provide a list of connectives that are used to show cause and effect (e.g., *so*, *because*, *since*, *hence*, *as a result*, *consequently*, *for*, *as a consequence*; see also *The Literacy Continuum* pp. 642–644 and resources.fountasandpinnell.com) for students to use as a resource for their own writing.

Writers use connectives to show cause and effect.

"Air temperature drops about three degrees Fahrenheit for every thousand feet of altitude, so the peaks of many tall mountains . . . are always cold . . ." (Mountains, p. 5)

"Because plants can be tough to digest, there's still lots of good nutrition left after a cow has finished lunch." (Rotten!, p. 8)

"Since the teeth were remarkably similar to a modern-day iguana's . . . , Waterhouse essentially sculpted a very large, modified iguana." (Scaly Spotted Feathered Frilled, p. 11)

Reading Minilesson Principle
Writers use connectives to show a different or opposite point of view.

Understanding Connectives

You Will Need

▶ a few familiar books that use a variety of connectives to show a different point of view, such as the following from Text Set: Life on Earth:

- *Grand Canyon* by Jason Chin
- *Mountains* by Seymour Simon
- *Rotten!* by Anita Sanchez

▶ chart paper prepared with example sentences from the chosen books

▶ a highlighter

Academic Language / Important Vocabulary

▶ connectives
▶ point of view

Continuum Connection

▶ Understand (when listening) some sophisticated connectives (words that link ideas and clarify meaning) that are used in written texts but do not appear often in everyday oral language: e.g., *although, however, meantime, meanwhile, moreover, otherwise, therefore, though, unless, until, whenever, yet* (p. 82)

▶ Understand the meaning of common (simple), sophisticated, and academic connectives when listening to a nonfiction text read aloud (p. 86)

Goal

Learn connectives that show a different or opposite point of view.

Rationale

When students notice connectives that show a different or opposite point of view, they understand that the author is describing contrasting ideas and better understand the ideas in the text.

Assess Learning

Observe students when they talk about connectives. Notice if there is evidence of new learning based on the goal of this minilesson.

▶ Can students identify connectives that show a different or opposite point of view?

▶ Do they understand and use the terms *connectives* and *point of view*?

Minilesson

To help students think about the minilesson principle, engage them in noticing connectives that show a different or opposite point of view. Here is an example.

▶ Show the cover of *Grand Canyon* and display the prepared chart. Read the first example.

> What do you notice about the beginning of the sentence and the end of the sentence?

> The author tells two different and opposite ideas. How does he show that?

▶ Highlight the word *while*.

▶ Show the cover of *Mountains* and read the second example.

> Why does the author use the word *however* in this sentence?

> The author uses the connective *however* to show two opposite ideas or points of view. He explains that, unlike a different kind of mountain, the magma does not come to the surface when a dome mountain is formed. What connective in the second sentence is used to show a different point of view?

▶ Highlight the words *However* and *Instead*.

Have a Try

Invite the students to talk with a partner about connectives that show a different or opposite point of view.

▶ Show the cover of *Rotten!* and read the third example.

> Turn and talk to your partner about what connective the author uses to show that she's showing two different points of view.

▶ After students turn and talk, invite a few pairs to share their thinking. Highlight the word *actually*.

Summarize and Apply

Summarize the learning and remind students to notice connectives that show a different or opposite point of view.

> Why do writers use connectives like *while, however, instead,* and *actually*?

▶ Write the principle at the top of the chart.

> When you read today, notice if the author of your book uses connectives to show a different or opposite point of view. If you find an example, bring it to share when we come back together.

Share

Following independent reading time, gather students together in the meeting area to talk about connectives.

> Who found an example of a connective that shows a different or opposite point of view?

Extend the Lesson (Optional)

After assessing students' understanding, you might decide to extend the learning.

▶ Provide a list of connectives that are used to show a different or opposite point of view (e.g., *despite, but, although, however, on the other hand, while, instead, actually, otherwise, whereas;* see also *The Literacy Continuum* pp. 642–644 and resources.fountasandpinnell.com) for students to use as a resource for their own writing.

Writers use connectives to show a different or opposite point of view.

> "Many of these creatures are permanent residents . . ., while others are visitors . . ." (Grand Canyon, p. 5)

> "However, in dome mountains, the magma does not come to the surface. Instead, the molten rock pushes the ground up . . ." (Mountains, p. 17)

> "More proof that dung beetles are sacred sun gods in disguise? Actually, the beetles are using the sun as a compass, to help them find their burrow." (Rotten!, p. 8)

Reading Minilesson Principle

Writers use connectives to show the connection of ideas in formal presentations.

Understanding Connectives

You Will Need

- a brief presentation about a familiar topic and that contains a variety of connectives written on chart paper or displayed via a document camera

- a highlighter

- a short video clip of a formal presentation (such as a TED Talk) that includes a variety of connectives

Academic Language / Important Vocabulary

- connectives
- formal presentation

Continuum Connection

- Understand (when listening) some sophisticated connectives (words that link ideas and clarify meaning) that are used in written texts but do not appear often in everyday oral language: e.g., *although, however, meantime, meanwhile, moreover, otherwise, therefore, though, unless, until, whenever, yet* (p. 82)

- Understand the meaning of common (simple), sophisticated, and academic connectives when listening to a nonfiction text read aloud (p. 86)

Goal

Learn connectives that are used in formal presentations.

Rationale

When students notice connectives in formal presentations, they better understand the connections between the ideas and details. They are also more likely to use connectives when they give their own presentations.

Assess Learning

Observe students when they talk about connectives. Notice if there is evidence of new learning based on the goal of this minilesson.

- Can students identify connectives used in a formal presentation?

- Can they explain how the identified connectives show the connections between ideas?

- Do they understand and use the terms *connectives* and *formal presentation*?

Minilesson

To help students think about the minilesson principle, engage them in noticing connectives in formal presentations. Here is an example.

> We've been talking about how writers use connectives to show the relationship of ideas. I've prepared a formal presentation summarizing some of the things we've been discussing about connectives. As you listen to my presentation, notice how I show how my ideas are connected.

- Deliver the formal presentation that you prepared before class. Then, display the text of the presentation on chart paper or project it so that everyone can see.

> What do you notice about how I showed the connections between my ideas?

> What connectives did I use?

- Highlight (or have students highlight) the connectives on the chart paper.

Have a Try

Invite the students to talk with a partner about connectives in formal presentations.

▶ Play a short clip from a video of a formal presentation (such as a TED Talk). Tell students to make a note of any connectives they hear.

> Turn and talk to your partner about how the presenter showed the connections between her ideas. What connectives did you hear?

▶ After students turn and talk, invite a few pairs to share their thinking.

Summarize and Apply

Summarize the learning and remind students to notice connectives in formal presentations.

> Why do writers use connectives in formal presentations?

▶ Write the principle at the top of the chart.

▶ During independent reading time, you can give your students the opportunity to listen to other formal presentations online. If so, provide them with the necessary technology and a list of trusted sources of age-appropriate presentations. Or, they can read a book as usual.

> Whether you listen to another formal presentation or read a book, pay attention to the connectives you notice. Be ready to share when we come back together.

Share

Following independent reading time, gather students together in the meeting area to talk about connectives.

> Who noticed a connective today? Share what you noticed and what it shows.

Extend the Lesson (Optional)

After assessing students' understanding, you might decide to extend the learning.

▶ Have students give a formal presentation about a familiar topic. Remind them to use connectives to show the connections between ideas, as appropriate.

▶ Provide a list of connectives that are frequently used in formal presentations (e.g., *despite, although, however, for example, as a result, in fact, ultimately, on the other hand*; see also *The Literacy Continuum* pp. 642–644 and resources.fountasandpinnell.com) for students to use as a resource.

> **Writers use connectives to show the connection of ideas in formal presentations.**
>
> Writers use connectives for different reasons. While some connectives are used to add on to an idea, others are used to show cause and effect or a different point of view. In addition, writers use connectives to show the passage of time or to sequence something. As a result, the connections between their ideas are clear. Furthermore, their writing flows smoothly. However, don't overuse them—not every sentence needs a connective!

Assessment

After you have taught the minilessons in this umbrella, observe students as they talk and write about their reading across instructional contexts: interactive read-aloud, independent reading, guided reading, shared reading, and book club. Use *The Literacy Continuum* (Fountas and Pinnell 2017) to guide the observation of students' reading and writing behaviors.

▶ What evidence do you have of new understandings related to understanding connectives?

 • Do students notice connectives and phrases that show relationships between and among ideas?

 • Do they understand that different connectives have different purposes?

 • Are they using connectives when they discuss their reading?

 • Do they use connectives when giving formal presentations?

 • Do they understand and use academic vocabulary, such as *connective, sequence, cause, effect,* and *point of view*?

▶ In what other ways, beyond the scope of this umbrella, are students paying attention to language?

 • Do students use context to read unfamiliar words?

Use your observations to determine the next umbrella you will teach. You may also consult Minilessons Across the Year (pp. 61–64) for guidance.

Link to Writing

After teaching the minilessons in this umbrella, help students link the new learning to their own writing:

▶ Encourage students to use a wide variety of connectives in their own writing. Display lists of various types of connectives in the classroom.

Reader's Notebook

When this umbrella is complete, provide a copy of the minilesson principles (see resources.fountasandpinnell.com) for students to glue in the reader's notebook (in the Minilessons section if using *Reader's Notebook: Advanced* [Fountas and Pinnell 2011]), so they can refer to the information as needed.

Minilessons in This Umbrella

RML1   Notice how the author wants you to read the sentence.

RML2   Make your reading sound smooth and interesting.

RML3   Use your voice to reflect the tone of the text you are reading.

RML4   Show in your voice when a writer means something different than the words alone indicate.

Before Teaching Umbrella 4 Minilessons

Read aloud and discuss books with a variety of punctuation marks and print features, such as commas, ellipses, dashes, colons, and italics. Include books that contain a wide array of ways that authors convey meaning, such as through tone and irony. Use a variety of large books, small books projected with a document camera, posters, or examples of shared writing—anything large enough for students to see the print. Your primary focus is first to support the meaning and enjoyment of the text before focusing on reading the text fluently. For this umbrella, use these suggested books from the *Fountas & Pinnell Classroom™ Interactive Read-Aloud Collection* text sets, or you can use books or student writing samples from your classroom.

Kindness and Compassion

Chachaji's Cup by Uma Krishnaswami

The Hundredth Name by Shulamith Levey Oppenheim

Wings by Christopher Myers

Memoir/Autobiography

Where Fireflies Dance by Lucha Corpi

Inspiration/Creativity

World Make Way: New Poems Inspired by Art from The Metropolitan Museum of Art, edited by Lee Bennett Hopkins

Steel Drumming at the Apollo: The Road to Super Top Dog by Trish Marx

Exploring Identity

Garvey's Choice by Nikki Grimes

As you read aloud and enjoy these texts together, help students

- notice the punctuation marks and font styles in sentences,

- think about how to make their voices sound when they read aloud,

- read fluently and with expression, and

- read in a way that represents the intentions of the writer.

Kindness and Compassion

Memoir/Autobiography

Inspiration/Creativity

Exploring Identity

Section 3: Strategies and Skills

RML1

SAS.U4.RML1

Reading Minilesson Principle
Notice how the author wants you to read the sentence.

Maintaining Fluency

You Will Need

- several familiar books with a variety of punctuation marks and font styles, such as the following:
  - *Chachaji's Cup* by Uma Krishnaswami and *The Hundredth Name* by Shulamith Levey Oppenheim, from Text Set: Kindness and Compassion
  - *World Make Way* edited by Lee Bennett Hopkins, from Text Set: Inspiration/Creativity
- chart paper prepared with the punctuation in red
- markers
- books students are reading independently or basket of books
- document camera (optional)

Academic Language / Important Vocabulary

- fluency
- punctuation
- dialogue
- ellipses
- dash
- italics

Continuum Connection

- Recognize and reflect punctuation with the voice: e.g., period, question mark, exclamation point, dash, comma, ellipses, when reading in chorus or individually (p. 152)
- Recognize and reflect variations in print with the voice (e.g., italics, bold type, special treatments, font size) when reading in chorus or individually (p. 152)

Goal

Understand how the voice changes to reflect the punctuation marks and font style in a sentence.

Rationale

When students adjust their voices for punctuation marks and font styles in order to read the way the writer intended, they gain confidence as readers and improve fluency.

Assess Learning

Observe students when they read aloud. Notice if there is evidence of new learning based on the goal of this minilesson.

- Do students' voices reflect the punctuation marks and font styles in sentences they read aloud?
- Are they using the terms *fluency, punctuation, dialogue, ellipses, dash,* and *italics*?

Minilesson

To help students think about the minilesson principle, engage them in noticing how to change their voices to reflect the writer's intention. Here is an example.

- Ahead of time, prepare chart paper with various examples of punctuation and font styles, leaving room next to each for further writing.
- Select examples of writing that show the different types of punctuation you want to cover, either from student writing samples or selections from texts enlarged so students can see the print.
- Show pages 3 and 15 from *Chachaji's Cup.*

  > Listen as I read the words aloud. Notice what my voice does.

- Read the print, emphasizing voice changes for punctuation mark and font changes.

  > Why did my voice change as I read?

- As students mention types of punctuation, ask them how your voice changed. Record responses next to the corresponding punctuation mark or font style on the prepared chart.
- Repeat with page 10 from *The Hundredth Name* and pages 29 and 37 from *World Make Way.* Continue filling in the chart using students' responses.

  > Authors use punctuation and different font styles to indicate how they want the text to sound when it is read.

Have a Try

Invite the students to practice fluency with a partner.

▶ Have students sit in pairs with books that they are reading or have them choose books from a basket.

Choose a few sentences or pages. Look for punctuation marks and font changes. Do you see any that we haven't yet discussed? Take turns reading a section. Read the sentences the way the author wants them to sound.

▶ After a few minutes, ask several students to share what they noticed. Add any new ideas to the chart.

Summarize and Apply

Summarize the learning and remind students to notice punctuation marks and font styles when they read.

▶ Add the principle to the chart.

Today when you read, notice different punctuation marks or font styles. Think about how your voice should sound when you see them. Bring the book when we meet so you can share.

Share

Following independent reading time, gather students in small groups to read aloud to one another.

In your group, read aloud one or more sentences the way the author wants you to read them. Show how the author wants your voice to sound.

Extend the Lesson (Optional)

After assessing students' understanding, you might decide to extend the learning.

▶ Point out, as appropriate, that italics and boldface do not always mean that a word should be read with emphasis. For example, titles (e.g., book, movie) and foreign words are set in italics to distinguish them from the surrounding print. Headings and glossary words are often in boldface.

▶ Have the students engage in a readers' theater activity to practice speaking the way an author intends.

Notice how the author wants you to read the sentence.

When you see ____, make your voice...

.	go down and come to a full stop	*Italics*	say the word a little louder
?	go up	**bold**	make the word sound important
!	show strong feeling	CAPITALS	say the word louder for emphasis
,	pause for a short breath		
—	come to a full stop	underline	say the word a little louder
...	drift away		
:	pause to prepare for what comes next	( )	sound like speaking directly to reader
;	pause to separate two parts of a sentence	font change	read a bit differently for emphasis
" "	sound like the character is speaking		

Section 3: Strategies and Skills

RML 2
SAS.U4.RML2

Reading Minilesson Principle
Make your reading sound smooth and interesting.

Maintaining Fluency

You Will Need

- several familiar books with a variety of punctuation marks, font styles, and dialogue, such as the following:
  - *Where Fireflies Dance* by Lucha Corpi, from Text Set: Memoir/Autobiography
  - *World Make Way* edited by Lee Bennett Hopkins, from Text Set: Inspiration/Creativity
- chart paper and markers
- books students are reading independently or basket of books
- document camera (optional)

Academic Language / Important Vocabulary

- voice
- fluency
- phrasing
- smooth
- emphasis
- expression

Continuum Connection

- Read orally with integration of all dimensions of fluency (e.g., pausing, phrasing, word stress, intonation, and rate) alone and while maintaining unison with others (p. 151)

Goal

Learn how to integrate pausing, phrasing, stress, intonation, and rate to demonstrate fluent reading.

Rationale

When students know how to use rising and falling tones, pitch, volume, and rate to integrate all dimensions of fluency, their oral reading will sound smooth. This will also transfer to silent reading, resulting in better understanding and more enjoyment. When students read sentences with proper phrasing so that their reading sounds like talking, they can reflect on the author's meaning and increase their understanding of the text.

Assess Learning

Observe students when they read aloud and notice if there is evidence of new learning based on the goal of this minilesson.

- ▶ Are students making their reading sound smooth and interesting?
- ▶ Are they beginning to integrate all aspects of fluent reading?
- ▶ Do they understand the terms *voice, fluency, phrasing, smooth, emphasis,* and *expression*?

Minilesson

To help students think about the minilesson principle, engage them in noticing the characteristics of fluent reading. Here is an example.

- ▶ Show page 12 from *Where Fireflies Dance* by projecting with a document camera or writing the sentences on chart paper.

   Listen to my voice and notice how it changes as I read.

- ▶ Read with appropriate rate, expression, pausing, and stress.

   What did you notice about how I made my reading sound smooth and interesting?

   How did my voice change when I read the dialogue and came to other punctuation marks?

- ▶ As students respond, make a list on chart paper.
- ▶ Repeat the activity, reading pages 20 and 22 from *World Make Way*.
- ▶ Continue adding student ideas to the chart.

Have a Try

Invite the students to practice fluency with a partner.

▶ Have students sit in pairs with books they are reading or have them choose books from a basket. Ensure that at least a few groups use books that contain dialogue.

> Choose a few sentences or pages to read to your partner. Try to make your reading sound smooth and interesting.

▶ After a few minutes, ask several students to share what they noticed. Add any new ideas to the chart.

Summarize and Apply

Summarize the learning and remind students to make their reading sound smooth and interesting.

> Changing your voice in ways to make your reading sound smooth and interesting is how to read with fluency.

▶ Add the principle to the chart. Then, review the list on the chart.

> When you read aloud, make your voice sound smooth and interesting. Think about that when you read today. Bring your book when we meet so you can share.

Share

Following independent reading time, gather students in pairs to read aloud to one another.

> Choose a page from the book you read today to read to your partner. Make your reading sound fluent.

Extend the Lesson (Optional)

After assessing students' understanding, you might decide to extend the learning.

▶ Provide professional models of fluency by playing recordings of books (e.g., audiobooks) or inviting members of a community acting group to read aloud to your class.

▶ Separate lessons can be taught on each of the dimensions of fluency (pausing, phrasing, stress, intonation, rate) if students need more support.

Make your reading sound smooth and interesting.

- Make your voice volume louder or softer.
- Make your voice go up or down.
- Read with expression.
- Stress the words appropriately.
- Read with rhythm.
- Use the right speed.
- Sound smooth, like you are talking.
- Read phrases together.
- Pause or stop the right amount of time.
- Sound like the character.

Reading Minilesson Principle

Use your voice to reflect the tone of the text you are reading.

You Will Need

- several familiar books that provide good examples of tone, such as the following:
  - *Wings* by Christopher Myers, from Text Set: Kindness and Compassion
  - *Steel Drumming at the Apollo* by Trish Marx and *World Make Way* edited by Lee Bennett Hopkins, from Text Set: Inspiration/Creativity
- chart and markers
- books students are reading independently or basket of books

Academic Language / Important Vocabulary

- fluency
- tone
- reflect
- word choice
- formal
- informal

Continuum Connection

- Understand the role of the voice in communicating meaning in readers' theater, choral reading, songs, and poetry (p. 152)

Goal

When reading aloud, reflect the tone of the text in the voice.

Rationale

When students learn to adjust their voices to indicate the tone that the author wishes to convey, they show that they understand the author's meaning beyond the surface of the words.

Assess Learning

Observe students when they read aloud. Notice if there is evidence of new learning based on the goal of this minilesson.

- Do students' voices reflect tone when they read aloud?
- Are they using the terms *fluency, tone, reflect, word choice, formal,* and *informal*?

Minilesson

To help students think about the minilesson principle, engage them in noticing how to reflect tone. Here is an example.

> As I revisit a few pages from *Wings*, think about how my voice changes.

- Read pages 5 and 9, using a somber tone, and then read pages 34–37, using an upbeat, joyful tone.

  > The attitude, view, or feeling that the author conveys through the words he chooses is the author's tone. In addition to the word choice, the way I read aloud helps identify and express the author's tone.

  > What statement could you make about the author's tone, or attitude toward the subject he is writing about, in this book?

- Prompt the conversation as needed to support students' understanding of tone:
  - *Thinking about word choice, is the author conveying a formal tone or an informal tone?*
  - *What do you notice about the characters, setting, details, and language choice that helps you identify the author's attitude toward the subject?*
  - *Are there any changes in tone in different parts of the book?*
- Begin a chart and add students' noticings about the way you read to convey tone.
- Repeat the activity with different examples, such as pages 17–18 from *Steel Drumming at the Apollo* and page 7 from *World Make Way*.
- Add responses to the chart.

Have a Try

Invite the students to practice reading in a way that reflects tone with a partner.

▶ Have students sit in pairs with books that they are reading or have them choose books from a basket.

Choose a few sentences or pages to read to your partner. Think about the way the author wants you to read and make your voice change to match the intended tone.

▶ After a few minutes, ask several students to share how they changed their voices to reflect tone.

Summarize and Apply

Summarize the learning and remind students to think about how to convey tone when they read.

When you read aloud, think about the tone conveyed by the author and use your voice to express that tone.

▶ Add the principle to the chart.

Today when you read, notice tone and practice how your voice should sound to convey tone. Bring the book when we meet so you can share.

Share

Following independent reading time, gather students in small groups to read aloud to one another.

In your group, read aloud one or more sentences in which you noticed the tone. Show how the author wants your voice to sound.

Extend the Lesson (Optional)

After assessing students' understanding, you might decide to extend the learning.

▶ Encourage students to identify the tone in a variety of books and to practice reading aloud and adjusting voices to convey tone.

Use your voice to reflect the tone of the text you are reading.

Title	Author's Tone	How should the words be read to convey tone?
WINGS	Informal — dejected, somber — joyful, hopeful	• In a little sad and solemn way • A bit slower • Upbeat and positive • A little faster
STEEL DRUMMING	Formal — detached, unemotional — Informal — jovial, whimsical	• In a serious, straightforward way • With an informal, almost playful voice for the quote
World Make Way "Paint Me"	Informal — impatient, agitated, superior	• With an annoyed or irritated tone to sound like the character

Section 3: Strategies and Skills

Reading Minilesson Principle
Show in your voice when a writer means something different than the words alone indicate.

Maintaining Fluency

You Will Need

- examples of sarcasm and/or irony, such as in *Garvey's Choice* by Nikki Grimes, from Text Set: Exploring Identity
- chart and markers
- books students are reading independently or basket of books

Academic Language / Important Vocabulary

- fluency
- intention
- indicate
- sarcasm
- irony

Continuum Connection

- Understand the role of the voice in communicating meaning in readers' theater, choral reading, songs, and poetry (p. 152)

Goal

When reading aloud, show in your voice when a writer means something different than the words alone indicate.

Rationale

When students pay attention to and adjust their voices to convey verbal irony, they show an understanding of the writer's intention, resulting in deeper comprehension, as well as improving their ability to infer a character's motivations.

Assess Learning

Observe students when they read aloud. Notice if there is evidence of new learning based on the goal of this minilesson.

- ▶ Do students' voices reflect verbal irony when they read aloud?
- ▶ Are they using the terms *fluency, intention, indicate, sarcasm,* and *irony*?

Minilesson

To help students think about the minilesson principle, engage them in noticing how to change the voice to reflect irony or sarcasm. Here is an example.

- ▶ Revisit page 7 in *Garvey's Choice*. As you read, reflect the sarcasm used by Mom when she asks about reading not being a good thing.

  What is the writer trying to convey in Mom's question? How did I show that in the way I read the dialogue? Turn and talk about that.

- ▶ After time for discussion, ask students to share their thinking.

  The writer has in mind a meaning beyond what the words say. Verbal irony is when a speaker wants to emphasize something, so she says the opposite of what she means. Mom really means that reading *is* a good thing.

- ▶ Begin a chart that includes the title and a labeled example from the book that has language that is intended to be read in a way that adds meaning.

  Think about the way I read another poem and whether you notice an example of language that means one thing on the surface but has added meaning in the way the author wants it to be read.

- ▶ Read the first section on page 28, emphasizing the sarcasm.

  What do you notice about the way I read this? What was I trying to convey?

- ▶ Sarcasm is a type of verbal irony when someone says something that is the opposite of what they mean in a mocking or funny way with the intention of being insulting.

Have a Try

Invite the students to practice reading in a way that reflects sarcasm and/or irony with a partner.

▶ Have students sit in pairs with books that they are reading or have them choose books from a basket.

Choose a few sentences or pages to read to your partner. Notice if the writer has used verbal irony or sarcasm. Then think about the way the author wants you to read and make your voice change to match the way the author intended.

▶ After a few minutes, ask several students to share what they noticed.

Summarize and Apply

Summarize the learning and remind students to notice when a writer uses verbal irony or sarcasm.

You learned that, sometimes, a speaker means something different than the words alone indicate and that you need to show the real meaning in your voice.

▶ Add the principle to the chart.

Today when you read, notice whether the book has examples of verbal irony, or sarcasm, which is a specific type of verbal irony. Place a sticky note on any pages you want to remember. Bring the book when we meet so you can share.

Share

Following independent reading time, gather students in the meeting area.

Did anyone find an example in the book you read when the speaker means something different than the words indicate? Tell us about that.

Extend the Lesson (Optional)

After assessing students' understanding, you might decide to extend the learning.

▶ Share examples of dramatic irony or situational irony and have students practice reading the way the writer intends.

Show in your voice when a writer means something different than the words alone indicate.

Title	Example	Kind of Language	How should the words be read?
"Mom Speaks"	"When was [reading] not a good thing?" (p. 7)	Verbal irony	With a slightly annoyed and questioning voice
"Too-Skinny-for-Words"	"It's kinda hard to squeeze by since you take up so much space." (p. 28)	Sarcasm	With a mean voice

Assessment

After you have taught the minilessons in this umbrella, observe students as they talk and write about their reading across instructional contexts: interactive read-aloud, independent reading, guided reading, shared reading, and book club. Use *The Literacy Continuum* (Fountas and Pinnell 2017) to observe students' reading and writing behaviors.

▶ What evidence do you have of new understandings related to fluency?

- Are students reading and responding appropriately to punctuation and the style of the font when they read aloud?
- Do they integrate the various elements of fluency, such as pausing, phrasing, word stress, intonation, and rate when they read aloud?
- Do they notice dialogue and try to read the way the character would say it?
- Are students able to identify tone and read aloud using the author's intended tone?
- Can students recognize sarcasm and irony in a text and alter their voices appropriately?
- Do they use terms such as *fluency, punctuation, dialogue, expression, tone, intention, sarcasm,* and *irony*?

▶ In what other ways, beyond the scope of this umbrella, are students demonstrating fluency?

- Are they using a confident and enthusiastic voice when they speak in front of others—for example, when giving book talks?

Use your observations to determine the next umbrella you will teach. You may also consult Minilessons Across the Year (pp. 61–64) for guidance.

Link to Writing

After teaching the minilessons in this umbrella, help students link the new learning to their own writing:

▶ Have students use dialogue in their writing. Encourage them to think about how the character would speak and then write the dialogue that way.

Reader's Notebook

When this umbrella is complete, provide a copy of the minilesson principles (see resources.fountasandpinnell.com) for students to glue in the reader's notebook (in the Minilessons section if using *Reader's Notebook: Advanced* [Fountas and Pinnell 2011]), so they can refer to the information as needed.

Minilessons in This Umbrella

RML1 Tell the important events in order to summarize a biography or memoir.

RML2 Tell about the theme and plot in an organized way to summarize a fiction story.

RML3 Tell the big idea and how the most important information is organized to summarize an informational text.

Before Teaching Umbrella 5 Minilessons

The minilessons in this umbrella do not need to be taught consecutively; rather, you can teach them in conjunction with relevant Literary Analysis minilessons: RML1 with Umbrella 14: Studying Biography, RML2 with Umbrella 27: Understanding Plot, and RML3 with Umbrella 17: Thinking About the Topic of Expository Nonfiction.

Read and discuss fiction texts with characters, settings, clear problems and solutions, and a message. Read and discuss informational texts with a variety of underlying text structures. Use the texts from the *Fountas & Pinnell Classroom*™ *Interactive Read-Aloud Collection* text sets listed below, or choose books from your classroom library to support students in their ability to summarize their reading.

Perseverance

The Memory Coat by Elvira Woodruff

Exploring Identity

A Different Pond by Bao Phi

Activists/Change Makers

Gordon Parks: How the Photographer Captured Black and White America by Carole Boston Weatherford

Genre Study: Biography (Pioneers)

Tiny Stitches: The Life of Medical Pioneer Vivien Thomas by Gwendolyn Hooks

Life on Earth

Grand Canyon by Jason Chin

Animal Adaptations

Neighborhood Sharks: Hunting with the Great Whites of California's Farallon Islands by Katherine Roy

As you read aloud and enjoy these texts together, help students

- notice and discuss the events that shaped the life of a character in a fiction text or a subject in a biography,

- think about the message or lesson the author is trying to convey,

- understand what makes the subject of a biography notable, and

- notice the important information and the underlying text structures presented in an informational text.

Perseverance

Exploring Identity

Activists/ Change Makers

Genre Study: Biography (Pioneers)

Life on Earth

Animal Adaptations

Section 3: Strategies and Skills

RML 1
SAS.U5.RML1

Reading Minilesson Principle
Tell the important events in order to summarize a biography or memoir.

Summarizing

You Will Need

- two familiar biographies or memoirs, such as the following:
  - *Gordon Parks* by Carole Boston Weatherford from Text Set: Activists/Change Makers
  - *Tiny Stitches* by Gwendolyn Hooks, from Text Set: Genre Study: Biography (Pioneers)
- chart paper prepared with a summary of *Gordon Parks*
- chart paper and markers

Academic Language / Important Vocabulary

- biography
- summary
- subject

Continuum Connection

- Present a concise, organized oral summary that includes all important information (pp. 588, 600, 612)
- Present a logically organized oral summary that includes important information expressing the main idea or larger message and reflects the overall structure (expository or narrative) as well as important underlying text structures: e.g., description, cause and effect, chronological sequence, temporal sequence, categorization, comparison and contrast, problem and solution, question and answer (nonfiction) (pp. 588, 600, 612)

Goal

Tell the important events in a biography or memoir in chronological order.

Rationale

A biography often follows a chronological or narrative structure. Learning how to summarize a biography helps students learn to summarize other texts with a narrative structure. This lesson can also be used to help students summarize narrative nonfiction and memoir.

Assess Learning

Observe students when they summarize a biography or memoir. Notice if there is evidence of new learning based on the goal of this minilesson.

- ▸ Can students give an organized oral summary of a biography or memoir?
- ▸ Can they distinguish between essential and nonessential details?
- ▸ Are they using language such as *biography, summary,* and *subject*?

Minilesson

To help students think about the minilesson principle, engage them in noticing the important characteristics of a summary of a biography. Here is an example.

- ▸ Read the written summary of *Gordon Parks*.

  What did you notice about the way I told you about this biography? What information did I include?

  What is important to tell in a summary of a biography?

- ▸ Record responses on the chart.

  What did you notice about how I organized the information in my summary?

  The information that you include in the summary of a biography would be very similar when you summarize a memoir.

Have a Try

Invite students to summarize *Tiny Stitches* with a partner.

> One of you will summarize *Tiny Stitches*. As you listen, notice the information your partner gives in the summary.

▶ If time allows, ask a student to share a summary with the class. Invite other students to share what they noticed.

Summarize and Apply

Summarize the learning and invite students to prepare to deliver an oral summary of a biography.

> What should you tell in the summary of a biography or memoir?

▶ Review the chart, adding any additional ideas. Write the principle at the top of the chart.

> When you read today, read a biography or memoir or think about the last one you read. Be prepared to tell a summary of the book when we come back together.

Share

Following independent reading time, gather students together in the meeting area to share their summaries.

▶ Choose two or three students to share a summary of a biography or memoir with the class.

Extend the Lesson (Optional)

After assessing students' understanding, you might decide to extend the learning.

▶ Use this lesson as a model for teaching students to summarize narrative nonfiction.

▶ During guided reading and individual conferences, ask students to summarize a biography or memoir.

▶ **Writing About Reading** After students have demonstrated the ability to deliver a strong oral summary of a biography or memoir, ask them to write a summary in a reader's notebook (see WAR.U5.RML4).

Summary

Gordon Parks: How the Photographer Captured Black and White America by Carole Boston Weatherford

Gordon was born in 1912. When magazine photos captured his attention, he bought a camera and learned how to use it. He became a government photographer in Washington, DC. His photos appeared in newspapers and magazines. His most famous photograph, American Gothic, shows the unfairness of segregation. Gordon Parks is remembered for being a humanitarian as well as an artist.

Tell the important events in order to summarize a biography or memoir.

What to Include in the Summary of a Biography

- Title and author
- The subject of a book
- Why the subject is important
- Where and when the subject lived
- The important events in order
- The problem(s) the subject encountered and how they were solved.
- The author's message

Section 3: Strategies and Skills

RML 2
SAS.U5.RML2

Tell about the theme and plot in an organized way to summarize a fiction story.

Summarizing

You Will Need

- two familiar fiction books, such as the following:
  - *The Memory Coat* by Elvira Woodruff, from Text Set: Perseverance
  - *A Different Pond* by Bao Phi, from Text Set: Exploring Identity
- chart paper prepared with a summary of *The Memory Coat*
- chart paper and markers

Academic Language / Important Vocabulary

- summary
- summarize
- character
- setting
- plot
- theme

Continuum Connection

- Present a concise, organized oral summary that includes all important information (pp. 588, 600, 612)

- Present an organized oral summary that includes the setting (if important), significant plot events including climax and resolution, main characters and supporting characters, character change (where significant), and one or more themes (fiction) (pp. 588, 600, 612)

Goal

Tell about the theme and plot in an organized way to summarize a fiction story.

Rationale

When summarizing a fiction text, students must organize details about the characters, setting, plot, and theme in a logical sequence. Summarizing helps readers remember what they read and think about the most important attributes of a story.

Assess Learning

Observe students when they summarize fiction texts. Notice if there is evidence of new learning based on the goal of this minilesson.

- ▸ Can students deliver an oral summary of a fiction text that tells about the theme and the important events of the story in a logical sequence?
- ▸ Can students distinguish between essential and nonessential information when they give a summary?
- ▸ Are they using language such as *summary, summarize, character, setting, plot,* and *theme*?

Minilesson

To help students think about summarizing fiction books, engage them in noticing the characteristics of a summary. Here is an example.

- ▸ Read aloud the written summary of *The Memory Coat*.

    What did you notice about the information in my summary of *The Memory Coat*?

    What parts of the story did I include?

    What else did I include in my summary?

    What didn't I include?

- ▸ Record students' responses on chart paper.

    When you tell the most important parts of a story, you summarize it, or give a summary. A summary is short but gives enough information so someone can understand what the story is mainly about. You need to organize the information so the summary makes sense. What did you notice about how I organized the information in my summary?

Have a Try

Invite the students to summarize *A Different Pond* with a partner.

> One of you will summarize *A Different Pond*. As you listen, notice the information your partner gives in the summary.

▶ If time allows, ask one or two students to share their summaries with the class. Invite other students to share what they noticed.

Summarize and Apply

Summarize the learning and invite students to prepare to deliver an oral summary of a book.

> What should you tell in the summary of a fiction book?

▶ Review the chart, adding any additional ideas. Write the principle at the top of the chart.

> Today, think about how you would summarize the last fiction book you finished reading. Be prepared to give a summary of that book to a partner when we come back together.

Share

Following independent reading time, gather students together in the meeting area to share their summaries.

> Give a summary to your partner of the last fiction book you read.

> What did you notice about your partner's summary?

Extend the Lesson (Optional)

After assessing students' understanding, you might decide to extend the learning.

▶ During guided reading and individual conferences, ask students to summarize the book they have just read.

▶ **Writing About Reading** After students have demonstrated the ability to deliver a strong oral summary, ask them to write a summary in a reader's notebook (see WAR.U5.RML4).

Summary

The Memory Coat
by Elvira Woodruff

This story takes place long ago in Russia. Grisha lives with his cousin Rachel's family. He wears an old tattered coat that his mother made. When the family flees Russia, Rachel worries that Grisha's coat will make it hard to pass inspection at Ellis Island. She has an idea to help Grisha keep his coat and help the family stay in America. This story explores themes of family, perseverance, and compassion.

Tell about the theme and plot in an organized way to summarize a fiction story.

What to Include in a Story Summary

- Title and author
- Main character(s)
- Setting
- Problem and solution
- Important events in the plot
- Ending
- Theme(s)

Section 3: Strategies and Skills

Reading Minilesson Principle

Tell the big idea and how the most important information is organized to summarize an informational text.

You Will Need

- two familiar informational texts, such as the following:
  - *Grand Canyon* by Jason Chin, from Text Set: Life on Earth
  - *Neighborhood Sharks* by Katherine Roy, from Text Set: Animal Adaptations
- chart paper prepared with a summary of *Grand Canyon*
- chart paper and markers

Academic Language / Important Vocabulary

- summarize
- summary

Continuum Connection

- Present a concise, organized oral summary that includes all important information (pp. 588, 600, 612)
- Present a logically organized oral summary that includes important information expressing the main idea or larger message and reflects the overall structure (expository or narrative) as well as important underlying text structures: e.g., description, cause and effect, chronological sequence, temporal sequence, categorization, comparison and contrast, problem and solution, question and answer (nonfiction) (pp. 588, 600, 612)

Goal

Tell the big idea and the most important information to summarize an informational text.

Rationale

When you teach students how to summarize an informational book, you help them organize and clearly articulate the most important information in the book. This also helps them learn and notice a variety of informational text structures, such as categorical, descriptive, and compare and contrast.

Assess Learning

Observe students when they summarize informational texts. Notice if there is evidence of new learning based on the goal of this minilesson.

- Can students distinguish between essential and nonessential information when summarizing?
- Can they notice the underlying text structure of an informational text?
- Are they using academic language, such as *summarize* and *summary*?

Minilesson

To help students think about the minilesson principle, engage them in noticing the important characteristics of a summary of an informational book. Here is an example.

- Read the written summary of *Grand Canyon*.

  What did you notice about the information I shared?

  What did I include in my summary?

- Record responses on the chart.

  A summary does not tell everything in a book—only enough important information to give someone an idea of what the book is about. What did you notice about how I organized the information in my summary?

Have a Try

Invite students to summarize *Neighborhood Sharks* with a partner.

> One of you will summarize *Neighborhood Sharks*. As you listen, notice the information your partner includes in the summary.

▶ If time allows, ask one or two students to share their summaries with the class. Invite other students to share what they noticed.

Summarize and Apply

Summarize the learning and invite students to prepare to deliver an oral summary of an informational book.

> What should you tell in the summary of an informational book?

▶ Review the chart, adding any additional ideas. Write the principle at the top of the chart.

> When you read today, read an informational book or think about the last one you read. Be prepared to tell a summary of the book when we come back together.

Share

Following independent reading time, gather students in pairs in the meeting area to share their summaries.

> Share your summary with a partner.

▶ After students turn and talk, invite two or three students to share with the class.

Extend the Lesson (Optional)

After assessing students' understanding, you might decide to extend the learning.

▶ During guided reading and individual conferences, ask students to summarize an informational book.

▶ **Writing About Reading** After students have demonstrated the ability to deliver a strong oral summary of an informational book, ask them to write a summary in a reader's notebook (see WAR.U5.RML4).

Summary

Grand Canyon by Jason Chin takes you on a "hike" through one of the largest and most fascinating canyons in the world. The Colorado River has been cutting away at the canyon for millions of years, exposing many different layers of rock. These layers tell the history of the canyon by showing what life was like when each layer was formed. Walking through this wondrous canyon from bottom to top is both a history lesson and a study in geology.

Tell the big idea and how the most important information is organized to summarize an informational text.

What to Include in the Summary of an Informational Book

• The title, author, and topic

• The most important information

• How the book is organized

• The main message or big idea

Assessment

After you have taught the minilessons in this umbrella, observe students as they talk and write about their reading across instructional contexts: interactive read-aloud, independent reading, guided reading, shared reading, and book club. Use *The Literacy Continuum* (Fountas and Pinnell 2017) to guide the observation of students' reading and writing behaviors.

▶ What evidence do you have of new understandings related to summarizing?

  • Can students articulate clear, well-organized summaries of fiction, informational, and biographical texts?

  • Are they able to distinguish between essential and nonessential information?

  • Do they use academic language, such as *summary, summarize, character, setting, theme, plot, biography,* and *subject*?

▶ In what other ways, beyond the scope of this umbrella, are students talking about fiction and nonfiction books?

  • Have students begun to notice and discuss underlying text structures in nonfiction?

  • Do they notice and comment on text features in nonfiction books?

  • Are they noticing elements of author's craft in fiction books?

Use your observations to determine the next umbrella you will teach. You may also consult Minilessons Across the Year (pp. 61–64) for guidance.

Link to Writing

After teaching the minilessons in this umbrella, help students link the new learning to their own writing:

▶ Have students write summaries to attach to some books in the classroom library to help other students choose a book they will enjoy reading.

Reader's Notebook

When this umbrella is complete, provide a copy of the minilesson principles (see resources.fountasandpinnell.com) for students to glue in the reader's notebook (in the Minilessons section if using *Reader's Notebook: Advanced* [Fountas and Pinnell 2011]), so they can refer to the information as needed.

Minilessons in This Umbrella

RML1 Prepare for reading by using the text features and resources.

RML2 Be persistent when you read a difficult text.

RML3 Notice when you don't understand what you're reading and take action.

RML4 Read short sections and stop to think about what the author is saying.

Before Teaching Umbrella 6 Minilessons

The minilessons in this umbrella are intended to encourage students to use a variety of techniques when approaching texts that are difficult for them to read. You will not only address focus and persistence, but also teach students to monitor their comprehension.

Unlike other minilessons in this book, these lessons do not rely on previously read texts. Instead, provide real-world examples of texts that are likely to be difficult for your students, such as material from disciplinary reading. Expose students to reading materials that are beyond their instructional levels and that can be enlarged (written on chart paper or projected). Examples include practice testing booklets, online informational material and directions, scientific articles, textbooks, or primary source documents. The texts should be tailored to your group of students and what they find difficult, so readings will vary from class to class.

Introduce, read, and discuss a variety of texts that your students may find difficult. When you do,

- discuss what the text is about,

- demonstrate how to reread and check if a word makes sense, sounds right, and looks right,

- model thinking about the important information and details when reading,

- show how to stop and reread if something is confusing, and

- show how to read short sections and then stop and think about what the author is trying to say.

Section 3: Strategies and Skills

Reading Minilesson Principle

Prepare for reading by using the text features and resources.

You Will Need

- prepared chart paper or projected documents with examples that may be difficult for your students and that include a variety of text features (e.g., titles, headings, an introduction, a summary, graphics, key words)
- chart paper and markers
- document camera (optional)
- texts (e.g., books, magazines, articles) that may be difficult for students and that include a variety of text features

Academic Language / Important Vocabulary

- monitoring
- comprehension
- text features
- resources
- summary

Continuum Connection

- Search for information in texts with multiple features and very dense print (pp. 586, 598, 610)
- Use organizational tools to search for information: e.g., title, table of contents, chapter title, heading, subheading, sidebar, callout (pp. 586, 598, 610)

Goal

Prepare to read difficult texts by previewing text features and resources.

Rationale

When students understand that text features and resources are tools to help comprehend a difficult text, they use the techniques to unlock meaning when approaching difficult reading material.

Assess Learning

Observe students when they navigate difficult texts and notice if there is evidence of new learning based on the goal of this minilesson.

- ▶ Are students able to identify and use text features and resources to navigate difficult texts?
- ▶ Do they use the terms *monitoring, comprehension, text features, resources,* and *summary*?

Minilesson

To help students think about the minilesson principle, engage them in generating a list of text features and resources to use when navigating difficult texts. Here is an example.

- ▶ Display a text that may be difficult for students and that has a variety of text features (e.g., title, table of contents, headings, graphics) that can be used to determine the content of the material.

  What text features might help you understand what you will be reading about?

- ▶ Guide students to identify key features. Begin a list on chart paper.

  Have a look at some other examples and think about the text features and resources that can help you comprehend something that is difficult.

- ▶ Continue showing difficult examples that include a variety of text features, such as headings, an introduction, a summary, graphics, illustrations, and key words. As students identify each, add to the list on chart paper. The following prompts may be useful:

  - *What text features might help you get a clue about what you are reading?*
  - *What do you notice about the introduction?*
  - *How does the author identify key words?*
  - *What are some ways that you can define unfamiliar key words?*
  - *In what ways is the summary useful?*

Have a Try

Invite the students to talk with a partner about using text features and resources to help read difficult material.

▶ Provide each pair of students with a difficult expository book or article.

> Talk about the text features and resources you can use to find out what this book or article is about.

▶ After time for brief discussion, ask students to share their thinking and add new ideas to the list.

Summarize and Apply

Summarize the learning and remind students to use text features and resources.

> When you approach something that is difficult to read, the text features and resources can help you understand the information.

▶ Add the principle to the chart.

> When you read today, choose a text that may be difficult for you to read. Look for text features and resources and use them to help you understand. Bring the text when we meet so you can share.

Share

Following independent reading time, gather students in small groups.

> In your group, share what you read today and talk about any text features or resources you noticed and any that helped you understand what you read.

Extend the Lesson (Optional)

After assessing students' understanding, you might decide to extend the learning.

▶ Continue to support techniques for approaching difficult texts during guided reading or independent reading. From the *Fountas & Pinnell Prompting Guide, Part 2, for Comprehension: Thinking, Talking, and Writing* (Fountas and Pinnell 2009), use prompts such as the following:

- *What does the (title, dust jacket, back cover, preface, chapter headings, dedication, opening page) tell you about the book?*

- *What print features does the book have (cartoons, speech bubbles, headings, special fonts)?*

- *What kind of illustrations and graphics are included?*

> **Prepare for reading by using the text features and resources.**
>
> title
> table of contents
> preface, introduction, author's note
> index
> headings
> sidebars
> charts, graphs, diagrams
> illustrations, photos, maps
> captions
> key words
> glossary
> summary

Section 3: Strategies and Skills

Reading Minilesson Principle
Be persistent when you read a difficult text.

You Will Need

- chart paper or projected document that shows a text that is difficult for your students, prepared with highlighting and notes to assist with comprehension
- chart paper and markers
- sticky notes
- document camera (optional)
- basket of texts that are difficult for students

Academic Language / Important Vocabulary

- monitoring
- comprehension
- persistent
- focused
- techniques

Continuum Connection

- Notice and ask questions when meaning is lost or understanding is interrupted (p. 79)
- Make connections between texts and personal experience, content learned in past reading, and disciplinary knowledge (pp. 589, 601)

Goal

Use techniques to stay focused and persistent when reading.

Rationale

When you teach students to access the content of a difficult text, you help them persist in reading the text. They learn that it is normal to sometimes encounter texts that are difficult but that with patience and perseverance there are ways to unlock the meaning.

Assess Learning

Observe students when they approach difficult texts and notice if there is evidence of new learning based on the goal of this minilesson.

- Are students able to generate a list of techniques to use when approaching difficult texts?
- Do they try multiple techniques to stay focused and persistent when reading a difficult text?
- Do they use the terms *monitoring, comprehension, persistent, focused,* and *techniques?*

Minilesson

To help students think about the minilesson principle, engage them in generating a list of techniques to help them stay focused before, during, and after reading difficult texts. Here is an example.

- Ahead of time, select a text that is beyond the instructional level of most of your students. Highlight, add notes in the margins, and attach sticky notes that will be helpful in comprehending the text.

  What does it feel like when you read something that is very difficult?

  One of the things I try to do before I read something difficult is to think about what I already know and what I might want to know about the topic. Let's look at this topic. What are some things you know and that you might be interested in finding out about this topic?

- Have a brief conversation about the topic.
- Show the prepared document.

  Here is something that is difficult to read. I have done some things to help me stay focused and persistent. What do you notice that I have done?

- As students provide ideas, create a list on chart paper of techniques that can be used before reading, while reading, and after reading. Prompt the conversation as needed.

Have a Try

Invite the students to talk with a partner about monitoring comprehension when reading difficult texts.

> What techniques do you use when you read something difficult? Which of these techniques on the chart will you try? Turn and talk about that.

▶ After time for discussion, ask students to share. Add new ideas to the chart.

Summarize and Apply

Summarize the learning and remind students to stay focused and persistent when reading something that is difficult.

> When you read something that is difficult, it is important to stay focused and persistent and try different ways of thinking about the meaning.

▶ Add the principle to the chart.

> When you read today, choose something to read that may be difficult for you. Try using one or more of the techniques we talked about. Bring what you read when we meet so you can share.

Share

Following independent reading time, gather students together to talk about techniques they used to read difficult text.

> What are some techniques you used when you read something that was difficult today? How did the techniques work?

Extend the Lesson (Optional)

After assessing students' understanding, you might decide to extend the learning.

▶ Continue to support techniques for approaching difficult texts during guided reading or independent reading. From the *Fountas & Pinnell Prompting Guide, Part 2, for Comprehension: Thinking, Talking, and Writing* (Fountas and Pinnell 2009), use prompts such as the following:

- *What do you know about the genre that might help you?*
- *What do you think the writer means when she says* _____?
- *Were there parts of the book that you didn't understand?*
- *How does that fit with what you know?*

Be persistent when you read a difficult text.

Before Reading
- Think about what you know about the topic.
- Think about the purpose for reading (what you want to learn or find out).
- Look through the print and graphics to get a quick overview.

While Reading
- Use a highlighter to mark important words, phrases, or sentences.
- Write a note in the margin on the page.
- Add sticky notes.
- Reread a sentence or paragraph to understand it.
- Don't give up.

After Reading
- Summarize or think about what you understood.
- Think about what you want to know more about.

RML 3
SAS.U6.RML3

Notice when you don't understand what you're reading and take action.

Monitoring Comprehension of Difficult Texts

You Will Need

- several examples of texts that are difficult for most students (e.g., complex novel, scientific or technology article, or medical journal)
- chart paper and markers
- document camera (optional)
- basket with examples of reading materials that are difficult for students

Academic Language / Important Vocabulary

- techniques
- self-monitor
- self-correct
- reread
- key vocabulary

Continuum Connection

- Notice and ask questions when meaning is lost or understanding is interrupted (p. 79)
- Slow down to search for or reflect on information or to enjoy language and resume reading with momentum (pp. 588, 600, 612)
- When needed, reread to search for and use information from the body text, sidebars, insets, and graphics (pp. 586, 598, 610)

Goal

Self-monitor and self-correct by rereading, finding the meaning of key vocabulary, and reading on to gain more information.

Rationale

When you teach students to self-monitor their comprehension while reading, they learn to self-correct by rereading and/or looking up or using context to solve key vocabulary to gain meaning.

Assess Learning

Observe students when they read text that is difficult and notice if there is evidence of new learning based on the goal of this minilesson.

- ▶ Do students notice when they do not comprehend what they are reading?
- ▶ Do they stop and take action when they do not comprehend a difficult text?
- ▶ Do they use the terms *techniques, self-monitor, self-correct, reread,* and *key vocabulary*?

Minilesson

To help students think about the minilesson principle, engage them in thinking about the actions that support their understanding a text. Here is an example.

> Everyone at one time or another encounters reading material that doesn't make sense or that is difficult to understand.

- ▶ Show or project an example of difficult reading material. Read the first paragraph or difficult section aloud with good momentum and no explanations.

> Did you understand what I read?

> I read that quickly. Sometimes, you realize that the first time you read, you are going too fast to understand what the author is writing about. What can you do when that happens?

- ▶ As students provide ideas, create a list on chart paper.

> It's important to notice when you don't understand what you are reading. The first thing to do is stop—and then try some different techniques to comprehend what the author is writing about.

Have a Try

Invite the students to talk with a partner about noticing when they don't understand what they are reading and taking action.

> ▶ Refer to the generated list.
>
> > We started a list of some things you can do when you don't understand what you are reading. Are there others? Turn and talk about that.
>
> ▶ After time for brief discussion, ask students if they have any new ideas to add to the list.

Summarize and Apply

Summarize the learning and remind students to notice when they don't understand what they are reading and to take action.

> ▶ Review the chart and add the principle to the top.
>
> > When you read today, choose something that might be difficult for you to understand. If you come to a difficult part, try one or more of the techniques that are listed on the chart. Bring the reading material when we meet so you can share.

Notice when you don't understand what you're reading and take action.

TAKE ACTION

- Slow down.

- Reread at a slower pace.

- Read ahead to see if the meaning is clarified.

- Look up key words in the glossary or dictionary.

- Look back at the table of contents and think about the topic of the book to figure out how the information fits.

- Look for information in sidebars or graphics, such as maps and diagrams.

Share

Following independent reading time, gather students in small groups.

> In your group, share what you read today and talk about any techniques you used to help you understand what you read.

Extend the Lesson (Optional)

After assessing students' understanding, you might decide to extend the learning.

> ▶ Continue to support techniques for approaching difficult texts during guided reading or independent reading. From the *Fountas & Pinnell Prompting Guide, Part 2, for Comprehension: Thinking, Talking, and Writing* (Fountas and Pinnell 2009), use prompts such as the following:
>
> > • *Does that make sense?*
> >
> > • *Were there parts that you didn't understand?*
> >
> > • *What do you think the author means when he says _____?*
> >
> > • *How do the graphics (diagrams, maps, sidebars) enhance your understanding of the topic?*

RML4

SAS.U6.RML4

Reading Minilesson Principle

Read short sections and stop to think about what the author is saying.

Monitoring Comprehension of Difficult Texts

You Will Need

- examples of text that may be difficult for students
- chart paper and markers
- document camera (optional)
- sticky notes
- basket of difficult reading materials

Academic Language / Important Vocabulary

- techniques
- section
- summarize

Continuum Connection

- Notice and ask questions when meaning is lost or understanding is interrupted (p. 79)

Goal

Read short sections and think about what the author is saying.

Rationale

While reading difficult material, students who learn to stop and think about what an author is saying begin to remember what they read, organize the information, and increase comprehension. In content-area studies and research, they will likely encounter difficult texts.

Assess Learning

Observe students when they encounter difficult texts and notice if there is evidence of new learning based on the goal of this minilesson.

- ▶ Do they read a short section and then think about what the author is trying to say?
- ▶ Do they use the terms *techniques, section,* and *summarize*?

Minilesson

To help students think about the minilesson principle, engage them in a discussion about how to read a short section of a difficult text and then pause to think about what the author is trying to say.

- ▶ Show or project an example of text that is difficult for most students.

  When you read something that is difficult to understand, you can use some techniques to help you understand what you are reading.

- ▶ Read a short section.

  What is the author trying to say?

  What questions or confusions do you have?

- ▶ As students generate ideas, write each on a sticky note and place in the margin.
- ▶ Briefly summarize the section with them and talk about techniques for answering any questions they have.
- ▶ Read another short portion of the text and then stop and repeat the process.

  What did you notice about this technique for comprehending difficult text?

- ▶ Engage students in a discussion and guide them to conclude that if you break a difficult text into short sections and pause to think about what each section means, you can work your way through a difficult text.

Have a Try

Invite the students to talk with a partner about navigating difficult texts.

▶ Show or project another paragraph from the difficult text you have been using as an example.

> With a partner, take turns reading a short section aloud. Then stop to talk about any questions you have and talk about what the author is trying to say.

Summarize and Apply

Summarize the learning and remind students to read a short section of a difficult text and think about what an author is trying to say.

> How could you summarize the technique you used today to understand a difficult text?

▶ Add the principle to the chart.

> When you read today, choose something that is difficult for you. When you come to a part you don't understand, read a short section and then stop and think about what the author is trying to say. Bring the text when we meet so you can share.

Share

Following independent reading time, gather students in pairs.

> With your partner, share what you read today and talk about what you did to understand what you read.

Extend the Lesson (Optional)

After assessing students' understanding, you might decide to extend the learning.

▶ Continue to support techniques for approaching difficult texts during guided reading or independent reading. From the *Fountas & Pinnell Prompting Guide, Part 2, for Comprehension: Thinking, Talking, and Writing* (Fountas and Pinnell 2009), use prompts such as the following:

- *What is the author really trying to say?*
- *Why did the author say _____?*
- *What are the most important concepts the writer told about?*
- *Did the writer compare (and contrast) anything?*

Read short sections and stop to think about what the author is saying.

The Domestication of Plants and Animals

Early humans were nomadic hunter-gatherers, using a set of diverse techniques to gather food. Approximately 12,000 to 11,000 years ago (10,000 to 8,000 BCE), the domestication of plants and animals began.

> Humans started raising animals and plants a very long time ago.

Dogs were one of the first animals domesticated by humans. Eventually goats, cattle, pigs, and other animals were also domesticated. The domestication of key plants and animals and the establishment of agricultural societies had huge consequences.

> Humans' lives changed a lot once they knew how to raise their own food.

Section 3: Strategies and Skills

Assessment

After you have taught the minilessons in this umbrella, observe students as they talk and write about their reading across instructional contexts: interactive read-aloud, independent reading, guided reading, shared reading, and book club. Use *The Literacy Continuum* (Fountas and Pinnell 2017) to observe students' reading and writing behaviors across instructional contexts.

▶ What evidence do you have of new understandings related to monitoring comprehension of difficult texts?

- Are students able to persist and stay focused when reading a difficult text?
- Are they using text features and resources when reading?
- Do students monitor their comprehension and take action when meaning is lost?
- Do they stop at the end of a short section to think about what the author is trying to say?
- Do they understand the terms *monitoring, comprehension, techniques, persistent, focused, text features, resources, self-monitor, self-correct, reread,* and *summarize*?

▶ In what other ways, beyond the scope of this umbrella, are students talking about ways to monitor comprehension of difficult texts?

- Are students engaging in conversations about difficult texts and providing support and ideas to classmates as they read text that is beyond their instructional level?

Use your observations to determine the next umbrella you will teach. You may also consult Minilessons Across the Year (pp. 61–64) for guidance.

Reader's Notebook

When this umbrella is complete, provide a copy of the minilesson principles (see resources.fountasandpinnell.com) for students to glue in the reader's notebook (in the Minilessons section if using *Reader's Notebook: Advanced* [Fountas and Pinnell 2011]), so they can refer to the information as needed.

Minilessons in This Umbrella

RML1 Search efficiently and effectively for information on the internet.

RML2 Evaluate whether you have found the information you need.

RML3 Stay focused while reading on the internet.

RML4 Evaluate the credibility of the source of the information you read on the internet.

RML5 Evaluate whether a website presents one perspective or multiple perspectives.

RML6 Notice when bloggers or website authors link to other sources to provide evidence for an argument.

Before Teaching Umbrella 7 Minilessons

With the constant explosion of new technologies, children and teenagers spend more and more time reading in digital environments. A 2015 report by Common Sense Media (https://www.commonsensemedia.org/sites/default/files/uploads/research/census_researchreport.pdf, 21) found that eight- to twelve-year-old children spend about two and a half hours per day using digital media (e.g., computers, tablets, and smart phones) outside of school. Although the growth of digital technologies offers myriad benefits to children and adults alike, this increase also presents a number of challenges. Reading in digital environments requires a different set of skills than reading print publications. Students need to learn how to effectively find the information they need, how to evaluate its relevance and credibility, and how to stay focused while doing so.

Before teaching the minilessons in this umbrella, determine how and when your students will have access to digital devices during the school day, and put structures in place for ensuring that they can use them safely. You might, for example, have students use a student-friendly search engine or give them lists of safe, trustworthy websites about different topics. Be sure to give your students numerous opportunities to use digital technology in different ways and for different purposes.

Section 3: Strategies and Skills

Reading Minilesson Principle
Search efficiently and effectively for information on the internet.

Reading in Digital Environments

You Will Need

- a computer or tablet with internet access (connected to a projector, if possible)
- chart paper and markers
- a list of possible questions for students to research on the internet (see Summarize and Apply)

Academic Language / Important Vocabulary

- internet
- website
- web page
- information
- search engine
- keywords

Continuum Connection

- Use different strategies to increase the effectiveness of your searches including key words, advanced search engine filters, and symbols (p. 355)
- Locate websites that fit one's needs and purpose (p. 355)

Goal

Use different search techniques to increase the effectiveness of searches including keywords, search engine filters, and symbols.

Rationale

Many students understand the basics of searching for information on the internet but often find it challenging to find the information they actually need. When students are armed with a toolkit of effective searching techniques—for example, using filters and symbols, knowing how to phrase inquiries, knowing how to perform multistep searches—they are more likely to find the information they need (for more resources on effective searching strategies, visit a website such as commonsense.org).

Assess Learning

Observe students when they search for information on the internet and notice if there is evidence of new learning based on the goal of this minilesson.

- Do students know how to phrase and revise search inquiries?
- Do they use and understand the terms *internet*, *website*, *web page*, *information*, *search engine*, and *keywords*?

Minilesson

Engage students in a discussion about how to search for information on the internet and provide an interactive demonstration. This lesson assumes the use of Google as a search engine.

- Display Google (or another search engine) on a projector or large screen.

    The internet is a wonderful resource, but it can be hard to find exactly what you're looking for. What are problems or challenges you've had?

- Make a list of students' responses on chart paper. Then discuss each problem one-by-one, inviting students to offer possible solutions. Add solutions to the chart in a second column. Offer your own search tips, as necessary.

    Now let's do a search together. I want to learn about the Grand Canyon.

- Search for the words *Grand Canyon*.

    The search engine found more than three million websites! I need to think about what exactly I want to find out. I'd like to know if Native Americans ever lived in or around the Grand Canyon. What should I search for?

- Search for *Native Americans Grand Canyon*.

    Here's a web page called "Native American Indian Tribes of the Grand Canyon." It says that the Havasupai tribe has been living in the Grand Canyon for the past eight hundred years. This result gives me what I'm looking for.

Have a Try

Invite the students to talk with a partner about another search inquiry.

> I have a challenge question for you: What river flows through the capital city of the country that won the 1998 World Cup? Turn and talk to your partner about how you could find the answer to this question on the internet.

▶ If necessary, explain that some topics need to be broken down into multiple steps. Demonstrate searching for the answer to this question by breaking it down into three steps (e.g., *1998 World Cup winner*, *capital of France*, *Paris river*).

Summarize and Apply

Summarize the learning and remind students to use these tips and techniques when searching for information on the internet.

▶ Ask students to summarize what they learned today. Write the principle at the top of the chart.

▶ Have students practice these search techniques. Give them a list of possible topics/ questions to search for. For example: What *was the favorite food of the eighth president of the United States? What important events happened in Canada one hundred years ago? What is the average lifespan of the biggest animal in the world?*

Share

Following independent reading time, gather students together in the meeting area to talk about their search techniques and results.

> What information did you search for? What techniques did you use to find the information you needed? What did you find out?

Extend the Lesson (Optional)

After assessing students' understanding, you might decide to extend the learning.

▶ Share additional techniques for searching for information on the internet. For example, you might talk about Google image search, show students how to narrow down results by date, or show them how to search for results within a particular website.

Search efficiently and effectively for information on the internet.

Problem	Solution
I don't know what to type in the search box.	• Type only the most important keywords.
I can't find what I'm looking for.	• Is there another way to say what you're looking for? Use synonyms. • Make your search terms more specific or less specific.
I don't know how to spell the thing I'm looking for.	• Don't worry about spelling. The search engine can often guess what word you mean, even if you spell it wrong!
I want to search for words in an exact order.	• Use quotation marks if you want to find websites that have your keywords in the same order "I have a dream that one day this nation will rise up"
The results are about something completely different from what I'm looking for.	• Use a minus sign (-) in front of words you want to exclude. If you are looking for websites about Mars—the planet, not the chocolate bar—type this: Mars -chocolate
The websites are too hard to read—they're for adults.	• Type the word kids after your search terms to find websites that are for kids. World War II kids

Reading Minilesson Principle
Evaluate whether you have found the information you need.

You Will Need

- a computer or tablet with internet access (connected to a projector, if possible)
- chart paper and markers

Academic Language / Important Vocabulary

- internet
- website
- web page
- information
- evaluate
- search engine

Continuum Connection

- Locate websites that fit one's needs and purpose (p. 355)
- Identify the purpose of a website (p. 355)

Goal

Evaluate whether you have found the appropriate information after doing a search.

Rationale

When students are able to evaluate whether they have found the information they need after conducting an internet search, they spend more time reading relevant, interesting information and less time searching for information or going off-task.

Assess Learning

Observe students when they search for information on the internet and notice if there is evidence of new learning based on the goal of this minilesson.

- ▶ Can students skim the website to determine if it contains the information they need?
- ▶ Do they understand and use the terms *internet, website, web page, information, evaluate,* and *search engine*?

Minilesson

To help students think about the minilesson principle, engage them in a demonstration and discussion about how to evaluate search results. Here is an example.

- ▶ Display Google (or another search engine) on a projector or large screen.

  I am concerned about how people are relying too much on fossil fuel. Today I'm going to search online for information about how I can use less fossil fuel. I'm going to search using the words *how to use less fossil fuel.*

- ▶ Think aloud as you choose a result to click on.

  Here's a web page called "Use Less Fossil Fuels." I can see that this web page has a list of ways to reduce the use of fossil fuel—for example, by buying food that is locally produced. I think this web page has the information I'm looking for. What did you notice about how I chose which search result to click on?

- ▶ Record students' responses on chart paper. Then click on the search result you chose, and think aloud as you evaluate the source for relevancy.

  To make sure that it has the information I need, I'll skim the web page.

- ▶ Read aloud and point to any important words or phrases, subheadings, and text features.

  This web page has what I need, so I'm going to read the whole page closely. What did you notice about what I did after I chose a web page to click on?

- ▶ Record responses on the chart.

Have a Try

Invite the students to evaluate the relevancy of a website with a partner.

> Now I would like to learn about gravity. I want to know more about how gravity works.

▶ Search for *gravity*. Click on a search result that is *not* relevant (e.g., a website about the movie *Gravity*).

> Does this website have the information I need? Turn and talk to your partner about what you think.

> This website clearly doesn't have the information I need, so I'm not going to waste my time reading the whole website. I need to go back to my search results and choose another website.

Summarize and Apply

Summarize the learning and remind students to evaluate the relevancy of search results.

> How can you evaluate whether you have found the information you need when you're searching on the internet?

▶ Add any new insights to the chart, and write the principle at the top.

> If you go online today, think about a topic that you would like to learn about or a question that you'd like to have answered. Evaluate whether you have found the information you need.

Share

Following independent reading time, gather students together in the meeting area to talk about how they evaluated their search results.

> Who searched for information online today?

> How did you evaluate whether the websites you found had the information you needed?

Extend the Lesson (Optional)

After assessing students' understanding, you might decide to extend the learning.

▶ Teach students how to recognize advertisements/sponsored links in search engine results and explain that they should generally be avoided.

Evaluate whether you have found the information you need.

1. Decide which website to click on.

  • Read the titles.
  • Read the short description.
  • Check out the web address/source. (Is it a website that you've heard of before?)
  • Click on the website that seems most likely to have the information you need.

2. Evaluate whether the website you clicked on has the information you need.

  • Skim the website (look for titles, subheadings, text features, and key words and phrases).
  • If it seems to have the information you need, read the website closely.
  • If it doesn't, go back to your search results and choose another website.

Section 3: Strategies and Skills

RML 3
SAS.U7.RML3

Reading Minilesson Principle
Stay focused while reading on the internet.

Reading in Digital Environments

You Will Need

▸ chart paper and markers

Academic Language / Important Vocabulary

▸ internet
▸ website
▸ information
▸ link
▸ focused

Continuum Connection

▸ Use a variety of digital resources such as websites, public and subscription-based databases, e-books, and apps to locate, evaluate, and analyze literary and informational content (p. 355)

Goal

Be aware of potential distractions and stay focused when reading online.

Rationale

With practically an endless array of links, videos, advertisements, and other distractions, websites offer an optimal environment for distracted reading. When students are aware of this potential and know strategies for staying focused, they are less likely to be distracted and will spend more time doing in-depth reading.

Assess Learning

Observe students when they use the internet and notice if there is evidence of new learning based on the goal of this minilesson.

▸ How well do students stay focused while reading on the internet?

▸ Do they understand and use the terms *internet, website, information, link,* and *focused*?

Minilesson

To help students think about the minilesson principle, engage them in a discussion about staying focused while reading on the internet.

▸ To introduce the idea of distracted reading online, use the following example or an authentic example from your personal experience.

> You can learn a lot of interesting information on the internet, but sometimes it is difficult to stay focused while reading. For example, once I went online to read about how volcanic eruptions work, but I ended up watching a trailer for a movie about a volcanic eruption! Has something like this ever happened to any of you?

> One thing that helps me stay focused is to make sure I always have a purpose for being online. For example, one day my purpose might be to learn about the Civil War. If I find myself getting tempted to click on a link, I'll ask myself, "Will this link help me learn more about the Civil War?" If the answer is no, I won't click on it. What are some other techniques you might use to stay focused while reading online?

▸ Record students' responses on chart paper. Offer additional ideas of your own, as needed.

▸ Note: Some web browsers offer a "reader view" feature, which strips away all the clutter—images, advertisements, links, etc.—from a website, making it easier to focus on reading. If you have such a feature on your classroom devices, show students how to use it, and add it to the chart.

Have a Try

Invite the students to talk with a partner about how to stay focused while reading online.

> Turn and talk to your partner about staying focused while reading online. You might talk about problems you've had, which of these ideas you would like to try, or any other ideas you have for staying focused.

▶ After students turn and talk, invite several pairs to share their thinking. Add any new ideas to the list.

Summarize and Apply

Summarize the learning and remind students to stay focused while reading online.

> What did you learn today about how to stay focused while reading on the internet?

▶ Write the principle at the top of the chart.

> If you go online today, remember to stay focused on what you're reading. If you find it difficult to stay focused, review the chart we made and try some of these ideas.

Share

Following independent reading time, gather students together in the meeting area to share how they stayed focused while reading on the internet.

> Who read something online today?
>
> What did you do to stay focused?

Extend the Lesson (Optional)

After assessing students' understanding, you might decide to extend the learning.

▶ Display the chart in the technology area of your classroom. Revisit it from time to time, and add new ideas that come up.

▶ Teach a minilesson about how to take notes while reading on the internet.

Stay focused while reading on the internet.

- Always have a purpose, or reason, for using the internet. Don't click on links that won't help you with that purpose.

- Read or skim the whole website first before deciding what links to click on next.

- Use the "reader view" option on the web browser.

- Try to have only one tab open at a time.

- Take notes about what you are reading.

RML4
SAS.U7.RML4

Reading Minilesson Principle
Evaluate the credibility of the source of the information you read on the internet.

Reading in Digital Environments

You Will Need

- a computer or tablet with internet access (connected to a projector, if possible)
- chart paper and markers

Academic Language / Important Vocabulary

- internet
- website
- information
- credibility
- source

Continuum Connection

- Determine when a website was last updated (p. 355)
- Consider information about a website author, as well as the author's credentials and affiliations, to determine level of expertise (p. 355)
- Determine the reliability of a website based on analysis of author expertise, accuracy of information, validity of sources, scientific evidence, etc. (p. 355)

Goal

Evaluate the credibility of sources of the information read on the internet.

Rationale

When you teach students how to evaluate the credibility of internet sources, they are more likely to access and acquire accurate information. Additionally, the ability to critically evaluate information will serve them in all aspects of their lives, whether they are reading print or digital publications or are engaged in discussions, and will help them develop into thoughtful and critical members of society.

Assess Learning

Observe students when they read information on the internet and notice if there is evidence of new learning based on the goal of this minilesson.

- Do students evaluate the credibility of the websites they read online?
- Can they explain how to evaluate the credibility of a website?
- Do they understand and use the terms *internet, website, information, credibility,* and *source?*

Minilesson

To help students think about the minilesson principle, model evaluating the credibility of a website. Here is an example.

- Display Google (or another search engine). Search for *Ruth Bader Ginsburg* (or another topic of your choice).

  I just read a great book about Ruth Bader Ginsburg, and now I want to learn more about her. I searched for her name on the internet, and I found these results. I want to make sure I choose a credible, or trustworthy, source that will give me accurate information about her. Which of these results do you think are credible? What makes you think that?

- If necessary, guide students to notice any results from well-known, credible publications. Click on one of them.

  What are some other things you would want to check to find out if this site is credible?

- Guide students to understand how to check the author's credentials, the bibliography, and the date updated (if available).

Have a Try

Invite the students to talk with a partner about how to evaluate the credibility of a website.

> What did we think about when we evaluated the credibility of a website? What questions did we ask ourselves? Turn and talk to your partner about those questions.

▶ After students turn and talk, invite several students to share their thinking. Use their responses to make a chart.

Summarize and Apply

Summarize the learning and remind students to evaluate the credibility of online sources.

> What did you learn today about how to evaluate the credibility of a website?

> Why is it important to determine whether a website is credible?

▶ Write the principle at the top of the chart.

> If you go online today, think about a topic that you would like to read about, and search for information about it. Remember to evaluate the credibility of the websites you find.

Share

Following independent reading time, gather students together in the meeting area to share how they evaluated the credibility of internet sources.

> Who searched for information online today?

> How did you evaluate the credibility of the websites you found?

Extend the Lesson (Optional)

After assessing students' understanding, you might decide to extend the learning.

▶ Involve students in creating and maintaining running lists of trusted internet sources about various topics. Display the lists in your classroom's technology area.

Evaluate the credibility of the source of the information you read on the internet.

- Who created this website?

- Are they a trusted source (for example, a government agency, a university, or a major publication)? Web addresses that end in **.gov** or **.edu** are usually trustworthy.

- Who is the author?

- Is the author an expert on the topic?

- Does the author list the sources (a bibliography)?

- When was the website last updated? Is the information current?

Section 3: Strategies and Skills

<table>
<tr>
<td>

RML 5
SAS.U7.RML5

</td>
<td>

Reading Minilesson Principle
Evaluate whether a website presents one perspective or multiple perspectives.

</td>
</tr>
</table>

Reading in Digital Environments

You Will Need

- a computer or tablet with internet access (connected to a projector, if possible)
- two student-friendly web articles about the same topic: one that presents a single perspective and one that presents multiple perspectives. For example, you might use an opinion piece in favor of allowing cell phones in schools and another article that explains both the pros and the cons. Unless the articles are very short, choose in advance key sentences or paragraphs to read aloud.
- a web article about a different topic
- chart paper and markers

Academic Language / Important Vocabulary

- internet
- website
- perspective
- evaluate

Continuum Connection

- Determine whether a website presents one perspective or multiple perspectives (p. 355)

Goal

Evaluate whether a website presents one perspective or multiple perspectives.

Rationale

When students are able to evaluate whether a website presents one perspective or multiple perspectives, they are less likely to indiscriminately believe everything they read on the internet—or elsewhere. They understand that an author's perspective influences what information they choose to include in their writing, and they begin to develop the ability to evaluate information analytically and forge their own perspectives.

Assess Learning

Observe students when they read information on the internet and notice if there is evidence of new learning based on the goal of this minilesson.

- ▶ Can students evaluate whether a website presents one perspective or multiple perspectives?
- ▶ Do they understand and use the terms *internet, website, perspective,* and *evaluate*?

Minilesson

To help students think about the minilesson principle, engage them in a demonstration and discussion about how to evaluate whether a website presents one or more perspectives. Here is an example.

- ▶ Display the single-perspective web article.
- ▶ Read the title of the article and a few important passages from the article that clearly show the author's perspective on the topic.

    How an author feels about a topic is her perspective. What is the author's perspective on allowing cell phones in schools? How can you tell?

    Does the author give reasons why cell phones in schools might be okay?

    Does this website present one perspective or multiple perspectives about cells phones in schools?

- ▶ Display the multiple-perspective web article. Read the title and then a few select passages that discuss multiple perspectives.

    How do you think the author of this article feels about allowing cell phones in schools?

    What reasons does the author give for why allowing them may be okay?

    What reasons does he give for why it may not be okay?

    Does this website give one perspective or multiple perspectives?

Have a Try

Invite the students to talk with a partner about another web article.

- Display the third web article. Read the title and a few important passages.

  Does this website present one perspective or multiple perspectives about the topic? Turn and talk to your partner about that. Be sure to give reasons for your thinking.

- After time for discussion, invite a few students to share their thinking.

Summarize and Apply

Summarize the learning and remind students to evaluate whether websites present one or multiple perspectives.

How can you tell if a website presents only one perspective on a topic or an issue?

How can you tell if a website presents multiple perspectives?

- Use students' responses to make a chart. Write the principle at the top.

  If you go online today, think about a topic or an issue that you would like to learn more about. Search for websites about that topic, and remember to evaluate whether each website you read presents one or multiple perspectives.

Share

Following independent reading time, gather students together in the meeting area to discuss how they evaluated websites.

Who searched for information online today?

How did you determine whether a website presented one perspective or multiple perspectives?

Extend the Lesson (Optional)

After assessing students' understanding, you might decide to extend the learning.

- Explicitly discuss how an author's perspective on a topic influences the writing and what information is included and omitted.

- Discuss why it is important to read multiple perspectives about a topic or an issue—not just online but also in print.

Evaluate whether a website presents one perspective or multiple perspectives.

One Perspective	• It is obvious how the author feels about the topic. • The author tells you that something is either GOOD or BAD (or right or wrong). • The author only gives reasons and evidence for ONE side of an issue. • The title tells you how the author feels.
Multiple Perspectives	• The title tells you what the website is about, but it doesn't tell you how the author feels. • You don't necessarily know how the author personally feels about the topic. • The author gives reasons and evidence for BOTH sides of an issue.

RML 6
SAS.U7.RML6

Reading Minilesson Principle
Notice when bloggers or website authors link to other sources to provide evidence for an argument.

Reading in Digital Environments

You Will Need

- a computer or tablet with internet access (connected to a projector, if possible)
- a student-friendly blog entry or web editorial (e.g., from *USA Today*) that provides links to external sources
- chart paper and markers

Academic Language / Important Vocabulary

- website
- blogger
- source
- evidence
- argument
- link

Continuum Connection

- Examine and think critically about the different strategies used by the media (TV, movies, news, video, multimedia blogs) and other content providers to engage and influence (p. 355)

Goal

Notice when bloggers and website authors link to other sources to provide evidence for an argument and think critically about the linked source.

Rationale

Noticing when website authors link to other sources to provide evidence for an argument helps students verify the accuracy of the information provided. This ability allows them to analyze the argument on a deeper level and to forge their own perspectives on the topic or issue.

Assess Learning

Observe students when they use the internet and notice if there is evidence of new learning based on the goal of this minilesson.

- ▶ Do students notice when website authors link to other sources to provide evidence for an argument?
- ▶ Do they click on such links and think critically about the linked source?
- ▶ Do they understand and use the terms *website, blogger, source, evidence, argument,* and *link*?

Minilesson

To help students think about the minilesson principle, engage them in a demonstration and discussion about linked sources.

- ▶ Display the blog entry or web editorial. Read aloud a paragraph that contains links to other sources. Point with the cursor to one of the links.

  What do you notice about this text?

  This text is a link to another website. Why do you think the author is linking to another website here?

  Sometimes bloggers and website authors link to other sources to give more or different information that can provide evidence for their arguments.

- ▶ Click on the link. Model evaluating the source of the information. Here is an example.

  I see that this website has the same fact that was in the opinion article we were reading. This must be where the author found this fact. I can also see that this website is a reliable source of information—the web address ends in *.gov*, which means that it's a government agency. That makes me think that this information is probably accurate.

  What did you notice about what I did after I clicked the link?

- ▶ Record responses on chart paper.

Have a Try

Invite the students to talk with a partner about another linked source.

▶ Read aloud another paragraph of the editorial and click on a link to another source.

> Turn and talk to your partner about how and why the author of this article uses links to other sources. Also, evaluate the linked source. Is this a reliable source of information? Why or why not?

▶ After time for discussion, invite several students to share their thinking.

Summarize and Apply

Summarize the learning and remind students to use linked sources to verify information.

> Why do bloggers and website authors sometimes link to other sources?
>
> How can these links help you as a reader?

▶ Write the principle at the top of the chart.

> If you read a blog or an editorial online today, notice if there are links to other sources to provide evidence for an argument. If so, you may want to click on one or more of the links to verify the information.

Share

Following independent reading time, gather students together in the meeting area to share how they used linked sources.

> Did anyone read something online that linked to other sources?
>
> Were the links useful?

Extend the Lesson (Optional)

After assessing students' understanding, you might decide to extend the learning.

▶ Show students how to open links in a new tab. This makes it easier to return to the original website.

▶ Start a class blog that students can contribute to, or have students start individual blogs. Teach students how to post entries and how to link to external sources. Have them write opinion pieces on the blog, and encourage them to link to other sources to provide evidence for their arguments.

Notice when bloggers or website authors link to other sources to provide evidence for an argument.

- Notice links to other sources. Links are usually a different color from the main text.

- If you want to verify the information, click on the link.

- Verify that the same information appears on the linked source.

- Evaluate the credibility of the linked source.

Section 3: Strategies and Skills

Assessment

After you have taught the minilessons in this umbrella, observe students as they use the internet. Use *The Literacy Continuum* (Fountas and Pinnell 2017) to guide the observation of students' reading and writing behaviors.

▶ What evidence do you have of new understandings related to reading in digital environments?

- Are students able to use search engines effectively?
- Are they able to evaluate whether they have found the information they need?
- Do they stay focused while reading on the internet?
- Do they evaluate the credibility of internet resources and whether a website presents one perspective or multiple perspectives?
- Do they notice when website authors link to other sources?
- Do they understand and use terms such as *internet, information, source, website, link, search engine, evaluate,* and *perspective*?

▶ In what other ways, beyond the scope of this umbrella, are students using technology?

- Do students do online research to evaluate the information in nonfiction books?

Use your observations to determine the next umbrella you will teach. You may also consult Minilessons Across the Year (pp. 61–64) for guidance.

Link to Writing

After teaching the minilessons in this umbrella, help students link the new learning to their own writing:

▶ If you have your students conduct online research for writing projects, remind them to use the skills they learned from this umbrella. Teach them how to record the sources they use to avoid plagiarizing.

Reader's Notebook

When this umbrella is complete, provide a copy of the minilesson principles (see resources.fountasandpinnell.com) for students to glue in the reader's notebook (in the Minilessons section if using *Reader's Notebook: Advanced* [Fountas and Pinnell 2011]), so they can refer to the information as needed.

Section 4 | Writing About Reading

Throughout the year, students will respond to what they read in a reader's notebook. These lessons help students use this important tool for independent literacy learning and make it possible for them to become aware of their own productivity, in the process building self-efficacy. All opportunities for writing about reading support the students in thinking about texts and articulating their understandings.

4 Writing About Reading

Minilessons in This Umbrella

RML1 Collect your thinking in your reader's notebook.

RML2 Record each book you read on your reading list.

RML3 Keep a tally of the kinds of books you read.

RML4 Follow the guidelines to help you do your best reading and writing work.

Before Teaching Umbrella 1 Minilessons

The minilessons in this umbrella are intended to introduce *Reader's Notebook: Advanced* (Fountas and Pinnell 2011) to your students; however, if you do not have it, a plain notebook can be used instead. The goal of a reader's notebook is for students to have a consistent place to collect their thinking about their reading (see pp. 52–53 for more on using a reader's notebook).

Students will do most of their writing about reading in a reader's notebook during the time set aside for independent reading and writing. To establish routines for that time, teach MGT.U2.RML1. For this umbrella, use the following books from the *Fountas & Pinnell Classroom™ Independent Reading Collection* or any other books from your classroom library.

Independent Reading Collection

Ancient Egypt by Ken Jennings

Bill Peet: An Autobiography by Bill Peet

Independent Reading

Reader's Notebook

Section 4: Writing About Reading

Reading Minilesson Principle
Collect your thinking in your reader's notebook.

You Will Need

- a reader's notebook for each student (if using a plain notebook, set up tabbed sections for Reading List, Genre Studies, Minilessons, Writing About Reading, and Glossary)
- chart paper prepared with a five-column chart
- markers

Academic Language / Important Vocabulary

- reader's notebook
- reading list
- genre studies
- minilessons
- writing about reading
- glossary

Continuum Connection

- Form and express opinions about a text in writing and support those opinions with rationales and evidence (pp. 209, 212)
- Compose notes, lists, letters, or statements to remember important information about a text (pp. 208, 211)

Goal

Understand that a reader's notebook is a special place to collect thinking about books read.

Rationale

Students need numerous opportunities to respond to reading in different forms. A reader's notebook is a special place for them to keep a record of their reading lives and to share their thinking about books they have read.

Assess Learning

Observe students when they use a reader's notebook and notice if there is evidence of new learning based on the goal of this minilesson.

- Do students understand the purpose of a reader's notebook and of each section?
- Do they understand the terms *reader's notebook, reading list, genre studies, minilessons, writing about reading,* and *glossary*?

Minilesson

Give each student a reader's notebook and introduce students to the contents and purpose of the notebook. Here is an example.

> You will use your reader's notebook throughout the school year. Take a moment to look through it and see what you notice about it.
>
> What do you notice about your reader's notebook? What do you think you will write in it?

- Draw students' attention to the tabs at the top of the reader's notebook.

> You can use the tabs at the top of your reader's notebook to find each of the five sections. First, open your notebook to the yellow Reading List tab.
>
> What do you think you will write in this section?
>
> What information will you record about each book?

- Record students' responses in the first column of the chart, under the heading *Reading List*.

- Continue in a similar manner with the four remaining sections: *Genre Studies, Minilessons, Writing About Reading,* and *Glossary*.

- You might also have students look at the different ways they will write about their reading on the Forms for Writing About Reading page and the Suggestions for Writing About Reading page in the Writing About Reading section.

Have a Try

Invite the students to talk with a partner about the reader's notebook.

> Turn and talk to your partner about how you will use your reader's notebook.

▶ After students turn and talk, invite a few students to share their thinking. Confirm their understanding of the reader's notebook and clear up any misconceptions that may have arisen.

Summarize and Apply

Summarize the learning and remind students to collect their thinking about their reading in their reader's notebook.

> Why do you think it's a good idea to use a reader's notebook?

▶ Write the principle at the top of the chart.

> After you read today, turn to the Writing About Reading section in your reader's notebook and write what you're thinking about the book you're reading. Be ready to talk about what you wrote when we come back together.

Share

Following independent reading time, gather students together in the meeting area to talk about what they wrote.

> What did you write about today in your reader's notebook?

Extend the Lesson (Optional)

After assessing students' understanding, you might decide to extend the learning.

▶ Have students personalize the covers of their reader's notebooks by drawing, adding stickers or cut-out paper shapes, etc.

▶ Have students establish a place to store their reader's notebooks.

Collect your thinking in your reader's notebook.

Reading List	Genre Studies	Minilessons	Writing About Reading	Glossary
A list of books you have read (title, author, genre, etc.)	What you have noticed about different genres	The minilesson principles and notes about minilessons	Your thinking about books you have read (letters, summaries, lists, etc.)	Definitions of important terms related to reading and writing

Section 4: Writing About Reading

RML 2
WAR.U1.RML2

Reading Minilesson Principle
Record each book you read on your reading list.

Introducing a Reader's Notebook

You Will Need

- two books, such as the following from *Independent Reading Collection*:
  - *Ancient Egypt* by Ken Jennings
  - *Bill Peet: An Autobiography* by Bill Peet
- chart paper prepared to look like the reading list in *Reader's Notebook: Advanced* [Fountas and Pinnell 2011] and partially filled in with a few books
- markers
- a reader's notebook for each student

Academic Language / Important Vocabulary

- reader's notebook
- reading list
- title
- author
- genre
- response

Continuum Connection

- Record in Reader's Notebook the titles, authors, illustrators, and genre of texts read independently, and dates read [pp. 208, 211]

Goal

Learn to record the book title, author, genre, the level of challenge the book provided, and the date it is completed in a reader's notebook.

Rationale

Recording the books they have read on a reading list helps students remember which books they have read and enjoyed. It also helps them remember which books they found difficult or did not enjoy, and those examples help them make better reading choices and develop self-awareness as readers.

Assess Learning

Observe students when they use a reader's notebook and notice if there is evidence of new learning based on the goal of this minilesson.

- ▶ Do students understand the purpose of the reading list and how to use it?
- ▶ Do they understand the terms *reader's notebook, reading list, title, author, genre,* and *response*?

Minilesson

To help students think about the minilesson principle, engage students in a demonstration and discussion about how to fill in the reading list in a reader's notebook. Here is an example.

- ▶ Have students turn to the yellow tab that says Reading List. Then direct them to turn to the white page titled Reading List.

  What will you record on this page in your reader's notebook?

- ▶ Display the prepared chart.

  What do you notice about how I listed some books on my reading list? What information did I provide?

  What do you think the letters *TL*, *F*, and *RF* mean?

- ▶ Direct students' attention to the Reading Requirements page on the front of the yellow tab and point out the genre codes. Hold up *Ancient Egypt*.

  If I were going to read this book today, how would I record it on my reading list? What would I write first?

- ▶ Demonstrate filling in the #, *Title*, and *Author* columns.

  What will I write on my list when I've finished reading it?

- ▶ Discuss the *Genre Code, Date Completed,* and *One-Word Response* columns. Demonstrate filling them in. Point out that students should mark graphic texts with an asterisk.

Have a Try

Invite the students to talk with a partner about how to record books.

▶ Display the cover of *Bill Peet: An Autobiography*.

   If I decide to read this book next, how should I list it on my reading list? Turn and talk to your partner about this.

▶ After time for discussion, invite a few pairs to share their thinking. Add the number, title, and author to the chart.

Summarize and Apply

Summarize the learning and remind students to list the books they read on their reading list.

   Why is it a good idea to keep a list of the books you read in your reader's notebook?

▶ Write the principle at the top of the chart.

   When you read today, write the title and author of the book you're reading on your reading list. When you finish reading it, fill in the rest of the information.

Share

Following independent reading time, gather students together in the meeting area to discuss their reading lists.

   What did you read today?

   How did you record that book on your reading list? What information did you write?

Extend the Lesson (Optional)

After assessing students' understanding, you might decide to extend the learning.

▶ Invite students to look at their reading lists and notice whether they are reading all one type of book or whether they are reading a variety of genres.

Record each book you read on your reading list.

#	Title	Author	Genre Code	Date Completed	One-Word Response
1	Greek Myths	Olivia Coolidge	TL	9/8	Difficult
2	Around the World	John Coy	F	9/17	Action-packed
3	Finally	Wendy Mass	RF	9/21	Funny
4	Ancient Egypt	Ken Jennings	I	9/26	Interesting
5	Bill Peet: An Autobiography	Bill Peet			

Section 4: Writing About Reading

RML 3
WAR.U1.RML3

Reading Minilesson Principle
Keep a tally of the kinds of books you read.

Introducing a Reader's Notebook

You Will Need

- two informational books
- chart paper prepared to mirror the Reading Requirements page from *Reader's Notebook: Advanced* (Fountas and Pinnell 2011) and filled in with the specific reading requirements you have chosen for your students (the requirements given in this lesson are merely intended as examples)
- markers

Academic Language / Important Vocabulary

- reader's notebook
- genre
- requirement
- realistic fiction
- informational

Continuum Connection

- Record in Reader's Notebook the titles, authors, illustrators, and genre of texts read independently, and dates read (p. 208, 211)

Goal

Keep track of how many books are read in a particular genre in the reader's notebook.

Rationale

When students read books from a variety of genres (and keep track of their progress), they become well-rounded readers. Reading books outside their preferred genres allows students to step outside their comfort zone and expand their reading interests, literary and general knowledge, and vocabulary.

Assess Learning

Observe students when they use a reader's notebook and notice if there is evidence of new learning based on the goal of this minilesson.

- ▶ Do students keep a tally in a reader's notebook of the genres of the books they have read?
- ▶ Do they use the terms *reader's notebook, genre, requirement, realistic fiction,* and *informational*?

Minilesson

To help students think about the minilesson principle, demonstrate tallying books on the Reading Requirements page of a reader's notebook (adjust to fit your specific reading requirements). Here is an example.

- ▶ Display the prepared chart.

   The title of this page in the reader's notebook is Reading Requirements. What is a requirement?

   A requirement is something that you're expected to do. Your reading requirement this year is to read at least forty-five books.

- ▶ Point to the numbers in the *Requirement* column.

   What do you think these numbers mean?

   You will be expected to read a certain number of books in each genre.

- ▶ Point to the *Tally* column.

   What do you think you'll write in this column?

   You'll keep track of how many books you have read in each genre by keeping a tally.

- ▶ Demonstrate adding six tally marks next to *Realistic Fiction*.

Have a Try

Invite the students to talk with a partner about how to tally books.

▶ Display two informational books.

Turn and talk to your partner about how to tally these books on the Reading Requirements page.

▶ After students turn and talk, invite a volunteer to share his or her thinking. Add two tally marks to the *Informational* row.

Summarize and Apply

Summarize the learning and remind students to tally the kind and number of books they read.

This year you will read books from many different genres, but most of the books you read can be from any genre you like.

Today, read any book you like and notice what genre it is. When you finish reading it, make a tally mark on your Reading Requirements page next to the genre of the book.

Share

Following independent reading time, gather students together in the meeting area to discuss their Reading Requirements pages.

What did you write on your Reading Requirements page today?

Extend the Lesson (Optional)

After assessing students' understanding, you might decide to extend the learning.

▶ You may want to talk with each student individually about personal reading requirements.

▶ Review students' tallies regularly to make sure they are on track to meet the requirements and are reading a variety of books.

Reading Requirements
Total Books: 45

Requirement	Genre	Tally
5	(RF) Realistic Fiction	HHH I
	(HF) Historical Fiction	
5	(TL) Traditional Literature	
5	(F) Fantasy	
3	(SF) Science Fiction	
3	(B) Biography/ Autobiography	
	(M) Memoir	
5	(I) Informational	//
1	(P) Poetry	
1	(H) Hybrid	

Section 4: Writing About Reading

Reading Minilesson Principle
Follow the guidelines to help you do your best reading and writing work.

Introducing a Reader's Notebook

You Will Need

- chart paper and markers

Academic Language / Important Vocabulary

- reader's notebook
- guidelines

Continuum Connection

- Listen with attention during instruction, and respond with statements and questions (p. 341)

Goal

Learn and/or develop the guidelines for working together in the classroom.

Rationale

When you teach students to follow guidelines, they are better equipped to do their best work. You might have students review the established guidelines in *Reader's Notebook: Advanced* (Fountas and Pinnell 2011) or construct their own. When students play an active role in developing guidelines, they take ownership of them.

Assess Learning

Observe students during literacy work and notice if there is evidence of new learning based on the goal of this minilesson.

- Do students follow the guidelines established during this minilesson?
- Do they use and understand the terms *reader's notebook* and *guidelines*?

Minilesson

To help students think about the minilesson principle, talk about the guidelines in *Reader's Notebook: Advanced* or create a list of guidelines together. Here is an example.

- Divide students into small groups.

  You have been learning about what to do when it's time to read and write independently and how to use a reader's notebook. Today we're going to make a list of guidelines for that time. What are guidelines?

  Guidelines are rules or suggestions about how something should be done. Talk with your group about what you should all agree to do so that you can do your best work.

- After time for discussion, invite each group to share their thinking. Record their responses on chart paper. If needed, prompt students with questions such as the following:

  - *What should you do when it's independent reading time?*
  - *What voice level should you use?*
  - *What should you do if you give a book a good chance but you're still not enjoying it?*
  - *What should you do each time you start a new book?*
  - *What should you think about while you're reading?*
  - *What does it mean to "do your best work"? How can you make sure that you're doing your best work?*

Have a Try

Invite the students to talk with a partner about the guidelines.

> Turn and talk to your partner about anything else you think we should add to our guidelines.

▸ After students turn and talk, invite several pairs to share their ideas. Add any new guidelines to the list, if appropriate.

Summarize and Apply

Summarize the learning and remind students to follow the guidelines for literacy work.

> Today we made a list of guidelines for independent reading. Why is it important to follow these guidelines?

▸ Direct students to look at the guidelines inside the front cover of *Reader's Notebook: Advanced* or provide copies for students to glue into a plain notebook.

> When you are reading or writing on your own today, be sure to follow the guidelines we created together. If you think of anything else that you'd like to add to the guidelines, bring your ideas to share when we come back together.

Share

Following independent reading time, gather students together in the meeting area to talk about the guidelines.

> How did the guidelines help you do your best work today?

> Does anyone have anything to add to our guidelines?

Extend the Lesson (Optional)

After assessing students' understanding, you might decide to extend the learning.

▸ Revisit the list of guidelines with your students from time to time to see how they are working and to consider whether they need to be revised.

Guidelines to Help You Do Your Best Reading and Writing Work

1. Read a book or write down your thoughts about your reading.

2. Work silently so that you and your classmates can do your best thinking.

3. Use a soft voice when conferring with a teacher.

4. Choose books that you think you'll enjoy and abandon books that aren't working for you after you've given them a good chance.

5. List the book information when you begin reading and record the date and a one-word response when you finish the book.

6. Think about the genre of the book you are reading and what you notice.

7. Always do your best work.

Section 4: Writing About Reading

Assessment

After you have taught the minilessons in this umbrella, observe students as they talk and write about their reading across instructional contexts: interactive read-aloud, independent reading, guided reading, shared reading, and book club. Use *The Literacy Continuum* (Fountas and Pinnell 2017) to guide the observation of students' reading and writing behaviors.

- ▶ What evidence do you have of new understandings related to using a reader's notebook?
  - Do students understand the purpose of a reader's notebook?
  - Do they understand the purpose of each section?
  - Do they record the title, author, and date completed of the books they read on their reading list?
  - How well do they keep a tally of the kinds of books they have read?
  - Do they follow the guidelines for working during the time for independent reading and writing?
  - Do they use the terms *reader's notebook, reading list, writing about reading,* and *genre*?
- ▶ What other parts of the reader's notebook might you have the students start using based on your observations?

Use your observations to determine the next umbrella you will teach. You may also consult Minilessons Across the Year (pp. 61–64) for guidance.

Reader's Notebook

When this umbrella is complete, provide a copy of the minilesson principles (see resources.fountasandpinnell.com) for students to glue in the reader's notebook (in the Minilessons section if using *Reader's Notebook: Advanced* [Fountas and Pinnell 2011]), so they can refer to the information as needed.

Minilessons in This Umbrella

RML1   Make a list of the books you want to read.

RML2   Keep a tally of the kinds of writing about reading that you use in your notebook.

RML3   Take minilesson notes in your reader's notebook so you can refer to information you need.

RML4   Write about the genres you study.

RML5   Use the glossary as a tool to support your writing about reading.

Before Teaching Umbrella 2 Minilessons

Before teaching the minilessons in this umbrella, students should be familiar with the purpose and structure of *Reader's Notebook: Advanced* (Fountas and Pinnell 2011). If you do not have it, a plain notebook can be used instead (pp. 52–53). It would also be helpful to have taught the minilessons in Umbrella 3: Living a Reading Life in Section One: Management.

    The minilessons in this umbrella do not have to be taught consecutively; instead, each one may be taught when it is relevant to the work students are doing in the classroom. However, before students begin to use a reader's notebook, they should have read and discussed a variety of high-quality books and participated in several writing lessons incorporating shared writing.

As you read aloud and discuss books together, help students

- talk about books they want to read and share their reasons for their choices,

- notice the characteristics of different genres, and

- write about their reading in different ways.

Section 4: Writing About Reading

Reading Minilesson Principle
Make a list of the books you want to read.

Using a Reader's Notebook

You Will Need

- a reader's notebook for each student (if using a plain reader's notebook, create copies of a Books to Read chart)
- chart paper prepared to look like the Books to Read page from *Reader's Notebook: Advanced* (Fountas and Pinnell 2011)
- a few books from your classroom library that your students might enjoy reading independently
- markers

Academic Language / Important Vocabulary

- reader's notebook
- title
- author
- list

Continuum Connection

- Record in Reader's Notebook the titles, authors, illustrators, genre of texts read independently, and dates read (pp. 208, 211)

Goal

Create and maintain a list of books to read in the future.

Rationale

When students keep a list of the books they would like to read, they are better able to make good book choices, and they develop an identity as a reader in a community of readers where books are recommended and shared.

Assess Learning

Observe students when they talk and write about books they want to read and notice if there is evidence of new learning based on the goal of this minilesson.

- ▶ Do students add books to their Books to Read list?
- ▶ Do they use vocabulary such as *reader's notebook, title, author,* and *list*?

Minilesson

To help students think about the minilesson principle, discuss ways to choose books and how to keep a list of books to read in a reader's notebook. Here is an example.

- ▶ Have students turn to the Books to Read chart on the back of the yellow tab in the reader's notebook.

    What do you notice about this page? What do you think you will use it for?

    Here, you will make a list of books that you want to read. Can anyone think of a book that you would like to read?

    _____ wants to read _____. How could he record this book on his Books to Read list? What should he write and where?

- ▶ Demonstrate writing the title, author, and genre code on the prepared chart.

    What should he do when he has finished reading the book?

- ▶ Demonstrate adding a checkmark to the *Check When Completed* column.

Have a Try

Invite the students to start their own Books to Read lists.

> Listen carefully as I tell you about a few books from our classroom library, and think about whether you would like to read each book.

▶ Give a brief book talk about a few books from your classroom library. Allow time for students to add the books to their Books to Read list if they would like to read the book.

> If you have thought of another book that you would like to read, feel free to add it to your list.

Summarize and Apply

Summarize the learning and remind students to add books they would like to read to their Books to Read list.

> Why is it a good idea to keep a list of books that you want to read?

> When you read today, you may want to start reading one of the books on your list. You can add books to your list whenever you learn about one you would like to read. Bring your list to share when we come back together.

Share

Following independent reading time, gather students together in the meeting area to discuss their Books to Read lists.

> Did anyone read one of the books on your Books to Read list or add a new book to your list? Which book?

Extend the Lesson (Optional)

After assessing students' understanding, you might decide to extend the learning.

▶ Refer to students' Books to Read lists during individual reading conferences to help them plan what to read next.

▶ Remind students of ways they can find out about good books to read (see MGT.U3.RML1).

Reading List

Books to Read

Title	Author	Genre	Check When Completed
The Thing About Jellyfish	Ali Benjamin	RF	✓

Reading Minilesson Principle
Keep a tally of the kinds of writing about reading that you use in your notebook.

You Will Need

- chart paper resembling the Forms for Writing About Reading page in *Reader's Notebook: Advanced* (Fountas and Pinnell 2011)
- markers
- document camera (optional)

Academic Language / Important Vocabulary

- reader's notebook
- writing about reading
- tally

Goal

Learn how to keep a tally of the different forms of writing about reading.

Rationale

When you teach students to keep a tally of the kinds of writing they do, they are more likely to write about their reading in a wide variety of ways. It would be best to help students do the recording and tallying after each form of writing is introduced (see Umbrella 5: Introducing Different Genres and Forms for Responding to Reading in this section).

Assess Learning

Observe students when they keep track of the kinds of writing they do and notice if there is evidence of new learning based on the goal of this minilesson.

- ▶ Do students keep a tally of the kinds of writing about reading they have used?
- ▶ Do they understand how to make and count tally marks?
- ▶ Do they use and understand the terms *reader's notebook, writing about reading,* and *tally*?

Minilesson

To help students think about the minilesson principle, demonstrate how to tally forms of writing in a reader's notebook. Discuss only the forms of writing that you have already introduced to your students. Here is an example.

- ▶ Display the prepared chart paper or project the Forms for Writing About Reading page from *Reader's Notebook: Advanced*.

  What do you think you will record on this page in your reader's notebook?

  This page lists some of the different ways to write about reading. Which of these forms of writing have you already tried?

- ▶ Based on students' responses, point to one form of writing (e.g., book review) on the chart and read its definition.

  What does the third column in the chart tell you?

  The third column gives the definition of each type of writing.

- ▶ Point to the first column and read the heading, *Tally*.

  What will you write in this column?

  In this column, you will keep a tally of the different forms of writing you use. How do you keep a tally?

- ▶ If necessary, review how to keep a tally and count tally marks.

Have a Try

Invite the students to enter tally marks for the forms of writing they have used.

> If you have already used any of these forms of writing about reading in your reader's notebook this year, add a tally mark on your list.

▶ Invite a volunteer to demonstrate how to add a tally mark next to one form of writing.

Summarize and Apply

Summarize the learning and remind students to keep track of the forms of writing they do.

> What did you learn how to do today in your reader's notebook?

> If you write about your reading today, remember to put a tally mark next to the form of writing that you use.

Share

Following independent reading time, gather students together in the meeting area to talk about their writing about reading.

> Did you write about your reading today?

> What form of writing did you use?

> How did you keep track of it in your reader's notebook?

Extend the Lesson (Optional)

After assessing students' understanding, you might decide to extend the learning.

▶ You will need to decide which forms of writing about reading are appropriate for your students. After teaching each new form of writing, read aloud its definition on the Forms for Writing About Reading page and remind students to keep track of the forms of writing they use.

Forms for Writing About Reading

Tally	Kind of Writing	Definition
卌	Summary	a few sentences that tell the most important information
//	Book Recommendation	writing that gives another reader some information and advice on a book
/	Book Review	an opinion and analysis that includes comments on the quality of a book and gives another reader advice
/	Poem	a poetic piece that responds to a book (characters, setting, story events)
/	Blog	a blend of the term "web log," a blog has entries of comments, descriptions of events, or other information

Section 4: Writing About Reading

RML2 WAR.U2.RML2

Umbrella 2: Using a Reader's Notebook   579

Reading Minilesson Principle
Take minilesson notes in your reader's notebook so you can refer to information you need.

You Will Need

- a chart from a recently taught minilesson (e.g., LA.U6.RML1)
- chart paper and markers
- document camera (optional)
- a reader's notebook for each student

Academic Language / Important Vocabulary

- reader's notebook
- minilesson
- principle
- information
- notes

Goal

Copy minilesson notes into a reader's notebook for future reference.

Rationale

Reader's Notebook: Advanced (Fountas and Pinnell 2011) includes a section for information from minilessons. When students keep information from previous minilessons for reference, they are better able to remember what they learned and to use and build on that knowledge. At the end of each minilesson, have students copy the minilesson principle into a reader's notebook and make notes about anything they want to remember. Or, download the minilesson principles (see p. 586).

Assess Learning

Observe students when they use the Minilessons section of the reader's notebook and notice if there is evidence of new learning based on the goal of this minilesson.

- Do students neatly write (or glue) the minilesson principles into the Minilessons section of the reader's notebook and write some notes?
- Do they understand the terms *reader's notebook, minilesson, principle, information,* and *notes*?

Minilesson

Teach students how to take notes about minilessons in the reader's notebook and engage them in a discussion about how and when they might use the notes. Here is an example.

- Have students turn to the Minilessons section (gray tab) of the reader's notebook. Direct them to read the page silently.

  What do you think you will write in this section of your reader's notebook?

- Display a chart from a recently taught minilesson.

  When we have minilessons, we usually make a chart together about what you are learning. Often, I write the minilesson principle at the top. The principle summarizes the important understanding you need to learn.

  At the end of each minilesson, you will have the opportunity to take notes in your reader's notebook about what you learned. Watch what I do.

- On a separate sheet of chart paper, copy the minilesson principle from the chart and write a few notes about the minilesson underneath it (e.g., examples of books, important terms and definitions) or project a reader's notebook page.

  What did you notice about the notes I wrote about the minilesson?

  Because you will put all your minilesson notes in the same section, you will always know where to find them.

Have a Try

Invite the students to talk with a partner about when and why they might use their notes from previous minilessons.

> The gray tab says "You can look back at what you learned when you need to." Turn and talk about when you might need to look back at the information from a minilesson.

▶ After time for discussion, invite several pairs to share their thinking.

Summarize and Apply

Summarize the learning and remind students to take notes about minilessons in the Minilessons section to refer to as needed.

> Let's make a chart summarizing what you learned from this minilesson. What should we write?

▶ After completing the chart with students' input, write the principle at the top.

> Now take a few minutes to make notes about what you learned from this minilesson in your reader's notebook. Then read your book! Bring your notes to share when we come back together.

Share

Following independent reading time, gather students together in the meeting area to talk about their notes.

> What did you write in your reader's notebook about today's minilesson?

> How might your notes help you in the future?

Extend the Lesson (Optional)

After assessing students' understanding, you might decide to extend the learning.

▶ If students are not up to writing the principles and notes for each umbrella, download the page of minilesson principles for each umbrella (see p. 586) and have students glue it into a reader's notebook.

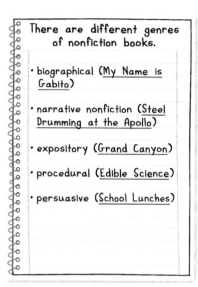

There are different genres of nonfiction books.

- biographical (<u>My Name is Gabito</u>)
- narrative nonfiction (<u>Steel Drumming at the Apollo</u>)
- expository (<u>Grand Canyon</u>)
- procedural (<u>Edible Science</u>)
- persuasive (<u>School Lunches</u>)

Take minilesson notes in your reader's notebook so you can refer to information you need.

- Write the minilesson principles in the Minilessons section of your reader's notebook.

- Write a few examples or brief notes to help you better remember the information.

- Reread the principles and notes when you need to.

Section 4: Writing About Reading

Reading Minilesson Principle
Write about the genres you study.

Using a Reader's Notebook

You Will Need

- charts from a recently taught genre studies umbrella (e.g., LA.U14.RML1 and RML2)
- chart paper resembling the Genre Studies form in *Reader's Notebook: Advanced* (Fountas and Pinnell 2011)
- markers
- a reader's notebook for each student

Academic Language / Important Vocabulary

- reader's notebook
- genre
- definition
- examples
- noticings

Continuum Connection

- Record the titles, authors, and genres of books to recommend (pp. 208, 211)

Goal

Write a working definition of the genre, book examples, and noticings about the characteristics of the genre.

Rationale

When students take notes about the genres they study, they are more likely to remember what they noticed and learned about the genre.

Assess Learning

Observe students when they write about genres in a reader's notebook and notice if there is evidence of new learning based on the goal of this minilesson.

- Can students write in a reader's notebook a working definition, noticings, and book examples for each genre they study?
- Do they understand the terms *reader's notebook, genre, definition, examples,* and *noticings*?

Minilesson

This minilesson should be taught immediately or shortly after finishing a genre studies umbrella. The following example addresses biography (Umbrella 14: Studying Biography in Section Two: Literary Analysis), but you can adapt the lesson to fit any genre your students have studied.

- Direct students to turn to the back of the orange Genre Studies tab in the reader's notebook.

    What do you think you will write in this section of your reader's notebook?

- Display a genre definition chart from a recently taught genre studies umbrella. Also display the chart prepared for this minilesson.

    We've been studying biography lately. I want to take some notes so I can remember what I've learned. What should I write on the line at the top of the Genre Studies page?

- Demonstrate writing the name of the genre on the line at the top of the enlarged page.

    What should I write under the *Working Definition* heading?

- Copy the definition from the definition chart onto the Genre Studies form. Then display the noticings chart from the genre studies umbrella.

    What should I write under the *Noticings* heading?

- Copy the noticings from the noticings chart onto the Genre Studies form.

Have a Try

Invite the students to talk with a partner about examples of the genre.

> Turn and talk to your partner about what we should write in the Book Examples section of the chart. What are some biographies that we have read?

▶ After time for discussion, invite a few pairs to share their thinking. Add book examples to the chart.

Summarize and Apply

Summarize the learning and remind students to write about the genres they study.

> Why is it a good idea to write in your reader's notebook about the genres you study?

▶ Write the principle at the top of the chart.

> Before you read today, take a few minutes to copy our notes about the biography genre onto the first blank page in the Genre Studies section of your reader's notebook. You can also make a note of anything else you've noticed about biography or any biographies that you've read. Bring your reader's notebook to share when we come back together.

Genre___Biography___

Working Definition	Noticings
A biography is a story about a person written by someone else.	• The author tells about a person's accomplishments and challenges.
	• The author chooses facts to include about the person's life.

Book Examples
• Talkin' About Bessie by Nikki Grimes
• When the Beat Was Born by Laban Carrick Hill
• Schomburg by Carole Boston Weatherford

• The author tells about the important things a person did or why the person why the person is interesting.
• The author gives an important message.
• The author includes the setting and the people who influenced the person's life.

Share

Following independent reading time, gather students together in the meeting area to discuss their notes.

> What did you write about biography in your reader's notebook today?

Extend the Lesson (Optional)

After assessing students' understanding, you might decide to extend the learning.

▶ At the end of each subsequent genre studies minilesson, give students time to make notes about their learning in a reader's notebook.

Section 4: Writing About Reading

RML 5
WAR.U2.RML5

Reading Minilesson Principle
Use the glossary as a tool to support your writing about reading.

Using a Reader's Notebook

You Will Need

- chart paper and markers
- a reader's notebook for each student

Academic Language / Important Vocabulary

- reader's notebook
- glossary
- term
- definition
- literary

Goal

Use the glossary as a tool to support writing about reading.

Rationale

When students are familiar with literary terms, they can communicate their ideas about their reading more clearly and precisely. *Reader's Notebook: Advanced* (Fountas and Pinnell 2011) includes a glossary of literary terms that students can use to remind themselves of academic language and important vocabulary.

Assess Learning

Observe students when they write about their reading and notice if there is evidence of new learning based on the goal of this minilesson.

- Do students use literary terms appropriately in their writing?
- Do they refer to the glossary in their reader's notebook when they are unsure about a literary term?
- Do they understand the terms *reader's notebook, glossary, term, definition,* and *literary*?

Minilesson

Discuss the Glossary of Terms in *Reader's Notebook: Advanced* and engage students in thinking about the ways they might use the glossary. Here is an example.

- Direct students to turn to the Glossary of Terms section (blue tab) of the reader's notebook. Give them a few minutes to review this section silently.

    What do you notice about this section of the reader's notebook?

- Guide students to notice that the glossary contains definitions of genres, literary terms, and different text structures.

    When and why might you use this section? How might it be helpful?

- Record students' responses on the chart paper.
- Ask students to read the definitions of a few of the genres listed in the glossary (e.g., fantasy, historical fiction, folktale).

    How might these definitions be a helpful resource?

- Record students' responses on the chart paper.
- Repeat the same process, drawing the students' attention to the parts of the glossary that address text structure.

Have a Try

Invite students to further explore the glossary with a partner.

> Find one or two literary terms that are either new to you or that you need clarified. Talk with your partner about the terms you find.

▶ After students turn and talk, invite a few students to share what they discovered.

> Are there any other ways that the glossary might be helpful for you?

▶ Record any additional ideas to the chart.

Summarize and Apply

Summarize the learning and remind students to use the glossary as a tool to support their writing about reading.

> Today you learned how you can use the glossary as a tool to support your writing about reading.

▶ Write the principle at the top of the chart.

> After you read today, write about your thinking in your reader's notebook.

> When appropriate, use literary terms you have learned. If you need help remembering a term, use the glossary in your reader's notebook.

Share

Following independent reading time, gather students together in the meeting area to talk about their writing about reading.

> Did anyone use the glossary in their reader's notebook when they wrote about their reading today?

> How did the glossary help you?

Extend the Lesson (Optional)

After assessing students' understanding, you might decide to extend the learning.

▶ During Literary Analysis lessons, you might have students highlight terms in the glossary as they are introduced.

▶ When doing shared writing, model using the glossary to look up literary terms.

Use the glossary as a tool to support your writing about reading.

Ways You Might Use Your Reader's Notebook Glossary

- Clarify what you know about a literary term.

- Look up literary terms to use in letters about reading.

- Check the definition of a particular genre.

- Use the genre definitions to determine the genre of the book for the reader's notebook reading list.

- Refresh your understanding of different text structures to analyze and critique the way writers use text structure when you write about reading.

- Check the spelling of literary terms.

Assessment

After you have taught the minilessons in this umbrella, observe students as they talk and write about their reading across instructional contexts: interactive read-aloud, independent reading, guided reading, shared reading, and book club. Use *The Literacy Continuum* (Fountas and Pinnell 2017) to guide the observation of students' reading and writing behaviors.

▶ What evidence do you have of new understandings related to using the reader's notebook?

- Are students continuing to add to the list of books they want to read?
- Do they keep a tally of the forms of writing about reading they have used?
- Do they take notes about minilessons in their reader's notebooks and refer to them when appropriate?
- Do they take notes about the genres they study?
- Do they use the glossary to support their writing about reading?
- Do they use the terms *title, author, list, minilesson, genre,* and *tally*?

▶ Based on your observations, what other ways might you have your students write about reading in a reader's notebook?

Use your observations to determine the next umbrella you will teach. You may also consult Minilessons Across the Year (pp. 61–64) for guidance.

Reader's Notebook

When this umbrella is complete, provide a copy of the minilesson principles (see resources.fountasandpinnell.com) for students to glue in the reader's notebook (in the Minilessons section if using *Reader's Notebook: Advanced* [Fountas and Pinnell 2011]), so they can refer to the information as needed.

Minilessons in This Umbrella

RML1   Write dialogue letters to your teacher and classmates to share your thinking about your reading.

RML2   Know the qualities of a strong dialogue letter.

RML3   Write formal letters to newspaper or magazine editors to respond to articles.

Before Teaching Umbrella 3 Minilessons

Writing letters about reading is an authentic way for students to discuss texts with another reader. We suggest having each student write one letter about reading each week. We believe it is important that their writing is read by you and that you provide a response, so you will need to develop a management system for receiving and responding to the letters. You might have all students turn in a reader's notebook on one day each week or stagger the due dates for four or five students each day so you can provide regular responses to their letters without being overwhelmed by a large stack. If you are in a middle school setting in which you see several classes of students each day, you might want to consider having students alternate between writing to you and to their classmates each week so you can stagger the workload of responding (see pp. 53–55 for more about letters about reading and the reading-writing connection).

Before teaching this umbrella, it would be helpful to introduce or review the structure of a letter with your students. Students will need to be familiar with the structure of both a friendly letter (for RML1, RML2) and a formal letter (for RML3).

To teach the minilessons in this umbrella, use letters that you have written as a model or letters from past students. For mentor texts, use the books from the *Fountas & Pinnell Classroom™ Interactive Read-Aloud Collection* text sets listed below or choose books from your own classroom library.

Kindness and Compassion

Wings by Christopher Myers

Babu's Song by Stephanie Stuve-Bodeen

Chachaji's Cup by Uma Krishnaswami

Handling Emotions/Positive Relationships

Bird by Zetta Elliott

As you read aloud and enjoy these texts together, help students

- think about, talk about, and express opinions about texts,

- discuss the author's message, and

- mark interesting parts of their reading that they want to include in a letter.

Kindness and Compassion

Handling Emotions/ Positive Relationships

Reader's Notebook

Section 4: Writing About Reading

RML1
WAR.U3.RML1

Reading Minilesson Principle
Write dialogue letters to your teacher and classmates to share your thinking about your reading.

You Will Need

- chart paper prepared with a student-written letter (written by a real past student or by you from the perspective of a student) about a book that you recently read aloud to your students, such as one of the following from Text Set: Kindness and Compassion:
  - *Babu's Song* by Stephanie Stuve-Bodeen
  - *Chachaji's Cup* by Uma Krishnaswami
  - *Wings* by Christopher Myers
- chart paper and markers
- a reader's notebook for each student

Academic Language / Important Vocabulary

- dialogue letter

Continuum Connection

- Compose notes, lists, letters, or statements to remember important information about a text (pp. 208, 211)
- Provide evidence from the text or from personal experience to support written statements about the text (pp. 208, 212)

Goal

Understand the characteristics of dialogue letters, the different ways to share thinking about books, and how to provide evidence for that thinking.

Rationale

Writing dialogue letters to share thinking about reading helps students to read more closely and to think more critically about their reading.

Assess Learning

Assess students' dialogue letters. Notice if there is evidence of new learning based on the goal of this minilesson.

- Do students share various kinds of thinking about their reading in their dialogue letters?
- Do they provide evidence from the text and/or personal experience?
- Do they understand and use the term *dialogue letter*?

Minilesson

Use a prepared letter as a model to help students learn about the kind of thinking they can share in their letters and how to provide evidence for their thinking. Here is an example.

> Today, I would like to share with you a letter that one of my past students wrote to share his thinking about his reading.

- Read the prepared letter aloud.

> What do you notice about what Antonio wrote in his letter? What kinds of things did he write about?
>
> How did he provide evidence for his thinking?

- Record students' responses on chart paper, generalizing them as necessary.

> What do you notice about the beginning and ending of Antonio's letter?
>
> In the beginning of his letter, Antonio responded to what I wrote to him in my last letter. At the end, he asked me a question. This letter is an example of a dialogue letter. When you write dialogue letters with someone, you are having an ongoing conversation with that person through your letters. It is important to respond to their questions and to ask them questions in order to keep the conversation going. This year, you will write dialogue letters with me and your classmates to share your thinking about your reading.

Have a Try

Invite the students to talk with a partner about what they might include in a letter about their reading.

▶ Show the cover of *Wings*.

> Turn and talk about *Wings*. What thinking might you share in a letter about this book?

▶ After time for discussion, invite several students to share their thinking. Record any new types of thinking on the chart, generalizing them as needed.

Summarize and Apply

Summarize the learning and remind students to write letters about their reading in a reader's notebook.

> After you read today, write a letter to me about a book you are reading. Use the chart for ideas. Remember to provide evidence for your thinking. Bring your reader's notebook when we come back together.

▶ Add the principle to the chart.

Share

Following independent reading time, gather students together in the meeting area to talk about their letters.

> Who would like to read aloud the letter you wrote today?

Extend the Lesson (Optional)

After assessing students' understanding, you might decide to extend the learning.

▶ You will find a list of starter ideas in the Writing About Reading section of *Reader's Notebook: Advanced* (Fountas and Pinnell 2011). Students can refer to the list if they need help deciding what to write about.

▶ If students need support in writing a letter, use shared writing to create one together.

October 14

Dear Mr. Baker,

I agree that a theme of Babu's Song is family. The author is saying that family is more important than anything you can buy, even more important than the music box.

Another book that deals with family and possessions is Chachaji's Cup. Chachaji has a teacup that symbolizes family, home, and overcoming adversity. As Neel gets older, he grows apart from his uncle. The teacup breaks, too. However, Neel manages to repair both the teacup and his relationship with his uncle.

This story shows that objects can have special meaning, but they are not as important as family. What do you think about the message in this book, Mr. Baker?

From,
Antonio

Write dialogue letters to your teacher and classmates to share your thinking about your reading.

- Give a well-organized short summary.
- Tell what you notice about the illustrations.
- Tell what you learned about the characters.
- Give opinions about the book.
- Explain the author's message or theme.
- Explain how the book reminds you of something in your life, another book, or something in the world.
- Describe the setting and why it's important.
- Give interesting examples of the writing.
- Provide evidence for your thinking.
- Pose questions or wonderings.
- Respond to any questions in the last letter you received.

RML 2
WAR.U3.RML2

Reading Minilesson Principle
Know the qualities of a strong dialogue letter.

Writing Letters to Share Thinking About Texts

You Will Need

- chart paper prepared with a strong student-written letter about a book that you recently read aloud, such as *Bird* by Zetta Elliott, from Text Set: Handling Emotions/Positive Relationships
- chart paper and markers
- a reader's notebook for each student

Academic Language / Important Vocabulary

- dialogue letter
- quality

Continuum Connection

- Compose notes, lists, letters or statements to remember important information about a text (pp. 208, 211)
- Provide evidence from the text or from personal experience to support written statements about the text (pp. 208, 212)

Goal

Identify the qualities of a strong letter including content and conventions.

Rationale

When students can identify the qualities of a strong dialogue letter and assess letters against those standards, they are able to think more deeply about the books they read and communicate their thinking clearly in writing. This minilesson should be taught after students have written at least three letters about their reading.

Assess Learning

Assess students' dialogue letters. Notice if there is evidence of new learning based on the goal of this minilesson.

- ▶ Can students identify the qualities of a strong dialogue letter?
- ▶ Do their own dialogue letters demonstrate those qualities?
- ▶ Do they understand the terms *dialogue letter* and *quality*?

Minilesson

To help students think about the minilesson principle, use a prepared letter to engage students in a discussion about the qualities of a strong dialogue letter. Here is an example.

- ▶ Display the prepared letter and read it aloud.

  Here's a letter a student wrote that shares her thinking about her reading. What makes it a strong letter?

- ▶ If necessary, prompt the discussion with questions such as the following:
  - *How does she share her thinking about the text?*
  - *What makes this letter interesting to read?*
  - *Does her letter make sense?*
  - *How does she let you know what book she is writing about?*
  - *Does it have all the parts of a letter?*
  - *What kinds of words does she use to talk about the book?*

- ▶ Use the students' noticings to create, on a separate sheet of chart paper, a list of the qualities of a strong letter.

Have a Try

Invite the students to talk with a partner about one of their own dialogue letters.

> Take a look at one of the dialogue letters you have already written. What makes it a strong letter? Are there parts that could be improved? Share these thoughts with a partner.

▶ After time for reflection and discussion, ask a few students to share their thinking. Add any new ideas to the chart.

Summarize and Apply

Summarize the learning and remind students to refer to the chart when assessing their own letters.

> Today you thought about the qualities of a strong letter. After you read today, start writing a new letter. Think about the qualities on our chart as you write. Bring that letter with you when we come back together.

Share

Following independent reading time, gather students together in the meeting area to talk about their letters.

> Turn and talk to a partner about the letter you wrote today. What parts show your best thinking? What makes it a strong letter?

Extend the Lesson (Optional)

After assessing students' understanding, you might decide to extend the learning.

▶ Invite students to choose a letter that shows their best thinking. Have them write a few sentences or a paragraph telling why they think it is a thoughtful letter.

▶ Use the form called Assessment of Letters in Reader's Notebook (p. 55) to assess your students' letters.

November 7

Dear Mr. Baker,

You asked what I thought about <u>Bird</u> by Zetta Elliott. I liked it, but it was sad. I think the author's writing is beautiful and poetic. On the first page, she writes that a bird was "perched on the rusty rail of the fire escape shivering in the winter wind." Descriptions like that made the story come alive for me.

The story is sad because a boy loses both his brother and his grandfather. After his brother dies, the boy wishes he could have fixed his brother. Uncle Son replies, "You can fix a broken wing with a splint, and a bird can fly again, but you can't fix a broken soul." I wonder if someone could've helped Marcus, or if he really couldn't be fixed. What do you think, Mr. Baker?

From,
Jennifer

Qualities of a Strong Letter

- Is enjoyable to read
- Includes the title and author
- Makes sense
- Uses letter format: date, greeting, and closing
- Shows thinking about the book with evidence from personal experience or the book
- Might use a quote from the book
- Is neat and easy to read
- Shows best spelling and punctuation
- Shares the parts of the text you enjoyed or found interesting
- Uses literary terms when appropriate
- Asks questions you have about the book
- Provides responses to questions

Section 4: Writing About Reading

Reading Minilesson Principle
Write formal letters to newspaper or magazine editors to respond to articles.

Goal

Write formal letters to newspaper or magazine editors to respond to articles.

Rationale

When students learn how to write formal letters to newspaper or magazine editors in response to articles, they develop their ability to think analytically about what they read and to express and justify their opinions about what they have read.

Assess Learning

Assess students' letters to the editor. Notice if there is evidence of new learning based on the goal of this minilesson.

- ▶ Can students write a formal letter to an editor in response to an article?
- ▶ Are their letters written in the correct format?
- ▶ Do they express and justify their opinions about the article?
- ▶ Do they understand the terms *editor, article,* and *formal letter*?

Minilesson

To help students think about the minilesson principle, use a model letter to engage students in noticing the characteristics of a letter to the editor. Here is an example.

- ▶ Display the article you chose before class. Read it aloud.

  After reading this article, a student wrote a letter to the editor to respond to the article.

- ▶ Display the letter and read it aloud.

  What do you notice about her letter?

- ▶ Record students' responses on chart paper. As needed, prompt the discussion with questions such as the following:

  - *What is a letter to an editor? Why would someone write a letter to an editor?*
  - *What do you notice about the format of her letter? What information does it include?*
  - *How long is her letter?*
  - *How do you know which article she is responding to?*
  - *What kinds of things does she write in response to the article?*
  - *What do you notice about how she shares her opinion?*
  - *What evidence does she provide for her thinking?*
  - *What do you notice about her writing style?*

Have a Try

Invite the students to talk with a partner about what they would write in a letter to the editor.

> Think about the article we just read together. What would you write in a letter to the editor about this article? Turn and talk to your partner about what you would write.

▶ After students turn and talk, invite several students to share their thinking.

Summarize and Apply

Summarize the learning and remind students to refer to the chart when writing their own letters.

▶ Provide students with several sources of student-friendly articles.

> Today, you will write your own letter to an editor. You can respond to the article we read together, or you can choose a different article for your response letter. Refer to the chart if you need help remembering how to write a letter to the editor. Bring your letter to share when we come back together.

▶ Add the principle to the chart.

Share

Following independent reading time, gather students together in the meeting area to talk about their letters.

> Who would like to read aloud the letter you wrote today?

Extend the Lesson (Optional)

After assessing students' understanding, you might decide to extend the learning.

▶ Help students send their letters to the editor, if they wish to do so.

▶ Explain that letters to online newspaper and magazine editors will usually be sent digitally. Discuss the differences between formal letters and formal emails.

Olivia Wilson
12 Pleasant Street
Hilldale, CA 91234

Hilldale Gazette
123 Main Street
Hilldale, CA 91234

November 14

To the Editor:

I am writing in response to "Meatless Mondays" published on November 11th. I am in sixth grade at Hilldale Middle School, and I think that adopting Meatless Mondays is a great idea! As the article mentions, the production of meat is bad for the environment. And, research shows that most of us eat more meat than is good for us.

Some Hilldale residents are against the proposal because they think students should have choice, but students will still be able to eat meat at school the other days. We should all eat less meat. Who knows . . . some students might prefer salad to salami!

Sincerely,

Olivia Wilson

Write formal letters to newspaper or magazine editors to respond to articles.

- Use the format of a formal letter.
- Keep it short: one or two paragraphs.
- Give the title and the date of the article you're responding to.
- State your opinion about the article.
- Provide reasons and evidence for your opinion.
- Be polite and respectful.
- Use formal language.
- Write with your best spelling and punctuation.
- Try to make your letter interesting and enjoyable to read.

Section 4: Writing About Reading

Assessment

After you have taught the minilessons in this umbrella, observe students as they talk and write about their reading across instructional contexts: interactive read-aloud, independent reading, guided reading, shared reading, and book club. Use *The Literacy Continuum* (Fountas and Pinnell 2017) to guide the observation of students' reading and writing behaviors.

▶ What evidence do you have of new understandings related to writing letters about reading?

- Do students share their thinking about their reading in dialogue letters to their teachers and/or classmates?
- Do their letters demonstrate the qualities of a good dialogue letter?
- Can they write formal letters in response to magazine or newspaper articles?
- Do they use terms such as *quality, evidence,* and *respond* when they talk about their letters about reading?

▶ In what other ways, beyond the scope of this umbrella, are students writing about books?

- Are students using other forms of writing to share their thinking about books?
- Are they writing about longer chapter books over the course of several letters?

Use your observations to determine the next umbrella you will teach. You may also consult Minilessons Across the Year (pp. 61–64) for guidance.

Reader's Notebook

When this umbrella is complete, provide a copy of the minilesson principles (see resources.fountasandpinnell.com) for students to glue in the reader's notebook (in the Minilessons section if using *Reader's Notebook: Advanced* [Fountas and Pinnell 2011]), so they can refer to the information as needed.

Minilessons in This Umbrella

RML1   Use a grid to organize, analyze, and compare information.

RML2   Use a web to show how ideas are connected.

RML3   Use an outline to show the main topic of a book and its subtopics.

RML4   Use diagrams to show and analyze how authors organize information.

RML5   Use a Venn diagram to compare and contrast books.

Before Teaching Umbrella 4 Minilessons

Because students should think and talk about the concepts before writing about them, coordinate these minilessons with relevant Literary Analysis minilessons. Each lesson provides one example of how to use a graphic organizer; however, the lessons can be used in other ways, some of which are mentioned in Extend the Lesson. For a description of graphic organizers appropriate for grade 6, see page 206 in *The Literacy Continuum* (Fountas and Pinnell 2017).

Use books from the *Fountas & Pinnell Classroom™ Interactive Read-Aloud Collection* text sets listed below or choose high-quality fiction and nonfiction books from your classroom library.

Leadership

Sitting Bull by S. D. Nelson

Equality

Nelson Mandela by Kadir Nelson

Activists/Change Makers

Ballots for Belva
   by Sudipta Bardhan-Quallen

Animal Adaptations

Glow by W. H. Beck

Life on Earth

Living Fossils by Caroline Arnold

Perseverance

The Memory Coat by Elvira Woodruff

Kindness and Compassion

Babu's Song by Stephanie Stuve-Bodeen

Chachaji's Cup by Uma Krishnaswami

Handling Emotions/Positive Relationships

The Banana-Leaf Ball
   by Katie Smith Milway

Illustrator Study: K. Y. Craft

Pegasus by Marianna Mayer

King Midas and the Golden Touch
   by Charlotte Craft

Genre Study: Epic Tales

The Adventures of Odysseus by Hugh Lupton and Daniel Morden

Prince of Fire by Jatinder Verma

As you read aloud and enjoy these texts together, help students notice the underlying text structures.

Leadership

Equality

Activists/ Change Makers

Animal Adaptations

Life on Earth

Perseverance

Kindness and Compassion

Handling Emotions

K.Y. Craft

Genre Study: Epic Tales

Reader's Notebook

Reading Minilesson Principle
Use a grid to organize, analyze, and compare information.

Using Graphic Organizers to Share Thinking About Books

You Will Need

- several familiar biographies, such as the following:
  - *Sitting Bull* by S. D. Nelson, from Text Set: Leadership
  - *Nelson Mandela* by Kadir Nelson, from Text Set: Equality
  - *Ballots for Belva* by Sudipta Bardhan-Quallen, from Text Set: Activists/Change Makers
- chart paper prepared with a grid that has the headings *Title and Subject*, *Traits*, and *Achievements*
- markers
- a reader's notebook for each student
- basket of biographies
- a copy of the Comparison Grid for each student (optional)
- To download the following online resource for this lesson, visit **resources.fountasandpinnell.com**: Comparison Grid

Academic Language / Important Vocabulary

- reader's notebook
- graphic organizer
- grid
- organize
- analyze
- compare

Continuum Connection

- Write about connections among texts by topic, theme, major ideas, authors' styles, and genres (pp. 208, 212)

Goal

Use a grid to organize, analyze, and compare information across texts.

Rationale

When students learn how to use a grid to compare books, they learn to look closely at texts and compare characteristics across texts. This lesson provides a model for teaching students to use a graphic organizer to organize, analyze, and compare subjects of biographies. Make sure students have read a variety of biographies before teaching this lesson.

Assess Learning

Observe students when they talk about and use grids and notice if there is evidence of new learning based on the goal of this minilesson.

- Are students able to use a grid to organize, analyze, and compare information from different books?
- Do they understand the terms *reader's notebook, graphic organizer, grid, organize, analyze,* and *compare*?

Minilesson

To help students think about the minilesson principle, use familiar texts to demonstrate how to use a grid to organize, analyze, and compare information (subjects of biographies) across texts. Here is an example.

- Show the prepared grid with headings.

  What do you notice about this grid?

  How do you think I can use this grid?

- As students respond, engage them in a discussion about grids so that they understand what should be written in each section of the grid and how the grid will help them consider the traits and achievements of the subjects of several biographies.

- Show the cover of *Sitting Bull* and revisit several pages.

  How can we fill in this grid for the subject of this biography, Sitting Bull?

- Ask volunteers to make suggestions. As students provide ideas, fill in the sections of the grid.

- Show the cover of *Nelson Mandela* and revisit several pages.

  Now let's fill in this grid for Nelson Mandela, thinking about his traits that connect to his achievements.

- Continue filling in the grid.

Have a Try

Invite the students to talk with a partner about adding a biography subject to the grid.

▶ Show the cover of *Ballots for Belva* and revisit several pages.

> Turn and talk to your partner about what would go in the grid for Belva Lockwood.

▶ After time for a brief discussion, ask students to share. Add to grid.

Summarize and Apply

Summarize the learning and remind students to try using a grid in a reader's notebook.

> You can use a grid like the one on the chart to compare and analyze biographies.

▶ Add the principle to the chart. Then provide a copy of the Comparison Grid graphic organizer for students to glue into a reader's notebook or have them make their own.

> Choose a biography to read today. Label two columns *Traits* and *Achievements*, just like on the chart, and then fill in one row of the grid about the subject of the biography you are reading. Bring the book and your reader's notebook when we meet so you can share.

Share

Following independent reading time, gather students in small groups.

> Share the grid you started in your reader's notebook. Talk about how the biographies your group looked at are similar and different.

Extend the Lesson (Optional)

After assessing students' understanding, you might decide to extend the learning.

▶ Have students return to the Comparison Grid to fill in the other rows as they read other biographical texts.

▶ **Writing About Reading** Encourage students to create grids to compare other types of information in fiction and nonfiction books, such as the following: theme, poetic technique, character, author's message or technique, or genre.

Use a grid to organize, analyze, and compare information.

Title and Subject	Traits	Achievements
Sitting Bull	• strong leader • confident • loyal • courageous • insightful • dignified	• named war chief • first person to be named leader of entire Sioux nation • resisted relocation efforts for many years
Nelson Mandela	• strong leader • confident • dedicated • brave • insightful • dignified	• led resistance to apartheid • awarded Nobel Peace Prize • elected first black president of South Africa
Belva Lockwood	• strong leader • confident • unwavering beliefs • courageous • persistent • determined	• became an attorney when it was very difficult for women • fought for the rights of underserved people • twice ran for president and became the first woman to receive votes

Reading Minilesson Principle
Use a web to show how ideas are connected.

Using Graphic Organizers to Share Thinking About Books

You Will Need

- several familiar books that have connected ideas, such as the following:
  - *The Memory Coat* by Elvira Woodruff, from Text Set: Perseverance
  - *Babu's Song* by Stephanie Stuve-Bodeen and *Chachaji's Cup* by Uma Krishnaswami, from Text Set: Kindness and Compassion
  - *The Banana-Leaf Ball* by Katie Smith Milway, from Text Set: Handling Emotions/Positive Relationships
- chart paper prepared with a blank web graphic organizer
- a copy of a web for each student (optional)
- To download the following online resource for this lesson, visit **resources.fountasandpinnell.com**: Web

Academic Language / Important Vocabulary

- graphic organizer
- compassion
- web
- connected

Continuum Connection

- Write about connections among texts by topic, theme, major ideas, authors' styles, and genres (pp. 208, 212)
- Use graphic organizers such as webs to show how a nonfiction writer puts together information related to the same topic or subtopic (p. 213)

Goal

Learn how to use webs as a graphic organizer to connect information within a text or across texts.

Rationale

When students learn to create a web as a way to connect ideas within or across texts, they learn to pay attention to common ideas both in books and in their own lives. This lesson provides a model for how you can teach students to use a graphic organizer to connect ideas.

Assess Learning

Observe students when they talk about webs to connect ideas and notice if there is evidence of new learning based on the goal of this minilesson.

- ▶ Do students participate in creating a web to connect ideas within or between books?
- ▶ Are students using the terms *graphic organizer, web, compassion,* and *connected*?

Minilesson

To help students think about the minilesson principle, use familiar texts to help students create a web to highlight an idea that connects several books. Here is an example.

- ▶ Display the blank web and a variety of books that have a theme or idea that connects them, such as symbolism (e.g., *The Memory Coat, Babu's Song, Chachaji's Cup, The Banana-Leaf Ball*).

    One element all of these books have in common is symbolism.

- ▶ Write the word *symbolism* in the center bubble.

    How would you describe symbolism?

    What is an example of symbolism from *The Memory Coat*?

- ▶ As students provide examples, build the web by writing the title of the story and a few words about the symbolism example in one of the web bubbles. Help students revise their wording so as to include only a few words to represent the symbolic object and what it represents.

- ▶ Repeat for *Babu's Song* and *Chachaji's Cup*.

Have a Try

Invite the students to talk with a partner about creating a web to connect ideas.

▶ Show the cover of *The Banana-Leaf Ball*.

What could you record in this web that centers around symbolism for *The Banana-Leaf Ball*? Turn and talk about that.

▶ After time for discussion, ask a few volunteers to share ideas and add to web.

Summarize and Apply

Summarize the learning and remind students to think about how to use a web to connect ideas.

Today you learned that you can use a web to connect ideas in different books.

▶ Add the principle to the chart. Then provide a copy of a web that students can fill out and glue into a reader's notebook, or have them draw their own webs.

If you are reading a fiction book today, think about any symbolism you notice. Choose one of those ideas and begin to fill in a web about that. Bring your web when we meet to share.

Share

Following independent reading time, gather students in the meeting area. Ask a few students to share.

Who would like to share the web you made?

Extend the Lesson (Optional)

After assessing students' understanding, you might decide to extend the learning.

▶ Have students continue filling in the symbolism web in a reader's notebook as they read other fiction books with examples of symbolism.

▶ Encourage students to use webs in other ways to show how ideas in fiction and nonfiction books are connected (e.g., connect nonfiction topics or subtopics in one or more books, create a character traits web, use a web to connect themes across several texts).

Use a web to show how ideas are connected.

The Memory Coat
• Grisha's Coat: Family memories, long journey

Babu's Song
• Music box: communication; family connection

The Banana-Leaf Ball
• Banana-leaf ball: memories; connection; friendship

Symbolism

Chachaji's Cup
• Old china cup: memories; family; journeys

Reading Minilesson Principle
Use an outline to show the main topic of a book and its subtopics.

You Will Need

- one or more familiar books that can be used to create an outline, such as *Glow* by W. H. Beck, from Text Set: Animal Adaptations
- chart paper prepared with I, IA, and IB of an outline filled out for the book you are using
- markers
- basket of nonfiction books, some of which are organized by related topics

Academic Language / Important Vocabulary

- reader's notebook
- graphic organizer
- outline
- main topic
- subtopics

Continuum Connection

- Write an outline by providing summaries of information learned using headings and subheadings that reflect a text's overall structure and simple categories (p. 213)
- Recognize that informational texts may present a larger topic with many subtopics (p. 85)

Goal

Create an outline with headings and subheadings that reflect the organization of a text.

Rationale

When students learn to use an outline, they learn to identify the main topic and subtopics of a nonfiction book, which reveals the organization of the text. It may be helpful to teach the following umbrellas prior to this one: Umbrella 16: Noticing How Nonfiction Authors Choose to Organize Information and Umbrella 20: Using Text Features to Gain Information, both in Section Two: Literary Analysis.

Assess Learning

Observe students when they talk about and create outlines and notice if there is evidence of new learning based on the goal of this minilesson.

- ▶ Can they use and create an outline to show the main topic of a book and its subtopics?
- ▶ Are they using the terms *reader's notebook, graphic organizer, outline, main topic,* and *subtopics*?

Minilesson

To help students think about the minilesson principle, engage students in discussion about how to make an outline. Here is an example.

- ▶ Depending on the experience of your students, you might want to adjust the number of entries to vary from those shown in the example.
- ▶ Display the prepared chart and the cover of *Glow*.

  What do you notice about the book and the chart? How are they related?

  Here is an outline I started for *Glow*. I wrote the outline to organize and help me remember the information in the book.

- ▶ Draw students' attention to section I.

  What do you notice about what I wrote?

- ▶ Guide students to understand that topics are listed from larger to smaller and organized with roman and arabic numerals and uppercase and lowercase letters. The information is listed very briefly, not in complete sentences.

  If I were to continue the outline, what could I write next?

- ▶ Guide them to complete section IC. If needed, explain that a different topic would start with roman numeral II and continue with the same type of organization as shown on the chart.

Have a Try

Invite the students to talk with a partner about using an outline.

> Turn and talk with your partner about how you could use an outline.

Summarize and Apply

Summarize the learning and remind students to use an outline to show the main idea and subtopics.

> Today you learned that an outline is useful for showing the main idea and subtopics from a book. Sometimes a book has headings. How might headings help you outline a book?

▶ Add the principle to the top of the chart.

> Today when you read, choose a nonfiction book to read with a partner. Work together to create an outline of the topics and subtopics of the book (or part of the book) that could be added to your reader's notebook. Bring your outline and the book you used when we meet.

Share

Following independent reading time, match up sets of partners to make groups of four.

> As you share with your group the outline you created, talk about the decisions you made about what to include in the outline and how to organize it.

Extend the Lesson (Optional)

After assessing students' understanding, you might decide to extend the learning.

▶ Use different nonfiction examples to create more expanded outlines with students, including the various outline subsections.

▶ **Writing About Reading** Encourage students to create an outline in a reader's notebook to help organize and remember information from a nonfiction book.

Use an outline to show the main topic of a book and its subtopics.

Glow: Animals with Their Own Night-Lights

I. Where bioluminescent organisms live
  A. Land (foxfire mushrooms)
  B. Air (fireflies)
  C. Ocean (majority)
    1. Anglerfish
    2. Portuguese man-of-war
    3. Vampire squid
II. Purpose of bioluminescence
  A. Hunt
    1. Lure prey with light near mouth
    2. Trick prey with light on tail
  B. Defense
  C. Find friends

Reading Minilesson Principle
Use diagrams to show and analyze how authors organize information.

Using Graphic Organizers to Share Thinking About Books

You Will Need

- a familiar nonfiction book that has clear examples of compare and contrast, such as the following:
  - *Living Fossils* by Caroline Arnold, from Text Set: Life on Earth
- chart prepared with one or two items in each column of a compare and contrast chart
- markers
- copy of How Nonfiction Writers Organize Information for each student
- basket of short nonfiction books with a variety of organizational structures
- To download the above online resource for this lesson, visit **resources.fountasandpinnell.com**: How Nonfiction Writers Organize Information

Academic Language / Important Vocabulary

- graphic organizer
- diagram
- organize

Continuum Connection

- Write about the connections among texts by topic, theme, major ideas, authors' styles, and genres (pp. 208, 212)

Goal

Use diagrams to show how authors organize information.

Rationale

Graphic organizers help students to think about the ways books are structured so they begin to internalize these structures and are able to identify them. It also gives them options for how to organize their own writing. Students should have an understanding of the underlying text structures in nonfiction books before you teach this minilesson. (See Umbrella 16: Noticing How Nonfiction Authors Choose to Organize Information in Section Two: Literary Analysis.)

Assess Learning

Observe students when they choose and create diagrams and notice if there is evidence of new learning based on the goal of this minilesson.

- ▶ Are students able to determine an appropriate diagram to show how an author organizes information?
- ▶ Are they using the terms *graphic organizer, diagram,* and *organize*?

Minilesson

To help students think about the minilesson principle, use familiar nonfiction texts to help them think about how to choose and use a diagram to show how authors organize information. Here is an example.

- ▶ Provide a copy for each student of the online resource How Nonfiction Writers Organize Information to glue into a reader's notebook or list the categories on chart paper and review prior to the lesson (chronological, temporal, categories/subcategories, problem/solution, compare/contrast, cause/effect).

- ▶ Display the prepared compare and contrast chart for *Living Fossils*.

  What do you notice about this graphic organizer?

  Why is this graphic organizer a good choice for showing how the author organized the information in *Living Fossils*?

  How does the graphic organizer help you think about the book's organizational structure?

- ▶ Guide the conversation so students focus on why a compare and contrast grid is the most appropriate way to show how the author decided to organize information in *Living Fossils*.

  What else could we add to the other sections of this compare and contrast grid?

- ▶ Revisit pages as necessary to refresh students' memories and gather information to add to the grid. Use their responses to continue filling in the grid.

Have a Try

Invite the students to talk with a group about choosing and using a diagram to show how authors organize information in a nonfiction book.

▶ Have students sit in groups. Provide each group with a nonfiction book. Ensure that there are a variety of organizational structures spread between the groups.

> Turn and talk to your group about which type of diagram would be most appropriate to show how the author organizes the information in the nonfiction book your group has.

▶ After time for discussion, ask a volunteer from each group to tell which type of diagram would be the most useful for the book they looked at and why.

Summarize and Apply

Summarize the learning and remind students to think about how to use a diagram to show how authors organize information in a nonfiction book.

▶ Review the chart and write the principle at the top.

▶ Provide baskets of nonfiction books that have a variety of organizational structures. Provide various graphic organizers for students to glue in a reader's notebook or have them make their own.

> With a partner, choose a book from the basket to read. Work together to fill in the most appropriate organizer to show how the author organized the nonfiction information. Bring your notebook when we meet so you can share.

Share

Following independent reading time, match up sets of partners to make groups of four.

> Share with your group the diagram you made.

Extend the Lesson (Optional)

After assessing students' understanding, you might decide to extend the learning.

▶ If students need more support, you could introduce each diagram on the online resource How Nonfiction Writers Organize Information through shared writing.

▶ **Writing About Reading** Encourage students to use an appropriate diagram to show the organizational structure of other nonfiction books they read.

Use diagrams to show and analyze how authors organize information.

Horseshoe Crabs Then	Horseshoe Crabs Now
• lived 150 million years ago	• lives today
• fossils remain of their bodies and their trails	• can survive wide range of temperatures and salt levels
• crawled from lagoon to land	• hundreds move from ocean to land
• ate worms and shellfish	• females drag the males to shore and lay eggs
	• eat worms and shellfish; can survive months with little food

RML5
WAR.U4.RML5

Reading Minilesson Principle
Use a Venn diagram to compare and contrast books.

Using Graphic Organizers to Share Thinking About Books

You Will Need

- familiar fiction books for comparing and contrasting genre, such as the following:

  - two myths: *Pegasus* by Marianna Mayer and *King Midas and the Golden Touch* by Charlotte Craft, from Text Set: Illustrator Study: K. Y. Craft

  - two epics: *The Adventures of Odysseus* by Hugh Lupton and Daniel Morden and *Prince of Fire* by Jatinder Verma, from Text Set: Genre Study: Epic Tales

- chart paper prepared with a blank Venn diagram

- a copy of a Venn diagram for each student (optional)

- To download the following online resource for this lesson, visit **resources.fountasandpinnell.com**: Venn Diagram

Academic Language / Important Vocabulary

- genre
- Venn diagram
- compare and contrast

Continuum Connection

- Notice and write about an author's use of underlying structural patterns to organize information and sometimes apply the same structure to writing nonfiction texts: description, temporal sequence, question and answer, cause and effect, chronological sequence, compare and contrast, problem and solution, categorization (p. 213)

Goal

Use a Venn diagram to compare and contrast books.

Rationale

When students create a Venn diagram to compare and contrast books, they notice similarities and differences across texts. This lesson provides a model for teaching students to use a graphic organizer to compare and contrast genres.

Assess Learning

Observe students when they create a Venn diagram and notice if there is evidence of new learning based on the goal of this minilesson.

- ▶ Are students able to compare and contrast two books?
- ▶ Can they create a Venn diagram to compare and contrast two texts?
- ▶ Do they use the terms *genre, Venn diagram,* and *compare and contrast*?

Minilesson

To help students understand how to use a Venn diagram, engage them in a demonstration of comparing two similar genres, myths and epics. Here is an example.

- ▶ Show the prepared chart paper.

  What do you know about this type of graphic organizer?

- ▶ As students respond, ensure that they understand that a Venn diagram is used to compare and contrast two things.

- ▶ Show the covers of several books from two genres that lend themselves to comparison and contrast using a Venn diagram, such as two myths (e.g., *Pegasus* and *King Midas and the Golden Touch*) and two epics (e.g., *The Adventures of Odysseus* and *Prince of Fire*). Add the genres to the Venn diagram.

  These books represent two different genres. How are the genres the same and how are they different?

- ▶ Revisit a few pages of each story as needed to prompt the conversation.

  What information is the same in each genre?

  Where does the similar information go on a Venn diagram?

- ▶ Add similar ideas to the center of the Venn diagram.

  What characteristics occur in myths but not (or not always) in epics?

- ▶ Add responses to the appropriate sections of the Venn diagram.

RML5

WAR.U4.RML5

Have a Try

Invite the students to talk with a partner about creating a Venn diagram.

> Turn and talk about what characteristics always occur in epics, but not (or not always) in myths. These are the things that will be placed on the right side of the Venn diagram.

▶ After time for discussion, ask students for ideas. Add ideas to the chart.

Summarize and Apply

Summarize the learning and remind students that they can use a Venn diagram to compare and contrast ideas.

> Today you created a Venn diagram to compare and contrast books of different genres.

▶ Add the principle to the top of the chart.

▶ Provide students with a Venn diagram that they can glue in a reader's notebook or have them make their own.

> Today when you read, choose two books to read with a partner. Work with your partner to fill in a Venn diagram. For example, you could compare and contrast genres, characters, or settings. Bring your diagram when we meet so you can share.

Share

Following independent reading time, match up sets of partners to make groups of four.

> Share the Venn diagrams that you made.

Extend the Lesson (Optional)

After assessing students' understanding, you might decide to extend the learning.

▶ Encourage students to use a Venn diagram to compare and contrast other ideas, such as the way a topic is presented in a fiction and a nonfiction book, comparing and contrasting two characters in a fiction story, or comparing and contrasting two animals using information from an expository text.

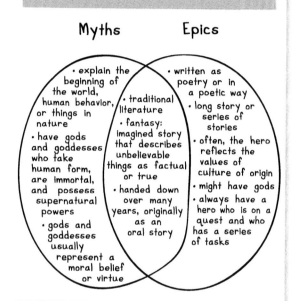

Use a Venn diagram to compare and contrast books.

Myths
- explain the beginning of the world, human behavior, or things in nature
- have gods and goddesses who take human form, are immortal, and possess supernatural powers
- gods and goddesses usually represent a moral belief or virtue

(overlap)
- traditional literature
- fantasy: imagined story that describes unbelievable things as factual or true
- handed down over many years, originally as an oral story

Epics
- written as poetry or in a poetic way
- long story or series of stories
- often, the hero reflects the values of culture of origin
- might have gods
- always have a hero who is on a quest and who has a series of tasks

Section 4: Writing About Reading

Assessment

After you have taught the minilessons in this umbrella, observe students as they talk and write about their reading across instructional contexts: interactive read-aloud, independent reading, guided reading, shared reading, and book club. Use *The Literacy Continuum* (Fountas and Pinnell 2017) to guide the observation of students' reading and writing behaviors.

▶ What evidence do you have of new understandings related to graphic organizers?

- Can students use a grid to represent ideas from books?

- Can they create a web to show how ideas from books are connected?

- Are they able to create an outline to organize ideas from nonfiction books?

- Are they able to use a diagram to show how authors organize information?

- Do they use a Venn diagram to compare and contrast books?

- Do they use academic vocabulary, such as *reader's notebook, graphic organizer, grid, outline, web, cause and effect*, and *Venn diagram*?

▶ In what other ways, beyond the scope of this umbrella, are students using a reader's notebook?

- Are students thinking about other ways to use a reader's notebook to write about fiction and nonfiction?

- Do they use a reader's notebook to share opinions about their reading?

Use your observations to determine the next umbrella you will teach. You may also consult Minilessons Across the Year (pp. 61–64) for guidance.

Reader's Notebook

When this umbrella is complete, provide a copy of the minilesson principles (see resources.fountasandpinnell.com) for students to glue in the reader's notebook (in the Minilessons section if using *Reader's Notebook: Advanced* [Fountas and Pinnell 2011]), so they can refer to the information as needed.

Minilessons in This Umbrella

RML1   Your writing about your reading shows your thinking about it.

RML2   A written sketch of the subject of a biography is a short description of his or her traits with supporting evidence.

RML3   A storyboard shows the significant events in a story.

RML4   A summary of a book gives the important information.

RML5   A short write shows your quick thinking about a book.

RML6   Two-column writing shows your response to a phrase or quote from a book.

Before Teaching Umbrella 5 Minilessons

Students need to be familiar with using a reader's notebook (see Umbrella 1: Introducing a Reader's Notebook in this section). They should be thinking and talking about concepts before they write about them, so consider teaching these minilessons alongside relevant Literary Analysis minilessons or to expand opportunities for reflecting on books.

Use these texts from the *Fountas & Pinnell Classroom™ Interactive Read-Aloud Collection* and *Independent Reading Collection* or choose high-quality books from your classroom library.

Interactive Read-Aloud Collection

Kindness and Compassion

Babu's Song by Stephanie Stuve-Bodeen

Perseverance

The Memory Coat by Elvira Woodruff

Handling Emotions/Positive Relationships

The Banana-Leaf Ball by Katie Smith Milway

Illustration Study: Mood

Teacup by Rebecca Young

Equality

Nelson Mandela by Kadir Nelson

Activists/Change Makers

Gordon Parks by Carole Boston Weatherford

Animal Adaptations

Exploding Ants by Joanne Settel

Poetry

Neighborhood Odes by Gary Soto

The Flag of Childhood selected by Naomi Shihab Nye

Independent Reading Collection

The Odyssey by Gareth Hinds

Interactive Read-Aloud
Kindness and Compassion

Perseverance

Handling Emotions

Illustration Study

Equality

Activists/ Change Makers

Animal Adaptations

Poetry

Independent Reading

Section 4: Writing About Reading

Reading Minilesson Principle

Your writing about your reading shows your thinking about it.

You Will Need

- chart paper and markers
- a reader's notebook for each student

Academic Language / Important Vocabulary

- reader's notebook
- brainstorm

Continuum Connection

- Have topics and ideas for writing in a list or notebook (p. 310)

Goal

Brainstorm a list of the different types of thinking you might share about books.

Rationale

When you teach students to think about the many ways they can write about books, they learn how to use writing as a tool to think more deeply about their reading. They reflect on common themes, messages, settings, and similar characteristics of literature. These understandings help students apply ideas and messages to their own lives, and they develop their understanding of the writer's craft in a variety of genres.

Assess Learning

Observe students when they think and talk about writing about reading and notice if there is evidence of new learning based on the goal of this minilesson.

- ▶ Do students participate in brainstorming ideas for what they can write about their reading in a reader's notebook?
- ▶ Are they able to select an idea from the list to use for writing about a book they are reading?
- ▶ Do they use the terms *reader's notebook* and *brainstorm*?

Minilesson

To help students think about the minilesson principle, engage them in brainstorming ideas for writing about reading in their reader's notebooks. Here is an example.

- ▶ Each student should have a reader's notebook to use during this lesson. If students have been keeping notes about reading or about minilessons in a reader's notebook, they can refer to those notes during the brainstorming portion of the lesson.

  When you talk about books, you share your thinking about books. You can also share your thinking by writing about what you read. Turn and talk about some different ideas you have for what you can think and write about in response to the books you read.

- ▶ Allow students a few moments to think or to refer to any notes they have about minilessons in the reader's notebook.

- ▶ As students share ideas, begin a list on chart paper. Remind them to think about both fiction and nonfiction books they have read and responded to.

- ▶ As needed, prompt the conversation to generate new categories of ideas. If you are using *Reader's Notebook: Advanced* (Fountas and Pinnell 2011), the Writing About Reading section has suggested ideas to help with the brainstorming session.

Have a Try

Invite the students to talk with a partner about the list of ways to write about reading in a reader's notebook.

> Look at the list of ideas for writing about your reading. Which ideas will you use? Do you have any ideas we didn't list? Turn and talk about that.

▶ After time for a brief discussion, ask a few students to share. Add any new ideas to the chart.

Summarize and Apply

Summarize the learning and remind students to use writing about their reading as a way to reflect on books.

> Today we made a list of different ways you can write about your reading in your reader's notebook.

▶ Review the ideas on the chart and add the principle.

> Today share your thinking by writing about the book you are reading. You may want to use some of the ideas from the list. Bring your reader's notebook and the book when we meet so you can share.

▶ If you are using *Reader's Notebook: Advanced* (Fountas and Pinnell 2011), have students write in the Writing About Reading section. If students are using another notebook, have them use a dedicated section of the notebook for responding to reading.

Share

Following independent reading time, gather students in small groups.

> Share in your group what you wrote in your reader's notebook. Did you use one of the ideas on the list, or did you write about something different?

Extend the Lesson (Optional)

After assessing students' understanding, you might decide to extend the learning.

▶ Keep the list posted and add to it as students experience new minilessons or as they generate new ideas for writing about reading. Encourage them to try new ideas from the list instead of repeating the same types of writing responses. Your feedback to their writing will also expand the possibilities.

▶ Remind students to keep a tally of the kinds of writing about reading they use (see WAR.U2.RML2).

Your writing about your reading shows your thinking about it.

- The genre and its characteristics
- Whether the main character is the narrator and how this affects the story
- Whether the characters are believable
- What you learned about the time period
- How the setting shapes the events in the story
- The author's point of view
- Whether there are twists or turns that surprised you
- How the events and action created tension in the story
- Your thoughts and feelings about the author's stated or implied message
- The kind of research that went into writing the book
- What the book makes you want to know more about
- How you might use what you learned
- What you notice about the word choice or style

Section 4: Writing About Reading

RML 2

WAR.U5.RML2

Reading Minilesson Principle
A written sketch of the subject of a biography is a short description of his or her traits with supporting evidence.

You Will Need

- several familiar biographies, such as the following:
  - *Nelson Mandela* by Kadir Nelson, from Text Set: Equality
  - *Gordon Parks* by Carole Boston Weatherford, from Text Set: Activists/Change Makers
- chart paper and markers
- a reader's notebook for each student

Academic Language / Important Vocabulary

- reader's notebook
- written sketch

Continuum Connection

- Compose notes, lists, letters, or statements to remember important information about a text (p. 211)
- Write to explore a writer's purpose and stance toward a topic (p. 212)

Goal

Write a sketch of the subject of a biography.

Rationale

When students write a sketch of the subject of a biography, they have to think about how the author portrays the subject and gain insight into why the author chose to write about the subject. Sometimes creating a drawing of the subject first can start their thinking. Before teaching this lesson, be sure students have learned about biographies (see Umbrella 14: Studying Biography in Section Two: Literary Analysis).

Assess Learning

Observe students when they write a sketch of the subject of a biography and notice if there is evidence of new learning based on the goal of this minilesson.

- ▶ Can students write a sketch of the subject of a biography that accurately reflects how the author depicts the subject?
- ▶ Are students using the terms *reader's notebook* and *written sketch*?

Minilesson

To help students think about the minilesson principle, engage them in thinking about what information to include in a written sketch. Here is an example.

- ▶ Show the cover of *Nelson Mandela*.

  A written sketch is a brief paragraph that helps someone get to know the subject of a biography or a character. Think about what you know about Nelson Mandela from reading this biography about him. Turn and talk about what he was like and how he did things.

- ▶ Provide a moment for discussion to refresh students' memories about Nelson Mandela.

  Let's work together to write a sketch of Nelson. What information should be included in the paragraph?

- ▶ As students provide ideas, write a brief sketch. As you write, help students stay focused on the traits of the subject and evidence of those traits.

  Let's look at what we wrote and think about what information is included. What do you notice?

- ▶ Read the written sketch. Then, engage students in an analysis of the written sketch. Prompt students to understand that a good written sketch will tell not only something about a subject's physical traits, but also personality traits. A good written sketch includes text evidence.

Have a Try

Invite the students to talk with a partner about information for a written sketch of the subject of a biography.

▶ Show the cover of *Gordon Parks*.

What might you include in a sketch of Gordon Parks, using what you learned about him in this biography? Turn and talk about that.

▶ After time for a brief discussion, ask students to share ideas.

Summarize and Apply

Summarize the learning and remind students to create a written sketch in a reader's notebook.

▶ Review the written sketch and add the principle to the chart.

Today, create a written sketch in a reader's notebook. You can use one of the subjects we discussed (Nelson Mandela or Gordon Parks), or you can choose someone from a biography you are reading. Bring your reader's notebook when we meet so you can share.

Share

Following independent reading time, gather students in groups of three to share their written sketches.

With your group, share the written sketch you wrote. Talk about the choices you made.

Extend the Lesson (Optional)

After assessing students' understanding, you might decide to extend the learning.

▶ Have students write a character sketch using a familiar fiction book and include a drawing of the character. Encourage students to be sure that details in the written sketch and drawing go beyond just physical traits so a person reading the sketch and looking at the drawing can determine other qualities about the character.

> **A written sketch of the subject of a biography is a short description of his or her traits with supporting evidence.**
>
> Nelson Mandela was a leader of human rights. He was born in Qunu in South Africa. As the smartest child in the family, he was the only one who attended school. After his father died, he was sent away to school in Johannesburg. There, he found powerless people who lived in great poverty. He later became an attorney and fought for those poor people. When the South African government began segregating people, he bravely spoke out against this practice, which was called apartheid. He had to work in hiding because of the threat of arrest and was eventually jailed for many years of hard labor, but he didn't give up. He got a message to the people that he would return, and he did. Eventually, people of all races were given the right to vote in South Africa, and Nelson Mandela was elected president.

Section 4: Writing About Reading

Reading Minilesson Principle

A storyboard shows the significant events in a story.

You Will Need

- an example of a graphic novel (e.g., *The Odyssey* by Gareth Hinds from *Independent Reading Collection*), or another book written in storyboard format (optional)

- several familiar books that have easy-to-follow events, such as the following:

  - *Babu's Song* by Stephanie Stuve-Bodeen, from Text Set: Kindness and Compassion

  - *The Memory Coat* by Elvira Woodruff, from Text Set: Perseverance

- chart paper and markers

- document camera (optional)

- a reader's notebook for each student

Academic Language / Important Vocabulary

- storyboard
- panel
- plot
- events

Continuum Connection

- Draw or sketch to represent or remember the content of a text and provide a basis for discussion or writing (p. 208)

- Represent a longer series of events from a text through drawing and writing (p. 208)

- Make notes or write descriptions to help remember important details about plot (p. 209)

Goal

Create a storyboard to represent the significant events in a plot.

Rationale

When students identify the most important events in stories and write about them in a sequential way, they recognize the pattern in narratives and are able to think deeply about the elements of plot. Storyboards provide an opportunity for students to use images to communicate their thinking about a book.

Assess Learning

Observe students when they create a storyboard and notice if there is evidence of new learning based on the goal of this minilesson.

- ▶ Are students able to identify and sequence the most important events in a plot?

- ▶ Can they create a storyboard that shows the events from a book they read?

- ▶ Are they using the terms *storyboard, panel, plot,* and *events*?

Minilesson

To help students think about the minilesson principle, guide them in creating a storyboard to show the plot events from a familiar book. Here is an example.

- ▶ If you have a comic book, graphic novel, or other book written in storyboard format, show a page.

  What do you notice about the format of this story?

- ▶ As needed, assist with the conversation so that students notice that each event is in a box (panel), there are pictures and just a few words, and the events go in order.

  This is similar to what is called a storyboard. A storyboard shows pictures of the important events in a story and has just a few words for each panel. Storyboards are often used to plan how to film a movie because they tell something about each main event that the director wants to show.

- ▶ Show the cover and review some pages of *Babu's Song*. As needed, guide them to think of which main events to show in a storyboard. The following prompts may be helpful.

  - *Which events from this story could be included in a storyboard?*

  - *How would you show the first event?*

  - *What could go in the next panel?*

- ▶ As students provide ideas, begin sketching the first few panels.

Have a Try

Invite the students to talk with a partner about how to create a storyboard using a familiar book.

> What would go in the first few panels of a storyboard to show the action in *The Memory Coat*? Turn and talk about that.

Summarize and Apply

Summarize the learning and remind students to think about the most important events as they read.

> Today you learned how to create a storyboard to show the important events in a story.

▶ Add the principle to the chart.

> Make a storyboard for the last fiction book you read or one you are reading. The storyboard can be for the part of the book you've read so far or for a chapter. Bring the book and your storyboard when we meet so you can share.

▶ To make the drawing easier, you might want to give students an unlined sheet of paper the size of the page in the reader's notebook to glue in when finished.

A storyboard shows the significant events in a story.

I wish I could go to school, too.

Share

Following independent reading time, gather students in pairs.

> Share your storyboard with your partner. If you are not finished, tell your partner what you will put in the next few panels, or ask for ideas if you are unsure about what to draw next.

Extend the Lesson (Optional)

After assessing students' understanding, you might decide to extend the learning.

▶ Have students create storyboards for other types of books that have a narrative structure (e.g., autobiography, biography, memoir, narrative nonfiction).

RML4

WAR.U5.RML4

Reading Minilesson Principle
A summary of a book gives the important information.

Introducing Different Genres and Forms for Responding to Reading

You Will Need

- several fiction books that are good examples for writing a summary, such as the following:
  - *The Banana-Leaf Ball* by Katie Smith Milway, from Text Set: Handling Emotions/Positive Relationships
  - *Teacup* by Rebecca Young, from Text Set: Illustration Study: Mood
- chart paper prepared with a book summary
- chart paper and markers
- a reader's notebook for each student

Academic Language / Important Vocabulary

- reader's notebook
- summary

Continuum Connection

- Select and include appropriate and important details when writing a summary of a text (p. 208)
- Provide details that are important to understanding how a story's plot, setting, and character traits are related (p. 208)

Goal

Write a brief summary of the most important information in a fiction text, including the characters, the setting, the problem and solution (when applicable), and the larger message of the text.

Rationale

Once students can give a good oral summary, they are ready to write book summaries. When students write a summary, they learn to think about the elements of fiction stories or nonfiction books and the big ideas in them. This is different from a retelling that gives most of the information. Prior to teaching this lesson, students need a good understanding of plot and summarizing (see Umbrella 5: Summarizing in Section Three: Strategies and Skills).

Assess Learning

Observe students when they write summaries and notice if there is evidence of new learning based on the goal of this minilesson.

- ▶ Can students write a concise summary of a book they have read?
- ▶ Do they use the terms *reader's notebook* and *summary*?

Minilesson

To help students think about the minilesson principle, engage them in thinking about what to write in a summary. Here is an example.

- ▶ Display the prepared summary and the cover of *The Banana-Leaf Ball*.

  I have written a summary of *The Banana-Leaf Ball*. What information do you notice I included in the summary?

- ▶ As students respond, prompt the conversation as needed so they notice the typical contents of a summary of a book: title and author, main characters, setting, problem, resolution, and the author's message, theme, or big idea.

- ▶ Record responses on chart paper.

  In what order did I write the information?

  What are some things from the book that I did *not* include in my summary?

  Why do you think I did not include that information?

  What is the difference between retelling and summarizing?

Have a Try

Invite the students to talk with a partner about writing a summary.

▶ Show *Teacup* and turn through a few pages.

> What would you include in a summary of *Teacup*? Turn and talk about that.

▶ After a brief time for discussion, ask students to share ideas.

Summarize and Apply

Summarize the learning and remind students to think about how they would summarize what they are reading.

> A summary is a few sentences that tell the most important information.

▶ Review the chart about summaries. Add the principle to the chart.

> Try writing a summary of a fiction book in your reader's notebook. You can write a summary of *Teacup*, or you can write about a book you recently finished reading. Bring your reader's notebook when we meet so you can share.

Share

Following independent reading time, gather students in pairs to share their summaries.

> Share with your partner the summary you wrote. As you listen, look at our chart and notice whether the summary includes *only* the important information. Then talk about that when your partner is finished.

Extend the Lesson (Optional)

After assessing students' understanding, you might decide to extend the learning.

▶ Guide students in writing a summary for a familiar nonfiction book. Then create an anchor chart together that lists the information that should be included in a nonfiction summary (e.g., title, author, topic, main points, information in order, essential details).

Summary

The Banana-Leaf Ball by Katie Smith Milway is about a boy named Deo who is forced from his home in Burundi to a refugee camp in Tanzania. Gang leader Remy and others steal things, and Deo becomes a target. When he is alone, he makes a soccer ball out of banana leaves. One day, a soccer coach arrives and the boys spend time playing soccer. Later, Deo teaches Remy and the other boys how to make banana-leaf balls. Eventually, Deo returns to his home and becomes a coach who teaches younger boys how to get along and trust each other by playing soccer together.

A summary of a book gives the important information.

Summary (Fiction)

- Has only important information
  - Title and author
  - Main characters
  - Setting
  - Problem and resolution
  - Author's message, theme, or big idea
- Tells information in order

Section 4: Writing About Reading

RML5
WAR.U5.RML5

Reading Minilesson Principle
A short write shows your quick thinking about a book.

Introducing Different Genres and Forms for Responding to Reading

You Will Need

- several books that are good candidates for doing a short write, such as the following:
  - *Teacup* by Rebecca Young, from Text Set: Illustration Study: Mood
  - *Exploding Ants* by Joanne Settel, from Text Set: Animal Adaptations
- chart paper and markers
- document camera (optional)
- a reader's notebook for each student

Academic Language / Important Vocabulary

- short write

Continuum Connection

- Understand writing as a vehicle to communicate something the writer thinks (p. 310)

Goal

Use a short write to share and deepen thinking about a book.

Rationale

When you teach students to do a short write, they learn how to share their thinking about a variety of aspects of their reading quickly. Before teaching this lesson, be sure students have learned about the ways authors organize nonfiction books (see Umbrella 16: Noticing How Nonfiction Authors Choose to Organize Information in Section Two: Literary Analysis).

Assess Learning

Observe students when they write to share their thinking and notice if there is evidence of new learning based on the goal of this minilesson.

- ❯ Can students do a short write to share their thinking?
- ❯ Do they use the term *short write*?

Minilesson

To help students think about the minilesson principle, provide a demonstration of how to do a short write. Then have students talk about what they notice. Here is an example.

- ❯ Show the cover of *Teacup*. On chart paper, begin a short write about the book. Write the title and author.

  > Let's see. One thing I noticed right away was the simplicity of the design and the color blue.

- ❯ Show the first few pages and model your thinking as you write.

  > The white print adds to the simple feeling of the design. When I think about what this book means, though, I realize that the themes are very big and complex. I find the contrast between the simplicity of design and the complexity of the ideas very interesting.

- ❯ Continue with the short write, modeling your thinking and writing aloud.

  > What did you notice about my short write?

- ❯ Guide students to notice that a short write is quick thinking in response to something they have read and that it can be about anything, though it should have a single clear point.

Have a Try

Invite the students to talk with a partner about doing a short write.

▶ Show the cover of *Exploding Ants*.

Here's a nonfiction book that you know. Turn and talk about what you might write in a short write about it. After time for a brief discussion, ask a few volunteers to share.

Summarize and Apply

Summarize the learning and remind students to do a short write in their reader's notebooks.

You can do a short write to share your quick thinking about any book.

▶ Add the principle to the top of the chart.

Today, do a short write about *Exploding Ants*. Use the ideas you talked about with your partner. Bring your notebook when we meet so you can share.

Share

Following independent reading time, gather students in pairs to share their writing.

Share your short write with a partner. Take turns reading to each other.

Extend the Lesson (Optional)

After assessing students' understanding, you might decide to extend the learning.

▶ **Writing About Reading** Encourage students to use the Writing About Reading page in their reader's notebooks for other short write ideas (also available from resources.fountasandpinnell.com). Examples include a character analysis, whether the illustrations or photographs successfully enhance the topic of a nonfiction book, aspects of the author's or illustrator's craft, how the author builds suspense, what thoughts, dialogue, and behaviors reveal about a character, how the setting affects the plot, how the author uses time in the story, or what could be changed about the book to increase your enjoyment of the story.

> ### A short write shows your quick thinking about a book.
>
> <u>Teacup</u>
> by Rebecca Young
>
> The design of this book is so simple looking but elegant. The print is in white, and there is very little of it on the pages. The illustrator used just a few colors for most of the book, mostly shades of blue. However, when the boy reached a new home, the illustrator used bright green and yellow. The whole feeling of the book is very simple, yet the ideas in the book— journeys, perseverance, and hope—are very complex.

Section 4: Writing About Reading

RML 6

WAR.U5.RML6

Reading Minilesson Principle

Two-column writing shows your response to a phrase or quote from a book.

Introducing Different Genres and Forms for Responding to Reading

You Will Need

- several familiar books that have memorable phrases and/or quotes, such as the following from Text Set: Poetry:
  - *The Flag of Childhood* selected by Naomi Shihab Nye
  - *Neighborhood Odes* by Gary Soto
- chart paper prepared with two columns
- markers
- a reader's notebook for each student
- document camera (optional)

Academic Language / Important Vocabulary

- phrase
- quote

Continuum Connection

- Draw and write about connections between the ideas in texts and students' own life experiences (p. 208)

Goal

Use a double-column entry with a phrase or quote from a text in the left column and responses in the right column.

Rationale

When students learn to respond to a phrase, quote, or question from their reading, they learn to express their responses to reading in a clear, organized way and to think deeply about language they encounter while reading.

Assess Learning

Observe students when they write responses to phrases, quotes, or questions and notice if there is evidence of new learning based on the goal of this minilesson.

- ▶ Can students write a response to an important phrase or quote?
- ▶ Are they using the terms *phrase* and *quote*?

Minilesson

To help students think about the minilesson principle, engage students in a discussion of how to respond to phrases, quotes, or questions that they encounter as they read. Here is an example.

> Sometimes when you read, you find a phrase or quote that stands out to you in some way. You might want to write about it in a way that helps you explore your thinking. Here's a sentence from *The Flag of Childhood* that I think is beautiful and interesting.

- ▶ Read aloud the first four lines from page 74 and write it in the left column.
- ▶ In the second column, begin writing a response to the phrase, reading aloud as you write.

> Turn and talk about my writing. What did you notice?

- ▶ After a brief discussion, ask a few volunteers to share.

> If you were writing a response to these sentences, what would you write?

- ▶ Add a few ideas from students to the right-hand column.

> Responding to this sentence helped me appreciate the writing even more. Writing about something is a way to think about it.

Have a Try

Invite the students to respond to a phrase, quote, or question from a book.

> ▶ Show or project page 4 from *Neighborhood Odes*. Write on chart paper or project the quote about the warm tortillas.
>
>> Think about this quote. What is your reaction to it? In your reader's notebook, write a quick response to this quote.
>
> ▶ After students have had a few minutes to write a response, ask a few volunteers to share.

Summarize and Apply

Summarize the learning and remind students to use a reader's notebook to write responses to phrases and quotes.

> ▶ Review the idea of creating two columns to respond to phrases or quotes.
>
>> Today, choose a phrase or quote that you like from the book you are reading. Make a two-column chart in your reader's notebook. Write the title of the book and the author at the top. Write the phrase or quote in the left column and write your response in the right column. Be ready to share what you wrote when we come together later.
>
> ▶ Add the principle to the chart.

Share

Following independent reading time, gather students in groups of three to share what they wrote.

> Share your quote or phrase and your response with your group.

Extend the Lesson (Optional)

After assessing students' understanding, you might decide to extend the learning.

> ▶ **Writing About Reading** Encourage students to respond to other types of language they notice (e.g., poetic language, memorable words, beautiful language, sensory details) in a two-column format.

Two-column writing shows your response to a phrase or quote from a book.

The Flag of Childhood selected by Naomi Shihab Nye	
"Thread by thread knot by knot like colonies of ants we weave a bridge" (p. 74)	I picture a group of women sitting together, doing embroidery. The teamwork required in working together is compared to the way ants tackle tasks much larger than themselves. Building a connection, or a bridge, between people with different backgrounds or experiences, and mending broken lives, is a difficult, large task. However, like ants who have great strength and can accomplish enormous tasks when they work together, this is what the women are doing.

Section 4: Writing About Reading

Assessment

After you have taught the minilessons in this umbrella, observe students as they talk and write about their reading across instructional contexts: interactive read-aloud, independent reading, guided reading, shared reading, and book club. Use *The Literacy Continuum* (Fountas and Pinnell 2017) to guide the observation of students' reading and writing behaviors.

▶ What evidence do you have of new understandings related to responding to reading?

- Are they able to write a sketch of the subject of a biography?
- Are they able to create a storyboard to represent significant events in a story?
- Do they write concise summaries of fiction books?
- Can they do a short write about a book?
- Can they respond in writing to an important phrase, quote, or question from a book?
- Are they using the terms *reader's notebook, brainstorm, storyboard, summary, written sketch, short write, response,* and *opinion*?

▶ In what other ways, beyond the scope of this umbrella, are students responding to reading?

- Are students using reader's notebooks in a variety of new ways?

Use your observations to determine the next umbrella you will teach. You may also consult Minilessons Across the Year (pp. 61–64) for guidance.

Reader's Notebook

When this umbrella is complete, provide a copy of the minilesson principles (see resources.fountasandpinnell.com) for students to glue in the reader's notebook (in the Minilessons section if using *Reader's Notebook: Advanced* [Fountas and Pinnell 2011]), so they can refer to the information as needed.

Minilessons in This Umbrella

RML1   Make an advertisement for a book.

RML2   Write a book review.

RML3   Make a persuasive poster based on an opinion you developed from reading.

Before Teaching Umbrella 6 Minilessons

The minilessons in this umbrella introduce students to different ways to write persuasively about their reading. We recommend that you teach Umbrella 15: Exploring Persuasive Texts, found in Section Two: Literary Analysis, before teaching this umbrella. For these minilessons, use the following books from the *Fountas & Pinnell Classroom™ Interactive Read-Aloud Collection* and the *Independent Reading Collection* or choose books from your classroom library.

Interactive Read-Aloud Collection

Memoir/Autobiography

Drawing from Memory by Allen Say

Life on Earth

Buried Sunlight: How Fossil Fuels Have Changed the Earth by Molly Bang and Penny Chisholm

Rotten! Vultures, Beetles, Slime, and Nature's Other Decomposers by Anita Sanchez

Independent Reading Collection

Phineas Gage: A Gruesome but True Story About Brain Science by John Fleischman

As you read aloud and enjoy these and other texts together, help students express their opinions about the topics discussed in the books and the books themselves.

Interactive Read-Aloud
Memoir/Autobiography

Life on Earth

Independent Reading

Section 4: Writing About Reading

Writing About Reading to Persuade

You Will Need

▶ a model advertisement that you have made about a book with which your students are familiar, such as *Drawing from Memory* by Allen Say, from Text Set: Memoir/Autobiography

▶ a book that you have read aloud recently with your class

▶ chart paper and markers

Academic Language / Important Vocabulary

▶ advertisement

▶ persuade

▶ effective

Continuum Connection

▶ Understand that argument and persuasive texts can be written in various forms: e.g., editorial, letter to the editor, essay, speech (p. 301)

Goal

Make an advertisement that tells about a text in an attention-getting or persuasive way.

Rationale

When students make book advertisements, they learn that there are genres that are well suited for certain purposes. Students also have the opportunity to express their opinions about books in a persuasive and creative way.

Assess Learning

Observe students when they create book advertisements and notice if there is evidence of new learning based on the goal of this minilesson.

▶ Can students create persuasive book advertisements?

▶ Do they understand the terms *advertisement, persuade,* and *effective*?

Minilesson

To help students think about the minilesson principle, use a book advertisement that you have created to engage them in noticing the characteristics of this type of persuasive writing. Here is an example.

▶ Display the book advertisement that you created before class.

After I read *Drawing from Memory* by Allen Say, I created a book advertisement for it. What do you think a book advertisement is? What is the purpose of a book advertisement?

The purpose of a book advertisement is to persuade other people to read the book. What does *persuade* mean?

Take a close look at my book advertisement. What do you notice about it? What elements did I include?

▶ Record students' noticings on chart paper.

Is this advertisement an effective way to persuade you to read the book? What makes it effective—or not?

Have a Try

Invite the students to talk with a partner about how to make a book advertisement.

▶ Show the cover of another book that you have read aloud recently with your class.

> If you were to make a book advertisement for this book, what would you write about it? Turn and talk to your partner about your ideas.

▶ After time for discussion, invite a few students to share their thinking.

Summarize and Apply

Summarize the learning and invite students to make a book advertisement.

> What did you learn today about how to make an effective book advertisement?

▶ Write the principle at the top of the chart.

> Today, make a book advertisement for a book that you have read recently and enjoyed. Think about what would appeal to someone who would like the book. Bring your book advertisement to share when we come back together.

Share

Following independent reading time, gather students together in the meeting area to share their book advertisements.

> Share your book advertisement with your partner. Discuss what you notice about each other's advertisements and what makes them persuasive.

Extend the Lesson (Optional)

After assessing students' understanding, you might decide to extend the learning.

▶ Share with students an assortment of official book advertisements. Invite them to discuss what they notice and whether the advertisements are effective.

Make an advertisement for a book.

From award-winning author and illustrator Allen Say . . .

Read Allen Say's own story of how he became the highly acclaimed artist he is today.

"Part memoir, part graphic novel, this book will inspire the hidden artist in all of us!"
—Ms. Grimes

DRAWING FROM MEMORY

by Allen Say

"I decided to become a cartoonist when I grew up. So I drew."

- Book title and author
- The book cover
- What the book is about
- A quote from a positive review of the book
- An attention-getting quote from the book
- The author's credentials

Section 4: Writing About Reading

RML2

Reading Minilesson Principle
Write a book review.

You Will Need

- chart paper prepared with a book review
- a book that you have read aloud recently with your class, such as *Phineas Gage* by John Fleischman, from *Independent Reading Collection*
- chart paper and markers
- To download the following online resources for this lesson, visit **resources.fountasandpinnell.com:** Book Reviews

Academic Language / Important Vocabulary

- book review
- opinion
- evidence

Continuum Connection

- Form and express opinions about a text in writing and support those opinions with rationales and evidence (pp. 209, 212)

Goal

Write a book review.

Rationale

When students write book reviews, they think critically about the books they read, express their opinions in writing, and support their opinions with rationales and evidence.

Assess Learning

Observe students when they write book reviews and notice if there is evidence of new learning based on the goal of this minilesson.

- ▶ Do students write effective book reviews?
- ▶ In their book reviews, do they express opinions about a book and support those opinions with rationales and evidence?
- ▶ Do they understand the terms *book review*, *opinion*, and *evidence*?

Minilesson

To help students think about the minilesson principle, engage them in noticing the characteristics of book reviews. Here is an example.

- ▶ Read aloud the book review on the prepared chart. Then divide students into small groups to notice the characteristics of a book review.
- ▶ After a brief time for the small-group discussions, bring the groups together to share what they noticed about book reviews. Ask questions such as the following to prompt discussion:
  - *What is a book review?*
  - *What did you notice about the book reviews you read?*
  - *What did the writers write about in their reviews?*
  - *What information did they provide about the books?*
  - *What kinds of opinions did the writers express?*
  - *What did you notice about how they expressed their opinions?*
  - *How did they support their opinions?*
- ▶ Record students' noticings on chart paper.

Have a Try

Invite the students to talk with a partner about what they would write in a book review.

▶ Show the cover of a book that you have read aloud recently with your class.

 If you were to write a book review about this book, what information would you include? What opinions would you express about this book, and how would you support them? Turn and talk to your partner about this.

▶ After students turn and talk, invite a few students to share their thinking.

Summarize and Apply

Summarize the learning and invite students to write a book review.

▶ Review the chart and write the principle at the top.

 Today, write a book review about the last book that you finished reading. Remember to support your opinions with reasons and evidence. Bring your book review to share when we come back together.

Share

Following independent reading time, gather students together in the meeting area to share their book reviews.

 Share your book review with your partner. Discuss what you notice about each other's reviews, and give your partner feedback about what he or she did well and what could be improved in the review.

Extend the Lesson (Optional)

After assessing students' understanding, you might decide to extend the learning.

▶ Give students numerous opportunities to write book reviews throughout the school year. Have students share their book reviews with each other and use each other's reviews as a means for choosing new books to read.

Book Review

Phineas Gage: A Gruesome but True Story About Brain Science by John Fleischman is a fascinating story about a man who had a terrible brain injury and what scientists learned about the brain. Fleischman begins the book by telling what will happen, which is unusual. He should have told the story in chronological order so that the accident was more of a surprise. Nevertheless, the author writes informatively and clearly about Phineas Gage. There is a glossary that explains the many medical terms. I definitely recommend this book if you are interested in learning about the human brain.

Write a book review.

Book Reviews

- Give the title and author of the book.
- Briefly tell what the book is about.
- Give the reviewer's opinions about the book.
- Give reasons and evidence for opinions.
- Often say both positive and negative things about the book.
- Say whether or not the reviewer recommends the book.
- Give the book a rating (for example, 5 out of 5 stars).

<table>
<tr>
<td>

RML 3
WAR.U6.RML3

</td>
<td>

Reading Minilesson Principle
Make a persuasive poster based on an opinion you developed from reading.

</td>
</tr>
</table>

Writing About Reading to Persuade

You Will Need

- a model persuasive poster that you have made about the topic of a book that your students are familiar with, such as *Buried Sunlight* by Molly Bang and Penny Chisholm, from Text Set: Life on Earth (see example on the following page)

- a different nonfiction book that you have recently read aloud, such as *Rotten!* by Anita Sanchez, from Text Set: Life on Earth

- chart paper and markers

- materials for poster making (poster board, markers, etc.)

Academic Language / Important Vocabulary

- persuasive

- opinion

Continuum Connection

- Express opinions about facts or information learned (p. 212)

Goal

Make a persuasive poster that reflects an opinion about a topic.

Rationale

When students create persuasive posters based on their reading, they think deeply about the topic of a book they have read, develop an opinion about that topic, and gain confidence in sharing their opinion with others.

Assess Learning

Observe students when they create persuasive posters and notice if there is evidence of new learning based on the goal of this minilesson.

- Do students create persuasive posters based on opinions they have developed from reading?

- Do they understand the terms *persuasive* and *opinion*?

Minilesson

To help students think about the minilesson principle, use a persuasive poster that you have created to engage them in noticing the characteristics of this type of writing. Here is an example.

- Display the cover of *Buried Sunlight* alongside the persuasive poster that you created before class.

  Reading *Buried Sunlight* helped me realize how our dependence on fossil fuels is harming the planet and why it's so important that we all do our part to reduce our consumption of fossil fuels. After reading this book and doing some research about how to use less fossil fuels, I decided to make a persuasive poster to share my opinion with others. What do you think a persuasive poster is?

  What do you notice about my persuasive poster?

  What am I trying to persuade people to do?

  Do you think that my poster is effective? Will it convince people to agree with my point of view? If not, what could I do differently to make it more persuasive?

Have a Try

Invite the students to talk with a partner about how to make a persuasive poster.

▶ Show the cover of *Rotten!*

Think about an opinion that you have about the topic of this book. How could you make a persuasive poster to get people to agree with your opinion? What would you write on your poster? Turn and talk to your partner to share your thinking.

▶ After time for discussion, invite a few students to share their thinking.

Summarize and Apply

Summarize the learning and invite students to make a persuasive poster.

What did you learn today about how to make an effective persuasive poster?

▶ Write the principle at the top of the chart.

Today, make a persuasive poster about an opinion that you developed from reading a book. Bring your poster to share when we come back together.

Share

Following independent reading time, gather students together in the meeting area to share their posters.

Who would like to share your persuasive poster?

What choices did you make and why?

Extend the Lesson (Optional)

After assessing students' understanding, you might decide to extend the learning.

▶ Have students express opinions they have developed through reading in other written formats (e.g., a persuasive pamphlet).

Make a persuasive poster based on an opinion you developed from reading.

Say NO to fossil fuels!
Burning fossil fuels harms Earth. The consequences—for our lives, animals, and the environment—could be severe if we don't make changes.

Do your part to reduce consumption of fossil fuels.

* Walk, ride your bike, or take public transportation.
* Turn off lights and electronics.
* Buy locally produced food.
* Shop with reusable bags.
* Recycle waste.

It's not too late to save our planet!

Assessment

After you have taught the minilessons in this umbrella, observe students as they talk and write about their reading across instructional contexts: interactive read-aloud, independent reading, guided reading, shared reading, and book club. Use *The Literacy Continuum* (Fountas and Pinnell 2017) to observe students' reading and writing behaviors.

> ▶ What evidence do you have of new understandings related to writing about reading to persuade?
>
> - Can students make an advertisement for a book that tells about it in an attention-getting or persuasive way?
> - Can they write a review of a book and support their opinions about the book with evidence?
> - Can they make a persuasive poster based on an opinion they developed through reading?
> - Do they understand and use vocabulary such as *advertisement*, *review*, *persuasive*, and *opinion*?
>
> ▶ In what other ways, beyond the scope of this umbrella, might you have your students write about their reading?
>
> - Do students use different forms of writing to respond creatively to their reading?

Use your observations to determine the next umbrella you will teach. You may also consult Minilessons Across the Year (pp. 61–64) for guidance.

Reader's Notebook

When this umbrella is complete, provide a copy of the minilesson principles (see resources.fountasandpinnell.com) for students to glue in the reader's notebook (in the Minilessons section if using *Reader's Notebook: Advanced* [Fountas and Pinnell 2011]), so they can refer to the information as needed.

Minilessons in This Umbrella

RML1 Notice the characteristics of a literary essay.

RML2 Write a thesis statement.

RML3 Write an introduction that hooks the reader and presents your argument.

RML4 Write examples to support your thesis statement.

RML5 Write a conclusion that restates the argument and shares a new understanding.

Illustrator Study:
K. Y. Craft

Illustration Study:
Mood

Before Teaching Umbrella 7 Minilessons

The minilessons in this umbrella are intended to introduce students to writing literary essays. For writing, they may use the *Reader's Notebook: Advanced* (Fountas and Pinnell 2011); however, if you do not have it, a plain notebook can be used instead. By using a reader's notebook for writing about reading, students have a consistent place to collect their thinking about their reading (see pp. 52–53 for more on using a reader's notebook).

Through inquiry, students learn to recognize the characteristics of an essay that analyzes a particular aspect of literature. Then, they practice formulating a thesis statement, writing an introduction and conclusion, and identifying and using examples from a text or multiple texts to support a thesis. For this umbrella, use the following books from the *Fountas & Pinnell Classroom™ Interactive Read-Aloud Collection* or any other books from your classroom library that students know well.

Illustrator Study: K. Y. Craft

King Midas and the Golden Touch by Charlotte Craft

Illustration Study: Mood

An Angel for Solomon Singer by Cynthia Rylant

RML1
WAR.U7.RML1

Reading Minilesson Principle
Notice the characteristics of a literary essay.

You Will Need

- prepared copies of sample literary essays (one copy per student) from online resources
- chart paper and markers
- reader's notebooks
- To download the following online resources for this lesson, visit **resources.fountasandpinnell.com**: Literary Essays

Academic Language / Important Vocabulary

- literary essay
- paragraphs
- introduction
- argument
- thesis
- conclusion
- evidence

Continuum Connection

- Write literary essays that present ideas about a text and may include examples and a summary of the text (p. 207)

Goal

Notice and understand the characteristics of a literary essay.

Rationale

When students learn to recognize the characteristics of a literary essay, they begin to identify aspects they will incorporate into their own essays and think about pieces of literature from an analytical perspective.

Assess Learning

Observe students when they think and talk about literary essays and notice if there is evidence of new learning based on the goal of this minilesson.

- Are students beginning to recognize the characteristics of a literary essay?
- Do they use academic language, such as *literary essay, paragraphs, introduction, argument, thesis, conclusion,* and *evidence*?

Minilesson

To help students think about the minilesson principle, engage them in an analysis of literary essays, followed by a discussion of the characteristics they notice. Here is an example.

- Ahead of time, print examples of literary essays from online resources or use literary essays written by you or by students. Make one copy of each essay per student. Have students read the essays prior to the lesson and identify what they notice about what is included in the essays. Encourage them to make notes on the copies to serve as reminders for the class discussion. (Keep the essays to use in RML3 and RML5.)

  What did you notice about the essays you looked at? Turn and talk about what you noticed.

- After students have had a chance to share, ask them how they would define a literary essay based on their noticings. Write a draft definition on the chart paper, using academic language such as *thesis* and *argument* as appropriate.

  A literary essay focuses on one aspect of literary analysis. For example, an essay might focus on themes within a book or across books, how a character changes in a story, a character's traits, or an aspect of the writer's craft.

  Let's look at the introductions of the essays you read. What do you notice about the introduction of a literary essay?

- As students share, write their noticings on the chart. Repeat the same question about the paragraphs in the body of the essay and the conclusion.

Have a Try

Invite the students to talk with a partner about any other noticings they have about literary essays.

> Turn and talk to your partner about anything else you notice about literary essays. Is there anything we should add to or omit from our definition?

▶ After students turn and talk, invite a few students to share their thinking. Add any new ideas to the definition on the chart.

Summarize and Apply

Summarize the learning and remind students about the characteristics of a literary essay.

> Look at the characteristics of a literary essay that we listed on the chart.

▶ Add the principle to the top of the chart.

> You noticed that writers of literary essays use evidence from a work of literature to prove their thesis or opinion. To do this analysis, you need to choose a book that makes you think and that you know well. Today during reading time, write a short list of books in your reader's notebook that you might be interested in analyzing in a literary essay. Bring your reader's notebook to share.

▶ If you think your students need more support, have them choose from a selection of books you have read aloud, discussed, and enjoyed together.

Share

Following independent reading time, gather students together in groups of three to talk about their book lists.

> Share the list of books you might choose for your literary essay.

Extend the Lesson (Optional)

After assessing students' understanding, you might decide to extend the learning.

▶ If students need additional practice identifying the characteristics of an essay, more sample essays can be provided. It is helpful to collect student essays in a scrapbook for future examples.

▶ If students need more support, consider having everyone write about the same familiar book that you have read and discussed in depth.

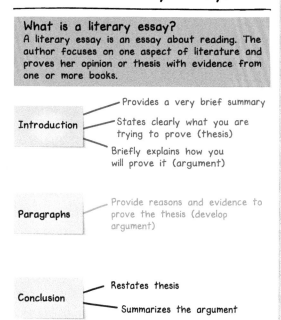

Notice the characteristics of a literary essay.

What is a literary essay?
A literary essay is an essay about reading. The author focuses on one aspect of literature and proves her opinion or thesis with evidence from one or more books.

Introduction
- Provides a very brief summary
- States clearly what you are trying to prove (thesis)
- Briefly explains how you will prove it (argument)

Paragraphs
- Provide reasons and evidence to prove the thesis (develop argument)

Conclusion
- Restates thesis
- Summarizes the argument

Section 4: Writing About Reading

Writing Literary Essays

You Will Need

- two familiar books that lend themselves to writing a literary essay, such as the following:
  - *An Angel for Solomon Singer* by Cynthia Rylant, from Text Set: Illustration Study: Mood
  - *King Midas and the Golden Touch* by Charlotte Craft, from Text Set: Illustrator Study: K. Y. Craft
- chart paper prepared with three or four thesis statements for one of the books you will be using
- markers
- reader's notebooks

Academic Language / Important Vocabulary

- literary essay
- thesis statement
- argument

Continuum Connection

- Write literary essays that present ideas about a text and may include examples and a summary of the text (p. 207)

Goal

Learn to write a thesis statement that states the main argument of an essay.

Rationale

When students learn the characteristics of a strong thesis statement and how to write one of their own, they become more confident in analyzing literature and in learning to focus before starting to write a literary essay.

Assess Learning

Observe students when they write thesis statements and notice if there is evidence of new learning based on the goal of this minilesson.

- ▶ Do students understand what a thesis statement is?
- ▶ Are students able to write a thesis statement for a literary essay?
- ▶ Do they understand the terms *literary essay, thesis statement,* and *argument*?

Minilesson

To help students think about the minilesson principle, engage them in thinking about how to write a thesis statement for a literary essay. Here is an example.

- ▶ Show the book *An Angel for Solomon Singer.*

  Turn and talk about some of the things we discussed when we read *An Angel for Solomon Singer* together.

- ▶ After students have had time to share briefly with a partner, reveal the three or four thesis statements you have written about the text. The thesis statements should relate to some of the big ideas you discussed about the book previously.

  I have written a few thesis statements about *An Angel for Solomon Singer* on the left side of the chart paper. What do you notice about these thesis statements?

- ▶ As students share their thinking, write their noticings on the right side of the chart.

  Now let's think about *King Midas and the Golden Touch.* What might you focus on in a literary essay about this book? Turn and talk about that in threes.

- ▶ After time for discussion, ask volunteers to share their thinking. As students respond, guide them to develop a thesis statement about the theme of the book. Write the statement on the chart paper. Use the following prompts as necessary to focus the discussion:

  - *What is the central theme of this book?*
  - *What argument do you want to make about this theme?*
  - *How will you prove it?*

Have a Try

Invite the students to talk with a partner about another possible thesis statement about *King Midas and the Golden Touch*.

> You have written a thesis statement about the theme of *King Midas and the Golden Touch*. Turn and talk about some of the other ideas you had about this book and then jot down another sample thesis statement in your reader's notebook.

▶ After time for discussion, invite students to share their thinking. Have students make suggestions for another thesis statement and write one of the examples on the chart.

Summarize and Apply

Summarize the learning and encourage students to write a sample thesis statement for a literary essay.

> A thesis statement describes for the reader what the literary essay will be about.

▶ Write the principle at the top of the chart.

> Today, choose the book you will use for writing a literary essay. In your reader's notebook, write one or more thesis statements. You might explore the theme or message of the book, argue something about the main character, or explore an aspect of craft. Bring your reader's notebook when we meet so you can share.

Share

Following independent reading time, gather students in groups of three.

> In groups, share your thesis statements. Talk about any suggestions for ways to improve the thesis statements and think about whether you could write an essay that focuses on the argument you present in your thesis statement.

Extend the Lesson (Optional)

After assessing students' understanding, you might decide to extend the learning.

▶ Work with students in small groups to further develop their thesis statements.

▶ Depending on the experience of your students, teach them how to prove a thesis statement using multiple texts.

Write a thesis statement.

Thesis Statements	Noticings About Thesis Statements
An Angel for Solomon Singer • Human contact and caring can transform a lonely life to one of connection and contentment. • One of the central messages of <u>An Angel for Solomon Singer</u> is that your attitude can change the way you view the world around you. • Cynthia Rylant uses imagery and symbolism throughout <u>An Angel for Solomon Singer</u> to convey the idea that anywhere can become home. **King Midas** • Greed can have painful consequences that can also teach a lesson about what is important in life. • People are not perfect, but kindness can overcome flawed decision making.	• Address the big ideas of the text (that is, they address many of the things you have discussed about the text) • State an opinion or argument • Can be proven with evidence from one book or from more than one book • Can be about • theme or message • writer's or illustrator's craft • symbolism • a character's change or traits • any other aspect of literary analysis

RML 3
WAR.U7.RML3

Reading Minilesson Principle
Write an introduction that hooks the reader and presents your argument.

Writing Literary Essays

Goal

Write an introduction for a literary essay.

Rationale

When students learn the characteristics of a strong literary essay introduction and how to write one of their own, they become more confident in analyzing literature and in learning to focus before starting to write a literary essay.

Assess Learning

Observe students when they write an introduction and notice if there is evidence of new learning based on the goal of this minilesson.

- Can students identify the qualities of a strong literary essay introduction?
- Are they able to write an introduction for a literary essay?
- Do they understand the terms *literary essay, introduction, hook,* and *argument*?

Minilesson

To help students think about the minilesson principle, engage them in thinking about how to write an introduction for a literary essay. Here is an example.

- Ahead of time, print out the literary essays from online resources or use samples from former students. Make a packet of essays per pair of students. You may choose to copy only the introduction of each essay. If you copy whole essays, save them for RML5.

- Before the lesson, write an introduction for *An Angel for Solomon Singer* on chart paper. Display the chart paper and the cover of the book.

  > Take a look at this sample introduction for a literary essay about *An Angel for Solomon Singer*. Read the introduction and then share what you notice.

- After a brief time, ask students to share their thoughts, guiding the conversation as needed. Begin a list on chart paper about what a strong literary essay introduction includes. Highlight the thesis statement when students identify it.

- Have students sit in pairs, and distribute the packets of literary essays.

  > With a partner, take a look at two other sample introductions. Talk about what you notice.

- After time for discussion, ask volunteers to share their thinking. Add any new ideas to the list.

Have a Try

Invite the students to talk with a partner about writing an introduction for a literary essay.

▶ Have students bring the book they have selected to use for writing a literary essay and sit with a partner.

> Think about your thesis and the book you will use to write your own literary essay. What might you include in your introduction? Turn and talk about that.

▶ After time for discussion, invite a few volunteers to share. Add any new ideas to the list.

Summarize and Apply

Summarize the learning and encourage students to write a sample introduction for a literary essay.

> What are some things you discovered about writing an introduction to a literary essay?

▶ Review the list on the chart and write the principle at the top.

> Today, in a reader's notebook, write an introduction for your literary essay. Bring your reader's notebook when we meet so you can share.

Share

Following independent reading time, gather students in groups of three to share their literary essay introductions.

> In groups, share your introductions. Talk about any suggestions for ways to improve the introductions and think about whether an essay could be written that supports everything stated in your introduction.

Extend the Lesson (Optional)

After assessing students' understanding, you might decide to extend the learning.

▶ Work with students in small groups to further develop their introductions.

▶ Ask your students to experiment with rewriting their introductions a few different ways and choosing the one they think works best for their thesis.

Introduction

"Home is where the heart is" is one of those classic expressions. You may have seen it written in needlepoint hanging in someone's kitchen or framed on the wall of an entry hallway, but what does it actually mean? Is home defined by where we feel love and are loved by others? In An Angel for Solomon Singer, Cynthia Rylant explores this idea as she writes about an older man living in a hotel in New York City. He is lonely and homesick for the fields and whispering pines of his home in Indiana. Just as his loneliness is about to take over, he discovers the Westway Cafe and begins to see New York with a new set of eyes. Through the characters of Solomon Singer and the cafe waiter, Angel, Rylant reveals that human contact and caring can transform a lonely life to one of connection and contentment.

Write an introduction that hooks the reader and presents your argument.

In the introduction to a literary essay, authors—
- state the book title and author
- write a solid thesis statement that shows the reader what the essay will be about
- include a brief summary of the book
- hook the reader/capture the reader's interest
- might begin with a quote, an interesting statement, something amusing, a controversial statement, etc.
- provide background information, if needed

Section 4: Writing About Reading

RML4
WAR.U7.RML4

Reading Minilesson Principle
Write examples to support your thesis statement.

Writing Literary Essays

- a familiar book that lends itself to writing a literary essay related to lessons learned by a character, such as:
  - *An Angel for Solomon Singer* by Cynthia Rylant from Text Set: Illustration Study: Mood
- chart paper prepared ahead of time with a thesis statement generated in RML2, along with *just* the beginning of an outline with text examples that support the thesis
- markers
- books students will be using to write literary essays
- sticky notes

Academic Language / Important Vocabulary

- literary essay
- thesis
- argument
- support

Continuum Connection

- Write literary essays that present ideas about a text and may include examples and a summary of the text (p. 207)

Goal

Provide evidence to support your thesis statement.

Rationale

When students learn to include text examples that support the thesis statement in a literary essay, they become more confident in analyzing literature and in learning to focus before starting to write a literary essay.

Assess Learning

Observe students as they select text examples to use in a literary essay and notice if there is evidence of new learning based on the goal of this minilesson.

- Are students aware that text examples in a literary essay need to support the thesis statement?
- Can they select appropriate text examples to include in a literary essay?
- Do they use and understand the terms *literary essay, thesis, argument,* and *support*?

Minilesson

To help students think about the minilesson principle, engage them in thinking about how to choose text examples for a literary essay that will support the thesis statement. Here is an example.

- Show the prepared thesis statement and text examples, along with the cover of *An Angel for Solomon Singer.*

  Take a look at what I have written on the chart. What do you notice?

- Guide the conversation as needed to help students notice that the outline you have started includes text examples that directly support the thesis in some way.

  Why do you think it is important to select text examples that support the thesis?

  In what ways do each of these text examples support the thesis?

- Support the conversation as needed to ensure that students understand that the selection of text examples is targeted to find only those examples that support the thesis statement. This ensures that the entire essay is focused.

  Think about what other text examples you might use from *An Angel for Solomon Singer* that would support the thesis statement. Turn and talk about that.

- After time for discussion, ask volunteers to share their thinking. Continue building the outline, using students' suggestions.

Have a Try

Invite the students to talk with a partner about selecting text examples to support a thesis statement.

▸ Have students bring books they will be using to write a literary essay and their prepared thesis statements and sit with a partner.

> Share the book you will be using to write a literary essay and the thesis statement. Talk about one or two examples you might use in your essay to support your thesis.

Summarize and Apply

Summarize the learning and remind students to include text examples to support their thesis when writing a literary essay.

> Why is it important to include text examples in a literary essay that supports your thesis statement?

▸ Add the principle to the chart.

> Today, use a sticky note to select text examples from the book you will use to write your literary essay that will support your thesis statement. Begin jotting down the examples in your reader's notebook, along with a quick note about how the example supports your thesis statement.

Share

Following independent reading time, gather students together in pairs.

> Share with a partner the examples you have selected and talk about how each example supports your literary essay thesis statement.

Extend the Lesson (Optional)

After assessing students' understanding, you might decide to extend the learning.

▸ If students need more support, repeat the lesson using additional books they are familiar with until they are ready to select targeted text examples independently.

▸ Work with students in small groups to have them share text examples and talk about how each supports their thesis statement, guiding them as needed to select appropriate examples and to connect each to their thesis statements.

Write examples to support your thesis statement.

Title and Thesis Statement	Text Examples
An Angel for Solomon Singer Human contact and caring can transform a lonely life to one of connection and contentment.	I. Solomon Singer is a sad, lonely man. 　A. Evidence: "Solomon Singer was lonely and had no one to love and not even a place to love . . ." (p. 10) 　B. Evidence: Some pictures show reflections, symbolizing his distance from people and happiness. 　C. Evidence: Wishing for home—fields, stars, conversation of crickets II. The waiter, Angel, is friendly and caring. 　A. Evidence: Rylant's description—eyes lined at corners from a life of smiling; voice like Indiana pines 　B. Evidence: Angel invites Solomon back each night with a warm smile. (p. 24) 　C. Evidence: Angel's name is symbolic. III. Solomon starts to become content. 　A. Evidence: NYC begins to feel like home: "voices sound like the conversations of friendly crickets." (p. 20) 　B. Evidence: Westway Cafe feels like home. (p. 24) 　C. Evidence: He doesn't feel lonely. (p. 28)

RML5

WAR.U7.RML5

Reading Minilesson Principle
Write a conclusion that restates the argument and shares a new understanding.

Writing Literary Essays

You Will Need

- a familiar book that lends itself to writing a literary essay, such as:
  - *An Angel for Solomon Singer* by Cynthia Rylant, from Text Set: Illustration Study: Mood
- essays from online resources (a set of copies per pair of students)
- chart paper prepared with a sample conclusion for the chosen book
- markers
- reader's notebooks
- books students have selected for writing literary essays
- To download the following online resources for this lesson, visit **resources.fountasandpinnell.com**: Literary Essays

Academic Language / Important Vocabulary

- literary essay
- conclusion
- summary
- argument

Continuum Connection

- Write literary essays that present ideas about a text and may include examples and a summary of the text (p. 207)

Goal

Write a conclusion to a literary essay.

Rationale

When students learn the characteristics of a strong literary essay conclusion, they learn how to summarize their analysis and use the conclusion to come to new understandings, apply those understandings to their own lives, or generate new questions for themselves or their readers.

Assess Learning

Observe students when they write an introduction and notice if there is evidence of new learning based on the goal of this minilesson.

- ▶ Can students identify the qualities of a strong literary essay conclusion?
- ▶ Are students able to write a conclusion for a literary essay?
- ▶ Do they understand the terms *literary essay, conclusion, summary,* and *argument*?

Minilesson

To help students think about the minilesson principle, engage them in thinking about how to write a conclusion for a literary essay. Here is an example.

- ▶ Ahead of time, print out the literary essays from online resources or use samples from former students. Make one copy per pair of students. You may choose to copy only the conclusion of each essay.

- ▶ Before the lesson, write a conclusion for *An Angel for Solomon Singer* on chart paper. Display the chart paper and the cover of the book.

  Take a look at this sample conclusion for a literary essay about *An Angel for Solomon Singer*. Read the conclusion and then share what you notice.

- ▶ After a brief time, ask students to share their thoughts, guiding the conversation as needed. Begin a list on chart paper about what a strong literary essay conclusion includes. Label the example essay as you highlight and discuss characteristics present in the sample conclusion.

- ▶ Have students sit in pairs, and distribute the packets of literary essays.

  With a partner, take a look at two other sample conclusions. Talk about what you notice.

- ▶ After time for discussion, ask volunteers to share their thinking. Add any new ideas to the list.

Have a Try

Invite the students to talk with a partner about writing a conclusion for a literary essay.

▶ Have students bring the book they have selected to use for writing a literary essay and sit with a partner.

> Think about your thesis and the book you will be using to write your own literary essay. What might you include in your conclusion? Turn and talk about that.

▶ After time for discussion, invite a few volunteers to share. Add any new ideas to the list.

Summarize and Apply

Summarize the learning and encourage students to write a sample conclusion for a literary essay.

> What are some things you discovered about writing a conclusion to a literary essay?

▶ Review the list on the chart.

> Today, in a reader's notebook, write a conclusion for your literary essay. Bring your reader's notebook when we meet so you can share.

Share

Following independent reading time, gather students in groups of three.

> In groups, share your conclusions. Talk about any suggestions for ways to improve them.

Extend the Lesson (Optional)

After assessing students' understanding, you might decide to extend the learning.

▶ Work with students in small groups to further develop their conclusions.

▶ Ask your students to experiment with rewriting their conclusions a few different ways and invite them to choose the one they think works best for the thesis.

Literary essay: An Angel for Soloman Singer
Conclusion

Solomon Singer's story shows that human connection and caring have the power to transform a life. Through Angel's simple acts of kindness, he helps Solomon to feel at home in his new surroundings. Instead of seeing the streets of New York as cold and lonely, he sees them as beautiful in their own way. As he walks into the Westway Cafe, he feels cared for and loved, just as he did at home in Indiana. Home is truly where the heart is. How might you make someone else feel at home? How might you change a life?

- Restates thesis
- Summarizes argument
- Loops back to introduction
- Gives reader something to ponder

Write a conclusion that restates the argument and shares a new understanding.

In the conclusion to a literary essay, authors

- summarize the argument and thesis statement
- usually demonstrate a new understanding
- often apply the thesis to their own lives
- sometimes restate the thesis
- sometimes loop back to the introduction
- sometimes offer the reader something to ponder

Assessment

After you have taught the minilessons in this umbrella, observe as they write literary essays. Use *The Literacy Continuum* (Fountas and Pinnell 2017) to guide the observation of students' reading and writing behaviors.

▶ What evidence do you have of new understandings related to writing a literary essay?

- Can students recognize and discuss the characteristics of a literary essay?
- Are they able to write a thesis statement that includes an argument?
- Can they write an introduction to a literary essay that hooks the reader and presents the argument?
- Do they identify and incorporate examples from a text to support the thesis?
- Are they able to write a conclusion to a literary essay that summarizes the thesis statement and arguments and offers a new idea or insight?
- Do they use academic language, such as *literary essay, characteristics, thesis statement, argument, introduction,* and *conclusion*?

Use your observations to determine the next umbrella you will teach. You may also consult Minilessons Across the Year (pp. 61–64) for guidance.

Reader's Notebook

When this umbrella is complete, provide a copy of the minilesson principles (see resources.fountasandpinnell.com) for students to glue in the reader's notebook (in the Minilessons section if using *Reader's Notebook: Advanced* [Fountas and Pinnell 2011]), so they can refer to the information as needed.

Minilessons in This Umbrella

RML1 Write a diary entry from the perspective of a character.

RML2 Write an interview to tell about the subject of a biography.

RML3 Create a poem in response to your reading.

Before Teaching Umbrella 8 Minilessons

The minilessons in this umbrella introduce students to different ways to respond creatively to reading in writing. Before teaching this umbrella, make sure that your students have had experience writing about their reading in a variety of ways. For the model responses in these minilessons, use the following books from the *Fountas & Pinnell Classroom™ Interactive Read-Aloud Collection* or choose high-quality, engaging books from your classroom library.

Exploring Identity

A Different Pond by Bao Phi

Genre Study: Biography (Pioneers)

Schomburg: The Man Who Built a Library by Carole Boston Weatherford

Hoaxes and Con Artists

Lon Po Po: A Red-Riding Hood Story from China by Ed Young

As you read aloud and enjoy these texts together, help students talk about what they learned from the books and/or share their emotional responses.

Exploring Identity

**Genre Study:
Biography (Pioneers)**

Hoaxes and Con Artists

Section 4: Writing About Reading

Reading Minilesson Principle
Write a diary entry from the perspective of a character.

You Will Need

- a model diary entry that you have written in response to a book your students are familiar with, such as *A Different Pond* by Bao Phi, from Text Set: Exploring Identity
- chart paper and markers

Academic Language / Important Vocabulary

- perspective
- diary entry
- character

Continuum Connection

- Describe character attributes as revealed through thought, dialogue, behavior, and what others say or think about them, and support with evidence (p. 209)
- Describe characters' intentions, feelings, and motivations as revealed through thought, dialogue, behavior, and what others say or think about them and support with evidence (p. 209)

Goal

Write a diary entry from the perspective of a character.

Rationale

Writing a diary entry from the perspective of a fictional character helps students connect with characters on a deeper level and better understand their emotions and motivations. This minilesson should be taught when students already have a good understanding of perspective and point of view. Before this minilesson we recommend teaching Umbrella 29: Understanding Characters' Feelings, Motivations, and Intentions and Umbrella 32: Analyzing Perspective and Point of View.

Assess Learning

Observe students when they write a diary entry from the perspective of a character and notice if there is evidence of new learning based on the goal of this minilesson.

- ▶ Can students write a diary entry from the perspective of a fictional character?
- ▶ Do they understand the terms *perspective*, *diary entry*, and *character*?

Minilesson

To help students think about the minilesson principle, use a diary entry that you have written from the perspective of a character to engage them in noticing the characteristics of this type of written response. Here is an example.

> After I read *A Different Pond*, I wanted to better understand the dad's feelings and thoughts. So I decided to write a diary entry from his perspective. What do you think it means to write a diary entry from the perspective of a character?
>
> Listen carefully as I read my diary entry aloud, and see what you notice.

- ▶ Display and read aloud the diary entry that you wrote before class.
- ▶ Use questions such as the following to elicit students' noticings:
  - *How can you tell that this is a diary entry?*
  - *How did I begin and end my diary entry?*
  - *How can you tell which character's perspective was used to write this entry?*
  - *What kinds of things did I write about in my diary entry?*
  - *What does this diary entry help you understand about the character?*
- ▶ Annotate the diary entry with students' noticings.

> To write from a character's perspective, you have to think about who the character is and what the character's life and experiences are like.

Have a Try

Invite the students to talk with a partner about writing a diary entry from the perspective of a character.

> If you were writing a diary entry from the perspective of the dad, what else might you include in your entry? What other details, thoughts, or feelings could you write about? Turn and talk to your partner about your ideas.

▶ After time for discussion, invite a few students to share their thinking.

Summarize and Apply

Summarize the learning and invite students to write a diary entry in a reader's notebook from the perspective of a character.

> How can writing a diary entry from a character's perspective help you better understand the character?

▶ Write the principle at the top of the chart.

> When you read today, choose a fiction book. Then write a diary entry from the perspective of a character in your story. Bring your diary entry to share when we come back together.

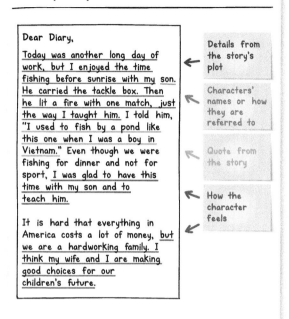

Share

Following independent reading time, gather students together in the meeting area to share their diary entries.

> Who would like to read aloud the diary entry you wrote today?

> How did writing a diary entry help you better understand the story you read?

Extend the Lesson (Optional)

After assessing students' understanding, you might decide to extend the learning.

▶ **Writing About Reading** Have students write in a reader's notebook two (or more) diary entries about the same event in a story—each from the perspective of a different character.

RML2

WAR.U8.RML2

Reading Minilesson Principle
Write an interview to tell about the subject of a biography.

**Responding Creatively
to Reading**

You Will Need

- a model interview that you have (partially) written with the author of a biography your students are familiar with, such as *Schomburg: The Man Who Built a Library* by Carole Boston Weatherford, from Text Set: Genre Study: Biography (Pioneers)

- chart paper prepared with part of an interview with an author (see blue print on chart)

- markers

Academic Language / Important Vocabulary

- interview
- subject
- biography

Continuum Connection

- Write interviews with an author or expert (questions and responses designed to provide information) (p. 207)

Goal

Write an interview with the author to provide information about the subject of a biography.

Rationale

Writing an interview with the author about the subject of a biography allows students to consolidate and summarize the key ideas and details in the biography.

Assess Learning

Observe students when they write interviews to tell about the subject of a biography and notice if there is evidence of new learning based on the goal of this minilesson.

- Can students write an interview with the author to tell about the subject of a biography?

- Are their interviews in the correct format?

- Do their interviews accurately summarize key points from the biography?

- Do they understand the terms *interview*, *subject*, and *biography*?

Minilesson

To help students think about the minilesson principle, use a fictitious interview with an author that you have written about the subject of a biography. Engage students in noticing the characteristics of this type of written response. Here is an example.

- Display the interview that you started before class.

  > After I read *Schomburg: The Man Who Built a Library*, I decided to write about Arturo Schomburg in my reader's notebook. I wrote it as an interview with the author, Carole Boston Weatherford. I imagined the interview responses, but I drew information from the book and also did some research. The interview is about the book. Take a few minutes to silently read what I wrote.

- Use questions such as the following to elicit students' noticings about the interview:

  - *What do you notice about what I wrote?*
  - *What do you think* Q *and* A *stand for?*
  - *What kind of writing is this?*
  - *What is the purpose of an interview?*
  - *What kind of information did I give about Arturo Schomburg?*

Have a Try

Invite the students to talk with a partner about the answer to the final question in the interview.

> I need you to help me finish writing this interview. I wrote the final question, but not the final answer. How could we answer the question "Why was Arturo Schomburg so important"? Turn and talk to your partner about what you think.

▶ After students turn and talk, invite a few pairs to share their thinking. Use their responses to write an answer to the final question.

Summarize and Apply

Summarize the learning and invite students to write an interview about the subject of a biography.

> One way to respond to your reading is to write an interview.

▶ Write the principle at the top of the chart.

> When you read today, choose a biography.
> Then, write an interview to tell about the subject of the biography. Write at least three questions and three answers. Bring your interview to share when we come back together.

Share

Following independent reading time, gather students together in the meeting area to share their interviews.

> Who would like to share your interview?

▶ Choose a volunteer and read (or have another student read) the interview with the volunteer so that two voices are heard.

Extend the Lesson (Optional)

After assessing students' understanding, you might decide to extend the learning.

▶ If there is an author living in your area, invite him or her to visit your class. Have students prepare questions to ask in an interview.

Write an interview to tell about the subject of a biography.

Q: Why did you want to write about Arturo Schomburg?

A: I've written about many African American heroes and Arturo is one of the most interesting. He was an Afro-Puerto Rican man who passionately collected books, letters, music, and art from Africa and the African diaspora. His personal library was so large, it eventually became part of the New York Public Library! He made a huge contribution.

Q: How did you learn so much about Arturo Schomburg?

A: From the research I did for my book Schomburg: The Man Who Built a Library and other books I've written about important African American men and women. I did a lot to learn about him before writing the book. I found out more while writing it. It was hard to decide what to include! I put in details I thought would interest kids and show what a great person he was.

Q: Why was Arturo Schomburg so important?

A: Arturo Alfonso Schomburg never tired of learning about the great contributions that people of African heritage made to society. His collection became the basis of the Schomburg Center for Research in Black Culture, which was named in his honor, at the New York Public Library branch in Harlem.

Reading Minilesson Principle
Create a poem in response to your reading.

Responding Creatively to Reading

You Will Need

- a model poem that you have written in response to a book that is familiar to your students, such as *Lon Po Po* by Ed Young, from Text Set: Hoaxes and Con Artists (see example poem on the following page)
- chart paper and markers
- sticky notes

Academic Language / Important Vocabulary

- poem
- response

Continuum Connection

- Write a poetic text in response to prose text, either narrative or informational (p. 302)

Goal

Create a poem in response to reading.

Rationale

Writing poems in response to reading gives students the opportunity to express their personal emotional response to a book. It also strengthens their understanding of the characteristics of poetry.

Assess Learning

Observe students when they write poems in response to reading and notice if there is evidence of new learning based on the goal of this minilesson.

- ▶ Do students write poems in response to their reading?
- ▶ Do their poems refer to specific details from the book?
- ▶ Do they understand the terms *poem* and *response*?

Minilesson

To help students think about the minilesson principle, use a poem that you have written in response to a book to engage them in noticing the characteristics of this type of written response. Here is an example.

- ▶ Display the poem that you prepared before class.

  After I read *Lon Po Po*, I decided to write a poem in response to my reading. Listen carefully as I read my poem aloud, and see what you notice about it.

- ▶ Read the poem aloud. Then use questions such as the following to prompt students' thinking about the poem:
  - *What did you notice about how I wrote a poem in response to my reading?*
  - *How can you tell that this is a poem?*
  - *How can you tell that I wrote this poem in response to* Lon Po Po?
  - *What do you notice about the lines in my poem?*
  - *What do you notice about the words?*
- ▶ Annotate the poem with students' noticings.

Have a Try

Invite the students to talk with a partner about writing a poem in response to reading.

> Take a moment to think about a book that might inspire you to write a poem. Then turn and talk to your partner about the book you would write about and why.

▶ After students turn and talk, invite a few students to share their thinking with the class.

Summarize and Apply

Summarize the learning and invite students to write a poem in response to their reading.

> What did you learn today about how to write a poem in response to your reading?

> Why is it a good idea to write a poem in response to a book you read?

▶ Write the principle at the top of the chart.

> Today, take some time to write a poem in response to your reading. You might write a poem in response to the book you read today or another book that you've read recently. Bring your poem to share when we come back together.

Share

Following independent reading time, gather students together in the meeting area to share their poems.

> Who would like to read aloud the poem you wrote in response to your reading today?

Extend the Lesson (Optional)

After assessing students' understanding, you might decide to extend the learning.

▶ Give students numerous opportunities to share their poems with each other and give and receive feedback. If any of the poems are suitable, prepare copies to use for shared reading—either chorally or in two or more voices.

Create a poem in response to your reading.

Po Po, Is It You?

Po Po, is it you? ← Repetition
  Arrived so late
  Voice of gravel
  Hidden in darkness
  Sleepy.

Po Po, is it you? ← Detail from the book
  Foot like a bush
  Hand like a thorn
  Revealed in light
  Hungry.

Po Po, is it you?
  Shang, "Po Po?" ← Characters' names
  Tao, "Po Po?"
  Paotze, "Po Po?"
  Silent.

Po Po, it is not you!
  Climbed down ← Line breaks
    Into the house
    Closed the door
    Locked the latch
    Peacefully asleep.

Assessment

After you have taught the minilessons in this umbrella, observe students as they talk and write about their reading across instructional contexts: interactive read-aloud, independent reading, guided reading, shared reading, and book club. Use *The Literacy Continuum* (Fountas and Pinnell 2017) to observe students' reading and writing behaviors.

> ▶ What evidence do you have of new understandings related to responding creatively to reading?
>
> > • Can students write a diary entry from the perspective of a character?
> >
> > • Do they write poems in response to their reading?
> >
> > • Can they write interviews to tell what they learned from a biography?
> >
> > • Do they use terms such as *perspective, diary entry, character, interview, subject,* and *biography?*
>
> ▶ In what other ways, beyond the scope of this umbrella, are students writing about books?
>
> ▶ Are students using other forms of writing to share their thinking about books?
>
> ▶ Are they writing about longer chapter books through a series of responses?

Use your observations to determine the next umbrella you will teach. You may also consult Minilessons Across the Year (pp. 61–64) for guidance.

Readers' Notebook

When this umbrella is complete, provide a copy of the minilesson principles (see resources.fountasandpinnell.com) for students to glue in the readers' notebook (in the Minilessons section if using *Readers' Notebook: Advanced* [Fountas and Pinnell 2011]), so they can refer to the information as needed.

Glossary

adventure/adventure story A contemporary realistic or historical fiction or fantasy text that presents a series of exciting or suspenseful events, often involving a main character taking a journey and overcoming danger and risk.

affix A letter or group of letters added to the beginning or end of a base or root word to change its meaning or function (e.g., *prefix* or *suffix*).

alphabet book/ABC book A book that helps children develop the concept and sequence of the alphabet by pairing alphabet letters with pictures of people, animals, or objects with labels related to the letters.

animal fantasy A modern fantasy text geared to a very young audience in which animals act like people and encounter human problems.

animal story A contemporary realistic or historical fiction or fantasy text that involves animals and that often focuses on the relationships between humans and animals.

assessment A means for gathering information or data that reveals what learners control, partially control, or do not yet control consistently.

beast tale A folktale featuring animals that talk.

behaviors Actions that are observable as children read or write.

biography A biographical text in which the story (or part of the story) of a real person's life is written and narrated by another person. Biography is usually told in chronological sequence but may be in another order.

bold/boldface Type that is heavier and darker than usual, often used for emphasis.

book and print features (as text characteristics) The physical attributes of a text (for example, font, layout, and length).

categorization A structural pattern used especially in nonfiction texts to present information in logical categories (and subcategories) of related material.

cause and effect A structural pattern used especially in nonfiction texts, often to propose the reasons or explanations for how and why something occurs.

character An individual, usually a person or animal, in a text.

chronological sequence An underlying structural pattern used especially in nonfiction texts to describe a series of events in the order they happened in time.

closed syllable A syllable that ends in a consonant: e.g., *lem*-on.

compare and contrast A structural pattern used especially in nonfiction texts to compare two ideas, events, or phenomena by showing how they are alike and how they are different.

comprehension (as in reading) The process of constructing meaning while reading text.

concrete poetry A poem with words (and sometimes punctuation) arranged to represent a visual picture of the idea the poem is conveying.

conflict In a fiction text, a central problem within the plot that is resolved near the end of the story. In literature, characters are usually in conflict with nature, with other people, with society as a whole, or with themselves. Another term for conflict is *problem*.

consonant digraph Two consonant letters that appear together and represent a single sound that is different from the sound of either letter: e.g., *sh*ell.

cumulative tale A story with many details repeated until the climax.

dialogue Spoken words, usually set off with quotation marks in text.

directions (how-to) A procedural nonfiction text that shows the steps involved in performing a task. A set of directions may include diagrams or drawings with labels.

elements of fiction Important elements of fiction include narrator, characters, plot, setting, theme, and style.

elements of poetry Important elements of poetry include figurative language, imagery, personification, rhythm, rhyme, repetition, alliteration, assonance, consonance, onomatopoeia, and aspects of layout.

endpapers The sheets of heavy paper at the front and back of a hardback book that join the book block to the hardback binding. Endpapers are sometimes printed with text, maps, or designs.

English language learners People whose native language is not English and who are acquiring English as an additional language.

epic A traditional tale or long narrative poem, first handed down orally and later in writing. Usually an epic involves a journey and a set of tasks or tests in which the hero triumphs. Generally the nature of the deeds and attributes of the hero have grown and become exaggerated over time.

essay An analytic or interpretive piece of expository writing with a focused point of view, or a persuasive text that provides a body of information related to a social or scientific issue.

expository text A nonfiction text that gives the reader information about a topic. Expository texts use a variety of text structures, such as compare and contrast, cause and effect, chronological sequence, problem and solution, and temporal sequence. Seven forms of expository text are categorical text, recount, collection, interview, report, feature article, and literary essay.

fable A folktale that demonstrates a useful truth and teaches a lesson. Usually including personified animals or natural elements such as the sun, fables appear to be simple but often convey abstract ideas.

factual text See *informational text*.

family, friends, and school story A contemporary realistic or historical fiction text focused on the everyday experiences of children of a variety of ages, including relationships with family and friends and experiences at school.

fantasy A fiction text that contains elements that are highly unreal. Fantasy as a category of fiction includes genres such as animal fantasy and science fiction.

fiction Invented, imaginative prose or poetry that tells a story. Fiction texts can be organized into the categories realism and fantasy. Along with nonfiction, fiction is one of two basic genres of literature.

figurative language Language that imaginatively compares two objects or ideas to allow the reader to see something more clearly or understand something in a new way. An element of a writer's style, figurative language changes or goes beyond literal meaning. Two common types of figurative language are metaphor (a direct comparison) and simile (a comparison that uses *like* or *as*).

flash-forward A literary device in which the action moves suddenly into the future to relate events that have relevance for understanding the present.

flashback A literary device in which the action moves suddenly into the past to relate events that have relevance for understanding the present.

fluency In reading, this term names the ability to read continuous text with good momentum, phrasing, appropriate pausing, intonation, and stress. In word solving, this term names the ability to solve words with speed, accuracy, and flexibility.

folktale A traditional fiction text about a people or "folk," originally handed down orally from generation to generation. Folktales are usually simple tales and often involve talking animals. Fables, fairy tales, beast tales, trickster tales, tall tales, realistic tales, cumulative tales, noodlehead tales, and pourquoi tales are some types of folktales.

font In printed text, the collection of type (letters) in a particular style.

form A kind of text that is characterized by particular elements. Mystery, for example, is a form of writing within the realistic fiction genre. Another term for form is *subgenre*.

fractured fairy tale A retelling of a familiar fairy tale with characters, setting, or plot events changed, often for comic effect.

free verse A type of poetry with irregular meter. Free verse may include rhyme, alliteration, and other poetic sound devices.

friendly letter In writing, a functional nonfiction text usually addressed to friends and family that may take the form of notes, letters, invitations, or e-mail.

genre A category of written text that is characterized by a particular style, form, or content.

graphic feature In fiction texts, graphic features are usually illustrations. In nonfiction texts, graphic features include photographs, paintings and drawings, captions, charts, diagrams, tables and graphs, maps, and timelines.

graphic text A form of text with comic strips or other illustrations on every page. In fiction, a story line continues across the text; illustrations, which depict moment-to-moment actions and emotions, are usually accompanied by dialogue in speech balloons and occasional narrative description of actions. In nonfiction, factual information is presented in categories or sequence.

haiku An ancient Japanese form of non-rhyming poetry that creates a mental picture and makes a concise emotional statement.

high-frequency words Words that occur often in the spoken and written language (for example, *the*).

humor/humor story A realistic fiction text that is full of fun and meant to entertain.

hybrid/hybrid text A text that includes at least one nonfiction genre and at least one fiction genre blended in a coherent whole.

illustration Graphic representation of important content (for example, art, photos, maps, graphs, charts) in a fiction or nonfiction text.

imagery The use of language—descriptions, comparisons, and figures of speech—that helps the mind form sensory impressions. Imagery is an element of a writer's style.

independent writing Texts written by children independently with teacher support as needed.

infer (as a strategic action) To go beyond the literal meaning of a text; to think about what is not stated but is implied by the writer.

infographic An illustration—often in the form of a chart, graph, or map—that includes brief text and that presents and analyzes data about a topic in a visually striking way.

informational text A nonfiction text in which a purpose is to inform or give facts about a topic. Informational texts include the following genres: biography, autobiography, memoir, and narrative nonfiction, as well as expository texts, procedural texts, and persuasive texts.

interactive read-aloud An instructional context in which students are actively listening and responding to an oral reading of a text.

interactive writing A teaching context in which the teacher and students cooperatively plan, compose, and write a group text; both teacher and students act as scribes (in turn).

intonation The rise and fall in pitch of the voice in speech to convey meaning.

italic (italics) A typestyle that is characterized by slanted letters.

label A written word or phrase that names the content of an illustration.

layout The way the print and illustrations are arranged on a page.

legend In relation to genre, this term names a traditional tale, first handed down orally and later in writing, that tells about a noteworthy person or event. Legends are believed to have some root in history, but the accuracy of the events and people they describe is not always verifiable. In relation to book and print features, this term names a key on a map or chart that explains what symbols stand for.

limerick A type of rhyming verse, usually surprising and humorous and frequently nonsensical.

limited point of view A method of storytelling in which the narrator knows what one character is thinking and feeling. The narrator may relate the actions of many characters but will not move between the points of view of different characters in a given scene or story.

literary essay An expository text that presents ideas about a work (or works) of literature in a formal, analytical way.

lyrical poetry A songlike type of poetry that has rhythm and sometimes rhyme and is memorable for sensory images and description.

main idea The central underlying idea, concept, or message that the author conveys in a nonfiction text. Compare to *theme, message.*

maintaining fluency (as a strategic action) Integrating sources of information in a smoothly operating process that results in expressive, phrased reading.

making connections (as a strategic action) Searching for and using connections to knowledge gained through personal experiences, learning about the world, and reading other texts.

meaning One of the sources of information that readers use (MSV: meaning, language structure, visual information). Meaning, the semantic system of language, refers to meaning derived from words, meaning across a text or texts, and meaning from personal experience or knowledge.

memoir A biographical text in which a writer takes a reflective stance in looking back on a particular time or person. Usually written in the first person, memoirs are often briefer and more intense accounts of a memory or set of memories than the accounts found in biographies and autobiographies.

mentor texts Books or other texts that serve as examples of excellent writing. Mentor texts are read and reread to provide models for literature discussion and student writing.

message An important idea that an author conveys in a fiction or nonfiction text. See also *main idea, theme.*

modern fantasy Fantasy texts that have contemporary content. Unlike traditional literature, modern fantasy does not come from an oral tradition. Modern fantasy texts can be divided into four more specific genres: animal fantasy, low fantasy, high fantasy, and science fiction.

monitoring and self-correcting (as a strategic action) Checking whether the reading sounds right, looks right, and makes sense, and solving problems when it doesn't.

mood The emotional atmosphere communicated by an author in his or her work, or how a text makes readers feel. An element of a writer's style, mood is established by details, imagery, figurative language, and setting. See also *tone*.

myth A traditional narrative text, often based in part on historical events, that explains human behavior and natural events or phenomena such as the seasons and the earth and sky.

narrative nonfiction Nonfiction texts that tell a story using a narrative structure and literary language to make a topic interesting and appealing to readers.

narrative text A category of texts in which the purpose is to tell a story. Stories and biographies are kinds of narrative.

narrative text structure A method of organizing a text. A simple narrative structure follows a traditional sequence that includes a beginning, a problem, a series of events, a resolution of the problem, and an ending. Alternative narrative structures may include devices, such as flashback or flash-forward, to change the sequence of events or have multiple narrators.

narrator The teller of the story of a text. The term *point of view* also indicates the angle from which the story is told, usually the first person (the narrator is a character in the story) or the third person (the unnamed narrator is not a character in the story).

nonfiction Prose or poetry that provides factual information. According to their structures, nonfiction texts can be organized into the categories of narrative and nonnarrative. Along with fiction, nonfiction is one of the two basic genres of literature.

nonnarrative text structure A method of organizing a text. Nonnarrative structures are used especially in three genres of nonfiction— expository texts, procedural texts, and persuasive texts. In nonnarrative nonfiction texts, underlying structural patterns include description, cause and effect, chronological sequence, temporal sequence, categorization, compare and contrast, problem and solution, and question and answer. See also *organization, text structure,* and *narrative text structure.*

open syllable A syllable that ends in a vowel sound: e.g., *ho*-tel.

oral tradition The handing down of literary material—such as songs, poems, and stories—from person to person over many generations through memory and word of mouth.

organization The arrangement of ideas in a text according to a logical structure, either narrative or nonnarrative. Another term for organization is *text structure.*

organizational tools and sources of information A design feature of nonfiction texts. Organizational tools and sources of information help a reader process and understand nonfiction texts. Examples include table of contents, headings, index, glossary, appendix, about the author, and references.

peritext Decorative or informative illustrations and/or print outside the body of the text. Elements of the peritext add to aesthetic appeal and may have cultural significance or symbolic meaning.

personification A figure of speech in which an animal is spoken of or portrayed as if it were a person, or in which a lifeless thing or idea is spoken of or portrayed as a living thing. Personification is a type of figurative language.

perspective How the characters view what is happening in the story. It is shaped by culture, values, and experience. See also *narrator* and *point of view*.

persuasive text A nonfiction text intended to convince the reader of the validity of a set of ideas—usually a particular point of view.

picture book An illustrated fiction or nonfiction text in which pictures work with the text to tell a story or provide information.

plot The events, action, conflict, and resolution of a story presented in a certain order in a fiction text. A simple plot progresses chronologically from start to end, whereas more complex plots may shift back and forth in time.

poetry Compact, metrical writing characterized by imagination and artistry and imbued with intense meaning. Along with prose, poetry is one of the two broad categories into which all literature can be divided.

point of view The angle from which a fiction story is told, usually the first person (the narrator is a character in the story; uses the pronouns *I*, *me*) or the third person (an unnamed narrator is not a character in the story; uses the pronouns *he*, *she*, *they*). See also *narrator*, *third-person limited point of view*, and *third-person omniscient point of view*.

pourquoi tale A folktale intended to explain why things are the way they are, usually having to do with natural phenomena.

predicting (as a strategic action) Using what is known to think about what will follow while reading continuous text.

prefix A group of letters placed in front of a base word to change its meaning: e.g., *pre*plan.

principle A generalization that is predictable.

print feature In nonfiction texts, print features include the color, size, style, and font of type, as well as various aspects of layout.

problem See *conflict*.

problem and solution A structural pattern used especially in nonfiction texts to define a problem and clearly propose a solution. This pattern is often used in persuasive and expository texts.

procedural text A nonfiction text that explains how to do something. Procedural texts are almost always organized in temporal sequence and take the form of directions (or "how-to" texts) or descriptions of a process.

prompt A question, direction, or statement designed to encourage the child to say more about a topic.

Prompting Guide, Part 1 A quick reference for specific language to teach for, prompt for, or reinforce effective reading and writing behaviors. The guide is organized in categories and color-coded so that you can turn quickly to the area needed and refer to it as you teach (Fountas and Pinnell 2012).

punctuation Marks used in written text to clarify meaning and separate structural units. The comma and the period are common punctuation marks.

purpose A writer's overall intention in creating a text, or a reader's overall intention in reading a text. To tell a story is one example of a writer's purpose, and to be entertained is one example of a reader's purpose.

question and answer A structural pattern used especially in nonfiction texts to organize information in a series of questions with responses. Question-and-answer texts may be based on a verbal or written interview, or on frequently arising or logical questions about a topic.

reader's notebook A notebook or folder of bound pages in which students write about their reading. A reader's notebook is used to keep a record of texts read and to express thinking. It may have several different sections to serve a variety of purposes.

readers' theater A performance of literature—i.e., a story, a play, or poetry—read aloud expressively by one or more persons rather than acted.

realistic fiction A fiction text that takes place in contemporary or modern times about believable characters involved in events that could happen. Contemporary realistic fiction usually presents modern problems that are typical for the characters, and it may highlight social issues.

repetition Repeated words or phrases that help create rhythm and emphasis in poetry or prose.

resolution/solution The point in the plot of a fiction story when the main conflict is solved.

rhyme The repetition of vowel and consonant sounds in the stressed and unstressed syllables of words in verse, especially at the ends of lines.

rhythm The regular or ordered repetition of stressed and unstressed syllables in poetry, other writing, or speech.

searching for and using information (as a strategic action) Looking for and thinking about all kinds of content to make sense of a text while reading.

self-correcting Noticing when reading doesn't make sense, sound right, or look right, and fixing it when it doesn't.

sequence See *chronological sequence* and *temporal sequence*.

series A set of books that are connected by the same character(s) or setting. Each book in a series stands alone, and often books may be read in any order.

setting The place and time in which a fiction text or biographical text takes place.

shared reading An instructional context in which the teacher involves a group of students in the reading of a particular big book to introduce aspects of literacy (such as print conventions), develop reading strategies (such as decoding or predicting), and teach vocabulary.

shared writing An instructional context in which the teacher involves a group of students in the composing of a coherent text together. The teacher writes while scaffolding children's language and ideas.

short write A sentence or paragraph that students write at intervals while reading a text. Students may use sticky notes, notepaper, or a reader's notebook to write about what they are thinking, feeling, or visualizing as they read. They may also note personal connections to the text.

sidebar Information that is additional to the main text, placed alongside the text and sometimes set off from the main text in a box.

small-group reading instruction The teacher working with children brought together because they are similar enough in reading development to teach in a small group; guided reading.

solving words (as a strategic action) Using a range of strategies to take words apart and understand their meanings.

sources of information The various cues in a written text that combine to make meaning (for example, syntax, meaning, and the physical shape and arrangement of type).

speech bubble A shape, often rounded, containing the words a character or person says in a cartoon or other text. Another term for *speech bubble* is *speech balloon*.

stance How the author feels about a topic; the author's attitude.

story A series of events in narrative form, either fiction or nonfiction.

story within a story A structural device occasionally used in fiction texts to present a shorter, self-contained narrative within the context of the longer primary narrative. See also *plot*.

strategic action Any one of many simultaneous, coordinated thinking activities that go on in a reader's head. See *thinking within, beyond, and about the text*.

stress The emphasis given to some syllables or words.

structure One of the sources of information that readers use (MSV: meaning, language structure, visual information). Language structure refers to the way words are put together in phrases and sentences (syntax or grammar).

style The way a writer chooses and arranges words to create a meaningful text. Aspects of style include sentence length, word choice, and the use of figurative language and symbolism.

subgenre A kind of text that is characterized by particular elements. See also *form*.

suffix A group of letters added at the end of a base word or word root to change its function or meaning: e.g., hand*ful*, hope*less*.

summarizing (as a strategic action) Putting together and remembering important information and disregarding irrelevant information while reading.

syllable A minimal unit of sequential speech sounds composed of a vowel sound or a consonant-vowel combination. A syllable always contains a vowel or vowel-like speech sound: e.g., *pen-ny*.

tall tale A folktale that revolves around a central legendary character with extraordinary physical features or abilities. Tall tales are characterized by much exaggeration.

temporal sequence An underlying structural pattern used especially in nonfiction texts to describe the sequence in which something always or usually occurs, such as the steps in a process. See also *procedural text* and *directions (how-to)*.

text structure The overall architecture or organization of a piece of writing. Another term for text structure is *organization*. See also *narrative text structure* and *nonnarrative text structure*.

theme The central underlying idea, concept, or message that the author conveys in a fiction text. Compare to *main idea*.

thesis a statement, proposition, or theory that is put forward as a premise to be maintained or proved, often by argument; the main idea or claim of an essay or nonfiction text.

thinking within, beyond, and about the text Three ways of thinking about a text while reading. Thinking *within* the text involves efficiently and effectively understanding what is on the page, the author's literal message. Thinking *beyond* the text requires making inferences and putting text ideas together in different ways to construct the text's meaning. In thinking *about* the text, readers analyze and critique the author's craft.

third-person omniscient point of view A method of storytelling in which the narrator knows what all characters are thinking and feeling. Omniscient narrators may move between the points of view of different characters in a given scene or story.

thought bubble A shape, often rounded, containing the words (or sometimes an image that suggests one or more words) a character or person thinks in a cartoon or other text. Another term for *thought bubble* is *thought balloon*.

tone An expression of the author's attitude or feelings toward a subject reflected in the style of writing. For instance, a reader might characterize an author's tone as ironic or earnest. Sometimes the term *tone* is used to identify the mood of a scene or a work of literature. For example, a text might be said to have a somber or carefree tone. See also *mood*.

tools As text characteristics, parts of a text designed to help the reader access or better understand it (table of contents, glossary, headings). In writing, references that support the writing process (dictionary, thesaurus).

topic The subject of a piece of writing.

traditional literature Stories passed down in oral or written form through history. An integral part of world culture, traditional literature includes folktales, tall tales, fairy tales, fables, myths, legends, epics, and ballads.

trickster tale A folktale featuring a clever, usually physically weaker or smaller, animal who outsmarts larger or more powerful animals.

understandings Basic concepts that are critical to comprehending a particular area of content.

visual information One of three sources of information that readers use (MSV: meaning, language structure, visual information). *Visual information* refers to the letters that represent the sounds of language and the way they are combined (spelling patterns) to create words; visual information at the sentence level includes punctuation.

wordless picture book A form in which a story is told exclusively with pictures.

writing Children engaging in the writing process and producing pieces of their own writing in many genres.

writing about reading Children responding to reading a text by writing and sometimes drawing.

Credits

Illustration: p. 347 (map) Rob Schuster

Cover image from *Above World*. Copyright © 2012 Jenn Reese. Reproduced by permission of the publisher, Candlewick Press, Somerville, MA.

Cover image from *The Adventures of Odysseus* by Hugh Lupton and Daniel Morden, illustrated by Christina Balit. Copyright © 2017 Hugh Lupton, Daniel Morden, and Christina Balit. Used by permission of Barefoot Books, Inc., Cambridge, MA.

Cover image from *Africa Is Not a Country* by Mark Melnicove and Margy Burns Knight, illustrated by Anne Sibley O'Brien. Text copyright © 2000 Margy Burns Knight, Mark Melnicove, and Anne Sibley O'Brien. Illustrations copyright © 2000 by Anne Sibley O'Brien. Reprinted with the permission of Millbrook Press, a division of Lerner Publishing Group, Inc. All rights reserved. No part of this excerpt may be used or reproduced in any manner whatsoever without the prior written permission of Lerner Publishing Group, Inc.

Cover image from *An Angel For Solomon Singer* by Cynthia Rylant. Copyright © 1992 Cynthia Rylant. Reprinted by permission of Scholastic, Inc.

Cover image from *Ancient Egypt* by Ken Jennings. Copyright © 2015 Ken Jennings. Reprinted with the permissions of Little Simon, an imprint of Simon & Schuster Children's Publishing Division. All rights reserved.

Cover image from *As Fast as Words Could Fly* by Pamela M. Tuck, illustrated by Eric Velasquez. Copyright © 2013 Pamela M. Tuck and Eric Velasquez. Permission arranged with Lee & Low Books, Inc., New York, NY 10016.

Cover image from *Babu's Song* by Stephanie Stuve-Bodeen, illustrated by Aaron Boyd. Copyright © 2008 Stephanie Stuve-Bodeen and Aaron Boyd. Permission arranged with Lee & Low Books, Inc., New York, NY 10016.

Cover image from *Ballots For Belva* by Sudipta Bardhan-Quallen, illustrated by Courtney A. Martin. Text Copyright © 2008 Sudipta Bardhan-Quallen. Illustrations Copyright © 2008 Courtney A. Martin. Used by permission of Abrams, an imprint of Harry N. Abrams, Inc., New York. All rights reserved.

Cover image from *The Banana-Leaf Ball* written by Katie Smith Milway, illustrated by Shane W. Evans. Cover illustration © 2017 Shane W. Evans. Used by permission of Kids Can Press, Toronto.

Cover image from *Bill Peet: An Autobiography*. Copyright © 1989 by William Peet. Reprinted with permission of Houghton Mifflin Harcourt.

Cover image from *Bird* by Zetta Elliott, illustrated by Shadra Strickland. Copyright © 2008 Zetta Elliott and Shadra Strickland. Permission arranged with Lee & Low Books, Inc., New York, NY 10016.